the Gendered Society

SIXTH EDITION

MICHAEL KIMMEL

Stony Brook University, State University of New York

New York   Oxford
OXFORD UNIVERSITY PRESS

For my Nordic colleagues and friends: Oysten, Jorgen, Lars, Klas, Robert, Dag, Ulla-Brit, Svend-Aage Kirsten, and Anna Sofie.

Oxford University Press is a department of the University of Oxford. It furthers the University's objective of excellence in research, scholarship, and education by publishing worldwide. Oxford is a registered trade mark of Oxford University Press in the UK and certain other countries.

Published in the United States of America by Oxford University Press
198 Madison Avenue, New York, NY 10016, United States of America.

Library of Congress Cataloging-in-Publication Data

Names: Kimmel, Michael S., author.
Title: The gendered society / Michael Kimmel, Stony Brook University, State
    University of New York.
Description: Sixth edition. | New York : xford University Press, [2017] |
    Includes bibliographical references and index.
Identifiers: LCCN 2016016501| ISBN 9780190260316 (pbk. : alk. paper) | ISBN
    9780190260323 (instructor edition : alk. paper)
Subjects: LCSH: Sex role. | Sex differences (Psychology) | Gender identity. |
    Sex discrimination. | Equality.
Classification: LCC HQ1075 .K547 2017 | DDC 305.3—dc23
LC record available at https://lccn.loc.gov/2016016501

9 8 7 6 5 4 3 2 1

Printed in the United States of America
Printed by R.R. Donnelley, United States of America

Contents

Preface *vii*

CHAPTER I **Introduction:** *Human Beings: An Engendered Species* *1*

Part 1 Explanations of Gender 17

CHAPTER 2 **Ordained by Nature:** *Biology Constructs the Sexes* *19*

CHAPTER 3 **Spanning the World:** *Culture Constructs Gender Difference* *58*

CHAPTER 4 **"So, That Explains It":** *Psychoanalytic and Developmental Perspectives on Gender* *87*

CHAPTER 5 **The Social Construction of Gender Relations** *114*

Part 2 Gendered Identities, Gendered Institutions 149

CHAPTER 6 **The Gendered Family** *151*

CHAPTER 7 **The Gendered Classroom** *204*

CHAPTER 8 **Gender and Religion** *234*

CHAPTER 9 **Separate and Unequal:** *The Gendered World of Work* *260*

CHAPTER 10 **The Gender of Politics and the Politics of Gender** *311*

CHAPTER II **The Gendered Media** *343*

Part 3 Gendered Interactions 371

CHAPTER 12 **Gendered Intimacies:** *Friendship and Love* *373*

CHAPTER 13 **The Gendered Body** *396*

CHAPTER 14 **The Gender of Violence** *448*

Epilogue: "A Degendered Society"? *483*
Notes *489*
Sources for Chapter Opening Art *531*
Index *533*

v

Preface

As this book enters its sixth edition, it's been adopted widely around the country and translated into several languages. It's personally gratifying, of course, but more gratifying is the embrace of the book's vision of a world in which gender inequality is but a distant anachronism, and a serious intellectual confrontation with gender inequality, and the differences that such inequality produces, is a central part of the struggle to bring such a world about. I'm proud to contribute to that struggle.

In this sixth edition, I've tried to incorporate the suggestions and to respond to the criticisms various reviewers and readers have offered. I've continued to expand and update the book, trying to take account of new material, new arguments, new data. In the last edition, I added a chapter on gender and politics and paid more and closer attention to issues surrounding bisexuality and transgenderism. This edition features a new section on transgender individuals. I also added box features throughout the book. "Oh Really?" dispels some myths about what I call the "interplanetary theory of gender"—that men are from Mars and women from Venus—with some critical questions about some often silly speculation. "Compared to What?" offers a wider context for some empirical phenomena that we observe in the United States, on the premise that seeing how we stack up compared to other nations will show the side variations in gendered experiences and, in so doing, underline further the "binary" opposition of Martians and Venusians. A new box feature called "Read All About It" directly links the text with the corresponding chapter in *The Gendered Society Reader*. Thus, readers can still use the text and the *Reader* separately, but those who want to adopt both have some connective tissue between them spelled out in the text.

This background suggests some of the ways that this book is a work in progress. Not a week goes by that I don't hear from a colleague or a student who is using the book and has a question, a comment, a suggestion, or a criticism. I wish I could have incorporated everyone's suggestions (well, not *everyone's!);* all engage me in the never-ending conversation about gender and gender inequality of which this book is but a small part.

It's ironic that as each edition comes close to completion, my identities as a writer and father are brought into sharper relief. As I completed the second edition, I remarked that people were constantly asking if having a son has forced me to change my views about biological difference. (It hasn't; if anything, watching the daily bombardment of messages about gender to which my son is constantly subjected, my constructionist ideas have grown stronger. Anything that was so biologically "natural" wouldn't need such relentless—and relentlessly frantic—reassertion.)

Let me share one experience to illustrate. As my son Zachary's eighth birthday approached, his mother and I asked what sort of theme he wanted for his party. For the previous two years, we'd had a skating party at the local rink—the rink where his hockey team skated early on Saturday mornings. He rejected that idea. "Been there and done that, Dad" was the end of that. "And besides, I skate there all the time."

Other themes that other boys in his class had recently had—indoor sports activities, a Red Bulls soccer game, secret agent treasure hunt—were also summarily rejected. What could he possibly want? "A dancing party," he said finally. "One with a disco ball."

His mother and I looked at each other. "A dancing party?" we asked. "But Zachary, you're only eight."

"Oh, no, not like a 'dancing' party like that," he said, making air quotation marks. "I mean like Cotton Eye Joe and the Virginia Reel and Cha-Cha Slide and like dance games."

So a dancing party it was—for twenty-four of his closest friends (his school encourages inviting everyone to the party). An even split of boys and girls. All twelve girls danced their heads off. "This is the best party ever!" shouted Grace. The other girls squealed with delight. Four of the boys, including Zachary, danced right along with the girls. They had a blast.

Four other boys walked in, checked out the scene, and immediately walked over to a wall, where they folded their arms across their chests and leaned back. "I don't dance," said one. "Yuck," said another. They watched, periodically tried to disrupt the dancing, seemed to make fun of the dancers, stuffed themselves with snacks, and had a lousy time.

Four other boys began the afternoon by dancing happily, with not a hint of self-consciousness. But then they saw the leaners, the boys propped up against the wall. One by one these dancers stopped, went over to the wall, and watched.

But they couldn't stay for long. They kept looking at the kids dancing their hilarious line dances, or the freeze dance, and they inched their way back, dancing like fiends, only to stop, notice the passive leaners again, and drift back to the wall.

Back and forth they went all afternoon, alternatingly exhilarated and exasperated, joyously dancing and joylessly watching. My heart ached for them as I watched them pulled between being children and being "guys."

Or is it between being *people* and being *guys*? People capable of a full range of pleasures—from smashing an opposing skater into the boards and that down-on-the-knee fist-pump after scoring a goal, to do-si-doing your partner or that truly inane faux lassoing in Cotton Eye Joe. Or guys, for whom pleasure now becomes defined as making fun of other people's joy.

Poised between childhood and adult masculinity, these boys were choosing, and one could see how agonizing it was. They hated being on the sidelines, yet stayed impervious until they could stand it no longer. But once they were back on the dance floor, they were piercingly aware that they were now the objects of ridicule.

This is the price we pay to be men: the suppression of joy, sensuality, and exuberance. It is meager compensation to feel superior to the other chumps who have the audacity to enjoy themselves. I pray my dancing fool of a son will resist the pull of that wall. His is the dance of childhood.

It is this "other" side of boys, lives—not that they will become men—but that they are boys, children, and we daily watch what is also so *naturally* and obviously hardwired systematically excised from boys' lives. The demands of boyhood, which have nothing whatever to do with evolutionary imperatives or brain chemistry, cripple boys, forcing them to renounce those feelings and suppress and deny the instinct to care. And those who deviate will be savagely punished.

This anecdote illustrates some of the issues in this book, in familial miniature—issues of *ideology, inequality,* and *identity.* I hope that this book contributes to exposing and exploring the full range of those issues. And that we enjoy ourselves along the way.

ACKNOWLEDGMENTS

The editorial and marketing team at Oxford University Press, and especially Sherith Pankratz, Katy Albis, Meredith Keffer, and Micheline Frederick, have been, as always, terrific to work with. I have relied on the critical reviews by colleagues who have adopted the book (and also by those who haven't) to help me try and say it clearly and correctly.

I would also like to thank the reviewers of the sixth edition, who provided me with helpful feedback and suggestions:

- Nena Sechler Craven, Delaware State University
- Kathryn Keller, Montclair State University
- Janet Lever, California State University, Los Angeles
- Gregory Maddox, Southern Illinois University Carbondale
- Kathleen O'Reilly, Three Rivers Community College
- Erin A. Smith, University of Texas at Dallas
- Gretta Stanger, Tennessee Technological University
- Michelle Tellez, Northern Arizona University

I would also like to thank Bethany Coston, Helana Darwin, Lisa Cox Hall, Julie Hartman-Linck, and Michelle Deming for their comments on specific parts of the manuscript.

I am grateful to Robert Cserni for research assistance.

And I rely constantly on the support of my colleagues and friends, and the love of my family.

I've been fortunate to spend a significant amount of time in Scandinavia, where a commitment to greater gender equality seems encoded in Nordic DNA. I'm grateful to the many colleagues I've met along the way, many of whom have become dear friends. I'm grateful for their warmth, hospitality, and the conviction that the phrase "activist-scholar" need not be an oxymoron. As a Visiting Professor at the University of Oslo, I look forward to continuing the conversation. Helan Går!

INTRODUCTION

Human Beings: An Engendered Species

In no country has such constant care been taken as in America to trace two clearly distinct lines of action for the two sexes, and to make them keep pace with the other, but in two pathways which are always different.

—ALEXIS DE TOCQUEVILLE, *DEMOCRACY IN AMERICA* (1835)

Daily, we hear how men and women are different. We hear that we come from different planets. They say we have different brain chemistries, different brain organization, different hormones. They say our different anatomies lead to different destinies. They say we have different ways of knowing, listen to different moral voices, have different ways of speaking and hearing each other.

You'd think we were different species, like, say, lobsters and giraffes, or Martians and Venusians. In his best-selling book, pop psychologist John Gray informs us that not only do women and men communicate differently, but also they "think, feel, perceive, react, respond, love, need, and appreciate differently."[1] It's a miracle of cosmic proportions that we ever understand one another!

Yet, despite these alleged interplanetary differences, we're all together in the same workplaces, where we are evaluated by the same criteria for raises, promotions, bonuses, and tenure. We sit in the same classrooms, eat in the same dining halls, read the same books, and are subject to the same criteria for grading. We live in the same houses, prepare and eat the same meals, read the same newspapers, and tune in to the same television programs.

What I have come to call this "interplanetary" theory of complete and universal **gender difference** is also typically the way we explain another universal phenomenon: **gender inequality**. Gender is not simply a system of classification, by which biological males and biological females are sorted, separated, and socialized into equivalent sex roles. Gender also expresses the universal inequality between women and men. When we speak about gender we also speak about hierarchy, power, and inequality, not simply difference.

So the two tasks of any study of gender, it seems to me, are to explain both difference and inequality or, to be alliterative, *difference* and *dominance*. Every general explanation of gender must address two central questions and their ancillary derivative questions.

First: *Why is it that virtually every single society differentiates people on the basis of gender?* Why are women and men perceived as different in every known society? What are the differences that are perceived? Why is gender at least one—if not the central— basis for the division of labor?

Second: *Why is it that virtually every known society is also based on male dominance?* Why does virtually every society divide social, political, and economic resources unequally between the genders? And why is it that men always get more? Why is a gendered division of labor also an unequal division of labor? Why are women's tasks and men's tasks valued differently?

It is clear, as we shall see, that there are dramatic differences among societies regarding the type of gender differences, the levels of gender inequality, and the amount of violence (implied or real) that are necessary to maintain both systems of difference and domination. But the basic facts remain: *Virtually every society known to us is founded upon assumptions of gender difference and the politics of gender inequality.*

On these axiomatic questions, two basic schools of thought prevail: **biological determinism** and **differential socialization**. We know them as "nature" and "nurture," and the question of which is dominant has been debated for a century in classrooms, at dinner parties, by political adversaries, and among friends and families. Are men and women different because they are "hardwired" to be different, or are they different because they've been taught to be? Is biology destiny, or is it that human beings are more flexible and thus subject to change?

Most of the arguments about gender difference begin, as will this book, with biology (in chapter 2). Women and men *are* biologically different, after all. Our reproductive anatomies are different, and so are our reproductive destinies. Our brain structures differ, our brain chemistries differ. Our musculature is different. Different levels of different hormones circulate through our different bodies. Surely, these add up to fundamental, intractable, and universal differences, and these differences provide the foundation for male domination, don't they?

The answer is an unequivocal maybe. Or, perhaps more accurately, yes and no. There are very few people who would suggest that there are no differences between males and females. At least, I wouldn't suggest it. What social scientists call *sex differences* refers precisely to that catalog of anatomical, hormonal, chemical, and physical differences between women and men. But even here, as we shall see, there are enormous ranges of femaleness and maleness. Though our musculature differs, plenty of women are physically stronger than plenty of men. Though on average our chemistries are different, it's not an all-or-nothing proposition—women do have varying levels of androgens, and men have varying levels of estrogen in their systems. And though our brain structure may be differently lateralized, males and females both do tend to use both sides of their brain. And it is far from clear that these biological differences automatically and inevitably lead men to dominate women. Could we not imagine, as some writers already have, a culture in which women's biological abilities to bear and nurse children might be seen as the expression of such ineffable power—the ability to create life—that strong men wilt in impotent envy?

In fact, in order to underscore this issue, most social and behavioral scientists now use the term "gender" in a different way than we use the term "sex." "Sex" refers to the biological apparatus, the male and the female—our chromosomal, chemical, anatomical organization. "Gender" refers to the meanings that are attached to those differences within a culture. "Sex" is male and female; "gender" is masculinity and femininity— what it means to be a man or a woman. Even the Supreme Court understands this distinction. In a 1994 case, Justice Antonin Scalia wrote:

> The word "gender" has acquired the new and useful connotation of cultural or attitudinal characteristics (as opposed to physical characteristics) distinctive to the sexes. That is to say, gender is to sex as feminine is to female and masculine is to male.[2]

And whereas biological sex varies very little, gender varies enormously. What it means to possess the anatomical configuration of male or female means very different things depending on where you are, who you are, and when you are living.

It fell to anthropologists to detail some of those differences in the meanings of masculinity and femininity. What they documented is that gender means different things to different people—that it varies cross-culturally. (I discuss and review the anthropological evidence in chapter 3.) Some cultures, like our own, encourage men to be stoic and to prove their masculinity. Men in other cultures seem even more preoccupied with demonstrating sexual prowess than American men. Other cultures prescribe a more relaxed definition of masculinity, based on civic participation, emotional responsiveness, and the collective provision for the community's needs. And some cultures encourage women to be decisive and competitive, whereas others insist that women are naturally passive, helpless, and dependent. What it meant to be a man or a woman in seventeenth-century France and what it means among Aboriginal peoples in the Australian outback at the turn of the twenty-first century are so far apart that comparison is difficult, if not impossible. The differences between two cultures are often greater than the differences between the two genders. If the meanings of gender vary from culture to culture and vary within any one culture over historical time, then to understand gender we must employ the tools of the social and behavioral sciences and history.

The other reigning school of thought that explains both gender difference and gender domination is *differential socialization*—the "nurture" side of the equation.

Men and women are different because we are taught to be different. From the moment of birth, males and females are treated differently. Gradually we acquire the traits, behaviors, and attitudes that our culture defines as "masculine" or "feminine." We are not necessarily born different: We become different through this process of socialization.

Nor are we born biologically predisposed toward gender inequality. Domination is not a trait carried on the Y chromosome; it is the outcome of the different cultural valuing of men's and women's experiences. Thus, the adoption of masculinity and femininity implies the adoption of "political" ideas that what women do is not as culturally important as what men do.

Developmental psychologists have also examined the ways in which the meanings of masculinity and femininity change over the course of a person's life. The issues confronting a man about proving himself and feeling successful will change, as will the social institutions in which he will attempt to enact those experiences. The meanings of femininity are subject to parallel changes, for example, among prepubescent women, women in childbearing years, and postmenopausal women, as they are different for women entering the labor market and those retiring from it.

Although we typically cast the debate in terms of *either* biological determinism *or* differential socialization—nature versus nurture—it may be useful to pause for a moment to observe what characteristics they have in common. Both schools of thought share two fundamental assumptions. First, both "nature lovers" and "nurturers" see women and men as markedly different from each other—truly, deeply, and irreversibly different. (Nurture does allow for some possibility of change, but it still argues that the process of socialization is a process of making males and females different from each other—differences that are normative, culturally necessary, and "natural.") And both schools of thought assume that the differences *between* women and men are far greater and more decisive (and worthy of analysis) than the differences that might be observed *among* men or *among* women. Thus, both nature lovers and nurturers subscribe to some version of the **interplanetary theory of gender difference**.

Second, both schools of thought assume that gender domination is the inevitable outcome of gender difference, that difference causes domination. To the biologists, it may be because pregnancy and lactation make women more vulnerable and in need of protection, or because male musculature makes men more adept hunters, or because testosterone makes them more aggressive with other men and with women, too. Or it may be that men have to dominate women in order to maximize their chances to pass on their genes. Psychologists of "gender roles" tell us that, among other things, men and women are taught to devalue women's experiences, perceptions, and abilities and to overvalue men's.

I argue in this book that both of these propositions are inadequate. First, I hope to show that the differences between women and men are not nearly as great as are the differences among women or among men. Many perceived differences turn out to be differences based less on gender than on the social positions people occupy. Second, I will argue that gender difference is the product of gender inequality and not the other way around. In fact, gender difference is the chief outcome of gender inequality, because it is through the idea of difference that inequality is legitimated.

As one sociologist recently put it, "the very creation of difference is the foundation on which inequality rests."[3]

Using what social scientists have come to call a "social constructionist" approach—I explain this in chapter 5—I will make the case that neither gender difference nor gender inequality is inevitable in the nature of things or, more specifically, in the nature of our bodies. Nor is difference—and domination—explainable solely by reference to differential socialization of boys and girls into sex roles typical of men and women.

When proponents of both nature and nurture positions assert that gender inequality is the inevitable outcome of gender difference, they take, perhaps inadvertently, a political position that assumes that inequality may be lessened or that its most negative effects may be ameliorated, but that it cannot be eliminated—precisely because it is based upon intractable differences. On the other hand, to assert, as I do, that the exaggerated gender differences that we see are not as great as they appear and that they are the result of inequality allows a far greater political latitude. By eliminating gender inequality, we will remove the foundation upon which the entire edifice of gender difference is built.

What will remain, I believe, is not some nongendered androgynous gruel, in which differences between women and men are blended and everyone acts and thinks in exactly the same way. Quite the contrary. I believe that as gender inequality decreases, the differences among people—differences grounded in race, class, ethnicity, age, sexuality, *as well as* gender—will emerge in a context in which all of us can be appreciated for our individual uniqueness as well as our commonality.

MAKING GENDER VISIBLE FOR BOTH WOMEN AND MEN

To make my case, I shall rely upon a dramatic transformation in thinking about gender that has occurred over the past thirty years. In particular, three decades of pioneering work by feminist scholars, both in traditional disciplines and in women's studies, have made us aware of the centrality of gender in shaping social life. We now know that gender is one of the central organizing principles around which social life revolves. Until the 1970s, social scientists would have listed only class and race as the master statuses that define and proscribe social life. If you wanted to study gender in the 1960s in social science, for example, you would have found but one course designed to address your needs—Marriage and the Family—which was sort of the "Ladies Auxiliary" of the social sciences. There were no courses on gender. But today, gender has joined race and class in our understanding of the foundations of an individual's identity. Gender, we now know, is one of the axes around which social life is organized and through which we understand our own experiences.

In the past thirty years, feminist scholars properly focused most of their attention on women—on what Catharine Stimpson has called the "omissions, distortions, and trivializations" of women's experiences—and the spheres to which women have historically been consigned, like private life and the family.[4] Women's history sought to rescue from obscurity the lives of significant women who had been ignored or whose work had been minimized by traditional androcentric scholarship and to examine the everyday lives of women in the past—the efforts, for example, of laundresses, factory workers, pioneer homesteaders, or housewives to carve out lives of meaning and dignity in a world controlled by men. Whether the focus has been on the exemplary or the ordinary, though, feminist scholarship has made it clear that gender is a central axis in women's lives.

But when we think of the word "gender," what gender comes to mind? It is not unusual to find, in courses on history of gender, psychology of gender, or sociology of gender, that the classroom is populated almost entirely by women. It's as if only women had gender and were therefore interested in studying it. Occasionally, of course, some brave young man will enroll in a women's studies class. You'll usually find him cringing in the corner, in anticipation of feeling blamed for all the sins of millennia of patriarchal oppression.

It's my intention in this book to build upon the feminist approaches to gender by also making masculinity visible. We need, I think, to integrate men into our curriculum. Because it is *men*—or rather masculinity—who are invisible.

"What?!" I can hear you saying. "Did he just say 'integrate men into our curriculum'? Men are invisible? What's he talking about?! Men aren't invisible. They're everywhere."

And, of course, that's true. Men are ubiquitous in universities and professional schools and in the public sphere in general. And it's true that if you look at the college curriculum, every course that doesn't have the word "women" in the title is about men. Every course that isn't in "women's studies" is de facto a course in "men's studies"—except we usually call it "history," "political science," "literature," "chemistry."

But when we study men, we study them as political leaders, military heroes, scientists, writers, artists. Men, themselves, are invisible *as men*. Rarely, if ever, do we see a course that examines the lives of men as men. What is the impact of gender on the lives of these famous men? How does masculinity play a part in the lives of great artists, writers, presidents, and so on? How does masculinity play out in the lives of "ordinary" men—in factories and on farms, in union halls and large corporations? On this score, the traditional curriculum suddenly draws a big blank. Everywhere one turns there are courses about men, but virtually no information on masculinity.

Several years ago, this yawning gap inspired me to undertake a cultural history of the idea of masculinity in America, to trace the development and shifts in what it has meant to be a man over the course of our history.[5] What I found is that American men have been very articulate in describing what it means to be a man and in seeing whatever they have done as a way to prove their manhood, but that we hadn't known how to hear them.

Integrating gender into our courses is a way to fulfill the promise of women's studies—by understanding men as gendered as well. In my university, for example, the course on nineteenth-century British literature includes a deeply "gendered" reading of the Brontës that discusses their feelings about femininity, marriage, and relations between the sexes. Yet not a word is spoken about Dickens and masculinity, especially about his feelings about fatherhood and the family. Dickens is understood as a "social problem" novelist, and his issue was class relations—this despite the fact that so many of Dickens's most celebrated characters are young boys who have no fathers and who are searching for authentic families. And there's not a word about Thomas Hardy's ambivalent ideas about masculinity and marriage in, say, *Jude the Obscure.* Hardy's grappling with premodernist conceptions of an apathetic universe is what we discuss. And my wife tells me that in her nineteenth-century American literature class at Princeton, gender was the main topic of conversation when the subject was Edith Wharton, but the word was never spoken when they discussed Henry James, in whose work gendered anxiety erupts variously as chivalric contempt, misogynist rage, and sexual ambivalence. James, we're told, is "about" the form of the novel, narrative technique, the stylistic powers of description and characterization. Certainly not about gender.

So we continue to act as if gender applied only to women. Surely the time has come to make gender visible to men. As the Chinese proverb has it, the fish are the last to discover the ocean.

This was made clear to me in a seminar on feminism I attended in the early 1980s.[6] In that seminar, in a discussion between two women, I first confronted this invisibility of gender to men. During one meeting, a white woman and a black woman were discussing whether all women are, by definition, "sisters," because they all have essentially the same experiences and because all women face a common oppression by men. The white woman asserted that the fact that they are both women bonds them, in spite of racial differences. The black woman disagreed.

"When you wake up in the morning and look in the mirror, what do you see?" she asked.

"I see a woman," replied the white woman.

"That's precisely the problem," responded the black woman. "I see a *black* woman. To me, race is visible every day, because race is how I am *not* privileged in our culture. Race is invisible to you, because it's how you are privileged. It's why there will always be differences in our experience."

At this point in the conversation, I groaned—more audibly, perhaps, than I had intended. Because I was the only man in the room, someone asked what my response had meant.

"Well," I said, "when I look in the mirror, I see a human being. I'm universally generalizable. As a middle-class white man, I have no class, no race, no gender. I'm the generic person!"

Sometimes, I like to think that it was on that day that I *became* a middle-class white man. Sure, I had been all those before, but they had not meant much to me. Until then, I had thought myself generic, universally generalizable. Since then, I've begun to understand that race, class, and gender don't refer only to other people, who are marginalized by race, class, or gender privilege. Those terms also describe me. I enjoyed the privilege of invisibility. The very processes that confer privilege to one group and not another group are often invisible to those upon whom that privilege is conferred. What make us marginal or powerless are the processes we see. Invisibility is a privilege in another sense—as a luxury. Only white people in our society have the luxury not to think about race every minute of their lives. And only men have the luxury to pretend that gender does not matter.

Consider another example of how power is so often invisible to those who have it. Many of you have e-mail addresses, and you send e-mail messages to people all over the world. You've probably noticed that there is one big difference between e-mail addresses in the United States and e-mail addresses of people in other countries: Their addresses end with a "country code." So, for example, if you were writing to someone in South Africa, you'd put "za" at the end or "jp" for Japan or "uk" for England (United Kingdom) or "de" for Germany (Deutschland). But when you write to people in the United States, the e-mail address ends with "edu" for an educational institution, "org" for an organization, "gov" for a federal government office, and "com" or "net" for commercial Internet providers. Why is it that the United States doesn't have a country code?

It is because when you are the dominant power in the world, everyone else needs to be named. When you are "in power," you needn't draw attention to yourself as a specific entity, but, rather, you can pretend to be the generic, the universal, the generalizable. From the point of view of the United States, all other countries are "other" and thus need to be named, marked, noted. Once again, privilege is invisible. In the world of the Internet, as Michael Jackson sang, "We are the world."

There are consequences to this invisibility: Privilege, as well as gender, remains invisible. And it is hard to generate a politics of inclusion from invisibility. The **invisibility of privilege** means that many men, like many white people, become defensive and angry when confronted with the statistical realities or the human consequences of racism or sexism. Because our privilege is invisible, we may become defensive. Hey, we may even feel like victims ourselves. Invisibility "creates a neurotic oscillation between a sense of entitlement and a sense of unearned privilege," as journalist Edward Ball put it, having recently explored his own family's history as one of the largest slave-owning families in South Carolina.[7]

The continued invisibility of masculinity also means that the gendered standards that are held up as the norm appear to us to be gender-neutral. The illusion of gender neutrality has serious consequences for both women and men. It means that men can maintain the fiction that they are being measured by "objective" standards; for women, it means that they are being judged by someone else's yardstick. At the turn of the twentieth century, the great sociologist Georg Simmel underscored this issue when he wrote:

> We measure the achievements and the commitments . . . of males and females in terms of specific norms and values; but these norms are not neutral, standing above the contrasts of the sexes; they have themselves a male character . . . The standards of art and the demands of patriotism, the general mores and the specific social ideas, the equity of practical judgments and the objectivity of theoretical knowledge . . . all these categories are formally generically human, but are in fact masculine in terms of their actual historical formation. If we call ideas that claim absolute validity objectivity binding, then it is a fact that in the historical life of our species there operates the equation: objective = male.[8]

Simmel's theoretical formulation echoes in our daily interactions. Recently, I was invited to be a guest lecturer in a course on sociology of gender taught by one of my female colleagues. As I entered the lecture hall, one student looked up from her notes and exclaimed, "Finally, an objective opinion." Now, I'm neither more nor less "objective" than my colleagues, but, in this student's eyes, I was seen as objective—the disconnected, disembodied, deracinated, degendered voice of scientific and rational objectivity. I am what objectivity looks like! (One ironic result is that I could probably say more outlandish things in a classroom than my female colleagues could.

If a female, or African American, professor were to make a statement such as, "White men are privileged in American society," our students might respond by saying, "Of course, you'd say that. You're biased." They'd see such a normative statement as revealing the inherent biases of gender or race, a case of special pleading. But when I say it? As objective fact, transmitted by an objective professor, they'll probably take notes.)

Such an equation that "objective = male" has enormous practical consequences in every arena of our lives, from the elementary school classroom to professional and graduate schools and in every workplace we enter. As Simmel writes, "Man's *position of power* does not only assure his relative superiority over the woman but it assures that his standards become generalized as generically human standards that are to govern the behavior of men and women alike."[9]

THE CURRENT DEBATE

I believe that we are, at this moment, having a national debate about masculinity in this country—but that we don't know it. For example, what gender comes to mind when I invoke the following current American problems: "teen violence," "gang violence," "suburban violence," "drug violence," "violence in the schools"? And what gender comes to mind when I say the words "suicide bomber" or "terrorist hijacker"?

Of course, you've imagined men. And not just any men—but younger men, in their teens and twenties, and relatively poorer men, from the working class or lower middle class.

But how do our social commentators discuss these problems? Do they note that the problems of youth and violence are really problems of young *men* and violence? Do they ever mention that everywhere ethnic nationalism sets up shop, it is young men who are the shopkeepers? Do they ever mention masculinity at all?

Now, imagine that these were all women—all the ethnic nationalists, the militias, the gay-bashers. Would that not be *the* story, the *only* story? Would not a gender analysis be at the center of every single story? Would we not hear from experts on female socialization, frustration, anger, premenstrual syndrome, and everything else under the sun? But the fact that these are men earns nary a word.

Take one final example. What if it had been young girls who opened fire on their classmates in West Paducah, Kentucky; in Pearl, Mississippi; in Jonesboro, Arkansas; or in Springfield, Oregon? And what if nearly all the children who died were boys? Do you think that the social outcry would demand that we investigate the "inherent violence" of southern culture? Or simply express dismay that young "people" have too much access to guns? And yet no one seemed to mention that the young boys who actually committed those crimes were simply doing—albeit in dramatic form at a younger age—what American men have been taught to do for centuries when they are upset and angry. Men don't get mad; they get even. (I explore the gender of violence in chapter 14.)

I believe that until we make gender visible for both women and men we will not, as a culture, adequately know how to address these issues. That's not to say that all we have to do is address masculinity. These issues are complex, requiring analyses of the political economy of global economic integration, of the transformation of social classes, of urban poverty and hopelessness, of racism. But if we ignore masculinity—if we let it remain invisible—we will never completely understand them, let alone resolve them.

THE PLURAL AND THE POWERFUL

When I use the term "gender," then, it is with the explicit intention of discussing both masculinity and femininity. But even these terms are inaccurate because they imply that there is one simple definition of masculinity and one definition of femininity. One of the important elements of a social constructionist approach—especially if we intend to dislodge the notion that gender differences alone are decisive—is to explore the differences *among* men and *among* women, because, as it turns out, these are often more decisive than the differences between women and men.

Within any one society at any one moment, several meanings of masculinity and femininity coexist. Simply put, not all American men and women are the same. Our experiences are also structured by class, race, ethnicity, age, sexuality, region. Each of these axes modifies the others. Just because we make gender visible doesn't mean that we make these other organizing principles of social life invisible. Imagine, for example, an older, black, gay man in Chicago and a young, white, heterosexual farm boy in Iowa. Wouldn't they have different definitions of masculinity? Or imagine a twenty-two-year-old wealthy, Asian-American, heterosexual woman in San Francisco and a poor, white, Irish Catholic lesbian in Boston. Wouldn't their ideas about what it means to be a woman be somewhat different?

If gender varies across cultures, over historical time, among men and women within any one culture, and over the life course, can we really speak of masculinity or femininity as though they were constant, universal essences, common to all women and to all men? If not, gender must be seen as an ever-changing fluid assemblage of meanings and behaviors. In that sense, we must speak of **masculinities** and **femininities** and thus recognize the different definitions of masculinity and femininity that we construct. By pluralizing the terms, we acknowledge that masculinity and femininity mean different things to different groups of people at different times.

At the same time, we can't forget that all masculinities and femininities are not created equal. American men and women must also contend with a particular definition that is held up as the model against which we are expected to measure ourselves. We thus come to know what it means to be a man or a woman in our culture by setting our definitions in opposition to a set of "others"—racial minorities, sexual minorities. For men, the classic "other" is, of course, women. It feels imperative to most men that they make it clear—eternally, compulsively, decidedly—that they are unlike women.

For most men, this is the "hegemonic" definition—the one that is held up as the model for all of us. The hegemonic definition of masculinity is "constructed in relation to various subordinated masculinities as well as in relation to women," writes sociologist R. W. Connell. The sociologist Erving Goffman once described this hegemonic definition of masculinity like this:

> In an important sense there is only one complete unblushing male in America: a young, married, white, urban, northern, heterosexual, Protestant, father, of college education, fully employed, of good complexion, weight, and height, and a recent record in sports . . . Any male who fails to qualify in any one of these ways is likely to view himself—during moments at least—as unworthy, incomplete, and inferior.[10]

Women contend with an equally exaggerated ideal of femininity, which Connell calls "emphasized femininity." **Emphasized femininity** is organized around compliance with gender inequality and is "oriented to accommodating the interests and desires of men." One sees emphasized femininity in "the display of sociability rather than technical competence, fragility in mating scenes, compliance with men's desire for titillation and ego-stroking in office relationships, acceptance of marriage and childcare as a response to labor-market discrimination against women."[11] Emphasized femininity exaggerates gender difference as a strategy of "adaptation to men's power" stressing empathy and nurturance; "real" womanhood is described as "fascinating," and women are advised that they can wrap men around their fingers by knowing and playing by the "rules." In one research study, an eight-year-old boy captured this emphasized femininity eloquently in a poem he wrote:

> If I were a girl, I'd have to attract a guy
> wear makeup; sometimes.
> Wear the latest style of clothes and try to be likable.
> I probably wouldn't play any physical sports like football or soccer.
> I don't think I would enjoy myself around men
> in fear of rejection
> or under the pressure of attracting them.[12]

GENDER DIFFERENCES AS "DECEPTIVE DISTINCTIONS"

The existence of multiple masculinities and femininities dramatically undercuts the idea that the gender differences we observe are due solely to differently gendered people occupying gender-neutral positions. Moreover, that these masculinities and femininities are arrayed along a hierarchy, and measured against one another, buttresses the argument that domination creates and exaggerates difference.

The interplanetary theory of gender assumes, whether through biology or socialization, that women act like women, no matter where they are, and that men act like men, no matter where they are. Psychologist Carol Tavris argues that such binary thinking leads to what philosophers call the "law of the excluded middle," which, as she reminds us, "is where most men and women fall in terms of their psychological qualities, beliefs, abilities, traits and values."[13] It turns out that many of the differences between women and men that we observe in our everyday lives are actually not *gender* differences at all, but rather differences that are the result of being in different positions or in different arenas. It's not that gendered individuals occupy these ungendered positions, but rather that the positions themselves elicit the behaviors we see as gendered. The sociologist Cynthia Fuchs Epstein calls these "**deceptive distinctions**" because, although they appear to be based on gender, they are actually based on something else.[14]

Here's a good example. Take math. Aggregate differences in girls' and boys' scores on standardized math tests have led people to speculate that whereas males have a natural propensity for arithmetic figures, females have a "fear of math." Couple this with their "fear of success" in the workplace and you might find that women manage money less effectively—with less foresight, less calculation, less care. The popular writer Colette Dowling, author of the best-selling 1981 book *The Cinderella Complex* (a book that claimed that underneath their apparent ambition, competence, and achievement, women "really" are waiting for Prince Charming to rescue them and carry them off into a romantic sunset, a future in which they can be as passive and helpless as they secretly want to be), interviewed sixty-five women in their late fifties about money matters and found that only two had *any* investment plans for their retirements. Broke and bankrupt after several best-sellers and single again herself, Dowling argues that this relates to "conflicts with dependency. Money savvy is connected with masculinity in our culture," she told an interviewer. "That leaves women with the feeling that if they want to take care of themselves and are good at it, the quid pro quo is they'll never hook up with a relationship." Because of ingrained femininity, women end up shooting themselves in the foot.[15]

But such assertions fly in the face of all available research, argues the financial expert Jane Bryant Quinn, herself the author of a best-seller about women and money. "It *is* more socially acceptable for women not to manage their money," she told the same interviewer. "But the Y chromosome is not a money management chromosome. In all the studies, if you control for earnings, age and experience, women are the same as men. At twenty-three, out in the working world staring at a 401(k) plan, they are equally confused. But if those women quit working, they will know less and less about finance, while the man, who keeps working, will know more and more."[16] So it is our experience, not our gender, that predicts how we'll handle our retirement investments.

What about those enormous gender differences that some observers have found in the workplace (the subject of chapter 9)? Men, we hear, are competitive social climbers who seek advancement at every opportunity; women are cooperative team-builders who shun competition and may even suffer from a "fear of success." But the pioneering study by Rosabeth Moss Kanter, reported in *Men and Women of the Corporation*, indicated that gender mattered far less than opportunity. When women had the same opportunities, networks, mentors, and possibilities for advancement, they behaved just as the men did. Women were not successful because they lacked opportunities, nor because they feared success; when men lacked opportunities, they behaved in stereotypically "feminine" ways.[17]

Finally, take our experiences in the family, which I examine in chapter 6. Here, again, we assume that women are socialized to be nurturing and maternal, men to be strong and silent, relatively emotionally inexpressive arbiters of justice—that is, we assume that women do the work of "mothering" because they are socialized to do so. And again, sociological research suggests that our behavior in the family has somewhat less to do with gender socialization than with the family situations in which we find ourselves.

Research by sociologist Kathleen Gerson, for example, found that gender socialization was not very helpful in predicting women's family experiences. Only slightly more than half the women who were primarily interested in full-time motherhood were, in fact, full-time mothers; and only slightly more than half the women who were primarily interested in full-time careers had them. It turned out that marital stability, husbands' income, women's workplace experiences, and support networks were far more important than gender socialization in determining which women ended up full-time mothers and which did not.[18]

On the other side of the ledger, research by sociologist Barbara Risman found that despite a gender socialization that downplays emotional responsiveness and nurturing, most single fathers are perfectly capable of "mothering." Single fathers do not hire female workers to do the typically female tasks around the house: They do those tasks themselves. In fact, Risman found few differences between single fathers and mothers (single or married) when it came to what they did around the house, how they acted with their children, or even their children's emotional and intellectual development. Men's parenting styles were virtually indistinguishable from women's, a finding that led Risman to argue that "men can mother and that children are not necessarily better nurtured by women than by men."[19]

These findings also shed a very different light on other research. For example, some recent researchers found significant differences in the amount of stress that women and men experience on an everyday basis. According to the researchers, women reported higher levels of stress and lower numbers of "stress-free" days than did men. David Almeida and Ronald Kessler sensibly concluded that this was not a biologically based difference, a signal of women's inferiority in handling stress, but rather an indication that women had more stress in their lives, because they had to juggle more family and work issues than did men.[20]

Almeida and Kessler's findings were reported with some fanfare in newspapers, which with few exceptions recounted new significant gender differences. But what Almeida and Kessler actually found was that women, as Kessler noted, "tend to the home, the plumber, their husband's career, their jobs, and oh yes, the kids." By contrast, for men, it's "How are things at work? The end."[21] And they found this by asking married couples, both husbands and wives, about their reactions to such "stressors." What do you think their findings would have been had they asked single mothers and single fathers the same questions? Do you think they would have found any significant gender differences at all? More likely, they would have found that trying to juggle the many demands of a working parent is likely to generate enormous stress both for men and for women. Again, it's the structure, not the gender, that generates the statistical difference.

Based on all this research, you might conclude, as does Risman, that "if women and men were to experience identical structural conditions and role expectations, empirically observable gender differences would dissipate."[22] I am not fully convinced. There *are* some differences between women and men, after all. Perhaps, as this research suggests, those differences are not as great, decisive, or impervious to social change as we once thought. But there are some differences. It will be my task in this book to explore both those areas where there appear to be gender differences but where there are, in fact, few or no differences, and those areas where gender differences are significant and decisive.

THE MEANING OF MEAN DIFFERENCES

Few of the differences between women and men are "hardwired" into all males to the exclusion of all females or vice versa. Although we can readily observe differences between women and men in rates of aggression, physical strength, math or verbal achievement, caring and nurturing, or emotional expressiveness, it is not true that all males and no females are aggressive, physically strong, and adept at math and science and that all females and no males are caring and nurturing, verbally adept, or emotionally expressive. What we mean when we speak of gender differences are mean differences, differences in the average scores obtained by women and men.

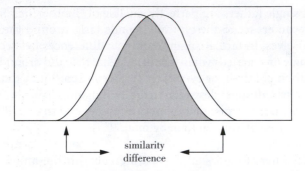

similarity
difference

Figure 1.1. Schematic rendering of the overlapping distributions of traits, attitudes, and behaviors by gender. Although mean differences might be evident on many characteristics, these distributions suggest far greater similarity between women and men and far greater variability among men and among women.

These mean scores tell us something about the differences between the two groups, but they tell us nothing about the distributions themselves, the differences *among* men or *among* women. Sometimes these distributions can be enormous: There are large numbers of caring or emotionally expressive men and of aggressive and physically strong women. (See figure 1.1.) In fact, in virtually all the research that has been done on the attributes associated with masculinity or femininity, the differences among women and among men are far greater than the mean differences between women and men. We tend to focus on the mean differences, but they may tell us far less than we think they do.

What we think they tell us, of course, is that women and men are different, from different planets. This is what I will call the "interplanetary theory of gender difference"—that the observed mean differences between women and men are decisive and that they come from the fact that women and men are biologically so physically different.

For example, even the idea that we are from different planets, that our differences are deep and intractable, has a political dimension: To call the "other" sex the "opposite" sex obscures the many ways we are alike. As the anthropologist Gayle Rubin points out:

> Men and women are, of course, different. But they are not as different as day and night, earth and sky, yin and yang, life and death. In fact from the standpoint of nature, men and women are closer to each other than either is to anything else— for instance mountains, kangaroos, or coconut palms . . . Far from being an expression of natural differences, exclusive gender identity is the suppression of natural similarities.[23]

The interplanetary theory of gender difference is important not because it's right—in fact, it is wrong far more often than it is right—but because, as a culture, we seem desperately to *want* it to be true. That is, the real sociological question about gender is not the sociology of gender differences—explaining the physiological origins of gender difference—but rather the sociology of knowledge question that explores why gender difference is so important to us, why we cling to the idea of gender difference so tenaciously, why, I suppose, we shell out millions of dollars for books that "reveal" the deep differences between women and men but will probably never buy a book that says, "Hey, we're all Earthlings!"

That, however, is the message of this book. Virtually all available research from the social and behavioral sciences suggests that women and men are not from Venus and Mars, but rather are both from planet Earth. We're not opposite sexes, but neighboring sexes—we have far more in common with each other than we have differences. We pretty much have the same abilities and pretty much want the same things in our lives.

THE POLITICS OF DIFFERENCE AND DOMINATION

Whether we believe that gender difference is biologically determined or is a cultural formation, the interplanetary theory of gender difference assumes that gender is a property of individuals, that is, that gender is a component of one's identity. But this is only half the story. I believe that individual boys and girls become gendered—that is, we learn the "appropriate" behaviors and traits that are associated with hegemonic masculinity and exaggerated femininity, and then we each, individually, negotiate our own path in a way that feels right to us. In a sense, we each "cut our own deal" with the dominant definitions of masculinity and femininity. That's why we are so keenly attuned to, and so vigorously resist, gender stereotypes—because we believe that they do not actually encompass our experiences.

But we do not cut our own deal by ourselves in gender-neutral institutions and arenas. The social institutions of our world—workplace, family, school, politics—are also gendered institutions, sites where the dominant definitions are reinforced and reproduced and where "deviants" are disciplined. We become gendered selves in a gendered society.

Speaking of a gendered society is not the same thing as pointing out that rocket ships and skyscrapers bear symbolic relationships to a certain part of the male anatomy. Sometimes function takes precedence over symbolic form. (Do you really think women would explore outer space in a machine shaped like a bagel?) It is also only partially related to the way we use metaphors of gender to speak of other spheres of activity—the way, for example, the worlds of sports, sex, war, and work each appropriate the language of the other spheres.

When we say that we live in a gendered society we imply that the organizations of our society have evolved in ways that reproduce both the differences between women and men and the domination of men over women. Institutionally, we can see how the structure of the workplace is organized around demonstrating and reproducing masculinity: The temporal organization and the spatial organization of work both depend upon the separation of spheres (distance between work and home and the fact that women are the primary child-care providers).

As it did with respect to the invisibility of gendered identity, assuming institutional gender neutrality actually serves to maintain the gender politics of those institutions. And it underscores the way we often assume that if you allow individuals to express a wider range of gender behaviors, they'll be able to succeed in those gender-neutral institutions. So we assume that the best way to eliminate gender inequality in higher education or in the workplace is to promote sameness—in other words, we're unequal only because we're different.

This, however, creates a political and personal dilemma for women in gendered institutions. It's a no-win proposition for women when they enter the workplace, the military, politics, or sports—arenas that are already established to reproduce and sustain masculinity. To the extent that they become "like men" in order to succeed, they are seen as having sacrificed their femininity. Yet to the extent to which they refuse to sacrifice their femininity, they are seen as different, and thus gender discrimination is legitimate as the sorting of different people into different slots.[24] Women who succeed are punished for abandoning their femininity—rejected as potential partners, labeled as "dykes," left off the invitation lists. The first women who entered the military or military colleges or even Princeton and Yale when these institutions went coeducational in the late 1960s were seen as being "less" feminine, as being unsuccessful as women. Yet had they been more "successful" as women, they would have been seen as less capable soldiers or students.[25] Thus gender inequality creates a double bind for women—a double bind that is based on the assumption of gender difference and the assumption of institutional gender neutrality.

There's a more personal side to this double bind. Often, men are perplexed by the way their wives have closets filled with clothes, yet constantly complain that they have "nothing to wear." Men often find this behavior strange, probably the behavior of someone who must have come from another planet. After all, we men typically alternate among only three or four different colors of shirts and suits, which we match with perhaps five or six different ties. Navy blue, charcoal gray, black—what could be so difficult about getting dressed?

But women who work enter a gendered institution in which everything they wear "signifies" something. So they look at one business-like dress and tell themselves, "No, this is too frumpy. They'll never take me seriously as a woman in this dress!" So they hold up a slinkier and tighter outfit and think, "In this little number, all they'll see in me is a woman, and they'll never take me seriously as an employee." Either way—corporate frump or sexy babe—women lose, because the workplace is, itself, gendered, and standards of success, including dressing for success, are tailored to the other sex.

Both difference and domination are produced and reproduced in our social interactions, in the institutions in which we live and work. Though the differences between us are not as great as we often assume, they become important in our expectations and observations. It will be my task in this book to examine those differences—those that are real and important—as well as to reveal those that are neither real nor important. I will explore the ways in which gender inequality provides the foundation for assumptions of gender difference. And, finally, I will endeavor to show the impact of gender on our lives—how we become gendered people living gendered lives in a gendered society.

KEY TERMS

Biological Determinism
Deceptive Distinctions
Differential Socialization
Emphasized Femininity
Femininities

Gender Difference
Gender Inequality
Interplanetary Theory
　of Gender Difference

Invisibility of Privilege
Masculinities

Explanations *of* Gender

ORDAINED *by* NATURE

Biology Constructs the Sexes

A devil, a born devil, on whose nature
Nurture can never stick! On whom my pains,
Humanely taken, all, all lost, quite lost!
— SHAKESPEARE, *THE TEMPEST* (ACT IV, SCENE 1)

Oprah: "Do you think society will change if it were proven beyond a shadow of a
doubt that you were born that way?"

Gay twin: "It would be easier . . . the acceptance, but you understand that people
still don't accept Blacks and Hispanics and handicapped . . . Gays are right in there
with them . . . people don't accept obese people."

Oprah (chagrined): "I forgot about that. Let's take a break."

Aside from his exasperated cry of "women—what do they want?" Sigmund
Freud's most famous line is probably the axiom "Anatomy is destiny."
Though it's not clear that Freud ever intended that it be taken literally, a large
number of people believe that the differences in male and female anatomy are
decisive and provide the basis for the differences in men's and women's experiences. One recent researcher proclaimed his belief that "the differences between
the males and females of our species will ultimately be found in the cell

arrangements and anatomy of the human."[1] To biologists, the source of human behavior lies neither in our stars nor in ourselves, as Caesar had suggested to Brutus—but rather in our cells.

Biological explanations hold a place of prominence in our explanations of both gender *difference* and gender *inequality*. First, biological explanations have the ring of "true" science to them: Because their theories are based on "objective scientific facts," the arguments of natural scientists are extraordinarily persuasive. Second, biological explanations seem to accord with our own observations: Women and men *seem* so different to us most of the time—so different, in fact, that we often appear to be from different planets.

There's also a certain conceptual tidiness to biological explanations, because the social arrangements between women and men (gender inequality) seem to stem directly and inevitably from the differences between us. Biological arguments reassure us that what *is* is what should be, that the social is natural. Finally, such reassurances tell us that these existing inequalities are not our fault, that no one is to blame, really. We cannot be held responsible for the way we act—hey, it's biological! (Such claims are made by conservatives and liberals, by feminists and misogynists, and by homophobes and gay activists.) What's more, if these explanations are true, no amount of political initiative, no amount of social spending, no great policy upheavals will change the relationships between women and men.

This chapter will explore some of the biological evidence that is presented to demonstrate the natural, biologically based differences between the sexes and the ways in which social and political arrangements (inequality) directly flow from those differences. Biological differences can tell us much about the ways in which men and women behave. The search for such differences can also tell us a lot about our culture—about what we want so desperately to believe and why we want to believe it.

BIOLOGICAL DIFFERENCES, THEN AND NOW

The search for the biological origins of the differences between women and men is not new. What is new, at least for the past few centuries, is that scientists have come to play the central role in exploring the natural differences between males and females.

Prior to the nineteenth century, most explanations of gender difference had been the province of theologians. God had created man and woman for different purposes, and those reproductive differences were decisive. Thus, for example, did the Reverend John Todd warn against woman suffrage, which would "reverse the very laws of God," and its supporters, who tried to convince woman that she would "find independence, wealth and renown in man's sphere, when your only safety and happiness is patiently, lovingly, and faithfully performing the duties and enacting the relations of your own sphere."[2]

By the late nineteenth century, under the influence of Darwin and the emerging science of evolutionary biology, scientists jumped into the debate, wielding their latest discoveries. Some argued that woman's normal biological processes made her unfit for the public world of work and school. For example, in his book *A Physician's Counsels to Woman in Health and Disease* (1871), Dr. W. C. Taylor cautioned women to stay home and rest for at least five or six days a month:

We cannot too emphatically urge the importance of regarding these monthly returns as periods of ill health, as days when the ordinary occupations are to be suspended or modified . . . Long walks, dancing, shopping, riding and parties should be avoided at this time of month invariably and under all circumstances.[3]

In his pathbreaking work *On the Origin of Species* (1859), Darwin had posed several questions. How do certain species come to be the way they are? Why is there such astonishing variety among those species? Why do some species differ from others in some ways and remain similar in other ways? He answered these questions with the law of **natural selection**. Species adapt to their changing environments. Those species that adapt well to their environments are reproductively successful, that is, their adaptive characteristics are passed on to the next generation, whereas those species that are less adaptive do not pass on their characteristics. Within any one species, a similar process occurs, and those individuals who are best suited to their environment pass on their genes to the next generation. Species are always changing, always adapting.

Such an idea was theologically heretical to those who believed that God had created all species, including human beings, intact and unchanging. And Darwin did believe that just as the species of the lower animal world evidence differences between males and females, so, too, do human beings. "Woman seems to differ from man in mental disposition, chiefly in her greater tenderness and lesser selfishness," he wrote in *The Descent of Man*. Men's competitiveness, ambition, and selfishness "seem to be his natural and unfortunate birthright. The chief distinction in the intellectual powers of the two sexes is shown by man's attaining to a higher eminence, in whatever he takes up, than can woman—whether requiring deep thought, reason, or imagination, or merely the uses of the senses and the hands."[4]

No sooner had the biological differences between women and men been established as scientific fact than writers and critics declared all efforts to challenge social inequality and discrimination against women to be in violation of the "**laws of nature**." Many writers argued that women's efforts to enter the public sphere—to seek employment, to vote, to enter colleges—were misguided because they placed women's social and political aspirations over the purposes for which their bodies had been designed. Women were not to be *excluded* from voting, from the labor force, or from higher education as much as they were, as the Reverend Todd put it, "to be exempted from certain things which men must endure."[5] This position was best summed up by a participant in a debate about woman suffrage in Sacramento, California, in 1880:

I am opposed to woman's sufferage [sic] on account of the burden it will place upon her. Her delicate nature has already enough to drag it down. Her slender frame, naturally weakened by the constant strain attendant upon her nature is too often racked [sic] by diseases that are caused by a too severe tax upon her mind. The presence of passion, love, ambition, is all too potent for her enfeebled condition, and wrecked health and early death are all too common.[6]

Social scientists quickly jumped on the biological bandwagon—especially social Darwinists, who shortened the time span necessary for evolution from millennia to one or two generations and who causally extended Darwin's range from ornithology to human beings. In their effort to legitimate social science by allying it with natural law, social Darwinists applied Darwin's theory in ways its originator had never imagined, distorting his ideas about natural selection to claim decisive biological differences among races, nations, families, and, of course, between women and men. For example, the eminent French sociologist Gustav LeBon, who would later become famous for his theory of the collective mind and the irrationality of the crowd, believed that the differences between women and men could be explained by their different brain structure. He wrote in 1879:

> In the most intelligent races, as among the Parisians, there are a large number of women whose brains are closer in size to those of gorillas than to the most developed of male brains . . . All psychologists who have studied the intelligence of women . . . recognize today that they represent the most inferior forms of human evolution and that they are closer to children and savages than to an adult civilized man. They excel in fickleness, inconstancy, absence of thought and logic, and incapacity to reason. Without doubt, there exist some distinguished women, very superior to the average man, but they are as exceptional as the birth of any monstrosity, as, for example, of a gorilla with two heads . . .[7]

Much of the debate centered on whether or not women could be educated, especially in colleges and universities. One writer suggested that a woman "of average brain" could attain the same standards as a man with an average brain "only at the cost of her health, of her emotions, or of her morale." Another prophesized that women would grow bigger and heavier brains and that their uteruses would shrink if they went to college. Perhaps the most famous social scientist to join this discussion was Edward C. Clarke, Harvard's eminent professor of education. In his best-selling book *Sex in Education: or; A Fair Chance for the Girls* (1873), Clarke argued that women should be exempted from higher education because of the tremendous demands made upon their bodies by reproduction. If women went to college, Clarke predicted, they would fail to reproduce, and it would require "no prophet to foretell that the wives who are to be mothers in our republic must be drawn from transatlantic homes."[8] (Clarke's invocation of the threat to civilization posed by immigrants reproducing faster than native-born whites is common to the conflation of racism and sexism of the era.)

The evidence for such preposterous biological claims? Simple. It turned out that college-educated women were marrying less often and bearing fewer children than were non-college-educated women. It must have been those shriveled wombs and heavier brains. And it also appeared that 42 percent of all women admitted to mental institutions were college-educated, compared with only 16 percent of the men. Obviously, college education was driving women crazy. Today, of course, we might attribute this difference in fertility or in mental illness among college-educated women to enlarged opportunities or frustrated ambitions, respectively, but not to shrinking wombs. Clarke's assertions remain a striking example of the use of correlational aggregate social science data for decidedly political purposes.

The implicit conservatism of such arguments was as evident at the beginning of the twentieth century as it is now. "How did woman first become subject to man as she is now all over the world?" asked James Long. "By her nature, her sex, just as the negro is and always will be, to the end of time, inferior to the white race, and therefore, doomed to subjection; but happier than she would be in any other condition, just because it is the law of her nature."[9] Such sentiments echo back across the centuries when political leaders invoke biological differences as the basis for **sex discrimination**. When Newt Gingrich became Speaker of the House of Representatives in 1995, he argued against women's participation in the military because "females have biological problems staying in a ditch for 30 days because they get infections and don't have upper body strength," whereas males "are basically little piglets, you drop them in the ditch, they roll around in it, doesn't matter . . . Males are biologically driven to go out and hunt giraffes."[10]

READ ALL ABOUT IT!

Nature and Nurture: Not an Either/Or, but a Both/And . . .

We tend to think that it's "nature" versus "nurture"—either that we're entirely born this way or that we're entirely the product of socialization and upbringing. In her brief essay "Where Does Gender Come From?" the eminent biologist Anne Fausto-Sterling makes clear that from the earliest moments of life, nature and nurture interact to produce the conditions in which we create and express our gendered selves.

Today, serious biological arguments generally draw their evidence from three areas of research: (1) **evolutionary theory**, from sociobiology to "evolutionary psychology," (2) **brain research**, and (3) **endocrinological research** on sex hormones, before birth and again at puberty. The latter two areas of research are also used to describe the biologically based differences between heterosexuals and homosexuals, differences that are, as we shall see, often expressed in gender terms.[11]

OH? REALLY •

Why are boys and girls color-coded? Why pink for girls and blue for boys? Did you know it was biological? After asking 171 British adult men and women to choose in a forced-choice experiment, two biologists proposed this grander evolutionary explanation: that women, as gatherers, developed a preference for red hues, like pink, because they needed to identify ripe berries and fruit. Further, women "needed to discriminate subtle changes in skin color due to emotional states and social-sexual signals" in "their roles as care-givers and 'empathizers'" (p. R625).

Not only is this dreadful history—for centuries, boys and girls were dressed identically, and when they were first gender-coded, in the 1870s and 1880s, in the United States, the preference was pink and red for *boys* and blue for *girls*—but it's also incredibly bad evolutionary science. What sorts of "subtle changes in skin color" were we likely to find on the African savannah, where the original humans hunted and gathered? Do these biologists think that those early humans were white Englishmen and women, who blushed when embarrassed?

Source: Anya Hurlbert and Yazhu Ling, "Biological Components of Sex Differences in Color Preference" in *Current Biology*, 17(16), August 21, 2007.

THE EVOLUTIONARY IMPERATIVE: FROM SOCIAL DARWINISM TO SOCIOBIOLOGY AND EVOLUTIONARY PSYCHOLOGY

Evolutionary biologists since Darwin have abandoned the more obviously political intentions of the social Darwinists, but the development of a new field of **sociobiology** in the 1970s revived evolutionary arguments. Edward Wilson, a professor of entomology at Harvard, helped to found this school of thought, expanding his original field of expertise to include human behavior as well as bugs. All creatures, Wilson argued, "obey" the "**biological principle**," and all temperamental differences (personalities, cultures) derive from the biological development of creatures undergoing the pressure of evolutionary selection. The natural differences that result are the source of the social and political arrangements we observe today. Eventually, he confidently predicted, the social sciences and humanities would "shrink to specialized branches of biology."[12]

One major area that sociobiologists have stressed is the differences in male and female sexuality, which they believe to be the natural outgrowth of centuries of evolutionary development. Evolutionary success requires that all members of a species consciously or unconsciously desire to pass on their genes. Thus males and females develop reproductive "strategies" to ensure that our own genetic code passes on to the next generation. Sociobiologists often use a language of intention and choice, referring to "strategies" that make it sound as if our genes were endowed with instrumental rationality and that each of our cells acted in a feminine or masculine way. Thus they seem to suggest that the differences we observe between women and men today have come from centuries of advantageous evolutionary choices. As Wilson and fellow sociobiologist Richard Dawkins put it, "Female exploitation begins here." Culture has little to do with it, as Wilson argues, because "the genes hold culture on a leash."[13]

Take, for example, the size and the number of the reproductive cells themselves. Add to that the relative cost to male and female in producing a healthy offspring, and—presto!—you have the differences between male and female sexual behavior at a typical college mixer this weekend. "He" produces billions of tiny sperm; "she" produces one gigantic ovum. For the male, **reproductive success** depends upon his ability to fertilize a large number of eggs. Toward this end, he tries to fertilize as many eggs as he can. Thus males have a "natural" propensity toward promiscuity. By contrast, females require only one successful mating before their egg can be fertilized, and therefore they tend to be extremely choosy about which male will be the lucky fellow. What's more, females must invest a far greater amount of energy in gestation and lactation and have a much higher reproductive "cost," which their reproductive strategies would reflect. Females, therefore, tend to be monogamous, choosing the male who will make the best parent. "A woman seeks marriage to monopolize not a man's sexuality, but, rather, his political and economic resources, to ensure that her children (her genes) will be well provided for," writes journalist Anthony Layng. As sociobiologist Donald Symons puts it, women and men have different "**sexual psychologies**":

> Since human females, like those of most animal species, make a relatively large investment in the production and survival of each offspring—and males can get away with a relatively small one—they'll approach sex and reproduction, as animals do, in rather different ways from males . . . Women should be more choosy and more

hesitant, because they're more at risk from the consequences of a bad choice. And men should be less discriminating, more aggressive and have a greater taste for variety of partners because they're *less* at risk.

Not surprisingly, Symons notes, this is "what we find":

Selection favored the basic male tendency to be aroused sexually by the sight of females. A human female, on the other hand, incurred an immense risk, in terms of time and energy, by becoming pregnant, hence selection favored the basic female tendency to discriminate with respect both to sexual partners and to the circumstances in which copulation occurred."[4]

The dilemma for these monogamous females, then, is how to extract parental commitment from these recalcitrant rogue males, who would much prefer to be out fertilizing other females than home with the wife and kids. Women's strategy is to "hold out" for emotional, and therefore parental, commitment *before* engaging in sexual relations. Thus not only are women predetermined to be monogamous, but also they link sexual behavior to emotional commitment, extracting from those promiscuous males all manner of promises of love and devotion before they will finally "put out." Thus males are hardwired genetically to be promiscuous sexual predators, ever on the prowl for new potential sexual conquests, whereas females have a built-in biological tendency toward monogamy, fantasies of romantic love and commitment coupled with sexual behavior, and a certain sexual reticence that can be overcome only by chivalric male promises of fealty and fidelity.

READ ALL ABOUT IT!

Millennia of Evolution Created the Gender Differences We See Today

After millennia, we think it's hardwired that men be aggressive and competitive, and women nurturing and demure. In her essay "Caveman Masculinity," sociologist Martha McCaughey argues that such assertions really read history backward, taking contemporary observations and reading them back into evolutionary history. In so doing, they make contemporary arrangements seem inevitable—which ignores all the myriad historical twists and turns, as well as the range of contemporary variations on the issue. But actually, it also disrespects our cave-dwelling ancestors, pigeonholing them into crass stereotypes and disregarding any information that doesn't fit our pat theories. Turns out Fred and Wilma had a more complex social structure than we give them credit for having.

Other evolutionary arguments examine other aspects of reproductive biology to spell out the differences between men and women and thereby explain the social inequality between them. For example, the separation of spheres seems to have a basis far back in evolutionary time. "In hunter-gatherer societies, men hunt and women stay at home. This strong bias persists in most agricultural and industrial societies, and, on that ground alone, appears to have a genetic origin," writes Edward Wilson. "My own guess is that the genetic bias is intense enough to cause a substantial division of labor in the most free and most egalitarian of future societies."[15] Lionel Tiger and Robin Fox emphasize the social requirements for the evolutionary transition to a hunting-and-gathering society. First, the hunting band must have solidarity and cooperation, which require bonding among the hunters. Women's biology—especially their menstrual cycle—puts them at a significant disadvantage for such consistent cooperation, and the presence of women would disrupt the cooperation necessary among the men and insinuate competition and aggression. They also are possessed of a "maternal instinct." Thus it would make sense for men to hunt and for women to remain back home raising the children.[16]

From such different reproductive strategies and evolutionary imperatives come different temperaments, the different personalities we observe in women and men. The newest incarnation of sociobiology is called "**evolutionary psychology**," which declares an ability to explain psychological differences between women and men through their evolutionary trajectories. Men are understood to be more aggressive, controlling, and managing—skills that were honed over centuries of evolution as hunters and fighters. After an equal amount of time raising children and performing domestic tasks, women are said to be more reactive, more emotional, "programmed to be passive."[17]

These differences lead us to completely different contemporary mating strategies as well. Psychologist David Buss surveyed more than ten thousand people from thirty-seven different cultures around the world and found strikingly similar things about what women and men want in a mate. It can't be culturally specific if they all agree, can it? In every society, females placed a high premium on signs of economic prosperity, whereas men placed their highest premium on youth and beauty, whose signal traits were large breasts and ample hips—in other words, signs of fertility. Sexual selection maximizes reproductive success, right? Well, maybe. Actually, Indian *men* ranked being a good financial provider higher than women did in Finland, Great Britain, Norway, Spain, and Australia (which are, incidentally, among the most "gender equal"

OH? **REALLY** • We all know that women are choosier than men.

And for evidence, just look at the world of "speed-dating"—sessions where you have about a dozen "dates" lasting about five minutes each. At these sessions, the women sit at tables, waiting to be approached, and the men circulate (or "rotate"), looking for a potential partner. Men are far less choosy, listing far more women on their potential date list than women list men. Men on the prowl, women being choosy.

Except it has nothing to do with gender at all. When psychologists Eli Finkel and Paul Eastwick reversed the roles, so that men stayed seated and women rotated, the results were exactly the opposite. Women were far less selective, and the men were far more selective.

It turns out, Finkel and Eastwick argued, that the mere fact of physically approaching someone as a potential date will make you less choosy and more likely to have a favorable impression of the person you approach.

Source: E. J. Finkel and P. W. Eastwick, "Arbitrary Social Norms and Sex Differences in Romantic Selectivity," *Psychological Science*, 20, 2009, pp. 1290–1295.

countries in the world). Does it interest you that although these traits were important, the single trait most highly valued by *both* women and men was love and kindness? Could it be that love, harmony, and kindness are even more important to our reproductive success than his sexual conquest and her monogamous reticence—that, in essence, **evolutionary success** depends more on our similarities than our differences?[18]

Finally, these differences also enable scientists to try to explain such behaviors as interspecies violence and aggression. In their book *A Natural History of Rape*, Thornhill and Craig Palmer amplify these arguments and make wildly unfounded assertions in the process. Rape, they write, is "a natural, biological phenomenon that is a product of human evolutionary heritage."[19] Males' biological predisposition is to reproduce, and their reproductive success comes from spreading their seed as far and wide as possible; women are actually the ones with the power because they get to choose which males will be successful. "But getting chosen is not the only way to gain sexual access to females," they write. "In rape, the male circumvents the females' choice."[20] Rape is the evolutionary mating strategy of losers, males who cannot otherwise get a date. Rape is an alternative to romance; if you can't always have what you want, you take what you need.

Don't blame the men, though—or even their genetic imperatives. It's really women's fault. "As females evolved to deny males the opportunity to compete at ovulation time, copulation with unwilling females became a feasible strategy for achieving copulation," write Richard Alexander and K. M. Noonan. Women, then, are biologically programmed to "hold out"—but they better not do it too long. If women were only a little bit more compliant, men wouldn't be forced to resort to rape as a reproductive tactic.[21]

EVOLUTIONARY PSYCHOLOGY—A JUST-SO STORY

Do these evolutionary arguments make sense? Does their evidence add up to basic, irreconcilable differences between women and men, made necessary by the demands of evolutionary adaptation? Although there is a certain intuitive appeal to these arguments—because they give our contemporary experiences the weight of history and science—there are simply too many convenient lapses in reasoning for us to be convinced.

The theory may tidily describe the intricate mating rituals of fruit flies or brown birds or *seem* applicable to an urban singles bar or the dating dynamics of high school and college students, but it is based on an interpretation of evidence that is selective and conforms to preconceived ideas. It is as if these sociobiologists observe what is normative—that men are more likely than women to separate love and sex, that men feel entitled to sexual contact with women, that men are more likely to be promiscuous—and read it back into our genetic coding. Such explanations always fall into teleological traps, reasoning backward to fill existing theoretical holes. It is so because it is supposed to be so. Besides, the time span is too short. Can we explain each single sexual encounter by such grand evolutionary designs? I would bet that most of our conscious "strategies" at college mixers have more immediate goals than to ensure our reproductive success.

Some arguments go far beyond what the data might explain and into areas that are empirically untestable. Biologist Richard Lewontin, a passionate critic of sociobiology, argues that "no evidence at all is presented for a genetic basis of these characteristics [religion, warfare, cooperation] and the arguments for their establishment by natural selection cannot be tested, since such arguments postulate hypothetical situations in human prehistory that are uncheckable." And fellow evolutionary biologist Stephen Jay Gould denies that there is "any direct evidence for genetic control of specific human social behavior."[22] "Genes don't cause behaviors," writes the neuroprimatologist Robert Sapolsky. "Sometimes, they influence them."[23]

Some sociobiological arguments seem to assume that only one interpretation is possible from the evidence. But there could be others. Psychologists Carol Tavris and Carole Wade, for example, ask why parents—women or men—would "invest" so much time and energy in their children when they could be out having a good time. Although sociobiologists argue that we are "hardwired" for such altruistic behavior, because our children are the repository of our genetic material, Tavris and Wade suggest that it may be simple economic calculation: In return for taking care of our offspring when they are young and dependent, we expect them to take care of us when we are old and dependent—a far more compact and tidy explanation.[24]

Some sociobiological arguments are based on selective use of data, ignoring those data that might be inconvenient. Which species should we use as the standard of measurement? Among chimpanzees and gorillas, for example, females usually leave home and transfer to new tribes, leaving the males at home with their mothers; among baboons, macaques, and langurs, however, it's the males who leave home to seek their fortune elsewhere. So which sex has the wanderlust, the natural predisposition to leave home? Sociobiologists tend to favor male-dominant species to demonstrate the ubiquity of male dominance. But there are other species. For example, baboons seem to be female-dominant, with females determining the stability of the group and deciding which males are trustworthy enough to be their "friends." Then there is the female chimpanzee. She has sex with lots of different males, often up to fifty times a day during peak estrus. She flirts, seduces, and does everything she can to attract males— whom she then abandons and moves on to the next customer. Would we say that such evidence demonstrates that females are genetically programmed toward promiscuity and males toward monogamy? Bonobos, our closest primate relatives, are remarkably communal, generous, and egalitarian—and very sexy.[25] And sociobiologists tend to ignore other behavior among primates. For example, sexual contact with same-sex others is "part of the normal sexual repertoire of all animals, expressed variously over the lifetime of an individual."[26] In fact, same-sex sexual contact is ubiquitous in the animal kingdom—ranging from bighorn sheep and giraffes, both of which have what can be described only as gay orgies, to dolphins, whales, manatees, and Japanese macaques and bonobos, which bond through "lesbian" sexual choices.[27] But few posit a natural predisposition toward homosexuality. "Simple minded analogies between human behavior and animal behavior are risky at best, irresponsibly goofy at worst," writes neurobiologist Simon LeVay, himself the author of some rather risky, at best, studies on gay brains (discussed later).[28]

Speaking of baboons, consider this. We all "know" that the so-called alpha male is the head of the pack, the guy who gets deference from the other males and sexual access to the choicest females. This is assumed to be the best evolutionary strategy: beat all the males and cavort with the most reproductively capable females. But actually, it's

Sociobiologists and evolutionary psychologists use a most gendered anthropomorphic language of motivation, cognition, and activity itself to describe our tiniest of cells. You've probably imagined sperm as hardy warriors swimming purposively upstream, against the current, on a suicide mission to fertilize that egg, or die. Here's what it *actually* looks like:

A wastefully huge swarm of sperm weakly flops along, its members bumping into walls and flailing aimlessly through thick strands of mucus. Eventually, through sheer odds of pinball-like bouncing . . . a few sperm end up close to an egg. As they mill around, the egg selects one and reels it in, pinning it down in spite of its efforts to escape. It's no contest, really. The gigantic hardy egg yanks the tiny sperm inside, distills out the chromosomes, and sets out to become an embryo.

Source: David Freedman, "The Aggressive Egg" in *Discover,* June 1, 1992.

also a recipe for high stress and the danger of an early death. Evolutionary biologist Laurence Gesquiere and his collegues studied so-called beta-male baboons, the guys who are a bit lower on the totem pole. They don't challenge the alphas (that would be suicidal), but they also have some status. As a result, they have far less stress. They don't fight much; they don't spend time guarding potential sexual mates. And they do get to mate with females, though not as much as the alphas. After all, as a journalist wrote, "When the alpha gets into another baboon bar fight, who's going to take the girl home?" As a result, they live longer and healthier lives—they do "pretty well for a long time," rather than "very well for a short time." Maybe the old Avis Rent-a-Car ad—that as the #2 car rental company "we try harder"—wasn't necessary. Maybe being #2 offers a longer and less stressful life.[29]

Some arguments are just plain wrong in light of empirical evidence. Take the argument about how women's menstrual cycle debilitates them so that they were inevitably and correctly left behind in the transition to hunting and gathering. Katherine Dalton's research on English schoolgirls showed that 27 percent got poorer test scores just before menstruation than at ovulation. (She does not say how much worse they did.) But 56 percent showed no change in test grades, and 17 percent actually performed better at premenstruation. And what about that "**maternal instinct**"? How do we explain the enormous popularity of **infanticide** as a method of birth control throughout Western history and the fact that it was women who did most of the baby killing? Infanticide has probably been the most commonly practiced method of birth control throughout the world. One historian reported that infanticide was common in ancient Greece and Rome and that "every river, dung heap and cesspool used to be littered with dead infants." In 1527, a priest commented that "the latrines resound with the cries of children who have been plunged into them."[30]

And finally, what is one to make of the argument that rape is simply sex by other means for reproductively unsuccessful males? Such arguments ignore the fact that most rapists are not interested in sex but rather in humiliation and violence, motivated more by rage than by lust. Most rapists have regular sex partners, quite a few are married. Many women well outside of reproductive age, either too young or too old, are raped. And why would some rapists hurt and even murder their victims, thus preventing the survival of the very genetic material that they are supposed to be raping in order to pass on? And why would some rapists be homosexual rapists, passing on their genetic material to those who could not possibly reproduce? And what about rape in prison? Using theories of selfish genes or evolutionary imperatives to explain human behavior cannot take us very far.

"Selection favored males who mated frequently," argue Thornhill and Palmer; therefore, "rape increased reproductive success."[31] But why should this be true? Might it not also be the case that being hardwired to be good lovers and devoted fathers enabled us to be reproductively successful? One might argue that selection favored males who mated *well*, because successful mating is more than spreading of seed. After all, human males are the only primates for whom skillful lovemaking, enhancing *women's* pleasure, is normative, at least in many societies. Being an involved father probably ensured reproductive success far better than did rape. After all, babies are so precious, so fragile that they need extraordinary—and extraordinarily long!—care and devotion. Infants conceived during rape would have a far lower chance of survival, which is probably one reason we invented love. Infants conceived in rape might well have been subject to infanticide—historically the most common form of birth control before the modern era.

The preposterous idea that rape is an evolutionary mating strategy for losers in the sexual marketplace is belied by the most common form of rape in the United States. Did you know that the majority of rapes in America have nothing whatever to do with reproduction? You know why? The victims are male. In January 2012, the U.S. Department of Justice released an estimate of the prevalence of sexual abuse in penitentiaries: 216,000. That's 216,000 *victims*, not incidences. These victims are often assaulted multiple times over the course of a year, meaning the number of actual rapes is significantly higher. Such rates make the United States the first country in the history of the world to count more men as rape victims than women. And Thornhill and Palmer's facile evolutionism is exposed as mere ideology.

But we can add an element to the equation that enables us to better explain why the United States has the highest rates of rape for *both* women and men. Psychologist Roy Baumeister and his colleagues suggest that a simplistic frustration-aggression model (he wants, can't have, and therefore takes) is inadequate to explain rape rates. There must be cultural permission—a sense of entitlement—that enables rape to take place. Their study of sexually coercive men showed that an inflated sense of entitlement, low empathy, and a view of heterosexuality as exploitive and competitive enabled the aggression. Men who may have been equally frustrated, but did not feel that sense of entitlement, were unlikely to rape. That sense of entitlement is not found in nature. It is carefully "nurtured" in culture. Thus nature and nurture must interact to produce the conditions and the motivation for sexual aggression.[32]

Is rape "natural"? Of course it is. As is *any* behavior or trait found among human primates. If it exists in nature, it's natural. Some "natural" beverages contain artificial—"social"—additives that give them their color, their texture, their taste, their "meaning" or "significance." This is equally true of rape. Telling us that it is natural tells us nothing about it except that it is found in nature.

Sociobiology and evolutionary psychology provide us with what Rudyard Kipling called a "just-so story"—an account that uses some evidence to tell us how, for example, an elephant got its trunk, or a tiger its stripes. Just-so stories are children's fables, understood by the reader to be fictions, but convenient, pleasant, and, ultimately, useful fictions.

Could we not use the same evidence and construct a rather different just-so story? Try this little thought experiment. Let's take the same evidence about sperm and eggs, about reproductive strategies, about different levels of parental investment that the sociobiologists use, and add a few others. Let's also remember that human females are the only primate females who do not have specified periods of estrus, that is, they are potentially sexually receptive at any time of their reproductive cycle, including when they are incapable of conception. What could be the evolutionary **reproductive "strategy"** of this? And let's also remember that the human clitoris plays no part whatsoever in human reproduction but is solely oriented toward sexual pleasure. And don't forget that in reality most women do not experience peaks of sexual desire during ovulation (which is what evolutionary biologists would predict, because women must ensure reproductive success) but actually just before and just after menstruation (when women are almost invariably infertile, though the ratio of female to male hormones is lowest).[33] And finally, let's not forget that when a baby is born, the identity of the mother is obvious, though that of the father is not. Until very recently, with the advent of DNA tests, fathers could never be entirely certain that the baby was theirs; after all, how do they know their partner had not had sexual contact with another male?

From this evidence one might adduce that human females are uniquely equipped biologically—indeed, that it is their sexual strategy—to enjoy sex simply for its physical pleasure and not for its reproductive potential. And if the reproductive goal of the female is to ensure the survival of her offspring, then it would make sense for her to deceive as many males as possible into thinking that the offspring was theirs. That way, she could be sure that all of them would protect and provide for the baby because none of them could risk the possibility of his offspring's death and the obliteration of his genetic material. So might not women's evolutionary "strategy" be promiscuity?[34]

One more bit of evidence is the difference between male and female orgasm. Whereas male orgasm is clearly linked to reproductive success, female orgasm seems to have been designed solely for pleasure; it serves no reproductive function at all. According to Elisabeth Lloyd, a philosopher of science at Indiana University, the capacity for female orgasm may be a holdover from parallel fetal development in the first eight or nine weeks of life. But its persistence may be that orgasm is a reproductive strategy for promiscuous females. Sexual pleasure and orgasm may encourage females to mate frequently and with multiple partners until they have an orgasm. The males, on the other hand, couldn't be sure the offspring was *not* theirs, so they would struggle to protect and provide. Thus, female orgasm might be part of women's evolutionary strategy—and making sure females do *not* enjoy sex too much might be males' evolutionary response![35]

Some of these issues seem to be present among the Bari people of Venezuela, where female promiscuity ensures that a woman's offspring stand a better chance of survival. Among the Bari, the man who impregnates the female is considered the primary father, but other men with whom the mother also has sex during her pregnancy consider themselves secondary fathers and spend a good deal of time making sure the child has enough fish or meat to eat.[36] And it may be not that far off from what we do as well. One recent study found that women reported that their partners increased their attentiveness and "monopolization" behavior—calling them often to check on their whereabouts, for example—just as they began to ovulate. But the women found that they fantasized far more about cheating on their partners at the same time. (They reported no increase whatever in sexual thoughts about their partners—so much for their evolutionary predisposition toward fidelity.) Although this suggests that the men had good reason to be more guarding and jealous, it also suggests that women "instinctively want to have sex with as many men as possible to ensure the genetic quality of their offspring, whereas men want to ensure that their own genes get reproduced," according to a journalist reporting on the story. Equally selfish genes and equally a "war between the sexes"—but one with a completely different interpretation.[37]

Another biological fact about women might make life even more confusing for males seeking to determine paternity. Martha McClintock's research about women's menstrual cycles indicated that in close quarters, women's cycles tend to become increasingly synchronous; that is, over time, women's cycles will tend to converge with those of their neighbors and friends. (McClintock noticed this among her roommates and friends while an undergraduate at Wellesley in the late 1960s.[38]) What's more, in cultures where artificial light is not used, all the women will tend to ovulate at the full moon and menstruate at the new moon. Although this might be an effective method of birth control in nonliterate societies (to prevent pregnancy, you must refrain from sex when the moon approaches fullness), it also suggests that unless women are controlled, paternity cannot be established definitively.[39]

If males were as promiscuous as females they would end up rather exhausted and haggard from running around hunting and gathering for all those babies who might *or might not* be their own. How were they to know, after all? In order to ensure that they did not die from exhaustion, males might "naturally" tend toward monogamy, extracting from women promises of fidelity before offering up a lifetime of support and protection to the potential offspring from those unions. Such males might invent ideals of female chastity, refuse to marry (sexually commit to) women who were not virgins, and develop ideologies of domesticity that would keep women tied to the household and children to prevent them from indulging in their "natural" disposition toward promiscuity.

In fact, there is some persuasive evidence on this front. Because getting pregnant is often difficult (it takes the average couple three or four months of regular intercourse to become pregnant), being a faithful and consistent partner would be a far better reproductive strategy for a male. "Mate guarding" would enable him to maximize his chances of impregnating the woman and minimize the opportunities for other potential sperm bearers.[40]

Of course, I'm not suggesting that this interpretation supplant the one offered by evolutionary psychologists. But the fact that one can so easily use the exact same biological evidence to construct an entirely antithetical narrative suggests that we should be very careful when the experts tell us there is only one interpretation possible from these facts. "Genes do not shout commands to us about our behavior," writes the celebrated ecologist Paul Ehrlich. "At the very most, they whisper suggestions."[41]

OH? REALLY•

Why do men want women to have an orgasm when they have sex? Here's a good example of how reliance on evolutionary theory leads to a rather circuitous argument. Psychologist William McKibbin and his colleagues found that the risk of "sperm competition"—when different men's sperm "compete" inside the woman to fertilize her egg—leads men who are happy in their relationships to be more concerned with their partner's orgasm (since female orgasm "may facilitate selective uptake"—that is, her orgasmic contractions may increase the possibility of conception). So let's get this straight: Since her orgasm *may* facilitate selective uptake, and since he may fear sperm competition (because, let's face it, sperm themselves do not experience anxiety or competition or any other emotion, because they are *cells*, for heaven's sake!), then, if he is emotionally invested in the relationship, he is more concerned with her sexual pleasure than had he just picked her up at a bar.

In science, we search for the most parsimonious explanation of some empirical phenomenon; that is, the simplest and least convoluted explanation. Evolutionary pseudoscience may lead us on a circuitous path, but I think we all know that a man is more likely to be concerned with his female partner's orgasm if he actually *likes* her, not if he's worried about some fantasized competitive sperm sprint.

Source: William F. McKibbin, Vincent M. Bates, Todd Shackelford, Christopher A. Hafen, and Craig W. LaMunyon, "Risk of Sperm Competition Moderates the Relationship Between Men's Satisfaction with Their Partner and Men's Interest in Their Partner's Copulatory Orgasm" in *Personality and Individual Differences*, 49, 2010, pp. 961–966.

"HIS" BRAIN AND "HER" BRAIN

Biologists have also focused on the brain to explain the differences between women and men. This approach, too, has a long history. In the eighteenth century, experts measured women's brains and men's brains and argued that because women's brains were smaller and lighter, they were inferior. Of course, it later turned out that women's brains were not smaller and lighter relative to body size and weight and thus were not predictive of any cognitive differences. The late nineteenth century was the first heyday of brain research, as researchers explored that spongy and gelatinous three-pound blob in order to discover the differences between whites and blacks, Jews and non-Jews, immigrants and "normal" or "real" Americans, criminals and law-abiding citizens. For example, the great sociologist Emile Durkheim succumbed to such notions when he wrote, "With the advance of civilization the brain of the two sexes has increasingly developed differently . . . This progressive gap between the two may be due both to the considerable development of the male skull and to a cessation and even a regression in the growth of the female skull." And another researcher argued that the brain of the average "grown-up Negro partakes, as regards his intellectual faculties, of the nature of the child, the female, and the senile White." (One can only speculate where this put older black women.) But despite the fact that none of these hypothesized differences turned out to have any scientific merit, they all satisfied political and racist assumptions.[42]

Brain research remains a particularly fertile field of study, and scientists continue their search for differences between women and men in their brains. One writes that "many of the differences in brain function between the sexes are innate, biologically determined, and relatively resistant to change through the influences of culture."

Popular books proclaim just how decisive these differences are. The male brain is "not so easily distracted by superfluous information"; it is a "tidier affair" than the female brain, which appears "less able to separate emotion from reason."[43] (Notice that these statements did not say—though they easily might have, based on the same evidence— that the female brain is capable of integrating *more* diverse sources of information and *better* able to synthesize feelings and thought.)

That brain research fits neatly into preconceived ideas about men's and women's roles is hardly a coincidence. In most cases, brain researchers (like many other researchers) find exactly what they are looking for, and what they are looking for are the brain-based differences that explain the observable behavioral differences between adult women and men. One or two historical examples should suffice. The "science" of **craniology** was developed in the late nineteenth century to record and measure the effect of brain differences among different groups. But the scientists could never agree on exactly which measures of the brain to use. They *knew* that men's brains had to be shown to be superior, but different tests yielded different results. For example, if one used the ratio of brain surface to body surface, then men's brains would "win"; but if one used the ratio of brain weight to body weight, then women's brains would appear superior. No scientist could rely on such ambiguity: More decisive methods had to be found to demonstrate that men's brains are superior.[44]

Test scores were no better as indicators. At the turn of the twentieth century, women were found to be scoring higher on comprehensive examinations at New York University. Because scientists "knew" that women are not as smart as men, some other explanation had to be sought. "After all, men are more intellectual than women, examination papers or no examination papers," commented the dean of the college, R. Turner. "Women have better memories and study harder, that's all. In tasks requiring patience and industry women win out. But when a man is both patient and industrious he beats a woman any day." (It is interesting to see that women's drive, ambition, and industriousness were used against them but that men were not faulted for impulsiveness, impatience, and laziness.) In the 1920s, when IQ tests were invented, women scored higher on those tests as well. So the experimenters changed the questions.[45]

Contemporary brain research has focused on three areas: (1) the differences between right hemisphere and left hemisphere, (2) the differences in the tissue that connects those hemispheres, and (3) the ways in which males and females use different parts of their brains for similar functions.[46]

Some scientists have noticed that the right and left hemispheres of the brain seem to be associated with different cognitive functions and abilities. Right-hemisphere dominance is associated with visual and spatial abilities, such as the ability to conceive of objects in space. Left-hemisphere dominance is associated with more practical functions, such as language and reading. Norman Geschwind and Peter Behan, for example, observed that sex differences begin in the womb when the male fetus begins to secrete testosterone that washes over the brain, selectively attacking parts of the left hemisphere and slowing its development. Thus, according to Geschwind, males tend to develop "superior right hemisphere talents, such as artistic, musical, or mathematical talent." Geschwind believes that men's brains are more lateralized, with one half dominating over the other, whereas women's brains are less lateralized, with both parts interacting more than in men's.[47]

One minor problem with this research, though, is that scientists can't seem to agree on which it is "better" to have and, not so coincidentally, which side of the brain dominates for which sex. In fact, they keep changing their minds about which hemisphere is superior and then, of course, assigning that superior one to men. Originally, it was the *left* hemisphere that was supposed to be the repository of reason and intellect, whereas the right hemisphere was the locus of mental illness, passion, and instinct. So males were thought to be overwhelmingly more left-brained than right-brained. By the 1970s, though, scientists had determined that the truth lay elsewhere and that the right hemisphere was the source of genius, talent, creativity, and inspiration, whereas the left hemisphere was the site of ordinary reasoning, calculation, and basic cognitive function. Suddenly males were hailed as singularly predisposed toward right-brainedness. One neuroscientist, Ruth Bleier, reanalyzed Geschwind and Behan's data and found that in over five hundred fetal brains from ten to forty-four weeks of gestation, the authors had found no significant sex differences—this despite the much-trumpeted testosterone bath.[48]

READ ALL ABOUT IT!

Male and female brains are wired so differently that there really are "his" and "her" brains. In "The Truth About Boys and Girls," neuroscientist Lise Eliot shows that tiny differences in the brain can become greater or lesser, depending on how different societies decide to treat boys and girls. Echoing the work of Fausto-Sterling, Eliot shows how some of these tiny differences are exaggerated, and some minimized, in contemporary society.

Perhaps it wasn't which half of the brain dominates, but rather the degree to which the brain was lateralized—that is, had a higher level of differentiation between the two hemispheres—that determined sex differences. Buffery and Gray found that female brains were more lateralized than male brains, which, they argued, interfered with spatial functioning and made women less capable at spatial tasks. That same year, Levy found that female brains were *less* lateralized than male brains, and so he argued that *less* lateralization interferes with spatial functioning. (There is virtually no current evidence for either of these positions, but that has not stopped most writers from believing Levy's argument.)[49] One recent experiment shows how the desperate drive to demonstrate difference actually leads scientists to misinterpret their own findings. In 1997, a French researcher, Jean Christophe Labarthe, tried to demonstrate sex differences in visual and spatial abilities. Two-year-old boys and girls were asked to build a tower and a bridge. For those of average birth weight or better (greater than 2,500 grams), there was no difference whatever in ability to build a tower, although 21 percent of the boys and only 8 percent of the girls could build a bridge. For children whose birth weight was less than 2,500 grams, though, there were no differences for either skill. From this skimpy data, Labarthe concludes that boys are better at bridge-building than girls—instead of the far more convincing (if less mediagenic) finding that birth weight affects visual and spatial functioning![50]

Some research suggests that males use only half their brains while performing some verbal tasks, such as reading or rhyming, whereas females draw on both sides of their brains. A recent experiment reveals as much about our desire for difference as about difference itself. Researchers from the Indiana University School of Medicine measured brain activity of ten men and ten women as they listened to someone read aloud a John Grisham thriller. A majority of the men showed exclusive activity on the left side of their brains, whereas the majority of the women showed activity on both sides of the brain. Although some might suggest that this provides evidence to women who complain that their husbands are only "half-listening" to them, the study mentions little about what the minority of males or females were doing—especially when the total number was only ten to begin with. Besides, what if they were listening instead to a Jane Austen novel? Might the males have "needed" both sides of their brain to figure out a plot that was a bit less action-packed? Would the females have been better able to relax that side of their brain that has to process criminal intrigue and murder?[51]

If these tacks weren't convincing, perhaps both males and females use both halves of their brains but use them *differently*. In their popular book detailing these brain differences, Jo Durden-Smith and Diane deSimone suggest that in the female left hemisphere, language tends to serve as a vehicle for communication, whereas for males that hemisphere is a tool for more visual-spatial tasks, like analytical reasoning. Similarly, they argue, in the right hemisphere males assign more neural space to visual-spatial tasks, whereas females have more room left over for other types of nonverbal communication skills, such as emotional sensitivity and intuition.[52]

But don't the differences in mathematical ability and reading comprehension provide evidence of different sides of the brain being more dominant among females and males? Although few would dispute that different sides of the brain account for different abilities, virtually all humans, both men and women, use both sides of their brains to reasonably good effect. If so, argues the neuropsychiatrist Jerre Levy, "then males may be at a double disadvantage in their emotional life. They may be emotionally less sophisticated. And because of the difficulty they may have in communicating between their two hemispheres, they may have restricted verbal access to their emotional world."[53]

It is true that males widely outnumber females at the genius end of the mathematical spectrum. But does that mean that males are, on average, more mathematically capable and females more verbally capable? Janet Hyde, a psychologist at the University of Wisconsin, has conducted a massive amount of research on this question. She reviewed 165 studies of verbal ability that included information about over 1.4 million people and included writing, vocabulary, and reading comprehension. She found no gender differences in verbal ability. But when she analyzed one hundred studies of mathematical ability, representing the testing of nearly four million students, she did find some modest gender differences. In the general studies, females outperformed males in mathematics, except in those studies designed only for the most precocious individuals.[54] What Hyde and her colleagues—and virtually every other researcher— found is that there is a far greater range of differences *among* males and *among* females than there is *between* males and females. That is to say that the variance within the group far outweighs the variance between groups, despite the possible differences between the mean scores of the two groups.

But what if it's not the differences between the hemispheres or even that males and females use the same hemispheres differently? Perhaps it's the connections *between* the hemispheres. Some researchers have explored the bundle of fibers known as the "corpus callosum" that connects the two hemispheres and carries information between them. A subregion of this connecting network, known as the "splenium," was found by one researcher to be significantly larger and more bulbous in shape in females. This study of fourteen brains at autopsy suggested that this size difference reflected less hemispheric lateralization in females than in males and that this affected visual and spatial functioning. But subsequent research failed to confirm this finding. One researcher found no differences in the size of the corpus callosum between males and females. What's more, in magnetic resonance imaging tests on living men and women, no differences were found between women and men.[55]

But that doesn't stop some popular writers from dramatic and facile extrapolation. Here's Robert Pool, from his popular work *Eve's Rib*: "Women have better verbal skills than men on average; the splenium seems to be different in women and men, in shape if not in size; and the size of the splenium is related to verbal ability, at least in women." And a recent popular book by psychologist Michael Gurian claims that only females with "boys' brains" can grow up to be architects because girls' brains are organized to promote nurturing, the love and caring for children. Not only is such a statement insulting to women—as if mathematical reasoning and spatial ability were somehow "beyond" them—but also it's insulting to men, especially to fathers who seem to be fully capable of nurturing children.[56]

But that's more or less typical. These sorts of apparent differences make for some pretty strange claims, especially about brain chemistry. For example, because boys' brains secrete slightly less serotonin, on average, than girls' brains, Michael Gurian claims that boys are "more impulsive" and "not as calm" as girls are in large classrooms. Although the variation among boys and among girls is significantly larger than any small difference between males and females, Gurian has no problem recommending educational policies that would "honor" that impulsivity. Even more astonishing is his claim, often echoed by John Gray, that during sex, males have a rush of oxytocin, a chemical that is linked to feelings of pleasure. In the throes of that "bonding hormone," a man is likely to blurt out "I love you," but it is only the effect of the chemical. If you're wondering why he doesn't call the next day, it's because the hormone's effect has worn off, not because, having scored, he's looking for the exit.[57]

The scientific evidence actually points in the other direction. In males, the amygdala, an almond-shaped part of the brain that responds to emotionally arousing information, is somewhat larger than it is in females. The neurons in this region, associated with emotions, make more numerous connections in males than in females, which produce some differences in the ways males and females react to stress. In one experiment, German researchers removed the newborn pups of degus, South American rodents akin to North American prairie dogs—an experience that is quite unsettling. The researchers measured the amount of serotonin in the pups. (Serotonin, a neurotransmitter, is a key chemical in mediating emotional behavior. Prozac and other selective serotonin reuptake inhibitors antidepressants increase serotonin functioning by inhibiting its reabsorption.) When the researchers allowed the pups to hear their mothers' calls during the separation, the males' serotonin levels rose, whereas the females' levels declined—that is, the females felt more anxiety, and their behavior was less calm and orderly during such a period of separation.[58]

Although this experiment might be interpreted to suggest why females are more often diagnosed with depression than are males—less serotonin to begin with and more reabsorbed into the brain—it also pays no attention to the different ways our cultures prescribe for males and females to express anxiety and cope with stress. If you tell one group, from day 1, that the way to handle stress and anxiety is to withdraw quietly, and you tell the other group that the only way to handle stress is to be loud and rambunctiously aggressive, it's a good guess that they will, by and large, follow orders. This may explain why depression is more likely to be diagnosed among girls and anxiety and aggression disorders more likely among boys.

Besides, the scientists themselves still don't agree. For example, one recent brain study at UC Irvine found differences in gray matter (which represents information processing centers) and white matter (which represents the connections between these centers) in males and females. Males had about 6.5 times more gray matter than females, and females had about 10 times more white matter than males. On the other hand, Simon Baron-Cohen, a British brain researcher, notes that the 9 percent difference in cerebrum size is due to the "larger total volume of white matter in men." Yet no one makes any claims that these differences lead to differences in general intelligence; indeed, the Irvine scientists insist there are none. Gray and white matter may be different, but the difference doesn't really make much of a difference.[59] Even neuropsychologist Doreen Kimura understands that "in the larger comparative context, the similarities between human males and females far outweigh the differences." And Jonathan Beckwith, professor of microbiology and molecular genetics at Harvard Medical School, argues that "even if they found differences, there is absolutely no way at this point that they can make a connection between any differences in brain structure and any particular behavior pattern or any particular aptitude."[60]

In her excellent dismantling of this brain pseudoscience, Lise Eliot, who actually *is* a neuroscientist, points to an even more "insidious" way that the real neuroscience of the brain is misused. Every credible researcher knows that brains change over a person's life, responding to social stimuli to actually change their neural pathways. So, over time, males, and females, brains diverge because of the activities that our societies ask them to do. But the research that posits these large innate differences are done on adults' brains, even *old* adults (postmortem), when the socially produced differences would be at their greatest—and then they are casually and uncritically "read" back onto the brains of infants, "ignoring the fundamental plasticity by which the brain learns anything."[61]

If there is no evidence for these arguments, why do they persist? One brain researcher, Marcel Kinsbourne, suggests that it is "because the study of sex differences is not like the rest of psychology. Under pressure from the gathering momentum of feminism, and perhaps in backlash to it, many investigators seem determined to discover that men and women 'really' are different. It seems that if sex differences do not exist, then they have to be invented."[62]

THE GAY BRAIN

One of the most interesting and controversial efforts by scientists who study the biological origins of behavior has been the search for origins of **sexual orientation**. Recent research on brain structure and endocrinological research on hormones have suggested a distinctly homosexual "essence," which will emerge regardless of the cultural conditions that shape its opportunities and experiences. This research on the origins of sexual *orientation* is related to research on the basis of sex differences between women and men because, culturally, we tend to understand sexuality in terms of gender. Gender stereotypes dominate the discussion of sexual orientation; we may assume, for example, that gay men are not "real" men, in other words, are not sufficiently masculine, identify with women, and even adopt feminine affects and traits. Similarly, we may assume that lesbians are insufficiently feminine, identify with and imitate men's behaviors, and so on. Homosexuality, our stereotypes tell us, is a *gender* "disorder."[63]

We have a century-long legacy from which we draw such stereotypic ideas. Homosexuality emerged as a distinct identity in the late nineteenth century, when it was regarded as an "inborn, and therefore irrepressible drive," according to one Hungarian physician. Earlier, there were homosexual *behaviors*, of course, but identity did not emerge from nor inhere in those behaviors. By the turn of the twentieth century, though, "the homosexual" was characterized by a form of "interior androgyny, a hermaphroditism of the soul," writes Foucault. "The sodomite had been a temporary aberration; the homosexual was now a species." Since Freud's era, we have assumed that male homosexuality, manifested by effeminacy, and lesbianism, manifested by masculine affect, might not be innate but are, nonetheless, intractable products of early childhood socialization and that differences between gays and straights, once established, prove the most telling in their lives' trajectories.[64]

In recent decades, biological research has emerged as central in the demonstration of the fundamental and irreducible differences between homosexuals and heterosexuals. And it should not surprise us that researchers have found what they hoped to find—that homosexual men's brains and hormone levels more closely resemble those of females than those of heterosexual males. Science, again, has attempted to prove that the stereotypes of gay men and lesbians are based not in cultural fears and prejudices, but in biological fact. For example, in the 1970s, Dorner and his associates found that homosexual men possess a "predominantly female-differentiated brain," which is caused by a "deficiency" of androgen during the hypothalamic organizational phase in prenatal life and which may be activated to homosexual behavior by normal or about-normal androgen levels in adulthood.[65]

More recently, Simon LeVay focused on the structure of the brain in an effort to uncover the etiology of homosexuality. Hoping that science can demonstrate "the origins of sexual orientation at a cellular level," LeVay gives no credence to environmental determination of sexuality. "If there are environmental influences, they operate very early in life, at the fetal or early-infancy stages, when the brain is still putting itself together," he argues. "I'm very much skeptical of the idea that sexual orientation is a cultural thing." LeVay noticed that, among primates, experimental lesions in the medial zone of the hypothalamus of monkeys did not impair sexual functioning but did suppress mounting attempts by the male monkeys on female monkeys. He also noticed that the size of this region of the brain is different in men and women. In his experiment, LeVay examined the brain tissues of forty-one deceased people. Nineteen of these had died of AIDS and were identified as part of the risk group "homosexual and bisexual men"; sixteen other men were presumed to be heterosexual because there was no evidence to the contrary (six had died of AIDS and the other ten from other causes); and six were women who were presumed heterosexual (one had died of AIDS). These brains were treated and compared. Three of the four sections revealed no differences, but a fourth section, the anterior hypothalamus, a region about the size of a grain of sand, was found to be different among the groups. LeVay found that the size of this area among the presumably heterosexual men was approximately twice the size of that area for the women and the presumably gay men.[66]

But several problems in his experiments give us pause. LeVay and his colleagues failed to measure the cell number or density because "of the difficulty in precisely defining the neurons belonging to INAH 3," the area of the brain involved. A number of the "homosexual" men (five of the nineteen) and of the women (two of the six) appeared to have areas of the brain as large as those of the presumed heterosexual men. And in three of the presumed heterosexual men, this area of the brain was actually very small. What's more, the sources of his data were widely varied. All the gay men in his sample died of AIDS, a disease known to affect the brain. (Reduced testosterone occurs among AIDS patients, and this alone may account for the different sizes.) And all the brains of the gay men were preserved in a formaldehyde solution that was of a different strength than the solution in which the brains of the heterosexual men were preserved, because of the fears of HIV transmission, although there was no effort to control for the effect of the formaldehyde on the organs. It is possible that what LeVay may have been measuring was the combined effect of HIV infection and preservation in high densities of formaldehyde solution on postmortem brain structure, rather than differences in brain structure between living heterosexuals and homosexuals. A recent effort to replicate LeVay's findings failed, and one researcher went further, suggesting that "INAH-3 is not necessary for sexual behavior in men, whether they chose men or women as their partners."[67]

More recently, researchers have found that the brains of male transsexuals more closely resembled the brains of women than those of heterosexual, "normal" men. Dutch scientists at the Netherlands Institute for Brain Research examined the hypothalamus sections of forty-two men and women, six of whom were known to be transsexuals and nine of whom were gay men, whereas the rest were presumed to be heterosexual. Again they found that the hypothalamus in the transsexual men and women was smaller than those in the heterosexual or homosexual men. Although they were careful *not* to interpret their findings in terms of sexual orientation because the heterosexual and homosexual men's brains were similar, they did take their research to signal sex differences because the male transsexuals were men who felt themselves to be women. However, it may also be a result of transsexual surgery and the massive amounts of female hormones that the male transsexuals took, which might have had the effect of shrinking the hypothalamus, just as the surgery and hormones also resulted in other anatomical changes (loss of facial and body hair, breast growth, etc.).[68]

Another recent study suggests that gay men are different from heterosexual men and more like heterosexual women. A group of Swedish researchers exposed heterosexual men and women and gay men to chemicals derived from male and female sex hormones (extracted from sweat glands in the armpit for males and urine for females) and recorded which parts of the brain were most visibly stimulated on a positron emission tomography scan. The brains of all three groups reacted similarly to various normal scents, like lavender or cedar: They recorded the information in the part of the brain that responds to olfactory sensations only. But when they were presented with testosterone, the part of the brain most closely associated with sexual activity (the hypothalamus) was triggered, but it remained quiescent among the heterosexual men; they responded only in the olfactory region. When presented with estrogen, by contrast, the females and gay men registered only in the olfactory area, whereas the heterosexual men responded strongly in the hypothalamus.[69] Although the response among journalists was a collective "Eureka! The gay brain," the researchers themselves were far more circumspect about the meaning of the results. The different pattern of activity could be a cause of sexual orientation—or a consequence, Dr. Savic told a reporter. "We cannot tell if the different pattern is cause or effect. The study does not give any answer to these crucial questions."[70] For another thing, the research did not measure anything about lesbians, so we don't know what sorts of armpit scents would drive their hypothalamus wild with desire.

Another recent study did examine lesbians' brain chemistry and found that the sounds emitted by the inner ears of lesbians fall in between the sounds emitted by the inner ears of men and heterosexual women, forming a sort of "intermediate" zone between the two groups. (Lesbian emissions were stronger than men's but weaker than heterosexual women's.) Before we get carried away, though, I should mention that the research found no differences whatever between gay men and heterosexual men on such emissions.[71] "You can't assume that because you find a structural difference in the brain that it was caused by genes," says researcher Marc Breedlove. "You don't know how the difference got there." Another adds that we "are still unsure whether these signs are causes or effects."[72] Personally, I'm more concerned about the sounds of bias and false difference that flow *into* our ears than the sounds that flow *out* of them.

THE SEARCH FOR THE GAY GENE

Other biological research has attempted to isolate a gay gene and thus show that sexual orientation has its basis in biology. For example, research on pairs of monozygotic twins (twins born from a single fertilized egg that splits in utero) suggests that identical twins have a statistically far higher likelihood of having similar sexualities (either both gay or both straight) than do dizygotic twins (twins born from two separate fertilized eggs). One genetic study involved eighty-five pairs of twins in the 1940s and 1950s. All forty pairs of monozygotic twins studied shared the same sexual orientation; if one twin was heterosexual, the other was also; if one twin was homosexual, so, too, was the other twin. Such data were so perfect that subsequent scientists have doubted their validity.[73]

More recently, Eckert and his colleagues found that in fifty-five pairs of twins, five had at least one gay member and that in a sixth pair, one twin was bisexual. Bailey and Pillard collected data on gay men who were twins, as well as on gay men who had adoptive brothers who lived in the same home before age two. The 161 respondents were drawn from responses to ads placed in gay periodicals and included 56 monozygotic twins, 54 dizygotic twins, and 57 adoptive brothers. Respondents were asked about their brother's sexuality and were asked for permission to contact those brothers. About three-fourths of the brothers participated in the study. Bailey and Pillard found that in 52 percent of the monozygotic pairs, in 22 percent of the dizygotic pairs, and in 11 percent of the adoptive pairs, both brothers were homosexual or bisexual.[74]

Such findings were widely interpreted to mean that there is some biological foundation for men's sexual contact with other men. But several problems remain. The study was generated from self-identified homosexuals, not from a sample of twins.[75] What's more, there was no independent measure of the environment in which these boys grew up, so that what Bailey and Pillard might have measured is the predisposition of the environments to produce similar outcomes among twins. After all, biological predisposition should be more compelling than one-half. And the fact that fraternal twins of homosexual men were twice as likely as other biological brothers would mean that environmental factors *must* be present, because dizygotic twins share no more genetic material than other biological brothers. The increase in concordance could be just as convincingly explained by a continuum of similarity of treatment of brothers— from adoptive to biological to dizygotic to monozygotic—without any genetic component whatever.

Actually, what is most interesting in the twin studies is how little concordance there actually is. After all, having identical genetic material and the same family and environmental conditions should produce a greater concordance than, at best, half. There is, however, some evidence that homosexual orientations tend to occur more frequently in family constellations. Psychiatrist Richard Pillard and psychologist James Weinrich questioned fifty heterosexual and fifty-one homosexual men and their siblings. Only 4 percent of the heterosexual men had brothers who were homosexual (the same percentage that had been found by Kinsey's studies in the 1940s), whereas about 22 percent of the gay men had gay or bisexual brothers. "This is rather strong evidence that male homosexuality clumps in families," said Weinrich, although there was no indication of the biological or genetic origin of this relationship. And the correlation, incidentally, did not hold true for women, as about the same percentage of the sisters of both groups said they had sisters who were lesbian. None said his or her parents were gay. This gender disparity might suggest that more than biology is at work here and that **gender identity** may have more to do with inequality than with genetics.[76]

Recently, sociologists Peter Bearman and Hannah Bruckner examined all the studies that purported that opposite-sex twins are more likely to be gay than twins who are not. They concluded that there are no hormonal connections whatever and that the level of sex stereotyping in early childhood socialization is a far better predictor of behavioral outcome than whether or not one has a twin of the opposite sex.[77]

ESTROGEN AND TESTOSTERONE: HORMONAL BASES FOR GENDER DIFFERENCES

Sex differentiation faces its most critical events at two different phases of life: (1) fetal development, when primary sex characteristics are determined by a combination of genetic inheritance and the biological development of the embryo that will become a boy or a girl; and (2) puberty, when the bodies of boys and girls are transformed by a flood of sex hormones that causes the development of all the secondary sex characteristics. Breast development for girls, lowering of voices for boys, the development of facial hair for boys, and the growth of pubic hair for both are among puberty's most obvious signs.

A significant amount of biological research has examined each of these two phases in an attempt to chart the hormonal bases for sex differentiation. Much of this research has focused on the links between sex hormones and aggression in adolescent boys and women and on problems of normal hormonal development and the outcomes for gender identity development. Summarizing his reading of this evidence, sociologist Steven Goldberg writes that because "men and women differ in their hormonal systems" and "every society demonstrates patriarchy, male dominance and male attainment," it is logical to conclude that "the hormonal renders the social inevitable."[78]

Earlier, we saw how Geschwind and Behan found that during fetal development it is the "testosterone bath" secreted by slightly more than half of all fetuses that begins sex differentiation in utero. (All embryos, remember, begin as "female.") Geschwind and Behan found that this testosterone bath selectively attacks the left hemisphere, which is why males favor the right hemisphere. But the implication of fetal hormonal research is that the secretion of sex hormones has a decisive effect on the development of gender identity and on the expressions of masculinity and femininity. We've all heard the arguments about how testosterone, the male sex hormone, is not only the driving force in the development of masculinity in males, but also the biological basis of human aggression, which is why males are more prone to violence than women. We should remember that women and men have both testosterone *and* estrogen, although typically in dramatically different amounts. On average, men do have about ten times the testosterone level that women have, but the level among men varies greatly, and some women have levels higher than some men.

In recent years, research has suggested some correlations between levels of testosterone and body mass, baldness, self-confidence, and even the ability and willingness to smile. But a recent survey found no correlations between testosterone levels and competitiveness.[79] In fact, it might go the other way. After administering a dose of testosterone to women, Christoph Eisenegger and his colleagues in Zurich found that it increased their levels of cooperation, not competition. But—and this is really interesting—those women who believed they had been given testosterone became more competitive than those who believed they'd received a placebo. Eisenegger and his colleagues conclude that the effect of testosterone on competition is a deeply ingrained folk wisdom that it increases competition—despite the evidence that it actually has the *opposite* effect![80] Some wildly inflated claims about the effects of testosterone have led to both popular misconceptions and a variety of medical interventions to provide remedies. In one recent book, for example, psychologist James Dabbs proclaims that "testosterone increases masculinity," which was translated by a journalist into the equation that "lust is a chemical" as he looked forward to his "biweekly encounter with a syringe full of manhood."[81] And, of course, today men can purchase testosterone patches to boost their daily testosterone level or AndroGel, a product that seems to promise masculinity in a tube.[82]

READ ALL ABOUT IT!

We all know that testosterone causes aggression, right? And since males have such higher levels of testosterone, males tend to be far more aggressive. Not exactly. In "Testosterone Rules," neuroprimatologist Robert Sapolsky recounts his experiments with monkey hierarchies, finding that the missing ingredient in testosterone studies is social permission: In order to use that testosterone-fueled aggression, you have to believe that the target of your aggression is a legitimate target. No matter how juiced on testosterone you might be, you probably won't attack your instructor. (Note: This is not a matter to be empirically tested!)

Although the claims made for testosterone are often ridiculous, ministering less to science and more to men's fears of declining potency, there are some experiments on the relationship between testosterone and aggression that appear convincing. Males have higher levels of testosterone and higher rates of aggressive behavior than females do. What's more, if you increase the level of testosterone in a normal male, his level of aggression will increase. Castrate him—or at least a rodent proxy of him— and his aggressive behavior will cease entirely. Though this might lead one to think that testosterone is the cause of the aggression, Stanford neuroprimatologist Robert Sapolsky warns against such leaps of logic. He explains that if you take a group of five male monkeys arranged in a dominance hierarchy from 1 to 5, then you can pretty much predict how everyone will behave toward everyone else. (The top monkey's testosterone level will be higher than that of the monkeys below him, and levels will decrease down the line.) Number 3, for example, will pick fights with numbers 4 and 5, but will avoid and run away from number 1 and number 2. If you give number 3 a massive infusion of testosterone, he will likely become more aggressive—but only toward number 4 and number 5, with whom he has now become an absolute violent torment. He will still avoid number 1 and number 2, demonstrating that the "testosterone isn't causing aggression, it's exaggerating the aggression that's already there."[83]

It turns out that testosterone has what scientists call a "permissive effect" on aggression: It doesn't cause it, but it does facilitate and enable the aggression that is already there. What's more, testosterone is produced *by* aggression, so that the correlation between the two may, in fact, have the opposite direction than previously thought. In his thoughtful book *Testosterone and Social Structure*, Theodore Kemper notes several studies in which testosterone levels were linked to men's experiences. In studies of tennis players, medical students, wrestlers, nautical competitors, parachutists, and officer candidates, winning and losing determined levels of testosterone, so that the levels of the winners rose dramatically, whereas those of the losers dropped or remained the same. Kemper suggests that testosterone levels vary depending upon men's experience of either dominance, "elevated social rank that is achieved by overcoming others in a competitive confrontation," or eminence, where elevated rank "is earned through socially valued and approved accomplishment." Significantly, men's testosterone levels prior to either dominance or eminence could not predict the outcome; it was the experience of rising status due to success that led to the elevation of the testosterone level. (These same experiences lead to increases in women's testosterone levels as well.)[84]

Several recent studies have made the earlier facile correlation quite a bit more interesting. A Finnish study found no difference in testosterone levels between violent and nonviolent men. But among the violent men, levels of testosterone did correlate with levels of hostility: The violent men with higher levels of testosterone were diagnosed with antisocial personality disorder. This supports the notion that testosterone has a permissive effect on aggression, because it correlates with hostility *only* among the violent men. And a UCLA researcher found that men with *low* testosterone were more likely to be angry, irritable, and aggressive than men with normal or high levels of testosterone. Although Sapolsky's statement that "testosterone is probably a vastly overrated hormone" may be an understatement, these last studies raise some troubling concerns, especially when compared with the questions about sexual orientation and hormone levels (see later).[85]

Some recent research approaches the relationship between testosterone and aggression from the other side. It turns out that marriage and fatherhood tend to depress the amount of testosterone in a man's body. In one study of fifty-eight Boston-area men (nearly all of whom were Harvard graduate or professional students), unmarried men had higher levels than did married men, and that difference increased only slightly when the married man had a child. Those married men with children who spent a lot of time doing child care had even lower levels. Actually, the testosterone levels differed only slightly, and only in the evening; samples taken in the morning, when one had rested, showed no differences at all. Yet from these results, massive leaps of logic followed. Because testosterone facilitates competition and aggression, fathers with children were opting out of this typically masculine activity. "Maybe it's very adaptive for men to suppress irritability," commented Peter Ellison, one of the study's authors. "Maybe the failure to do that places the child at risk." Maybe. Or maybe Harvard graduate students have lower testosterone levels than other men in Boston. Or maybe by the end of the day, trying to balance work and family life, an involved father is simply depleted. (Stress reduces levels of testosterone.) From such tiny and inconsistent differences, one should leap to no conclusions whatever.[86]

Some therapists, though, go much further and prescribe testosterone for men as a sort of chemical tonic, designed to provide the same sort of pep and "vim and vigor" that tonics and cure-alls promised at the turn of the twentieth century. Happy consumers swear by the results, and some therapists have even diagnosed a medically treatable malady (which should enable it to be covered by insurance) called "**andropause**" or "**male menopause**," treatable by hormone-replacement therapy for men.[87]

Much of the research on hormones and gender identity has been done by inference—that is, by examining cases where hormones did not work properly or where one biological sex got too much of the "wrong" hormone.[88] In some of the more celebrated research on fetal hormone development, Money and Ehrhardt reported on girls who had androgenital syndrome (AGS)—a preponderance of male hormones (androgens) in their systems at birth—and on another set of girls whose mothers had taken progestins during pregnancy. All twenty-five girls had masculine-appearing genitalia and had operations to "correct" their genitals. The AGS girls also were given constant cortisone treatments to enable their adrenal glands to function properly.[89]

Money and Ehrhardt's findings were interesting. The girls and their mothers reported a higher frequency of tomboy behavior in these girls. They enjoyed vigorous

Can Food Make Us Gay?

That might not be as crazy as it sounds, at least according to evangelical preacher Jim Rutz. He argues that homosexuality is caused by insufficient amounts of the appropriate sex hormone and that therefore gay men are more "feminine" than straight men. And, he claims, soy products, like tofu, contain large amounts of estrogen, so "when you feed a baby soy formula, you're giving him or her the equivalent of *five birth control pills a day*." Eating tofu can turn you gay. "Soy is feminizing," he claims, "and commonly leads to a decrease in the size of the penis, sexual confusion and homosexuality." This idea was recently translated into a commercial for Hummers, the ultimate compensation for insecure gender identity.

Despite the fact that these assertions are biologically preposterous (and, in the case of penis size, simply untrue, as you'll see in a few pages), there is one fascinating implication of this assertion for a student of gender. Notice that soy is to be avoided because it contains female hormones, which will turn you gay. Well, who is the "you" in that sentence? A male! If homosexuality is a gender disorder (males who are feminized, females who are masculinized), why does the earnest Reverend Rutz not *prescribe* soy products for girls, to make sure they don't become lesbians? Are there only gay *men*?

This concern about homosexuality turns out to be another moment of gender inequality. And although all of us should watch what we eat for health reasons, it's unlikely that there is any food that can make you gay—or straight.

Source: Jim Rutz, "Soy Is Making Kids 'Gay'" in *World Net Daily*, December 12, 2006.

---

outdoor games and sports, preferred toy cars and guns to dolls, and attached more importance to career plans than to marriage. However, they showed no more aggression or fighting than other girls. Later research seemed to confirm the notion that "prenatal androgen is one of the factors contributing to the development of temperamental differences between and within the sexes."[90]

Appearances, however, can be deceiving. Medical researcher Anne Fausto-Sterling argues that several problems make Ehrhardt and her colleagues' research less convincing than it at first may seem. The research suffered from "insufficient and inappropriate" controls: Cortisone is a powerful drug, and the AGS girls underwent calamitous surgery (including clitoridectomy), and there were no independent measures of the effects. Further, the "method of data collection is inadequate" because it was based entirely on interviews with parents and children, with no impartial direct observation of these reported behaviors. Finally, "the authors do not properly explore alternative explanations of their results," such as parental expectations and differential treatment of their very "different" children.[91]

Another set of experiments examined the other side of the equation—boys who received higher-than-average doses of prenatal estrogen from mothers who were treated with estrogen during their pregnancies. Yalom, Green, and Fisk found that boys who received "female" hormones in utero were less active and less athletic than other boys. However, all the boys' mothers were chronically and seriously ill during their infancy and childhood (which was not true for the control sample of normal boys). Perhaps the boys had simply been admonished against loud and boisterous play in the house so as not to disturb their mothers and had simply *learned* to be content while playing quietly or reading.[92]

"As Nature Made Him"?

One of the most famous cases that purports to prove how biological sex is the sole foundation for gender identity concerned a Canadian boy, Bruce Reimer. In 1966, Bruce and his identical twin Brian underwent routine circumcisions in a hospital. Brian's circumcision went smoothly, but Bruce's went terribly wrong, and his penis was severed. His distraught parents brought him to Johns Hopkins University Medical Center, where, under the aegis of Dr. John Money, he was surgically "transformed" into a girl. Over the next decades "Brenda" was faced with several more surgical procedures, annual visits to Dr. Money's clinic, and massive doses of female sex hormones, while her parents struggled to raise Brenda as a girl. And not just "a" girl—but a very frilly, feminine, and dainty girl at that. (Even though she described herself as a tomboy as a child, Brenda's mother was determined that her "daughter" be "polite and quiet" and "ladylike.")

Despite their becoming poster children for Money's claims that gender identity is more malleable than originally thought and, indeed, that it can be changed, both twins grew up depressed and unhappy on the Canadian prairie, with parents who were both naïve and uncommunicative and deeply ashamed of what had happened. Eventually, Brenda's situation was revealed to a sexologist, Dr. Milton Diamond at the University of Hawaii, a longtime foe of John Money's unorthodox ideas and practices. Under Diamond's supervision, Brenda reclaimed his male gender identity, renamed himself "David," and became the man he said he felt he always was. "Suddenly it all made sense why I felt the way I did," he told a journalist who eventually wrote a best-selling book about his life. "I wasn't some sort of weirdo. I wasn't crazy." David eventually married and adopted three children.[93]

His story, passionately told by journalist John Colapinto, became a book, *As Nature Made Him: The Boy Who Was Raised as a Girl*, and a TV documentary. Colapinto argues forcefully that David's case demonstrates that nature trumps nurture, that biology is destiny, and that meddling with Mother Nature is always disastrous. The case "provides stark evidence that a person's brain predetermines sexual identity—not one's anatomy or social environment," was how a writer in the *Los Angeles Times* put it.[94]

But is the case that simple, that no matter how much tinkering one does, nature always trumps nurture? Any scientist should be wary of generalizing from a single case—especially a case with so many other factors that might have influenced the outcome. How would you feel about yourself, and your gender identity, if you were constantly being dragged to some hospital every few months throughout your early childhood, had your genitals poked and prodded and surgically "repaired," and if everyone paid what would no doubt feel like an inordinate amount of attention to your genitalia? Would it change your opinion, for example, if I also told you that David's father became an uncommunicative alcoholic, that his mother attempted suicide and was clinically depressed, and that his twin brother, Brian, became a drug addict and a criminal and eventually committed suicide himself? Or that even David killed himself as well, in part because, despite his hopes, he never fully felt comfortable as a male either? Confused and depressed, who wouldn't want a magical explanation for all of one's pain and suffering, that single "A-ha! That's the reason I feel so weird!"

It's not so simple. For one thing, the case's assertions rest on the dubious premise that a child without a penis could not possibly be a boy and that a girl must be feminine—demure, restrained, and dressed in frilly clothes. Were our gender roles more elastic, we wouldn't try so obsessively to coerce such behaviors from our children, who express far more variability than our norms about proper gender behavior. Surely our gender identity is the result of a complex interaction of genetics, brain chemistry, hormones, and our immediate familial environment, nestled within a more general social and cultural milieu. No one cause of something so complex and variable as gender identity could possibly be extracted, especially from one such troubling case.[95]

About the relationship between women's hormones and behaviors, we have the research on premenstrual syndrome (PMS). During the days just before menstruation, some women seem to exhibit symptoms of dramatic and wildly unpredictable mood changes, outbursts of violence, anger, and fits of crying. Alec Coppen and Neil Kessel studied 465 women and observed that they were more irritable and depressed during the premenstrual phase than during midcycle. Such behaviors have led physicians to label this time "premenstrual syndrome." In fact, PMS has been listed as a disease in the *Diagnostic and Statistical Manual of Mental Disorders (DSM-5)* of the American Psychiatric Association, which guides physicians (and insurance companies) in treating illnesses. And PMS has even been successfully used as a criminal defense strategy for a woman accused of violent outbursts. Two British women, arguing that PMS is a form of temporary insanity, have used PMS as a successful defense in their trials for the murder of their male partners.

The politics of PMS parallels the politics of testosterone. "If you had an investment in a bank, you wouldn't want the president of your bank making a loan under those raging hormonal influences at that particular period," one physician noted. "There are just physical and psychological inhabitants that limit a female's potential." Happily, PMS occurs for only a few days a month, whereas unpredictably high levels of testosterone in men may last all month. Perhaps these presumed bank investors might want to rethink their investment strategies. Or consider this observation by feminist writer Gloria Steinem: During those days immediately preceding her menstrual period (the PMS days), a woman's estrogen level drops to its lowest point in the monthly cycle. Thus, just before menstruation, women, at least hormonally, more closely resemble men than at any other point in their cycle![96] Perhaps, then, the only sensible purely biological solution would be to have every corporation, government office, and—especially—military operation run by gay men, whose levels of testosterone would presumably be low enough to offset the hormone's propulsion toward aggression, while they would also be immune to the "raging hormonal influences" of PMS.

HORMONES AND HOMOSEXUALITY

The research on the relationship between hormones and homosexuality might lead us in that direction, were we politically disposed to go there. However, most research on the relationship between prenatal hormones and sexual orientation has had exactly the opposite political agenda. At the turn of the twentieth century, many theorists held that homosexuals were "inverts," creatures of one sex (their "true" sex) trapped in the body of the other. Some argued that homosexuality was "caused" by hormonal imbalances in utero that left males effeminate and therefore desiring men and left women masculine and therefore desiring women. In the 1970s, the German researcher Gunter Dorner, director of the Institute for Experimental Endocrinology at Humboldt University in Berlin, and his associates argued that low levels of testosterone during fetal development, a rather tepid hormonal bath, would predispose males toward homosexuality. If rats did not receive enough of their appropriate sex hormone during fetal development, "then something would go wrong with the formation of the centers and with later sexual behavior," reported two journalists. "Adult rats would behave in ways like members of the opposite sex. They would become, in a sense, 'homosexual.'"[97]

Such research fit neatly with the era's antigay political agenda, suggesting as it did that male homosexuality was the result of insufficient prenatal masculine hormones or inadequate masculinity. Treatment of homosexuality—indeed, perhaps its cure—might be effected simply by injecting higher doses of testosterone into these men, whose recharged virility would transform them into heterosexuals with higher sex drives. When such an experiment was attempted, researchers found that the men's sex drive did indeed increase as a result of the testosterone injections. However, the object of their lusts did not change: They simply desired more sex with men! Hormone levels may affect sexual urges, and especially the intensity or frequency of sexual activity, but they are empirically and logically irrelevant to studies of sexual object choice.

Could prenatal stress account for a disposition toward homosexuality? In another series of studies, Dorner and his colleagues argued that more homosexual men are born during wartime than during peacetime. Their evidence for this claim was that a high proportion of the 865 men treated for "venereal disease" in six regions of the German Democratic Republic were born between 1941 and 1947. They theorized that because prenatal stress leads to a "significant decrease in plasma testosterone levels" among rat fetuses, which also leads to increased bisexual or homosexual behaviors among the adult rats, why not among humans? Dorner theorized that war leads to stress, which leads to a lowering of androgens in the male fetuses, which encourages the development of a homosexual orientation. Based on this trajectory, Dorner concluded that the prevention of war "may render a partial prevention of the development of sexual deviation."[98] (Well, perhaps—but only because wartime tends to place men together in foxholes without women, where they may engage in homosexual activity more frequently than during peacetime.[99])

Even if these data were convincing, a purely endocrinological account fails to satisfy. For example, one could just as easily construct a purely psychodynamic theory. For example: In wartime, children tend to grow up more often without a father or to be separated from other members of the family. If homosexuality really occurs more frequently during wartime, it would be just as reasonable to take this as "proof" of certain psychodynamic theories of homosexuality, for example, the lack of a father or a particularly close bond between mother and son.

Another just-so story? Perhaps. But, then, so are explanations about aggregate levels of testosterone during wartime. Although these arguments may not be convincing, they continue to exert significant influence over our commonsense explanations of gender difference.

Another body of research on prenatal hormones examines hormonal anomalies as a clue to normal development. Take, for example, congenital adrenal hyperplasia (CAH), a genetic defect that causes female fetuses to be exposed to extremely high levels of testosterone in utero. Girls with CAH really enjoy playing with boys' toys and show decidedly masculine affective styles. But does that mean that there is "something in them that's innately male," as television celebrity and advocate of biological determinism John Stossel thinks?[100] Hardly.

The most interesting recent research on the relationship between prenatal hormones and sexual orientation has been carried out by psychologist Marc Breedlove and his students. Breedlove is a far more careful researcher than most, and he is also far more cautious in the claims he makes. Breedlove measured the lengths of the index and ring fingers (second and fourth digits) and calculated the ratios between them for both heterosexual women and lesbians and for gay and heterosexual men. It's well known that for average women, the two fingers are usually the same length, whereas among average men, the index finger is more often significantly shorter than the fourth. This is assumed to be an effect of prenatal androgens on male fetuses. Breedlove found that the ratio between the two fingers was more "masculine" among the lesbians than the heterosexual women; that is, that lesbians' index fingers were significantly shorter than their ring fingers. He found no differences between gay and straight men (both were equally "masculine"), although another study did find significant differences between the two, with gay men's finger ratios being somewhat more "masculine" than those of heterosexual men.[101]

Breedlove believed that the difference between lesbians and heterosexual women was due to the effect of increased prenatal androgens among the lesbians—thus rendering them more "masculine." Now this accords with traditional stereotypes that suggest that homosexuality is related to gender nonconformity. But one must be careful about overstating these stereotypes, because Breedlove found the exact opposite among men. Breedlove also found a relationship between birth order and sexual orientation for men. The greater the number of older brothers a man had, the higher the likelihood that he would be homosexual. In fact, subsequent researchers have suggested that each additional elder brother that a man has increases the likelihood that he will be gay by about 30 percent. Breedlove hypothesized that this also was the result of prenatal androgenization of subsequent children. Although this might not appear controversial, it accords with other studies that find that gay men's levels of testosterone are significantly *higher* than those of heterosexual men. That is, gay men are more "real men" than are straight men. (Other research that supports the argument that gay men are "hypermasculine" includes studies that find that gay men's penis size is greater than that of straight men, despite the fact that gay men undergo puberty a bit earlier and are therefore slightly shorter than straight men and that gay men report significantly higher amounts of sexual behavior.) "This calls into question all of our cultural assumptions that gay men are feminine," said Breedlove in an interview—a thought that biological determinists and their political allies will not find especially comforting.[102]

This sort of research does give us pause. Anthony Bogaert did a similar study in which he found that there was no effect on sexual orientation by unrelated siblings in the same household (they had to be biological) but that older brothers who did not live with a person did influence the chances of that person being gay. This seems to rule out socialization effects (older nonrelated brothers "recruiting" the youngest through sexual coercion) or the outcome of seemingly harmless sexual play. Bogaert offers no speculation about why this might be the case or even about exactly what sorts of physiological mechanisms cause it. It might be nature's way of reducing the number of males competing for increasingly scarce (with large broods of males) females. If so, it not only signals some biological elements to the origins of sexual orientation, but also makes a strong case for the naturalness of homosexuality.[103] At least male homosexuality. No birth order phenomena have been posited as predictors of lesbianism.

THE RESEARCH ON INTERSEXUALITY

One of the most intriguing tests of hormonal research has been carried out on intersex people. Here, at the boundaries of biological sex, we can observe more clearly the processes that are often too difficult to see in "normal" biological development. Intersex people are organisms that have both male and female characteristics. True intersex people have either one ovary and one testicle or else a single organ with both types of reproductive tissue. They are exceedingly rare. Less rare, however, are those whose biological sex is ambiguous.[104]

Take the most celebrated case: Two relatively isolated villages in the Dominican Republic seemed to produce a larger-than-expected set of cases of genetically male intersex for at least three generations. These were babies born with internal male structures but with sex organs that resembled a clitoris more than they did a penis. Moreover, the testes had not descended at all, leaving what appeared to be a scrotum that resembled labia, as well as an apparently closed vaginal cavity. Their condition was the result of an extremely rare deficiency in a steroid, 5-alpha reductase. Eighteen of these babies were raised as girls and studied by a team of researchers from Cornell University.[105]

After these children had relatively uneventful childhoods, during which they played and acted like other little girls, their adolescence became somewhat more traumatic. They failed to develop breasts and noticed a mass of tissue in their groins that turned out to be testicles beginning a descent. At puberty, their bodies began to produce a significant amount of testosterone, which made their voices deepen, their muscles develop, and facial hair appear. Suddenly, these youngsters were no longer like the other girls! And so all but one of them switched and became males. One remained a female, determined to marry and have a sex change operation. (Another decided he was a male but continued to wear dresses and act as a female.) All the others were successful in making the transition; they became men, found typically masculine jobs (woodchoppers, farmers, miners), and married women.

Imperato-McGinley and her colleagues interpreted these events as a demonstration of the effect of prenatal and pubertal sex hormones. They argued that a prenatal dose of testosterone had created "male" brains, which had remained dormant within ambiguous and female-appearing physiological bodies. At puberty, a second secretion of testosterone activated these genetically masculine brains, and the youngsters made the transition without too much psychological trauma.

They didn't, however, do it alone. The other villagers had made fun of them, calling them *guevadoches* ("eggs [testicles] at twelve") or *machihembra* ("first woman, then man"). But after they had made the move to become males, their neighbors were more encouraging and offered advice and gifts to ease the transition. Moreover, one might argue that these children had a less fixed relationship between early gender development and adolescent gender patterns precisely because of their ambiguous genital development. After three generations, they might have come to assume that a girl does not always develop into a woman. Anthropologist Gilbert Herdt argues that such "gender polymorphic" cultures have the ability to deal with radical gender changes across the life cycle far more easily than do "gender dimorphic" cultures, such as the United States, where we expect everyone to be either male or female for his or her entire life.[106] One might also ask what would have happened had these been little boys who, it turned out, had actually been female and were therefore invited to make a transition to being adult women. Who would choose to stay a girl if she could end up becoming a boy, especially in a culture in which the sexes are highly differentiated and males enjoy privileges that females do not? Would boys find a transition to becoming girls as easy?

THE POLITICS OF BIOLOGICAL ESSENTIALISM

Biological arguments for sex differences have historically tended to be politically conservative, suggesting that the social arrangements between women and men—including social, economic, and political discrimination based on sex—are actually the inevitable outcome of nature working in its mysterious ways. Political attempts to legislate changes in the gender order or efforts to gain civil rights for women or for gay men and lesbians have always been met with **biological essentialism**: Don't fool with Mother Nature! James Dobson, a former professor of pediatrics and founder of Focus on the Family, a right-wing advocacy group, puts the case starkly:

> I feel it is a mistake to tamper with the time-honed relationship of husband as loving protector and wife as recipient of that protection . . . Because two captains sink the ship and two cooks spoil the broth, I feel that a family must have a leader whose decisions prevail in times of differing opinions . . . That role has been assigned to the man of the house.[107]

Social scientists have also jumped onto the biological bandwagon. For example, sociologist Steven Goldberg, in his book *The Inevitability of Patriarchy,* argues that because male domination is ubiquitous, eternal, it simply has to be based on biological origins. There is simply too much coincidence for it to be social. Feminism, Goldberg argues, is therefore a war with nature:

> Women follow their own physiological imperatives . . . In this, and every other society [men] look to women for gentleness, kindness, and love, for refuge from a world of pain and force . . . In every society basic male motivation is the feeling that the women and children must be protected . . . The feminist cannot have it both ways: if she wishes to sacrifice all this, all that she will get in return is the right to meet men on male terms. She will lose.[108]

Politically, unequal social arrangements are, in the end, ordained by nature.[109]

But the evidence—occasionally impressive, often uneven—is far from convincing. If male domination is natural, based on biological imperatives, why, asks sociologist Cynthia Fuchs Epstein, must it be coercive, held in place by laws, traditions, customs, and the constant threat of violence for any woman who dares step out of line? Why would women want to enter male spheres, like colleges and universities, politics and the labor force, the professions, and the military, for which they are clearly biologically ill-suited?

Ironically, in the past decade, conservatives who argue that biological bases account for both sex differences and sexuality differences have been joined by some women and some gay men and lesbians who have adopted an essentialism of their own. Some feminists, for example, argue that women should be pleased to claim "the intuitive and emotional strengths given by their right-hemisphere, in opposition to the over-cognitive, left-hemisphere-dominated, masculine nature."[110] Often a feminist essentialism uses women's experiences as mothers to describe the fundamental and irreducible differences between the sexes, rather than evolution, brain organization, or chemistry. Sociologist Alice Rossi argues that, because of their bodies, "women have a head start in easier reading of an infant's facial expressions, smoothness of body motions, greater ease in handling a tiny creature with tactile gentleness."[111]

Similarly, research on the biological bases of homosexuality suggests some unlikely new political allies and a dramatic shifting of positions. Gay brain research may have shed little light on the etiology of sexual orientation, but it has certainly generated significant political heat. In a way, the promotion of gay essentialism is a political strategy to normalize gayness. "It points out that gay people are made this way by nature," observes Robert Bray, the director of public information of the National Gay and Lesbian Task Force. "It strikes at the heart of people who oppose gay rights and who think we don't deserve our rights because we're choosing to be the way we are." Michael Bailey and Richard Pillard, the authors of the gay twin study, opined in a *New York Times* op-ed essay that a "biological explanation is good news for homosexuals and their advocates." "If it turns out, indeed, that homosexuals are born that way, it could undercut the animosity gays have had to contend with for centuries," added a cover story in *Newsweek*. Such an understanding would "reduce being gay to something like being left handed, which is in fact all that it is," commented gay journalist and author Randy Shilts in the magazine. And Simon LeVay, whose research sparked the recent debate, hoped that homophobia would dissipate as the result of this research, because its basis in prejudice about the unnaturalness of homosexual acts would vanish. Gays would become "just another minority," just another ethnic group, with an identity based on primordial characteristics.[112]

This political implication is not lost on conservatives, who are now taking up the social constructionist "nurture" theory of sexual orientation as firmly as they argue for intractable biologically based differences between women and men. More than a decade ago, then–vice president Dan Quayle argued that homosexuality is a matter of choice—"the wrong choice," he added quickly. Former attorney general John Ashcroft agreed that it is "a choice which can be made and unmade." Such thinking leads to the politically volatile though scientifically dubious "conversion" movement that holds that, through intensive therapy, gay men and lesbians can become happy and "healthy" heterosexuals.[113]

Others are less convinced. Gay historian John D'Emilio wondered if "we really expect to bid for real power from a position of 'I can't help it.' "[114] Even if we are, as Lady Gaga sings, "born this way," such naturalization efforts are vulnerable to political subversion by the very forces they are intended to counteract. Antigay forces could point to a brain defect and suggest possible prenatal interventions for prevention and postnatal "cures." The headline in the *Washington Times* heralding LeVay's research shouted: "Scientists Link Brain Abnormality, Homosexuality." LeVay himself acknowledges this danger, commenting that "the negative side of it is that with talk of an immutable characteristic, you then can be interpreted as meaning a defect or a congenital disorder. You could say that being gay is like having cystic fibrosis or something, which should be aborted or corrected in utero." And no sooner did he say that than James Watson, Nobel laureate for his discovery of the double helix in genetics, suggested that women who are found to be carrying the gene for homosexuality ought to be allowed to abort the child. "If you could find the gene which determines sexuality and a woman decides she doesn't want a homosexual child, well, let her," he said in an interview.

What this debate ignores is what we might call the *sociology* of gay essentialism: the ways in which gender remains the organizing principle of the homosexual essence.

Notice how essentialist research links homosexuality with **gender inversion**, as if *women* were the reference point against which gay and straight men were to be measured. Gay men, it turns out, have "female" brain structures, thus making gay men into **hermaphrodites**—women's brains in men's bodies—a kind of neurological third sex. But if gay men and women had similar brain structures, then the headline in the *Washington Times* cited earlier might have more accurately problemized heterosexual men, the numerical minority, as the deviant group with the brain abnormalities.

More significantly, though, these studies miss the social organization of gay sex—the ways in which the who, what, where, when, how, and how many are governed by gender norms. In their sexual activities, rates of sexual encounters, and variations, gay men and lesbians are far greater gender *conformists* than they are nonconformists. Gay men's sexuality looks strikingly like straight men's sexuality—except for the not completely incidental detail of the gender of their object choice. Regardless of sexual orientation, virtually all sex research points to one conclusion: Gender, *not sexual orientation*, is the organizing principle of sexual behavior. Gay men and straight men seek masculine sex; sex is confirmation of masculinity. Straight women and lesbians experience feminine sex; sex is confirmation of femininity.[115]

The gender organization of sexuality also explains who believes it. Recent surveys have shown that, overwhelmingly, it is gay *men* who believe that their homosexuality is natural, biological, and inborn. Lesbians are more likely to believe that their homosexuality is socially constructed.[116] Gay men lean toward essentialist explanations, Vera Whisman argues, because gender privilege gives them the possibility of access to higher-status positions; if their homosexuality is biological, it can be overlooked and they can claim their "rightful" (read: masculine) status. Lesbian sexuality is seen by lesbians as more socially and historically contingent because lesbians are doubly marginalized, and their sexuality and gender identity are often, but not always, conditioned by an ideological connection to feminism. As lesbian-feminist writer Charlotte Bunch argues:

> Woman identified Lesbianism is, then, more than a sexual preference, it is a political choice. It is political because relationships between men and women are essentially political, they involve power and dominance. Since the Lesbian actively rejects that relationship and chooses women, she defies the established political system.[117]

For lesbians, sexual behavior implies a political statement about living outside the mainstream; gay men see it as an accident of birth to be overcome by being overlooked.

CONCLUSION

Biological research holds significant sway over our thinking about the two fundamental questions in the study of gender: the *differences* between women and men and the gendered *inequalities* that are evident in our social lives. But from the perspective of a social scientist, the biologists may have it backward. Innate gender differences do not automatically produce the obvious social, political, and economic inequalities we observe in contemporary society. In fact, the reverse seems to be true: Gender inequality, over time, ossifies into observable differences in behaviors, attitudes, and traits. If one were to raise a person in a dark room and then suddenly turn the lights on, and the person had a difficult time adjusting to the light, would you conclude that the person had genetic eye problems compared with the population that had been living in the light all that time?

There are many problems with the research on biological bases for gender difference and more and greater problems with the extrapolation of those differences to the social world of gender inequality. Consider the problem of what we might call **"anthropomorphic hyperbole."** Neurobiologist Simon LeVay writes that "genes demand instant gratification."[118] What are we to make of such an obviously false statement? Genes do not "demand" anything. And which genes is he talking about anyway? Some genes simply control such seemingly unimportant and uninteresting things as eye color or the capacity to differentiate between sweet and sour tastes. Others wait patiently for decades until they can instruct a man's hair to begin to fall out. Still others are so undemanding that they may wait patiently for several generations, until another recessive mate is found after multiple attempts at reproduction. Genes may play a role in the sexual decision making of a species or even of individual members of any particular species; they do so only through an individual's interaction with his or her environment. They cannot possibly control any particular decision made by any particular individual at any particular time. With whom you decide to have sex this weekend—or even if you *do* have sex—is not determined by your genes, but rather by you.

Another problem in biological research has been the casual assumption that causation always moves from physiology to psychology. Just because one finds a correlation between two variables doesn't permit one to speculate about the causal direction. As biologist Ruth Hubbard argues:

> If a society put[s] half its children into short skirts and warns them not to move in ways that reveal their panties, while putting the other half into jeans and overalls and encouraging them to climb trees, play ball, and participate in other vigorous outdoor games; if later, during adolescence, the children who have been wearing trousers are urged to "eat like growing boys" while the children in skirts are warned to watch their weight and not get fat; if the half in jeans runs around in sneakers or boots, while the half in skirts totters about on spike heels, then these two groups of people will be biologically as well as socially different.[119]

We know, then, what we *cannot* say about the biological bases for gender difference and gender inequality. But what *can* we say? We can say that biological differences provide the raw materials from which we begin to create our identities within culture, within society. "Biological sexuality is the necessary precondition for human sexuality," writes historian Robert Padgug. "But biological sexuality is only a precondition, a set of potentialities, which is never unmediated by human reality, and which becomes transformed in qualitatively new ways in human society."[120]

At the conclusion to his powerful indictment of **social Darwinism**, first published in 1944, the eminent historian Richard Hofstadter pointed out that biological ideas such as survival of the fittest,

> whatever their doubtful value in natural science, are utterly useless in attempting to understand society; that the life of man in society, while it is incidentally a biological fact, has characteristics that are not reducible to biology and must be

explained in the distinctive terms of a cultural analysis; that the physical well-being of men is a result of their social organization and not vice versa; that social improvement is a product of advances in technology and social organization, not of breeding or selective elimination; that judgments as to the value of competition between men or enterprises or nations must be based upon social and not allegedly biological consequences . . ."[121]

In his presidential address to the American Sociological Association, Troy Duster warned of the "increasing authority of reductionist science" informing public conversations. A recent article by psychologist Deena Skolnick Weisberg and her colleagues suggest just how prescient is Duster's comment. Weisberg and her colleagues gave three groups—regular adults, students in a neuroscience course, and neuroscience experts—a set of descriptions of psychological phenomena, followed by different types of explanations for those phenomena. These explanations were either good or bad explanations, though one of each type also had utterly irrelevant neuroscientific information randomly thrown in.

Everyone thought the good explanations were better than the bad ones. But the nonexpert groups also found the explanations—good and bad—with the trumped up neuroscience information more satisfying than those without the information—even though the information was utterly useless. It was especially helpful in making bad explanations sound more reasonable.[122] (I suppose that sly students might have determined that adding a dollop of irrelevant scientific jargon to an answer on an exam might obscure the fact that they don't really know what they are talking about, but that would work only in a class that wasn't using this book. Sorry.)

Figure 2.1. © Mike Shapiro Cartoons.

Scientists have yet to discover the gene that carries the belief in nature over nurture; it is not yet clear which half of the brain blots out evidence of cultural or individual variation from evolutionary imperatives. Is human gullibility for pseudo-scientific explanations carried on a particular chromosome? Scientists—social, behavioral, natural, biological—will continue to disagree as they hunt for the origins of human behavior. What they must all recognize is that people behave differently in different cultures and that even similar behaviors may mean different things in different contexts.

Americans seem to want desperately to believe that the differences between women and men are significant and that those differences can be traced to biological origins. A cover story in *Newsweek* promised to explain "Why Men and Women Think Differently," although the story revealed problems with every bit of evidence and concluded that "the research will show that our identities as men and women are creations of both nature and nurture. And that no matter what nature deals us, it is we—our choices, our sense of identity, our experiences in life—who make ourselves what we are."[123]

How we do that, how we create identities out of our experiences, how we understand those experiences, and the choices we make—these are the province of social science, which tries to explore the remarkable diversity of human experience. Although biological studies can suggest to us the basic building blocks of experience and identity, it is within our cultures, our societies, and our families that those building blocks are assembled into the astonishingly diverse architecture that constitutes our lives.

KEY TERMS

Andropause	Evolutionary Success	Natural Selection
Anthropomorphic Hyperbole	Evolutionary Theory	Reproductive Strategies
Biological Essentialism	Gender Identity	Reproductive Success
Biological Principle	Gender Inversion	Sex Discrimination
Brain Research	Hermaphrodites	Sexual Orientation
Craniology	Infanticide	Sexual Psychologies
Endocrinological Research	Laws of Nature	Social Darwinism
Evolutionary Psychology	Male Menopause	Sociobiology
	Maternal Instinct	

3

SPANNING *the* WORLD
Culture Constructs Gender Difference

If a test of a civilization be sought, none can be so sure as the
condition of that half of society over which the other half has power.
—HARRIET MARTINEAU, *SOCIETY IN AMERICA* (1837)

Biological models assume that biological sex determines gender, that innate
biological differences lead to behavioral differences, which in turn lead to
social arrangements. By this account, social inequalities are encoded into our
physiological composition. Biological anomalies alone should account for variation. But the evidence suggests otherwise. When children like the Dominican
pseudohermaphrodites are raised as the other *gender* they can easily make the
transition to the other *sex*. And how do we account for the dramatic differences
in the definitions of masculinity and femininity around the world? And how
come some societies have much wider ranges of gender inequality than others?
On these questions, the biological record is mute.

What's more, biology is not without its own biases, though these have been
hard to detect. Some anthropologists argue that biological models projected
contemporary Western values onto other cultures. These projections led evolu-
tionists like Steven Goldberg to ignore the role of women and the role of colonialism in establishing gender differences in traditional cultures. Anthropologists
like Karen Brodkin suggest that biological researchers always assumed that

gender *difference* implied gender *inequality*, because Western notions of difference do usually lead to and justify inequality. In other words, gender difference is the *result* of gender inequality—not the other way around.[1]

Anthropological research on cultural variations in the development of gender definitions arose, in part, in response to such casual biological determinism. The more we found out about other cultures, the more certain patterns emerged. The evolutionary world and ethnographic world offer a fascinating diversity of cultural constructions of gender. Yet some themes do remain constant. Virtually all societies manifest some amount of difference between women and men, and virtually all cultures exhibit some form of male domination, despite variations in gender definition. So anthropologists have also tried to explore the link between the near-universals of gender difference and gender inequality. Some search for those few societies in which women hold positions of power; others examine those rituals, beliefs, customs, and practices that tend to increase inequality and those that tend to decrease it.

THE VARIATIONS IN GENDER DEFINITIONS

When anthropologists began to explore the cultural landscape, one of the first things they found was far more variability in the definitions of masculinity and femininity than any biologist would have predicted. Men possessed of relatively similar levels of testosterone, with similar brain structure and lateralization, seemed to exhibit dramatically different levels of aggression, violence, and, especially, aggression toward women. Women with similar brains, hormones, and ostensibly similar evolutionary imperatives had widely varying experiences of passivity, PMS, and spatial coordination. One of

Figure 3.1. *Source:* Courtesy Malcolm Evans Cartoons.

the most celebrated anthropologists to explore these differences was Margaret Mead, whose research in the South Seas (Samoa, Polynesia, Indonesia) remains, despite some significant criticism, an example of engaged scholarship, clear writing, and important ideas. Mead was clear that sex differences are "not something deeply biological," but rather are learned and, once learned, become part of the ideology that continues to perpetuate them. Here's how she put it:

> I have suggested that certain human traits have been socially specialized as the appropriate attitudes and behavior of only one sex, while other human traits have been specialized for the opposite sex. This social specialization is then rationalized into a theory that the socially decreed behavior is natural for one sex and unnatural for the other, and that the deviant is a deviant because of glandular defect, or developmental accident.[2]

In *Sex and Temperament in Three Primitive Societies* (1935), Mead explored the differences in those definitions, whereas in several other books, such as *Male and Female* (1949) and *Coming of Age in Samoa* (1928), she explored the processes by which males and females become the men and women their cultures prescribe. No matter what she seemed to be writing about, though, Mead always had one eye trained on the United States. In generating implicit comparisons between our own and other cultures, Mead defied us to maintain the fiction that because it is so here, it must be right and cannot be changed.

In *Sex and Temperament*, Mead directly took on the claims of biological inevitability. By examining three very different cultures in New Guinea, she hoped to show the enormous cultural variation possible in definitions of masculinity and femininity and, in so doing, to enable Americans better to understand both the cultural origins and the malleability of their own ideas. The first two cultures exhibited remarkable similarities between women and men. Masculinity and femininity were not the lines along which personality differences seemed to be organized. Women and men were not the "opposite" sex. For example, all members of the Arapesh culture appeared gentle, passive, and emotionally warm. Males and females were equally "happy, trustful, confident," and individualism was relatively absent. Men and women shared child rearing; both were "maternal," and both discouraged aggressiveness among boys and girls. Both men and women were thought to be relatively equally sexual, though their sexual relationships tended to be "domestic" and not "romantic" or apparently what we might call passionate. Although female infanticide and male polygamy were not unknown, marriage was "even and contented." Indeed, Mead pronounced the political arrangements "utopian." Here's how she summed up Arapesh life:

> quiet and uneventful co-operation, singing in the cold dawn, and singing and laughter in the evening, men who sit happily playing to themselves on hand-drums, women holding suckling children to their breasts, young girls walking easily down the centre of the village, with the walk of those who are cherished by all about them.[3]

By contrast, Mead describes the Mundugumor, a tribe of headhunters and cannibals who also viewed women and men as similar but expected both sexes to be equally aggressive and violent. Women showed little "maternal instinct"; they detested pregnancy and nursing and could hardly wait to return to the serious business of work and war. "Mundugumor women actively dislike child-bearing, and they dislike children," Mead writes. "Children are carried in harsh opaque baskets that scratch their skins, later, high on their mother's shoulders, well away from the breast." Among the Mundugumor, there was a violent rivalry between fathers and sons (there was more infanticide of boys than of girls), and all people experienced a fear that they were being wronged by others. Quite wealthy (partly as a result of their methods of population control), the Mundugumor were, as Mead concludes, "violent, competitive, aggressively sexual, jealous, ready to see and avenge insult, delighting in display, in action, in fighting."[4]

Here, then, were two tribes that saw gender differences as virtually nonexistent. The third culture Mead described was the Tchambuli, where, as in the United States, women and men were seen as extremely different. This was a patrilineal culture in which polygyny was accepted. Here, one sex was composed primarily of nurturing and gossipy consumers who spent their days dressing up and going shopping. They wore curls and lots of jewelry, and Mead describes them as "charming, graceful, coquettish." These, incidentally, were the men, and they liked nothing better than to "go off resplendent in feathers and shell ornaments to spend a delightful few days" shopping. The women were dominant, energetic, economic providers. It was they who fished, an activity upon which the entire culture depended, and it was they "who have the real positions of power in the society." Completely unadorned, they were efficient, business-like, controlled all the commerce and diplomacy of the culture, and were the initiators of sexual relations. Mead notes that the Tchambuli were the only culture she had ever seen "where little girls of ten and eleven were more alertly intelligent and more enterprising than little boys." She writes that "what the women will think, what the women will say, what the women will do lies at the back of each man's mind as he weaves his tenuous and uncertain web of insubstantial relations with other men." By contrast, "the women are a solid group, confused by no rivalries, brisk, patronizing, and jovial."[5]

What Mead found, then, were two cultures in which women and men were seen as similar to each other and one culture in which women and men were seen as extremely different from each other—but exactly the opposite of the model familiar to us. Each culture, of course, believed that women and men were the way they were because their biological sex *determined* their personality. None of them believed that women and men were the outcome of economic scarcity, military success, or cultural arrangements (figure 3.2).

Mead urged her readers to "admit men and women are capable of being molded to a single pattern as easily as a diverse one."[6] She demonstrated that women and men are *capable* of similar or different temperaments, but she did not adequately explain *why* women and men turn out to be different or the same. These, then, are the questions for anthropologists: What are the determinants of women's and men's experiences? Why should male domination be nearly universal? These questions have been taken up by other anthropologists.

THE CENTRALITY OF THE GENDER DIVISION OF LABOR

In almost every society, labor is divided by gender (as well as age). Certain tasks are reserved for women, others for men. How do we explain this gender division of labor, if not by some biologically based imperatives?

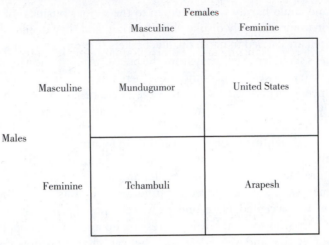

Figure 3.2. From Margaret Mead's *Sex and Temperament in Three Primitive Societies* (New York: William Morrow, 1935) (plus her implicit fourth case).

One school of thought, functionalism, maintains that a sex-based division of labor was necessary for the preservation of the society. As society became increasingly complex, there arose a need for two kinds of labor: hunting and gathering. Functionalists differ as to whether this division of labor had any *moral* component, whether the work of one sex was more highly valued than the work of the other. But they agree that the sex-based division of labor was functionally necessary for these societies. Such models often assume that because the sex-based division of labor arose to meet certain social needs at one time, its preservation is an evolutionary imperative, or at least an arrangement that is not to be trifled with casually.

On the other hand, because the sex-based division of labor has a history, it is not biologically inevitable; societies have changed and will continue to change. And it's a very recent history at that. "The sexual division of labor as we know it today probably developed quite recently in human evolution," writes anthropologist Adrienne Zihlman.[7] Moreover, this sex-based division of labor is far more varied than we might have assumed. In some cultures, women build the house; in others, they do the cooking. But in a few, it's the reverse. In most cultures, women are responsible for child care. But not in all cultures, and women are certainly not doing it all. In some cultures, tasks are dramatically skewed and labor rigidly divided; others offer far more flexibility and fluidity. Today, a sex-based division of labor is functionally anachronistic, and the biological bases for specific social tasks being assigned to either men or women have long been eroded. In the place of such foundations, though, lie centuries of social customs and traditions that today contribute to our gender ideologies about what is appropriate for one sex and not the other. The gender-based division of labor has become a part of our culture, not a part of our physical constitutions.

In fact, our physical constitutions have become less determinative in the assignment of tasks and the choosing of careers. It may even be true that the less significance there is to real physical differences, the more emphasis we place on them ideologically. For example, men no longer need to have physical strength to be powerful and dominant. The most highly muscular men, in fact, appear in cultural side-shows of body-building competition, but they do no more physical labor than the average suburban husband mowing the lawn and shoveling snow. As for women, the technologies of family planning and sexual autonomy—birth control technology, legal abortion, and institutional child care—have freed them from performing only child-care duties and enabled them to participate in the institutions of the public sphere.

Once free, women have entered every area of the public sphere. A century ago, women campaigned to enter the college classroom, the polling place, the professions, and the work world. More recently, it's been the military and military colleges that have opened their doors to women, the latter by court order. Today, very few occupations exist for which only women or only men are strictly biologically suited. Ask yourselves: What occupations do you know of that *biologically* only women or only men can perform? Offhand, I can think of only three: for women, wet nurse and surrogate mother; for men, professional sperm donor. None of these is exactly a career of choice for most of us.

If a sex-based division of labor has outlived its social usefulness or its physical imperatives, it must be held in place by something else: the power of one sex over the other. Where did that power come from? How has it developed? How does it vary from culture to culture? What factors exaggerate it; what factors diminish it? These are among the questions that anthropologists have endeavored to answer.

THEORIES OF GENDER DIFFERENTIATION AND MALE DOMINATION

Several theorists have tried to explain the **sexual division of labor** and gender inequality by reference to large, structural forces that transform societies' organizing principles. They've pointed to the impact of private property, the demands of war, and the importance of male bonding to hunting and gathering as possible explanations (figure 3.3).

Private Property and the Materialism of Male Domination

In the late nineteenth century, Friedrich Engels applied ideas that he developed with his collaborator, Karl Marx, and assigned to private property the role of central agent in determining the division of labor by sex. In *The Origin of the Family, Private Property and the State*, Engels suggested that the three chief institutions of modern Western society—a capitalist economy, the nation-state, and the nuclear family—emerged at roughly the same historical moment—and all as a result of the development of private property. Prior to that, Engels asserts, families were organized on a communal basis, with group marriage, male-female equality, and a sexual division of labor without any moral or political rewards going to males or females. The birth of the capitalist economy created wealth that was mobile and transferable—unlike land, which stays in the same place. Capitalism meant private property, which required the establishment of clear lines of inheritance. This requirement led, in turn, to new problems of sexual fidelity. If a man were to pass his property on to his son, he had to be sure that his son was, indeed, *his*. How could he know this in the communal group marriage of precapitalist families?

"We've gathered enough. Let's hunt."

Figure 3.3. Stuart Leeds/The New Yorker Collection/The Cartoon Bank.

OH? REALLY•

The origins of gender inequality date back to caveman days.

We like to think that gender inequality was found among our most ancient ancestors, as if that would somehow justify contemporary inequality. Images of cavemen dragging women by their hair, or of Fred Flintstone heading off to work in the slag heap while Wilma stays at home in Bedrock with Pebbles and Dino, dominate our consciousness.

Turns out it's all wrong. Actually, those first hunter-gatherers were far more gender-equal. Gender equality gave those hunting-gathering bands an evolutionary advantage, according to research by Mark Dyble and his colleagues. Wider social networks brought closer cooperation among unrelated people, and a higher likelihood of innovation. And it also meant less inbreeding.

Gender inequality began in earnest when people settled down. Settled agriculture meant that people could accumulate resources and save them, which led to hierarchies and imbalances, and men sought to solidify their gains by taking multiple wives. So it was farmers, not cavemen, who introduced patriarchy.

Source: M. Dyble, G. D. Salini, N. Chaudhary, A. Page, D. Smith, J. Thompson, L. Vinicius, R. Mace, and A. B. Migliano, "Sex Equality Can Explain the Unique Social Structure of Hunter-Gatherer Bands" in *Science*, 348(6236), May 15, 2015, pp. 796–798.

Out of this need to transmit inheritance across generations of men the traditional nuclear family emerged, with monogamous marriage and the sexual control of women by men. And if inheritance were to be stable, these new patriarchs needed to have clear, binding laws, vigorously enforced, that would enable them to pass their legacies on to their sons without interference from others. This required a centralized political apparatus (the nation-state) to exercise sovereignty over local and regional powers that might challenge them.[8]

Some contemporary anthropologists continue in this tradition. Eleanor Leacock, for example, argues that prior to the rise of private property and social classes, women and men were regarded as autonomous individuals who held different positions that were held in relatively equal esteem. "When the range of decisions made by women is considered," she writes, "women's autonomous and public role emerges. Their status was not as literal 'equals' of men…but as what they were—female persons, with their own rights, duties and responsibilities, which were complementary to and in no way secondary to those of men." In her ethnographic work on the Labrador peninsula, Leacock shows the dramatic transformation of women's former autonomy by the introduction of the fur trade. The introduction of a commercial economy turned powerful women into home-bound wives. Here again, gender inequality, introduced by economic shifts, resulted in increasing differences in the meanings of masculinity and femininity.[9]

Karen Sacks (now Karen Brodkin) examined four African cultures and found that the introduction of the **market economy** shifted basically egalitarian roles toward male dominance. As long as the culture was involved in producing goods for its own use, men and women were relatively equal. But the more involved the tribe became in a market exchange economy, the higher the level of gender inequality and the lower the position of women. Conversely, when women and men shared access to the productive elements of the society, the result was a higher level of sexual egalitarianism.[10]

Warfare, Bonding, and Inequality

Another school of anthropological thought traces the origins of male domination to the imperatives of warfare in primitive society. How does a culture create warriors who are fierce and strong? Anthropologist Marvin Harris has suggested two possibilities. The culture can provide different rewards for the warriors, based on their dexterity or skill. But this would limit the solidarity of the fighting force and sow seeds of dissent and enmity among the soldiers. More effective would be to reward virtually all men with the services of women, excluding only the most inadequate or cowardly men. Warrior societies tend to practice female infanticide, Harris observes, ensuring that the population of females remains significantly lower than that of males (and thus the males will be competing for the women). Warrior societies also tend to exclude women from the fighting force, because their presence would reduce the motivation of the soldiers and upset the sexual hierarchy. In this way, warfare leads to female subordination as well as patrilinearity, because the culture will need a resident core of fathers and sons to carry out its military tasks. Males come to control the society's resources and, as a justification for this, develop patriarchal religion as an ideology that legitimates their domination over women.[11]

Two other groups of scholars use different variables to explain the differences between women and men. **Descent theorists**, like Lionel Tiger and Robin Fox, stress the invariance of the mother-child bond. Men, by definition, lack the tie that mothers have with their children. How, then, can they achieve that connection to the next generation, the connection to history and society? They form it with other men in the hunting group. This is why, Tiger and Fox argue, women must be excluded from the hunt. In all societies, men must somehow be bound socially to the next generation, to which they are not inextricably, biologically connected. Male solidarity and monogamy are the direct result of men's needs to connect with social life.[12] **Alliance theorists** like Claude Levi-Strauss are less concerned with the need to connect males to the next generation than they are with the ways that relationships among men come to organize social life. Levi-Strauss argues that men turn women into sex objects whose exchange (as wives) cements the alliances among men. Both descent and alliance theorists treat these themes as invariant and natural, rather than as the outcomes of historical relationships that vary dramatically not only over time but also across cultures.[13]

DETERMINANTS OF WOMEN'S STATUS

Virtually every society of which we have knowledge claims some differentiation between women and men, and virtually every society exhibits patterns of gendered inequality and male domination. Yet the variety within these universals is still astounding. Gender differences and gender inequality may be more or less pronounced. It is not simply the case that the higher the degree of gender differentiation, the greater the gender inequality, although this is generally the pattern. One could, conceivably, imagine four such possibilities—high or low levels of gender differentiation coupled with either high or low levels of gender inequality.

What, then, are the factors that seem to determine women's status in society? Under what conditions is women's status improved, and under what conditions is it minimized? Economic, political, and social variables tend to produce different cultural

Figure 3.4. *Source:* Kim Warp/The New Yorker Collection/The Cartoon Bank.

configurations. For example, one large-scale survey of different cultures found that the more a society needs physical strength and highly developed motor skills, the larger will be the differences in socialization between males and females. It also seems to be the case that the larger the family group, the larger the differences between women and men. In part this is because the isolation of the nuclear family means that males and females will need to take the other's roles on occasion, so that strict separation is rarely enforced.[14]

One of the key determinants of women's status has been the division of labor around child care. Women's role in reproduction has historically limited their social and economic participation. Although no society assigns all child-care functions to men, the more that men participate in child care and the freer women are from child-rearing responsibility, the higher women's status tends to be. There are many ways to free women from sole responsibility. In non-Western societies, several customs evolved, including employing child nurses who care for several children at once, sharing child care with husbands or with neighbors, and assigning the role of child care to tribal elders whose economic activity has been curtailed by age.[15]

Relationships between children and their parents have also been seen as keys to women's status. Sociologist Scott Coltrane found that the closer the relationship between father and son, the higher the status of women is likely to be. Coltrane found that in cultures where fathers are relatively uninvolved, boys define themselves *in opposition* to their mothers and other women and therefore are prone to exhibit traits of **hypermasculinity**, to fear and denigrate women as a way to display masculinity. The more mothers and fathers share child rearing, the less men belittle women. Margaret Mead also emphasized the centrality of fatherhood. Most cultures take women's role in child rearing as a given, whereas men must learn to become nurturers. There is much at stake, but nothing is inevitable: "Every known human society rests firmly on the learned nurturing behavior of men."[16]

That men must learn to be nurturers raises the question of masculinity in general. What it means to be a man varies enormously from one culture to another, and these definitions have a great deal to do with the amount of time and energy fathers spend with their children. Such issues are not simply incidental for women's lives either;

OH? REALLY. Everyone knows that cavemen and cavewomen were hunters and gatherers, respectively, and that she was entirely responsible for child care. Except it may not be true. Anthropologist Lee Gettler found that fathers in early human species coparented—they were involved in bathing, feeding, playing, and teaching. (Only about 10 percent of all mammals find males helping out around the "house.") Male involvement in such harsh conditions also helped ensure the likelihood of survival, while a strict division of labor was probably a much riskier proposition. (And with fathers helping out, mothers didn't have to expend as much energy and could therefore reproduce again sooner, leading to more children.) Even way back then, dads were huggers as well as hunters.

Source: L. T. Gettler, "Direct Male Care and Hominin Evolution: Why Male-Child Interaction Is More Than a Nice Social Idea," in *American Anthropologist*, 112(1), 2010, pp. 7–21.

it turns out that the more time men spend with their children, the less gender inequality is present in that culture. Conversely, the freer women are from child care—the more that child care is parceled out elsewhere and the more that women control their fertility—the higher will be their status. Coltrane also found that women's status depends upon their control over property, especially after marriage. A woman's status is invariably higher when she retains control over her property after marriage.

Interestingly, recent research on male bonding, so necessary to those theories that stress warfare or the necessity of attaching males to the social order, also seems to bear this out. Sociologist and geographer Daphne Spain argues that the same cultures in which men developed the most elaborate sex-segregated rituals were those cultures in which women's status was lowest. Spain mapped a number of cultures spatially and found that the greater the distance the men's hut was from the center of the village, the more time the men spent at their hut, and the more culturally important the men's rituals were, the lower women's status was. "Societies with men's huts are those in which women have the least power," she writes. If you spend your time away from your hut, off at the men's hut with the other men, you'll have precious little time, and even less inclination, to spend with your family and to share in child rearing![17]

Similarly, anthropologist Thomas Gregor found that all forms of spatial segregation between males and females are associated with gender inequality. The Mehinaku of central Brazil, for example, have well-institutionalized men's huts where the tribal secrets are kept and ritual instruments are played and stored. Women are prohibited from entering. As one tribesman told Gregor, "This house is only for men. Women may not see anything in here. If a woman comes in, then all the men take her into the woods and she is raped."[18]

These two variables—the father's involvement in child rearing (often measured by spatial segregation) and women's control of property after marriage—emerge as among the central determinants of women's status and gender inequality. It is no wonder that they are also determinants of violence against women, because the lower women's status in a society, the higher the likelihood of rape and violence against women. In one of the most wide-ranging comparative studies of women's status, Peggy Reeves Sanday found several important correlates of women's status. Contact was one. **Sex segregation** was highly associated with women's lower status, as if separation were "necessary for the development of sexual inequality and male dominance." (By contrast, a study of a sexually egalitarian society found no ideology of the desirability of sex segregation.) Of course, women's economic power, that crucial determinant, is "the result of a sexual division of labor in which women achieve self-sufficiency and establish an independent control sphere." In addition, in cultures that viewed the environment as relatively friendly, women's status was significantly higher; cultures that saw the environment as hostile were more likely to develop patterns of male domination.[19]

Finally, Sanday found that women had the highest levels of equality, and thus the least frequency of rape, when both genders contributed about the same amounts to the food supply. When women contributed equally, men tended to be more involved in child care. Ironically, when women contributed a lot, their status was also low. So women's status tended to be lower when they contributed either very little or a great deal and more equal when their contribution was about equal.

We can now summarize the findings of cross-cultural research on female status and male dominance.

1. Male dominance is lower when men and women work together with little sexual division of labor. Sex segregation of work is the strongest predictor of women's status.

2. Male dominance is more pronounced when men control political and ideological resources that are necessary to achieve the goals of the culture and when men control all property.

3. Male dominance is "exacerbated under **colonization**"—both capitalist penetration of the countryside and industrialization generally lower women's status. Male dominance is also associated with demographic imbalances between the sexes: The higher the percentage of marriageable men to marriageable women, the lower is women's status.

4. Environmental stresses tend to exaggerate male domination.[20]

THE CROSS-CULTURAL EXPLANATIONS OF RAPE

The earlier quotation, cited by Gregor, and the research of Peggy Reeves Sanday and others suggest that rape is not the evolutionary reproductive strategy of less successful males, as was suggested by some evolutionary psychologists. Rather, rape is a cultural phenomenon by which relations between men are cemented. Rape may be a strategy to ensure continued male domination or a vehicle by which men can hope to conceal maternal dependence, according to ethnographers, but it is surely not an alternative dating strategy.

Think, for example, of the way that rape is used in warfare. The mass rape of Bosnian women or the current mass rapes of women in the Sudan or the Congo are not some product or convoluted expression of evolutionary mating strategies, but rather a direct and systematic effort on the part of one militarized group of males to express and sustain the subordination of a conquered group of males. Mass rape in warfare is about the final humiliating appropriation of the conquered group's property. It is as if to say: "We burn your houses, eat your chickens, and rape your women. We have fully and completely conquered you."

And what about rape not as a crime to be punished but as the *restitution* for a crime that has been committed? In June 2002, a Pakistani woman, Mukhtar Mai, was gang-raped in a small village in southern Punjab. She was ordered to be raped by a local judicial council as punishment for nonmarital sex. Except she didn't actually have nonmarital sex—her brother did. Or so they believed. Mukhtar was ordered raped because of a crime her brother was said to have committed. (It was later revealed that her brother, age twelve, had himself been abducted and sodomized by three elder tribesmen, who fabricated the sex story as a cover-up.) Were these elder tribesmen tried and convicted of the rape of the twelve-year-old boy? No. Were the men who sentenced Mukhtar Mai to be gang-raped themselves brought to justice? Eventually, after a world outcry against such obvious injustice. Although obviously neither of these rapes could even be remotely tied to some evolutionary strategy for reproductive success, together they reveal the way that rape serves to reproduce male domination. Both the dominance hierarchies among men and the hierarchies that place men over women were revealed in this horrific moment.[21]

In her ethnographic study of a gang rape at the University of Pennsylvania, Peggy Reeves Sanday underscores how a campus gang rape looks surprisingly like this Pakistani judicial council. She suggests that gang rape has its origins both in the gender inequality that allows men to see women as pieces of meat and in men's needs to demonstrate their masculinity to one another. Gang rape cements the relations among men. But more than that, gang rape permits a certain homoerotic contact between men. When one participant reported his pleasure at feeling the semen of his friends inside the woman as he raped her, Sanday sensed a distinct erotic component. The woman was the receptacle, the vehicle by which these men could have sex with one another and still claim heterosexuality. Only in a culture that degrades and devalues women could such behaviors take place. Rape, then, is hardly an evolutionary strategy by which less successful males get to pass on their reproductive inheritance. It is an act that occurs only in those societies where there is gender inequality and by men who may be quite "successful" in other forms of mating but believe themselves entitled to violate women. It is about *gender*, not about *sex*, and it is a way in which gender inequality produces gender difference.[22]

RITUALS OF GENDER

One of the ways by which anthropologists have explored the cultural construction of gender is by examining specific gender rituals. Their work suggests that the origins of these rituals lie in nonbiological places. Because questions of reproduction and child rearing loom so large in the determination of gender inequality, it makes sense that a lot of these rituals are concerned with reproduction. And because spatial segregation seems to be highly associated with gender difference and gender inequality, ritual segregation—either in space or time—may have also been a focus of attention. For example, the initiation of young males has been of particular concern, in part because of the relative disappearance of such formal cultural rituals in the contemporary United States. **Initiation rituals** provide a sense of identity and group membership to the men who participate in them. Many cultures, especially settled agricultural and pastoral societies, include **circumcision**, the **excision** of the foreskin of a boy's penis, in a ritual incorporating a male into the society. The age of this ritual varies; one survey of twenty-one cultures that practice circumcision found that four perform it in infancy, ten when the boy is about ten years old (before puberty), six perform it at puberty, and one waits until late adolescence.

Why would so many cultures determine that membership in the world of adult men requires **genital mutilation**? Indeed, circumcision is the most common medical procedure in the United States. Theories, of course, abound. In the Jewish Bible, circumcision is a visible sign of the bond between God and man, a symbol of man's obedience to God's law. (In Genesis 17:10–11, 14, God commands Abraham to circumcise Isaac as part of a covenant.) But circumcision also seems to have been seen as a way of acquiring a trophy. Successful warriors would cut off their foes' foreskins to symbolize their victory and to permanently disfigure and humiliate the vanquished foe. (In I Samuel 18:25, King Saul demands that David slay one hundred enemies and bring back their foreskins as a bride-price. David, a bit overeager, brings back two hundred.)

In other cultures, ethnographers suggest that circumcision creates a visible scar that binds men to one another and serves as a rite of passage to adult masculinity.

Whiting, Kluckhohn, and Anthony argue that it symbolically serves to sever a boy's emotional ties to his mother and therefore to ensure appropriate masculine identification. Other writers point out that cultures that emphasize circumcision of young males tend to be those where both gender differentiation and gender inequality are greatest. Circumcision, which is always a public ceremony, simultaneously cements the bonds between father (and his generation) and son (and his generation), links the males together, and excludes women, visibly and demonstrably. Circumcision, then, tends to be associated with male domination,[23] as do other forms of male genital mutilation. In a very few cultures, for example, the penis is ritually bled by cutting. Such cultures still believe in bleeding as a cure for illness—in this case, illness brought about by sexual contact with women, who are believed to be impure and infectious. And we know of four cultures that practice hemicastration, the removal of one testicle. In one culture, people believe it prevents the birth of twins.[24]

Female circumcision is also practiced in several cultures, though far fewer than practice male circumcision. This circumcision consists either of **clitoridectomy**, in which the clitoris is cut away, or infibulation, in which the labia majora are sewn together with only a very small opening left to allow for urination. It is interesting that female circumcision is often performed by adult women. In other cultures, it is performed by the brother of the girl's father. Clitoridectomy is widespread in Africa but few other places, and it invariably takes place in societies that also practice male circumcision. Infibulation seems to be most widely practiced in East Africa and Somalia, and its goal is to prevent sexual intercourse, whereas the goal of clitoridectomy is simply to prevent sexual pleasure and thereby sexual promiscuity. It is estimated by the World Health Organization that 130 million girls and women have undergone some form of cutting of the clitoris (figure 3.5).[25]

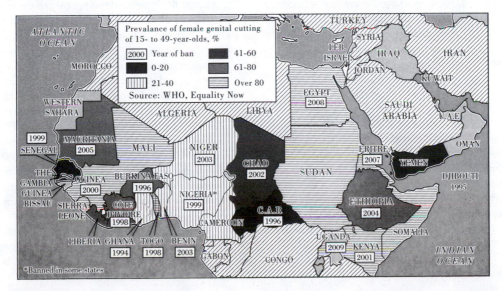

Figure 3.5.

READ ALL ABOUT IT!

Female genital mutilation (FGM) is becoming a global public health and human rights issue. But while it initially seemed to be a problem linked to Muslim societies in which women's status is remarkably low, it turns out to be far more widespread than Muslim cultures. In fact, according to Thomas von der Osten-Sacken and Thomas Uwer, who together are directors of a German-based human rights organization, the variations in dynamics of organization of FGM make it impossible to treat with a one-size-fits-all policy. A coordinated effort to promote human rights is, they argue, necessary to fully address the issue.

It is interesting that both cultures that circumcise men and those that circumcise women tend to be those where men's status is highest. The purpose of the ritual reveals the reason for some of this difference. For men, the ritual is a marking that simultaneously shows that all men are biologically *and culturally* alike—and that they are different from women. Thus it can be seen as reinforcing male dominance. Historically, there was some evidence that male circumcision was medically beneficial, because it reduced

Female Circumcision

Here is a description of female circumcision from one who underwent it, a Sudanese woman now working as a teacher in the Middle East:

I will never forget the day of my circumcision, which took place forty years ago. I was six years old. One morning during my school summer vacation, my mother told me that I had to go with her to her sisters' house and then to visit a sick relative in Halfayat El Mulook [in the northern part of Khartoum, Sudan]. We did go to my aunt's house, and from there all of us went straight to [a] red brick house [I had never seen].

While my mother was knocking, I tried to pronounce the name that was on the door. Soon enough I realized that it was Haija Alamin's house. She was the midwife [who performed circumcisions on girls in my neighborhood]. I was petrified and tried to break loose. But I was captured and subdued by my mother and two aunts. They began to tell me that the midwife was going to purify me.

The midwife was the cruelest person I had seen . . . [She] ordered her young maid to go buy razors from the Yemeni grocer next door. I still remember her when she came back with the razors, which were enveloped in purple wrappings with a crocodile drawing on it.

The women ordered me to lie down on a bed [made of ropes] that had a little hole in the middle. They held me tight while the midwife started to cut my flesh without anesthetics. I screamed till I lost my voice. The midwife was saying to me "Do you want me to be taken into police custody?" After the job was done I could not eat, drink, or even pass urine for three days. I remember one of my uncles who discovered what they did to me threatened to press charges against his sisters. They were afraid of him and they decided to bring me back to the midwife. In her sternest voice she ordered me to squat on the floor and urinate. It seemed like the most difficult thing to do at that point, but I did it. I urinated for a long time and was shivering with pain.

It took a very long time [before] I was back to normal. I understand the motives of my mother, that she wanted me to be clean, but I suffered a lot.[26]

the possibilities of penile infection by removing the foreskin, a place where bacteria could congregate. This is no longer the case; rates of penile infection or urethral cancer show only minuscule differences between those men who have and have not been circumcised. There is some evidence, however, that in Africa, male circumcision is associated with a lower risk of HIV infection and therefore recommended to reduce HIV infections among both women and men. But there is no medical justification for male circumcision in the United States, which is the only nation in which the majority of male babies are still medically circumcised (not due to religious beliefs). Rates in the United States have dropped from about 85 percent in the 1960s to about 58 percent today. Thus, health organizations may be in the ironic position of discouraging routine medical circumcision in some regions and encouraging it in others.[27]

For women, circumcision has never been justified by medical benefits; it directly impedes adequate sexual functioning and is designed to curtail sexual pleasure. Female circumcision is nearly always performed when women reach the age of puberty, that is, when they are capable of experiencing sexual pleasure, and seems to be associated with men's control over women's sexuality. Currently, political campaigns are being waged to prohibit female circumcision as a violation of women's human rights. In Kenya, some women have developed alternative rituals to enable girls to come of age without any form of genital mutilation. For example, "Cutting Through Words" is one ritual that provides a celebration of adulthood that honors the girl and her family. "We need to tread carefully since female genital mutilation is deeply rooted into the culture," says Priscilla Nangurai, headmistress of a church-sponsored girls, boarding school, who has been one of the advocates of change. "We can end it through education, advocacy and religion."[28]

However, many defenders of female circumcision suggest that such campaigns are motivated by Western values. They insist that afterward women are revered and respected as members of the culture. (There are no widespread political campaigns against male circumcision, though some individuals have recently begun to rethink the ritual as a form of genital mutilation, and a few men are even undergoing a surgical procedure designed to replace the lost foreskin.[29]) Others counter that the right to control one's own body is a fundamental human right and that cultures that practice such behaviors must conform to universal standards.

One of the more interesting theories about the prevalence of these reproductive and sexual rituals has been offered by Jeffrey and Karen Paige in their book *The Politics of Reproductive Ritual*. Paige and Paige offer a materialist interpretation of these rituals, locating the origins of male circumcision, couvade, and purdah in the culture's relationship with its immediate material environment. Take **couvade**, for example (figure 3.6). This is a ritual that men observe when their wives are having babies. Generally, the men observe the same food taboos as their wives, restrict their ordinary activities, and even seclude themselves during their wives' delivery and postpartum period. What could possibly be the point of this? Some might think it is anthropologically "cute," as the men often even imitate the symptoms of pregnancy, in apparent sympathy for their wives. But Paige and Paige see it differently. They argue that couvade is significant in cultures where there are no legal mechanisms to keep the couple together or to assure paternity. Couvade is a way for men to fully claim paternity, to know that the baby is theirs. It is also a vehicle by which the men can control women's sexuality by appropriating control over paternity.[30]

Figure 3.6. Courtesy of Kathleen Moore/moorestories.com.

 Women everywhere adorn themselves with jewelry, makeup, and other fashion accessories in order to be more attractive to men. Actually, there are many cultures in which it's the *males* who adorn themselves and parade around for women's approval. In one culture, the Wodaabe of Niger, each year the men dress up in ceremonial garb, paint their faces and lips, and parade in front of the unadorned women, who sit in judgment of the men, deciding which one they will sleep with. (The opening photo of this chapter shows a dancer applying makeup.) The Wodaabe prize height, white teeth, and white eyes—all signs of health—so the men desperately try to set off their teeth (by staining their lips black), stand on tiptoes, and open their eyes as wide as possible.

Figure 3.7. *Source:* Courtesy of Photography Collection, Harry Ransom Center, The University of Texas at Austin.

Paige and Paige also examine the politics of **purdah**, the Islamic requirement that women conceal themselves at all times (figure 3.7). Ostensibly, this requirement is to protect women's chastity and men's honor—women must be completely covered because they "are so sexy, so tempting, so incapable of controlling their emotions and sexuality, the men say, that they are a danger to the social order." It is as if by concealing women, men can harness women's sexuality. But this is only half the story. It also suggests that *men* are so susceptible to temptation, so incapable of resistance, such easy prey, that they are likely to fall into temptation at any time. In order to protect women from *men's* sexual rapaciousness, men must control women and take away the source of the temptation.[31]

HOW MANY GENDERS ARE THERE?

We've explored the relationship between levels of gender difference and levels of inequality. But in some cultures, gender itself doesn't seem to be that important, certainly not the central organizing principle of social life. In fact, it hardly matters at all. What accounts for that difference?

READ ALL ABOUT IT!

We tend to think we are either men or women (and that, biologically, this corresponds to being male or female). Yet the cross-cultural record demonstrates that gender is not nearly as fixed and categorical as we might believe. Instead, it is fluid, and not only do people move between poles, but societies can use gender as a way to respond to ecological or political crises. When a society loses a significant number of men (e.g., in war) or women (e.g., in some environmental calamity), it is not uncommon for members of one sex to live as the other, with complete social approval, as sociologist Judith Lorber shows in her essay "Men as Women and Women as Men." Indeed, this isn't as foreign a concept as we might at first think. Just remember Joan of Arc or Molly Pitcher (who fought bravely against the British in the American Revolution).

The discussion of gender difference often assumes that differences are based on some biological realities that sort physical creatures into their appropriate categories. Thus we assume that because there are two biological sexes (male and female), there must only be two genders (men and women). But some research challenges such bipolar assumptions. Some societies recognize more than two genders—sometimes three or four. Research on Native American cultures is particularly fascinating and provocative. The Navajo, for example, appear to have three genders—one for masculine men, one for feminine women, and another, called the **nadle**, for those whose sex is ambiguous at birth. One can be born a *nadle* or decide to become one; either way, *nadles* perform tasks assigned to both women and men and dress as the gender whose tasks they are performing, though they are typically treated as women and addressed using feminine kinship terms. But let's not jump to conclusions: Being treated as a woman is a promotion, not a demotion, in Navajo society, where women historically have had higher status than men and are accorded special rights and privileges, including sexual freedom, control over property, and authority to mediate disputes. *Nadles* are free to marry either males or females, with no loss of status (figure 3.8).[32]

Another custom among some Native American cultures is the **two-spirit person**, which is also found in Southeast Asia and the South Pacific. (Two-spirit people have historically been called *berdache*, but they prefer the new term since "berdache" was the term the French colonialists used.) Two-spirit people are members of one biological sex who adopt the gender identity of the other sex, although such a practice is far more common for males than for females. In his pathbreaking study *The Spirit and the Flesh*, anthropologist Walter Williams explored the world of the two-spirit person in detail. These are men who dress, work, and generally act as women—though everyone knows that they are biologically males. Among the Crow in North America, the two-spirit people are simply males who do not want to become warriors.[33]

In southern Mexico, indigenous communities in the state of Oaxaca allow for a **third gender**, called **muxe** (a Zapotec word derived from the Spanish word *mujer* or woman). Like the others, these are males who feel themselves, from an early age, to be more like women. Not only does the community accept them, but they are embraced as especially gifted, artistic, and intelligent.[34]

Figure 3.8. This remarkable photograph is titled "Squaw Jim and His Squaw." On the left is Squaw Jim, a biological male in woman's attire—a Crow berdache afforded distinctive social and ceremonial status within the tribe. In addition to the special attributes that distinguished the berdache or *bote*, Squaw Jim served as an enlisted scout at Fort Keogh and achieved a reputation for bravery when he saved the life of a tribesman at the Battle of the Rosebud, on June 17, 1876. This image is the earliest known photograph of a North American two-spirit person. Photograph by John H. Fouch, 1877.

Source: Courtesy of Dr. James S. Brust.

Some grow up to be gay, some straight. What is clear, and most important to us here, is that the *muxe* represent a distinct *gender*, not necessarily a gay masculinity. In that sense, they might be considered transgender, but not necessarily homosexual.

Consider how we treat males who dress and act like women. We treat them like freaks or deviants or assume they must be homosexual. They are outcasts; acting like a two-spirit in this culture is not recommended if you value your health and your life. Among the Native American cultures of the Great Plains, though, two-spirit people are revered as possessed of special powers, enjoy high social and economic status, and frequently control the tribe's ritual life. The reasoning is straightforward and logical: By being men who act like women, the two-spirit people are sexually in-different to women, something that other men are not capable of being. Surely, they must be possessed of some supernatural power to be able to resist the charms of females! Only a two-spirit person can be counted on to administer fairly without seeking to advance his claim on a specific woman whom he might fancy.

And what about the other way around? Native American poet and author Paula Gunn Allen argued that among the Sioux there were warrior women who married other women and were known as "manly-hearted women." Among the Cherokee, these women were called "beloved women" and they were "warriors, leaders and influential council members."[35]

The Mohave seemed to have four genders and permitted both women and men to cross genders to carefully demarcated roles. A boy who showed preferences for feminine clothing or toys would undergo a different initiation at puberty and become an *alyha*. He would then adopt a female name, paint his face as a woman, perform female roles, and marry a man. When they married, the *alyha* would cut his upper thigh every month to signify "his" menstrual period, and he would learn how to simulate pregnancy and childbirth. Martin and Voorhies suggest how this was accomplished:

> Labor pains, induced by drinking a severely constipating drug, culminate in the birth of a fictitious stillborn child. Stillborn Mohave infants are customarily buried by the mother, so that an alyha's failure to return to "her" home with a living infant is explained in a culturally acceptable manner.[36]

If a Mohave female wanted to cross genders, she would undergo an initiation ceremony to become a **hwame**. *Hwame* lived men's lives—hunting, farming, and the like—and assumed paternal responsibility for children, though they were prohibited from assuming positions of political leadership. Neither a *hwame* nor an *alyha* was considered deviant.

In the Middle East, we find a group of Omani males called **xanith** who are biologically males, but whose social identity is female. They work as skilled domestic servants, dress in men's tunics (but in pastel shades more associated with feminine colors), and sell themselves in passive homosexual relationships. They are permitted to speak with women on the street (other men are prohibited). At sex-segregated public events, they sit with the women. However, they can change their minds—and their gender experiences. If they want to be seen as males, they are permitted to do so, and they then may engage in heterosexual sex. Others simply grow older and eventually quit the homosexual prostitution; they are then permitted to become "social men." Some "become" women, even going as far as marrying men. And still others move back and forth between these positions throughout their lives, suggesting a fluidity of gender identity that would be unthinkable to those who believe in biological determinism.

Gender fluidity can be associated with greater gender equality, if people believe that the relationship between biological sex and socially constructed gender is more porous and that one can move readily between them. Or it can be associated with less gender equality, as if any variation from the expected norm can be cause to invent a whole new gender. In Afghanistan, boys are so highly prized and gender inequality so extreme that it is not uncommon for a family with no sons to raise one of their daughters as if she were a boy. They are called neither daughter nor son, but *bacha posh*, which means "dressed as a boy," a specific identity that remains until she hits puberty. And it's not a bad deal for the daughter, since the life of a girl is pretty well circumscribed. "Do you want to look like a boy and dress like a boy, and do more fun things like boys do, like bicycling, soccer and cricket?" one little girl was asked. She answered yes immediately. Wouldn't you?[37]

Figures 3.9a and 3.9b. Photographer Shahria Sharmin photographed the *hijra* community in Bangladesh after meeting a young *hijra* named Heena. Here is how Heena described herself: *"I feel like a mermaid. My body tells me that I am a man but my soul tells me that I am a woman. I am like a flower, a flower that is made of paper. I shall always be loved from a distance, never to be touched and no smell to fall in love with."*

Source: Photos courtesy of Shahria Sharmin.

SEXUAL DIVERSITY

Studies of **gender fluidity** are complemented by studies of sexual variation. Taken together, they provide powerful arguments about the cultural construction of both gender and sexuality. Anthropologists have explored remarkable sexual diversity and thus have suggested that biological arguments about the naturalness of some activities and arrangements may be dramatically overstated. Take homosexuality, which evolutionary biologists would suggest is a biological "aberration" if ever there were one, because homosexuality is not reproductive, and the goal of all sexual activity is to pass on one's genetic code to the next generation. Not only is homosexual activity ubiquitous in the animal kingdom, but also it is extraordinarily common in human cultures—so common, in fact, that it would appear to be "natural." What varies is not the presence or absence of homosexuality—those are pretty much constants—but the ways in which homosexuals are treated in those cultures. We've already seen that many cultures honor and respect those who transgress gender definitions and adopt the gender of the other sex. Some of these might be considered "homosexual," if your definition of "homosexual" has to do only with the biological sex of your sex partner.

Even by that definition, though, we find astonishing variation in the ways in which homosexuals are regarded. In 1948, anthropologist Clyde Kluckhohn surveyed North American Indian tribes and found homosexuality accepted by 120 of them and rejected by 54. Some cultures (Lango in East Africa, Koniag in Alaska, and Tanala in Madagascar) allow homosexual marriages between men. Some cultures have clearly defined homosexual roles for men and women, with clearly defined expectations.[38]

READ ALL ABOUT IT!

Many societies construct elaborate rituals by which boys *become* men and girls *become* women. Even when they believe that gender identities are biologically based, the culture still has a responsibility to ensure safe passage between these two age-related states. These rituals vary enormously, as anthropologist Gilbert Herdt shows in his essay "Coming of Age and Coming Out Ceremonies Across Cultures." Herdt did the original research on the Sambia that we'll discuss, here he takes us inside the world of the Sambia—and other cultures, including our own—to discuss the rich diversity of initiation rituals.

In a remarkable ethnography, Gilbert Herdt described the sexual rituals of the Sambia, a mountain people who live in Papua New Guinea. The Sambia practice **ritualized homosexuality** as a way to initiate young boys into full adult manhood. Young boys ritually daily fellate the older boys and men so that the younger boys can receive the vital life fluid (semen) from the older men and thus become men. "A boy must be initiated and [orally] inseminated, otherwise the girl betrothed to him will outgrow him and run away to another man," was the way one Sambia elder put it. "If a boy doesn't eat semen, he remains small and weak." When they reach puberty, these boys are then fellated by a new crop of younger boys. Throughout this initiation, the boys scrupulously avoid girls and have no knowledge of heterosexuality until they are married. Neither the boys nor the older men think of themselves as engaging in homosexual behavior: The older men are married to women and the younger men fully expect to be. There is no adult homosexuality among the Sambia. But these young boys must become, as Herdt puts it, "reluctant warriors." How else are the boys to receive the vital life force that will enable them to be real men and warriors?[39]

Nearby, also in Melanesia, are the Keraki, who engage in a related practice. There, the boys are sodomized by older men, because the Keraki believe that without the older men's semen, the boys will not grow to be men. This ritual practice occurs until the boys enter puberty and secondary sex characteristics appear—facial hair, dropped voice—at which point the ritual has accomplished its task. When an anthropologist asked Keraki men if they had been sodomized, many responded by saying, "Why, yes! Otherwise how should I have grown?" Other ritualized homosexual practices have been reported from other cultures.[40] Interestingly, such ritual practices, as those among the Sambia and Keraki, are more evident in cultures in which sex segregation is high and women's status is low. This conforms to other ethnographic evidence that suggests that elaborate rituals of male bonding have the effect of excluding women from ritual life and thus correlate with women's lower status. Sex segregation is almost always associated with lower status for women—whether among the Sambia or among cadets at the Citadel.[41]

If all this sounds extraordinarily exotic, remember this: In every major city in the United States, there is a group of young men, many of whom are married and virtually all of whom consider themselves to be heterosexual, who have sex with other men for money. These gay hustlers will perform only certain acts (anal penetration) or will allow only certain acts (they permit their clients to fellate them but will not reciprocate). By remaining the "insertor" in homosexual acts, these men do not identify as homosexual, but rather as men. Men are insertors, whether with women or with men, so as long as they remain insertors, they believe their masculinity is not compromised. "Objectively," you may argue, they are engaging in gay sex. But by their definition, homosexuality equals passivity in sexual contact, having sex like a woman. And by that definition, they are not having gay sex. Whatever you might make of this, though, suddenly the Sambia do not look completely alien; they look more like distant cousins.

Some cultures take permissiveness regarding homosexuality to a remarkable level. Among the Aranda of Australia, Siwans of northern Africa, and Keraki of New Guinea, already described here, every male is homosexual during adolescence and bisexual after marriage. The purpose of this is to divert adolescent sex away from young girls and prevent teenage pregnancy and therefore to keep the birth rate down in cultures that have very scarce resources. The well-studied Yanomamö have an institutionalized form of male homosexuality as well as female infanticide. This warrior culture fears population explosion and the depletion of resources to females.[42]

The Etero and the Marind-anim, both in New Guinea, prefer homosexuality to heterosexuality, even though they maintain heterosexual marriages. How, you might ask, do they solve the problem of reproduction? The Etero place a taboo on heterosexual sex for most of the year but prohibit gay sex when the moon is full (and thus when all the women are ovulating). For the Marind-anim, even that much sexual contact with the opposite sex is undesirable. Their birth rate is so low that this warrior culture organizes raids every year, during which it kidnaps the babies of other cultures, raising them to be happy, healthy—and, of course, homosexual—Marind-anim.[43]

One Melanesian society, called "East Bay" in William Davenport's ethnographic study, practices full adult bisexuality. Nearly every male has extensive homosexual sexual contact throughout his life, though all are also heterosexual and married to women. (None is exclusively homosexual, and only a few exclusively heterosexual.) Women and men are seen as relatively equal in terms of sexual drive, and there are no taboos against contact with women.[44]

SEXUAL CUSTOMS AS GENDER DIVERSITY

Sexual customs display a dizzying array that, all elements taken together, implies that sexual behavior is anything but organized around reproduction alone. Where, when, how, and with whom we have sex vary enormously from culture to culture. Ernestine Friedel, for example, observed dramatic differences in sexual customs between two neighboring tribes in New Guinea. One, a highland tribe, believes that intercourse makes men weaker and that women are naturally prone to tempt men, threatening them with their powerful sexuality. They also find menstrual blood terrifying. These sexual ideologies pit women against men, and many men would rather remain bachelors than risk contact with women. As a result, population remains relatively low, which this culture needs because it has no new land or resources to bring under cultivation. Not far away, however, is a very different culture. Here, both men and women enjoy sex and sex play. Men worry about whether women are sexually satisfied, and they get along relatively well. They have higher birth rates, which is manageable because they live in a relatively abundant and uncultivated region, where they can use all the hands they can get to farm their fields and defend themselves.[45]

Sex researchers have explored the remarkable cultural diversity of sexual behaviors and in so doing have exposed the **ethnocentrism** of those arguments that stress the inevitability and naturalness of our own behaviors. Take the typical American couple, Mr. and Mrs. Statistical Average. They're white, middle-aged, married, and have sex about twice a week, at night, in their bedroom, alone, with the lights off, in the "missionary position"—the woman on her back, facing the man, who lies on top of her. The encounter—from the "Do you want to?" to kissing, foreplay, intercourse (always in that order), and finally to "Goodnight, sweetheart"—lasts about fifteen minutes. Now consider other cultures: Some cultures never have sex outside. Others believe that having sex indoors would contaminate the food supply (usually in the same hut). What about our rates of sexual contact? The Zande have sex two or three times a night and then once again upon awakening. Chaga men have about ten orgasms a night, and Thonga men try to have sex with as many as three or four of their wives each night. But few beat the Marquesa: Although it's not uncommon for a Marquesan man to have thirty or more orgasms a night, it is normal to have at least ten. Older married men are exempted: They have only about three or four a night. By contrast, the Yapese have sex only once a month or so. During this encounter, the man sits with his back against the side of the hut and his legs straight out. The woman straddles him, and he inserts his penis into her vagina a little bit and then proceeds to stimulate her for several hours while she has dozens of orgasms.[46]

Whereas for us kissing is a virtually universal initiation of sexual contact—"first base," as it were—other cultures find it disgusting because of the possibility of exchanging saliva. "Putting your lips together?" say the Thonga or the Siriono. "But that's where you put food!" Some cultures practice almost no foreplay at all, but instead go directly to intercourse; others prescribe several hours of touching and caressing, in which intercourse is a necessary but sad end to the proceedings. Some cultures include oral sex in their lovemaking; others have never even considered it. Alfred Kinsey found that 70 percent of the American men he surveyed in 1948 had had sex only in the missionary position and that 85 percent had an orgasm within two minutes of penetration. In his survey of 131 Native American cultures, Clyde Kluckhohn found the missionary position preferred in only 17.[47]

In our culture, it is men who are supposed to be the sexual initiators and women who are supposed to be sexually resistant. We've all heard stories about men giving women aphrodisiacs to make them more sexually uninhibited. The latest is **Rohypnol**, the "date rape drug," which men apparently put into unsuspecting women's drinks to make them more "compliant" or at least unconscious (which, in these men's minds, may amount to the same thing). How different are the Trobriand Islanders, to whom women are seen as sexually insatiable and as those who take the initiative. Or the Tukano-Kubeo in Brazil. Here, women are the sexual aggressors and may even avoid getting pregnant or abort a pregnancy because pregnancy would mean forgoing sex. Women, not men, commit adultery, but women justify it by saying that it was "only sex." Tukano-Kubeo men secretly give the women anaphrodisiacs to cool them down.[48]

These are but a few examples. When questioned about their practices, people in these cultures give the same answers we would. "It's normal," they'll say. And they've developed the same kind of self-justifying arguments that we have. The Bambara, for example, believe that having sex during the day will produce albino children, whereas the Masai believe daytime sex can be fatal. So members of these cultures have sex only at night, and apparently, there are no albinos born and no fatalities during sex. The Chenchu, by contrast, believe that sex at night will lead to the birth of blind babies. So they have sex only during the day and thus avoid having blind children. The Yurok believe that practicing cunnilingus would keep the salmon from running. No oral sex, no shortage of salmon. Such sexual variety suggests that the biological imperative toward reproduction can take many forms but that none is more "natural" than any other.

ANTHROPOLOGY AS HISTORY

Anthropological research has helped to expose the faulty logic of those who argue that the universality of gender difference or of male domination is somehow natural and inevitable. By exploring the variety of meanings that has accompanied the cultural definitions of masculinity and femininity and by examining cultural configurations that either magnify or diminish gender inequality, cross-cultural research has taken us beyond apparent biological imperatives. In another sense, anthropological research on our human ancestors has also provided a historical retort to biological inevitability. Take, for example, the arguments we saw earlier that male domination was a natural development in the shift to hunting-and-gathering societies. Remember the story: Men's superior physical strength led them naturally toward hunting, whereas weaker women stayed home and busied themselves with gardening and child rearing. Tidy and neat—but also, it appears, historically wrong.

It turns out that such stories actually read history backward, from the present to the past, seeking the historical origins of the patterns we find today. But recent research suggests that meat made up a rather small portion of the early human diet, which meant that all that celebrated hunting didn't count for much at all. And those weapons men invented, the great technological breakthrough that enabled cultures to develop—placing cultural development squarely on the backs of men? Turns out that the great technological leap was more likely slings that women with babies developed so they could carry both baby and food. It may even be true that the erect posture of human beings derives not from the demands of hunting, but rather from the shift from foraging for food to gathering and storing it. Although celebrants of "masculinist" evolution credited the demands of the hunt for creating the necessity of social (male) bonding for the survival of the community, surely it is the bond between mother and infant that literally and materially ensures survival. Painting a more accurate anthropological picture would require that we acknowledge that females were not simply passive and dependent bearers of children, but rather were active participants in the technological and economic side of life.[49]

Another way to look at this is suggested by Helen Fisher. She notes startling similarities between contemporary American culture and early human cultures. The elements we have inherited as the biologically natural system—nuclear families, marriages with one partner for life, the dramatic separation of home and workplace—all seem to be relatively recent cultural inventions that accompany settled agricultural societies. On the other hand, divorce and remarriage, institutionalized child care, and women and men working equally both at home and away are more typical of the hunting-and-gathering societies that preceded ours—and lasted for millions of years. It may be, Fisher suggests, that after a brief evolutionary rest stop in settled agricultural domain (during which time male domination, warfare, and monotheism all developed), we are returning to our "true" human evolutionary origins. "As we head back to the future," she suggests, "there's every reason to believe the sexes will enjoy the kind of equality that is a function of our birthright."[50]

If this sounds a bit too mythical, there is a school of feminist anthropology that goes much further. Most anthropologists agree with Michelle Rosaldo, who concluded that "human cultural and social forms have always been male dominated," or with Bonnie Nardi, who finds "no evidence of truly egalitarian societies. In no societies do women participate on an equal footing with men in activities accorded the highest prestige."[51] But one school of feminist anthropologists sees such universality as "an ethnological delusion," and this school argues that there have been, and are, societies in which women and men have been, and are, equal. What's more, there also may have been societies in which women were the dominant sex. Based on archeological excavations in Crete and elsewhere, Marija Gimbutas and Riane Eisler and others have argued that Neolithic societies were goddess-worshipping, gender-equal, virtual Gardens of Eden, in which women and men may have occupied separate spheres but were equal and mutually respectful. Symbolized, Eisler writes, by the chalice—the symbol of shared plenty—these ancient peoples evidenced a "partnership" model of human interaction.[52]

Then, the story goes, the barbarians invaded, instituting male domination, introducing a single omnipotent male God, and unleashing "the lethal power of the blade"—a violent and hierarchical world drenched in the blood of war and murder. We've been living under such a brutal dominator model—"in which male dominance, male violence, and a generally hierarchic and authoritarian social structure was the norm"—ever since. In such a world, "having violently deprived the Goddess and the female half of humanity of all power, gods and men of war ruled," Eisler writes, and "peace and harmony would be found only in the myths and legends of a long lost past."[53]

Another just-so story? Perhaps. I'm always skeptical of arguments that point to a dimly lit historical past for our models of future social transformation, because they so often rely on selective evidence and often make for retrogressive politics. And I'm equally uneasy with sweeping categorizations of "female" peace-loving cultures being swept aside by brutally violent "male" ones. After all, the contemporary world, for all its murderous, rapacious, and bloodthirsty domination, is *far* less violent than hunter-gatherer societies. Ethnographic data suggest that only about 10 percent of societies rarely engage in war; most cultures are engaged in conflict either continuously or more than once a year. The !Kung bushmen celebrated by Eisler as the "harmless people" have a murder rate higher than that of Detroit or Washington, D.C. "The sad archeological evidence," writes Francis Fukuyama, "indicates that systematic mass killings of men, women, and children occurred in Neolithic times. There was no age of innocence."[54]

On the other hand, why would we want to believe that male domination is somehow natural and inevitable? Some of Eisler's arguments are on firm evolutionary footing: It is likely, for example, that descent was originally traced through **matrilinearity**. This would make descent far more certain in cultures that did not understand the relationship between sexual intercourse and birth nine months later. And one can believe the credible evidence that women played a greater role in early human societies, without assuming one momentous calamity of invasion when that Edenic world was forever lost.

There is even some evidence of cultures that, although not fully female-dominated, evince women's power in all public and private arenas. Maria Lepowsky's impressive ethnography of the Vanatinai, a matrilineal, decentralized culture in New Guinea, found no evidence of male domination—no men's huts, no special ceremonial cults. Boys as well as girls care for their younger siblings. Men do child care. And both women and men exercise sexual freedom. Women have, Lepowsky writes, "equal opportunities of access to the symbolic capital of prestige derived from success in exchange." That is, both women's and men's economic participation gives everyone equal possibilities of prestige and honor. It depends on what you do, not what biological sex you are.[55]

Peggy Sanday's fascinating study of the matrilineal Minangkabau of western Sumatra, one of the largest ethnic groups in Indonesia, is a case in point. Instead of looking for a mirror-image world, in which women wield power as men do, Sanday finds instead a culture in which women's ways of governing parallel men's ways and at times even supplant men's ways. Here, women are self-confident and independent of their husbands, and although men hold many of the formal political offices, women "rule without governing." They "facilitate social bonding outside the machinations of political power," which enables "the men's job of adjudicating disputes according to the rules of adat [customs] and consensus decision-making."[56]

Women's status varies widely, depending on many cultural factors. And that alone makes it clear that male domination is not inevitable.

THE VALUES OF CROSS-CULTURAL RESEARCH

If anthropologists have demonstrated anything, it is the rich diversity in human cultural arrangements and the disparate definitions of gender and sexuality that we have produced within our cultures. Several theories explain the historical origins of these patterns and suggest ways we can modify or abandon some historically coercive or exploitative practices without doing damage to our evolutionary legacy. Cultural relativism also suggests that, in this enormous cultural variety and historical evolution of custom and culture, we shed those customs we no longer need, even if once they served some societal purpose. "Assertions of past inferiority for women should therefore be irrelevant to present and future developments," writes Eleanor Leacock.[57] Still, questions linger. Given such diversity of sexuality and gender, why is male dominance so universal? If it's not inevitable, how do we explain its persistence? Here, the answers may be a bit closer to home.

KEY TERMS

Alliance Theory	Gender Fluidity	Pseudohermaphrodite
Circumcision	Genital Mutilation	Purdah
Clitoridectomy	*Hwame*	Ritualized Homosexuality
Colonization	Hypermasculinity	Rohypnol
Couvade	Initiation Rituals	Sex Segregation
Descent Theory	Market Economy	Sexual Division of Labor
Ethnocentrism	Matrilinearity	Third Genders
Excision	*Muxe*	Two-Spirit People
Female Circumcision	*Nadle*	*Xanith*

Oh, so that explains the difference in our salaries!

"SO, THAT EXPLAINS IT"

Psychoanalytic and Developmental Perspectives on Gender

Upon no subject has there been so much dogmatic assertion based on so little scientific evidence, as upon male and female types of mind.
—JOHN DEWEY, "*IS COEDUCATION INJURIOUS TO GIRLS?*" (1911)

The cartoon above adopts a popular idea about the theories of Sigmund Freud, the founder of psychoanalysis. Freud believed that the anatomical differences between males and females led them toward different personalities, that sex did determine temperament. However, he did not believe that such differences were biologically programmed into males and females at birth. On the contrary, Freud saw his work as challenging those who held that the body contained all the information it needed at birth to become an adult man or woman. He believed that the observed differences between women and men were traceable to our different experiences from infancy onward, especially in the ways we were treated in our families.

Gender identity, Freud maintained, was a crucial part of personality development—perhaps *the* most crucial part. Gender was acquired, molded through interactions with family members and with the larger society. And it wasn't an easy acquisition; the route to appropriate gender identity was perilous and included the constant possibility of gender identity failure, which was manifested most clearly in sexual nonconformity, especially homosexuality. Of course, biology did play some role here: Freud and his followers believed that visible anatomical differences were decisive in the development of the child and especially that sexual energy, located in the body, propelled the child's experiences that determined gender identity. But the essence of psychological development was "not based on any premise of inherent differences between the sexes, but solely on the different nature of their experiences."[1]

FREUD'S THEORY OF PSYCHOSEXUAL DEVELOPMENT

Freud proposed a stage theory of individual gender development, one in which each individual passes through a number of stages on his or her path to adult gender identity. These stages are set into motion by two factors: the composition or structure of the psyche and the realities of life. Four elements comprise Freud's model of the psyche: id, ego, super-ego, and the external world. These elements together form the basic architecture of the self, and each has a decisive role to play in the formation of personality. The id represents our desire to satisfy our basic animal needs for food, shelter, and pleasure. Id is energy, drive, craving. Id "knows" only that it wants gratification but has neither morality nor the means to acquire what it wants. Freud calls the id "a cauldron filled with seething excitations."[2]

Unfortunately, the external world possesses limited possibilities for instinctual gratification; the id's desires are constantly thwarted. How we cope with those frustrations determines personality development. The ego, the rational, problem-solving portion of our personality, takes the impulses of the id and translates them into strategies for gratification that will be effective. The ego must discipline the id, tame it, and seek possible sources of gratification for it. Another part of the psyche, the super-ego, is an outgrowth of ego's efforts to seek socially effective and appropriate outlets for gratification of id's desires. Freud calls the super-ego an "internalized externality"—it sees the limited possibilities for gratification offered by society as legitimate. Super-ego is the seat of morality, and it assists the ego in selecting effective strategies to achieve socially approved goals.

These different components of the self emerge gradually through a child's development as the ego tries to navigate its way through the narrow straits presented by the incessant demands of the id and the imperious claims of the super-ego. In a way, Freud's theory of development is a rather sad story, as each successive stage does not provide nearly the pleasures of the one it replaces—we grow by giving up things that give us pleasure—and, because the ego is often not strong enough to undertake such a struggle, there are the omnipresent dangers of temporary backsliding to earlier stages in our fantasies (neurosis) or a dramatic break with reality and the attempt to live in that earlier stage (psychosis).

Prior to birth, Freud believed, all the infant's desires are gratified; in the womb we are sensuously content. But birth expels us from this enveloping Eden; hungry and alone, we can take nothing for granted. Now the infant transfers gratification to the mother's breast, seeking pleasure through ingesting food. This Freud calls the "oral stage." But just as the ego accommodates itself to this source of gratification, it's removed by weaning. In the next stage, the "anal stage," gratification is achieved not by taking food in but rather by giving food back, as in urination and defecation. These bodily functions are now a source of pleasure, but no sooner do we discover the joys of excretory creation that can compensate for the loss of the breast than we are toilet-trained, forced to repress that source of gratification until it is socially appropriate to do it, until, that is, it's convenient for grown-ups. Finally, after oral denial and anal repression, we reach what Freud calls the "phallic stage." And here's where gender comes in.

Until now, both boys and girls experience roughly the same things. But after the resolution of the anal crisis, our paths diverge sharply. In this stage it is our task to "become" either masculine or feminine. Freud believed that this process is more difficult for boys than for girls, because from the beginning a girl learns to identify with her mother as a female, and this identification remains continuous into adulthood. In contrast, a boy must detach himself from his identification with his mother, *disidentify* with her, and identify with his father, a process that requires unlearning one attachment and forming a new one. This is made more difficult because mothers commonly offer a great deal of affection and caring, whereas fathers are often less affectionate and more authoritarian.

This critical moment for the boy is called the "**Oedipal crisis**," after the play by Sophocles, *Oedipus, the King*. The resolution of the Oedipal crisis is vital—the boy learns to desire sex with women and to identify as a man. This is crucial in Freudian theory: *The boy achieves gender identity and sexual orientation at the same moment in time*. During the Oedipal stage, the boy desires sexual union with his mother, but he also realizes that he is in competition with his father for her affections. With his sexual desire for his mother thwarted by his father, the little boy sexualizes his fear of the father, believing that if he were to compete sexually with his father, his father would castrate him. The boy's ego resolves this state of terror of castration by transferring the boy's identification from mother to father, so that, symbolically, he can have sexual access to his mother. Thus the boy must break the identification with his mother, repudiate her, and identify with his father. This is a great shock—the mother has been the source of warmth and love and is the object of his desire; the father has been a more distant source of authoritarian power and is the source of the boy's terror. But by identifying with the father the little boy ceases being "feminine" (identified with the mother) and becomes masculine, as he simultaneously becomes heterosexual, symbolically capable of sexual relations with mother-like substitutes. Almost literally, as the 1930s popular song put it, he will "want a girl just like the girl that married dear old Dad."

For girls, Freud believed, the path is complementary but not nearly as traumatic. Girls retain their identification with the mother but must renounce their sexual desire for her. They do this by acknowledging that they are incapable of sexual relations with the mother, because they lack the biological equipment that makes such relations possible. This is why Freud believed that women experience "**penis envy**." The little girl understands that her only chance for sexual gratification is to retain her identification with the mother and to be sexually possessed by a man who can satisfy her so that she can have a baby, which will be her source of feminine gratification. In the process, she transfers the location of sexual gratification from the clitoris (an "atrophied penis," in Freud's terms) to the vagina, in other words, she develops feminine, passive sexuality. Again, gender identity and sexual orientation go hand in hand. (Freud did acknowledge that his "insight into these developmental processes in girls is unsatisfactory, incomplete, and vague"—given how it was really an effort to derive some complementary comparison with boys' development and was not a theory of girls' development itself.[3])

Three issues are worth noting in this account of gender identity and sexuality. First, Freud dislocates gender and sexuality from the realm of biology. There is nothing inevitable about males becoming masculine or females becoming feminine. Gender identity and sexuality are psychological achievements—difficult, precarious, and full of potential pitfalls (an absent father may prevent a boy from transferring his identification from his mother, for example). Gender and sexuality are accomplished within the family, Freud argues, not activated by internal biological clocks.

Second, Freud links gender identity to sexual orientation, making homosexuality a developmental *gender* issue rather than an issue of immorality, sin, or biological anomaly. Homosexuals are simply those who have either failed to renounce identification with the mother in favor of the father (gay men) or those who have failed to retain their ties of identification to the mother (lesbians). (This idea also served as the basis for therapeutic interventions designed to "cure" homosexuals by encouraging gender-appropriate behaviors.) Homosexuality is a kind of proof that something went wrong in the gender identity acquisition path.

Third, Freud restates with new vigor traditional **gender stereotypes** as if they were the badges of successful negotiation of this perilous journey. A boy must be the sexual initiator and scrupulously avoid all feminine behaviors, lest he be seen as having failed to identify with the father. A girl must become sexually passive, wait for a man to be attracted to her, so that she can be fulfilled as a woman. Femininity means fulfillment not as a lover, but as a mother.

It's important to remember that though Freud postulated that homosexuality is the failure of the child to adequately identify with the same-sex parent and is therefore a problem of gender identity development, he did not believe in either the criminal persecution or the psychiatric treatment of homosexuals. In fact, when Freud was contacted by a woman whose son was homosexual, he patiently explained why he did not think her son needed to be "cured":

> Homosexuality is assuredly no advantage, but it is nothing to be ashamed of, no vice, no degradation; it cannot be classified as an illness; we consider it to be a variation of the sexual function . . . Many highly respectable individuals of ancient and modern times have been homosexuals, several of the greatest men among them . . . It is a great injustice to persecute homosexuality as a crime—and a cruelty too . . .
>
> What analysis can do for your son runs in a different line. If he is unhappy, neurotic, torn by conflicts, inhibited in his social life, analysis may bring him harmony, peace of mind, full efficiency, whether he remains homosexual or gets changed.[4]

It took another forty years before the American Psychiatric Association declassified homosexuality as a mental illness.

Today, many popular stereotypes about homosexuality continue to rely on Freudian theories of gender development. Many people believe that homosexuality is a form of gender nonconformity; that is, effeminate men and masculine women are seen in the popular mind as likely to be homosexual, whereas masculine men's and feminine women's gender-conforming behavior leads others to expect them to be heterosexual.

In fact, we often believe we can "read" someone's sexual orientation by observing his or her gender stereotypic behavior, as if really masculine men or really feminine women couldn't possibly be gay or lesbian.

Freud's theories have been subject to considerable debate and controversy. He based his theories about the sexuality of women on a very small sample of upper-middle-class women in Vienna, all of whom were suffering from psychological difficulties that brought them to treatment with him in the first place. (Freud rejected the idea that they had been the victims of sexual abuse and incest, although many of them claimed they had been.) His theories of male development were based on even fewer clinical cases and on his own recollections of his childhood and his dreams. These are not the most reliable scientific methods, and his tendency to make sexuality the driving force of all individual development and all social and group processes may tell us more about his own life, and perhaps contemporary Vienna, than about other societies and cultures. Some researchers have argued that many of Freud's patients were actually telling the truth about their sexual victimization and not fantasizing about it and that, therefore, it is not the fantasies of children but rather the actual behaviors of adults that form the constituent elements in the construction of children's sexual view of the world.[5]

Although many today question Freud's theories on methodological, political, or theoretical grounds, there is no question that these theories have had a remarkable impact on contemporary studies and on popular assumptions about the relationship between gender identity and sexual behavior and sexual orientation. If gender identity and sexual orientation were *accomplished*, not inherent in the individual, then it was the parents' fault if things didn't turn out "right." Magazine articles, child-rearing manuals, and psychological inventories encouraged parents to do the right things and to develop the right attitudes, traits, and behaviors in their children; thus the children would achieve appropriate gender identity and thereby ensure successful acquisition of heterosexual identity.

THE M-F TEST

In the early 1930s, just three decades after Freud developed his theories, Lewis Terman, a psychology professor at Stanford, and his associate, Catherine Cox Miles, tried to codify masculinity and femininity into their component parts—traits, attitudes, and behaviors. Marshalling all the available diagnostic methods of their time, they produced a survey, published in 1936 as *Sex and Personality*. Their book presented an inventory of behaviors, attitudes, and traits that enabled parents and teachers to monitor a child's successful acquisition of masculinity or femininity.[6]

Terman and Miles utilized a broad range of empirical measures to test gender identity and constructed a continuum from masculinity to femininity, along which any individual could be placed according to answers on a series of questions. (The systematic—even obsessive—enterprise to find all possible measures of gender identity is itself an indication of the perceived significance of successful gender identity.) As a result of inventories like the M-F test, gender identity came to be associated with a particular bundle of attitudes, traits, and behaviors, which, once acquired, could be seen as indicators of successful gender acquisition. When embraced by social science in the 1940s, these inventories became the basis for sex-role theory.

The **M-F test** was perhaps the single most widely used means to determine successful acquisition of gender identity and was still being used until the 1960s. The test was quite wide-ranging, including Rorschach-like interpretations of inkblots, which were coded for gender appropriateness, as well as identification, sentence completion, and some empirical questions. Here is a small sample of the questions on the M-F test. (If you want to keep your own score on these few items—to make sure that your own gender identity is progressing "normally"—you should score it the way that Terman and Miles suggested in 1936: If the response is "masculine," give yourself a "1"; if feminine, score with a "2." Interesting how these little value judgments creep into scientific research!)

Gendered Knowledge: In the following completion items there are right and wrong answers, and it was assumed that the more "boyish" would know the right answer to questions 2, 3, and 5 and that the more "girlish" would know the answers to items 1 and 4. Girls who knew the answers to 2, 3, and 5 would be scored as more "masculine."

1. Things cooked in grease are: boiled (+), broiled (+), fried (−), roasted (+).
2. Most of our anthracite coal comes from: Alabama (−), Colorado (−), Ohio (−), Pennsylvania (+).
3. The "Rough Riders" were led by: Funston (−), Pershing (−), Roosevelt (+), Sheridan (−).
4. Red goes best with: black (−), lavender (+), pink (+), purple (+).
5. The proportion of the globe covered by water is about: 1/8 (−), 1/4 (−), 1/2 (−), 3/4 (+).

Gendered Feelings: The test also included a variety of stimuli that were thought to provoke certain emotions. Respondents were to answer whether these things caused (a) a lot, (b) some, (c) little, or (d) none of the expected emotion. For example:

- Does: being called lazy; seeing boys make fun of old people; seeing someone cheat on an exam make you ANGRY?
- Does: being lost; deep water; graveyards at night; Negroes [this is actually on the list!] make you AFRAID?
- Does: a fly caught on sticky fly paper; a man who is cowardly and can't help it; a wounded deer make you feel PITY?
- Does: boys teasing girls; indulging in "petting"; not brushing your teeth; being a Bolshevik make you feel that a person is WICKED?

To score this section, give yourself a minus (2) for every answer in which you said the thing caused a lot of the emotion, except for the answer "being a Bolshevik," which was obviously serious enough for men to get very emotional about. On all others, including being afraid of "Negroes," however, high levels of emotion were scored as feminine.

Gendered Occupations, Appearances, Books: The test also included possible careers and their obvious sex-typing, such as librarian, auto racer, forest ranger, florist, soldier, and music teacher. There were lists of character traits (loud voices, men with beards, tall women) that those tested were asked to like or dislike and a list of children's books (*Robinson Crusoe, Rebecca of Sunnybrook Farm, Little Women, Biography of a Grizzly*) that they either liked, didn't like, or had not read.

Gendered People: There was a list of famous people whom one either liked, disliked, or did not know (Bismarck, Lenin, Florence Nightingale, Jane Addams). (Obviously, not having read a book or not knowing about a famous person could be seen as gender confirming or nonconfirming.)

There were also questions about what you might like to draw if you were an artist (ships or flowers), what you might like to write about if you were a newspaper reporter (accidents or theater), and where you might like to travel if you had plenty of money (hunt lions in Africa or study social customs; learn about various religions or see how criminals are treated). Finally, the test included some self-reporting about the respondent's own behaviors and attitudes. Such yes or no items (here listed with the scoring of a yes answer) included:

- Do you rather dislike to take your bath? (+)
- Are you extremely careful about your manner of dress? (−)
- Do people ever say you talk too much? (+)
- Have you ever been punished unjustly? (+)
- Have you ever kept a diary? (−)

The research by Terman and Miles enabled a new generation of psychologists to construct a continuum between masculinity and femininity, along which any individual could be located, and thereby to chart the acquisition of gender identity by examining the traits, attitudes, and behaviors appropriate to each gender. If a boy or girl exhibited the appropriate traits and attitudes, parents could be reassured that their child was developing normally. If, however, the child scored too high on the "inappropriate" side of the continuum, intervention strategies might be devised to facilitate the adoption of more appropriate behaviors. Artistic boys would be pushed toward rough-and-tumble play; tomboys would be forced into frilly dresses to read quietly a book like *Rebecca of Sunnybrook Farm* instead of climbing a tree. Behind these interventions lay the spectre of the sissy, the homosexual male, who, Terman and Miles and other psychologists believed, had gender identity problems. Following Freud, they believed that homosexuality was a gender disorder. As another psychologist, George W. Henry, wrote in 1937:

> In a large majority of . . . cases the tendencies to homosexuality as shown by attitude and behavior can be observed in early childhood . . . To the extent that his interests, attitude and behavior are out of harmony with his actual sex he is likely to meet with circumstances which will accentuate his deviation. Boys appear to be somewhat more vulnerable than girls and if they show undue feminine tendencies special care should be exercised to give them opportunity to develop masculine characteristics.[7]

This notion that gender nonconformity is an indicator of sexual orientation remains a most common assumption. If a boy acts "feminine," or a girl acts "masculine," we assume this reveals his or her sexuality—not some expression of his or her gender identity. For decades it has served as the basis for pop psychologists' warnings about "growing up straight" and how to prevent your son from "turning gay." (Pop psychologists seem far less concerned about girls becoming lesbians.) Today, it's often the religious right that offers such neo-Freudian warnings.[8]

How Parents Can Tell . . .

The evangelical Christian organization Focus on the Family offers parents several warning signs that might indicate "gender confusion," which, if left unattended, might lead them on the path toward homosexuality. For boys age 5 to 11, these may include:

1. A strong feeling that they are "different" from other boys.
2. A tendency to cry easily, be less athletic, and dislike the roughhousing that other boys enjoy.
3. A persistent preference to play female roles in make-believe play.
4. A strong preference to spend time in the company of girls and participate in their games and other pastimes.
5. A susceptibility to be bullied by other boys, who may tease them unmercifully and call them "queer," "fag," and "gay."
6. A tendency to walk, talk, dress, and even "think" effeminately.
7. A repeatedly stated desire to be—or insistence that he is—a girl.

If your child is experiencing these symptoms, the organization urges you to seek professional help.

Source: See www.focusonyourchild.com/develop/artl/A0000684.html.

Post-Freudian Theories of Gender Development

Freudian psychoanalytic theory spawned several different traditions in psychology. Some developmental psychologists sought to chart the sequences or stages of gender and sexual development, as children pass through psychological stages that correspond to physical changes. Other psychologists used various statistical tests to more precisely measure the differences between males and females at certain ages. Feminist psychoanalysts took Freud and his followers to task for their implicit or explicit use of masculinity as the normative reference against which all developmental stages were plotted and understood. And, finally, some psychologists sought to specify the social requirements for both masculine and feminine sex roles.

Cognitive development theories locate the trigger of gender development and gender identity formation slightly later in life than early childhood. Psychologists of this school argue that children are born more or less gender neutral; that is, no important biological differences between boys and girls at birth explain later gender differences. As they grow, children process new information through "cognitive filters" that enable them to interpret information about gender. Swiss psychologist Jean Piaget examined the developmental sequences in children's self-perception and their views of the world. Children are active participants in their own socialization, Piaget argued, not simply the passive objects of social influence. Piaget applied this model to cognitive development, pointing out the sequences of tasks and mental processes appropriate to children of various ages.[9]

Lawrence Kohlberg applied this Piagetian model of sequential cognitive development to the acquisition of a stable gender identity. One of the central developmental tasks of early childhood, Kohlberg argued, is to label oneself as either male or female. The point in time at which children learn "I am a boy" or "I am a girl" is a point after which self-identification seems fixed. The decision is _cognitive_, part of the pattern of mental growth in the organism. Early in life, children develop a gendered mental filter, after which new information from the social world is interpreted and acted upon in terms of its appropriateness to their gender identity. Even by age two, children have relatively stable and fixed understandings of themselves as gendered, and this categorization, Kohlberg argues, "is basically a cognitive reality judgment rather than a product of social rewards, parental justifications, or sexual fantasies." Things, persons, and activities are labeled "this is appropriate to who I am" or "this is not appropriate to who I am." Messages coded in certain ways get through to boys; those coded in other ways get through to girls.[10]

According to this theory, children's early gender identities depend on concrete, physical cues like dress, hairstyle, and body size in their categorization of the world into two genders. Boys never wear dresses and have short hair; girls do wear dresses and have long hair. Many children believe that they can change their gender by getting haircuts or changing their clothing, because they believe gender identity is concrete and attached to physical attributes. Some children become upset if their parents engage in gender-inappropriate conduct (Daddy carries Mommy's purse, Mommy changes the tire). It is not until age five or six that most children have the cognitive machinery to recognize gender as an attribute of the person and not the result of the material props that we use to display gender.

By this view, the acquisition of a gender identity is a switching point in the child's life. After age six, the child sees the world in *gender* terms. The child cannot go back, because the process of acquiring gender identity is irreversible after age three or four. All gender-role performances that are socially coded as appropriate for men or women become, thereafter, more easily acquired by the child who possesses the "correct" filter. Because so many aspects of behavior depend on gender identity, the acquisition of an irreversible filter is necessary to human development and is to be expected in all societies.

Social learning of gender does not end in childhood. Acquisition of gender identity may begin early, but it continues throughout the life cycle. Young children label themselves "boy" or "girl" at an early age, after which they actively begin to use the label to make sense of the world. However, this label, demonstrated by the capacity to express the sentence "I am a boy (girl)" in a number of ways and situations, does not exhaust the content of gender roles or pick out unerringly the appropriate gender-typed stimuli. A child does not know most of the things that an adult knows or believes or likes or feels. The two- or three-year-old girl does not know that a woman is not likely to become president. She knows only that she uses the word "girl" to label herself and that she is comfortable with that label. Gender identity is more fluid than young children believe, and our gender socialization continues throughout our lives. And, equally important, we are active agents in our own socialization, not simply the passive receptors of cultural blueprints for appropriate gender behaviors.

Because there is no "natural" relationship between gender identity and gender-role performances, the young child who "knows" his or her gender possesses a label with very little content. However, the label is used to organize the new things that are experienced. This is done by observing who (in gender terms) leaves the house to go to work, who is in charge of the labor of the household, and who plays with cars or dolls (or at least who the child sees playing with these toys in the media). All of these activities are more or less gender-typed, mostly by who does them rather than by what is done. In addition, all children hear verbal exhortations of what boys do/don't do and what girls do/don't do. Children naturally tend to imitate models of behavior, even if that imitation is not reinforced, and this includes the vast amount of gender-typical behavior that is performed in front of them. Children swim in an ocean of gendered conduct, and it is terribly difficult to swim against the tide.[11]

From this point of view, the stability of the sense of a gendered self does not depend on biological differences at birth, the experiences of early childhood, or a cognitive filter. It depends on the way that a child's day-to-day situations continuously stabilize his or her sense of being a boy or a girl. Because men and women each have different social learning histories, we find gender differences in the behaviors and values of children and adults. To understand our own sexuality, we must first look at the kinds of arrangements we have made for the ways in which men and women are supposed to behave in our society and the ways they conceive of themselves. If you conceive of yourself as a woman, and you are put into circumstances in which people in your society expect women to react in a certain way, the fact that you think of yourself as a woman shapes the way you react to those circumstances. Thus in a society there are always two factors that affect gendered behavior: the demands of the social situation and one's prior experience of being a girl or a boy or a woman or a man.

FEMINIST CHALLENGES TO PSYCHOANALYSIS AND DEVELOPMENTAL PSYCHOLOGY

Freud's theory of **psychosexual development** offered a very different kind of challenge to assumptions of biological inevitability. Rather than focus on variation, as did anthropologists, Freud stressed the universality of sex differences but argued that such differences were produced—learned by children in interactions with their families and the larger society. He saw nothing inevitable about becoming either masculine or feminine, or about becoming heterosexual. Sexual orientation and gender identity were achievements.

Many women have dismissed Freud's arguments because he argued that their development was the result of their coming to terms with the shame that would naturally follow from the realization that they did not have penises. Not only did his arguments place an absurd emphasis on a little flap of tissue, but also penis envy meant that women would always see themselves as inferior to men. What's more, Freud asserted that female development required the repudiation of the clitoris, the source of sexual agency and pleasure, for the more "mature" sexuality of vaginal receptivity.

No sooner had Freud published his theories than women challenged the centrality of penis envy in girls' development. Karen Horney's 1922 essay "On the Genesis of the **Castration Complex** in Women" suggested that a theory that posited one-half of the human race to be unsatisfied was itself theoretically problematic. It was, rather, "the actual social subordination of women" that provided the context for women's development. Since then, women have patiently explained that it was men, not women, who saw the possession of a penis as such a big deal. After all, without one, how could women know what it felt like? As one psychoanalyst put it:

OH? REALLY •

Boys wear blue and girls wear pink—and that's how the natural biological differences between the two are clearly marked for everyone to see.

You'd think that's the way it's always been, right—that boys and girls are color-coded from infancy? But the historical reality of such color coding is far from straightforward. Before the twentieth century, Americans believed that boys and girls were pretty much the same, and so they were all dressed the same: in flowing white dresses. The photo here shows one such boy.

Recognize him? It's Franklin Delano Roosevelt, who would one day be president. (You can almost see his cigarette holder clenched in his teeth if you look closely!)

In a historical study of infant and toddler dress codes, historian Jo Paoletti found that when color coding first came into vogue, it was exactly the opposite of our current style. In 1890, *Ladies Home Journal* recommended pink for boys because it was a stronger color! Others said that pink was more flattering for dark-haired children, and blue for the fair-haired, regardless of their biological sex. It wasn't until the 1920s that the current fashion of pink = feminine and blue = masculine was established.

Source: Jo Paoletti, *Pink and Blue: Telling the Boys from the Girls in America* (Bloomington: Indiana University Press, 2012).

> It is the male who experiences the penis as a valuable organ and he assumes that women also must feel that way about it. But a woman cannot really imagine the sexual pleasure of a penis—she can only appreciate the social advantages its possessor has.[12]

Perhaps women had a more political and social "privilege envy" than any envy to do with the body.

In fact, some argued, Freud had it backward. Women did not have penis envy as much as men had "**womb envy**." Women, after all, can produce babies, apparently (at least in those cultures in which a rather uneventful moment nine months earlier is not remembered or not considered as significant) all by themselves! No matter what men do, they cannot create life. Bruno Bettelheim and several others suggested that the origins of women's subordination stemmed from men's fears of women's reproductive powers, and these researchers pointed to male initiation rituals that imitated birth throes as an indication of ritual appropriation masking significant envy.[13]

Another line of critique has been to reverse Freud's initial proposition. Instead of asking how and why women come to see themselves as inferior to men, why not ask how men come to see themselves as superior to women? Several feminist writers such as Nancy Chodorow, Lillian Rubin, Dorothy Dinnerstein, and Jessica Benjamin have posed that question.[14] Inspired by the object-relations school of psychoanalytic thought, these theorists pointed to the more deeply embedded masculine biases in Freud's formulation. Freud argued that the final achievement of gender development was individual autonomy—freedom from dependency on the mother and thus freedom from the need for group identification. Autonomy was achieved in the boy's renunciation of identification with his mother and subsequent identification with his father. However, in *The Reproduction of Mothering*, Chodorow argued that Freud inadvertently revealed the sources of men's sense of superiority and, thus, of male domination.[15]

What if, she argued, we were to suggest that the capacities for intimacy, connection, and community were healthy adult experiences? That would mean that the stage *before* the Oedipal crisis—when both boys and girls are deeply attached to their mother—is crucial. What happens is that boys lose that capacity for connection and intimacy in the break with the mother and the shift to the father, whereas girls retain that capacity. What's more, such a shift is so traumatic for boys—and yet so necessary in our culture—that they must demonstrate constantly that they have successfully achieved it. Masculinity comes to be defined as the distance between the boy and his mother, between himself and being seen as a "mama's boy" or a sissy. So he must spend a significant amount of time and energy demonstrating his successful achievement of this distance, which he does by devaluing all things feminine—including girls, his mother, femininity, and, of course, all emotions associated with femininity. Male domination requires the masculine devaluation of the feminine. As Chodorow puts it:

> A boy, in his attempt to gain an elusive masculine identification, often comes to define his masculinity in largely negative terms, as that which is not feminine or involved with women. There is an internal and external aspect to this. Internally, the boy tries to reject his mother and deny his attachment to her and the strong dependency on her that he still feels. He also tries to deny the deep personal identification with her that has developed during his early years. He does this by repressing whatever he takes to be feminine inside himself, and, importantly, by denigrating whatever he considers to be feminine in the outside world.

Thus Freud provided a decidedly "feminist" reading of male domination. He just didn't know it, so fixated was he on the break with the mother as the crucial moment in *human* development.[16]

Kohlberg's ideas about the stages of cognitive and moral development have also come under critical scrutiny from feminist scholars. Kohlberg's stages proceeded from very concrete and practical rules to the application of universal ethical principles. But when girls and boys were evaluated, girls seemed "arrested" at the third stage of moral development, a stage that stresses mutual interpersonal expectations and relationships. (Kohlberg argued that this difference followed logically from the more remote and abstracted nature of the boy's relationship with his father, compared with the girl's more interdependent relationship with her mother.) Carol Gilligan, one of Kohlberg's students, was not persuaded and believed the different types of moral reasoning ought not be hierarchically ranked. In her pathbreaking book *In a Different Voice*, Gilligan suggested that such stages appear only when men's lives are regarded as the norm. In her interviews with Harvard women undergraduates, Gilligan found very different criteria for moral decision making. She heard another moral voice besides the "ethic of justice"—that abstract, universal, ethical paradigm Kohlberg proposed as the final stage of moral development. There is also an "ethic of care," stressing intimacy and connectedness, that seems to be followed more often by women. From this, Gilligan suggested that the origins of aggression might be different for women and men.

For men, the ethic of justice demands the blind and indifferent application of sanctions; aggression stems from constraints on individual autonomy. Women, Gilligan writes, hear a different voice, wherein "lies the truth of an ethic of care, and the tie between the relationship and responsibility, and the origins of aggression in the failure of connection."[17]

Gilligan's work unleashed a broad controversy among feminist psychologists that has continued to ripple through the larger culture. Gilligan's work *seemed* to support arguments that women and men are fundamentally, irretrievably, and irreconcilably different. Other work building on that premise followed quickly, including works on cognition and epistemology and popular works that emphasized differences between women's and men's linguistic and mythical spheres.[18] Ironically, groups that sought to exclude women from various arenas attempted to use Gilligan's arguments to legitimate discrimination. If women and men are so obviously different, their reasoning went, then excluding women from certain positions would not be discrimination, but rather really a way to honor and respect differences. Historically, men who argued against woman suffrage made exactly the same case that Gilligan made. Here, for example, is an antisuffragist, writing in 1914:

> One practical difficulty in the way of the participation of women in public affairs we might as well put bluntly. They do not seem to be intellectually fit for it . . . [I]t is very rare to find a woman who has a statesmanlike mind. The ordinary woman is interested in persons rather than in principles. Only when a principle is embodied in a person is she aroused to any enthusiasm. She sees the picturesque aspects of a cause, but does not readily follow an economic process . . . She is more likely to be interested in little things which touch her own life than in great things which determine the destinies of nations.

More recently, the Citadel and Virginia Military Institute cited the differences between women and men as justifications for excluding women from their state-supported corps of cadets (figure 4.1), and fire departments sought to exclude women from entering their ranks. (Given that the legal code requires the indifferent application of the law and adherence to abstract principles, one might have also predicted a move to exclude women from serving as judges.)[19]

Gilligan herself was more circumspect and deplored efforts to use her findings "to rationalize oppression." What she found is that "educationally advantaged North American males have a strong tendency to focus on issues of justice when they describe an experience of moral conflict and choice; two thirds of the men in our studies exhibited a 'justice focus.' One third of the women we studied also showed a justice focus. But one third of the women focused on care, in contrast to only one of the 46 men." Moreover, "one third of both females and males articulate justice and care concerns with roughly equal frequency." The psychological patterns Gilligan observed, she argued, are "not based on any premise of inherent differences between the sexes, but solely on the different nature of their experiences." To extrapolate from these data to claim that *men* and *women* differ on moral voices would be to distort her findings into stereotypes; she writes:

> The title of my book was deliberate; it reads, "in a *different* voice," not "in a *woman's* voice." In my introduction, I explain that this voice is not identified by gender but by theme. Noting as an empirical observation the association of this voice with women,

Figure 4.1. Upperclass cadets "socialize" a young woman at Virginia Military Institute after the Supreme Court demanded that VMI admit women to its Corps of Cadets.

Source: AP Photo/Steve Helber.

I caution the reader that "this association is not absolute, and the contrasts between male and female voices are presented here to highlight a distinction between two modes of thought and to focus a problem of interpretation rather than to represent a generalization about either sex." In tracing development, I "point to the interplay of these voices within each sex and suggest that their convergence marks times of crisis and change." No claims, I state, are made about the origins of these voices or their distribution in a wider population, across cultures or time (. . .). Thus, the care perspective in my rendition is neither biologically determined nor unique to women. It is, however, a moral perspective different from that currently embedded in psychological theories and measures, and it is a perspective that was defined by listening to both women and men describe their own experience.[20]

Subsequent research has failed to replicate the binary gender differences in ethics; most researchers "report no average differences in the kind of reasoning men and women use in evaluating moral dilemmas, whether it is care-based or justice-based."[21]

Feminist psychologists did, however, expose an androcentric bias in the psychological literature of gender identity and development. With men as the normative standard against which both men and women were evaluated, women always seemed to be coming up short. As Gilligan demonstrated, when psychologists began to shift their framework and to listen closely to the voices of women, new patterns of development emerged. This bias also had consequences in the lives of real people. For example, the ***Diagnostic and Statistical Manual of Mental Disorders (DSM)***, published by the American Psychiatric Association, is the diagnostic bible of mental illness professionals. For some time, the *DSM* has listed such mental illnesses as "premenstrual dysphoric disorder," which is its version of PMS. So each woman potentially suffers from a specific mental illness for up to one week a month—which adds up to about 25 percent of her adult life. (Homosexuality was removed from the manual.) Psychologist Paula Caplan suggested that the *DSM* instead consider adding a new set of diagnoses, including "Delusional Dominating Personality Disorder" (DDPD) to classify sexist behavior as symptomatic of mental illness. And what about "John Wayne syndrome" or "macho personality disorder"? she asks. Her quiz to identify DDPD goes a long way toward exposing the gender biases in those ostensibly gender-neutral manuals (figure 4.2).

DEVELOPMENTAL DIFFERENCES

So what are the real—and not the imagined or produced—psychological differences between women and men? Developmental psychologists have pointed to some significant differences between males and females that emerge as we grow. Yet even these are differences between the means of two distributions, in which there is more variation *among* men and *among* women than there is *between* women and men. When psychologist Janet Hyde reviewed forty-six meta-analyses—studies that reviewed *all* the available studies on a certain topic—in a sort of "meta-meta-analysis," she found that the size of the gender difference for 78 percent of all the traits, attitudes, and behaviors measured by these studies was "small or close to zero."[22] And when psychologists Eleanor Maccoby and Carol Jacklin surveyed over 1,600 empirical studies from 1966 to 1973, they found only four areas with significant and consistent sex differences: (1) Girls have relatively higher verbal ability; (2) boys have better visual and spatial ability; (3) boys do better on mathematical tests; (4) boys were consistently more aggressive than girls. In fact, Maccoby and Jacklin conclude that their work

> revealed a surprising degree of similarity in the rearing of boys and girls. The two sexes appear to be treated with equal affection, at least in the first five years of life (the period for which most information is available); they are equally allowed and encouraged to be independent, equally discouraged from dependent behavior; . . . there is even, surprisingly, no evidence of distinctive parental reaction to aggressive behavior in the two sexes. There ARE differences, however. Boys are handled and played with somewhat more roughly. They also receive more physical punishment. In several studies boys were found to receive both more praise and more criticism from their caretakers—socialization pressure, in other words, was somewhat more intense for boys—but the evidence on this point is inconsistent. The area of greatest differentiation is in very specifically sex-typed behavior. Parents show considerably more concern over a boy's being a "sissy" than over a girl's being a tomboy. This is especially true of fathers, who seem to take the lead in actively discouraging any interest a son might have in feminine toys, activities, or attire.[23]

DO YOU RECOGNIZE THIS MAN?*

A quiz you'll never see in *Cosmo* and *Redbook*

Men who meet at least six of the following criteria may have Delusional Dominating Personality Disorder! Warning: DDPD is pervasive, profound, and a maladaptive organization of the entire personality! (Check as many as apply.)

1. Is he . . .

☐ unable to establish and maintain meaningful interpersonal relationships?

☐ unable to identify and express a range of feelings in himself (typically accompanied by an inability to identify accurately the feelings of other people)?

☐ unable to respond appropriately and empathically to the feelings and needs of close associates and intimates (often leading to the misinterpretation of signals from others)?

☐ unable to derive pleasure from doing things for others?

2. Does he . . .

☐ use power, silence, withdrawal, and/or avoidance rather than negotiation in the face of interpersonal conflict or difficulty?

☐ believe that women are responsible for the bad things that happen to him, while the good things are due to his own abilities, achievements, or efforts?

☐ inflate the importance and achievements of himself, males in general, or both?

☐ categorize spheres of functioning and sets of behavior rigidly according to sex (like believing housework is women's work)?

☐ use a gender-based double standard in interpreting or evaluating situations or behavior (considering a man who makes breakfast sometimes to be extraordinarily good, for example, but considering a woman who sometimes neglects to make breakfast deficient)?

☐ feel inordinately threatened by women who fail to disguise their intelligence?

☐ display any of the following delusions:

- the delusion that men are entitled to the services of any woman with whom they are personally associated;

- the delusion that women like to suffer and be ordered around;

- the delusion that physical force is the best method of solving interpersonal problems;

- the delusion that men's sexual and aggressive impulses are uncontrollable;

  the delusion that pornography and erotica are identical;

- the delusion that women control most of the world's wealth and/or power but do little of the world's work;

- the delusion that existing inequalities in the distribution of power and wealth are a product of the survival of the fittest and that, therefore, allocation of greater social and economic rewards to the already privileged are merited.

3. Does he have . . .

☐ a pathological need to affirm his social importance by displaying himself in the company of females who meet any three of these criteria:

- are conventionally physically attractive; **or**

- are younger;

- are shorter;

- weigh less;

- appear to be lower on socioeconomic criteria; **or**

- are more submissive . . . than he is?

☐ a distorted approach to sexuality, displaying itself in one or both of these ways:

- a pathological need for flattery about his sexual performance and/or the size of his genitalia;

- an infantile tendency to equate large breasts on women with their sexual attractiveness.

☐ emotionally uncontrolled resistance to reform efforts that are oriented toward gender equity?

The tendency to consider himself a "New Man" neither proves nor disproves that the subject fits within this diagnostic category.

Some women also fit many of these criteria, either because they wish to be as dominant as men or because they feel men should be dominant.

Freely adapted, with permission, from *They Say You're Crazy:*
How the World's Most Powerful Psychiatrists Decide Who's Normal (Addison-Wesley, 1995) by Paula J. Caplan.

Figure 4.2. *Hypothetical Diagnostic Tool for Delusional Dominating Personality Disorder (DDPD)* by Paula J. Caplan. Used with permission.

Relying on parents for signals about what is appropriate turns out to be more decisive than the sex of the children. In one experiment, half of sixty preschool children were told that a tool set was for boys and a kitchen set was for girls. The children were also asked what they thought their mothers and fathers would say if they played with the toys: Would their parents say it was good, bad, or that it didn't matter?

How much time did they play with each of the toys (figure 4.3)? The results of the experiment were interesting. For the boys, it depended less on the type of toy and more

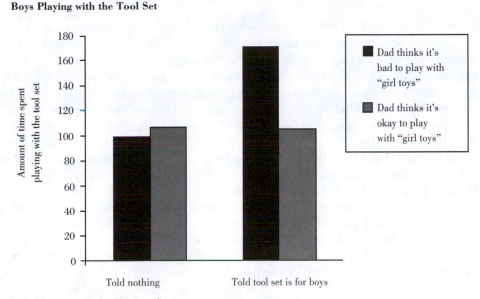

Boys Playing with the Tool Set

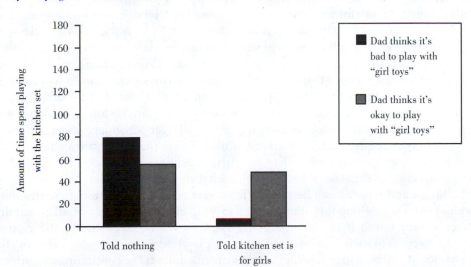

Boys Playing with the Kitchen Set

Figure 4.3. "Boys Playing with the Tool Set" and "Boys Playing with the Kitchen Set" graphs. *Sex Roles*, "Preschoolers' Awareness of Social Expectations of Gender: Relationships to Toy Choices," Vol. 38 Issue 9, 1998, pp. 695–696, Tarja Raag and Christine L. Rackliff.

Source: © 1998 Plenum Publishing Corporation. With permission of Springer.

READ ALL ABOUT IT!

Forget Mars and Venus, says psychologist Janet Hyde. We're all Earthlings! And in her "Gender Similarities Hypothesis" she reviews all the empirical evidence that women and men are far more similar than we are different. Turns out there is way more evidence for similarity than there is for difference—except, of course, for outdated stereotypes.

on what they were told about it—and what they thought their fathers would think. When boys were told nothing about the toys, they spent the same amount of time playing with both the tools and the kitchen set. When the tools were labeled "for boys," those who thought their fathers would consider cross-gender play as "bad" spent a lot more time playing with the tools. And when the kitchen set was labeled "for girls," not one boy who thought his father would say that such play was "bad" even touched it.

Now, remember that when the toys were not labeled, the boys spent as much time with the tools as they did with the kitchen set. Clearly there was nothing intrinsic about tools or kitchen sets that was more or less attractive to the boys. What mattered is how they were labeled—and what they thought their fathers would say. (It's equally interesting that the kids didn't think the fathers would care which toys their daughters played with or that their mothers would care what *either* the boys or the girls played with. Only the sons, and only the fathers.)[24]

Given the amount of attention we have been paying to the gender of children's toys, it is perhaps ironic that they've actually become *more* gendered in recent years, not less. Or, perhaps, not so ironic after all. (Remember that baby boys' and girls' outfits are increasingly gendered as well.) The chart in figure 4.4 shows the ratio of toys advertised as especially for boys or toys advertised as particularly for girls in relationship to the total number of toys for children. Two things stand out. First, notice that between 1910 and 1940, more toys for girls were gender-coded than toys for boys. This coincides with the feminist campaigns for women to work, join unions, serve on juries, attend universities, and, of course, vote. (Suffrage was granted in 1920.) Perhaps there was more anxiety about women's roles at that time, and gender-coded toys were a way to suppress that interest in breaking out of those roles? And second, notice that after a relatively stable period from 1940 to 1970, during which the ratios were relatively low, toys have begun to diverge again, with both boys and girls getting a larger percentage of gender-coded toys than ever before. And, what's more, while both are increasing, the coding of toys for boys is significantly higher than for girls, indicating, perhaps, increased anxiety about making sure that boys don't "stray" from their prescribed roles.

Males and females can be trained for a vast array of characteristics, and individual variations along this array overlap extensively. Because only small actual differences are found between girls and boys, how do we account for the relative ineffectiveness of socialization activities (toys, play, television, schools) in shaping the behavior of children in psychological experiments, and yet the continuing assignment to children and adults of roles on the basis of gender typing? Our answer can be only speculative. It appears that most psychological experiments offer boys and girls an opportunity to perform similar tasks without labeling the tasks as gender-appropriate.

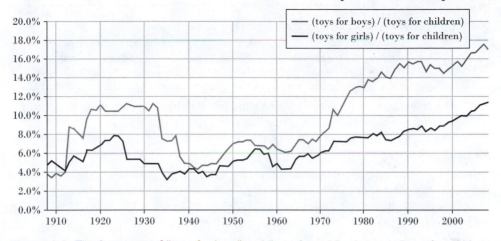
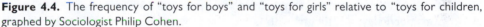

Figure 4.4. The frequency of "toys for boys" and "toys for girls" relative to "toys for children," graphed by Sociologist Philip Cohen.

Source: Google Books Ngram Viewer, http://books.google.com/ngrams; http://socimages.tumblr.com/post/105142152260/gender-segregation-of-boys-and-girls-toys-in.

In these contexts, males and females perform mostly alike. It would appear that the real power of gender typing resides less in the child than in the environments in which the child finds him- or herself. The social environment is filled with gendered messages and gendered activities. Even if the child possesses no fixed and permanent gender role, social arrangements will continually reinforce gender differences. In a gender-neutral experiment, social requirements are removed, and so the child does not behave in accord with a gender stereotype. Perhaps it is not internalized beliefs that keep us in place as men or women, but rather our interpersonal and social environments. Because there is considerable variation in what men and women actually do, it may require the weight of social organization and constant reinforcement to maintain gender-role differences.

READ ALL ABOUT IT!

As we grow up, we pass through different stages when gender expression is more or less rigid—and more or less relentlessly applied. While we often begin our childhoods dressed more or less the same—overalls, running shoes—it's not too long before the opposite sex is said to have "cooties" and we become rigidly insistent on exaggerated stereotypic forms of dress. Some girls go all "girly girl"—that sudden desire to wear ballet outfits to school— and some boys go all rough and tumble, avoiding any outfit that might be even remotely associated with girls. In "Pink Frilly Dresses and the Avoidance of All Things 'Girly' . . . ," psychologist May Ling Halim and her colleagues chart this rigidity and examine how committed children are to such rigid notions of gender identity. Do you think boys or girls are more gender rigid? Why?

Boys like to play with guns, and girls like to play house.

Actually, it depends. Boys and girls, aged three to seven, were presented with three possible toys to play with: a gun and holster (traditionally male), a tea set (traditionally female), and a ball (neutral). After establishing that certain characteristics were gender-coded—hard, sharp, angular (masculine), soft and smooth (feminine)—the researchers altered the toys. The gun was adorned with rhinestones in a purple holster. The camouflage-colored tea set was covered with sharp spikes.

And both the boys and girls were certain that the tea set was for boys and the gun and holster were for girls.

Source: Rosalind Chait Barnett, "Understanding the Role of Pervasive Negative Gender Stereotypes: What Can Be Done?" Paper presented at The Way Forward, Heidelberg, Germany, May 2007.

Resistance to such constricting gender arrangements comes in many shapes and sizes. Consider Riley, a little girl who is frustrated with the color coding of toys for boys and girls. In a well-watched YouTube video (seen four million times), she says, utterly exasperated, "Why do all the girls have to buy pink stuff and all the boys have to buy different color stuff?" (Watch her one-minute video at: http://www.youtube .com/watch?v=-CU04oHqbas)

READ ALL ABOUT IT!

Much of our childhood socialization—from infancy through adulthood, actually—is a form of gender policing, a way that our peers, families, and the larger culture all remind us, all the time, what is expected of us as women and men. Step out of line and you're likely to hear it—and loudly. "Dude, you're a fag!" is what sociologist C. J. Pascoe heard from high school students in one California school. It so perfectly captured the ways that young boys police gender performances from other boys, extracting conformity so that no one could possibly get the wrong idea about you.

And then there are Sasha's parents, Beck Laxton and Kieran Cooper in Cambridge, England. For five years, they kept Sasha's biological sex a secret, letting Sasha dress as Sasha wanted—hand-me-downs from older brothers and sisters mostly—referring to Sasha as "the child" or "the infant," and playing with dolls, trucks, and whatever else Sasha liked. It drove other folks nuts, but Sasha is a completely happy child, who, at age five, had his sex revealed to the world because it was required by the school authorities. A Toronto couple recently did the same with their baby. Despite all the dire predictions, the kids seem to be doing well. "As long as he has good relationships and good friends," Laxton says, "then nothing else matters, does it?"[25]

THE SOCIAL PSYCHOLOGY OF SEX ROLES
In their effort to understand the constellation of attitudes, traits, and behaviors that constitutes appropriate **gender identity**, some social psychologists elaborated and

Creating Little Martians and Venusians

The goal of gender socialization is not to enable little boys and little girls to express their natural gender differences, but to create those differences in the first place and then make them seem natural. And how better than to make sure boys and girls get the message than through fashion?

Here's a good one. In 2013, after years of Lara Croft and Dora the Explorer, Marvel Comics came out with new Avengers T-shirts for boys and girls. For boys, royal blue; for girls, bright red and tapered.

Source: http://www.huffingtonpost.com/2013/04/11/sexist-avengers-t-shirts-n_3063942.html.

Source: Disney Store (left); SuperHeroStuff.com (right).

extended the original classifications of the M-F scale offered by Terman and Miles. If masculinity and femininity could be understood as points on a continuum, a variety of abnormal behaviors could possibly be understood as examples of gender-inappropriate behavior.[26] In the years after World War II, for example, some psychologists hypothesized that the propensity toward fascism and Nazism stemmed from distorted assertions of gender identity. The authors of *The Authoritarian Personality* posited a typology of behaviors, based on the M-F scale, a scale that suggested that femininity and masculinity can describe both an internal psychological identification and an external behavioral manifestation. Their typology thus created four possible combinations instead of two:

		Internal Psychological Organization	
		Masculine	**Feminine**
External Behavioral Manifestation	**Masculine**	MM	MF
	Feminine	FM	FF

Two of the cells, upper left and lower right, would be considered "gender appropriate"—males and females whose internal psychological identification matches their external behaviors. Those males whose scores placed them in the upper right cell—internally feminine, externally masculine—also scored highest on measures of racism, authoritarianism, and hypermasculinity. The authors proposed that such attitudes were the means for those who were insecure about their masculinity to cover up their insecurities—by more rigid adherence to the most traditional norms.[27]

This notion became common wisdom in 1950s America and was used to study juvenile delinquency, Southern resistance to integration and civil rights, and male resistance to feminism. A more recent study has included homophobia. It resonated in popular advice about schoolyard bullies—that they are the *least* secure about their masculinity, which is why they have to try to prove it all the time. One's response to a bully—"Why don't you pick on someone your own size?"—will always fall on deaf ears, because the goal is not to compete but to win, so that insecure masculinity can be (however momentarily) *reaffirmed*. It doesn't work, of course, because the opponent is no real match, and so the bully has to do it all over again.

Interestingly, Sanford and his colleagues found that the men who scored in the lower left cell—externally feminine and internally masculine—were the most creative, artistic, and intelligent. It took a very secure man, indeed, to stray from the behavioral norms of masculinity, they suggested. And a recent study confirmed this trend. Cognitive biologist Qazi Rahman and his colleagues at the University of London administered a series of tests to heterosexual men and women. They found that higher levels of childhood gender nonconformity correlated with higher IQ and reading ability in both males and females. That is, higher levels of childhood femininity in *males* and lower levels in *females* were correlated with higher levels of intelligence and academic achievement.[28]

READ ALL ABOUT IT!

If you're perceived as "feminine," you can be pretty vulnerable to gender policing, bullying, and the like. This, argues Robb Willer and his colleagues in "Overdoing Gender," is what leads some guys to completely go overboard in proving their masculinity. Willer et al. argue that when guys feel their masculinity is vulnerable, being questioned or even threatened, they'll dramatically overcompensate and be more homophobic, bellicose, and, well, more likely to buy an SUV. Willer's study gives some credence to the idea that those muscle cars, dude SUVs, and Hummers are not expressions of a secure manhood, but exactly the opposite—one of several ways that men can compensate for not feeling masculine enough.

A recent effort to revisit this thesis found that men who felt that their masculinity was more "threatened" would overcompensate; they showed higher rates of support for the Iraq War, more negative attitudes toward homosexuals, and a greater interest in purchasing a sport utility vehicle. That old adage that the bigger the car, the smaller the . . . well, you know, may turn out to have some empirical validity.[29]

Whereas Sanford and his colleagues had developed a typology of inner identities and external behaviors, Miller and Swanson saw a developmental sequence. All children, both males and females, begin their lives as "FF"—totally identified with and behaving like the mother. Boys then pass through the Oedipal stage, or "FM," during which they continue to identify with the mother but begin to make a break from that identification, while they simultaneously acquire superficial masculine traits and behaviors. Finally, males arrive at "MM," both internal identification and external behaviors that are gender-appropriate. Thus authoritarianism, racism, sexism, and homophobia might now be seen as examples of psychological immaturity, a kind of arrested development. (The potential fourth stage, "MF," was dropped from the study.)[30]

A second trajectory that coincided with these studies was the work of Talcott Parsons and other sociologists who sought to establish the societal necessity for masculinity and femininity. Parsons argued that society had two types of major functions—production and reproduction—and that these required two separate institutional systems—the occupational system and the kinship system—which, in turn, required two types of roles that needed to be filled in order for it to function successfully. **Instrumental roles** demanded rationality, autonomy, and competitiveness; **expressive roles** demanded tenderness and nurturing so that the next generation could be socialized. In this way, Parsons shifted the emphasis of sex-role identity development away from the "need" of the infant to become either masculine or feminine to the need of society for individuals to fill specific slots. Fortunately, Parsons argued, we had two different types of people who were socialized to assume these two different roles.

Parsons suggested, however, that the allocation of roles to males and females did not always work smoothly. For example, in Western societies, the isolation of the nuclear family and the extended period of childhood meant that boys remained identified with the mother for a very long time. What's more, the separation of spheres meant that girls had their appropriate role model immediately before them, whereas boys did not have adequate role models. Thus, he argued, boys' break with the mother and their need to establish their individuality and masculinity often were accompanied by violent protest against femininity, and angry repudiation of the feminine became a way for the boy to purge himself of feminine identification. He "revolts against identification with his mother in the name of masculinity," Parsons writes, equating goodness with femininity, so that becoming a "bad boy" becomes a positive goal. This, Parsons suggests, has some negative consequences, including a "cult of **compulsive masculinity**":

> Western men are peculiarly susceptible to the appeal of an adolescent type of assertively masculine behavior and attitudes which may take various forms. They have in common a tendency to revolt against the routine aspects of the primarily institutionalized masculine role of sober responsibility, meticulous respect for the rights of others, and tender affection towards women. Assertion through physical prowess, with an endemic tendency toward violence and hence the military ideal, is inherent in the complex and the most dangerous potentiality.[31]

For the girl, the process is somewhat different. She has an easier time because she remains identified with the mother. Her rebellion and anger come from recognizing "masculine superiority"—"the fact that her own security like that of other women is dependent on the favor—even 'whim'—of a man." Suddenly she realizes that the qualities that she values are qualities that may handicap her. She may express the aggression that would invariably follow upon such frustration by rebelling against the feminine role altogether: She may become a feminist.

By the 1970s, sex-role theory was, itself, facing significant critical scrutiny. Some thinkers found the binary model between roles, system needs, and males and females just a bit too facile and convenient, as well as politically conservative—as if changing roles meant disrupting the needs that *society* had. Others stressed the coercive nature of these roles: If they were natural and met readily evident needs, why did so many people rebel against them, and why did they need to be so rigorously enforced?

Two significant challenges came from social psychologists themselves. Sandra Bem and others explored the *content* of sex roles. The **Bem Sex Role Inventory** tested respondents on their perception of sixty different attributes, twenty of which were coded as "feminine," twenty as "masculine," and twenty more as "fillers" (table 4.1). Although this replaced a continuum with categorical sex roles, Bem discovered that the most psychologically well adjusted and intelligent people were those who fell in between the polar oppositions of masculinity and femininity. It was, she argued, **androgyny,** "the combined presence of socially valued, stereotypic, feminine and masculine characteristics," that best described the healthily adjusted individual. What's more, Bem argued, is that given where most of us actually fall on the continuum, masculinity and femininity are hardly opposites.

Table 4.1. Items on the Masculinity, Femininity, and Social Desirability Scales of the BSRI

Masculine items	Feminine items	Neutral items
49. Acts as a leader	11. Affectionate	51. Adaptable
46. Aggressive	5. Cheerful	36. Conceited
58. Ambitious	50. Childlike	9. Conscientious
22. Analytical	32. Compassionate	60. Conventional
13. Assertive	53. Does not use harsh language	45. Friendly
10. Athletic	35. Eager to soothe hurt feelings	15. Happy
55. Competitive	20. Feminine	3. Helpful
4. Defends own beliefs	14. Flatterable	48. Inefficient
37. Dominant	59. Gentle	24. Jealous
19. Forceful	47. Gullible	39. Likable
25. Has leadership abilities	56. Loves children	6. Moody
7. Independent	17. Loyal	21. Reliable
52. Individualistic	26. Sensitive to the needs of others	30. Secretive
31. Makes decisions easily	8. Shy	33. Sincere
40. Masculine	38. Soft spoken	42. Solemn
1. Self-reliant	23. Sympathetic	57. Tactful
34. Self-sufficient	44. Tender	12. Theatrical
16. Strong personality	29. Understanding	27. Truthful
43. Willing to take a stand	41. Warm	18. Unpredictable
28. Willing to take risks	2. Yielding	54. Unsystematic

Note: The number preceding each item reflects the position of each adjective as it actually appears on the Inventory.

Several empirical studies seemed to bear out the desirability of an androgynous personality constellation over a stereotypically feminine or masculine one. But subsequent studies failed to confirm the validity of these measures, and androgyny was discredited as a kind of wishy-washy nonpersonality, rather than the synthesis of the best of both worlds.[32] What's more, conceptually, dividing male and female traits into two categories makes it impossible to integrate power and gender inequality in the discussion; twenty years after her initial studies, Bem notes that the scale "reproduces . . . the very gender polarization that it seeks to undercut."[33]

Whereas proponents of androgyny challenged the content of sex-role theory, Joseph Pleck challenged the form. In a series of articles that culminated in his book *The Myth of Masculinity*, Pleck advanced the idea that the problem was not that men were having a hard time fitting into a rational notion of masculinity but rather that the role itself was internally contradictory and inconsistent. Instead of simply accepting the sex role as a package, Pleck operationalized what he called the "Male Sex Role Identity" model into a discrete set of testable propositions. These included:

1. Sex-role identity is operationally defined by measures of psychological sex typing, conceptualized in terms of psychological masculinity and/or femininity dimensions.
2. Sex-role identity derives from identification-modeling and, to a lesser extent, reinforcement and cognitive learning of sex-typed traits, especially among males.
3. The development of appropriate sex-role identity is a risky, failure-prone process, especially for males.
4. Homosexuality reflects a disturbance of sex-role identity.
5. Appropriate sex-role identity is necessary for good psychological adjustment because of an inner psychological need for it.
6. Hypermasculinity indicates insecurity in sex-role identities.
7. Problems of sex-role identity account for men's negative attitudes and behavior toward women.
8. Problems of sex-role identity account for boys' difficulties in school performance and adjustment.
9. Black males are particularly vulnerable to sex-role identity problems.
10. Male adolescent initiation rites are a response to problems of sex-role identity.
11. Historical changes in the character of work and the organization of the family have made it more difficult for men to develop and maintain their sex-role identities.

When virtually all of these propositions turned out to be empirically false, Pleck argued that the male sex role itself was the source of strain, anxiety, and male problems. Psychology was thus transformed from the vehicle that would help problematic men adapt to their rational sex role into one of the origins of their problems, the vehicle by which men had been fed a pack of lies about masculinity. The sex-role system itself was the source of much of men's anxieties and pain. In its place, Pleck proposed the Male Sex Role Strain model:

1. Sex roles are operationally defined by sex-role stereotypes and norms.
2. Sex roles are contradictory and inconsistent.

3. The proportion of individuals who violate sex roles is high.
4. Violating sex roles leads to social condemnation.
5. Violating sex roles leads to negative psychological consequences.
6. Actual or imagined violation of sex roles leads individuals to overconform to them.
7. Violating sex roles has more severe consequences for males than females.
8. Certain characteristics prescribed by sex roles are psychologically dysfunctional.
9. Each gender experiences sex-role strain in its work and family roles.
10. Historical changes cause sex-role strain.

The net effect of this new model is to shift the understanding of problems from the men themselves to the roles that they are forced to play.[34] Subsequent research has explored the grappling with these contradictory role specifications by different groups of men and the problematic behaviors (such as sexual risk taking) that are expressions of men's efforts to reconcile contradictory role demands.[35]

But there remain problems with sex-role theory that even these two ambitious efforts could not resolve. For one thing, when psychologists discussed the "male" sex role or the "female" sex role, they posited a single, monolithic entity, a "role," into which all boys and all girls were placed. Through a process of socialization, boys acquired the male sex role; girls, the female one. Imagine two large tanks, into which all biological males and females are placed. But all males and all females are not alike. There are a variety of different "masculinities" or "femininities" depending on class, race, ethnicity, age, sexuality, and region. If all boys or all girls were to receive the same socialization to the same sex role, differences in the construction of black masculinity, or Latina femininity, or middle-aged gay masculinity, or midwestern older white femininity, and so on, would all be effaced. Sex-role theory is unable to account for the differences *among* men or *among* women because it always begins from the normative prescriptions of sex *roles*, rather than the experiences of men and women themselves. (Remember that the differences among men and among women—not the differences between women and men—provide most of the variations in attitudes, traits, and behavior we observe.)

A second problem with sex-role theory is that the separate tanks into which males and females are sorted look similar to each other. When we say that boys become masculine and girls become feminine in roughly similar ways, we posit a false equivalence between the two. If we ignore the power differential between the two tanks, then both privilege and oppression disappear. "Men don't have power," writes pop therapist Warren Farrell; "men and women have roles."[36] Despite what men and women may *feel* about their situation, men as a group have power in our society over women as a group. In addition, some men—privileged by virtue of race, class, ethnicity, sexuality, and so on—have power over other men. Any adequate explanation of gender must account not only for gender difference but also for male domination. Theories of sex roles are inadequate to this task.[37]

This theoretical inadequacy stems from the sorting process in the first place. Sex-role theorists see boys and girls sorted into those two separate categories. But what we know about being a man has everything to do with what it means to be a woman; and what we know about being a woman has everything to do with what it means to be a man. Constructions of gender are *relational*—we understand what it means to be a man or a woman in relation to the dominant models as well as to one another. And those who are marginalized by race, class, ethnicity, age, sexuality, and the like also measure their gender identities against those of the dominant group.

Finally, sex-role theory assumes that only individuals are gendered, that gendered individuals occupy gender-neutral positions and inhabit gender-neutral institutions. But gender is more than an attribute of individuals; gender organizes and constitutes the field in which those individuals move. The institutions of our lives—families, workplaces, schools—are themselves gendered institutions, organized to reproduce the differences and the inequalities between women and men. If one wants to understand the lives of people in any situation, the French philosopher Jean-Paul Sartre once wrote, one "must inquire first into the situation surrounding [them]."[38] Theorists of sex roles and androgyny help us move beyond strictly psychological analyses of gender. But the inability to theorize difference, power, relationality, and the institutional dimension of gender means that we will need to build other elements into the discussion. Sociological explanations of gender begin from these principles.

KEY TERMS

Androgyny

Bem Sex Role Inventory

Castration Complex

Cognitive Development Theories

Compulsive Masculinity

Diagnostic and Statistical Manual of Mental Disorders (DSM)

Expressive Roles

Gender Identity

Gender Stereotypes

Instrumental Roles

M-F Test

Oedipal Crisis

Penis Envy

Psychosexual Development

Womb Envy

CHAPTER

5

The SOCIAL CONSTRUCTION *of* GENDER RELATIONS

Society is a masked ball, where every one hides his real character, and reveals it by hiding.

—RALPH WALDO EMERSON, "WORSHIP" (1860)

In one of the most thoughtful definitions, C. Wright Mills defined sociology as the intersection of biography and history. In his view, the goal of a sociological perspective would be to locate an individual in both time and space, to provide the social and historical contexts in which a person constructs his or her identity. In that sense, sociology's bedrock assumption, upon which its analyses of structures and institutions rest, is that individuals shape their lives within both historical and social contexts. We do not do so simply because we are biologically programmed to act in certain ways, nor because we have inevitable human tasks to solve as we age. Rather, we respond to the world we encounter, shaping, modifying, and creating our identities through those encounters with other people and within social institutions.

Thus sociology takes as its starting points many of the themes raised in earlier chapters. Sociological perspectives on gender assume the variability of gendered identities that anthropological research has explored, the biological "imperatives" toward gender identity and differentiation (though sociology locates the source of these imperatives less in our bodies and more in our environments), and the psychological imperatives toward both autonomy and connection that modern society requires of individuals in the modern world. To a sociologist, both our biographies (identities) and histories (evolving social structures) are gendered.

Like other social sciences, sociology begins with a critique of biological determinism. Instead of observing our experiences as the expressions of inborn, interplanetary differences, the social sciences examine the variations among men and among women, as well as the differences between them. The social sciences thus begin with the explicitly social origin of our patterns of development.

Our lives depend on social interaction. Literally, it seems. In the thirteenth century, Frederick II, emperor of the Holy Roman Empire, decided to perform an experiment to see if he could discover the "natural language of man." What language would we speak if no one taught us language? He selected some newborn babies and decreed that no one speak to them. The babies were suckled and nursed and bathed as usual, but speech and songs and lullabies were strictly prohibited. All the babies died. And you've probably heard those stories of "feral children"—babies who were abandoned and raised by animals became suspicious of people and could not be socialized to live in society after age six or so. In all the stories, the children died young, as did virtually all the "isolates," those little children who were locked away in closets and basements by sadistic or insane parents.[1]

What do such stories tell us? True or apocryphal, they suggest that biology alone—that is, our anatomical composition—doesn't determine our development as we might have thought. We need to interact, to be socialized, to be part of society. It is that interaction, not our bodies, that makes us who we are.

Isolated Children

Some children have been isolated from almost all human contact by abusive caregivers. One of the best-documented cases of an isolated child was "Isabelle," who was born to an unmarried, deaf-mute teenager. The girl's parents were so afraid of scandal that they kept both mother and daughter locked away in a darkened room, where they had no contact with the outside world. In 1938, when she was six years old, Isabelle escaped from her confinement. She was unable to speak except to make croaking sounds, she was extremely fearful of strangers, and she reacted to stimuli with the instinct of a wild animal. Gradually she became used to being around people, but she expressed no curiosity about them; it was as if she did not see herself as one of them. But doctors and social scientists began a long period of systematic training. Within a year she was able to speak in complete sentences, and soon she was able to attend school with other children. By the age of fourteen, she was in the sixth grade, happy and well-adjusted. She managed to overcome her lack of early childhood socialization, but only through exceptional effort.

Studies of other isolated children reveal that some can recover, with effort and specialized care, but that others suffer permanent damage. It is unclear exactly why, but no doubt some contributing factors are the duration of the isolation, the child's age when the isolation began, the presence of some human contacts (like Isabelle's mother), other abuse accompanying the isolation, and the child's intelligence. The 1994 film *Nell* starred Jodie Foster as a near-isolate who gradually learns language and social interaction well enough to fall in love with her doctor (played by Liam Neeson).

Often, the first time we hear that gender is socially constructed, we take it to mean that we are, as individuals, not responsible for what we do. "'Society' made me like this," we might say. "It's not my fault." (This is often the flip side of the other response one often hears: "In America an individual can do anything he or she wants to do," or "It's a free country, and everyone is entitled to his or her own opinion.") Both of these rhetorical strategies—what I call "**reflexive passivity**" and "**impulsive hyperindividualism**"—are devices that we use to deflect individual accountability and responsibility. They are both, therefore, misreadings of the sociological mandate. When we say that gender identity is socially constructed, what we do mean is that our identities are a fluid assemblage of the meanings and behaviors that we construct from the values, images, and prescriptions we find in the world around us. Our gendered identities are both voluntary—we choose to become who we are—and coerced—we are pressured, forced, sanctioned, and often physically beaten into submission to some rules. We neither make up the rules as we go along nor fit casually and without struggle into preassigned roles.

For some of us, becoming adult men and women in our society is a smooth and almost effortless drifting into behaviors and attitudes that feel as familiar to us as our skin. And for others of us, becoming masculine or feminine is an interminable torture, a nightmare in which we must brutally suppress some parts of ourselves to please others—or, simply, to survive. For most of us, though, the experience falls somewhere in between: There are parts we love and wouldn't part with, and other parts where we feel we've been forced to exaggerate one side at the expense of others. It's the task of the sociological perspective to specify the ways in which our own experiences, our interactions with others, and institutions combine to shape our sense of who we are. Biology provides the raw materials, whereas society and history provide the context, the instruction manual, that we follow to construct our identities.

A SOCIAL CONSTRUCTIONIST PERSPECTIVE

In the first chapter, I identified the four elements of a social constructionist perspective on gender. Definitions of masculinity and femininity vary, first, from culture to culture, and, second, in any one culture over historical time. Thus social constructionists rely on the work of anthropologists and historians to identify the commonalities and the differences in the meanings of masculinity and femininity from one culture to another and to describe how those differences change over time.

Gender definitions also vary over the course of a person's life. The issues confronting women when they are younger—their marketability in both the workplace and the marriage market, for example—will often be very different from the issues they face at menopause or retirement. And the issues confronting a young man about proving himself and achieving what he calls success and the social institutions in which he will attempt to enact those experiences will change throughout his life. For example, men often report a "softening," the development of greater interest in care giving and nurturing, when they become grandfathers than when they became fathers—often to the puzzlement and distress of their sons. But in their sixties and seventies, when their children are having children, these men do not feel the same pressures to perform, to leave a mark, to prove themselves. Their battles are over, and they can relax and enjoy the fruits of their efforts. Thus we rely on developmental psychologists to specify the normative "tasks" that any individual must successfully accomplish as he or she matures and develops, and we also need scholars in the humanities to explore the symbolic record that such men and women leave us as evidence of their experiences.

Finally, definitions of masculinity and femininity will vary within any one culture at any one time—by race, class, ethnicity, age, sexuality, education, region of the country, and so on. You'll recall that it seems obvious that an older, gay, black man in Chicago will have a different idea of what it means to be a man than will a heterosexual white teenager in rural Iowa.

Social constructionism thus builds on the other social and behavioral sciences, adding specific dimensions to the exploration of gender. What sociology contributes are the elements that the social psychology of sex roles cannot explain adequately: difference, power, and the institutional dimensions of gender. To explain difference, social constructionism offers an analysis of the plurality of gender definitions; to explain power, it emphasizes the ways in which some definitions become normative through the struggles of different groups for power—including the power to define. Finally, to explain the institutional dimension, social constructionism moves beyond the socialization of gendered individuals who occupy gender-neutral sites to the study of the interplay between gendered individuals and gendered institutions.

BEYOND SEX-ROLE THEORY

As we saw in the last chapter, social psychologists located the process of acquisition of gender identity in the developmental patterns of individuals in their families and in early childhood interaction. Specifically, sex-role theorists explored the ways in which individuals come to be gendered and the ways in which they negotiate their ways toward some sense of internal consistency and coherence, despite contradictory role definitions. Still, however, the emphasis is on the gendering of individuals and occasionally on the inconsistent cultural blueprints with which those individuals must contend. Sociological understandings of gender begin, historically, with a critique of sex-role theory, with sociologists arguing that such theory is inadequate to fully understand the complexities of gender as a social institution. Sociologists have identified four significant problems with sex-role theory—problems that require its modification.

First, the use of the idea of roles has the curious effect of actually minimizing the importance of gender. Role theory uses drama as a metaphor—we learn our roles through socialization and then perform them for others. But to speak of a gender role makes it sound almost too theatrical and thus too easily changeable. Gender, as Helena Lopata and Barrie Thorne write, "is not a role in the same sense that being a teacher, sister, or friend is a role. Gender, like race or age, is deeper, less changeable, and infuses the more specific roles one plays; thus, a female teacher differs from a male teacher in important sociological respects (e.g., she is likely to receive less pay, status and credibility)." *To make gender a role like any other role is to diminish its power in structuring our lives.*[2]

Second, sex-role theory posits singular normative definitions of masculinity and femininity. If the meanings of masculinity and femininity vary across cultures, over historical time, among men within any one culture, and over the life course, we cannot speak of masculinity or femininity as though each were a constant, singular, universal essence. Personally, when I read what social psychologists wrote about the "male sex role" I always wondered whom they were writing about. "Who, me?" I thought. Is there really only *one* male sex role and only *one* female sex role?

One key theme about gender identity is the ways in which other differences—race, class, ethnicity, sexuality, age, region—all inform, shape, and modify our definitions of gender. To speak of one male or one female sex role is to compress the enormous variety of our culture's ideals into one and to risk ignoring the other factors that shape our identities. In fact, in those early studies of sex roles, social psychologists did just that, suggesting that, for example, black men or women or gay men or lesbians evidenced either "too much" or "too little" adherence to their appropriate sex role. In that way, homosexuals or people of color were seen as expressing sex-role problems; because their sex roles differed from the normative, it was they who had the problem. (As we saw earlier, the most sophisticated sex-role theorists understand that such normative definitions are internally contradictory, but they still mistake the normative for the "normal.")

By positing this false universalism, sex-role theory assumes what needs to be explained—how the normative definition is established and reproduced—and explains away all the differences among men and among women. Sex-role theory cannot fully accommodate these differences among men or among women. A more satisfying investigation must take into account these different definitions of masculinity and femininity constructed and expressed by different groups of men and women. Thus we speak of *masculinities* and *femininities*. What's more, sociologists see the differences among masculinities or femininities as expressing exactly the opposite relationship than do sex-role theorists. Sex-role theorists, if they can accommodate differences at all, see these differences as aberrations, as the failure to conform to the normal sex role. Sociologists, on the other hand, believe that the differences among definitions of masculinity or femininity are themselves the outcome of the ways in which those groups interact with their environments. Thus sociologists contend that one cannot understand the differences in masculinity or femininity based on race or ethnicity without first looking at the ways in which institutional and interpersonal racial inequality structure the ways in which members of those groups actively construct their identities. Sex-role theorists might say, for example, that black men, lesbians, or older Latinas experience discrimination because their definitions of masculinity and femininity are "different" from the norm. To a sociologist, that's only half right. A sociologist would add that these groups develop different definitions of masculinity and femininity in active engagement with a social environment in which they are discriminated against. Thus their differences are more the product of discrimination than its cause.

This leads to a third arena in which sociologists challenge sex-role theory. Gender is not only plural, it is also relational. A related problem with sex-role theory is that it posits two separate spheres, as if sex-role differentiation were more a matter of sorting a herd of cattle into two appropriate pens for branding. Boys get herded into the masculine corral, girls the feminine. But such a static model also suggests that the two corrals have virtually nothing to do with one another. "The result of using the role framework is an abstract view of the *differences* between the sexes and their situations, not a concrete one of the *relations* between them."[3] But what surveys indicate is that men construct their ideas of what it means to be men *in constant reference* to definitions of femininity. What it means to be a man is to be unlike a woman; indeed, social psychologists have emphasized that although different groups of men may disagree about other traits and their significance in gender definitions, the "antifemininity" component of masculinity is perhaps the dominant and universal characteristic.

Fourth, because gender is plural and relational, it is also situational. What it means to be a man or a woman varies in different contexts. Those different institutional contexts demand and produce different forms of masculinity and femininity. "Boys may be boys," cleverly comments feminist legal theorist Deborah Rhode, "but they express that identity differently in fraternity parties than in job interviews with a female manager."[4] Gender is thus not a property of individuals, some "thing" one has, but rather a specific set of behaviors that is produced in specific social situations. And thus gender changes as the situation changes.

Sex-role theory cannot adequately account for either the differences among women and men or their different definitions of masculinity and femininity in different situations without implicitly assuming some theory of deviance. Nor can it express the relational character of those definitions. In addition, sex-role theory cannot fully account for the power relationships between women and men and among different groups of women and different groups of men. Thus the fourth and perhaps most significant problem in sex-role theory is that it *depoliticizes* gender, making gender a set of individual attributes and not an aspect of social structure. "The notion of 'role' focuses attention more on individuals than on social structure, and implies that 'the female role' and 'the male role' are complementary (i.e., separate or different but equal)," write sociologists Judith Stacey and Barrie Thorne. "The terms are depoliticizing; they strip experience from its historical and political context and neglect questions of power and conflict."[5]

But how can one speak of gender without speaking of power? As I pointed out in the book's introduction, a pluralistic and relational theory of gender cannot pretend that all masculinities and femininities are created equal. All American women and all American men must also contend with a singular vision of both masculinity and femininity, specific definitions that are held up as models against which we all measure ourselves. These are what sociologist R. W. Connell calls the "hegemonic" definition of masculinity and the "emphasized" version of femininity. These are normative constructions, the ones against which others are measured and, almost invariably, found wanting. (Connell's trenchant critique of sex-role theory, therefore, hinges on her contention that sex-role psychologists do not challenge but in fact reproduce the hegemonic version as the "normal" one.) **Hegemonic masculinity** is a "particular variety of masculinity to which others—among them young and effeminate as well as homosexual men—are subordinated."[6] We thus come to know what it means to be a man or a woman in American culture by setting our definitions in opposition to a set of "others"—racial minorities, sexual minorities, and so on. One of the most fruitful areas of research in sociology today is trying to specify exactly how these hegemonic versions are established and how different groups negotiate their ways through problematized definitions.

Sex-role theory proved inadequate to explore the variations in gender definitions, which require adequately theorizing the variations *within* the category of men or women. Such theorizing makes it possible to see the relationships between and among men or between and among women as structured relationships as well. Tension about gender was earlier theorized by sex-role theory as a tension between an individual and the expectations that were established by the sex role—that is, between the individual and an abstract set of expectations.

This leads to the fifth and final problem with sex-role theory—its inadequacy in comprehending the dynamics of change. Movements for social change, like **feminism** or **gay liberation**, become movements to expand role definitions and to change role expectations. Their goal is to expand role options for individual women and men, whose lives are constrained by stereotypes. But social and political movements are not only about expanding the opportunities for individuals to break free of the constraints of inhibiting sex roles, to allow their "true" selves to emerge: They are also about the redistribution of power in society. They demand the reallocation of resources and an end to forms of inequality that are embedded in social institutions as well as sex-role stereotypes. Only a perspective that begins with an analysis of power can adequately understand those social movements. A social constructionist approach seeks to be more concrete, specifying tension and conflict not between individuals and expectations, but rather between and among groups of people within social institutions. Thus social constructionism is inevitably about power.

What's wrong with sex-role theory can, finally, be understood by analogy. Why is it, do you suppose, no reputable scholars today use the terms "race roles" or "class roles" to describe the observable aggregate differences between members of different races or different classes? Are such "race roles" specific behavioral and attitudinal characteristics that are socialized into all members of different races? Hardly. Not only would such a term flatten all the distinctions and differences among members of the same race, but also it would ignore the ways in which the behaviors of different races—to the extent that they might be seen as different in the first place—are the products of racial inequality and oppression and not the external expression of some inner essence.

The positions of women and blacks have much in common, as sociologist Helen Hacker pointed out in her groundbreaking article "Women as a Minority Group," which was written more than a half century ago. Hacker argued that systematic structural inequality produces a "culture of self-hatred" among the target group. And yet we do not speak of "race roles." Such an idea would be absurd, because (1) the differences within each race are far greater than the differences between races; (2) what it means to be white or black is always constructed in relationship to the other; and (3) those definitions make no sense outside the context of the racially based power that white people, as a group, maintain over people of color, as a group. Movements for racial equality are about more than expanding role options for people of color.

Ultimately, to use role theory to explain race or gender is to blame the victim. If our gendered behaviors "stem from fundamental personality differences, socialized early in life," suggests psychologist David Tresemer, then responsibility must lie at our own feet. This is what R. Stephen Warner and his colleagues call the "Sambo theory of oppression"—"the victims internalize the maladaptive set of values of the oppressive system. Thus behavior that appears incompetent, deferential, and self-degrading is assumed to reflect the crippled capabilities of the personality."[7] In this worldview, social change must be left to the future, when a more egalitarian form of childhood socialization can produce children better able to function according to hegemonic standards. Social change comes about when the oppressed learn better the ways of their oppressors. If they refuse, and no progress is made—well, whose fault is that?

A NOTE ABOUT POWER

One of the central themes of this book is that gender is about difference and also about inequality, about power. At the level of gender relations, gender is about the power that men as a group have over women as a group, and it is also about the power that some men have over other men (or that some women have over other women). It is impossible to explain gender without adequately understanding power—not because power is the consequence of gender difference, but rather because power is what produces those gender differences in the first place.

To say that gender is a power relation—the power of men over women and the power of some men or women over other men or women—is among the more controversial arguments of the social constructionist perspective. In fact, the question of power is among the most controversial elements in all explanations of gender. Yet it is central; all theories of gender must explain both difference and domination. Whereas other theories explain male domination as the result of sex differences, social constructionism explains differences as the result of domination.

Yet a discussion about power invariably makes men, in particular, uncomfortable or defensive. How many times have we heard a man say, when confronted with women's anger at gender-based inequality and discrimination, "Hey, don't blame me! I never raped anyone!" (This is analogous to white people's defensive response denying that their family ever owned or continues to own slaves when confronted with the contemporary reality of racial oppression.) When challenged by the idea that the gender order means that men have power over women, men often respond with astonishment. "What do you mean, men have all the power? What are you talking about? I have no power at all. I'm completely powerless. My wife bosses me around, my children boss me around, my boss bosses me around. I have no power at all!" Most men, it seems, do not feel powerful.

Here, in a sense, is where feminism has failed to resonate for many men. Much of feminist theory of gender-based power derived from a symmetry between the structure of gender relations and women's individual experiences. Women, as a group, were not *in* power. That much was evident to anyone who cared to observe a corporate board, a university board of trustees, or a legislative body at any level anywhere in the world. Nor, individually, did women *feel* powerful. In fact, they felt constrained by gender inequality into stereotypic activities that prevented them from feeling comfortable, safe, and competent. So neither were women in power, nor did they feel powerful.

That symmetry breaks down when we try to apply it to men. Because although men may be *in* power everywhere one cares to look, individual men are not "in power," and they do not feel powerful. Men often feel themselves to be equally constrained by a system of stereotypic conventions that leaves them unable to live the lives to which they believe they are entitled. Men as a group are in power (when compared with women) but do not feel powerful. The feeling of powerlessness is one reason why so many men believe that they are the victims of reverse discrimination and oppose affirmative action. Or why some men's movement leaders comb through the world's cultures for myths and rituals to enable men to claim the power they want but do not feel they have. Or even why many yuppies took to wearing "power ties" while they munched their "power lunches" during the 1980s and early 1990s—as if power were a fashion accessory for those who felt powerless.

Pop psychologist Warren Farrell called male power a "myth" because men and women have complementary roles and equally defamatory stereotypes of "sex object" and "success object." Farrell often uses the analogy of the chauffeur to illustrate his case. The chauffeur is in the driver's seat. He knows where he's going. He's wearing the uniform. You'd think, therefore, that he is in power. But from his perspective, someone else is giving the orders; he's not powerful at all. This analogy does have some limited value: Individual men are not powerful, at least none but a small handful of individual men. But what if we ask one question of our chauffeur and try to shift the frame just a little. What if we ask him: What is the gender of the person who *is* giving the orders? (The lion's share of riders in chauffeur-driven limousines are, after all, upper-class white men.) When we shift from the analysis of the individual's experience to a different context, the relations between and among men emerge also as relations of power—power based on class, race, ethnicity, sexuality, age, and the like. "It is particular groups of men, not men in general, who are oppressed within patriarchal sexual relations, and whose situations are related in different ways to the overall logic of the subordination of women to men."[8]

Like gender, power is not the property of individuals—a possession that one has or does not have—but rather a property of group life, of social life. Power *is*. It can neither be willed away nor ignored. Here is how the philosopher Hannah Arendt put it:

> Power corresponds to the human ability not just to act but to act in concert. Power is never the property of an individual; it belongs to a group and remains in existence only so long as the group keeps together. When we say of somebody that he is "in power" we actually refer to his being empowered by a certain number of people to act in their name. The moment the group, from which the power originated to begin with . . . disappears, "his power" also vanishes.[9]

To a sociologist, power is not an attitude or a possession; it's not really a "thing" at all. It cannot be "given up" like an ideology that's been outgrown. Power creates as well as destroys. It is deeply woven into the fabric of our lives—it is the warp of our interactions and the weft of our institutions. And it is so deeply woven into our lives that it is most invisible to those who are most empowered.

In general, sociology adds three crucial dimensions to the study of gender: (1) the life course perspective, (2) a macrolevel institutional analysis, and (3) a microlevel interactionist approach.

GENDER THROUGH THE LIFE COURSE

I've suggested that role theory is ill-equipped to account for the significant differences among different groups of women or men—differences of class, race, ethnicity, sexuality, and so on. Gender identities and expressions vary far more than the prescriptive roles to which we are presumably assigned. Nor can role theory fully embrace the changes in gender identity over the course of our lives. Sex-role theory overemphasizes the developmental decisiveness of early childhood as the moment that gender socialization happens. Developmental psychologists have provided compelling evidence concerning the acquisition of gender identity in early childhood. Through socialization, especially in families and schools, the basic elements of gender identity are established, the foundation laid for future elaboration and expression.

But the story doesn't stop there. At its least convincing, some developmental psychology proposes that once one acquires gender identity it is fixed, permanent by age five or six. Sociologists embraced some of that idea, although they often pushed the age limit up to that tumultuous period called "adolescence." Surely, though, gender identity was fixed indelibly by puberty, which is marked, after all, by all the physical changes that mark the full-fledged assumption of adult masculinity and femininity.

Sociologists used to think that the three primary institutions of socialization were the family, school, and church; the three primary bearers of their socializing message were parents, teachers, and religious figures (priests, ministers, rabbis, imams, and the like). This model has proved inaccurate for two reasons. First, it assumes that socialization is a smooth process that is accomplished by the end of childhood, when family, school, and church have receded in significance in a person's life. Second, it views the socialization process from the point of view of the socializer, not the socialized. That is, from the point of view of the child, the chief **agents of socialization**—parents, teachers, and religious figures—translate as grown-ups, grown-ups, and grown-ups.

Kids know better. They also know that a primary agent of their socialization is their peer group—the other boys and girls, and later men and women—with whom they interact. They also know that the images and messages that daily surround them in the media are constantly giving them messages about what men and women are supposed to look and act like. Media and peer groups are, today, part of the pentagram of socializing institutions.

Media and peer groups, however, do not recede after early childhood; indeed, one might say they pick up where family, church, and school leave off. Some of the messages from peer groups and media reinforce what we've learned; other messages directly contradict those earlier messages. And it's up to us to sort it out.

Gender socialization continues throughout the life course. The process is neither smooth nor finite—it's bumpy and uneven and continues all our lives. What masculinity or femininity might mean to us in our twenties will mean something dramatically different to us in our forties or our sixties. And although a small part of that explanation has to do with biological stages of development—puberty, reproductive years, menopause, physical decline—these stages vary so significantly from culture to culture that sociologists search for the meaning of such biological shifts in the ways in which those aging bodies interact with their social context. The institutions in which we find ourselves change, and with those changes come different meanings of masculinity and femininity.

Take, for example, a well-known "factoid" about the differences between male and female sexuality. We hear, for example, that males reach their sexual "peak" at age eighteen or so but that women reach their sexual peak somewhat later, perhaps as late as their mid-thirties. This biological mismatch in hitting our sexual stride is often attributed to different maturational trajectories or different evolutionary strategies. He reaches his sexual peak when he is capable of producing the highest quantity of fertile sperm and thus is capable of fertilizing the highest number of females. She reaches her sexual peak when she is leaving fertility behind and, in all likelihood, has already had all the children she will have.

To be sure, these different moments correspond with some hormonal shifts, especially for women as they end their childbearing years and enter menopause. But can we explain this divergence solely on the basis of different rates of maturation, hormones, and bodies? I don't think so. This divergence in sexualities is far more easily and convincingly explained by putting male and female sexuality in context. And that context is the relationship to marriage and family life. For men, what's experienced as sexy is unknown, mysterious, even a bit dangerous. Men reach their sexual peak early because that's when their sex life is unconstrained by marriage. By contrast, women often feel that they need the security of a stable relationship to really let themselves explore their sexuality: They reach their peak because marriage provides that trust and intimacy that activate women's pleasure. What's more, women's fertility is frequently accompanied by a certain "danger"—unwanted pregnancy—that is hardly an aphrodisiac. Could it be that women reach their sexual peak when they are in a stable and secure relationship with someone they trust enough to give full voice to their desires and don't have to worry about the possibility of unwanted pregnancy as a result?

Or take that staple of daytime self-help talk shows: the **midlife crisis**. In the 1970s, two best-selling books, *Seasons of a Man's Life* (D. J. Levinson, Darrow, Klein, M. H. Levinson, and McKee, 1978) and *Passages* (Sheehy, 1976), popularized the belief that middle-aged men (and, to a lesser extent, women) go through a developmental "crisis" characterized by a pressure to make wholesale changes in their work, relationships, and leisure. For men, stereotypical responses to this pressure might include divorcing their wives to date younger women, pursuing lifelong ambitions, changing jobs, buying a sports car, growing a ponytail, and piercing an ear or taking up adventurous and risky hobbies and suddenly professing a newfound love of hip-hop (figure 5.1).

Figure 5.1. Male midlife crises often provide fodder for popular films. In *City Slickers* (1991), Billy Crystal (center) flanked by Daniel Stern and Bruno Kirby play three middle-class guys who bring in a herd of steer on a dude ranch adventure.

Source: © Columbia Pictures/Courtesy Everett Collection.

The idea of midlife crisis was embraced by a large segment of mainstream American culture. Middle-aged people found the concept intuitively compelling as a way of understanding changes in their own feelings and behaviors. Others employed it as a useful explanation of erratic behavior in their middle-aged adult parents or friends. Thirty years later, it remains a popular concept, the subject of pop psychology books and websites offering advice to people who struggle with the symptoms of the "crisis": depression, angst, irrational behavior, and strong urges to seek out new partners.

Careful research clearly demonstrates that this so-called crisis is not typical. Most men do not experience any sort of crisis in their middle adult years. Disconfirming research became available shortly after the concept was introduced, and more recent research finds no empirical support for midlife crisis as a universal experience for either men or women. Midlife does present a series of developmental challenges, and some middle-aged men do respond in ways that fit the stereotype. However, people go through challenges and crises in every life stage. The triggers are usually changes in work, health, or relationships rather than a mere accumulation of birthdays.[10]

In the largest study to date on midlife, Elaine Wethington demonstrated that the midlife crisis is far from inevitable. Yet more than 25 percent of those over age thirty-five surveyed (all residing in the United States) *believed* that they have had such a crisis. Upon further investigation, about half of these reports reflected only a time of stressful life events, not a sustained period of loss of balance and searching.[11]

Belief in midlife crisis may partially hinge on what's called "**confirmation bias**," whereby a single case or a few cases of the expected behavior confirm the belief, especially when the behavior is attention-getting or widely reported. Less-obvious disconfirming behavior is easier to ignore. In other words, if we happen to know a man who spent the year after his forty-fifth birthday getting a divorce, dating a twenty-two-year-old, buying a sports car, and taking up skydiving, we might believe in the midlife crisis, even though we know a dozen other middle-aged men who have done none of these things.

GENDER AND AGING

Gender is a lifelong project. As people age in the contemporary West, men experience a great deal less stigma than do women. On men, gray hair and wrinkles are signs of maturity; on women, they are signs of "getting old." It's not uncommon for a man to date or marry a woman twenty years younger, but rare—and labeled bizarre—when an older woman dates or marries a younger man. In 1991, comedienne Martha Raye, age seventy-five, married forty-two-year-old Mark Harris, and the media was scandalized. Speculation ran rampant about Mark's ulterior motives. Surely he was just after her money. How could a forty-two-year-old man find a seventy-five-year-old woman attractive? But when Tony Randall, also age seventy-five, married Heather Harlan, a full fifty years his junior, he was universally praised for his vigor, and no one questioned Heather's motives. (Both couples stayed married until the older partner's death.)

In the media, much older men are commonly paired as romantic leads with much younger women. Michael Douglas was fifty-four when he played the husband of twenty-six-year-old Gwyneth Paltrow in *A Perfect Murder* (1998). Harrison Ford was fifty-seven when he romanced thirty-nine-year-old Kristin Scott Thomas in *Random Hearts* (1999). In *Entrapment* (1999), thirty-year-old Catherine Zeta-Jones played an insurance agent who falls in love with a jewel thief played by Sean Connery. He was sixty-nine, old enough to be her grandfather.

But women are almost never paired romantically with younger men in the movies (unless the women are around twenty-three and the "younger man" is fifteen, as in *Private Lessons, Tadpole*, and *Summer of '42*). In fact, most actresses have trouble finding any work at all after age forty. In the 2002 documentary *Searching for Debra Winger*, Rosanna Arquette interviews many actresses on the problems they have experienced being "old" in Hollywood. Debra Winger temporarily retired from acting in her late thirties when the offers stopped coming, even though she had won three Academy Award nominations. Daryl Hannah was in her mid-thirties when she was cast as the mother of a sixteen-year-old. Even superstars like Jane Fonda and Cher now find themselves relegated to supporting roles as mothers and grandmothers, while women under thirty play most of the romantic leads. Deciding who is old, and who is too old, seems to be a matter of cultural expectations, not biology.

As the meaning of age varies by gender, so, too, does the experience of aging. The meanings of masculinity and femininity that we take into adulthood and beyond resonate in different ways as we age. For example, men and women face retirement differently. Men value independence and stoic resolve, and so in retirement might end up with a more attenuated friendship and support network, fewer friends, and a greater sense of isolation—which in turn might lead to earlier death because loneliness and isolation are risk factors for aging people. Women are far more likely to have maintained close contact with children, with workplace colleagues, and with friends and head into retirement with their larger friendship and support network intact. Buttressed by that support, women will be less isolated and lonely and therefore likely to live longer. Could this different expression of different gender ideologies partly explain the difference in women's and men's life expectancies? Not entirely, to be sure. But it probably pushes a bit.

And just as gender shapes our lives, so, too, should it structure our deaths. And gender is just as salient at the end of our lives as it was during them. Take, for example, when we die. Because women live longer than men, the elderly are more likely to be female. In the United States, the ratio of women to men is about 10:8 for those sixty-five to seventy-five, and by eighty-five, it decreases to 10:4.[12]

But why do women live longer? Earlier, I speculated that some small part of the reason has to do with the ways that gender ideology structures our sustaining networks of friends and kin. But some part is surely physical: Physicians have long speculated that women have stronger constitutions and more immunity to disease. They are less likely to fall victim to heart disease, because testosterone increases the level of "bad" cholesterol (low-density lipoprotein), whereas estrogen increases the level of "good" cholesterol (high-density lipoprotein). British researcher David Goldspink (2005) found that men's hearts weaken much more rapidly as they age: Between the ages of eighteen and seventy, their hearts lose one-fourth of their power (but don't worry, regular cardiovascular exercise can slow or stop the decline), but healthy seventy-year-old women have hearts nearly as strong as those of twenty-year-olds.

Because the gap is decreasing, one cannot attribute this difference to biology alone. What sociological reasons might account for women living longer? Between the ages of eighteen and twenty-four, men are four to five times more likely to die than women, mostly from accidents: During this period of late adolescence and early adulthood, men often prove their masculinity through reckless and risky behavior, whereas women do not. At every age, men spend more time in the public sphere, where they are more likely to get into accidents, commit violent crimes, be victimized by crime, and be exposed to illnesses and hazardous material. Meanwhile, women spend more time at home. So as gender inequality lessens and more women work outside the home, we would predict that the gap will decrease.

The problem is that the life expectancy gap is decreasing everywhere, in both gender-polarized and egalitarian countries: five years in Norway and eight years in Sri Lanka, seven years in France and seven years in Mongolia. In fact, it seems to be decreasing more rapidly in gender-polarized countries: two years in Ethiopia, one year in Pakistan; and in Swaziland, men outlive women.[13]

Sociologists explain this by pointing out that rich and poor countries are diverging far more than women and men are in those countries. In poor countries, both women and men are increasingly susceptible to poor nutrition or health care, HIV, or violence and war and women to problem pregnancies. In wealthy countries, better health care and nutrition mean that both women and men are living longer. By 2040, European and American women will live to be about one hundred, and men will live to be ninety-nine.[14]

GENDER AS AN INSTITUTION

My earlier argument that power is the property of a group, not an individual, is related to my argument that gender is as much a property of institutions as it is part of our individual identities. One of the more significant sociological points of departure from sex-role theory concerns the institutional level of analysis. As we've seen, sex-role theory holds that gender is a property of individuals—that gendered people acquire their gender identity and move outward, into society, to populate gender-neutral institutions. To a sociologist, however, those institutions are themselves gendered. Institutions create gendered normative standards, express a gendered institutional logic, and are major factors in the reproduction of gender inequality. The gendered identity of individuals shapes those gendered institutions, and the gendered institutions express and reproduce the inequalities that compose gender identity.

To illustrate this, let us undertake a short thought experiment. To start with, let's assume that (1) men are more violent than women (whether biologically derived or socialized, this is easily measurable by rates of violent crime); that (2) men occupy virtually all the positions of political power in the world (again, easily measurable by looking at all political institutions); and that (3) there is a significant risk of violence and war at any moment.

Now, imagine that when you awaken tomorrow morning each of those power positions in all those political institutions—every president and prime minister; every mayor and governor; every state, federal, or local official; every member of every House of Representatives; and every Parliament around the world—was filled by a woman. Do you think the world would be any safer from the risk of violence and war? Do you think you'd sleep better that night?

Biological determinists and psychologists of sex roles would probably answer yes. Whether from fundamental biological differences in levels of testosterone, brain chemistries, or evolutionary imperatives, a biological perspective would probably conclude that because females are less violent and aggressive than men, the world would be safer. (It is ironic, then, that the same people who believe these biological differences are also among the least likely to support female candidates for political office.) And those who observe that different socialization produces women who are more likely to avoid hierarchy and competition and to search instead for peaceful solutions by another gendered value system would also breathe a collective sigh of relief.

"But," I hear some of you saying, "what about the women who have already *been* heads of state? What about Golda Meir, Indira Gandhi, and Margaret Thatcher? They're not exactly poster girls for a pacific ethic of care, are they?"

Indeed, not. And part of the reason why they were so unladylike in political office is that the office itself demands a certain type of behavior, independent of the gender of the person who holds it. Often it seems that no matter who occupies those positions, he—or she—can do little to transform them.

This observation is the beginning of a sociological perspective—the recognition that the institutions themselves express a logic—a dynamic—that reproduces gender relations between women and men and the gender order of hierarchy and power. Men *and* women have to express certain traits to occupy a political office, and their failure to do so will make the officeholder seem ineffective and incompetent. (That these criteria apply to men also, anyone who witnessed the gendered criticisms launched against Jimmy Carter for his being frightened by a scurrying rabbit or for his failure to invade Iran during the hostage crisis in 1979–1980 can testify.)

To argue that institutions are gendered is *only* the other half of the story. It's as simplistic to argue that the individuals who occupy those positions are genderless as it is to argue that the positions they occupy are gender-neutral. Gendered individuals occupy places within gendered institutions. And thus it is quite likely that if all the positions were filled with the gender that has been raised to seek peaceful negotiations instead of the gender that is accustomed to drawing lines in the sand, the gendered mandates of those institutions would be affected, modified, and moderately transformed. In short, if all those positions were filled with women, we might sleep more peacefully at night—at least a little bit more peacefully.

Another example will illustrate this in a different way. Take the work of Barbara McClintock, the Nobel Prize–winning research cytogeneticist. McClintock came upon her remarkable discovery of the behavior of molecules by a very different route than that used by her male colleagues. Whereas earlier models had always assumed a hierarchically ordered relationship, McClintock, using what she called "feminine methods" and relying on her "feeling for the organism," discovered that instead of each cell being ruled by a "master molecule," cells were driven by a complex interaction among molecules. In this case, the gender of the person collided with the gendered logic of scientific inquiry to generate a revolutionary—and Nobel Prize–winning—insight.[15]

To say, then, that gender is socially constructed requires that we locate individual identity within a historically and socially specific and equally gendered place and time and that we situate the individual within the complex matrix of our lives, our bodies, and our social and cultural environments. A sociological perspective examines the ways in which gendered individuals interact with other gendered individuals in gendered institutions. As such, sociology examines the interplay of those two forces—identities and structures—through the prisms of socially created difference and domination.

Gender revolves around these themes—identity, interaction, institution—in the production of gender difference and the reproduction of gender inequality. These themes are quite complex, and the relationships between and among them are also complex. These are the processes and experiences that form core elements of our personalities, our interactions with others, and the institutions that shape our lives. These experiences are shaped by our societies, and we return the favor, helping to re-shape our societies. We are gendered people living in gendered societies.

A social constructionist perspective, however, goes one step further than even this. Not only do gendered individuals negotiate their identities within gendered institutions, but also those institutions produce the very differences we assume are the properties of individuals. Thus "the extent to which women and men do different tasks, play widely disparate concrete social roles, strongly influences the extent to which the two sexes develop and/or are expected to manifest widely disparate personal behaviors and characteristics." Different structured experiences produce the gender differences that we often attribute to people.[16]

Let me illustrate this phenomenon first with a mundane example and then with a more analytically complex one. At the most mundane level, think about public restrooms (figure 5.2). In a clever essay on the "arrangement between the

Figure 5.2. This mural from a men's room in New Zealand makes fun of men's anxieties about penis size, even as it increases their anxiety.

Source: http://thesocietypages.org/socimages/2012/03/18/more-urinals/.

sexes," the late sociologist Erving Goffman playfully suggested the ways in which these public institutions produce the very gender differences they are supposed to reflect. Though men and women are "somewhat similar in the question of waste products and their elimination," Goffman observes, in public, men and women use sex-segregated restrooms, clearly marked "gentlemen" and "ladies." These rooms have very different spatial arrangements, such as urinals for men and more elaborate "vanity tables" and other grooming facilities for women. We think of these as justifiably "separate but equal."

But in the privacy of our own homes, we use the same bathrooms and feel no need for separate space. What is more, virtually no private homes have urinals for men, and few have separate and private vanity tables for women. (And, of course, in some cultures, these functions are performed publicly, with no privacy at all.) If these needs are biologically based, Goffman asks, why are they so different in public and in private? The answer, of course, is that they are not biologically based at all:

> The *functioning* of sex differentiated organs is involved, but there is nothing in this functioning that biologically recommends segregation; *that* arrangement is a totally cultural matter . . . Toilet segregation is presented as a natural consequence of the difference between the sex-classes when in fact it is a means of honoring, if not producing, this difference.[17]

In other words, by using separate facilities, we "become" the gentlemen and ladies who are supposed to use those separate facilities. The physical separation of men and women creates the justification for separating them—not the other way around.

At the less mundane but certainly no less important level, take the example of the workplace. In her now-classic work *Men and Women of the Corporation*, Rosabeth Moss Kanter demonstrated that the differences in men's and women's behaviors in organizations had far less to do with men's and women's characteristics as individuals than it had to do with the structure of the organization. Organizational positions "carry characteristic images of the kinds of people that should occupy them," she argued, and those who occupied them, whether women or men, exhibited those necessary behaviors. Though the criteria for evaluation of job performance, promotion, and effectiveness seem to be gender-neutral, they are, in fact, deeply gendered. "While organizations were being defined as sex-neutral machines," she writes, "masculine principles were dominating their authority structures." Once again, masculinity—the norm—was invisible.[18]

In a series of insightful essays, sociologist Joan Acker has expanded on Kanter's early insights and specified the interplay of structure and gender. It is through our experiences in the workplace, Acker maintains, that the differences between women and men are reproduced and through which the inequality between women and men is legitimated. Institutions are like factories, and what they produce is gender difference. The overall effect of this is the reproduction of the gender order as a whole. Thus an institutional level cannot be left out of any explanation of gender—because institutions are fundamentally involved in both gender difference and gender domination. "Gender is not an addition to ongoing processes, conceived as gender neutral," she argues. "Rather, it is an integral part of those processes."[19]

Institutions accomplish the creation of gender difference and the reproduction of the gender order, Acker argues, through several "gendered processes." These gendered processes mean that "advantage and disadvantage, exploitation and control, action and emotion, meaning and identity, are patterned through and in terms of a distinction between male and female, masculine and feminine." She observes five of these processes:

1. The production of gender divisions—the ways in which "ordinary organizational practices produce the gender patterning of jobs, wages, and hierarchies, power and subordination." In the very organization of work, gender divisions are produced and reinforced, and hierarchies are maintained—often despite the intentions of well-meaning managers and supervisors.

2. The construction of symbols and images "that explain, express, reinforce, or sometimes oppose those divisions." Gender images, such as advertisements, reproduce the gendering of positions so that the image of a successful manager or business executive is almost always an image of a well-dressed, powerful man.

3. The interactions between individuals—women and men, women and women, men and men, in all the forms and patterns that express dominance and submission. For example, conversations between supervisors and subordinates typically involve power dynamics, such as interruptions, sentence completion, and setting the topic for conversation, which, given the gendered positions within the organization, will reproduce observable conversational gender differences.

4. The internal mental work of individuals "as they consciously construct their understandings of the organization's gendered structure of work and opportunity and the demands for gender-appropriate behaviors and attitudes." This might include patterns of dress, speech, and general presentation of self.

5. The ongoing logic of organizations themselves—how the seemingly gender-neutral theories of organizational dynamics, bureaucracy, and organizational criteria for evaluation and advancement are actually very gendered criteria masquerading as "objective" and gender-neutral.[20]

As we've seen, sex-role theory assumed that gendered individuals enter gender-neutral sites, thus maintaining the invisibility of gender-as-hierarchy and specifically the invisible masculine organizational logic. On the other hand, many organizational theories assume that genderless "people" occupy those gender-neutral sites. The problem is that such genderless people are assumed to be able to devote themselves single-mindedly to their jobs, have no children or family responsibilities, and perhaps even have familial supports for such single-minded workplace devotion. Thus the genderless jobholder turns out to be gendered as a man. Once again, the invisibility of masculinity as the unexamined norm turns out to reproduce the power differences between women and men.

A few more examples should suffice. Many doctors complete college by age twenty-one or twenty-two, medical school by age twenty-five to twenty-seven, and then endure three more years of internship and residency, during which time they are occasionally on call for long stretches of time, sometimes even two or three days straight. They thus complete their residencies by their late twenties or early thirties. Such a program is designed for a male doctor—one who is not pressured by the ticking of a biological clock, one for whom the birth of children will not disrupt these time demands, and one who may even have someone at home taking care of the children while he sleeps at the hospital. No wonder women in medical school—who number nearly one-half of all medical students today—began to complain that they were not able to balance pregnancy and motherhood with their medical training. (The real wonder is that the male medical school students had not noticed this problem earlier!)

Similarly, lawyers just out of law school who take jobs with large corporate law firms are expected to bill up to fifty to sixty hours per week—a process that probably requires working eighty to ninety hours per week. Assuming at least six hours of sleep per night, a one-hour round-trip commute, and one half-day of rest, these young lawyers are going to have a total of about seventeen hours per week to eat, cook, clean their house, talk with and/or make love with their spouse (or date if they're single), and spend time with their children. Without that half-day off on the weekend, they have about one hour per day for everything else. Failure to submit to this regime places a lawyer on a "mommy track" or a "**daddy track**," which means that everyone will think well of that lawyer for being such an involved parent but that he or she is certain never to be promoted to partner, to join all the rest of the lawyers who made such sacrifices for their careers.

Or, finally, take academic tenure. In a typical academic career, a scholar completes a PhD about six to seven years after the BA, or roughly by the early thirties. Then he or she begins a career as an assistant professor and has six more years to earn tenure and promotion. This is usually the most intense academic work period of a scholar's life—he or she works night and day to publish enough scholarly research and prepare and teach courses. The early thirties are also the most likely childbearing years for professional women. The academic tenure clock is thus timed to a man's rhythms—and not just any man, but one who has a wife or other family supports to relieve him of family obligations as he works to establish his credentials. Remember the adage "publish or perish"? Often, to academics struggling to make tenure, it feels as though publishing requires that family life perish.

Observing the institutional dimension also offers the possibility to observe adjustment and readjustment within institutions as they are challenged. Sometimes, their boundaries prove more permeable than originally expected. For example, what happens when the boundaries between work and home become permeable, when women leave the home and enter the gendered workplace? Judith Gerson and Kathy Peiss suggest that boundaries "*within* the workplace (e.g., occupational segregation) and interactional microlevel boundaries assume increased significance in defining the subordinate position of women." Thus occupational segregation can reproduce gender difference *and* gender inequality by assigning women to secondary statuses within organizations. For those women who enter nontraditional positions, though, microlevel boundary maintenance would come into play—"the persistence of informal group behavior among men (e.g., after-work socializing, the uses of male humor, modes of corporate attire)—act to define insiders and outsiders, thus maintaining gender-based distinctions."[21]

Embedded in organizational structures that are gendered, subject to gendered organizational processes, and evaluated by gendered criteria, then, the differences between women and men appear to be the differences solely between gendered individuals. When gender boundaries seem permeable, other dynamics and processes can reproduce the gender order. When women do not meet these criteria (or, perhaps more accurately, when the criteria do not meet women's specific needs), we see a gender-segregated workforce and wage, hiring, and promotional disparities as the "natural" outcomes of already present differences between women and men. It is in this way that those differences are generated and the inequalities between women and men are legitimated and reproduced.

(One should, of course, note that it is through these same processes that the "differences" between working-class and professional men, between whites and people of color, and between heterosexuals and homosexuals are also produced and that the inequalities based on class or race or sexuality are legitimated and reproduced. Making gender visible in these organizational processes ought not to blind us to the complex interactions with other patterns of difference and principles of inequality. Just as a male pattern becomes the unexamined norm, so, too, does a white, heterosexual, and middle-class pattern become the unexamined norm against which others' experiences and performances are evaluated.)

The idea of organizational **gender neutrality**, then, is the vehicle by which the gender order is reproduced. "The theory and practice of gender neutrality," writes Acker, "covers up, obscures, the underlying gender structure, allowing practices that perpetuate it to continue even as efforts to reduce gender inequality are also under way."[22] Organizations reflect and produce gender differences; gendered institutions also reproduce the gender order by which men are privileged over women and by which some men—white, middle-class, heterosexual—are privileged over other men.

"DOING" GENDER

There remains one more element in the sociological explanation of gender. According to **sex-role theory**, we acquire our gender identity through socialization, and afterward we are socialized to behave in masculine or feminine ways. It is thus the task of society to make sure that the men act in the masculine manner and that the women act in the feminine manner. Our identity is fixed, permanent, and—now—inherent in our personalities. We can no more cease being men or women than we can cease being human.

READ ALL ABOUT IT!

We tend to think of gender identity as something one "has." One "acquires" gender identity through socialization, and then, at some culturally appointed time, one "becomes" a woman or a man. Not true, write sociologists Candace West and Donald Zimmerman in their classic article "Doing Gender." Gender isn't something one "has"; it's what we "do"—in every interaction with others, every time we engage with some institution, every time we look in the mirror. Gender is a lifelong process, based in interaction, where we are constantly being asked to credit other people's gender performance and also asking them to credit ours.

In an important contribution to the social constructionist perspective, sociologists Candace West and Don Zimmerman argued that gender is less a component of identity—fixed, static—that we take with us into our interactions than it is the product *of* those interactions. They argued that "a person's gender is not simply an aspect of what one is, but, more fundamentally, it is something that one *does*, and does recurrently, in interaction with others." We are constantly **"doing" gender**, performing the activities and exhibiting the traits that are prescribed for us.[23]

If our sex-role identity were inherent, West and Zimmerman might ask, in what does it inhere? What are the criteria by which we sort people into those sex roles to begin with? Typically, our answer returns us to biology and, more specifically, to the primary sex characteristics that we believe determine which gender one will become. Biological sex—externally manifested genitalia—becomes socialized gender role. Those with male genitalia are classified in one way; those with female genitalia are classified in another way. These two sexes become different genders, which are assumed to have different personalities and require different institutional and social arrangements to accommodate their natural—and now socially acquired—differences.

Most of the time we carry around these types of commonsense understandings. We see **primary sex characteristics** (those present at birth) as far more decisive than **secondary sex characteristics** (those that develop at puberty) for the assignment of gender-role identity. But how do we know? When we see someone on the street, it is his or her *secondary* sex characteristics that we observe—breast development, facial hair, musculature. Even more than that, it is the behavioral presentation of self—how someone dresses, moves, talks—that signals to us whether that someone is a man or a woman. It would be a strange world, indeed, if we had constantly to ask to see people's genitals to make sure they were who they appeared to be!

One method that sociologists developed to interrogate this assumption was to imagine that primary and secondary sex characteristics did not match. In many cases, "intersex" infants, or hermaphrodites—whose primary sex characteristics cannot be easily discerned visually—have their genitals surgically reconstructed, depending upon the size of the penis and not on the presence or absence of Y chromosomes. To these surgeons, "chromosomes are less relevant in determining gender than penis size." Therefore, to be labeled "male" does not necessarily depend on having one Y and one X chromosome, nor on the production of sperm, but rather on "the aesthetic condition of having an appropriately sized penis." The surgeons assume that no "male" would want to live as a man with such minute genitals, and so they "correct" what will undoubtedly be perceived as a problem. (These surgically constructed females go on to live their lives as women.) It would appear, then, that size really does matter—at least to the doctors![24]

This procedure has come under increasingly withering criticism from scientists, feminists, and intersexuals themselves, who are more interested in being happy with their bodies than in having someone "reassign" them because of some social idea that there can be only two sexes. **Intersexuality**, which affects about one thousand babies a year, pushes us to reconsider the genitals as the defining feature of biological sex. Gender, as William Reiner, a urologist and psychiatrist who treats intersex children, says, "has far more to do with other important structures than external genitals."[25]

Perhaps, but the genitals remain the commonsense "location" of biological sex. In a brilliantly disconcerting study, *Gender: An Ethnomethodological Approach*, Suzanne Kessler and Wendy McKenna proposed two images in which primary and secondary sex characteristics did not match (see figures 5.3 and 5.4). Which one is the "man," and which is the "woman"? How can you tell? If you base your decision on primary sex characteristics—the genitals—you would have to conclude that many of the people with whom you interact in daily life might be hiding their "true" selves. But, if you base your decision on what you see "above the waist," which is more visible in daily life, you would have to conclude that many people may actually be a different sex from that which they appear to be.

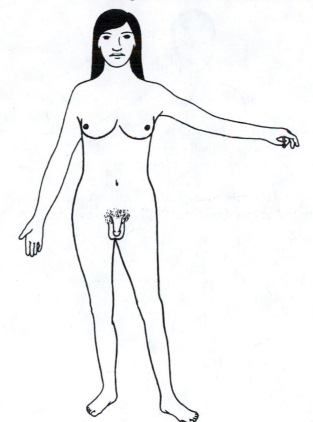

Figure 5.3. Figure with penis, breasts, hips, no body hair, and long hair.

Source: From *Gender: An Ethnomethodological Approach* by Kessler and McKenna. Copyright © 1985 by University of Chicago Press. Reprinted by permission of John Wiley & Sons, Inc.

Looking at those images, one might be tempted to dismiss this as the stuff of fantasy. After all, in real life, people's genitals match their secondary sex characteristics, and we are always easily able to tell the difference, right? Well, maybe not always. Recall the consternation in the popular film *The Crying Game* when it was revealed, to both the audience and the film's protagonist simultaneously, that Dil, the woman the lead was in love with, was actually a man. And remember everyone's reaction when Dustin Hoffman revealed that Emily Kimberly was, in fact, Edward Kimberly in *Tootsie*; or the Broadway play *M Butterfly*, which was about a man who lived with a woman for more than thirty years *without ever realizing that the woman was actually a man*. And think of the commotion and confusion about Marilyn Manson in recent years. And what about the consternation and disgust expressed by men who pay **cross-dressing** prostitutes for oral sex and then find out that "she" is actually "he"? Such confusion is often the basis for comedy. Knowing whether someone is male or female is far more important to the observer than it often is to the observed, as fans of the television program *Saturday Night Live* will recall with the ambiguous character "Pat." People who interacted with Pat were constantly trying to trick him/her into revealing

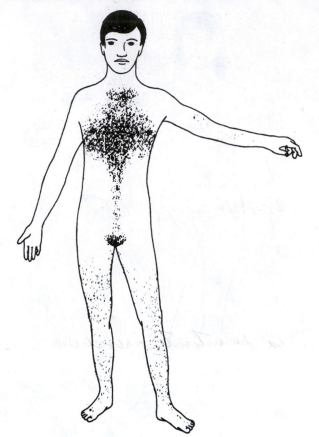

Figure 5.4. Figure with vulva, no breasts, no hips, body hair, and short hair.

Source: From *Gender: An Ethnomethodological Approach* by Kessler and McKenna. Copyright © 1985 by University of Chicago Press. Reprinted by permission of John Wiley & Sons, Inc.

what he/she "really" was, while Pat nonchalantly answered their questions and eluded every rhetorical trap.

READ ALL ABOUT IT!

Not only are we constantly "doing" gender through all our interactions, but we are also constantly classifying and sorting people, making sure that there are two—and only two—genders out there. In "Doing Gender, Determining Gender," sociologists Laurel Westbrook and Kristen Schilt take us inside those moments when it's not clear—and when we feel uncomfortable that it's not clear—about who is a man and who is a woman—and how you know in the first place! It's no surprise that the areas in which gender is being challenged as a simple, binary sex-based construction make us so uncomfortable. What is the "sex" on your driver's license? Which bathroom do you use? These are the sorts of questions that make us anxious.

Figure 5.5. The real story of Brandon Teena, a biological female (named Teena Brandon) who identified and passed as a boy in a small town in Nebraska, offers a less humorous side of gender indeterminacy. Brandon hung out and was accepted by a group of guys, but when he was exposed, he was beaten, raped, and eventually murdered. His story was made into an Oscar-winning movie, *Boys Don't Cry*, in 2006.
Source: AP Photo.

Of course, these are all media creations, and in real life, "passing" is far more difficult and far less common. But one reason we enjoy such a parade of such ambiguous characters is because gender certainty is so important to us. Without it, we feel as if we have lost our social bearings in the world and are threatened with a kind of "gender vertigo," in which the dualistic conceptions that we believe are the foundations of our social reality turn out to be more fluid than we believed or hoped.[26] It's as though our notions of gender are anchored in quicksand. One sociologist reported how she became disturbed by the **sexual ambiguity** of a computer salesperson:

> The person who answered my questions was truly a salesperson. I could not categorize him/her as a woman or a man. What did I look for? (1) Facial hair: She/he was smooth skinned, but some men have little or no facial hair. (This varies by race, Native Americans and Blacks often have none.) (2) Breasts: She/he was wearing a loose shirt that hung from his/her shoulders. And, as many women who suffered through a 1950s adolescence know to their shame, women are often flat-chested. (3) Shoulders: His/hers were small and round for a man, broad for a woman. (4) Hands: Long and slender fingers, knuckles a bit large for a woman, small for a man. (5) Voice: Middle range, unexpressive for a woman, not at all the exaggerated tones some gay males affect. (6) His/her treatment of me: Gave off no signs that

Okay, you convinced me in chapter 3 that there are more than only two genders. But surely there are two, *and only two*, biological sexes, right? Male and female. Well, no. The National Institutes of Health has four categories of "intersex" people:

XX intersex: A person with the chromosomes and ovaries of a woman, but with the external genitalia that appear male. (Usually the result of exposure to male hormones in utero or CAH). The person has a normal uterus, but the labia fuse and the clitoris is large and "penis-like."

XY intersex: A person with XY chromosomes, but with ambiguous or clearly female genitalia. Internally, testes may be absent, malformed, or normal. In the most famous cases of male pseudo-hermaphrodites in the Dominican Republic, this is caused by a specific deficiency in 5-alpha reductase. The children appear female until puberty, when their bodies are "transformed" into male bodies.

True gonadal intersex: A person with both ovarian and testicular tissue in one or both gonads. The cause of true gonadal intersexuality is unknown.

Complex or undetermined intersex: Other chromosomal combinations, such as XXY, XXX, or XO (only one chromosome) can also result in ambiguous sex development.

would let me know if I were of the same or different sex as this person. There were not even any signs that he/she knew his/her sex would be difficult to categorize and I wondered about this even as I did my best to hide these questions so I would not embarrass him/her while we talked of computer paper. I left still not knowing the sex of my salesperson, and was disturbed by that unanswered question (child of my culture that I am).[27]

Transvestites and cross-dressers reveal the artifice of gender. Gender is a performance, a form of drag, by which, through the successful manipulation of props, signs, symbols, behaviors, and emotions, we attempt to convince others of our successful acquisition of masculinity or femininity.

By contrast, there are nearly one million **transgender** individuals in the United States—individuals whose gender identity does not match up with the sex they were assigned at birth.[28] Gender identity is someone's internal, personal sense of being a man or a woman (or, as we'll discuss below, existing outside that binary). Trying to change a person's gender identity is no more successful than trying to change a person's sexual orientation—it doesn't work! As such, sometimes transgender people seek to bring their bodies—that is, their "sex"—more into alignment with their gender identity. This can happen through a variety of medical and nonmedical options: voice therapy, top surgery, makeup, hormone therapy, vaginoplasty, tattoos, hair replacement, binding, phalloplasty, breast implants, piercing, metoidioplasty, prosthetic breasts, artificial facial hair, name and/or pronoun change, psychotherapy, change of sex designation, hair removal, gendered dress . . . of course, this is a partial list![29]

People under the transgender umbrella are incredibly diverse. Terms like nonbinary (NB) and genderqueer (GQ) are intended to encompass individuals who feel that "man" and "woman"—and/or "male" and "female"—are insufficient to describe the way they experience their gender and/or the way they outwardly present it. Some

The "Social Construction" of Biology: The Case of Caster Semenya

We're led to believe that males and females are biologically different—Martians and Venusians—and that these differences are fixed, permanent, and categorical. After all, Martians can't survive on Venus, and vice versa. But how do we know—really know—who belongs where?

For most of us, it's a simple anatomical glance at either primary or secondary sex characteristics. Giveaway secondary sex-characteristic markers: Adam's apple, breasts, facial hair. Not perfect, I grant you, but they roughly correlate with what we consider biologically male or female.

But what if someone doesn't neatly fall into those categories? In 2009, the sports world was rocked by an eighteen-year-old South African sprinter named Caster Semenya. She was the first-place finisher in the eight-hundred-meter race at the World Track and Field championships held that year in Berlin—by a lot. By so much, in fact, that people wondered if she was, perhaps, not a "she" after all. One Italian runner, who finished sixth in the race, said, "These kind[s] of people should not run with us. For me, she is not a woman. She's a man."

Let's consider that last sentence for a moment, shall we? "She's a man."

As we've seen earlier, about one American in sixteen hundred is born clinically "intersex"—that is, with genetic, anatomical, or other conditions that render simple classification impossible. That's about two hundred thousand of us. But one medical specialist believes that this number only covers those at the extreme ends and the precise middle of the continuum. "For 99 percent of the population, it's easy to determine," Dr. Richard Auchus said. "But one percent of the population are not so straightforward." That's one in a hundred, not one in sixteen hundred—three million of us.

Caster Semenya was forced to undergo a series of tests to determine her biological sex. In the end, an anatomist, an endocrinologist, a neuroscientist, a gynecologist, and a psychotherapist deliberated for several weeks before determining her sex. That is, all five scientists had to agree on her biology. Rarely is biological sex so obviously "socially constructed"!

In 2012, Caster Semenya carried the South African flag in the opening of the Summer Olympics. She won a silver medal in the eight-hundred-meter-race.

Caster Semenya is a gold and silver medalist from South Africa whose achievements were questioned when genetic tests revealed that she carries XY chromosomes as a female athlete. It was claimed that this gives her an "unfair" advantage over cisgender female athletes.

Source: AP Photo/Mark Allan.

NBGQ individuals undergo medical/surgical transitioning or continue to identify partially with one gender, but many others believe their bodies don't define or dictate their gender. What they share is an understanding that the binary sex and gender systems are problematic, limiting, and not aligned with their personal sense of self. Just as with trans men and women, there is an ever-expanding terrain of identities under the NBGQ umbrella: agender, bigender, neutrois, genderfluid, transmasculine/feminine, masculine of center, boi, demiboy/girl, and androgyne, just to name a few.[30]

The fact that there are transgender, gender nonconforming, nonbinary, and genderqueer individuals who are ardent biological determinists and others who are social constructionists suggests that there is something imperfect and vague about

Figure 5.6. The transgender umbrella is a big one. When it comes to gendered presentation in everyday life, some trans people conform to gender norms for femininity or masculinity, while others—particularly those who identify as non-binary or genderqueer—play around with the gender binary, mixing and matching aspects of both masculinity and femininity or choosing to disavow both entirely.

Photo by D Dipasupil/Getty Images for Logo TV

the "choice" between biology and social construction. Despite a prolific literature in women's, feminist, and anthropological studies that proves the socially constructed nature of sex and gender, our society tends to understand sex and gender in terms of mutually exclusive hierarchical categories. As such, many transgender men and women are bound to play the "game of categories" with the rest of us. (Figure 5.6) But, beyond the rigid duality of sex and gender, there exists a broad diversity of identities and experiences. While the sex and gender binary arguably works fine for most people, who are we to impose it on those for whom it does not?

Most of us find the walls of those boxes enormously comforting. We learn gender performance early in childhood, and it remains with us virtually all our lives. When our gender identities are threatened, we will often retreat to displays of exaggerated masculinity or exaggerated femininity. And when our sense of others' gender identity is disrupted or dislodged, we can become anxious, even violent. "We're so invested in being men or women that if you fall outside that easy definition of what a man or woman is, a lot of people see you as some kind of monster," commented Susan Stryker, who is a male-to-female transsexual. Many transsexuals are murdered or attacked every year.[31]

The fascinating case of "Agnes" reported by Harold Garfinkle also demonstrates these themes. Agnes was first encountered in the late 1950s by a psychiatrist, Robert Stoller, and by Garfinkle, a sociologist. Though Agnes appeared in every way to be a very

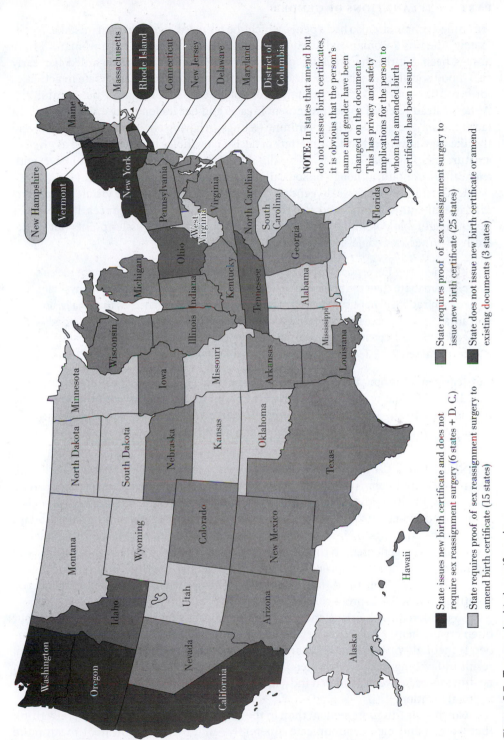

Figure 5.7. Transgender birth certificate laws.

Copyright © 2015 Movement Advancement Project.

Massachusetts

Rhode Island

Connecticut

New Jersey

Delaware

Maryland

District of Columbia

New Hampshire

Vermont

Maine

New York

Pennsylvania

Virginia

North Carolina

South Carolina

Florida

West Virginia

Ohio

Kentucky

Tennessee

Georgia

Alabama

Michigan

Indiana

Illinois

Mississippi

Louisiana

Wisconsin

Iowa

Missouri

Arkansas

Minnesota

North Dakota

South Dakota

Nebraska

Kansas

Oklahoma

Texas

Montana

Wyoming

Colorado

New Mexico

Idaho

Utah

Arizona

Nevada

California

Oregon

Washington

Hawaii

Alaska

NOTE: In states that amend but do not reissue birth certificates, it is obvious that the person's name and gender have been changed on the document. This has privacy and safety implications for the person to whom the amended birth certificate has been issued.

■ State issues new birth certificate and does not require sex reassignment surgery (6 states + D. C.)

▨ State requires proof of sex reassignment surgery to amend birth certificate (15 states)

▨ State requires proof of sex reassignment surgery to issue new birth certificate (25 states)

■ State does not issue new birth certificate or amend existing documents (3 states)

141

feminine woman, she also had a penis, which she regarded as a biological mistake. Agnes "knew" she was a woman and acted (and demanded to be treated) as a woman. "I have always been a girl," she proclaimed to her interviewers, and she regarded her early childhood socialization as a relentless trauma of being forced to participate in activities for boys, like sports. Because genitals were not "the essential signs of her femininity," Agnes instead referred to her prominent breasts and her lifelong sense that she was, in fact, female. "Her self-described feminine feelings, behavior, choices of companions, and the like were never portrayed as matters of decision or choice but were treated as *given* as a natural fact," writes Garfinkle. (Revealingly, Garfinkle refers to Agnes, as I have, with a feminine pronoun, although biologically Agnes possessed male genitalia.)[32]

Understanding how we do gender, then, requires that we make visible the performative elements of identity and also the audience for those performances. It also opens up unimaginable possibilities for social change; as Suzanne Kessler points out in her study of "intersex people" (hermaphrodites):

> If authenticity for gender rests not in a discoverable nature but in someone else's proclamation, then the power to proclaim something else is available. If physicians recognized that implicit in their management of gender is the notion that finally, and always, people construct gender as well as the social systems that are grounded in gender-based concepts, the possibilities for real societal transformations would be unlimited.[33]

Kessler's gender utopianism does raise an important issue in the sociological perspective. In saying that we "do" gender, we are saying that gender is not only something that is done to us. We create and re-create our own gendered identities within the contexts of our interactions with others and within the institutions we inhabit.

GENDERED COMMUNICATION

The multilayered approach offered by social constructionism emphasizes three levels of analysis: the individual, the institutional, and the interactive. First, through socialization, individuals acquire a gender identity, which they then proceed to adapt through the course of their lives. Second, the institutions in which we find ourselves are, themselves, gendered, so that seemingly "objective" or "gender-neutral" rules and regulations and operating procedures reproduce gender relations and reinforce gendered identities. And, third, our interactions themselves not only reflect gendered identities, but actually produce them.

So gendered interactions and gendered institutions do not reflect difference, but often create them. And the material with which these differences are created, remember, is inequality. So institutional arrangements often, without any malign intention, result in favoring men over women. That means that sometimes what we perceive to be differences between gendered individuals may actually be differences in their institutional location.

Nowhere is this more evident than in the way we communicate. We generally think that women and men communicate differently—and by communicate, I mean more than simply how we talk, but also how we use language, how we use nonverbal types of communication, when we speak, where we speak, and under what circumstances.

Figure 5.8. Schwartz HA, Eichstaedt JC, Kern ML, Dziurzynski L, Ramones SM, Agrawal M, et al. (2013) Personality, Gender, and Age in the Language of Social Media: The Open-Vocabulary Approach. PLoS ONE 8(9): e73791. doi:10.1371/journal.pone.0073791.

Do young men and women communicate differently? Of course they do. Andrew Schwartz and his colleagues analyzed seven hundred million words, phrases, and topics collected from the Facebook messages of seventy-five thousand volunteers. Figure 5.8 depicts the two word clouds—hers and his—of the words and phrases most commonly used. But do these differences exist because men and women communicate differently—or because people who occupy different positions communicate differently?

Take, for example, the well-known differences in communication patterns observed by Deborah Tannen in her best-selling book . . . *You Just Don't Understand.* Tannen argues that women and men communicate with the languages of their respective planets—men employ the competitive language of hierarchy and domination to get ahead; women create webs of inclusion with softer, more embracing language that ensures that everyone feels okay. At home, men are the strong, silent types, grunting monosyllabically to their wives, who want to use conversation to create intimacy. Men, she argues, use language to establish their position in a hierarchy. To men, conversations "are negotiations in which people try and achieve and maintain the upper hand if they can, and protect themselves from some others' attempts to put them down and push them around." Men interrupt more often, ignore comments from others, and make more declarations of facts and opinions. Women, by contrast, use conversation to establish and maintain relationships. To women, conversations are "negotiations for closeness in which people try and seek and give confirmation and support, and to reach consensus." Women negotiate in private, ask more questions to maintain the flow of conversation, use more personal pronouns. Often when women speak, they end a declarative sentence with a slight rise in tone, as if ending it with a question mark.[34]

Like Gilligan, Tannen claims that she has simply identified two distinct patterns and that one is not "better" than the other. Unlike Gilligan, though, Tannen ascribes the difference between these patterns entirely to gender. Nor are her biases as concealed as she might have thought. For example, Tannen writes that men's need for autonomy and independence can be a "hindrance" because "there are times when they do not have all the information needed to make a decision." By contrast, women "make better managers because they are more inclined to consult others and involve employees in decision making."[35]

But are such observed differences between women and men real? Here, the evidence is less conclusive. Studies of interruption suggest a far more complicated picture, that women interrupt women and men interrupt men at about the same rates, whereas men interrupt women far more than women interrupt men—a finding that led researchers to conclude that it's not the gender of the speaker, but rather the gender of the person to whom one is speaking that makes the difference. This also seems to be the case with silence—that the same man, silent and uncommunicative at home, is quite talkative at work, where he uses conversation to make sure everyone feels all right. Again, it is not the gender of the silent one, but rather his or her relative power in the situation. Tannen's argument that men and women use language differently is another version of Mars and Venus pop psychology—and just as riddled with misattributions. In the workplace, for example, employers and employees use language differently—regardless of whether they are women or men. Are bosses from Mars and secretaries from Venus? When we actually look at interactions, one's social position is far more important than one's gender.

Or think of the differences in communication patterns among women and men in hospitals. Men tend to be strong and silent, giving orders, but are not particularly nurturing or emotionally sensitive. Women, by contrast, are very empathic, and they listen carefully, speak more softly and kindly. Except, of course, when those women are doctors or those men are nurses. It is medically important for doctors not to become too emotionally expressive because, medical schools teach them, to do so might compromise the quality of care. (An odd concept, and a gendered one, that adequate care depends on emotional disengagement, i.e., forgetting or ignoring that both patient and caregiver are human beings with actual emotions.) And it is part of the quality of care that nurses are more emotionally attuned (perhaps to shield the doctors from messy feelings). So these ideas that "men" and "women" communicate differently turn out to be about people in different positions—and we are coming to see this as the "gender" of the professions breaks down and women enter medicine and men enter nursing. These are qualities of gendered positions, not expressions of gendered people, women and men are entering. I suppose doctors are from Mars and nurses are from Venus?[36]

Or take one more example: When he examined the recorded transcripts of women's and men's testimony in trials, anthropologist William O'Barr concluded that the witnesses' occupation was a more accurate predictor of their use of language than was gender. "So-called women's language is neither characteristic of all women, nor limited only to women," O'Barr writes. If women use "powerless" language, it may be due "to the greater tendency of women to occupy relatively powerless social positions" in society.[37] Communication differences turn out to be "deceptive distinctions" because rarely do we observe the communication patterns of dependent men and executive women.

READ ALL ABOUT IT!

Linguist Deborah Tannen caused a big stir with her best-seller *You Just Don't Understand*. Women and men use language differently, Tannen asserted: women to create connections, men to establish and maintain competitive hierarchies. No wonder men and women ended up in different positions at work, with women taking a backseat to the men getting all the promotions. Except it turns out to be untrue, a confusing of people's actual positions and their gender. In "Men and Women Are from Earth," their scathing critique of Tannen and others, Rosalind Barnett and Caryl Rivers dismantle this interplanetary theory of language and offer a far more grounded idea that people's language styles also depend on their positions: parents—male or female—with young children tend to use language to make peace, not draw lines in the sand. Corporate executives—male or female—can be monosyllabic and inexpressive, while their underlings—again, male or female—will use language to make everyone feel the conversation is progressing smoothly.

A SOCIOLOGY OF RAPE

In previous chapters, we illustrated theoretical perspectives by observing how each perspective deals with one specifically gendered phenomenon—rape. We've seen, for example, how some evolutionary biologists explain rape as an evolutionary reproductive strategy for "losers" who are unable to pass on their genetic inheritance by old-fashioned seduction. (It is therefore evolutionary biologists, not mainstream feminists, who insist that rape and sex are the same thing!) And we've seen how anthropologists undermine such biological arguments, suggesting instead that rape varies dramatically from one culture to another and that what causes the differences between rape-prone and rape-free societies is the status of women. Where women are valued and honored, rape rates are exceptionally low. Where women are degraded and devalued, rape rates are high.

Psychologists enable us to differentiate between rapists and nonrapists by understanding the psychodynamic processes that lead an individual man to such aberrant behavior. Whether because of childhood trauma, unresolved anger at his mother, or a sense of inadequate gender identity, rapists are characterized by their deviance from the norm. "Rape is always a symptom of some psychological dysfunction, either temporary and transient, or chronic and repetitive." In the popular view, rapists are "sick individuals."[38]

As we have seen, the sociological perspective builds upon these other perspectives. But it also offers a radical departure from them. Rape is particularly illustrative because it is something that is performed almost exclusively by one gender—men—although it is done to both men and women. Thus it is particularly useful for teasing out the dynamics of both difference (because only men do it) and dominance (because its primary function is the domination of either women or men). Instead of seeing a collection of sick individuals, sociologists look at how ordinary, how normal, rapists can be—and then at the culture that legitimates their behaviors. It also assesses the processes and dynamics that force all women to confront the possibility of sexual victimization—a process that reproduces both gender division and gender inequality.

Sociological studies of rapists have found that many are married or have steady, regular partners. Studies of gang rape reveal an even more "typical" guy who sees himself simply as going along with his friends. Rapists see their actions in terms that express power differentials between women and men. They see what they do to women as their "right," a sense of entitlement to women's bodies. And they often see their behavior in light of their relationship with other men. For example, the members of Spur Posse, a group of teenage boys in Southern California accused of numerous acts of date rape and acquaintance rape, kept score of their "conquests" using athletes' uniform numbers—which only the other members could understand. And during wartime, the rape of vanquished women becomes a form of communication between the victor and the loser, and women's bodies are the "spoils of war."

Although rape is an act of aggression by an individual man, or a group of men, it is also a social problem that women, as a group, face. Women may deal with rape as individuals—by changing their outfits, their patterns of walking and talking, their willingness to go to certain places at certain times—but rape affects all women. Rape is a form of "**sexual terrorism**," writes legal theorist Carol Sheffield, a "system of constant reminders to women that we are vulnerable and targets solely by virtue of our gender. The knowledge that such things can and do happen serves to keep all women in the psychological condition of being aware that they are potential victims."[39]

To the sociologist, then, rape expresses both a structure of relations and an individual event. At the individual level, it is the action of a man (or group of men) against a woman. It is sustained by a cultural apparatus that interprets it as legitimate and justified. It keeps women in a position of vulnerability as potential targets. In this way, rape reproduces both gender difference (women as vulnerable and dependent upon men for protection, women afraid to dare to enter male spaces such as the street for fear of victimization) and gender inequality.[40]

TOWARD AN EXPLANATION OF THE SOCIAL CONSTRUCTION OF GENDER RELATIONS

So how shall we think about gender from a **sociological perspective**? The elements of a definition seem clear enough. We shall explore three related levels—(1) identity, (2) interaction, and (3) institution—and, of course, the interactions among them, in order to explain the related phenomena—gender difference and gender inequality.

First, we understand that gender is not a "thing" that one possesses, but rather a set of activities that one *does*. When we do gender, we do it in front of other people; it is validated and legitimated by the evaluations of others. Gender is less a property of the individual than it is a product of our interactions with others. West and Zimmerman call gender a "managed property," which is "contrived with respect to the fact that others will judge and respond to us in particular ways." Women and men are distinct social groups, constituted in "concrete, historically changing—and generally unequal—social relationships." What the great British historian E. P. Thompson once wrote about class applies equally to gender. Gender "is a relationship, not a thing"—and, like in all relationships, we are active in its construction. We do not simply inherit a male or female sex role, but we actively—interactively—constantly define and redefine what it means to be men or women in our daily encounters with one another. Gender is something one *does*, not something one *has*.[41]

Second, we understand that we do gender in every interaction, in every situation, in every institution in which we find ourselves. Gender is a situated accomplishment, as much an aspect of interaction as it is of identity. As Messerschmidt puts it, "Gender is a situated accomplishment in which we produce forms of behavior seen by others in the same immediate situation as masculine or feminine." Gender is what we bring to these interactions and what is produced in them as well.[42]

Nor do we do gender in a genderless vacuum but, rather, in a gendered world, in gendered institutions. Our social world is built on systemic, structural inequality based on gender; social life reproduces both gender difference and gender inequality. We need to think of masculinity and femininity "not as a single object with its own history, but as being constantly constructed within the history of an evolving social structure." As Karen Pyke defines it, gender is:

> an emergent property of situated interaction rather than a role or attribute. Deeply held and typically nonconscious beliefs about men's and women's essential natures shape how gender is accomplished in everyday interactions. Because those beliefs are molded by existing macrostructural power relations, the culturally appropriate ways of producing gender favor men's interests over those of women. In this manner, gendered power relations are reproduced.[43]

In short, sociology is uniquely equipped to understand both what is really different between women and men and what is not really different but only seems to be, as well as the ways in which gender difference is the product of—and not the cause of—gender inequality. We are gendered people living gendered lives in a gendered society—but we do actually live on the same planet. (In fact, it may be that only on this planet would such differences make a difference.)

In the remainder of this book, we'll look at some of the institutions that create gender difference and reproduce gender inequality—families, schools, workplaces—and observe some of the ways in which those differences and that inequality are expressed through our interactions with one another—in love, sex, friendship, and violence.

KEY TERMS

Agents of Socialization	Gender Socialization	Secondary Sex
Confirmation Bias	Hegemonic Masculinity	Characteristics
Cross-Dressing	Impulsive	Sex-Role Theory
Daddy Track	Hyperindividualism	Sexual Ambiguity
"Doing" Gender	Intersexuality	Sexual Terrorism
Feminism	Midlife Crisis	Sociological Perspective
Gay Liberation	Primary Sex Characteristics	Transgender
Gender Neutrality	Reflexive Passivity	Transvestite

Gendered Identities, Gendered Institutions

The GENDERED FAMILY

Nobody has ever before asked the nuclear family to live all by itself in
a box the way we do. With no relatives, no support, we've put it in an
impossible situation.

—MARGARET MEAD

A mother of five children, one a newborn with Down's syndrome, leaves
home to pursue a career as the CEO of a major organization. She has a taste
for high fashion. Her husband, a union worker and part-time fisherman, goes
along for the ride. Her unwed sixteen-year-old daughter is pregnant and the
baby's father is another sixteen-year-old whose MySpace profile says he is a "red-
neck" who loves dirtbikes, "lives to play hockey," and does "not want kids." Then
his mother is arrested for selling illegal drugs.

Who is this paragon of bad mothering, this feckless father, this slutty teenager, her randy boyfriend with the felonious mother? Who is this poster family
of dysfunctionality? Why it's Sarah Palin, of course, the then-governor of Alaska
and the Republican candidate for vice president in the 2008 election, and her
husband Todd, their daughter Bristol, Bristol's boyfriend, Levi Johnston, and his
mother, Sherry. And remember that one of the major planks in her campaign to
become the country's Second Family was a return to "**family values.**"

The barrage of criticisms and defenses of the Palin family was dizzying in
its confusion. Some questioned her putting career over family, and others

defended her as a working mom. The religious right was ashamed of her daughter's "condition" but applauded her decision to keep the baby, and some feminists defended her sexual decision making but decried the fact that in Alaska she could not legally obtain an abortion without one of her parents' permission. And while many found Levi Johnston's postings distasteful, adoring fans of this hockey hunk proliferated instantly on Facebook and MySpace. (I don't think anyone rose to his mother's defense.)

Americans are confused about the family. On the one hand, it seems so fragile: Divorces skyrocket. Teenagers have babies out of wedlock. Feckless fathers abandon their family responsibilities to pursue other pleasures. Moms leave home and go off to work, leaving their children in the hands of strangers. Middle-class couples adopt babies from all over the world. Young people are living together, without marrying. And now even gay men and lesbians want to get married and raise families!

But, on the other hand, the family has proved a most resilient institution, able to adapt to changing economic, social, and cultural circumstances and remain the foundation of society. It has most decidedly not gone the way of the horse and buggy. It's survived the massive social mobility of modern society, which has meant the geographic dispersal of extended kin. It's survived the entry of women—including mothers of young children—into the labor force. New family forms abound: step-families, blended families, adoptive families. People who divorce often remarry quickly, indicating that they still believe in the institution, just not the person they married! And even gay men and lesbians believe in the family enough to want to have one of their own!

And Americans have been confused about the family for decades. Did I just say "decades"? Make that "over a century." Since the late nineteenth century, we've debated about whether or not the family is in crisis. In the nineteenth century, pundits warned that men were so dedicated to their work they were becoming absentee landlords at home. They fretted that if women entered the workplace or got the vote, the family would collapse.

Both sides of the debate have some merit. The data on the crisis of the family seem overwhelming: Married people do seem less happy than they did a generation ago. We're more isolated, have fewer close confidants and friends, and have little social support for family life, save a heaping helping of "family values." And you can't eat that. Marriage rates have consistently declined; less than two-thirds (62.6 percent) of American women aged 35–44 were legally married in 2013; the marriage rates in 2010 and 2011 (6.8 per 1,000 in both years) were the lowest in more than forty years. Cohabitation (both prior to marriage and in lieu of marriage) has increased dramatically in the past two decades, from 1.1 million in 1977 to 8.1 million in 2011 (7.6 million opposite-sex couples and 514,735 same-sex couples); the cohabiting population includes all age groups, but the average cohabiting age group is between twenty-five and thirty-four. Current estimates of divorce indicate that about half of first marriages end in divorce and 60 percent of those marriages involve children. Forty-one (40.7) percent of all births are to unmarried mothers (1.6 million in 2012). Among whites, the proportion of births to unmarried women rose from 5 percent in 1964–1969 to 35.9 percent in 2012; among black women, the proportion rose from 35 percent to 71.6 percent. Twenty-four percent of children live without their biological fathers. And children who are raised by only one parent are more likely to be poor, commit a crime, drop out of school, earn lower grades, and experience emotional problems.[1]

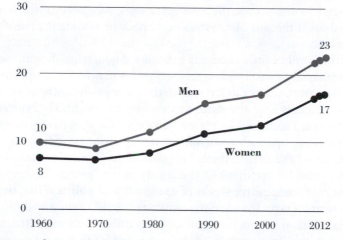

Figure 6.1. Percent of men and women ages twenty-five and older who have never been married, 1960–2012.

Source: "Record Share of Americans Have Never Married," Pew Research Center, Washington, DC (September 2014) http://www.pewsocialtrends.org/2014/09/24/record-share-of-americans-have-never-married/.

Though the family feels like one of the most fragile of social institutions, it is also perhaps among the most resilient. It's never been ossified into a static form, except in some mythic constructions that the family has "always" looked like this or that. American families have changed dramatically over the course of our history, and the family form continues to adapt to changing circumstances. There is, however, only modest evidence that the family is in decline or decay. Marriage remains quite popular, with more than nine in ten Americans taking the plunge. The proportion of women who remain single all their lives is actually lower today than it was at the start of the twentieth century. That almost half of all marriages in the United States are remarriages indicates both the increasing numbers of divorces and the continued belief in the institution of marriage. More men than ever are identifying themselves as fathers, and there are more single fathers raising children than ever before as well. And virtually everyone wants to get married—including gay men and lesbians, whose campaigns for the right to marry are currently on the political agenda (and are, ironically, opposed by the very people who want to "defend" marriage).[2]

If the nuclear family is not exactly in crisis, then what is all the noise about? Some part of the family values debate rests on what we might call "misplaced nostalgia"—a romanticized notion that the family form of the 1950s (the era of many of the debaters' adolescence) is a timeless trope that all family forms ought to emulate. In the 1960s, anthropologist Raymond Birdwhistell labeled this "the sentimental model" when he described the way people in rural Kentucky talked about or "remembered" their families—which, as he pointed out, bore little resemblance to the families in which they actually lived. Often our descriptions of the family conform more to this mythic model than to our actual experiences. When transformed into public policy, this blurred and ahistorical vision is often accompanied by a hearing disorder that seeks to block out the unpleasant sounds of modernity—the cacophonous chorus of different groups of people in a democracy, the hum of the workplace toward which both women and men are drawn, the din of television and rock or rap music, the moans of the sexual revolution.

Much of the family values debate is a displaced quarrel with feminism, which is often wrongly blamed or wrongly credited with what may be the single greatest transformation of American society in the twentieth century—the entry of women into the workplace. This process long antedates modern feminism, although the attack on the **"feminine mystique"** launched by the women's movement in the 1960s gave working women a political peg upon which to hang their aspirations and longings.

Finally, much of the debate about the crisis of the family is based on a misreading of history. Although we think of the family as the "private" sphere, a warm respite from the cold competitive world of economic and political life, the family has never been a world apart. The modern family was built upon a wide foundation of economic and political supports; it is today sustained by an infrastructure that includes public funding for roads, schools, and home buying and the legal arrangements of marriage and divorce. The workplace and family are deeply interconnected; the **"family wage"** organizes family life as well as economic life, expressing an idealized view of what the family is and should be. This public component of the private sphere is often invisible in current debates about the family, in part because it is so deeply ingrained in our historical development. The current "crisis" dates back to the beginning of the twentieth century, but the origins of the current dilemma lie much further back in our nation's past.

A BRIEF HISTORY OF THE AMERICAN FAMILY

From the start, American families were the beneficiaries of dramatic changes in family morality that swept Europe and the colonies in the mid-eighteenth century. Though paternal authority was still the core of the "well-ordered family," a new morality of "affective individualism" led to an ideal of warmer and more intimate relationships between husbands and wives and between parents and children. In a "surge of sentiment," men and women were encouraged to marry on the basis of mutual affection; marriage was regarded as the "union of individuals" rather than as the "union of two lineages." Husbands became less brutal to their wives—there was a decline in husbands beating wives and in men insisting on their conjugal "rights"—and parents less harsh toward their children, measured by a decline in corporal punishment.[3]

American women had greater freedom than their European counterparts. Without dowries to tie them economically to their families, and with the right to own property in their own names after marriage, American women had an easier time both marrying and remarrying. Thus the eighteenth- and early nineteenth-century American family looked less like a miniature monarchy and more like a "little commonwealth" in which husbands, wives, and children "worked together as participants in common enterprise." There was far less differentiation between "his" and "her" spheres: Women and men both worked in and around their homes; women produced many of the things needed for the family; and men worked to a rhythm of family time, not industrial time. Just as women and men were involved in the worlds of work, fathers and mothers were both involved in child rearing; historian John Demos writes of an "active, encompassing fatherhood, woven into the whole fabric of domestic and productive life." In fact, at the dawn of the nineteenth century, child-rearing manuals were written to fathers, not mothers, and children were largely raised by their same-sex parent in an informal but common sex-segregated pattern.[4]

In the first decades of the nineteenth century, however, this world was transformed. By the middle of the century, a gap between work and home grew dramatically, both in reality and in ideology, to create the separation of spheres. Family life "was wrenched apart from the world of work," and the workplace and the home clearly demarcated as *his* and *hers*. In 1849, Alfred Lord Tennyson expressed this separation of spheres in a poem, "The Princess":

> Man for the field and woman for the hearth:
> Man for the sword and for the needle she:
> Man with the head and woman with the heart:
> Man to command and woman to obey;
> All else confusion.[5]

Men experienced this separation in two ways. First, paid work shifted from home and farm to mill and factory, shop and office. Men now marched to a different beat as the day's rhythm shifted to the incessant pounding of industry. Second, men's share of the work around the home was gradually industrialized and eliminated as such tasks as fuel gathering, leather working, and grain processing shifted to the external world. This further "liberated" men to exit their homes and leave the rearing of both sons and daughters to their wives.

If men were liberated, women's position was as exalted in popular literature as it was potentially imprisoning in reality. In popular literature, from the nation's pulpits, and in high art, women's work was reconceptualized, not as "work" at all, but rather as a God-given mission. Although some home-based work was eliminated, such as spinning and weaving, much of women's sphere remained intact; women still cooked meals and baked bread, even if their husbands no longer grew and milled the grain or butchered the meat they cooked. Housecleaning and child rearing were increasingly seen as "**women's work**."

Though men's and women's spheres were symmetrical and complementary, they were not equal. As Catharine Beecher and Harriet Beecher Stowe wrote in their celebrated book *The American Woman's Home* (1869):

> When the family is instituted by marriage, it is man who is head and chief magistrate by the force of his physical power and requirement of the chief responsibility; not less is he so according to the Christian law, by which, when differences arise, the husband has the deciding control, and the wife is to obey.[6]

Many historians argue that this new ideology actually represented a historical decline in women's status. Historian Gerda Lerner, for example, points out that there were fewer female storekeepers and businesswomen in the 1830s than there had been in the 1780s. "Women were," she argues, "excluded from the new democracy." Democracy meant mobility—geographic, social, economic—and women were "imprisoned" in the home by the new ideology of feminine domesticity. Little wonder women's sphere needed the ideological buttressing of rhapsodic poetry and religious sermons to keep it in place. But men's "liberation" from the home was also partly illusory, because they were also in exile from it. As early as the 1820s and 1830s, critics were complaining that men spent too little time at home. "Paternal neglect at the present time is one of the most abundant sources of domestic sorrow," wrote the Reverend John S. C. Abbott in *Parents Magazine* in 1842. The father, "eager in the pursuit of business, toils early and late, and finds no time to fulfill . . . duties to his children." Theodore Dwight attempted to persuade men to resume their responsibilities at home in *The Father's Book* (1834), one of the nation's first advice books for men.[7]

The family had now become the "haven in a heartless world" that the great French writer Alexis de Tocqueville observed when he visited the United States in the early 1830s. "Shorn of its productive functions, the family now specialized in child-rearing and emotional solace, providing a much-needed sanctuary in a world organized around the impersonal principles of the market."[8]

Of course, this ideology and reality of the separation of spheres in mid-nineteenth-century America were largely white and middle class, but they were imposed on others as the norm, as the "American" family form. Working-class women and women of color continued to work outside the home, while the men shared housework and child care more readily out of economic necessity if not because of ideological commitment. Cast "primarily as workers rather than as members of family groups, [minority] women labored to maintain, sustain, stabilize and reproduce their families while working in both the public (productive) and private (reproductive) spheres."[9]

Having been relegated to women, the family's importance also declined, its integration into the community attenuated. As if to compensate for this shift, the family's symbolic importance increased. Events that had been casually organized were routinized as family events; community celebrations became household celebrations. "The Family" as the site of sentimentalized romantic longing was an invention of the nineteenth century, as families tried to shore up what they were, in fact, losing. Historian John Gillis writes:

> When men had worked at home, mealtimes had seldom been private, or even very regular. Holidays had revolved around community festivals and visiting rather than home-cooked meals and private family celebrations. Leisurely dinner hours, Sunday family time, and nuclear family togetherness on holidays such as Christmas were invented during the mid-nineteenth century.[10]

The rapid industrialization of the American economy in the decades following the Civil War only reinforced earlier trends. By 1890, only about 2 percent of married women were employed outside the home. And probably just as few men were working inside it. As motherhood came to be seen as women's sole "calling," the importance of fatherhood declined. "The suburban husband and father is almost entirely a Sunday institution," one writer in *Harper's Bazaar* put it in 1900. Articles with titles like "It's Time Father Got Back in the Family" appeared with some regularity in popular magazines. "Poor father has been left out in the cold," observed Progressive reformer Jane Addams in 1911. "He doesn't get much recognition. It would be a good thing if he had a day that would mean recognition of him." (This noble idea had to wait another sixty-one years to be implemented.)[11]

Commentators at the turn of the twentieth century fretted about the crisis of the family. The divorce rate had been steadily climbing since soldiers returned from the

Civil War—from seven thousand in 1860 to fifty-six thousand in 1900 and one hundred thousand in 1914. In 1916, one in every four marriages in San Francisco ended in divorce; in Los Angeles the number was one in five, and, in the more traditional and Catholic Chicago, one in seven. A 1914 survey of women graduates of Barnard, Bryn Mawr, Cornell, Mount Holyoke, Radcliffe, Smith, Vassar, Wellesley, and Wells colleges showed that fewer than 40 percent had married. Of Harvard graduates during the 1870s, almost one-third between the ages of forty and fifty were still single. "In fifty years, there will be no such thing as marriage," predicted the esteemed Harvard psychologist John Watson at the dawn of the new century.[12]

The crisis of the family was so pressing that President Theodore Roosevelt convened the first White House Conference on Children in 1909. Roosevelt believed that men needed to be encouraged to become more active fathers and that white, native-born women needed encouragement to have more children, lest white people commit what he called "**race suicide**." And he also believed that poverty, especially the poverty of widowed mothers, was the primary problem in the lives of children and that it was the government's obligation to help. Roosevelt advocated giving money to single mothers who had been certified as capable of providing decent care to their children if only they had a little more cash in their pocketbooks.[13]

The separation of spheres provided the foundation for a virtual perpetual crisis of the family throughout the twentieth century. Women's efforts to leave the home—to go to college, enter the labor force, join unions, attend professional schools—were met with significant resistance, and men's interest in returning home waxed and waned through the 1940s. World War II disrupted this pattern, as women entered the labor force in dramatic numbers. But the postwar economic boom, which was fueled by massive government expenditures in highway and school construction and the G.I. Bill that made single-family suburban home ownership a reality for an increasing number of American families, also stabilized this aberrant family form: the nuclear family of June and Ward Cleaver and their children Wally and the Beaver.[14]

This massive infusion of public expenditures to shore up the nuclear family ideal—breadwinner husband, housewife mother, and their children—was accompanied by a dramatic increase in marriage rates and a sharp decline in the ages of first marriage. Whereas today's marriage rates and marriage ages are in keeping with the rest of the twentieth century, the era 1945–1960 stands out as dramatically different, as "young men and women . . . reacting against the hardships and separations of depression and war . . . married unusually early." In 1867, there were 9.6 marriages per 1,000 people in the United States; a century later, the number was 9.7. In 1946, by contrast, the number hit an all-time high of 14.2. Thus the 1950s pattern of family life—characterized by high rates of marriage, high fertility, and low and stable rates of divorce, which many continue to regard as an ideal—"was the product of a convergence of an unusual series of historical, demographic and economic circumstances unlikely to return again," in the words of two leading family historians.[15]

As soon as this new family form emerged it was declared to be natural—that is, both biologically inevitable and morally appropriate. The effort to reinforce it became a constant hum in the nation's ears. "The effort to reinforce traditional norms seemed almost frantic," writes historian William Chafe, "as though in reality something very different was taking place." In academia, the structural-functionalist school of social science gave it legitimacy, arguing that the isolated suburban nuclear family, with distinct separation of spheres, served the needs of both children and society. The family system required both expressive (female) and instrumental (male) components to function appropriately, wrote sociologist Talcott Parsons, and this could be accomplished only in a family in which the housewife mother maintained the home for her breadwinner husband who worked outside it. Here's how another sociologist described this domestic paradise in 1955:

> Father helps mother with the dishes. He sets the table. He makes formula for the baby. Mother can supplement the income of the family by working outside. Nevertheless, the American male, by definition, *must* "provide" for his family. He is *responsible* for the support of his wife and children. His primary area of performance is the occupational role, in which his status fundamentally inheres; and his *primary* function in the family is to supply an "income," to be the "breadwinner." There is simply something wrong with the American adult male who doesn't have a "job."
>
> American women, on the other hand, tend to hold jobs *before* they are married and to quit when "the day" comes; or to continue in jobs of a lower status than their husbands. And not only is the mother the focus of emotional support for the American middle class child, but much more exclusively so than in most societies . . . The cult of the warm, giving "Mom" stands in contrast to the "capable," "competent," "go-getting" male. The more expressive type of male, as a matter of fact, is regarded as "effeminate," and has too much fat on the inner side of his thigh.[16]

A generation of middle-class men tried to toe the line of bland conformity as suburban breadwinners; here was the corporate clone of countless satires, the "man in the gray flannel suit" who drove his late-model car down to the suburban train station to catch the same train every morning—with every other man in the neighborhood. And a generation of women cooked and cleaned, dusted and mopped, washed and ironed, toiling to meet ever-increasing standards of cleanliness.

For many parents and children of the baby boom, this family form worked well. Suburban life was safer and simpler than life in the crowded cities from which many fifties families fled, and family life gave postwar men a secure anchor in an increasingly insecure corporate world. The home front centered on the kids' homework and a plethora of hobbies and leisure-time pursuits—hiking and camping, concerts and theater, sailing and photography. Middle-class Americans took family vacations, hung out together in family rooms, and purchased family-sized packages of prepared foods—when they weren't practicing gourmet French cooking. They walked together to the local library or movie theater. Some husbands doted on their wife-companions, and together they built lives more stable, comfortable, child-centered, and companionable—divorce being a last resort—than anything their own parents had ever envisioned.

The veneer of domestic bliss only partially concealed an increasing restlessness on the part of both husbands and wives (not to mention their children, for whom the 1960s would provide many creative [and not so creative] outlets for their discontent). Many women and men felt frustrated and unhappy with this supposedly "natural" family form. Some fathers felt alienated from their families, and especially from their children. Though they watched Ward Cleaver, Jim Anderson, and other devoted dads on television sitcoms, a large number of middle-class American men were better fathers in theory than in practice; they talked more about spending more time with their children than they actually did. Full-time housewifery and motherhood were "something new and historically unprecedented," and wives, laboring under the "senseless tyranny of spotless shirts and immaculate floors," swallowed their growing resentment as the world passed them by. In his 1957 panorama of American culture, *America as a Civilization*, historian Max Lerner discussed the "ordeal" of the modern woman, arguing that "the unhappy wife has become a characteristic culture type."[17]

Such unhappiness also fueled an increasingly politicized anger. In 1963, Betty Friedan's feminist call to arms, *The Feminine Mystique*, rang like a tocsin across those neatly manicured suburban lawns and campus quadrangles. Calling the suburban home a "comfortable concentration camp," Friedan declared that real life lay outside worrying about dishpan hands and diaper rash. Beatniks, playboys, and juvenile delinquents presented three alternatives to the suburban breadwinner. And the era's popular music exposed the ironies of such "well-respected men" and their wives, gulping vast quantities of "mother's little helper."[18]

In fact, no sooner was it fully established and acknowledged than this "traditional" family began to crack under the enormous weight put on it. The family was supposed to be the sole source of comfort and pleasure in an increasingly cold, bureaucratic world; the marital union was the single most important and sustaining bond of intimacy and friendship that a person could have. Gone were the more "traditional" supports of community networks, civic participation, and extended kinship ties—now the family was supposed to provide for all psychological and emotional needs.

It was almost too much to bear: The "traditional" family was an anachronism from the moment of its birth. In the 1960s, fewer than half (43 percent) of American families conformed to the traditional single-earner model; one-fourth (23 percent) were dual-earner couples. Yet nearly nine out of ten (88 percent) white children under the age of eighteen lived with both parents, 9 percent lived with one parent, and 3 percent with neither parent. Among black families, two-thirds (67 percent) lived with both parents, and one-fifth lived in mother-only households.

The family of the 1970s and early 1980s was actually stronger and more resilient because of its increasing diversity of form. In the early 1970s, Theodore Caplow and a team of sociologists returned to Middletown (Muncie, Indiana) fifty years after a landmark historical study of small-town America conducted by Robert and Helen Lynd. They found the family in better shape than it had been in the 1920s. Much of the credit was given to economic and social conditions—better pay, more leisure time, improved housing. Parents spent more time with their children than they had a half-century earlier. More flexible gender roles, women's increased opportunities, and increased knowledge about birth control and sexuality had markedly enhanced husbands' relationships with their wives.[19]

OH? REALLY. The idealized traditional family of the 1950s—breadwinner father and housewife mother with at least two school-aged kids at home—is still considered the norm in the United States. Actually, fewer than one out of every ten families looks like that. Does yours?

But since the early 1980s, the family has indeed been in trouble, partly because of the dramatic withdrawal of public supports. Decreased and depressed wages, especially for men, decreased leisure time, decreased funding for public housing, greater needs for both parents to work, and the return to earlier restrictions on access to birth control and to abortion have all led to dramatic declines in the quality of family life. Many of the problems associated with the family are really problems that are attendant upon economic downturn. In 1970, 15 percent of all children under age eighteen were living in families defined as "poor"; today that number is 21.2 percent.[20]

For middle-class families, the erosion of leisure time and the increasing demands of work have added strain to already attenuated family relationships. The "five o'clock dad" of the 1950s family has become "an endangered species." Over 10 percent of men with children under six years old work more than sixty hours a week, and 25 percent work between fifty and sixty hours. (Less than 8 percent of women with children that young work such long hours.) Ever resilient and responsive to the progressive erosion of the family foundation, American families have responded with a host of changes and modifications—as well as a host of prophets and pundits promoting false solutions.[21]

Since the 1960s, the median age of first marriage has crept steadily upward, increasing by five or six years for both women (26.9) and men (28.8). The number of children has steadily declined as couples have delayed childbearing so that both women and men could attend college and establish themselves in the labor force. Today 62 percent of American children live in nuclear families with both birth parents. Five percent live in step-families, and more than 25 percent live in a single-parent home. The number of single parents has increased about 6 percent a year.[22]

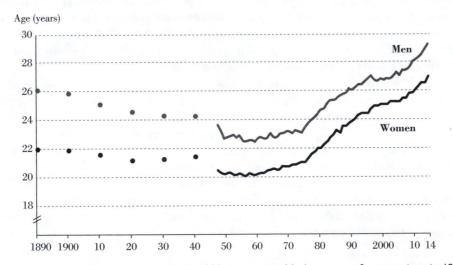

Figure 6.2. Median age at first marriage, 1890 to present. Median age at first marriage in 1950 for men was 22.8 and for women was 20.3. Median age at first marriage in 2013 for men was 29.0 and for women was 26.6.

Source: U.S. Census Bureau, Decennial Censuses, 1890 to 1940, and Current Population Survey, Annual Social and Economic Supplements, 1947 to 2014, http://www.census.gov/hhes/families/data/marital.html, table MS-2.

Table 6.1. Types of Households, 2012

Living alone	27.5 %
Married couples with children	19.6 %
Married couples without children	29.1 %
Other family households[1]	17.8 %

[1] Families whose householder was living with children or other relatives but had no spouse present.

Source: *America's Families and Living Arrangements 2012* (Washington, DC: U.S. Census Bureau, 2012).

Though single parents living with their children counted for only 13 percent of all families in 1970, they represented more than one-fourth (27.1) of all families by 2011. Fathers currently head 3.5 percent of all single-headed households with children. These U.S. percentages are the highest among industrial nations (see table 6.1). While the number of people who had not married by age thirty was 11 percent of women and 19 percent of men in 1970, today 65.6 percent of men and 55.6 percent of women ages twenty to thirty-four have never married, while 23.3 percent of men and 18 percent of women ages thirty-five to forty-four have never married. The number of women ages twenty-five to forty-four who had never married in 1950 was 9 percent for women of color and 10 percent for white women; by 1979, those numbers were 23 percent for women of color and 10 percent for white women. Cohabitation is increasingly common, and not simply as a phenomenon among college students and young people. (In fact, most cohabiters have never attended college and represent the least educated sector of society; cohabitation is replacing early marriage among poor and working-class people.) And around 39 percent of all cohabiting households include children.[23]

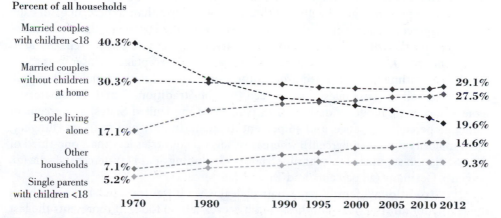

Figure 6.3. Changing Families, Changing Households, America's Families and Living Arrangements in 2012.

Source: U.S. Census Bureau: Current Population Survey.

At the same time, divorce rates have soared. There were only about two divorces per one thousand married women age fifteen and older in 1860 and about four in 1900; there are over twenty-two today. Nearly half of all marriages begun in 1980 and 1990 will end in divorce. These divorce rates are the highest in the industrial world. Most divorces occur after only a few years of marriage. As a result, it might be fair to say that the family is less the "haven in a heartless world" of nostalgic sentimentalism and more the "shock absorber" of contradictory pressures from the world outside it.[24]

An article in *Newsweek* asserted that "the American family does not exist." Rather, the article suggested, "we are creating many American families, of diverse styles and shapes . . . We have fathers working while mothers keep house; fathers and mothers working away from home; single parents; second marriages . . . childless couples; unmarried couples with and without children; gay and lesbian parents." Such family diversity is well illustrated by one prominent contemporary political figure: A white, middle-class, Southern boy, born into a single-parent family, raised by his mother alone, who divorced his first wife, has never paid alimony or child support, has no contact with his children, had an affair, and has a lesbian sister who is starting her own family. Who could such a model of diversity be? It's Newt Gingrich, former Speaker of the House of Representatives—who ran for president in 2012 proclaiming "family values."[25]

As the family has changed, so, too, have our ideas about it. Family sociologist Scott Coltrane writes that "support for separate spheres and the automatic dominance of men has weakened dramatically in the past few decades, though a substantial minority of Americans still clings to the so-called traditional view." Consider one or two examples: In the mid-1970s, one man being interviewed by sociologist Lillian Rubin said that "if a man with a wife and kids needs a job, no woman ought to be able to take it away from him." Few men today would express such a sense of entitlement to those jobs as to consider them "his" property. In 1977, two-thirds of Americans agreed with the statement that "it is much better for everyone involved if the man is the achiever outside the home and the woman takes care of the home and family." Twenty years later, fewer than two out of five (38 percent) agreed with that statement, and fewer than 30 percent of all baby boomers agreed. In 1977, more than half agreed with the statement that "it is more important for the wife to help her husband's career than to have one herself." By 1985, 36 percent agreed, and by 1991, 29 percent did. Today the percentage is closer to 25.[26]

These sentiments are echoed around the world. In an international Gallup poll, fewer than half of those questioned agreed that the "traditional" male breadwinner/ female housewife model is desirable: 48 percent in the United States, 49 percent in Chile, 46 percent in France, and 46 percent in Japan. In only one country, Hungary, did a majority agree (66 percent); whereas in several countries less than one-third of the population supported this family structure, including Spain (27 percent), India (28 percent), Germany (28 percent), and Taiwan (26 percent).

The **"traditional" family**, a normative ideal when it was invented, has never been the reality for all American families. And it is even less so today. It represents the last outpost of traditional gender relations—gender differences created through gender inequality—that are being challenged in every observable arena. Families are gendered institutions; they reproduce gender differences and gender inequalities among adults and children alike. Families raise children as gendered actors and remind parents to perform appropriate gender behaviors. It is no wonder, then, that each specific aspect of family life—marriage, child rearing, housework, divorce—expresses the differences and the inequalities of gender.

GENDERED MARRIAGE

Consider, for a moment, how we think about marriage. A woman devises some clever scheme to "trap" a man. When she's successful, her friends all celebrate the upcoming nuptials with delighted anticipation at a bridal shower. Women celebrate their weddings—they have finally "landed" a man. Their future is secure. By contrast, men "mourn" their upcoming nuptials. They've been trapped, and the future that stretches out before them is now heavy with responsibilities laid upon them by the "old ball and chain," the smiling warden of their personal prison. The bachelor party, traditionally held the night before the wedding, exudes a mournful, elegiac quality underneath its raucous exterior as the groom goes out with his male friends for his "last night of freedom," a night that often consists of smoking fat cigars, getting rip-roaring drunk, and watching porn movies and/or hiring lap dancers or prostitutes.

If you believed this cultural definition of marriage—something she wants and he has to be coerced or tricked into—you would think that marriage benefited women, that it was "their" domain. Yet according to much social science research, you would be mistaken. In the early 1970s, sociologist Jessie Bernard identified two distinct marriages, "his" and "hers." And, she argued, "his is better than hers."

Marriage benefits *men*. All psychological measures of indices of happiness and depression suggest that married men are much happier than unmarried men, whereas unmarried women are somewhat happier than married women. (The greatest difference is between married and unmarried men.) A greater proportion of men than women eventually marries; husbands report being more satisfied than wives with their marriages; husbands live longer and enjoy better health benefits than unmarried men, as well as better health than women (married or unmarried); and fewer men than women try to get out of marriage by initiating divorce. After divorce, men remarry much more quickly than women, and widowers die sooner than widows after the death of a spouse. Married men earn more than single men. And single men are less likely to be employed, tend to have lower incomes than married men, and are more prone to crime and drug use.[27]

All this suggests that marriage is a better deal for men than it is for women. And how could it be otherwise? Given the traditional division of labor in the family (she works, he doesn't) and the nontraditional division of labor outside the family (he works, and she probably does, too), the husband who works outside the home receives the emotional and social and sexual services that he needs to feel comfortable in the world. His wife, who (probably) works as well, also works at home providing all those creature comforts—and receives precious few of them in return. As *New York Times* writer Natalie Angier summed up this research, "Marriage is pretty good for the goose much of the time, but golden for the gander practically all of the time."[28]

To be sure, marriage also benefits women and is therefore positive for both men and women. According to sociologist Linda Waite, married people have more sex more often than unmarried people and enjoy it more. Married people have longer life expectancies and fewer health problems and lower levels of risky behavior, suicide, depression, and other psychological problems. And married people save more money.

Some of these benefits are explained by other factors that have little, if anything, to do with the matrimonial state. For example, married men's higher incomes seem to come from the unequal politics of housework (the wife's doing the housework frees the married man to work longer hours), and the fact that married couples save more has more to do with women in the labor force than it does with being married. And the fact that the benefits of marriage fall far more readily toward men would suggest that marriage increases, not diminishes, gender inequality. Women and men are unequal going into their marriages, and marriage only exacerbates this inequality by benefiting men more than women.[29]

READ ALL ABOUT IT!

Gender roles in the family are changing rapidly. Does it make a difference which partner earns more? How do we navigate turning the traditional stereotypes upside down? In "At Home Fathers and Breadwinning Mothers . . ." communications scholars Caryn Medved and William Rawlings ask what happens in families when men stay home and women go off to work as the family breadwinner. The authors identify several different types of reactions, but the major finding is that the couple's reaction has more to do with their already existing relationship. That is, it's not this new role reversal that changes things, but it's just one more expression of how the couple handles all sorts of issues together.

In recent years, some of the subjective measures of marital happiness have declined for both women and men. The sharp reversal of young men's economic prospects—the declining wages of white men in the Reagan era and since—combined with the increased tension in work-family negotiations, changing attitudes about child care and housework, and the absence of governmental provision of a structural foundation of adequate health care, child care, and family-friendly workplace policies, have all led to increased strains on marriage. Can the family continue to absorb the shock, as these forces buffet an institution that is at once so enduring and so fragile?

OH? REALLY •

Having a baby is the best way to ensure a happy marriage.

Actually, marital happiness decreases, often dramatically, after the transition to parenthood.

But that drop is not true across the board. Parents who slide into parenthood, disagree about it, or are ambivalent experience a really steep drop in marital happiness. Parents who equally welcome the baby often increase their marital happiness. The more equal the parents—in both planning and welcoming the baby—the more likely the baby is an actual "bundle of joy."

Source: Stephanie Coontz, "Till Children Do Us Part," in *New York Times*, February 5, 2009.

Another cause of the decline in marital happiness is, surprisingly, children. Children tend to put a damper on marital bliss. Couples who remain childless report higher levels of marital satisfaction than do those with children. They're better educated and more likely to live in cities, and the wives are more committed to their careers. They have more savings and investments, of course, and are more apt to buy an expensive home in their fifties. Marital happiness sinks with the arrival of the first baby, plunges even further when the first child reaches school age, and drops further when the child reaches the teenage years. Husbands begin to feel better about their marriages once their children turn eighteen, but wives don't feel better about their marriages until after the children leave home, according to Mary Bebin, a sociologist at Arizona State University.[30] Yet having and raising children are two of the major purposes of the family, its raison d'être. If one of the chief purposes of the family is to maintain both gender inequality and gender difference between the parents, then its other chief purpose is to ensure that those gendered identities are imparted to the next generation. It is in the family that the seeds of gender difference are planted, that we first understand that being a man or a woman, a boy or a girl, has different, and unequal, meanings.

THE GENDERED POLITICS OF HOUSEWORK AND CHILD CARE

We are living through a historic, fundamental transformation of family life. Perhaps the greatest single shock the family has had to absorb has been the entry of women into the workplace. This is, perhaps, the most profound and dramatic social change in recent American society, rippling outward to transform every other social institution. That women now work outside the home as a matter of course, of economic necessity, and of ambition and will has dramatically altered the life of the modern family. Some would like to turn back the clock to the rather unusual and short-lived family form that emerged in the 1950s and reassert it as the norm. Such a vision is unlikely to be embraced by most men, let alone most women, who today work outside the home because they want to and because they have to—and because it's good for them, good for their husbands, and good for their children.

Working mothers report higher levels of self-esteem and are less depressed than full-time housewives. Yet they also report lower levels of marital satisfaction than do their husbands, who are happier than the husbands of traditional housewives. Why would this be so? In part, because women's workload actually increases at home, whereas the men benefit by having almost the same amount of work done for them at home and having their standard of living buttressed by an additional income.[31]

So women today are working more but enjoying family life less. Consistently, and in every industrial country, women report higher levels of stress than do men.[32] Perhaps one reason women are so tired and unhappy is that they remain responsible for what sociologist Arlie Hochschild has called "the **second shift**," the housework and child care that every family must do to function properly. The movement of women from the home to the workplace has not been accompanied by a comparable movement of men back into the home. The transformation of American life promised by women's entry into the labor force is a "stalled revolution," a revolution that depends, now, on changes in men's attitudes and behaviors.

In 1970, a young feminist writer described what she saw as "the politics of housework." In the spirit of the feminist slogan "the personal is political," Pat Mainardi argued that the separation of spheres that defined the traditional family and made housework "women's work" was a reflection of male domination, not the expression of some feminine biological predisposition toward laundry or dishwashing. Women did housework and child care because they *had* to, she argued, not because they *wanted* to or because of some genetic master plan. And men didn't do housework because they could get out of it.[33]

Few people actually *like* doing housework. "A woman's work is never done, and happy she whose strength holds out to the end of the [sun's] rays," wrote Martha Moore Ballard in her diary in 1795. Nearly a century later, Mary Hallock Foote wrote: "I am daily dropped in little pieces and passed around and devoured and expected to be whole again next day and all days and I am never *alone* for a single minute." And in 1881, Helen Campbell wrote that spring housecleaning was "a terror to every one, and above all to gentlemen, who resent it from beginning to end." Perhaps Emily Dickinson said it best (using the passive voice). " 'House' is being 'cleaned,' " she wrote. "I prefer pestilence." (Of course, she wasn't the one cleaning it; Bridget and her other servants simply disturbed her peace.)[34]

Dozens of studies have assessed the changing patterns of housework, child care, and the different amounts of investments in family life. Who does what? How do people decide? Are men doing more now than they used to? Can they be encouraged/asked/cajoled/forced to do more? One statistic about family involvement is revealing of a larger pattern. Most studies, as you will see, suggest how little men's participation in family life has changed. In one respect, though, it has changed dramatically and completely. Thirty years ago, virtually no fathers were present at the births of their children; today, more than 90 percent are present in the delivery room. If men *want* to change their involvement in the family, there is evidence that they are capable of doing so quickly and relatively easily.[35]

The way mothers and fathers spend their time has changed dramatically in the past half century. Dads are doing more housework and child care; moms more paid work outside the home. Neither has overtaken the other in their "traditional" realms, but their roles are converging. For their part, fathers now spend more time engaged in housework and child care than they did half a century ago. Fathers' time spent doing household chores has more than doubled since 1965, from an average of about four hours per week to about ten hours in 2011. Mothers' time doing housework has gone down significantly over the same period, from thirty-two hours per week in 1965 to eighteen hours per week in 2011. Fathers have by no means caught up to mothers in terms of time spent caring for children and doing household chores, but there has been some gender convergence in the way they divide their time between work and home.[36]

And what men do is dramatically different from what women do. It's as if our houses were divided into discrete "zones"—his and hers—and husbands and wives had their own sphere of responsibility. "His" domain is outdoors—the yard, the driveway—or an outdoor space moved indoors, like the basement, garage, trash receptacles, and den; "her" domain is always indoors—the kitchen, laundry room, bedrooms, and bathroom. (If she moves outdoors, it is often with an "indoor" element—hanging laundry, tending the garden.) These two domains demand different types of activities. In one study, women and men were asked to list all the different things they do around the house. The total number of items on each list was roughly equivalent. But when the specific tasks were examined, the men listed items like "wash the car" and "mow the lawn," whereas the women listed "cook the meals" and "make the beds." As Arlie Hochschild explains:

> Even when couples share more equitably in the work at home, women do two-thirds of the daily jobs at home, like cooking and cleaning up—jobs that fix them into a rigid routine. Most women cook dinner and most men change the oil in the family car. But, as one mother pointed out, dinner needs to be prepared every evening around six o'clock, whereas the car oil needs to be changed every six months, any day around that time, any time that day.[37]

What's more, men tend to see their participation in housework *in relation* to their wives' housework; women tend to see their work as necessary for family maintenance. That's why men use terms like "pitch in" or "help out" to describe the time they spend in housework—as if the work was their wives' to do. "When men do the dishes it's called helping," Anna Quindlen, op-ed writer for the *New York Times*, observed wryly. "When women do dishes, that's called life."[38] And it may not even be all that helpful. According to the Center for Talent Innovation, 40 percent of professional wives felt that their husbands actually create *more* work around the house than they perform.[39]

It is true that men's share of housework has increased; "husbands of working wives are spending more time in the family than in the past." In 1924, 10 percent of working-class women said their husbands spent "no time" doing housework; today that figure is less than 2 percent. Between the mid-1960s and the mid-1970s, men's housework increased from 104 to 130 minutes a day, whereas women's decreased from 7.4 to 6.8 hours a day. In another survey of forty-five hundred married dual-career couples between the ages of twenty-five and fourty-four, 15 percent of the men admitted that they performed less than one hour of housework per week. The median amount for men was about five hours a week; for women it was about twenty hours. Men reported that they did 10 percent of the housework in 1970 and 20 percent in 1990—which, depending upon how you look at it, represents double the percentage in only twenty years or still only one-fifth the amount that needs to be done.[40]

Although men report that they currently do between one-fifth and one-fourth of all domestic labor, there is some evidence that asking people how much housework they do leads to rather large inaccuracies, because people often report how much they think they ought to be doing, not how much they actually do. Both women and men overreport the amount of housework they do—men overreport by about 150 percent, more than double the overreporting by women (68 percent). Interestingly, more privileged husbands with egalitarian gender attitudes tend to overreport at a higher rate than more traditional husbands, who probably believe that they should not be doing so much housework. Less privileged "supermoms" are more likely to overreport their housework than more privileged working mothers because only such inflated hours could justify their staying at home. The overreporting by men was so significant that the researchers doubt "that husbands have increased their supply of domestic labor to the household in the past 25 years."[41]

Other survey methodologies have yielded results that make me confident that men's participation in housework has increased somewhat over the past quarter-century, though probably not as much as men themselves might claim. When couples were asked to keep accurate records of how much time they spent doing which household tasks, men still put in significantly less time than their wives. Recent figures from the National Survey of Families and Households at the University of Wisconsin show that husbands were doing about fourteen hours of housework per week (compared with thirty-one hours for wives). In more traditional couples in which she stays home and the husband is the sole earner, her hours jump to thirty-eight and his decline slightly to twelve. This is reasonable, because they've defined housework as "her" domain. But when both work full time outside the home, the wife does twenty-eight hours and the husband does sixteen. (This is four times the amount of housework that Japanese men do, but only two-thirds of the housework that Swedish men do.) Men's increased participation has not been a steady progressive rise; rather, it increased from 1965 to 1985 and has leveled off since.[42]

Actually, the major finding of these recent studies is not that men are doing more housework but rather that less housework is being done—by anyone. In 1965, women did forty hours a week; now they do twenty-seven, so the amount of total time that men and women spend doing housework has decreased from fifty-two hours to forty-three hours per week. And marriage tends to exacerbate the differences between women and men. It turns out that men reduce their housework when they form a couple and increase it when they leave; women increase their time spent on housework when they form a couple and reduce it when they leave.[43]

Housework turns out to fluctuate a lot by timing, season, and marital status and among different groups of men. Not all men are doing more housework; or, rather, some men are doing more of it than others. Men's changing experience of family life depends on age, race, class, and level of education. Younger men, for example, are doing far more around the house than their fathers did—though their wives still do a lot more. A poll of women younger than thirty in *Ladies Home Journal* in May 1997 found that 76 percent said they do most of the laundry; 73 percent do most of the cooking; 70 percent do most of the housecleaning; 67 percent do most of the grocery shopping; and 56 percent pay most of the bills. In Canada, the numbers are similar: 77 percent of women prepare meals on an average day, compared with 29 percent of the men, and 54 percent of the women clean up after meals, compared with 15 percent of the men.[44]

While men's share of housework has increased modestly, the changes have been more pronounced in some younger dual-career families. Both ideologically and practically, there is increasing gender convergence, especially at the front of this new wave. According to the Pew Research Center, 62 percent of married adults said "sharing household chores" was the third most important ingredient (after faithfulness and sex) in a successful marriage in 2007—up from 47 percent in a comparable study in 1990. So, it seems more men are walking their talk. According to the U.S. Bureau of Labor Statistics, men and women in 2010 who were married, childless, and working full time (defined by the BLS as more than thirty-five hours a week) had combined daily totals of paid and unpaid work that were almost exactly the same: eight hours and eleven minutes for men, eight hours and three minutes for women. For those who had children under the age of eighteen, women employed full time did just twenty minutes more of combined paid and unpaid work than men did, the smallest difference ever reported, noted *Time* magazine writer Ruth Konigsberg.[45]

Ironically, working men are feeling more pressure as a result, as they find their workplaces less flexible. In one survey from Boston College's Center for Work and Family, nearly three-fifths of the fathers agreed with the statement "In the past three months, I have not been able to get everything done at home each day because of my job." Brad Harrington, executive director of the Center for Work and Family, points out that men may be feeling particularly squeezed because they never anticipated having so much domestic responsibility. "It's a surprise for them. They weren't prepared that this would be expected of them, and they have no role models of how to do it," he says. And a 2011 report from the Families and Work Institute concluded that long hours and increasing job demands are conflicting with more exacting parenting norms. "Men are feeling enormous pressure to be breadwinners and involved fathers," says Ellen Galinsky, the institute's director. "Women expect more of men, and men expect more of themselves."[46]

More work, more housework, less flexibility at work. Sounds pretty grim. So it may come as a surprise that the more housework and child care fathers do, the happier they are! In a 2010 study in Britain, fathers who shared housework and child care reported the highest levels of marital satisfaction and life satisfaction and the least stress. Maybe equality—sharing the burdens and the joys—just makes people feel better about their lives.[47]

Though we tend to think that sharing housework is the product of ideological commitments—progressive, liberal, well-educated, middle-class white families with more egalitarian attitudes—the data suggest a more complicated picture that has less to do with ideological concerns. In every single subcategory (meal preparation, dishes, cleaning, shopping, washing, outdoor work, auto repair and maintenance, and bill paying), for example, black men do more housework than white men. In more than one-fourth of all black families, men do more than 40 percent of the housework, in other words, men's "share" of housework comes closer to an equal share. In white families, only 16 percent of the men do that much. And blue-collar fathers, regardless of race—municipal and service workers, policemen, firefighters, maintenance workers—are twice as likely (42 percent) as those in professional, managerial, or technical jobs (20 percent) to care for their children while their wives work. A 2009 study found that lower-income, less educated male EMT workers did more housework and child care than did high-earning, highly educated physicians. The doctors congratulated themselves on being "good fathers" because they attended special school events and soccer games. The EMT workers didn't label themselves at all; their flexible schedules enabled them to attend to all the routine tasks of parenthood, like cooking, cleaning, and taking care of kids when they're sick.[48] This difference comes less from ideological commitments and more from an "informal flex time," a split-shift arrangement with one's spouse, which is negotiated by about one-fourth of all workers in the United States and by one-third of all workers with children under age five.[49]

The presence of children increases the gender gap. Mothers spend far more time with children than fathers do, especially when the children are infants, during which time families report "very low levels of paternal engagement." Mothers spend 50 percent more time with kindergarten to fourth-grade children than do fathers. Men's share of child care increases as the children get older, both requiring a different type of engagement and also perhaps offering more "fun" for dad. But when researchers

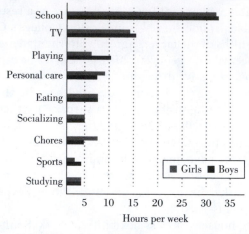

Figure 6.4. Average time U.S. children ages 6–17 spent on activities, 2002–2003.

Source: ISR Research Update, Number 4, January 2007. University of Michigan Institute for Social Research.

asked about how much time each parent spends *alone* with the children, fathers averaged only 5.5 hours a week, while mothers averaged closer to 20 (19.5) hours a week—a 350 percent difference. When they have children, men tend to spend longer hours at work, in part because they have to earn more to support their children and in part because they either want to or simply are able to. Their wives, of course, spend less time at work, thus exaggerating the gender gaps both at work and at home. "The gender gap is present even with no children," notes sociologist Beth Ann Shelton, "but it is exacerbated by the presence of children in the household."[50]

Children learn the gender expectations that their parents teach them. One 1991 study found that daughters of women working full time did more than ten hours a week of housework; sons did less than three hours a week. A recent study found that one of the best predictors of men's participation in child care was whether or not their fathers did housework and child care. One consultant who runs workshops called "Grateful Dad" found a more seasonal fluctuation in men's participation around the house. Although pundits fished around for possible explanations, he had a more parsimonious answer: Football season was over.[51]

More than with housework, there is consistent evidence of change in men's participation in child care. The major pull toward increasing men's participation in domestic work is as fathers, not as husbands. Men seem to maintain the contradictory ideas that they want to shield and protect their wives from life's unpleasantness, although they steadfastly refuse to perform a task as degrading as washing out the toilet. According to demographer Martha Farnsworthe Riche, "The great lesson of the past 15 to 20 years is that men don't care if the house is clean and neat, by and large." Or, as one wife noted, wearily, "I do my half, I do half of [my husband's] half, and the rest doesn't get done."[52]

But when it comes to being fathers, men are evidently willing to do more. A poll in *Newsweek* magazine found that 55 percent of fathers say that being a parent is more important to them than it was to their fathers, and 70 percent say they spend more

"And then Winnie the Pooh decided that it was time to check Daddy's e-mail again."

Figure 6.5. *Source:* Paul Noth/The New Yorker Collection/The Cartoon Bank.

time with their children than their fathers spent with them. A 1995 survey sponsored by the Families and Work Institute found that 21 percent of the 460 men surveyed said that they would prefer to be home caring for their families if they had enough money to live comfortably. (This is actually a fairly low percentage because the amount these men believed they needed in order to live comfortably was over $200,000.)[53]

Still, American men's rate of participation in child care lags behind the rates of participation of men in other industrial countries. In Australia, Canada, and the Netherlands men's rates are about double the rates in the United States, whereas in Britain the rates are about 40 percent higher.[54]

In Sweden, for example, there are so many men who either stay home to care for their children or split their time with their partners and wives that they have a special name for it: the "latte pappas." And data from Denmark suggest that child-care arrangements are rarely the cause of marital strife; it's housework. One study asked three thousand Danish married dual-career couples how often they fight about various things.[55] Here's what they found:

How often do you fight about . . .	Once a week	Once a month	Once every 6 months	Rarely
Housework	9	31	22	39
Child care	2	10	13	74
Child rearing ideas	7	19	17	58

These Danish couples seem to get along pretty well!

Men consistently report that they would *like* to spend more time with their children and families, *if they only could.* "No man, on his deathbed, ever regretted spending too much time with his family" is the way Senator Paul Tsongas put it when he left the Senate. Many men say they want to do more, but demands of work continue to get in their way. Others fear being seen by their colleagues and bosses as less committed to their careers and fear being placed on a "daddy track" from which there will be no advancement. Still others continually bump up against inflexible ideas of what it means to be a man. "The person whom I damaged most by being away when [my children] were growing up was me," observed one man sadly. "I let my nurturing impulse dry up."

For some men (and women), these desires are spilling over into action. In a study sponsored by the Dupont Corporation, 47 percent of managerial women and 41 percent of managerial men had told their supervisors that they would not be available for relocation; 32 percent of women and 19 percent of men had told their bosses that they would not take a job that required extensive travel; and 7 percent of women and 11 percent of men had already turned down a promotion they had been offered. To want to spend more time with the family is an old and tired male lament; to actually sacrifice career ambitions to do so is a new development, a most visible way to walk one's talk.[56]

Men often say that they want to be involved fathers and to spend more quality time with their children. But rarely are they willing to make such sacrifices in order to do it. The payoffs, however, when they do can turn out to be great. Men who do more housework are also better fathers. And men who have closer relationships with

"My wife is about to have a baby, so I was wondering if you could make me work late for the next eighteen years or so."

Figure 6.6. John Donohue/The New Yorker Collection/The Cartoon Bank.

their children report greater marital satisfaction and better health. They feel less stress (if you can believe that!) and less pressure to be successful, powerful, and competitive. They also live longer, causing the normally staid British financial magazine *The Economist* to quip, "Change a nappy, by God, and put years on your life." "When males take full responsibility for child care," sociologist Barbara Risman points out, "they develop intimate and affectionate relationships with their children." Nurturing their children is good for men's health. And, of course, increased family involvement by men benefits women, freeing them from the obligations of the second shift. And that enhances gender equality: Recall that anthropologists found consistently that women's economic and political status is highest in those cultures in which men do more domestic work.[57]

The Rise of the Stay-at-Home Dad

Countless stories seem to pour out of media outlets about stay-at-home dads. It seems every time there is even a ripple of interest in how much more housework and child care men might actually be doing, there are stories either extolling the virtues or questioning the masculinity of these new (usually) urban pioneers. Is there a "surge" in stay-at-home dads?

Yes and no. On the one hand, especially since the economic recession of 2008 and 2009, when many men lost their jobs, there has been an increase in stay-at-home dads. Here's one chart:

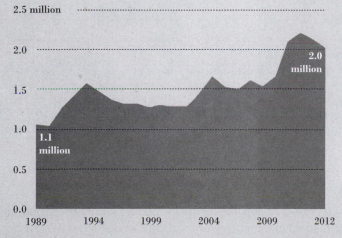

Rising number of stay-at-home dads. Number of fathers living with child(ren) younger than 18 who do not work outside the home.

Note: Based on fathers ages 18–69 with own children younger than 18 in the household. Fathers who live apart from their children are not included. Fathers are categorized based on employment status in the year prior to the survey.

Source: "Growing Number of Dads Home with the Kids," Pew Research Center, Washington, DC (June, 2014) http://www.pewsocialtrends.org/2014/06/05/growing-number-of-dads-home-with-the-kids/.

(Continued)

But at the same time, such graphs can be deceptive—in the same way that the "hordes" of women were "opting out" of the workforce a few years ago. In both cases, their time at home is rarely permanent; rather, it's a temporary respite while job hunting or while the kids are very little. And besides, stay-at-home moms are far more prevalent:

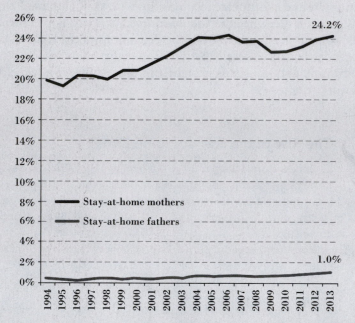

Stay-at-home mothers and stay-at-home fathers as percent of married-couple families with children under 15, 1994–2013.

Note: Stay-at-home parents are those who were out of the labor force for the previous year for the purpose of "taking care of home and family," while their spouse was in the labor force all of the previous year.

Source: Alex Williams, "Just Wait Until Your Mother Gets Home" in *New York Times*, August 12, 2012, Styles, p. 1.

There are, however, lots of payoffs for greater family participation by men. Obviously, when men do more housework and child care, their wives are happier. But it also has a significant impact on their children. In one study, girls raised in families where gender did not determine housework responsibilities were likely to be more ambitious as they considered their own occupational prospects. The study's lead author told a journal that "girls grow up with broader career goals in households where domestic duties are shared more equitably by parents."[58]

Increasing men's participation in housework and child care will require a combination of microlevel and macrolevel supports. Individually, men have to *want* to do more, and they will also need support from their wives and from their male friends, co workers, and colleagues. They'll need to know *how* to do it, as well, learning the set of

OH? **REALLY** •   **Does a More Equal Marriage Mean Less Sex?**

A cover story in the *New York Times Magazine* in February 2014 concluded, sadly, that when married couples deviated from a more traditional arrangement—that is, when men did "women's work" or women did "men's work"—or even when the balance shifted and he did more or she did less, they also reported having less sex. The writer, a psychotherapist, suggested that we'd better return to Mars and Venus—a consciously gendered division of household labor, both in terms of who does what and how much time we spend doing it—for the sake of our sex lives.

Except it turns out that the author leapt to erroneous conclusions based on a misreading of some very sketchy data. The study, by sociologist Sabino Kornrich and his colleagues, was based on data from the 1990s—but the couples in the study were married in the 1950s and 1960s, a time when men's household participation would have been seen as very disruptive to traditional gender arrangements. And child care wasn't included—it was just housework. And cohabiters weren't included, though their relationships tend to be far more egalitarian—and cohabiters have a lot more sex than married couples. (That's because they tend to be younger; stable cohabiters usually end up getting married.)

A better study, drawing on more recent and more comprehensive data, found no significant differences in sexual frequency between traditional and egalitarian couples. But, more significantly, they found that women in more traditional relationships expressed far lower sexual satisfaction.

So quantity doesn't go down, and quality goes up. Which may be why most men's advice columns these days advise men to engage in "choreplay." As *Men's Health* magazine put it, "Housework makes her horny." Well, perhaps not when she does it . . .

Sources: Sabino Kornrich, Julie Brines, and Katrina Leupp, "Egalitarianism, Housework, and Sexual Frequency in Marriage" in *American Sociological Review*, 78(1), 2013, pp. 26–50; Daniel L. Carlson, Amanda Miller, Sharon Sassler, and Sarah Hanson, "The Gendered Division of Routine Housework and Couples' Sexual Relationships: A Re-examination," manuscript, Georgia State University, 2014.

skills that, taken together and performed regularly, constitutes nurturing and caring—cooking, cleaning, laundry. "Unless fathers do a greater share of the work at home, mothers will remain disadvantaged in working outside the home. Mothers can't win unless fathers change, too."[59]

Working couples will also need to have structural, macrolevel supports, such as **family-friendly workplace policies**, paid parental leave, and adequate health care. The United States is one of the few countries in the world without a national policy of paid **maternity leave**; some Nordic countries include additional **paternity leave** as well. Nearly every Western European country has a child allowance—a payment to families for each child they have, regardless of income or whether the mother is employed or not. And U.S. corporations have not stepped into the institutional breach created by such governmental indifference to the plight of working parents (figure 6.7). Only 8 percent of American workers have any child-care benefits provided by their employers. Enacting corporate and governmental policies to promote the health and well-being of working families is a tall order, to be sure, but leaving

Figure 6.7. "First of all, Harrington, let me tell you how much we all admire your determination not to choose between job and family."

Source: Lee Lorenz/The New Yorker Collection/The Cartoon Bank.

individual family members to sort it out for themselves guarantees that little will change. The "failure to invest in children can lead to economic inefficiency, loss of productivity, shortages in needed skills, high health care costs, growing prison costs, and a nation that will be less safe, less caring, and less free."[60]

Perhaps the most interesting trend is the gradual separation of housework and child care over the last decade. Whereas mothers and fathers are spending from four to six hours *more* per week with their children, women have dramatically decreased the amount of housework they do, and men have not exactly jumped in to fill the void. "Either the house is clean or I see my kids," is how one female doctor in Milwaukee put it. Evidently, choosing between housework and child care is easier than choosing between career and family.[61]

Of course, there are wrinkles. Dads' increases in "family time" may actually push moms back into more traditional roles. In some places, Dad has become the "fun parent." Dad takes the kids to the park on Saturday morning to play soccer while mom washes the breakfast dishes, makes the beds, does the laundry, and prepares lunch. "What a great time we had with Dad," the kids will sing merrily when they return home. "He's such an involved parent!" (Well, they might not say it exactly like that, but you get the point.)

That women continue to perform the lion's share of the second shift puts enormous strains on marriage. Balancing work and family pulls working women in different directions, and either way they move, they are bound to feel guilty and frustrated. Even Karen Hughes, who was President George W. Bush's senior counselor and the architect of his policies, decided to return to Texas and her family because she couldn't have it all. One high-level executive who recently quit her job confessed that she "had as much going my way as any working mother could have. And I was absolutely flat-out. All I managed to do were the kids and my job. I could have continued to do this indefinitely, but I would have been a shell of myself."[62]

THE "CONSTRUCTED PROBLEMS" OF CONTEMPORARY FAMILY LIFE

Obviously, a woman or a man who feels like a "shell of myself" cannot provide a strong foundation on which to build a family, with a vibrant marriage and healthy children who are nourished physically and emotionally. Yet, increasingly, that's how parents feel, and their relationships with each other and with their children suffer as a result. Without a concerted national policy to assist working women and men to balance work and family obligations, we continue to put enormous strains on two sets of bonds, between husbands and wives and between parents and children, and virtually guarantee that the "crisis" of the family will continue. And we will also continue to face a series of "constructed problems"—problems that stem from the strain felt by individual families as they negotiate the increased pressures of sustaining dual-career couples and dividing housework and child care in the absence of help from the outside.

In the 1950s, the government stepped in where once the community and extended kinship networks had sustained family life and created an infrastructure (schools, hospitals, roads, and suburban homes) that supported and sustained family life. Today, we expect families to accomplish far more—expect them, for example, to support children often beyond high school and college and to provide for virtually all of an adult's emotional needs—on far less. It is from this widening chasm between what we expect from our families and what support we offer them that several "constructed problems" emerge. These problems are also the result of gender inequality—both its persistence and the efforts by women to remedy it. Only when we develop a sustained national effort—both individually and politically—to reduce the gender inequality in both the home and the workplace will these constructed problems begin to ease.

The "Problem" of Day Care

Take, for example, the "problem" of day care. Many Americans are reluctant to place their children in day care, the government has no national funding for day-care centers, and employers contribute about 1 percent of the total spent on child care. There is virtually no quality care available for infants and toddlers, and the costs of private care are staggering to parents at all income levels. Yet the most common conclusion from the research on the impact of day care on children's development is that there are no negative psychological, intellectual, developmental, or emotional consequences to being in day care. In fact, there is some evidence that quality child care has positive effects on children's curiosity, ability to share, ability to create friendships, and preparation for school. What's more, a 1996 National Institutes of Health study found that children's attachment to their mothers is not affected by whether or not they are in day care, what age they enter, or how many hours they spend there.[63]

So there really is a "problem" with day care: Despite its positive effects, there's not enough of it, it's not affordable, and the government and our employers don't seem to care very much about our children. But that is not the "problem" that we are asked to worry about. Almost daily, we seem to be bombarded with headlines that remind us of negative consequences of such care, including child sexual abuse at day-care centers. The implication of such terrifying stories is that if these children were home with their mothers, where they "belong," such terrible things would not be happening to them. The "problem" of day care turns out to be a debate about whether or not women should be working outside the home. "Having a nanny read you a story isn't the same as having your mother do so," writes William R. Mattox, a senior writer for the conservative Family Research Council. "A mother's worth cannot be reduced to the cost of what a paid substitute might command. To suggest that it can is like saying that the value of a woman making love to her husband is equal to the going rate for prostitutes in the area."[64]

To ask whether or not women should work outside the home is, of course, to ask the wrong question. For one thing, it poses a class-based contradiction, because we encourage poor women to leave the home and go to work and ask middle-class women to leave the workplace and return home. The landmark welfare reform legislation of 1996 requires that welfare recipients start working within two years of going on welfare. "It is difficult to argue that poor mothers should find jobs but that middle class mothers should stay home," writes family researcher Andrew Cherlin. And when they can find jobs, working-class and middle-class women are simply not going to stop working.[65]

Nor is there any reason why they should, because there is no evidence whatsoever that mothers' working outside the home adversely affects children. In fact, most of the evidence indicates that both direct and indirect benefits accrue to children of working mothers. Such children tend to have expanded role models, more egalitarian gender-role attitudes, and more positive attitudes toward women and women's employment. Daughters of employed women are more likely to be employed, and in jobs similar to those of their mothers, than are daughters of nonemployed women. Moreover, adolescent children of working mothers assume more responsibility around the home, which increases their self-esteem.[66]

Working outside the home also increases women's self-esteem and sense of personal efficacy and well-being, so working mothers tend to be happier in their marriages—which makes divorce less likely. One study found that the happier wives were in their jobs, the happier they were in their marriages. In a four-year study sponsored by the National Institute for Mental Health, Rosalind Barnet observed three hundred dual-career families and found that the women were neither depressed nor stressed out but rather that they had good marriages and good relationships with their children. Another survey of more than eight hundred two-career couples found similar results.[67]

A comparison with other industrial nations is instructive here. The United States is the only industrial country that does not have a national system of day care. Throughout the European Union, for example, child care is available, affordable, and expedient. Parents still balance career and family, albeit uncertainly—but they do it with far more social support than American parents do. In neither Europe nor the United States do women show any inclination to leave the labor force, but rather they seem to be demanding that the work world accommodate their family needs—and not the other way around.

Not only *will* women continue to work outside the home, but also they *should* work outside the home, argues Joan Peters. "If they do not, they cannot preserve their identities or raise children" who are able to be both independent and family-oriented. But, "women can do so successfully only if men take half the responsibility for child care." Again, the "solution" turns out to be social and political. Only one-third of all employees in large and midsize U.S. companies can receive even unpaid parental leave. Both nationally and in each family, the solution turns out to be greater gender equality—not women working less outside the home, but rather men working more inside it.[68]

The "Problem" of "Babies Having Babies"

The problem of day care is related to the problem of "babies having babies"—the increasing fertility of teenage women. Although the number of teen pregnancies has declined significantly since 1990, the number of teenage girls giving birth every year remains remarkably high—in fact, the United States has the highest rate of births to teenage mothers of all industrial nations—double that of the next highest country, the United Kingdom (which includes all of Ireland in its tabulation).

That decline hasn't quelled the debate. Some of the same people who complain about women *delaying* childbearing while they wallow in unbridled sexual consumerism are also among the loudest critics of teen pregnancy. Is it a problem of a sort of "Goldilocks" mentality—you should have children when you are not too young and not too old, but rather "just right" in terms of age? Actually, it often seems that the problem of teenage motherhood is a mask for what is really bothering its critics— women's sexual agency. Some concern stems from a disguised critique of feminism, which enables women to explore a healthy and safer sexuality. Efforts to stop teen

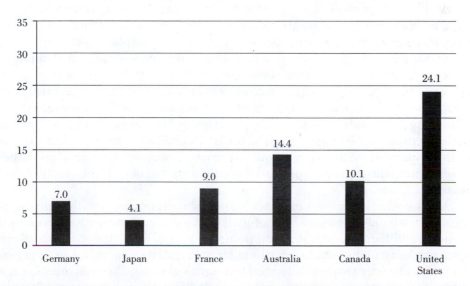

Figure 6.8. Teen birth rates (per 1,000 women aged 15–19, 2014).

Source: World Bank: World Development Indicators, Adolescent fertility rate (births per 1,000 women ages 15–19) (SP.ADO.TFRT). United Nations Population Division, World Population Prospects.

motherhood have included, for example, increasing restrictions on access to birth control and even birth control *information* and restrictions on abortion, including parental consent and waiting periods.

Take, for example, the statistics on rates of teenage motherhood (figure 6.8). In the mid-1950s, 27 percent of all girls had sexual intercourse by age eighteen; in 1988, 56 percent of girls and 73 percent of boys had sexual intercourse by age eighteen. In 1991, the rate of adolescent childbearing—births to teen mothers per one thousand girls—was 62.1, the highest rate since 1971, which was the year before abortion was legalized. This accounts for 9 percent of all births in the nation. Sixty-six percent of these young women were unmarried, compared with 1960, when only 15 percent were unmarried.[69]

Such numbers can be "read" in several ways. For some, such numbers illustrate a calamitous increase in teen motherhood, attributable to wanton teenage sexuality and rampant immorality, an erosion of respect for the institution of marriage, and the growing crisis of fatherlessness. But for others, such numbers illustrate the erosion of access to adequate birth control information, the steady attacks on women's right to choose that restrict women's access to abortion and other means of birth control, and the increased freedom of young people from their parents' insistence on "shotgun weddings."

On these questions, the research is unanimous: Restricting access to information about birth control, access to birth control, and access to abortion has little bearing on rates of sexual activity. In fact, virtually all studies of the effect of sex education indicate a *decrease* in rates of sexual activity, greater sexual selectivity, and higher rates of safer sex practices. Young people will continue to become sexually active in their mid-teens, whether or not they have access to birth control or information about it. In fact, restricting access is the surest way to encourage unwanted pregnancy.

The problem of babies having babies is also a way to blame women for men's irresponsibility. Politically, we are saying to young women that if they are going to dance (become sexually active), they will have to pay the piper (bear the consequences of unwanted pregnancies). But if, as we also know, it takes two to tango, perhaps the solution to the crisis of young motherhood lies in both increasing the abilities of these young women to become responsible (adequate health care, birth control information, and access to birth control) and fostering a more responsible young manhood. In fact, casting the crisis as "babies having babies" masks another serious problem—young girls' sexual victimization by men. Most of the fathers of babies born to teenage mothers are *not* themselves teenagers, but rather are adult men whose predatory sexual behavior goes unnoticed when the problem is cast in this way.

Occasionally, the problem of babies having babies is merged into the problem of unwed parenthood in general. Out-of-wedlock births in America have increased 600 percent in the past three decades, from 5 percent of all births in 1960 to about 40 percent today. Out-of-wedlock births to black parents have increased from 22 percent in 1960 to over two-thirds today. Doomsayers abound. David Blankenhorn, a conservative policy pundit, claims that the United States is moving toward "a post-marriage society" in which marriage is no longer a dominant institution. Again, one can attribute this to the increased freedom of both women and men from shotgun weddings, which certainly kept down the number of out-of-wedlock births. And Andrew Cherlin points out that much of this increase is not to single mothers or welfare cheats, but rather to cohabiting white mothers. That is, most of the births are to people in committed relationships who just don't happen to be married.[70]

But this controversy also illustrates the way family life and public policy are intimately connected. The percentage of out-of-wedlock births in the Nordic countries—Sweden, Norway, Denmark—is significantly higher than that *rate* in the United States. But in Nordic countries, with adequate child care, universal health care, and access to free education, the "need" of children to be born to married parents—access to parental health care programs, for example—is eliminated by a concerted policy of state spending to ensure the health and well-being of its citizens. So women and men marry when they want the additional sanctioning of religious authority, not because they need to be married for economic reasons.

The "Problem" of Fatherlessness

The question of men's responsibility also surfaces in the debates about fatherlessness. In recent years, commentators have noticed that fathers are not around, having left their children either through divorce or cavalier indifference. Recent works such as David Blankenhorn's *Fatherless America* or David Popenoe's *Life Without Father* have blamed absent fathers for causing myriad social problems, ranging from juvenile delinquency to crime and violence to unemployment. We read, for example, that 70 percent of all juveniles in state reform institutions come from fatherless homes. This bodes especially ill for young boys, because without a father, we are told, these young boys will grow up without a secure foundation for manhood: "In families where the father is absent, the mother faces an impossible task: she cannot raise a boy into a man. He must bond with a man as he grows up," writes psychologist Frank Pittman. It is a mistake to believe that "a mother is able to show a male child how to be a man." "Boys raised by traditionally masculine fathers generally do not commit crimes," adds Blankenhorn. "Fatherless boys commit crimes." In a home without a father, Robert Bly writes somewhat more poetically, "the demons have full permission to rage." This has consequences for both the fathers and the boys, creating in one moment two sets of unattached and unconstrained males roaming around the streets. "Every society must be wary of the unattached male," family researcher David Popenoe reminds us, "for he is universally the cause of numerous social ills."[71]

It is true that more children of both sexes are being raised in single-parent homes and that the "single parent" doing that child raising is more often than not a woman. Whereas just over one-tenth (11 percent) of children were being raised by unmarried mothers in 1970, just under one-fourth (24.6 percent) were being raised that way as of 2013. Almost half (41 percent) of all births are to unmarried women. But the number of single fathers has increased from about 393,000 in 1970 (10 percent of all single parents raising children) to more than two and a half million today (around 13 percent of single parents raising children)—without much appreciable decrease in raging demons.[72]

It's also true that the other side of the "feminization of poverty" coin is the "masculinization of irresponsibility"—the refusal of fathers to provide economically for their children. What is less certain, however, is the impact of fathers on the myriad social problems with which their absence seems to be correlated. Involvement by nonresident fathers does provide some benefits to children and consistently predicts higher academic achievement—which argues for maintaining fathers' connection to their children. And although fatherlessness may be correlated with high crime rates, that does not mean that fatherlessness *causes* the criminality. In fact, it might just be the other way around. To be sure, high crime rates and fatherlessness are indeed correlated. But it turns out that they are *both* products of a larger and more overwhelming problem: poverty.[73]

The National Academy of Sciences reports that the single best predictor of violent crime is not fatherlessness but rather "personal and neighborhood income." And, it turns out, fatherlessness also varies with income; the higher the income bracket, the more likely that the father is home—which suggests that the crisis of fatherlessness is actually a crisis of poverty. In his impressive ethnographic research on street gangs in Los Angeles, Martin Sanchez-Jankowski found "as many gang members from homes where the nuclear family was intact as there were from families where the father was absent" and "as many members who claimed close relationships with their families as those who denied them." Clearly something other than the mere presence or absence of a father is at work here.[74]

Occasionally public policy actually discourages fathers from maintaining contact with their children after separation or divorce. Or from paying child support in the first place. If a poor man pays child support to the state government, the state typically keeps the money to pay itself back for welfare payments paid to its children, on the logic that poor children might otherwise double-dip. But as a result, the mother and children see no tangible evidence of the father's efforts to support his children. So he might decide to give them money directly, under the table, which tangibly supports them but does nothing to offset his allocated payments, so the state may still have his wages garnished, arrest him, or otherwise penalize him. (Only Wisconsin allows the father's payments to go directly to the family without a reduction in welfare benefits—a policy that motivates fathers to pay and reduces the amount of time that mothers stay on welfare.)[75]

The confusion of correlation and causation also reveals a deeper confusion of consequence and cause. Fatherlessness may be a consequence of those larger, deeper, more structural forces that drive fathers from the home and keep them away—such as unemployment or increased workplace demands to maintain a standard of living. Pundits often attempt to transform the problem of fatherlessness into another excuse to blame feminism, and specifically women working outside the home. They yearn for a traditional nuclear family, with traditional gender inequality. For example, David Popenoe writes nostalgically about the family form of the 1950s—"heterosexual, monogamous, life-long marriage in which there is a sharp division of labor, with the female as the full-time housewife and the male as primary provider and ultimate authority"—without pausing to underscore that such a family form was also dramatically unequal when viewed from a gender perspective. Such a vision substitutes form for content, apparently under the impression that if only the family conformed to a specific form, then the content of family life would dramatically improve.[76]

This emphasis on form over content is most evident in the prescriptions about fatherlessness. You would think, naturally, that the solution is for fathers to be truly and deeply involved in family life, to share child care, if not housework, and to become a passionate presence in the lives of their children. You'd be wrong. Blankenhorn and others who lament fatherlessness do not issue a clarion call for a new fatherhood, based on emotional receptivity and responsiveness, compassion and patience, care and nurture (which are, after all, the *human* qualities one needs to be a good father in the first place). Instead he rails against him:

> He is nurturing. He expresses his emotions. He is a healer, a companion, a colleague. He is a deeply involved parent. He changes diapers, gets up at 2:00 A.M. to feed the baby, goes beyond "helping out" in order to share equally in the work, joys, and responsibilities of domestic life.[77]

How utterly "selfish" of him. Obviously, this sensitive father does all this because he "reflects the puerile desire for human omnipotentiality in the form of genderless parenthood, a direct repudiation of fatherhood as a gendered social role for men."[78] Let's assume for the moment that this sentence is actually sensible. It means that the *real* father is neither nurturing nor expressive; he is neither a partner nor a friend to his wife, and he sleeps through most of the baby's infantile helplessness, oblivious to the needs of his wife and child. This guy is a selfless, giving father simply because he has a Y chromosome.

THE "PROBLEM" OF GAY AND LESBIAN FAMILIES

Another recent constructed problem is that of gay and lesbian families. It's ironic that the same political commentators who fret about the decline of the family are the very people who would prevent gay men and lesbians from creating them. But the problems of gay families—marriage, child rearing—are actually less about families and more about the legal status of homosexuals. As soon as the Hawaii Supreme Court indicated the likelihood that it would recognize gay and lesbian marriages in 1997, for example, several states rescinded their adherence to the "full faith and credit" clause of the U.S. Constitution, the clause that requires one state to recognize contracts concluded in another state, such as those relating to marriage, voting, education, or driving. Soon thereafter, the U.S. Congress passed the **Defense of Marriage Act**, as if the institution of marriage were under attack by those who sought to enter it.

The Defense of Marriage Act (DOMA) was a hodgepodge of intolerance and discrimination masquerading as concern for the sanctity of marriage. It was only a matter of time before the U.S. Supreme Court found it to be unconstitutional, and, in 2013, the Court struck down a key part of DOMA so that same-sex couples married in states that allow it are now entitled to federal benefits afforded to heterosexual couples. On June 25, 2015, after the Supreme Court decision in *Obergefell* v. *Hodges*, same sex marriage is permitted in all 50 states.[79]

Although the U.S. Supreme Court ruled in *Obergefell v Hodges* that prohibiting same-sex marriage was unconstitutiona–that it denied to some people a right enjoyed by others based solely on their gender–there are many other grounds for discrimination that are still unevenly distributed across the country. Some states have lifted obstacles to full equality just as other states invent ways to add new ones (figure 6.9).

It is expressly prohibited to discriminate against gay men and lesbian couples in adoption procedures in only eleven states and the District of Columbia (New Jersey, New York, Indiana, Maine, California, Connecticut, Illinois, Massachusetts, Oregon, Vermont, and Florida).[80]

Although many political observers see **same-sex marriage** as a political football, tossed around when the socially conservative base of the Republican Party seemed poised to drift away from full allegiance, the issues that are raised by the controversy speak to the core issues about gender difference and gender inequality. What appears

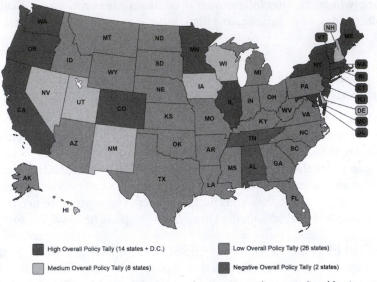

States with high equality offer solid protections across the six major policy areas (i.e., Marriage and Relationship Recognition, Adoption and Parenting, Non-Discrimination, Safe Schools, Health and Safety, and Ability for Transgender People to Correct the Gender Marker on Identity Documents).

States with medium equality often offer positive parenting laws, but fall short on safe schools, non-discrimination laws, health and safety laws, or laws and policies that help transgender people update the gender marker on their identity documents.

States with low or negative equality offer few or no protections.

Figure 6.9. This map shows the overall equality tallies for each state and the District of Columbia. A state's "policy tally" counts the number of positive laws and policies within the state that help drive equality for LGBT people.

In general laws covering sexual orientation affect lesbian, gay and bisexual people, while laws covering gender identity affect transgender people, although there is significant overlap. A state that has good protections on the basis of sexual orientation, but does not have good protections on the basis of gender identity, may not be considered a "high equality state" in overall state policy.

Source: http://www.lgbtmap.org/equality-maps/legal_equality_by_state

to be a concern for the sanctity of marriage is often accompanied by a discomfort with the idea of gay and lesbian families, based on misinformation about the quality of those relationships and their impact on children.

One reason why many gay and lesbian couples want to marry is because so many benefits accrue to married couples—benefits that heterosexual couples often take for granted. These benefits include the right to inherit from a spouse who dies without a will; the right to consult with doctors and make crucial medical decisions if the partner is incapacitated; the right of residency of a foreign spouse; the right to Social Security benefits; the right to include a spouse on one's health plan; the right to visit a spouse in a government institution like a prison or hospital; and the right to immunity from having to testify against one's spouse in a legal proceeding.[81]

It is no longer true that gay male relationships are more fragile than heterosexual relationships or that gay men are more "promiscuous" (i.e., have a greater number of different sexual partners) than do heterosexuals and lesbians. Some of the reasons for this can be found in masculine gender socialization, which discourages men from commitment to domestic life in the first place; exclusion from formal, legal marriage, which cements heterosexual relationships and increases the couple's likelihood of staying together despite disagreement; lack of children, who are often the reason why heterosexual couples continue to work on their relationships; and social disapproval and institutionalized homophobia, which can destabilize any couple. "It is paradoxical that mainstream America perceives gays and lesbians as unable to maintain long term relationships while at the same time denying them the very institutions that stabilize such relationships," argues Craig Dean, executive director of the Equal Marriage Rights Fund.[82]

Marriage is more than a legal right, more than a relationship. It is an institution, the bedrock institution of our ideal of the family. Without the right to marry, it is codified into law that gay relationships are less valuable, less important, than heterosexual ones. Such a devaluation leads to the very promiscuity that is used as the rationale for denying the right to marry in the first place.

In many cases, gay and lesbian couples provide a model of family life. For one thing, gay and lesbian couples are "less likely to fall into patterns of inequality" that define heterosexual marriages. By bringing together two people of the same gender, gender inequality is neutralized and gender difference eliminated. Compared with heterosexual couples, gay and lesbian couples are more likely to share housework; lesbian couples are the most egalitarian of all couple arrangements.[83] And, it turns out, gay men and lesbians often make excellent parents. In the late 1960s, one woman lamented her position, not as a lesbian, but rather as a nonparent:

> One of my mother's big disappointments was the fact that there would be no grandchildren. I love both of my parents a great deal, and I would do almost anything for their happiness, but I couldn't do that. I think I was saddened too, when . . . I knew that I wasn't ever going to have children. And I would like to have some . . . for myself.[84]

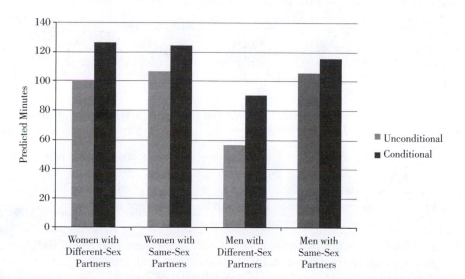

Figure 6.10. Unconditional and conditional predicted minutes spent engaged with children by family structure.

Source: Figure 1 from Kate Prickett, Alexa Martin-Storey, and Robert Crosnoe, "A Research Note on Time with Children in Different- and Same-Sex Two Parent Families" in *Demography* 52:3, pp. 905–918. With kind permission from Springer Science and Business Media.

Just as heterosexual women once felt they were forced to choose between having a career and having a family, many gay men and lesbians feel forced to choose between acknowledging their sexuality and having a family. And just as women today are unwilling to make that choice, wanting to "have it all," so, too, are gays and lesbians, who have decided that their homosexuality ought not to disqualify them as good parents. In 1976, there were between three hundred thousand and five hundred thousand gay and lesbian parents; today, there are an estimated one and a half to five million lesbian mothers and between one and three million gay fathers. Currently, between eight million and thirteen million children (about 5 percent of all children in the United States) are being raised by at least one gay parent.[85]

None of the fears of gay parenting has materialized. There is no evidence that gay fathers or lesbian mothers exert any special negative influence on child development or that they sexually abuse their children. In fact, the few studies that have been conducted show that "the outcomes for children in these families tend to be better than average." The research on lesbian mothers suggests that their children, both boys and girls, have patterns of gender identity development similar to those of children of heterosexual parents at comparable ages and display no differences in intelligence or adjustment. And 0 percent—as in none—physical or sexual abuse, compared with 26 percent of American adolescents who report parent or caregiver physical abuse and 8.3 percent who report sexual abuse, according to a national longitudinal study. "Quality of mothering," rather than sexual orientation, is the crucial determinant of children's development.[86] Cambridge University psychologist Michael Lamb reviewed more than one hundred studies from the last thirty years and concluded that the "research shows that the children and adolescents of same-sex parents are as emotionally healthy, and as educationally and socially successful, as children and adolescents raised by heterosexual parents."[87] As the fifteen-year-old daughter of a lesbian mother put it:

> I think I am more open-minded than if I had straight parents. Sometimes kids at school make a big deal out of being gay. They say it's stupid and stuff like that. But they don't really know, because they aren't around it. I don't say anything to them, but I know they are wrong. I get kind of mad, because they don't know what they are talking about.

This statement echoed a recent New Jersey court decision, which found that children in gay and lesbian families

> emerge better equipped to search out their own standards of right and wrong, better able to perceive that the majority is not always correct in its moral judgments, and better able to understand the importance of conforming their beliefs to the requirements of reason and tested knowledge, not the constraints of currently popular sentiments or prejudice.

Such sentiments, as family sociologist Judith Stacey points out, might well "serve as child-rearing ideals for a democracy."[88]

A recent meta-analysis of social science studies of gay and lesbian parenting suggests that children of these parents are more accepting of homosexuality and may be more likely to indicate a willingness to consider homosexual relationships themselves, although they are no more likely to identify themselves as "gay" than are children of heterosexual parents. More interestingly, however, are the *gender* consequences, as opposed to the sexual ones: Daughters of lesbian and gay parents are more assertive, confident, and ambitious, and sons are less conforming to traditional notions of masculine aggression and domination and more fluid in their gender identities.[89]

READ ALL ABOUT IT!

How do LGBT people decide to become parents and create families? Is it the same way that heterosexual couples do? Or do different communities navigate the routes to pregnancy and parenthood differently? In their compelling study of black lesbians, psychologist Sarah Reed and her colleagues found that sexual orientation and race matter significantly in how this community understands the opportunities and challenges of pregnancy and the process of becoming parents.

And Americans seem to finally be getting the message that same-sex marriage is not a real threat to the stability of heterosexual marriage. Opposition has been dropping significantly, especially among those under thirty, while support has steadily grown (figure 6.11). I make this prediction based on the demographic data, not some ideological agenda: It is only a matter of time before same-sex marriages are legal in all fifty states, ratified by a Supreme Court that cannot find any constitutional justification for preventing people who love each other from marrying. Eventually, I imagine, the opposition to LGBT families will go the way of opposition to mixed-race marriages—the attitude of a small but significant minority, but with no legal foundation.

That many of the "crises" turn out to be manufactured political efforts to push back the gains of women or LGBT people doesn't mean that there aren't some real and serious problems in our gendered families. I'll focus on three here, both because they illustrate the ways in which gender inequality often leads us to see gender difference, and also because gender offers us a way to think about these problems in new and different ways.

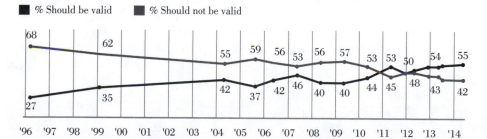

Figure 6.11. Do you think marriages between same-sex couples should or should not be recognized by the law as valid, with the same rights as traditional marriages?

Note: Trend shown for polls in which same-sex marriage question followed questions on gay/lesbian rights and relations. 1996–2005 wording: "Do you think marriages between homosexuals . . ."

Source: Justin McCarthy, 2014. Same-Sex Marriage Support Reaches New High at 55%, nearly eight in 10 young adults favor gay marriage. Copyright © 2014 Gallup, Inc. All rights reserved. The content is used with permission; however Gallup retains all rights of republication.

DIVORCE

It's hard to deny that divorce *is* a real problem. The divorce rate in the United States is astonishingly high. Around half of all marriages end in divorce—considerably more than in other industrialized countries (table 6.2). The U.S. rate is more than double the rate in Germany and France and nearly double the rate in Sweden and Britain—countries where individuals remain supported by national health care and children specifically benefit from adequate access to education and health care, while their custodial parents receive regular governmental stipends. (These, of course, ameliorate the harsh economic impact of divorce.) According to the Census Bureau, the number of divorced people more than quadrupled from 4.3 million in 1970 to 19.3 million in 1997. This represents 10 percent of all adults aged eighteen or over, up from 3 percent in 1970.[90]

Divorce may be a serious social problem—but not exactly for the reasons that many political commentators claim it is: These high divorce rates are not shattering the family. Rates of marital dissolution are roughly the same as they have been for a very long time. Looked at historically, high rates of divorce are merely accomplishing by conscious action what higher mortality rates had accomplished in an earlier period. As historian Lawrence Stone put it, "The median duration of marriage today is almost exactly the same as it was 100 years ago. Divorce, in short, now acts as a functional substitute for death: both are means of terminating marriage at a premature stage." (Of course, he adds, the psychological effects are not the same.)[91] Nor does the number of divorces necessarily indicate a loss of faith in marriage. Ninety-five percent of men and 94 percent of women between the ages of forty-five and fifty-four have been married. In fact, writes sociologist Constance Ahrons, author of *The Good Divorce*, "we like marriage so much that many of us will do it two, three, or more times." Remarriages now comprise about half of all marriages every year.[92]

The problem with divorce is more accurately linked to the constructed problem of fatherlessness and the real problem of gender inequality. Divorce reform was promoted, after all, by women who at the turn of the last century sought to provide legal recourse to those who wanted to escape marriages that were desperately unhappy and others that were brutally, even violently oppressive. The option of divorce loosened the marital knot to keep it from choking women. Like birth control and abortion, both of which have also generated heated debates, divorce undermined men's power over women and reduced gender inequality in the family.

Although liberalized divorce laws may have reduced gender inequality within marriage, they seem neither to have reduced it entirely nor to have reduced it after the marriage is dissolved. One recent study found that three of four women listed

The United States has the highest divorce rate in the world.

Actually, that's not true. Russia is the divorce capital of the world. According to the United Nations Demographic Yearbook, there are 5 divorces for every 1,000 people. The United States comes in fifth, with 3.4 divorces per 1,000 people.

Source: Ashley Reich, "Highest Divorce Rates in the World" in *Huffington Post*, May 25, 2011, http://www.huffingtonpost.com/2010/12/21/highest-divorce-rates-in_n_798550.html?

COMPARED *to* WHAT?

U.S. Marriage and Divorce Rates in Comparative Perspective

Table 6.2. Crude Marriage and Divorce Rates by Country: 1960–2012 (per 1,000 Population)

Country	Marriage rate						
	1960	1970	1980	1990	2000	2010	2012
United States[1]	8.5	10.6	10.1	9.8	8.2	6.8	6.8
Canada[2]	N/A	8.8	7.3	5.5	4.7	4.4	N/A
Japan[3]	N/A	9.9	6.1	6.3	5.6	5.5	N/A
France	7	7.8	6.2	5.1	5	3.9	3.7
Germany	9.5	7.4	6.3	6.5	5.1	4.7	4.8
Italy	7.7	7.3	5.7	5.6	5	3.7	3.5
Netherlands	7.7	9.5	6.4	6.5	5.5	4.5	4.2
Sweden	6.7	5.4	4.5	4.7	4.5	5.3	5.3
United Kingdom	7.5	8.5	7.4	6.6	5.2	N/A	4.4

Country	Divorce rate						
	1960	1970	1980	1990	2000	2010	2012
United States[1]	2.2	3.5	5	4.7	4	3.4	3.6
Canada[2]	N/A	1.4	2.5	2.6	2.2	2.1	N/A
Japan[3]	N/A	0.9	1.4	1.6	2	2	N/A
France	0.7	0.8	1.5	1.9	1.9	2.1	N/A
Germany	1	1.3	1.8	1.9	2.4	2.3	2.2
Italy	1.2	1.2	1.2	0.5	0.7	0.9	N/A
Netherlands	0.5	0.8	1.8	1.9	2.2	2	2.1
Sweden	1.2	1.6	2.6	2.7	2.6	2.5	2.5
United Kingdom	N/A	1	1.9	1.9	1.9	2.1	N/A

Notes: N/A = Not available. Marriage and divorce figures for most years include some estimated data. [1]Data are for 1985 instead of 1980 and 2011 instead of 2012. [2]Data are for 1985 instead of 1980, 1995 instead of 1990, 2002 instead of 2000, and 2008 instead 2010. [3]Data are for 1985 instead of 1980, 1995 instead of 1990, and 2005 instead of 2000.

Sources: NVSS National Marriage and Divorce Rate Trends, "Marriages and Crude Marriage Rates," United Nations Statistical Division (UNSTAT), 2011; "Divorces and Crude Divorce Rates," United Nations Statistical Division (UNSTAT), 2011; Eurostat (demo_nind) and Eurostat (demo_ndivind); U.S. Department of Health and Human Services, National Center for Health Statistics.

pathological behaviors by male partners (adultery, violence, substance abuse, abandonment) as their reason for divorce. Just as there are "his" and "her" marriages, there are also "his" and "her" divorces because divorce affects wives and husbands differently. Divorce exaggerates gender differences in the marriage, exacerbating gender inequality. In the mid-1980s, family researcher Leonore Weitzman calculated that following divorce, the woman's income drops a precipitous 73 percent, whereas her ex-husband's income increases 42 percent. In recent years, these data have been revised as overly dramatic, but no research suggests that the economic and social statuses of women and men after divorce are equivalent, and researchers still agree that women's resources decline somewhat more than men's. (Men's income goes down if their wives had careers.) As sociologist Paul Amato writes, "The greater the inequality between men and women in a given society, the more detrimental the impact of divorce on women."[93]

Divorce has different impacts on women and on men. Many divorced fathers "lose almost all contact with their children over time," writes David Popenoe. "They withdraw from their children's lives." Over half of all divorced fathers have no contact with their children; even one-third of the noncustodial fathers who have written visitation provisions have not seen their children in the past year. Noncustodial mothers, however,

Does feminism cause divorce? That's what John Gray, proponent of the interplanetary theory of gender (Men are from Mars . . .) thinks. "The reason why there's so much divorce is that feminism promotes independence in women," he told a journalist. "I'm very happy for women to find greater independence, but when you go too far in that direction, then who's at home?"

Actually, the more the divorce rate goes down, the more egalitarian the marriage. And the more gender equal, the more stable.

A study by Laurie Rudman and Jo Phelan found that having a feminist partner was linked to healthier and more stable heterosexual relationships for both women and men. Oh, yeah, and greater sexual satisfaction.

So, what are the best predictors of likely divorce? Age, income, and education.

College-educated middle-class people who get married later have the best chance of staying together. Non-college-educated, early-marrying working-class people are the most likely to divorce. (Oh, and those are the most likely to subscribe to the interplanetary theory of gender.)

Of college graduates who got married in the early 2000s, only about 11 percent were divorced by their seventh anniversary, while 17 percent of non–college graduates were divorced. Over 80 percent of 1980s college graduates who got married at age twenty-six or later were still married two decades later, compared with less than two-thirds (65 percent) who got married before age twenty-six. And while both working-class and middle-class women are working outside the home, middle-class women are more likely to couple that work with a more egalitarian view of marriage—dual career—than working-class women, who work because their husbands cannot earn enough to support the family, but who retain a more traditional notion of the male-breadwinner–female-homemaker model.

That is, John Gray has it exactly backward! Gender equality keeps marriages together. It's the interplanetary theory of gender that leads to higher divorce rates.

Sources: "Feminism and Free Porn Are Ruining Relationships–Author" in *NZHerald.co.nz*, June 6, 2014, http://www .nzherald.co.nz/lifestyle/news/article.cfm?c_id=6&objectid=11268800; Laurie Rudman and Jo Phelan, "The Interpersonal Power of Feminism: Is Feminism Good for Romantic Relationships?" in *Sex Roles*, 57 (11–12), 2007, pp. 787–799.

rarely lose contact with their children after divorce, maintaining family connections over employment possibilities and new relationships. In addition, divorced men exhibit increased symptoms of psychological and emotional distress. Divorce seems to affect women more adversely in material and financial terms and men more adversely in emotional and psychological terms.[94]

What predicts continued involvement of parents in their children's lives after a divorce is the quality of the relationship between the ex-spouses prior to the divorce. And ironically, it also appears that it is the men who were more involved with their children prior to the divorce who are most likely to disappear after it, whereas those men who were relatively uninvolved prior to divorce tend to become more active with their children afterward. In part, as Edward Kruk observes, this counterintuitive difference stems from the less involved fathers also being more "traditional" in their outlooks, which would increase their sense of commitment to family life even after divorce; whereas more "liberal" men are more likely to see themselves as "free" from family responsibilities.[95]

The debate about divorce in contemporary America often has less to do with the divorcing couple and far more to do with the anticipated outcome on children. In a widely publicized study, psychologist Judith Wallerstein found that a significant number of children "suffer long-term, perhaps permanent detrimental effects from divorce," whereas other children repress these effects, only to have them emerge years later. Children, she argues, lose the "scaffolding" upon which they construct their development. "When that structure collapses," she writes, "the children's world is temporarily without supports. And children, with a vastly compressed sense of time, do not know that the chaos is temporary." Ten years after divorce, Wallerstein found a significant number still adrift, troubled, and achieving less than expected. Many were having trouble establishing and sustaining relationships of their own. Twenty-five years after divorce, those problems had not disappeared—in fact, they may have been exacerbated. "When people decide to divorce, it has a short-term and long-term traumatic effect upon the children that makes their subsequent life journey more difficult," she writes. A lousy marriage, she now concludes, beats a good divorce. And a "good enough" marriage will dramatically enhance children's lives.[96]

Although such dire warnings as Wallerstein's have claimed countless magazine covers and public discussion, there is far less social science in her work than first meets the eye. After following sixty-one families in an affluent California suburb, she concluded that about half the women and two-thirds of the men carried serious emotional problems through to adulthood, including the inability to form cohesive relationships, distrust of the opposite sex, and associated problems. But Wallerstein had no control group, even of similarly affluent white families. So how do we know that the divorce was the cause of these later emotional problems? What's more, about one-third of the original children were not interviewed for this survey—are they the ones who adjusted successfully and moved on with their lives? We cannot know. And finally, and most damning, the original participants in the study were recruited through a promise of free therapy for divorcing couples who were having a difficult time of it. Wallerstein herself tells us (in *Surviving the Breakup*, though she fails to mention this in subsequent volumes) that most of them were having serious psychological problems *to begin with.* Only one-third were functioning adequately; half the fathers and close to half the mothers were "moderately disturbed or frequently incapacitated by disabling neuroses or addictions." She goes on:

> Here were the chronically depressed, sometimes suicidal individuals, the men and women with severe neurotic difficulties or with handicaps in relating to another person, or those with long-standing problems in controlling their rage or sexual impulses.

Hardly the sort of nationally representative sample that would provide convincing evidence. What Wallerstein has found is that the children of seriously psychologically impaired divorcing parents will have some difficulties themselves down the road.[97]

Consistently, though, the public discussion has been informed by these simple axiomatic assertions that divorce has a deleterious effect on children's well-being. And, to be sure, all other things being equal, having two parents in a happy, stable, intact family is pretty much certain to produce happier, healthier, and better-adjusted children than are families that are unhappy, unstable, or separated. The question is which of those variables—unhappy, unstable, separated—is the most crucial in producing the outcome.

Perhaps the most level-headed researcher to weigh in on these issues is Andrew Cherlin, a sociologist and demographer at Johns Hopkins University. In his 1999 Presidential Address to the Population Association of America, Cherlin made clear that his research found that the line of causation ran exactly counter to Wallerstein's clinical assertions. "We found that children whose parents would later divorce *already* showed more emotional problems at age 7 than children from families that would stay together," he notes. Divorce "occurs in families that are already troubled." In other words, divorce is the *outcome* of the problem, not its cause.[98]

Most research on divorce actually finds that after the initial emotional upset that affects nearly all children, over the long term, "most children settle down and return to a normal process of maturation." Another recent book found that about three-fourths of children of divorce are "coping reasonably well and functioning in the normal range." Most children recover from the stress of divorce and show few adverse signs a few years later if they have adequate psychological supports and economic resources.[99]

No one doubts that divorce is difficult for children or that being raised by two parents is probably better than being raised by one. For starters, with two parents, each is less likely to be tired and overworked. This makes higher levels and a higher quality of parent-children interaction more likely. And there is little doubt that, all else being equal, two people raising children together, whatever the parents' sexual orientation, is better for the children than one. The debate really concerns what we mean by "all else being equal." If we compare, for example, the educational achievement scores, sense of well-being, or levels of psychological and emotional adjustment of children who are raised in intact families with those of children raised in single-parent, postdivorce families, we find that those children in single-parent families manifest lower levels of well-being, self-esteem, educational attainment, and adjustment than those in two-parent homes.

But such comparisons are misdirected, because they compare two types of families—divorced and intact—as if they were equivalent. Divorce is not a remedy for

OH? REALLY •

Conventional wisdom has it that if your marriage is in trouble, you should stay together for the sake of the children. Although it's true that all things being equal, two-parent intact families are better for children's emotional well-being, things are rarely equal. In fact, as family sociologist Paul Amato has shown, children in intact, high-conflict families fare far worse than children in divorced families. Instead of staying together "for the sake of the children," if your marriage is in serious trouble, and conflict is constant, it might be better to divorce—for the sake of the children!

Source: Paul Amato, Laura Spencer Loomis, and Alan Booth, "Parental Divorce, Marital Conflict, and Offspring Well-Being During Early Adulthood" in *Social Forces*, 1995, 73 (3): 895–915.

marriage; it is a remedy for a *bad* marriage. And when researchers compare the outcomes for children being raised in a postdivorce family with the outcomes for children being raised in an intact—*but unhappy*—family, the evidence is clear. The consequences of divorce on children depend on the level of marital conflict prior to the divorce. One study found that children in divorced families did, indeed, feel lonely, bored, and rejected more often than those in intact families—but that children in unhappily married families felt the highest levels of neglect and humiliation.[100]

A longitudinal study begun in 1968 by psychologists Jeanne and Jack Block tracked a group of three-year-olds for several years. When the children were fourteen, the Blocks looked back at their data and found that some of the children whose parents would eventually divorce, especially the boys, were observed to be more aggressive and impulsive and more likely to be in conflict with their parents. Although, as sociologist Arlene Skolnick observes, it is impossible to discern whether parental conflict led to problems for these children, or vice versa, it is clear that "these children's problems did not result from the divorce itself." Another British study tracking seventeen thousand families also found that children's problems long antedate divorce and that problems among young children can, in fact, be a good predictor of eventual divorce.[101]

The most systematic research on these issues has been undertaken by family sociologists Paul Amato and Alan Booth and their colleagues. Amato and Booth found the single best predictor of a child's happiness and well-being to be the quality of the parents' marriage. Those children who grow up in homes where parental conflict is high and a divorce ensues do as well as those who grow up in happily married, intact homes. What's more, parents who are jealous, moody, inclined to fly off the handle, critical, and prone to dominate their spouse have a far worse effect on their children's eventual marriages than whether or not the parents are divorced. Further, these researchers found that in high-conflict families, children had higher levels of well-being if their parents divorced than if they stayed together; whereas in low-conflict families, children had higher levels of well-being if their parents stayed together than if they divorced. Divorce, Amato and Booth conclude, "is beneficial for children when it removes them from a high conflict marriage." But, like marriage, divorce ought not be entered into casually or without thought, because the consequences can be deleterious "when it removes them from a low-conflict marriage" (figure 6.12).[102]

The preponderance of research echoes these themes. Levels of family conflict are far more important in the lives of children than whether or not families stay together.

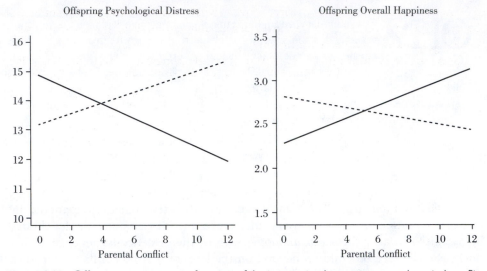

Figure 6.12. Offspring outcomes as a function of the interaction between parental marital conflict and parental divorce while controlling for parents' age, sex, race, and education and offspring's sex and age.

Source: Fig. 1. Paul R. Amato et al. "Parental Divorce, Marital Conflict, and Offspring Well-Being During Early Adulthood." *Social Forces* (1995) 73(3):895–915. Reprinted by permission of Oxford University Press and the Department of Sociology at the University of North Carolina at Chapel Hill.

Most research has found that "frequent marital and family conflict in so-called intact families is detrimental to children's physical health and that divorce may, in fact, insulate some children and adolescents from prolonged exposure to health-threatening family interactions." And it turns out that parent-child relations prior to marriage are the key determinant of whether the divorce is psychologically catastrophic. Content, it would appear, is more important than form.[103]

But this may be yet another case of mistaking correlation for causation. Although it may be true that children from divorced families experience more severe problems than children in intact families, it may be that *both* the divorces and the problems are caused by something else—the greater marital conflict. A longitudinal study found that children in families that eventually divorce manifest problems long before the actual divorce. The authors argue that many of the consequences attributed to divorce may, in fact, derive from the marital conflict and family stress that precede a divorce, rather than from the divorce itself. Blaming the problems of children on their parents' divorce "is a bit like stating that cancer is caused by chemotherapy," argues the president of the Family and Divorce Mediation Council of Greater New York. "Neither divorce nor chemotherapy is a step people hope to have to take in their lives, but each may be the healthiest option in a given situation."[104]

The solution that some propose to the problem of divorce is, of course, simple: Make divorce harder to obtain. The state of Louisiana has instituted "**covenant marriages**," which, unlike the contractual legal marriage, demand that couples take literally and seriously the provision of "'til death do us part." Several other states are now considering such a distinction. Yet most family researchers agree that such a triumph of form over content—making divorce harder to get without changing the content of the marriage—would "exacerbate the bitterness and conflict that are associated with the *worst* outcomes of divorce for kids."[105]

Divorce is a serious undertaking and not to be undertaken casually. But it is a "necessary 'safety-valve' for children (and parents) in high conflict households." From the standpoint of the children, "an end to an unhappy marriage is probably preferable to living in a household characterized by tension and acrimony," whereas forcing unhappy families to stay together would have the most deleterious outcomes for children, as well as for the adults. After divorce, most families "adjust," and some even "thrive." Divorce might better be seen as a social indicator that something is wrong not with one-half of all marriages, taken individually, but rather with the institution of marriage, that the foundation upon which marriage rests cannot sustain and support one-half of all the marriages that take place—without some serious efforts on the part of policymakers. Family therapist Betty Carter pointed out that if any other social institution were failing over half the people who entered it, we would demand that the institution change to fit people's new needs, not the other way around.[106]

CHILD CUSTODY

Whether or not divorce has simply accomplished by social policy what high mortality rates used to accomplish "naturally," there is one significant difference between the two methods to dissolve a marriage. With a divorce often comes the problem of child custody. Prior to the Industrial Revolution, children were seen as an economic "good," and courts utilized an economic means test to determine who would receive custody, and custody was regularly and routinely given to fathers. In the early years of the twentieth century, though, children came to be seen as a luxury, and so a new test, based on care and nurture, was used to determine custody arrangements—a policy that favored mothers. Today, the "best interests of the child" is the criterion employed to provide the foundation for custody decisions, although in practice, the best interests of the child are presumed to be better served by staying with the mother, not the father, because the presumption is that mothers provide better child care—especially for young children—than do fathers.

Such a policy makes a certain amount of sense, because women perform most of the tasks that provide the care and nurturing that children need. And yet, in the late 1970s, 63 percent of fathers who requested custody received it, a significant increase from the 35 percent and 37 percent who requested and received it in 1968 and 1972, respectively. In a recent study of one thousand divorces in two California counties, psychologist Eleanor Maccoby and law professor Robert Mnookin found that a majority of mothers and fathers wanted joint legal custody, whereas those who didn't preferred that they, and not their spouse, be given custody. Nearly 82 percent of mothers and 56 percent of fathers requested the custody arrangement they wanted, whereas 6.7 percent of women and 9.8 percent of men requested more than they wanted, and 11.5 percent of women and 34.1 percent of men requested less than they wanted. This suggests that "gender still matters" in what parents ask for and what they do to get it. That mothers were more likely to act on their desires by filing for a specific request also indicates that men need to ask for more up front to avoid feeling bitter later.[107]

Maccoby and Mnookin's research is notable for another finding. Children living with mothers generally did as well as children living with fathers; "the welfare of kids following a divorce did not depend a lot on who got custody," Maccoby told a journalist, "but rather on how the household was managed and how the parents cooperated." But one consequence of current custody arrangements is paternal withdrawal. Whether this is because the father is bereft to be kept from regular contact with his children or because after the marital bond is severed he experiences a euphoria of "freedom" and considers himself to have escaped from a conflict-ridden family situation, it appears that many men "see parenting and marriage as part of the same bargain—a package deal," write sociologists Frank Furstenberg and Andrew Cherlin. "It is as if they stop being fathers as soon as the marriage is over." In one nationally representative sample of eleven- to sixteen-year-old children living with their mothers, almost half had not seen their fathers in the previous twelve months. Nearly half of all divorced fathers in the United States pay no child support; in Europe the comparable number is about one-fourth.[108]

Paternal withdrawal, it turns out, actually affects the father-daughter relationship most significantly, even more than the much-touted father-son relationship, whereas the mother-daughter relationship seems to be the most resilient to divorce and custody disputes. This may surprise those who believe that the father-son bond is the most fragile and most hard-hit by postdivorce fatherlessness, but it illustrates how frequently daughters are ignored in that literature and how both boys and girls benefit from paternal responsibility and continued presence in their children's lives.[109]

In recent years, postdivorce fatherhood has become a political issue, as "father's rights" organizations have sprouted up, declaring men to be the victims of inequality in custody decisions. It is true that most court decisions grant custody to the mother, based on the "best interests of the child" standard. Father's rights groups challenge this assumption and claim that, invariably, joint custody is preferable for children. Sometimes, it appears that their rhetoric substitutes these aggrieved fathers' vindictiveness against their ex-wives, or their bewilderment at the entire divorce proceeding, for the "best interests" of children, but it also appears to be the case that all things being equal, joint physical and legal custody ought to be the norm in custody decisions. Here, of course, "all things being equal" means that there is no discernible danger to the child of sexual or physical abuse; that the parents can manage to contain their own postdivorce conflict and prevent the children from becoming pawns in a parental power struggle; and that the parents agree to equally support the children financially and emotionally. Such arrangements may be more difficult for parents than for children, who often report "a sense of being loved by both parents," as well as "feeling strongly attached to two psychological parents, in contrast to feeling close to just one primary parent." Contrary to some popular opinion, joint custody "does not create uncertainty or confusion" and seems to benefit children, who say they are more satisfied with the arrangement than those in single-custody homes and consider having two homes advantageous.[110]

We know, too, that joint custody will benefit men, who will, by maintaining a legal connection to their children, be far more likely to continue to share financial responsibilities for their development. What's more, joint custody may relieve the deep sense of loss, disengagement, and depression often experienced by men who are cut loose from continued involvement with their families. On the other hand, mandated joint legal custody may not be so good for women. Feminist legal theorist Martha Fineman argues that mandated joint legal custody may appear to be gender-neutral but that gender "neutrality" in one arena in a system of overall gender inequality may actually perpetuate gender discrimination, much the way the abandonment of affirmative action sounds race- or gender-neutral but actually favors white males over others by withdrawing from explicit challenges to historical discrimination. As Fineman writes:

> What may have started out as a system which, focusing on the child's need for care, gave women a preference *solely* because they had usually been the child's primary caretaker, is evolving into a system which, by devaluing the content or necessity of such care, gives men more than an equal chance to gain the custody of their children after divorce if they choose to have it, because biologically equal parents are considered as equal in expressive regards. Nonnurturing factors assume importance which often favors men.[111]

Perhaps the most judicious system of child custody will be one that recognizes the difference in "inputs" between fathers and mothers in the actual experiences of the children—time spent in child care, level of parental involvement in child development—while at the same time presuming that both parents are capable of and interested in (absent any evidence to the contrary) continued committed and involved relationships with their children. Men's becoming more involved in predivorce child care ought to be reflected in custody arrangements, as should women's continuing to shoulder the overwhelming majority of such care, despite their commitments to work. Fathers' "rights" after divorce will come more readily if the fathers have recognized their responsibilities during the marriage.[112]

THE PROBLEM OF FAMILY VIOLENCE

For too many Americans—children and parents alike—the family bears only a passing resemblance to the "haven in a heartless world" of nostalgic myth. Far from shielding their members from the cold and violent world outside its doors, the family *is* that cold and violent world. Violence tears at the fabric of the family. Although I will discuss some forms of family violence, particularly the violence between women and men, in chapter 13, here I want to discuss violence between parents and children, as well as violence among children. Family violence is remarkably gendered, reproducing and reinforcing gender inequality. The overwhelming amount of family violence is perpetrated by males—husbands beating wives, fathers hitting children, sons hitting their parents, or boys hitting their brothers or their sisters. "The actual or implicit threat of physical coercion is one of many factors underlying male dominance in the family," writes sociologist Murray Straus.[113]

Violence against children by parents is among the most controversial type of family violence. Although widespread support exists for corporal punishment—over two-thirds of Americans believe that it is all right for a parent to spank a child—that support disappears when such violent behavior by parents against children becomes systematic or extreme. Most Americans have hit their children, and most children have been hit by their parents. But the costs may outweigh the obvious benefits of immediate compliance from the child. Spanking is associated with several negative

Everyone spanks their kids.

Actually, the global trend is away from spanking—especially in advanced industrial countries. In 1979, Sweden banned corporal punishment in the home. As of 2014, thirty-eight other countries—including most of Europe and Brazil—have joined Sweden, and another twenty are about to follow suit.

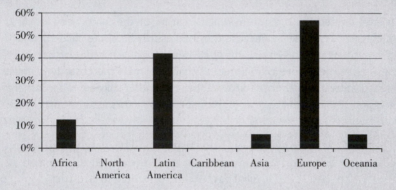

Percent of countries where corporal punishment is prohibited in the home, by region.

Information provided by the Global Initiative to End All Corporal Punishment of Children, www.endcorporalpunishment.org, 2015.

The effect of the ban has been enormous—and fast. A 2009 study found that thirty years after banning it, only 10 percent of Swedes approved of corporal punishment and only 10 percent used it. In less than two generations, the use of violence against children dropped from almost 100 percent to about 10 percent.

Source: http://www.endcorporalpunishment.org/pages/pdfs/GlobalProgress.pdf.

behaviors in children, including aggression, antisocial behavior, and mental health problems. The American Academy of Pediatrics has taken an official stand against spanking.[114]

Although the most common forms of parental violence against children are spanking or slapping, 20 percent of parents have hit their child with an object, almost 10 percent have kicked, bit, or hit their child with their fist, and almost 5 percent of families have experienced a parent beating up a child. And although mothers as well as fathers commit this violence, they are not equivalent. In one study, Bergman and his colleagues found that men are over ten times more likely to inflict serious harm on their children and that every perpetrator of the death of a child in this limited sample was either a father or a father surrogate.[115]

The most evident consequence of parental violence against children is observed in the behaviors of children. Children see that violence is a legitimate way to resolve disputes and learn to use it themselves. Violence against siblings is ubiquitous in American families. As Straus writes:

Violence between siblings often reflects what children see their parents doing to each other, as well as what the child experiences in the form of discipline. Children of non-violent parents also tend to use non-violent methods to deal with their siblings and later with their spouses and children. If violence, like charity, begins at home, so does non-violence.[116]

(Parents wondering how to discourage violence among their children might begin by resisting the temptation to hit them and by settling marital problems without resorting to violence.)

The long-term consequences of **parental violence** against children are also evident. The greater the corporal punishment experienced by the child, the greater the probability that the child will hit a spouse as an adult. And the likelihood is also higher that children hit by their parents will strike back. Child-to-parent violence is also serious; nearly one in ten (9 percent) of all parents of children aged ten to seventeen is a victim of violence perpetrated by his or her own children. Mothers are more likely to be victims of such violence, especially in the more severe cases.

The antecedent causes of children hitting their parents, and especially their mothers, are directly related to the severity of the violence experienced by the children and the severity of the spousal violence that the children observe. Children see their mothers hit by their fathers, and they "learn that mothers are an appropriate and acceptable target for intrafamily violence," writes sociologist Richard Gelles. Nowhere is the gender inequality of the family more evident than when a young boy hits his mother because he has learned by watching his father that violence against women is acceptable behavior for a boy coming into manhood.[117]

THE FAMILY OF THE FUTURE

Perhaps the most consistent finding to emerge from the literature on divorce, custody, and sexual orientation is that the form of the family—intact, divorced, single-parent, lesbian, or gay—matters far less for children than its content. This is the key issue, and we distract ourselves from developing policies and personal relationships built to nurture and sustain children because we are so preoccupied with the size and shape of the package. A home filled with love and support, where parents spend both quality time and quantity time with their children and with each other, is the strongest predictor of future physical, emotional, and psychological health of both the children and their parents. Family sociologist Arlene Skolnick writes that the most reliable studies "find that family structure—the number of parents in the home or the fact of divorce—is not in itself the critical factor in children's well-being. In both intact and other families, what children need most is a warm, concerned relationship with at least one parent."[118]

For example, a recent longitudinal study followed 126 Harvard undergraduates since their student days in the 1950s. Thirty-five years later, 116 of them were reevaluated. Of these, 25 percent who had rated their parents as loving and caring had developed major illnesses, whereas 87 percent of those who had rated their parents as uncaring had experienced at least one serious health problem. (The researchers controlled for other potential causes, such as family history of illness, parental death or divorce, smoking habits, and marital experiences.) Men who had a low perception of the parental care and love that they received as children had a far greater risk of becoming ill in midlife.[119]

The crisis of the family appears less a crisis of form than a series of challenges to its content. It is true that both marital happiness and children's well-being have declined over the past two decades. But it seems equally true that, as David Demo writes, "the negative consequences attributed to divorce, single-parent family structure and maternal unemployment have been greatly exaggerated." As a gendered institution, the family rests on assumptions about gender difference and the reality of gender inequality at both interpersonal and structural levels. At the structural level, gender inequality is maintained by governmental indifference to the plight of working families—from inadequate child care and parental leave provisions to a failure to support and sustain different types of families, in which children may grow up sensing that their lives are not as valuable and worthwhile as those of others.[120]

Family-friendly workplace policies would enable and encourage families to balance their working lives and their family commitments. In the United States, slightly more than 33 percent of workers at companies with more than one hundred employees get unpaid maternity leave, and, although 83 percent of all working men say that they feel the need to share the responsibilities of parenting, only 18 percent of all such corporations actually offer parental leave to men, and only 9 percent of all companies do. Compare these figures with those in Sweden or Norway, for example, where couples are offered one full year of paid parental leave at 80 percent of their salary. Norway and Sweden have even instituted what they call "daddy days," when fathers can take parental leave after the mother has returned to work, to ensure that the fathers have special time to spend with their children. In these countries, even grandparents get financial support to take time away from work to spend with their new grandchildren! These sorts of policies proclaim that a nation loves and cherishes its children so much that it is willing to use its resources to foster and facilitate that love. To me, *that's* "family values."[121]

Yet despite our claims to be a society that values the next generation, American governmental policy actually makes effective parenting more difficult for rich and poor alike. Inadequate funding for education, inadequate health care for children and adults, inadequate corporate policies regarding parental leave, and "family-unfriendly" workplaces—with inflexible hours, rigid time schedules, and lack of on-site child-care facilities—place too great a burden on already fragile and strained marital bonds and bonds between children and their parents. "We're trying to do what women want of us, what children want of us, but we're not willing to transform the workplace," notes an anthropologist who studies men's lives in several different cultures.[122]

The family as a gendered institution also depends on interpersonal relationships among family members, on the gendered division of household labor that reproduces male domination in society. Gender inequality is expressed in the different amounts of housework and child care performed by men and by the different trajectories of men's and women's lives after divorce. It is maintained too often by the real or implicit threat of violence.

Often we believe that forcing families to stay together will benefit the children, even if the parents are unhappy. "We stayed together for the sake of the children" is the way parents often put it. Sociologist Frank Furstenberg suggests instead that we place the welfare of children at the center of the discussion, not as the assumed outcome. "By directing more resources to low-income children, regardless of the family form they live in, through such mechanisms as access to quality child care, health care, schooling, and income in the form of tax credits, it may be possible to increase the level of human, social and psychological capital that children receive." In other words, do we "invest in strengthening marriage and hope that children will benefit, or invest in children and hope that marriages will benefit?"[123] Like Furstenberg, I place my bet on the latter option.

In my opinion, gender equality in the family does not require a large "dose of androgyny," nor do I prescribe, as does sociologist Andrew Greeley, that "men become more like women." Just as it is possible for women to enter the workplace without becoming "masculinized," it is also possible for men to return home from their long exile without becoming "feminized." If present trends continue, it seems inevitable that men will be doing an increasing amount of what used to be called "women's work" inside the home, just as women are doing an increasing amount of what used to be called "men's work" outside it. One can easily accommodate changes in one's activities without transforming one's identity or self-image.[124]

It was in the nineteenth century that the ideology of the separation of spheres was invented and imposed, "imprisoning" women in the home and "exiling" men from it. In the latter half of the twentieth century, the structural foundations of that ideology eroded, and it came under increasing ideological attack. My prediction is that the twenty-first century will witness a "reintegration of spheres," in which home and work will become increasingly similar, and men and women will be more active participants in both spheres. We should "insist on a closer integration between people's professional lives and their domestic lives," writes social critic Christopher Lasch. "Instead of acquiescing in the family's subordination to the workplace, [we] should seek to remodel the workplace around the needs of the family." And on the home front, an increasing number of people are "telecommuting" to work, traveling from bedroom to home office, and using laptops, cell phones, and fax machines to conduct paid work, while they cook for their children and clean the house during breaks.[125]

The most dramatic shift in family life in the twenty-first century will surely be the changing roles of men, just as the most dramatic demographic shift in the workplace in the twentieth century was the entry of women. Family sociologist Scott Coltrane predicts that as wives are employed longer hours, identify more with their jobs, and provide a larger share of family income, men will do increasing amounts of housework. What's more, he argues, as "fathers become more involved in baby care, they will begin to take more responsibility for routine child care, and a significant minority will move beyond the role of household helper." In the workplace, men will increasingly identify as fathers, just as within the home, women have increasingly identified as workers.[126]

READ ALL ABOUT IT!

What's Your "Plan B"?

A fascinating study of young people by sociologist Kathleen Gerson found that both women (80 percent) and men (70 percent) want a balanced, egalitarian marriage, where both work outside the home and both are involved parents. But such an arrangement is difficult to achieve, right? Both family and work take enormous amounts of time, and, unlike in other countries, our social policies provide virtually no support. So, Gerson asked these same people what they would prefer if it didn't work out, if they couldn't have the egalitarian relationships they wanted. In other words, what's your Plan B?

It was here that women and men diverged. About 70 percent of the men said they'd opt for a more traditional family arrangement: They'd work outside the home and their wives would keep house and raise the kids. But nearly three-quarters of the women said they'd rather divorce and go it alone with their kids than return to that 1950s family model.

Look at the difference:

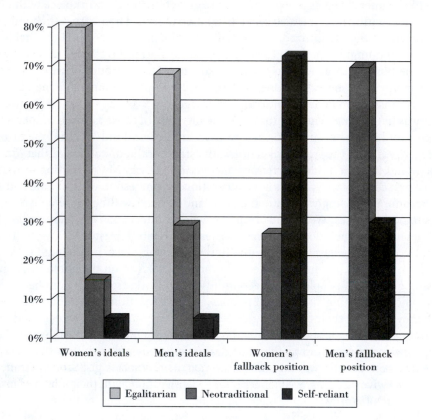

Here is one guy from Gerson's study:

> If I could have the ideal world, I'd like to have a partner who's making as much as I am—someone who's ambitious and likes to achieve. [But] if it can't be equal, I would be the breadwinner and be there for helping with homework at night.

And here is what one woman thinks of that plan:

> My mother is such a leftover from the fifties and did everything for my father. I'm not planning to fall into that trap. I'm really not willing to take that from any guy at all.

The question is, can we develop family policies that enable *both* women *and* men to have the family lives they actually want?

Source: Kathleen Gerson, *The Unfinished Revolution* (New York: Oxford University Press 2010); Lisa Wade, "Most Women Would Rather Divorce Than Be a Housewife" in *Huffington Post*, January 29, 2013, http://www .huffingtonpost.com/lisa-wade/housewife_b_2568187.html. Graph reproduced by permission of Oxford University Press, USA.

When men and women fully share housework and the raising of children, gender inequality in the family will gradually decrease, and the gender stereotypes and gender differences that were presumed to be the source of that inequality will also gradually begin to dissolve. After all, as we learn from anthropologists, those societies in which men take a larger role in child care are those in which women's status tends to be highest. Plus, a society in which women and men share parenting will be a society in which they are also equally active in the labor force. A change in the private sphere will bring about dramatic changes in the public sphere.

Think, for a moment, about the implications of shared parenting and housework, about the full impact of the reintegration of spheres. A child who experiences love and nurturing from his or her father and mother will come to see that nurturing is something that *adults* do, not something that women do and that men may or may not do, depending on whether there's a good game on the television. So all children, both boys and girls, will expect to be nurturing when they become adults. Similarly, a child will also see that working is something that *adults* do, not something that men do and that women may or may not do, depending on whether their husband "allows" it or whether they're raising children. In this sense, shared parenting might be a crucial step in "degendering" the two most highly gendered experiences we have, the two experiences that Freud himself identified as the most crucial elements of healthy adult life: love and work.

Robert Frost wrote these oft-quoted lines:

Home is the place where, when you go there
they have to take you in.

Our families are places in which we are both constrained by duty and obligation and inspired by love, respect, and honor. Love, we've found, can abide in traditional families, in single-parent families, and in gay and lesbian families. It can sustain children in intact families or after divorce. What matters is the content of the family, not its form. Love can abide, nourish, and sustain—wherever it lives and in whatever form.

KEY TERMS

Covenant Marriage	Feminine Mystique	Second Shift
Defense of Marriage Act	Maternity Leave	Traditional Family
Family Values	Parental Violence	Women's Work
Family Wage	Paternity Leave	
Family-Friendly Workplace	Race Suicide	
Policies	Same-Sex Marriage	

The GENDERED CLASSROOM

The Higher Education of Women is one of the great world battle-cries
for freedom; for right against might. It is the cry of the oppressed
slave. It is the assertion of absolute equality.

—Henry Fowle Durant, President
Wellesley College, "*The Spirit of the College*" (1877)

"Math class is tough" were among the first four words Barbie ever spoke.
When Mattel introduced the talking Barbie in 1992, a new group of her
nearly eight hundred million owners heard more than a teenager's complaint—
even if that teenager was the buxom blond bombshell whose feet were designed
to fit into high heels. That group heard the way gender inequality and gender
differences are reproduced.[1]

The interplanetary theory of gender tells us that boys and girls are fundamentally and categorically different: that boys excel in science and math, play
violently on the playground, and shout out in class; that girls, on the other hand,
sit quietly, speak softly, play gingerly, and excel in French and in literature. At the
same time, of course, we sit in the same classroom, read the same books, listen
to the same teachers, and are supposedly graded by the same criteria.

But are we having the same experience in those classes? Not exactly. Our gendering experiences begin even before we get to school. By the time we enter our first
classroom, we are learning more than our ABCs, more than spelling, math, and
science, more than physics and literature. We learn—and teach one another—what

it means to be men and women. And we see it all around us in our schools—who teaches us, what they teach us, how they teach us, and how the schools are organized as institutions. Schools are like old-fashioned factories, and what they produce is gendered individuals. Both in the official curriculum—textbooks and the like—and in the parallel "**hidden curriculum**" of our informal interactions with both teachers and other students, we become gendered. This is reinforced in the parallel curriculum presented by the mass media. And the message that students get—from both the content and the form of education—is that women and men are different and unequal, that the inequality comes from those differences, and that, therefore, such inequality is justified. Consider, though, the opposite position—that the differences we observe are the *products*, not the cause, of gender inequality. As law professor Deborah Rhode writes, "What schools teach and tolerate reinforces inequalities that persist well beyond childhood."[2]

TRADITIONAL EDUCATION FOR MANHOOD

Since the eighteenth century in America, education had been reserved for upper-class boys and men. We've seen earlier how opponents of women's equality used biological arguments to maintain gender exclusion—how, for example, they argued that higher education for women would result in "monstrous brains and puny bodies" with "flowing thought and constipated bowels," because it would violate the "plan" women's bodies held for them. Harvard professor Edward Clarke cited cases of "pale, weak, neuralgic, dyspeptic, hysterical, menorraghic, dysmenorrhoeic" educated women with "arrested development of the reproductive system."[3]

Many of the Victorian opponents of women's education believed that women could not withstand and would not wish to subject themselves to the rigors of higher education. By contrast, some opponents of **co-education** also believed that bringing women and men together would have disastrous effects on both sexes. Because the "minds of men and women are radically different," wrote one editorialist in the University of California at Berkeley *Daily Californian* in the 1890s, men and women must be taught separately. When the University of Michigan first debated co-education in 1858, its president opposed it because "men will lose as women advance, [and] we shall have a community of defeminated women and demasculated men." A local paper applauded the trustees' decision, arguing that to educate women would "unwoman the woman and unman the man."[4]

Some worried that educating women and men together would "emasculate" the collegiate curriculum, watering it down by forcing the inclusion of subjects and temperaments better omitted, slowing down the pace, or otherwise reducing standards that would allow women to keep up. In his influential treatise on adolescence, the great psychologist G. Stanley Hall warned against co-education because it "harms girls by assimilating them to boys' ways and work and robbing them of their sense of feminine character," whereas it harms boys "by feminizing them when they need to be working off their brute animal element." By making boys and girls more alike, he warned, co-education would "dilute" the mysterious attraction of the opposite sex— that is, co-education would cause homosexuality. (Of course, Hall could not yet have previewed Alfred Kinsey's studies of human sexuality, which found that most homosexual experimentation among males occurred precisely in those single-sex institutions—all-male schools, summer camps, Boy Scouts, the military, and prisons— that Hall believed would be palliatives against homosexuality.)

Of course, there were also strong supporters of women's education, such as the founders and first presidents of historically women's colleges, like Matthew Vassar and Milo Jewett (Vassar), Henry Durant (Wellesley), and L. Clark Seelye (Smith). Durant went as far as to argue that the real meaning of women's education is "revolt"— "against the slavery in which women are held by the customs of society—the broken health, the aimless lives, the subordinate position, the helpless dependence, the dishonesties and shams of so-called education."[5]

Women's physical weakness and helpless dependency were thus *consequences* of gender inequality, not their cause. The great British physician Henry Maudsley elaborated this more sociological explanation for women's difference in 1874:

> There are other reasons which go to make up the languid young-ladyhood of the American girl. Her childhood is denied the happy out-door sports of her brothers. There is a resolute shutting out of everything like a noisy romp; the active games and all happy, boisterous play, by field or roadside, are not *proper* to her! She is cased in a cramping dress, so heavy and inconvenient that no boy could wear it for a day without falling into gloomy views of life. All this martyrdom to propriety and fashion tells upon strength and symmetry, and the girl reaches womanhood a wreck. That she reaches it at all, under these suffering and bleached out conditions, is due to her superior elasticity to resist a method of education which would have killed off all the boys years before … There are abundant statistics to prove that hard study is the discipline and tonic most girls need to supplant the too great sentimentality and useless day dreams fostered by fashionable idleness, and provocative of "nerves," melancholy, and inanition generally, and, so far as these statistics can, that the women-graduates of these colleges make as healthy and happy wives and mothers as though they had never solved a mathematical problem, nor translated Aristotle.[6]

Official policies promoting co-education did not deter its male opponents. In 1900, the University of Rochester promised to open the door to women—if women could raise enough money to construct new dormitories and facilities. When they did—after Susan B. Anthony sold her life insurance policy to overcome the final monetary hurdle—and women tried to enter the classrooms, male students responded by stamping their feet, physically blocking classroom doors, and jeering at the women whenever they appeared on campus. The administration responded by physically segregating the women in a separate, but clearly less-than-equal, college of their own. The collegiate classroom that women had struggled so hard to enter did not exist so much to train them intellectually as to ensure social obedience to gender difference. They had entered another gendered classroom.

THE GENDERED CLASSROOM

The formal educational gendering process begins the moment we enter school and continues throughout our educational lives. In nursery schools and kindergarten classes, we often find the heavy blocks, trucks, airplanes, and carpentry tools in one area and the dolls and homemaking equipment in another area. Although they may be officially "open" to anyone for play, the areas are often sex-segregated by invisible but real boundaries. In the elementary school years, the informal play during out-of-school hours involves different sports, different rules, and different playground activities.

The nursery school where I taught in the late 1970s was divided into three zones. Indoors was a place for quiet play, and there were shelves of books, a small sandbox with cups and saucers, a quiet room, and a set of easels for painting. Immediately outside the building was the "near yard," which included two larger sandboxes with several larger pots and pans arrayed around them and an area marked off for foot games like hopscotch. Beyond this lay the "far yard," which included jungle gyms, a large, unenclosed sandbox, and other gross motor skill activities.

In the morning, the three-year-old girls would come into school quietly, place their coats neatly in their open locker, and walk slowly and uncertainly into the inside room. There they would look for a friend and sit quietly looking at books, talking, or playing at the interior sandbox while they adjusted to a new day at school. The boys would race in, throw their coats into their lockers (missing half the time), dash outside, grab a truck, and run to the far yard, shouting all the way.

All the boys, that is, except "Brad." Brad was a quiet and thoughtful three-year-old, kind and considerate, and one of the brightest students I ever taught—at any age! Each morning, Brad would walk in and head right for the easels, where he would spend his entire day happily painting. Some days he would go into full-scale production, producing painting after painting; on other days he would paint for a while and then stare dreamily outside at the trees.

When his parents saw me—the new male teacher—they were thrilled. "You *must* get Brad to go out to the far yard!" they pleaded with me, a look of terror in their eyes. "Please," Brad's mother repeated, softly. "Please."

One didn't need a PhD in elementary education to understand what was so terrifying to Brad's parents. The specter of homosexuality hovered in the air. Brad was not acting like the other boys, and his gender nonconformity was seen as a signal of his future sexual orientation. I tried to reassure his parents that Brad seemed genuinely happy painting and that he was very good at it, but they were not satisfied until I also promised that I would encourage Brad to play with trucks. They were certain that the nursery school could produce a masculine—and heterosexual—son. (Brad, I think, was hoping that they'd leave him alone and let him become an artist. As for me, I would occasionally come over to the easel where Brad was painting and ask if he wanted to come with me to the far yard. Invariably, he'd smile broadly and decline and return to his art.)

Although there are some signs of change, this nursery school experience is reproduced in every classroom in every town in America every day. Boys and girls learn—and teach each other—what are the appropriate behaviors and experiences for boys and girls and make sure that everyone acts according to plan. What's less visible are the ways the teachers and curriculum overtly and subtly reinforce not only gender difference, but also the inequalities that go along with and even produce that difference.

The classroom setting reproduces gender inequality. "From elementary school through higher education, female students receive less active instruction, both in the quantity and in the quality of teacher time and attention," note education professors Myra and David Sadker, summarizing the research in their important book *Failing at Fairness*. Many teachers perceive boys as being active, capable of expressing anger, quarrelsome, punitive, alibi-building, and exhibitionistic, and they perceive girls as being affectionate, obedient, responsive, and tenacious. When boys "put girls down," as they often do at that age, teachers (female usually) often say and do nothing to correct them, thus encouraging the boys' notion of superiority. Many teachers assume that girls are likely to "love" reading and "hate" mathematics and sciences, and they expect the opposite of boys.[7]

Teachers call on boys more often and spend more time with them. They ask boys more challenging questions than they do girls and wait longer for boys to answer. They urge boys to try harder, constantly telling boys that they can "do it." One study found that in all ten of the college classrooms observed, boys were more active, regardless of the gender of the teacher, though a female teacher increased girls' participation significantly. A report sponsored by the American Association of University Women summarized these studies when it concluded that whether "one is looking at preschool classrooms or university lecture halls…research spanning the past twenty years consistently reveals that males receive more teacher attention than do females." Part of the reason for this is that boys demand more attention, and part of the reason is that teachers also treat boys and girls differently. When the Sadkers were doing research for their book, they asked teachers why they paid more attention to the boys. The teachers told them things like: "Because boys need it more" and "Boys have trouble reading, writing, doing math. They can't even sit still."[8]

Here's a particularly evocative example from *Failing at Fairness*, a book that documents the myriad ways in which gender inequality permeates the classroom. One fifth-grade classroom the Sadkers observed was having a particularly noisy and rambunctious discussion about who was the best president in American history. "Just a minute," the teacher told the class. "There are too many of us here to all shout out at once. I want you to raise your hands, and then I'll call on you. If you shout out, I'll pick somebody else." This restored order for a moment. Then one boy enthusiastically called out:

STEPHEN: I think Lincoln was the best president. He held the country together during the war.
TEACHER: A lot of historians would agree with you.

> # OH?
> ## REALLY •
> Boys don't like girls who are "too smart."
>
> How many female readers have heard something like that? "Don't be too smart, you'll never find a husband!"
>
> This is just one of the ways that gender inequality creates the very differences we then believe are the cause of the inequality. But it turns out not to be true. Once, if a woman had a higher level of education than her husband, the odds were that the marriage would be more fragile, and divorce more likely. Not anymore. In a recent study, sociologists Christine Schwartz and Hongyun Han found that marriages in which the wife's educational level outstripped that of her husband had no increased risk of marital dissolution. (It's also true that the most stable marriages are the ones where the couple are relatively equal in their educational attainment— that is, stability no longer comes when his level is higher than hers.) Two pretty smart women, huh?
>
> *Source:* Christine Schwartz and Hongyun Han, "The Reversal of the Gender Gap in Education and Trends in Marital Dissolution" in *American Sociological Review*, 79(4), 2014, pp. 605–629.

MIKE (seeing that nothing happened to Stephen, calls out): I don't. Lincoln was okay, but my Dad liked Reagan. He always said Reagan was a great president.

DAVID (calling out): Reagan? Are you kidding?

TEACHER: Who do you think our best president was, Dave?

DAVID: FDR. He saved us from the Depression.

MAX (calling out): I don't think it's right to pick one best president. There were a lot of good ones.

TEACHER: That's interesting.

KIMBERLY (calling out): I don't think that presidents today are as good as the ones we used to have.

TEACHER: Okay, Kimberly. But you forgot the rule. You're supposed to raise your hand.[9]

Journalist Peggy Orenstein observed another junior high school class where boys "yelled out or snapped the fingers of their raised hands when they wanted to speak, [while the] girls seemed to recede from class proceedings." As one girl told her, "Boys never care if they're wrong."[10]

Here's an innovative way to try and correct these cultural biases. At one preschool in Stockholm, Sweden, named the "Egalia School" to proclaim its belief in equality, everything is organized to eliminate gender bias. Kids call each other "friends," not "boy" and "girl." No one uses gender pronouns like "his" or "her." Boys and girls play together; there is no gender segregation at all. Books focus on a wide range of subjects, but you won't find "Cinderella" or "Snow White" there—too sexist and heteronormative! "Society expects girls to be girlie, nice and pretty, and boys to be manly, rough and outgoing," explains one teacher. "Egalia gives them a fantastic opportunity to be whoever they want to be." The school doesn't deny anatomical differences—all the dolls are "correct"—but the educators insist that such differences "don't mean boys and girls have different interests and abilities. This is about democracy. About human equality."[11]

READ ALL ABOUT IT!

Schools are more than institutions in which we learn reading, writing, and 'rithmetic. They are factories of gender, and what they produce are gender-conforming boys and girls. From the curriculum to classroom configurations to the ways children interact with each other and with teachers, a central goal is to inculcate appropriate gender behavior from gendered children to appropriate gender identities. Think I used the word "gender" too often? Just think about how often you use it—or gendered language to talk about yourself and your friends. In two separate articles—"'Cool Boys,' 'Party Animals,' 'Squids' and 'Poofters'" and "Spice Girls, Nice Girls, Girlies and Tomboys"—sociologists Diane Reay and Wayne Martino respectively discuss the various languages that boys and girls use to police each other, to make sure that everyone does gender "right." How do you and your friends police gender behavior among your friends? What sorts of punishments do kids get if they "stray"?

OH? REALLY.

Everyone knows that boys are better at math. It's biological.

Except it turns out not to be true. Psychologist Janet Hyde found virtually no differences at all in a survey of over seven million American students. Perhaps all those reforms to encourage girls in math and science are actually succeeding. Or perhaps there really weren't such big differences to begin with. Here's what the distributions look like:

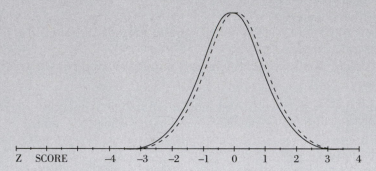

Figure 7.1a. Two normal distributions that are 0.15 standard deviations aparts (i.e., $d = 0.15$; this is the approximate magnitude of the gender difference in mathematics performance, averaging over all samples).

Source: Hyde, J; Fennema, E; Lamon, S. "Gender differences in mathematics performance: A meta-analysis." *Psychological Bulletin* Vol 107(2), Mar 1990, 139–155. Published by APA and reprinted with permission.

Maybe it's not the mean differences, but the differences at the extremes. In 2005, Lawrence Summers, then president of Harvard, speculated that it wasn't that *average* scores were all that different, but that the shape of the distributions was different, that males were overrepresented at both ends of the continuum—that is, there were more male math geniuses *and* more males at the extreme low end. That, he suggested, was why there were so many more male professors in math and science at the highest-prestige universities.

Except that turned out not to be true either. Using a massive data set drawn from eighty-six countries, Jonathan Kane and Janet Mertz found that this greater male variability is not present in some countries, meaning that, as Kane puts it, "it is reasonable to attribute difference in male performance primarily to country-specific social factors."

No Mars and Venus here. Just different cultures on planet Earth. In fact, we might even go further. Perhaps the differences we observe are not the *cause* of gender inequality, but the *result* of gender inequality. In a comparative study of several countries, boys had higher math scores in some countries, girls had higher scores in others, and in most cases boys' and girls' scores were virtually identical. What accounted for the difference? Those countries where girls did better in math also tended to be the countries that score higher on other measures of gender equality, like labor force participation, women in public office, and work–family balance policies.

Even in the United States, the gender differences in math performance are not nearly as great as the race or class differences. Look at the differences in math scores by class:

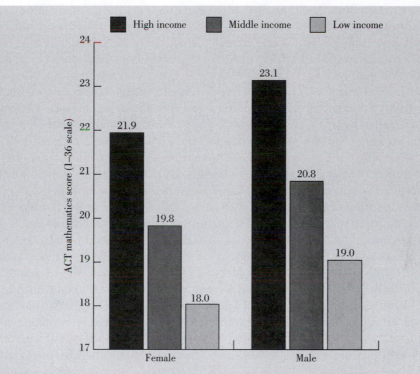

Figure 7.1b. Mathematics mean score, by gender and family income level, 2007.

Note: Low-income students reported an annual family income of less than $30,000, middle-income students reported an annual family income of $30,000 to $60,000, and high-income students reported an annual family income of more than $60,000.

Source: Unpublished data provided to the AAUW Education Foundation by the ACT Statistical Research Department. © The American Association of University Women.

Would anyone seriously argue that rich people are from Mars and poor people are from Venus? Of course not.

Sources: Janet Hyde, Sara Lindberg, Marcia Linn, Amy Ellis, and Caroline Williams, "Gender Similarities Characterize Math Performance" in *Science*, 321, July 25, 2008, pp. 494–495; Sara Lindberg, Janet Shibley Hyde, Jennifer Petersen, and Marcia Linn, "New Trends in Gender and Mathematics Performance: A Meta-Analysis" in *Psychological Bulletin*, November 2010, pp. 1123–1135; Jonathan Kane and Janet Mertz, "Debunking Myths About Gender and Mathematics Performance" in *Notices of the American Mathematical Society*, 59(1), January 2012, pp. 10–21.

The "chilly classroom climate" for girls also takes place within a sexually "hostile environment." In recent years, **sexual harassment** has become a significant problem in more than our workplaces; it's also a problem in our classrooms. In 1980, the nation's first survey of sexual harassment in schools, conducted by the Massachusetts State Department of Education, found widespread sexual harassment of girls. A 1986 Minnesota survey of predominantly white and middle-class juniors and seniors in vocational schools found that between one-third and three-fifths of the girls had experienced sexual harassment.

Lawsuits followed, and finally the issue began to get the attention it deserved. In 1991, nineteen-year-old Katy Lyle was awarded $15,000 to settle a lawsuit she brought against her Duluth, Minnesota, school district, because school officials failed to remove explicit graffiti about her from the walls of the boys' bathrooms, even after her parents complained several times. The next year, Tawnya Brawdy was awarded $20,000 from her Petaluma, California, junior high school, which had taken no action to stop boys from making obscene sounds and gestures about her breasts. (Tawnya had reached puberty early and had developed large breasts at a young age. The boys' behavior made her life so miserable that she could not eat, sleep, or function in class.) That same year, the U.S. Supreme Court unanimously sided with a young girl, Christine Franklin, in her case against the Gwinnett County, Georgia, school board, and awarded her $6 million in damages resulting from a violation of Title IX.

By the spring of the next year, 1993, almost half of all the sexual harassment cases then being investigated by the U.S. Department of Education's Office of Civil Rights involved elementary and secondary schools. And sexual harassment continues to plague our nation's schools. The Supreme Court found one school liable for the harassment of one girl by other students. In a landmark case (*Davis v. Monroe County Board of Education*), a mother sued the school board because her ten-year-old daughter suffered a constant "barrage of sexual harassment and abuse" from one of her classmates while her teachers and other school officials ignored it. According to a study commissioned by the American Association of University Women, nearly four-fifths of girls (78 percent) and over two-thirds of boys (68 percent) have been subjected to harassment (Figure 7.2).

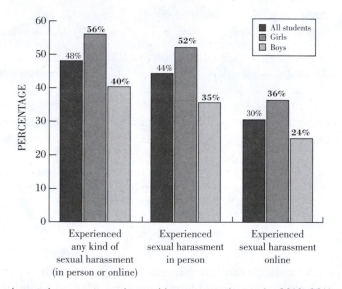

Figure 7.2. Students who experienced sexual harassment during the 2010–2011 school year, by gender.

Notes: Students were asked if they had experienced any of ten types of sexual harassment since the beginning of the school year. Bold numbers indicate statistically significant gender differences at the 95 percent level. Base = survey respondents (*n* = 1,965 students), 1,002 girls and 963 boys in grades 7–12.

Source: AAUW sexual harassment survey, May–June 2011. © The American Association of University Women.

In both cases, it's almost invariably other boys who are the perpetrators. As Bernice Sandler puts it:

> Sexual persecution starts at a very early age. In some elementary schools there is skirt flip-up day; in others girls refuse to wear clothes with elastic waistbands because the boys pull down their slacks and skirts. In junior high schools boys tape mirrors to the tops of their shoes so they can look up girls' dresses. Groups of boys in some high schools claim tables near the line where food is purchased. Whenever a female student walks by, they hold up a card with a number on it: one for an unattractive girl and ten for a superstar. In other schools there is "Grab a Piece of Ass Week" or lists circulate, such as "The Twenty Sluttiest Girls in School."[12]

WHAT ABOUT THE BOYS?

Given these dramatically divergent patterns, you might think that the systematic demolition of girls' self-esteem, the denigration of their abilities, and the demotion of their status would yield positive effects for young boys, that boys would rise as the girls declined. But that isn't what happens. In the elementary grades, boys are about four times more likely to be sent to child psychologists and far more likely to be diagnosed with dyslexia and attention deficit disorder than are girls. Beginning in elementary school and continuing throughout their schooling, boys receive poorer report cards; they are far more likely to repeat a grade. Nine times more boys than girls are diagnosed as hyperactive; boys represent 58 percent of those in special education classes for the mentally retarded, 71 percent of the learning disabled, and 80 percent of the emotionally disturbed. Nearly three-fourths of all school suspensions are of boys. By adolescence, boys are more likely to drop out, flunk out, and act out in class. Their self-esteem also drops during adolescence—not, admittedly, as much as girls' self-esteem, but it does drop.[13]

These data are often used to suggest that boys, not girls, are the new victims of significant gender discrimination in schools. After all, what happens to boys in schools? They have to sit quietly, take naps, raise their hands, be obedient—all of which does extraordinary violence to their "natural," testosterone-inspired, rambunctious playfulness. "Schools for the most part are run by women for girls. To take a high spirited second or third grade boy and expect him to behave like a girl in school is asking too much," comments Christina Hoff Sommers, author of *The War Against Boys*. The effect of education is "pathologizing boyhood." "On average, boys are physically more restless and more impulsive (than girls)," comments school consultant Michael Thompson. "We need to acknowledge boys' physical needs, and meet them." While we've been paying all this attention to girls' experiences—raising their self-esteem, enabling them to take science and math, deploring and preventing harassment and bullying—we've ignored the boys. "What about the boys?" asks the backlash chorus.[14]

Make no mistake: Boys' needs do merit our serious attention. We've already observed the consequences of ignoring them. But the classroom is hardly the feminizing environment that critics charged at the turn of the twentieth century as well as today. In my classroom, women students dress in flannel shirts, blue jeans and T-shirts, leather bomber jackets, and athletic shoes. They call each other "guys" constantly, even if the group is composed entirely of women. The classroom, like the workplace, is a public sphere institution, and when women enter the public sphere, they often have to dress and act "masculine" in order to be taken seriously as competent and capable. (I will detail this workplace process in chapter 9). A recent advertising campaign for Polo by Ralph Lauren children's clothing pictured young girls, aged about five or six, in Oxford button-down shirts, blazers, and neckties. Who is being feminized, and who is being masculinized?

As we've seen, there is little evidence that boys' aggression is biologically based. Rather, we understand that the negative consequences of boys' aggression are largely the social by-product of exaggerating otherwise healthy and pleasurable boisterous and rambunctious play. And it is exaggerated by boys so that they may better fit in with other boys; they overconform to the expectations of their peers. Instead of un-critically celebrating "boy culture," we might inquire instead into the experience of boys when they cease being boys themselves and begin to posture and parade their masculinity before the evaluative eyes of other boys.

At that moment we might find a psychological "disconnect," equivalent to that observed by Carol Gilligan with young girls. Gilligan and her associates described the way that assertive, confident, and proud young girls "lose their voices" when they hit adolescence. It is the first full-fledged confrontation with gender inequality that produces the growing gender gap in adolescence.[15] By contrast, boys become more con-fident, even beyond their abilities, just as girls grow less confident. Gender inequality means that just at the moment when girls lose their voice, boys *find* one—but it is the inauthentic voice of bravado, of constant posturing, of foolish risk taking and gratu-itous violence. According to psychologist William Pollack, boys learn that they are sup-posed to be in power and thus begin to act like it. "Although girls' voices have been disempowered, boys' voices are strident and full of bravado," he observes. "But their voices are disconnected from their genuine feelings." Thus, he argues, the way we bring boys up leads them to put on a "mask of masculinity," a posture, a front. They "ruffle in a manly pose," as the poet William Butler Yeats put it, "for all their timid heart."[16]

That girls "lose their voice" means that girls are more likely to undervalue their abilities, especially in the more traditionally "masculine" educational arenas such as math and science and the more traditionally masculine employment arenas such as medicine, the military, or architecture. Only the most able and most secure women take such courses or pursue those career paths. Thus their numbers tend to be few and their grades high. Boys, however, possessed of this false voice of bravado (and many facing strong family pressure to enter traditionally masculine arenas), are likely to *overvalue* their abilities, to remain in programs though they are less qualified and capable of succeeding. In one recent study, sociologist Shelley Correll compared thousands of eighth-graders in similar academic tracks and with identical grades and test scores. Boys were much more likely—remember, their scores and grades were identical—to say, "I have always done well in math" and "Mathematics is one of my best subjects" than were the girls. The boys were no better than the girls—they just thought they were.[17]

This difference, and not some putative discrimination against boys, is the reason why girls' mean test scores in math and science are now, on average, approaching those of boys. Too many boys who overvalue their abilities remain in difficult math and science courses longer than they should; they pull the boys' mean scores down. By contrast, few girls whose abilities and self-esteem are sufficient to enable them to "trespass" into a male domain skew female data upward.

A parallel process is at work in the humanities and social sciences. Girls' mean test scores in English and foreign languages, for example, also outpace boys' scores. But this is not because of "reverse discrimination," but rather because the boys bump up against the norms of masculinity. Boys regard English as a "feminine" subject. The research by Shelley Correll, for example, found that those same boys who had inflated their abilities in math suddenly rated themselves as worse than their female classmates in English and languages.[18]

Pioneering research in Australia by Wayne Martino and his colleagues found that boys are uninterested in English because of what an interest might say about their (inauthentic) masculine pose. "Reading is lame, sitting down and looking at words is pathetic," commented one boy. "Most guys who like English are faggots," commented another. The traditional liberal arts curriculum is seen as feminizing; as Catharine Stimpson recently put it sarcastically, "Real men don't speak French."[19]

Boys tend to hate English and foreign languages for the same reasons that girls love them. In English, boys observe, there are no hard-and-fast rules, but rather one expresses one's opinion about the topic, and everyone's opinion is equally valued. "The answer can be a variety of things, you're never really wrong," observed one boy. "It's not like maths and science where there is one set answer to everything." Another boy noted:

> I find English hard. It's because there are no set rules for reading texts…English isn't like maths where you have rules on how to do things and where there are right and wrong answers. In English you have to write down how you feel and that's what I don't like.

Compare this with the comments of girls in the same study:

> I feel motivated to study English because…you have freedom in English—unlike subjects such as maths and science—and your view isn't necessarily wrong. There is no definite right or wrong answer and you have the freedom to say what you feel is right without it being rejected as a wrong answer.[20]

It is not the school experience that "feminizes" boys, but rather the ideology of traditional masculinity that keeps boys from wanting to succeed. "The work you do here is girls' work," one boy commented to a researcher. "It's not real work." Added another, "When I go to my class and they [other boys] bunk off, they will say to me I'm a goody goody."

One English teacher at Central High School in St. Paul, Minnesota, says she sees this phenomenon all the time. "Boys don't want to look too smart and don't want to look like they're pleasing the teacher," she said. "Girls can negotiate the fine line between what peers want of them and excelling at school. Boys have a harder time balancing being socially accepted and academically focused." And sociologist Andrew Hacker notes that girls "are proving themselves better at being good students and scholars" than boys are. "It's not in the genes," he continues. "It's almost as if being a man and being a good student" are antithetical. Such comments echo the consistent findings of social scientists since James Coleman's pathbreaking 1961 study that identified the "hidden curriculum" among adolescents in which good-looking and athletic boys were consistently more highly rated by their peers than were good students.[21]

In one international study, researchers compared middle schoolers in twelve countries and found that girls reported themselves more engaged in school and that this engagement accounted for gender differences in academic performance. The more engaged the students, the better they did. But what accounts for this level of engagement by girls or boys' disengagement? Parental support and teacher support mattered a little, but the absence of peer support had an independent effect on school performance. The less peers thought doing well in school was important, the poorer students did—regardless of what their parents or teachers thought.[22]

In fact, such sentiments echo dire warnings from the turn of the twentieth century, when parents worried that the combination of co-education, female teachers, and increased mothering (and father absence) was turning hardy boys into a bunch of wimpy pantywaists. Then, as now, pundits worried that boyhood was being diluted in a feminizing sea, and groups sprang up to rescue and defend boyhood. It was at the turn of the twentieth century, for example, that collegiate sports were developed and the strenuous life was proclaimed by President Theodore Roosevelt. Boys' groups proliferated. One earnest reformer, Ernest Thompson Seton, was so concerned that modern life was turning "robust, manly, self-reliant boyhood into a lot of flat chested cigarette smokers of shaky nerves and doubtful vitality" that he founded the Boy Scouts as a sort of boys' liberation movement to enable boys to regain that hardy boyishness of the frontier.[23] And schools, too, had to be changed. Consider this diagnosis next to the comments of the boys in Martino's study (cited earlier):

> Literature is becoming emasculated by being written mainly for women and largely by women. The majority of men in this country, having been co-educated by women teachers, are unaware of this...I call it the sissification of literature and life. The point of view of the modern "important" novel like *Ulysses* is feminine in its preoccupation with the nastiness of sex.[24]

That was written in 1927!

Gender disparities—both numerical and experiential—are also evident on college campuses. Women now constitute the majority of students on college campuses, passing men in 1982, so today, 60 percent of all college students are female, and there are three women for every two men at the nation's community colleges. One reporter, obviously a terrible statistics student, tells us that if present trends continue, "the graduation line in 2068 will be all females." (That's like saying that if the enrollment of black students at Ole' Miss was one in 1964, twenty-four in 1968, and four hundred in 1988, by 1994 there would have been no white students there.) Women now outnumber men in the social and behavioral sciences by about three to one, and they've invaded such traditionally male bastions as engineering, where they now make up about 20 percent of all students, and biology and business, where the genders are virtually on par (figure 7.3).[25]

But the numbers cited by these critics just don't add up. For one thing, more *people* are going to college than ever before (see figure 7.4 on page 218). In 1960, 54 percent of boys and 38 percent of girls went directly to college; today the numbers are

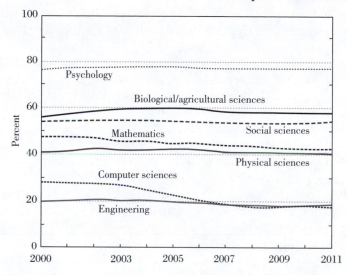

Figure 7.3. Women's share of science and engineering bachelor's degrees, by field: 2000–2011.

Note: Physical sciences include Earth, atmospheric, and ocean sciences.

Sources: National Center for Education Statistics, Integrated Postsecondary Education Data System, Completions Survey; and National Science Foundation, National Center for Science and Engineering Statistics, WebCASPAR database, http://webcaspar.nsf.gov. See appendix table 2–18.

64 percent of boys and 70 percent of girls. Here is the always reliable sociologist Joel Best (who has made a career out of explaining how to read statistics) on this manufactured crisis:

> Does this mean that males have stopped going to college? No. Overall, the number of males enrolled in college rose by 33 percent from 1970 to 2000. However, female enrollments rose much faster—143 percent during the same period. Well, does it mean that a smaller proportion of males are attending college? Again, no—male enrollments outstripped population growth (the number of resident males in the U.S. population 15–24 increased only about 14 percent during those years).[26]

And while some college presidents fret that to increase male enrollments they'll be forced to lower standards (which is, incidentally, exactly the opposite of what they worried about twenty-five years ago when they all went co-educational), no one seems to find gender disparities going the other way all that upsetting. Many of the top colleges and universities tilt toward higher male enrollments—like Princeton (53 percent), Columbia (53 percent), and MIT (55 percent). Nor does anyone seem driven to distraction about the gender disparities in nursing, social work, or education, traditionally far lower-paid occupations than those professions where men still predominate (engineering and computer sciences). "The idea that girls could be ahead is so shocking that they think it must be a crisis for boys," says Sara Mead, author of a report for Education Sector, a policy research center. "I'm troubled by this tone of crisis. Even if you control for the field they're

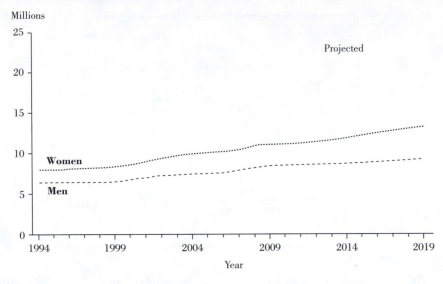

Figure 7.4. Actual and projected numbers for enrollment in all degree-granting institutions, by sex: fall 1994 through fall 2019.

Note: Some data have been revised from previously published figures. Mean absolute percentage errors of selected education statistics can be found in table A-2, appendix A.

Source: U.S. Department of Education, National Center for Education Statistics, Integrated Postsecondary Education Data System, "Fall Enrollment Survey" (IPEDS-EF 94–99), and Spring 2001 through Spring 2008; and Enrollment in Degree-Granting Institutions Model, 1973–2008. http://nces.ed.gov/pubs2011/2011017.pdf. (This figure was prepared April 2010.)

in, boys right out of college make more money than girls, so at the end of the day, is it grades and honors that matter, or something else the boys may be doing?"[27]

Much of the great gender difference we hear touted is actually what sociologist Cynthia Fuchs Epstein calls a "**deceptive distinction**," a difference that appears to be about gender but is actually about something else—in this case, class or race. The shortage of male college students is also actually a shortage of *nonwhite* males. The gender gap between college-age white males and white females is rather small. But only 36 percent of low-income black college students are male, and only 39 percent of low-income Hispanic students are male. (See table 7.1.)

Those who suggest that feminist-inspired reforms have been to the detriment of boys seem to believe that gender relations are a zero-sum game and that if girls and women gain, boys and men lose. But the reforms that have been initiated to benefit girls in class—individualized instruction, attention to different learning pathways, new initiatives, classroom configurations, teacher training, and more collaborative team-building efforts—have also been to the benefit of boys as well, as such methods also target boys' specific experiences. Perhaps instead of fretting about the numbers alone, we ought to pay attention to the *effect* of this gender imbalance. A UCLA higher education professor, Linda Sax, says such a discussion should address what effect, if any, the gender composition of a college has on men and women. To find out, she examined data from more than seventeen thousand students at 204 four-year colleges. Preliminary

Table 7.1. How Male Representation Breaks Down by Race and Income

About 9.9 million women (57.4%) and 7.4 million men (42.6%) were enrolled in colleges eligible for federal student aid in 2003–2004. The percentage of undergrads (18–24) who are male, by race and income:

	Low-income (less than $30,000)		Middle-income ($30,000 to $69,999)		Upper-income ($70,000 or more)	
	1995–1996	2003–2004	1995–1996	2003–2004	1995–1996	2003–2004
White	46	42	50	43	52	49
Black	32	36	48	42	41	48
Hispanic	43	39	46	42	50	49
Asian	53	47	57	50	52	51
All	44	40	50	44	51	49

Source: U.S. Department of Education, National Center for Education Statistics, National Postsecondary Student Aid Studies, 1995–1996, 1999–2000, 2003–2004.
Income ranges adjusted for inflation to 1995–1996 dollars.
Source: ACE Center for Policy Analysis.

results show that on campuses that were predominantly female, both men and women got higher grades. Predominantly female campuses also led to a "significant increase" in men's commitment to promoting racial understanding and led males to more liberal views on abortion, homosexuality, and other social issues, her research found.[28]

And the efforts to make the classroom safer and more hospitable to girls have also redounded to boys' benefit. Take, for example, classroom decorum. In 1940, the top disciplinary problems identified by high school teachers were (in order): talking out of turn, chewing gum, making noise, running in the hall, cutting in line, committing dress code violations, and littering. In 2010, the top problems were: bullying, gang activities, abuse of teachers other than verbal, verbal abuse of teachers, sexual harassment, cult or extremist group activities, and, last, student racial/ethnic tensions.[29] Challenging stereotypes, decreasing tolerance for school violence, and decreasing bullying enable both boys and girls to feel safer at school. Those who would simply throw up their hands in resignation and sigh that "boys will be boys" would have you believe that nothing can or should be done to make those classrooms safer. To my mind, those four words, "boys will be boys," may be the most depressing words in educational policy circles today.[30]

The "battle of the sexes" is not a zero-sum game—whether it is played out in our schools, our workplaces, or our bedrooms. Both women *and* men, girls *and* boys will benefit from real gender equality in the schools. "Every step in the advancement of woman has benefited our own sex no less than it has elevated her" was how an editorial in the Amherst College campus newspaper, the *Amherst Student*, put it when the school first debated co-education at the turn of the twentieth century.[31]

THE GENDER POLICE

Perhaps the central mechanism that maintains gender inequality in schools is the way we see educational success in terms of gender conformity. Consistently, when girls are asked questions about school success, they see high achievement, ambition, and competence as ungendered—that is, as not especially related to either masculinity or femininity. And just as consistently, boys see any connection to school as "feminine." To be successful in school is to be seen as not acting like a real boy. And anyone who does that risks a lot—losing self-esteem, losing one's friends, being targeted by bullies. It's through peer culture that students learn appropriate gender behavior. Peers establish the rules and enforce them—constantly, relentlessly, and mercilessly.

Just about every student reading this book knows that the most common put-down in middle school and high school in America today is, "That's so gay." And every student reading this book knows that such a statement has less to do with presumed sexual orientation and more to do with performance of gender conformity. But don't believe me. Here is Dave, explaining how he "knows" if a guy is gay: "If they show any sign of weakness or compassion, then other people jump to conclusions and bring them down. So really it's a survival of the fittest. It's not very good to be sensitive. If you have no feeling or compassion or anything like that, you will survive." Or listen to the words of one of my favorite gender theorists in the United States today, Eminem. When asked in 2001 why he was always rapping about "faggots," Eminem replied that calling someone a "faggot" is not a slur on his sexuality, but rather on his gender. "The lowest degrading thing that you can say to a man...is to call him a faggot and try to take away his manhood. Call him a sissy. Call him a punk. 'Faggot' to me doesn't mean gay people. 'Faggot' just means taking away your manhood."[32]

The fear of being tainted with homosexuality—the fear of emasculation—has morphed into a generic put-down. These days, "That's so gay" has far less to do with aspersions of homosexuality and far more to do with "**gender policing**"—making sure that no one contravenes the rules of masculinity.

High schools have become far more than academic testing grounds; they're the central terrain on which gender identity is tested and demonstrated. And unlike the standardized tests for reading and arithmetic, the tests of adequate and appropriate gender performance are administered and graded by your peers, by grading criteria known only to them. Bullying has become a national problem in high schools, in part because of the relentlessness and the severity of the torments. Verbal teasing and physical bullying exist along a continuum stretching from hurtful language through shoving and hitting to criminal assault and school shootings. Harmful teasing and bullying happen to more than one million schoolchildren a year.

In one study of middle and high school students in Midwestern towns, 88 percent reported having observed bullying, and 77 percent reported being a victim of bullying at some point during their school years. In another, 70 percent had been sexually harassed by their peers, 40 percent had experienced dating physical violence, 66 percent had been victimized by emotional abuse in a dating relationship, and 54 percent had been bullied. Another national survey of 15,686 students in grades six to ten published in the *Journal of the American Medical Association* (*JAMA*) found that 29.9 percent reported frequent involvement with bullying—13 percent as bully, 10.9 percent as victim, and 6 percent as both. One-quarter of kids in primary school, grades four to six, admitted to bullying another student with some regularity in the three months before the survey. And yet another survey found that during one two-week period at two Los Angeles middle schools, nearly half the 192 kids interviewed reported being bullied at least once. More than that said they had seen others targeted.[33]

Many middle and high school students are afraid to go to school; they fear locker rooms, hallways, bathrooms, lunch rooms, and playgrounds, and some fear even their classrooms. They fear being targeted or bullied in hostile high school hallways. Among young people aged twelve to twenty-four, three-tenths report that violence has increased in their schools in the past year, and nearly two-fifths have worried that a classmate was potentially violent. More than half of all teens know somebody who has brought a weapon to school. And nearly two-thirds (63 percent) of parents believe a school shooting is somewhat or very likely to occur in their communities.[34]

If bullying creates hostile high school hallways, those homosocial preserves within the school can be even more terrifying. Clubs, sports teams, and even the school band are plagued by increasingly dangerous and harmful incidents of **hazing**. There were over one hundred hazing-related deaths on high school and college campuses between 1995 and 2005. A national survey of high school students found that hazing is ubiquitous. Nearly half (48 percent) of all students who belonged to a group reported being subjected to hazing. Forty-three percent were subjected to humiliating activities, and fully 30 percent performed possibly illegal acts as part of their initiation. Hazing was so universal that there were virtually no groups that were safe. One-fourth of all students involved in church groups were subjected to hazing. Substance abuse in hazing is prevalent in high school (23 percent) and increases in college, where over half of all hazing activities (51 percent) involve substance abuse.

Most of the kids who are targeted cope; they're resilient enough or have enough emotional resources to survive reasonably intact. Many try valiantly, and often vainly, to fit in, to conform to these impossible standards that others set for them. Some carry psychological or even physical scars for the rest of their lives. Some withdraw or become depressed, alienated, or despondent. Some self-medicate with drugs or alcohol. And a few explode. As every adolescent knows, "doing a Columbine" means exploding in a murderous rage—and taking as many classmates and teachers as you can with you.

Between 1992 and 2006, there were twenty-nine cases of random school violence in which a young boy (or boys) opened fire on classmates.[35] All twenty-nine were committed by boys. Contrary to many stereotypes, all but one of those cases took place in a rural or suburban school—not an inner-city school. And all but two of the shooters were white. Yet we seem to have missed this in all the discussion about these school shootings. We continue to call the problem "teen violence," "youth violence," "gang violence," "suburban violence," "violence in the schools." Just who do we think is doing it—girls? Imagine if the shooters in schools in Littleton, Colorado; Pearl, Mississippi; Paducah, Kentucky; Springfield, Oregon; and Jonesboro, Arkansas, were instead black girls from poor families who lived in New Haven, Newark, Detroit, Compton, or South Boston. *Then* we'd notice race and class and gender! We'd likely hear about the culture of poverty, life in the inner city, and racial violence. Someone, I'd bet, would blame feminism for encouraging girls to become violent in vain imitation of boys.[36] Yet the obvious fact that these school killers were all middle-class white boys seems to have escaped almost everyone's notice.

More startling, though, is not that they were overwhelmingly middle-class white boys but that so many also had the same story. Virtually every single one of the shooters had a story about being gay-baited, bullied, and harassed—not every now and then, but constantly, daily. Why? It was *not* because they were gay (at least there is no evidence to suggest that any of them were gay), but rather because they were *different* from the other boys—shy, bookish, honor students, artistic, musical, theatrical, nonathletic, "geekish," or weird. It was because they were unathletic, overweight or underweight, or wore glasses.

Take Luke Woodham, a bookish, overweight sixteen-year-old in Pearl, Mississippi. An honor student, he was part of a little group that studied Latin and read Nietzsche. Students teased him constantly for being overweight and a nerd, taunted him as "gay" or "fag." Even his mother called him fat, stupid, and lazy. Other boys bullied him routinely, and, according to one fellow student, he "never fought back when other boys called him names." On October 1, 1997, Woodham stabbed his mother to death in her bed before he left for school. He then drove her car to school, carrying a rifle under his coat. He opened fire in the school's common area, killing two students and wounding seven others. After being subdued, he told the assistant principal, "The world has wronged me." Later, in a psychiatric interview, he said, "I am not insane. I am angry... I am not spoiled or lazy; for murder is not weak and slow-witted; murder is gutsy and daring. I killed because people like me are mistreated every day. I am malicious because I am miserable."

Or recall Michael Carneal, a fourteen-year-old freshman at Heath High School in Paducah, Kentucky. Shy and skinny, Carneal was barely five feet tall and weighed about 110 pounds. He wore thick glasses and played in the high school band. He felt alienated, pushed around, picked on. Boys stole his lunch and constantly teased him. In middle school, someone pulled down his pants in front of his classmates. He was so sensitive and afraid that others would see him naked that he covered the air vents in the bathroom and was devastated when students called him a "faggot" and the school gossip sheet labeled him as "gay." On Thanksgiving Day, 1997, he stole two shotguns, two semiautomatic rifles, a pistol, and seven hundred rounds of ammunition and, after a weekend of showing them off to his classmates, brought them to school hoping that they would bring him some instant recognition. "I just wanted the guys to think I was cool," he said. When the cool guys ignored him, he opened fire on a morning prayer circle, killing three classmates and wounding five others. Now serving a life sentence in prison, Carneal told psychiatrists weighing his sanity, "People respect me now."[37]

At Columbine High School, the site of the nation's most infamous school shooting, this connection was not lost on Evan Todd, a 255-pound defensive lineman on the Columbine football team, an exemplar of the jock culture that Dylan Klebold and Eric Harris found to be such an interminable torment. "Columbine is a clean, good place, except for those rejects," Todd said. "Sure we teased them. But what do you expect with kids who come to school with weird hairdos and horns on their hats? It's not just jocks; the whole school's disgusted with them. They're a bunch of homos... If you want to get rid of someone, usually you tease 'em. So the whole school would call them homos." Ben Oakley, a soccer player, agreed. "Nobody liked them," he said, "the majority of them were gay. So everyone would make fun of them." Athletes taunted Klebold and Harris and would throw rocks and bottles at them from moving cars. The school newspaper had recently published a rumor that Harris and Klebold were lovers.[38]

Actually, both boys sailed under the radar. Harris's parents were a retired army officer and a caterer, decent, well-intentioned people. Klebold's father was a geophysicist who had recently moved into the mortgage services business, and Klebold's mother worked in job placement for the disabled. Harris had been rejected by several colleges; Klebold was due to enroll at Arizona in the fall. But the jock culture was relentless. "Every time someone slammed them against a locker and threw a bottle at them, I think they'd go back to Eric or Dylan's house and plot a little more—at first as a goof, but more and more seriously over time," said one friend.[39]

The rest is now tragically familiar. Harris and Klebold brought a variety of weapons to their high school and proceeded to walk through the school, shooting whomever they could find. Students were terrified and tried to hide. Many students who could not hide begged for their lives. The entire school was held under siege until the police secured the building. In all, twenty-three students and faculty were injured, and fifteen died, including one teacher and the perpetrators.

Of course, these explosions are rare; most bullying victims manage to survive reasonably intact. But the fears of being targeted, the fears that others will shun you because of your stepping outside the boundaries of "appropriate" gender behavior, are pervasive. Gender conformity is demanded and extracted through such fear; it is often what keeps us in line.

THE SCHOOL AS GENDERED WORKPLACE

Just as historically women and girls were excluded from the classroom as students, so, too, were women excluded from the profession of teaching. Remember Ichabod Crane in Washington Irving's "The Legend of Sleepy Hollow"? In the eighteenth and nineteenth centuries, teaching had been seen as a respectable profession for a man. But the mid- to late-nineteenth-century gender ideology of the "separation of spheres" meant that women were pushed out of other arenas of work, and they soon began to see elementary education as a way they could fulfill both their career aspirations and their domestic functions of maternal nurturance.

This coincided conveniently with the expansion of public elementary school education, and especially the age segregation of students. (Remember that from the sixteenth to the eighteenth centuries, the educational norm was the one-room schoolhouse in which all ages were schooled together.) By segregating students into age categories, women's specific appropriateness with the younger students became apparent. Besides, administrators could pay these women teachers much lower salaries than they paid men. As a result, elementary education became "feminized." This meant that the occupational prestige and salaries of teachers dropped, discouraging men from entering the field and ensuring that it would become even more populated by women. Teaching was "women's work." But not, of course, school administration, which has remained largely a masculine arena. Thus the school came to resemble every other social institution in American society (table 7.2).

The frightful consequences were much debated at the start of the twentieth century. Some warned of the "invasion" of women teachers as if it were the "Invasion of the Boy Snatchers." One of the founders of American psychology, J. McKeen Cattell, worried about this "vast horde of female teachers" to whom boys were exposed. This had serious consequences; a boy taught by a woman, one admiral believed, would "render violence to nature," causing "a feminized manhood, emotional, illogical, noncombative." Another worried that "the boy in America is not being brought up to punch another boy's head or to stand having his own punched in a healthy and proper manner."[40]

In the second half of the twentieth century, women still held most of the primary education positions and virtually all positions in prekindergarten and special education. In 1994, 74 percent of all public and private school teachers were women. The number of women teachers decreases as students progress through the educational ranks. Most male teachers end up in secondary and postsecondary educational positions, whereas most female teachers end up in elementary grades.[41]

The sex composition of the labor force is related to its salary structure. It is virtually axiomatic that the greater the proportion of women in the field, the lower the salary. Within the educational field, women continue to earn less money than men doing the same jobs. The average female prekindergarten teacher in 1980 earned $8,390, whereas her male counterpart earned $14,912. (Data since then are consistent.) Ninety-eight percent of all prekindergarten teachers are women. As one progresses through the educational system the salary discrepancies become even more pronounced, in part because raises are based on years of experience, and women take more time off for childbearing.

Table 7.2. The Gender of Teaching

	Number (thousands)	Percentage of women
Preschool and kindergarten	695	98
Elementary and middle school	3,038	81
Secondary school	1,063	57
Postsecondary	1,313	50
Special education	377	80
Other teachers and instructors	753	64

Source: Current Population Survey, 2013, http://www.bls.gov/cps/cpsaat11.pdf.

OH? REALLY •

The "shortage" of male teachers is a major reason that boys are not succeeding in school; boys need a good male role model.

Actually, it's a myth. In a serious empirical examination of whether the sex of the teacher makes any difference at all, Martin Neuebauer and his colleagues used a large-scale data set and found virtually no evidence of a benefit from having a same-sex teacher. Other factors—like resources, class size, teacher preparation, and peer effects—are far more important, it turns out. The sex of the teacher is far less important than how the teacher teaches and with what sorts of resources and support.

Source: Martin Neuebauer, Marcel Helbig, and Andreas Landmann, "Unmasking the Myth of the Same-Sex Teacher Advantage" in *European Sociolgical Review*, October 2011, pp. 669–689.

Change has been more evident in higher education. A study in 1975 found that eight-tenths of all college teachers were men; by 1989 about one-third of all college teachers were women. But the implications of such evidence are not necessarily that gender equity is even close to having been achieved. When ranked by quality of school, women made up less than 10 percent of the faculty at high-prestige colleges, but nearly 25 percent at community colleges. More than two-thirds of women teach at two- and four-year colleges; men are equally divided between research universities and all other institutions. And the "uneven distribution of the sexes within academia," noted by sociologist Martin Trow in 1975, continues. Men continue to dominate in the sciences, where teaching loads are lower and the number of research and teaching assistants is highest. For example, women make up 45 percent of all lecturers, 35 percent of all assistant professors, 25 percent of all associate professors, and about 10 percent of all professors in the sciences and engineering. By contrast, women dominate in the semi-professions (nursing, social work, education) and those fields that require significant classroom contact, like languages.[42]

And that's not all. The slight trickling down of salary increases among college teachers has also been soaked up mainly by men. Between 1970 and 1980, female salaries increased 66 percent; men's salaries increased 70 percent. In 1970, women were making 84 percent of men's salaries; but in 1980, they were making only 70 percent. Today, women at all ranks receive lower salaries than do men at the same rank, in the same field, in the same department.

Women also dominate the ranks of the most populous arena of college teaching—adjunct lecturers and instructors. Part-time instructors, victims of both an

OH? REALLY.

Knowledge is knowledge. It doesn't matter whether the professor is male or female. What matters is that he or she can communicate effectively.

At least that's what most of us think. But it turns out that the gender of the professor matters in our assessments. A lot.

Benjamin Schmidt, a history professor at Northeastern University, built some interactive charts by analyzing the adjectives used by students in reviews on the Rate My Professor website. What interested Professor Schmidt was the way that students evaluated how smart the professor was: the more lofty the adjective—smart, brilliant, genius—the more the gender divide grew between female and male teachers. Each step was "more strongly gendered male than the previous one was," he said.

Far more male teachers were described with adjectives like "awesome," "a star," or "best professor ever," while more women were described with adjectives like "disorganized," "helpful," "annoying," or "playing favorites." (There was no gender difference with adjectives like "easy," "lazy," or "inspiring.") One of the largest differences was with the word "funny"—it seems that many students think their male professors are hilarious and their female professors have no sense of humor.

Go ahead, try it yourself. Go to http://benschmidt.org/profGender.

Type in some adjectives and watch the chart change.

Source: Claire Cain Miller, "Is the Professor Bossy or Brilliant? Much Depends on Gender" in *New York Times*, February 6, 2015, available at http://nyti.ms/1zgUOkg.

educational glut and covert gender discrimination, currently teach about one-half of all college classes, yet they are paid by the course, even if hired on yearly contracts, with neither health nor retirement benefits, and with paltry salaries. Well over half of them are women. Men are dramatically overrepresented at the top of the educational pyramid. In 1972, fewer than 3 percent of all top-level college and university administrators were women, and the typical relationship held that the more women administrators, the lower the prestige of the school. (This was modified, but only slightly, at the historically all-women colleges.) Only in the late 1990s, as women assumed the presidencies at Duke, the University of Pennsylvania, Princeton, Harvard, Yale, and SUNY at Stony Brook—as well as the presidencies at historically women's colleges like Vassar, Smith, Wellesley, and Bryn Mawr—did this equation begin to break down.

One reason for this disparity, of course, is that just like in all other workplaces, the efforts to balance work and family fall disproportionately on women's shoulders. At all ranks, and in all types of educational institutions, female professors and teachers with children spend much more time on family life (child care, care for aging parents and relatives, housework) than do their male counterparts.[43]

This disparity might help explain why so few women have risen to the ranks of the very top positions in science and engineering at the most prestigious schools (table 7.3). In January 2005, Lawrence Summers, then president of Harvard, set off a controversy by suggesting that women are simply not biologically suited to put in the eighty-hour work week required of these top-flight scientists. President Summers was soon enlightened by scores of female scientists who explained that working eighty-hour weeks makes having a family virtually impossible—unless one has someone else who will do it.

Just do the math. Let's assume you sleep seven hours a night (one hour less than you should). And let's say it takes you half an hour, door to door, to get to work every day. And let's assume that you spend two and a half hours a day getting showered and dressed, preparing and eating all your meals, and exercising. And let's just say that once a week you have a "date" with your spouse and have dinner, see a movie, and maybe even make love (total five hours). That accounts for 78.5 hours. Add that to your eighty-hour work week, and you've accounted for 158.5 hours—out of a 168-hour week. That leaves you less than ten hours—about an hour and a half a day for reading, relaxing, watching television, doing housework, and spending time with your family. In fact, the only sensible response to Summers's claim is to ask not what *women* can have such a life, but rather what rational human being could possibly want to live such an

Table 7.3. Women in Science and Mathematics

	Assistant professor	Associate professor	Full professor	All ranks
Computer and information	25%	17%	12%	17%
Physics	30%	25%	13%	22%
Biology	43%	31%	23%	37%
Mathematics	32%	28%	17%	26%

Note: Figures are for 2010.

Source: National Science Foundation report, "Women, Minorities, and Persons with Disabilities in Science and Engineering: 2013," http://www.nsf.gov/statistics/wmpd/2013/pdf/nsf13304_full.pdf, p. 204.

unbalanced life. Although we often imagine education to be a more sedentary and relaxed workplace, balancing work and family remains an obstacle to women's advancement in education—just as it does in every other workplace.

ARE SINGLE-SEX SCHOOLS THE ANSWER?

One might think that, after so many years of educational reform, and especially attention to the differences between girls and boys, things would be getting better. But the National Assessment of Educational Progress found that the gender differences for thirteen-year-olds actually increased in all the sciences except biology, as boys' skills improved and girls' skills declined. One educator sadly concluded that it is still true today that "co-educational schools are male-dominated and male-controlled institutions."[44]

Simple enumeration of equality may not be the answer. One teacher told journalist Peggy Orenstein that after learning that teachers paid more attention to boys than to girls, she explained to the class that henceforth she was going to call on both sexes exactly equally and that to make sure she did, she would hold the attendance roster in her hand. What happened next surprised her. "After two days the boys blew up," she told Orenstein. "They started complaining and saying that I was calling on the girls more than them. I showed them it wasn't true and they had to back down. I kept on doing it, but for the boys, equality was hard to get used to; they perceived it as a big loss."[45]

(Of course, equality is virtually always seen as a loss by the privileged group. If a teacher gives exactly equal time to heterosexuality and to homosexuality, to people of color and to white people, to women and to men, he or she is invariably going to be criticized as being biased in favor of the minority group. When one is used to being the center of attention all the time, being out of the limelight for a moment or even an hour can feel like complete rejection.)

So what is the answer? A return to single-sex schools? Some educators have thought so. In the early 1970s, as virtually all previously all-male colleges and many previously all-female colleges became co-educational, several studies indicated that single-sex colleges still held significant benefits. A study by Elizabeth Tidball in 1973 looked at the educational backgrounds of women listed in *Who's Who of American Women* and concluded that women's colleges with large numbers of women faculty provided the most beneficial environment for educating women.[46]

Although it is true that most of the women listed in *Who's Who* from the 1960s and before had gone to Vassar, Radcliffe, Bryn Mawr, Smith, and the other Seven Sisters colleges, Tidball's study had several serious flaws. First, her data came from the 1960s, before any formerly all-male Ivy League and other prestigious all-male schools were opened to women, and the actual number of women in the study was so small as to defy efforts at generalization. Second, there were far more women's colleges at the time—nearly three hundred in 1960, compared with just eighty-four in 1990. Third, many of the women listed in *Who's Who* were there because of the accomplishments of their fathers or their husbands; that is, they were not accomplished in their own right, but rather only in their connection to a man—which couldn't have been the result of attending an all-women's college. (For example, until the 1980s, most women who were in the U.S. Senate or House of Representatives or who were governors of states were the daughters or widows of men who had held those offices.)[47]

Perhaps the most glaring error in the Tidball research was that she assumed that it was attendance at a single-sex college that led to wealth and fame. However, most of the women who attended such prestigious colleges were *already* wealthy and had likely gone to single-sex boarding schools (or at least private preparatory schools). What Tidball had inadvertently measured was not the effect of single-sex schools on women's achievement, but rather the correlation between social class and attendance at all-female colleges. Here was a reported gender difference that turned out not to be a gender difference at all. Social class turned out to be the far better predictor of women's achievement than whether their college was single-sex or co-educational. Subsequent research found that co-educational colleges produced a higher percentage of women earning bachelor's degrees in the sciences, engineering, and mathematics.[48]

There was, additionally, some evidence that men's achievement was improved by attending a single-sex college. Again, many of these supposed gains in achievement vanished when social class and boys' secondary school experiences were added to the equation. In fact, when one discusses gender equality, the outcome of attending an all-male college, according to sociologist David Riesman, is "usually unfortunate. Stag undergraduate institutions are prone to a kind of excess." Although Jencks and Riesman "do not find the arguments against women's colleges as persuasive as the arguments against men's colleges," they conclude:

> The all-male college would be relatively easy to defend if it emerged from a world in which women were established as fully equal to men. But it does not. It is therefore likely to be a witting or unwitting device for preserving tacit assumptions of male superiority—assumptions for which women must eventually pay. So, indeed, must men...[who] pay a price for arrogance vis-à-vis women. Since they almost always commit a part of their lives into a woman's hands anyway, their tendency to crush these women means crushing a part of themselves. This may not hurt them as much as it hurts the woman involved, but it does cost something. Thus while we are not against segregation of the sexes under all circumstances, we are against it when it helps preserve sexual arrogance.[49]

In short, what women often learn at all-women's colleges is that they can do anything that men can do. By contrast, what men learn is that women cannot do what men do. In this way, women's colleges may constitute a challenge to gender inequality, whereas men's colleges reproduce that inequality.

Consider an analogy with race here. One might justify the continued existence of historically all-black colleges on the grounds that such schools challenge racist ideas that black students cannot achieve academically and provide a place where black students are free of everyday racism and thus free to become serious students. But one would have a more difficult time justifying maintaining an all-white college, which would, by its existence, reproduce racist inequality. Such a place would be more like "David Duke University" than Duke University. Returning to gender, as psychologist Carol Tavris concludes, "there is a legitimate place for all-women's schools if they give young women a stronger shot at achieving self-confidence, intellectual security, and professional competence in the workplace." On the other hand, because co-education is based "on the premise that there are few genuine differences between men and women, and that people should be educated as individuals, rather than as members of a gender," the question is "not whether to become co-educational, but rather when and how to undertake the process."[50]

Single-sex education for women often perpetuates detrimental attitudes and stereotypes about women, such as "by nature or situation girls and young women cannot become successful or learn well in co-educational institutions."[51] Even when supported by feminist women, the idea that women cannot compete equally with men in the same arena, that they need "special" treatment, signals an abandonment of hope, the inability or unwillingness to make the creation of equal and safe schools a national priority. "Since we cannot do that," we seem to be telling girls, "we'll do the next best thing—separate you from those nasty boys who will only make your lives a living hell."[52]

In some cases, making one's life a living hell was sort of the pedagogical point. Virginia Military Institute and the Citadel, both state-supported military-style institutions, fought women's entry because, they claimed, their "adversative" educational methodology—cadets are regimented and uniformed, heads are shaved, privacy is entirely removed, and stress is intentionally induced by incessant drilling, merciless harassment, and rigid discipline—is effective only for males. Women, the schools claimed, are "not capable of the ferocity requisite to make the program work." They are "physically weaker...more emotional, and cannot take stress as well as men." If admitted, VMI averred, female cadets would "break down crying" and suffer "psychological trauma" from the rigors of the system.[53] Whereas males "tend to need an environment of adversativeness or ritual combat in which the teacher is a disciplinarian and a worthy competitor," females "tend to thrive in a cooperative atmosphere in which the teacher is emotionally connected with the students," was the way the Citadel's lawyers put it.[54]

The Citadel also argued that women's entry would destroy the mystical bonding experience among the male cadets. One of the Citadel's expert witnesses, Major General Josiah Bunting III (a VMI graduate who became superintendent at VMI), suggested that women would be "a toxic kind of virus" that would destroy the Citadel. "Adolescent males benefit from being able to focus exclusively on the task at hand, without the intrusion of any sexual tension," he claimed.[55]

Instead of admitting women, VMI and the Citadel proposed funding women's "leadership" training at nearby private, all-female colleges. Such separate programs for men and women were not to be "**separate but equal**"—the fiction maintained by segregated schools to maintain segregation, which was ruled unconstitutional in 1954—but, as VMI protested, "distinct but superior," because educational methodologies would be tuned to the needs of males and females, respectively. The Supreme Court saw through this charade and overwhelmingly determined that these women's programs would be but a "pale shadow" of VMI; women were admitted in 1997.

In reality, the "rigors" of the adversative system are attractive to only a small number of men to begin with and probably to an even smaller number of women. In autumn 2002, forty women cadets enrolled at VMI. There has also been an increase in applications from men.

Such proposals to maintain sex segregation in education also seem to be based on faulty understandings of the differences between women and men, the belief in an unbridgeable chasm between "them" and "us" based on different styles of learning, qualities of mind, structures of brains, and ways of knowing, talking, or caring. John Dewey, perhaps America's greatest theorist of education and a fierce supporter of women's equal rights, was infuriated at the contempt for women suggested by such programs. Dewey scoffed at "'female botany,' 'female algebra,' and for all I know a 'female multiplication table,'" he wrote in 1911. "Upon no subject has there been so much dogmatic assertion based on so little scientific evidence, as upon male and female types of mind." Co-education, Dewey argued, is beneficial to women, opening up opportunities previously unattainable. Girls, he suggested, become less manipulative and acquire "greater self-reliance and a desire to win approval by deserving it instead of by 'working' others. Their narrowness of judgment, depending on the enforced narrowness of outlook, is overcome; their ultra-feminine weaknesses are toned up." What's more, Dewey claimed, co-education is beneficial to men. "Boys learn gentleness, unselfishness, courtesy; their natural vigor finds helpful channels of expression instead of wasting itself in lawless boisterousness," he wrote.[56] Another educational reformer, Thomas Wentworth Higginson, also opposed single-sex schools. "Sooner or later, I am persuaded, the human race will look upon all these separate collegiate institutions as most American travelers now look at the vast monastic establishments of Southern Europe; with respect for the pious motives of their founders, but with wonder that such a mistake should ever have been made."[57] Although Higginson predicted correctly for the collegiate level—there are today only three all-male colleges and fewer than half the number of all-female colleges that there were forty years ago—there are also some efforts to revive the single-sex ideal, at both the collegiate and the secondary levels.

The proposals for single-sex schools seem to be based either on a facile, and incorrect, assessment of some biologically based different educational "needs" or learning styles or on some well-intentioned efforts to help at-risk groups (black boys or girls). Listen to a statement from the National Association for Single Sex Public Education:

> Girls and boys differ fundamentally in the learning *style* they feel most comfortable with. Girls tend to look on the teacher as an ally. Given a little encouragement, they will welcome the teacher's help. A girl-friendly classroom is a safe, comfortable, welcoming place. Forget hard plastic chairs: put in a sofa and some comfortable beanbags . . . The teacher should never yell or shout at a girl. Avoid confrontation. Avoid the word "why" . . . Girls will naturally break up in groups of three and four to work on problems. Let them. Minimize assignments that require working alone.[58]

I assume that most female readers of this statement will be as offended by this insulting and condescending message as students in my classes were. And what does it assume is a sound pedagogical philosophy for boys? Answer: Make the classroom dangerous and inhospitable, seat students on uncomfortable chairs, yell at them, confront them, and always ask why. To put it as charitably as possible, I am sure that such organizations believe they have the best interests of children at heart. They base their claims, though, on the flimsiest of empirical evidence and the wildest of stereotypical assertions. Every day, real boys and girls prove such insulting stereotypes wrong.

In truth, the calls for single-sex schooling are based on "pseudo-science"—the rehashing of outmoded gender stereotypes as if they were based on anything more than anecdotal observation. In one short research note, several noted empirical researchers made clear that single-sex schools confer virtually no academic advantages, are not based on any credible evidence from brain research, and in fact may increase gender stereotyping instead of breaking it down.[59]

Such proposals also mistake consequence for cause, or, perhaps better put, emphasize form over content. Let me ask the question this way: Which sort of school would you choose: a really great co-educational school or a really terrible single-sex school? Odds are you would choose the co-ed school, because you know what some of these misguided educational reformers do not: The form of the school—co-ed or single-sex—is less important than its content. It turns out that single-sex schools tend to be private, small, with lots of resources, dedicated faculty, and low student-teacher ratios—not to mention wealthier students, with better educational backgrounds. And it is *those* qualities—not the single-sexedness—that yield the better outcomes.

In some sense, proposals for single-sex schools offer a resigned defeatism: Because we cannot fix the large co-ed public schools because the resources aren't there, let's retreat to single-sex schools. Surely, educational policy can set the bar higher than that.

TOWARD GENDER EQUALITY IN SCHOOLS

Many school districts are experimenting with **single-sex schools or single-sex classrooms**, especially to teach math and science to girls. There have been notable experiments with single-sex schools for black boys in Detroit and Newark and for black girls in New York City to teach math and science. In Detroit, for example, city officials tried to respond to a crisis in the black community: Of twenty-four thousand males enrolled in the Detroit public schools, only 30 percent had grade point averages better than 2.0; boys were suspended three times more often than girls; 60 percent of the drug offenses were committed by eighth- and ninth-grade dropouts. The city of Detroit proposed an all-male academy to offer boys "self-esteem, rites of passage, role model interaction and academic improvement." Although these goals were worthy, many parents objected that the project was ignoring the needs of girls, and, faced with likely lawsuits and public opposition, the city officials withdrew the proposal. Similar programs were canceled or withdrawn in Philadelphia and Miami, though one is still in operation in Baltimore. President Bush also advocated some forms of single-sex schools.[60]

The evidence to support such innovations is inconsistent and discouraging. In a sense, such schools propose a "racial" or "gender" remedy for a problem of "class"—because *children*, both boys and girls, would no doubt thrive in schools with lots of resources, small classes, and fabulously trained teachers. In addition, much of the celebrated "need" for positive role models and the excoriation of black men for abandoning their families take no account of the economic uncertainties that black males face or of the economic pressures that tear families apart. Economic hope for a real future would probably go a lot further in keeping families together and keeping boys in school and off the streets.[61]

And for girls? At the new Young Women's Leadership School in Harlem, 160 middle-school girls are doing somewhat better than their counterparts at co-educational schools. Ninety percent of them scored at or above grade level on math tests; 63 percent read at or above grade level (compared with 51 percent and 44 percent, respectively, for the rest of New York City). And their attendance rates exceed city averages by 3 percent. "Our intention is to give inner-city kids a choice which in the past has only been reserved for the wealthy and parochial school children," said Ann Rubenstein Tisch, one of the school's founders.[62]

But that school is currently being opposed legally by the American Civil Liberties Union and by the National Organization for Women on the grounds that it discriminates against boys. And the claims of benefits are being challenged empirically by a recent study by the American Association of University Women (AAUW), which found that although many girls report that they feel single-sex classrooms are more conducive to learning, they also show no significant gains in achievement in math and science. Another researcher found some significant differences between co-educational and single-sex classes—but only in Catholic schools, not in private single-sex schools, and only for girls. A third researcher found no advantages of one or the other type of school for middle-class and otherwise advantaged students but found some positive outcomes for black or Hispanic girls from low socioeconomic homes. "Separating by sex is not the answer to inequities in the schools," noted Maggie Ford, president of the AAUW Educational Foundation. And Kenneth Clark, the pioneering African-American educator, was equally unequivocal. "I can't believe that we're actually regressing like this. Why are we still talking about segregating and stigmatizing black males?" he asked. He should know: His research provided the empirical argument against "separate but equal" schools in the U.S. Supreme Court's landmark **Brown v. Board of Education** civil rights decision in 1954.[63]

The findings of the only systematic study of a pilot program for single-sex schools in California reported rather depressing results. Traditional gender stereotypes remained in full effect; in fact, such schools actually perpetuated stereotypes that girls are good and boys are bad, which should prompt some reconsideration from those who want to "rescue" boys from meddling feminists. In the end, after three years, five of the six school districts closed their single-sex academies.[64]

TITLE IX AND ATHLETIC EQUALITY

Another arena in which gender inequality in education is today being challenged is in extracurricular activities, especially sports. Here, girls once received the clear message that their place was on the sidelines, cheering for the boys, whose programs received the lion's share of funding. The passage of amendments to the Education Act of 1972 contained **Title IX**, which abolished sex discrimination in public schools and has since been taken to mandate that women's sports be funded equally with men's (excluding football, which is extraordinarily expensive for schools to fund and which virtually no women are able to play). Since then, girls' participation in interscholastic sports has soared from three hundred thousand to nearly three million, and the involvement of college-age women has expanded by more than 600 percent.[65]

The benefits of female participation in sports, spurred by Title IX, redound to everyone's benefit—and for the long term as well. Sociologist Don Sabo has studied these benefits for the past ten years and finds that female athletes are less likely than nonathletes to have unwanted pregnancies and less likely to take drugs, smoke cigarettes, or drink alcohol to excess, but are more likely to wear seat belts, to have a positive outlook on life, and to achieve higher grades.[66]

Predictably, this clear and unequivocal success has been met with loud and vociferous criticism that adequate enforcement of Title IX programs has rendered males the "second sex" of college sports, the new victims of reverse discrimination, because a number of men's teams have been cut to achieve the proportionality mandated by Title IX. The Commission on Opportunity in Athletics has offered a plan that would dilute the law so much that it would "significantly undermine the equality that Title IX has always stood for," according to an editorial in the *New York Times*.[67]

Such short-sighted criticism fails to note several important ways in which equality in sports is good for both women and men. By maintaining a zero-sum approach, for example, critics miss the ways in which both male and female sports programs are utterly disfigured by the salaries paid to male coaches in big-revenue college sports. When many college football and basketball coaches earn salaries—not including endorsement bonuses from athletic footwear companies—that are often ten times higher than the salary of their college's president, then clearly revenues for college sports need not mandate the cutting of a men's team, but rather demand the reallocation of funds throughout the entire athletic program. Simple fairness would dictate that girls and boys have equal opportunities to participate in sports, as in the rest of their lives, and the dramatic success of Title IX demonstrates that when such opportunities are offered, women take them. Besides, what could be more of a benefit to a guy than a woman who is strong and capable and appreciates the physicality of her own body?[68]

Across the country, state governments are mandating gender equity programs for elementary and secondary education. These programs are designed to reduce the obstacles that continue to stand in the way of girls', *as well as boys'*, achievement—the harassment and bullying from other boys and the brutal enforcement of rigid stereotypes of masculine and feminine behavior by both teachers and classmates. Because the same assumptions—that males and females are so fundamentally different that we could not possibly learn equally and together—plague both boys and girls. Gender inequality in education produces the gender differences we assume, with deleterious consequences for both genders; it impairs both boys' and girls' efforts to find their voices, discipline their minds, and prepare themselves for their futures.

KEY TERMS

Brown v. Board of Education	Hazing	Single-Sex Schools/
Co-education	Hidden Curriculum	Classrooms
"Deceptive Distinction"	Separate but Equal	Title IX
Gender Policing	Sexual Harassment	

GENDER *and* RELIGION

God is a man! was the full-page headline of the *New York Post*, a local tabloid newspaper, on June 17, 1991. Apparently, during a Father's Day sermon, John Cardinal O'Connor, then the archbishop of New York City, had excoriated radical feminists who had suggested the possibility of a more androgynous, all-embracing deity.[1]

The headline was actually a bit of a hyperbolic overstatement, typical of the tabloid press. Actually, O'Connor had said that "in the fatherhood of the Almighty God is, of course, all personhood, the personhood of mother and father simultaneously." And he went on to quote a Vatican official who said that "we are not authorized to change the 'Our Father' into an 'Our Mother.'" (That Vatican official, incidentally, was Joseph Cardinal Ratzinger, who became Pope Benedict XVI in 2005.)

Critical reaction was nonetheless swift. Many felt that again, women were being reminded that they were not equal in the church. One German theologian dismissed the statement facetiously by drawing this analogy: "A donkey thinks God is a donkey because in the eyes of a donkey, the donkey is the top of creation. O'Connor seems to me to be a combination of a man and a theological donkey."[2]

This little flare-up was actually only the latest skirmish in a centuries-long struggle. In Western societies, religion has long been bound up with questions about gender. Is God a man? Why do most of the world's great religious traditions have male prophets? What sorts of relationships does God prescribe, and which ones does God proscribe? Do men and women have equal roles in the various religious ministries?

Monotheistic religious traditions—Judaism, Christianity, and Islam—have been especially concerned with gender issues. Both in theological doctrine and as a social institution, religion has, for many centuries, played a dominant role in the idea that women and men are fundamentally different and that such difference is part of a divine plan. From that difference, these religious traditions hold, women and men are to perform different tasks, are assigned different roles, and are placed in subordinate and superordinate positions in a hierarchy. Most simply said, religious doctrine has been a consistent wellspring of claims of essential and eternal gender difference and, institutionally, a foundation justifying gender inequality.

READ ALL ABOUT IT!

We tend to think that religion is conservative when it comes to gender issues: that traditional religious beliefs reinforce a divinely ordained separation of spheres and the subordination of women. But what are the constellations of values and ideas, and what are their actual impact on people's gender attitudes? Are some religions worse or better about this? Are there factors that accentuate or minimize the way these doctrinal tenets are received? Stephanie Seguino, an economist at the University of Vermont, has examined the effect of religion on gender attitudes globally.

It needn't be this way, of course. One can imagine religious doctrines and rituals that celebrate equality. Perhaps a more Buddhist notion of complementarity, of yin and yang, heaven and earth, masculine and feminine, that values each as necessary *and equal*. Or perhaps a more pantheistic understanding in which various gods, some gendered and some not, are responsible for a wide variety of earthly phenomena.

THE HISTORICAL GENDERING OF RELIGION

Indeed, the historical record suggests that it wasn't always this way at all. In premodern societies, goddesses proliferated; as far back as human societies existed there were goddesses, especially of fertility, reproduction, and, later, plentiful harvests. Many of the great historical anthropologists of the nineteenth and early twentieth centuries proposed that primitive matriarchies and polytheistic cultures were gradually replaced—either by conquest or contact.[3] This is a matter of significant debate.

Historically, the Great Goddess was known by so many names that it is impossible to count them all: Astarte, Anat, Anahita, Asherah, Attoret, Attar, and Au—and that's just the "A's"![4] There are hundreds, if not thousands, of goddesses who have occupied the pantheon of deities throughout world history. In *Female Power and Male Dominance*, for example, anthropologist Peggy Reeves Sanday traces the origins of male domination in Europe and the Middle East to the triumph of sky gods over earth goddesses—that is, the triumph of the invisible and all-powerful over the more visible, immediate, and pragmatic.

Yet many cultures today continue to worship goddesses—with significant crossovers. For example, animist religions like the Yoruba in Africa have influenced religious cult traditions in the Western hemisphere such as Voodoo and Santeria, traditions that maintain women's spiritual power.[5]

Greek and Roman mythology paired up gods and goddesses, and while Zeus thundered angrily, goddesses like Athena and Hera proved able problem solvers. Mesopotamians worshipped Ishtar; Isis and Demeter were goddesses of law and justice in Egypt and Greece, respectively. Ancient cultures in the Near East and Middle East routinely included fertility goddesses, who controlled life forces such as birth and death. Some cultures even developed matriarchal religions in which the Great Mother was the source of all life.

Many contemporary nonindustrial cultures that have been less tainted by incorporation into Western networks still maintain such female deities, which suggests that seeing the female as both equal and divine answers some important cultural needs across historical time—needs that are largely unmet in our culture, perhaps to our detriment. For example, in South America, contemporary Andean peoples such as the Quechua and Aymara believe in the Mother Earth *Pachamama*, whose worship cult is found in rural areas and towns in Ecuador, Peru, Bolivia, northern Chile, and northwestern Argentina. Andean migrants carried the Pachamama cult to cities and many other extra-Andean places, including metropolitan Buenos Aires.

Among those religions such as Hinduism and Buddhism, which are older than Judaism (which is the oldest of the three major monotheistic religions), there is far more spiritual "diversity." Hinduism holds that there are many gods and goddesses (although the practice of the religion allows for significant gender inequality). And Buddhists don't believe in any titular "god" who stands above, but rather in the godlike potential of all humans.[6]

Shaktism, the worship of the female force that animates the world, is one of the three major sects of Hinduism. And in Tibetan Buddhism, the highest level any person can achieve is to become like the great female Buddhas (e.g., Arya Tara), who are depicted as being supreme protectors, fearless and filled with compassion for all beings.

Monotheism changed all that. There has never been much of a question that the single unitary God who first spoke to Abraham was a male God. God has had many personalities—merciful, vengeful, fraternal helper or angry judge, patient and paternal, or proud and patriarchal—but ever since Abraham heard that voice, that voice has been male.

Can you imagine what you might have thought if Charlton Heston had gone up to the top of the mountain in Cecil B. DeMille's epic movie *The Ten Commandments* and it was a sweetly feminine voice that spoke to him from the burning bush? My guess is that people would never have taken it seriously; indeed, even to suggest such a thing might have been so heretical that you might have been burned at the stake.

The monotheistic assertion of a male God, and a normative code that demanded that women be subordinate to men, had practical historical implications. It meant not only elevating men over women, but stamping out and suppressing all those other religious traditions that posited the equality of women, celebrated women's reproductive power as divine, or envisioned women as goddesses.

Indeed, much of the history of religion in Europe over the course of its first two millennia has been a history of purification, of a search for finer and finer expression of doctrinal truth through the suppression of all who might deviate from it. Many of the norms concerning gender relations—the commandments for the subordination of women, the deference of women to men—are not encoded into the initial scriptures,

Figure 8.1. Snake Goddess, Crete, seventh century BCE. This image is from "Goddess Tours," which organizes women-only tours to ancient goddess sites.

Source: Archaeological Museum, Heraklion, Crete, Greece. Anna Pakutina/Shutterstock.com.

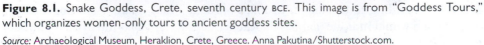

but came along later as commentaries on it. That is to say, they are not the word of God, but the words of mortal men, interpreting those scriptures within a specific historical context.

And not all are scriptures, either. Entire doctrinal traditions have been suppressed as heresy, including gospels that were contemporaneous to the New Testament but suggested far more egalitarian relations between the sexes and the divinity of women. These notions simmer just below the surface because they also suggest the eternal human desire for equality and the elevation of women to an equal station. Most recently, these ideas crept into the pop potboiler *The Da Vinci Code*, the tenth best-selling book of all time (the Bible is number one). A quasi-feminist text, it turns out that the entire Vatican hierarchy was determined to use all available methods, including murder, to suppress the possibility that Jesus and Mary Magdalene were more than "just friends."

Some scholars argue that as these **goddess traditions** were suppressed, they went **underground** and reemerged as **witchcraft**. (The word *witch* means "wise one.")

Witches were often healers, ritually in charge of medicine, and midwives, in charge of birth. These were powerful women, often independent of the rule of men (which, of course, made them especially threatening to the consolidation of patriarchal power). As Carol Christ writes:

> The wise woman was summoned at the crises of the life cycle before the priest; she delivered the baby, while the priest was called later to perform the baptism. She was the first called upon to cure illness or treat the dying, while the priest was called in after other remedies had failed, to administer the last rites . . . It is not difficult to see why she was persecuted by an insecure misogynist Church which could not tolerate rival power.[7]

Women's spirituality (to which I will return later) has also been the other side of patriarchal religions.

THEOLOGIES OF DIFFERENCE, THEOLOGIES OF INEQUALITY

Not only when it comes to the gender of God, but in so many areas the Bible and other canonical texts are normative, prescribing the appropriate relationship between men and women, husbands and wives, parents and children. It's estimated that four-fifths of the Qur'an is concerned with prescribing and proscribing the appropriate relations between women and men.[8] The Bible, both the New and Old Testaments, has a lot to say about domestic relationships.

What is perhaps most interesting is that the sacred texts, and their prophets, are far more equinanimous—or at least ambiguous—than their subsequent male interpreters have indicated. Those conflicting interpretations have provided the basis for centuries of conflict and discord. For example, Jesus seemed equally concerned with women as with men and made it a point to single out some women who were scorned by others for special devotion. (One woman, Junia, is referred to in Romans 16:7 as an apostle.) According to theologian Leonard Swidler, "Jesus neither said nor did anything which would indicate that he advocated treating women as intrinsically inferior to men, but . . . on the contrary, he said and did things which indicated he thought of women as the equals of men."[9]

And Mohammed insisted that women's consent had to be obtained before marriage—a startling reform at the time; women were also entitled to initiate divorce, to inherit, to maintain their own property, and to exercise certain conjugal rights. Women were also subject to the same requirements for prayer and fasting during the holy month of Ramadan. At the same time, men were permitted to have up to four wives (provided they could adequately provide for them), and women were subservient to men because men were to be "a degree above" women, because "God has made one to excel over the other."[10]

It is more often in the commentaries on these canonical texts that the religious imperative for gender inequality seems to have been most firmly instituted. It was not inevitable, and one could imagine that such textual ambiguity might have been interpreted to allow for greater gender inequality. This inequality is almost universally evident in the language of the Bible. Whenever the text uses the second person, singular or plural, it assumes the actor is male. In fact, although "you" must do this or that, some texts go on to explain that women "may not" do them.

"We've been wandering in the desert for forty years. But he's a man—would he ever ask directions?"

Figure 8.2. Peter Steiner/The New Yorker Collection/The Cartoon Bank.

So, for example, St. Paul's epistle to the Ephesians leaves no doubt about where he stood on gender equality (itself a comment that something must have been perceived as amiss for him to even comment on it):

> Let the wives be subject to their husbands as to the Lord; because a husband is head of the wife, just as Christ is head of the Church . . . But just as the Church is subject to Christ, so let wives also be subject in everything to their husbands. (Ephesians 5:22–24)

And in 1 Corinthians 11:3, again, a similar theme: "The head of every man is Christ, and the head of a woman is her husband." (Of all the apostles, Paul seemed most obsessed with women's subordination.) Just to be sure there was no misunderstanding, in 1998, in the wake of several decades of intense feminist campaigns, the Southern Baptist Convention amended its official statement of beliefs to insist that a wife should "submit graciously" to her husband and assume her "God-given responsibility to respect her husband and to serve as his 'helper.' "[11]

(Of course, what the religion *says* and what people actually *do* varies enormously. For example, though the Catholic Church forbids birth control, nearly all American Catholic women use some form of birth control. And while the man is supposed to be the head of the household, many evangelical Christians have—and support—egalitarian marriages.[12])

Orthodox Judaism certainly enshrines gender inequality: Women may not be rabbis, read the Torah during worship, sing in synagogue, or lead a service.[13] Indeed, only men count toward a *minyan*, the quorum of ten Jews who must be present in order to hold a prayer service. A hundred women and nine men? No service. Jewish women may not initiate marriage or divorce, may not pray at the Western Wall (they've been physically attacked by Orthodox men when they've tried), and there's a sort of informal morality brigade of Orthodox men who publicly chastise women who are dressed "immodestly" or who sit where they like on public buses. This sounds awfully similar to the roving bands of Muslim purification groups that roamed Afghanistan under the Taliban, enforcing its gendered code of conduct on Afghanis.

Such conflicts over the interpretations of sacred texts may be, at their heart, doctrinal, but they are often expressed as secular policies. For example, in the nineteenth century, it was the Protestant clergy that led the charge against women's rights, whether the right to vote, go to college, or enter professions such as medicine or law. It wasn't that women should have the "right" to these activities, wrote Rev. John Todd, but rather their divinely created frail constitutions required that they be "exempted from certain things which men must endure."[14]

But on the other side, though, many Protestant ministers were among the most fervent supporters of women's suffrage. Rev. Samuel B. May's 1846 sermon "The Rights and Condition of Women" argued that the disenfranchisement of women "is as unjust as the disenfranchisement of the males would be; for there is nothing in their moral, mental, or physical nature, that disqualifies them to understand correctly the true interests of the community, or to act wisely on reference to them."[15]

Similarly, while across Islamic societies today men are the heads of the household and women are often relegated to the private sphere, these practices are not at all consistent. In some of the world's largest Muslim countries, like Indonesia, women wear Western clothing and are engaged in every profession. Girls go to school unimpeded, and women and men are equally enfranchised.

In most religions, gender inequality is enshrined and enforced through a politicization of the body. All the monotheistic religions prescribe some bodily practices and proscribe others. For example, Christian men are not supposed to cover their heads, but Christian women are—and for similar reasons. (It is probable that Christian men were prohibited from covering their heads because Jews were required to do so, and this differentiated them from Jews.) As Paul explained to the Corinthians:

> A man indeed ought not to cover his head, because he is the image and glory of God. But woman is the glory of man. For man is not from woman, but woman from man. For man was not created for woman, but woman for man. (1 Corinthians 11:7–9)

In some more fundamentalist Islamic societies, women's bodies are to be completely concealed at all times; even if she must venture out in public in the first place (and then accompanied by a male relative) she must remain hidden under a **burka**. She may show no part of her body or face in public. Even today, women who defy these strictures in Afghanistan risk having acid thrown on their face to permanently disfigure them, public shaming of themselves and their families, and even ritual stonings.

READ ALL ABOUT IT!

France has banned the wearing of any head covering in its public schools—a practice that affects Muslim women and Jewish men, as well as members of other faiths. Why do people choose to wear these religious garments in public? More important, why do they choose to do so when their own parents and families do not? In "Veiled Submission," sociologists John Bartkowski and Jen'nan Ghazal Read interviewed evangelical women and Muslim women on college campuses to try to understand how they viewed gender inequality and identity.

Men's bodies are also policed. Since the prophet wore a beard, Muslim men, these moral enforcers believe, are required to wear a beard. Any man caught shaving could be executed—and barbers who shaved them could have their hands cut off. (Again, this by no means applies to all Islam; indeed, in those countries with the largest Muslim populations, such as Indonesia, such requirements are virtually unheard of.)

One of the hallmarks of women's second-class status among Orthodox Jews has always been the ritual cleansing. Menstruation makes women ritually unclean; for twelve days a month—that is, about 40 percent of every month—a woman is considered unclean; anything she touches becomes impure, and she must be physically segregated from men. Seven days after her menstrual cycle ends, she goes to a ritual bath called a *mikvah* where she is purified and thus able to rejoin social life.

You might think that women might chafe at such elaborate and lengthy reminders of their inequality. But in a fascinating study of young women who convert to Orthodox Judaism, sociologist Debra Kaufman discovered that what might be seen as "oppression" to an outsider might carry alternative meanings to the participants. Women who had converted to Orthodoxy, or become significantly more orthodox, actually valued the experience and found it "empowering." Participation, Kaufman writes, "put them in touch with their own bodies, in control of their own sexuality, and in a position to value the so-called feminine virtues of nurturance, mutuality, family and motherhood."[16]

Another study of Orthodox Jewish women in Israel found a wide range of responses to these ceremonies of **ritual purification**. One woman chafed at the oppression she felt, that she had "this feeling that it is the long hands of the rabbis of hundreds of years literally entering my body to check me." But another woman cherished her sense of "renewal," feeling "that I enter the water as a religious person who is accepted for who I am, without makeup, without colours: I have an intrinsic net worth, without any props."

And it's a decidedly sexual power, since the *mikvah* purifies her for sex, and Jewish law guarantees her rights to pleasure. One woman says:

> The *mikveh* gives me a wonderful feeling, when I go I feel like my husband is waiting for me like an honored guest, like he waits Friday night for the Sabbath angels . . . it makes me feel like our relationship moves to a higher level.

While another says:

> A woman can also initiate physical things. It's good to say that I want this or that, especially because the woman is supposed to enjoy. In fact, the husband is not ful-filling his commandment of *onah* if you don't enjoy. So that means that if you want sex, or whatever, then he has to agree and you have the right to ask for it.[17]

Actually, so, too, the veil—or ***hijab***—among Muslim women. Some have argued that wearing the *hijab* is a political statement, a statement of solidarity with other immigrant Muslims in more secular Western societies. Despite its denunciation as oppressive by feminist women worldwide, many young Muslim women embrace the *hijab* as an act of solidarity and community. For example, young Muslim women in France refused to remove their veils in schools, despite a French law that requires all head coverings to be removed, since education is a secular institution.

In one study in the United States, Muslim women saw wearing the *hijab* as an expression of their opposition to colonialism in the Middle East and an affirmation of gender differences as prescribed by their religion. In a fascinating dissertation in my department, one of our PhD students, Etsuko Maruoka, interviewed young Muslim students at Stony Brook who had decided to begin to wear the veil—much to their parents' discomfort! For them it was an act of rebellion against parents who were too eager to "Americanize" them, as well as an act of solidarity with Muslims all over the world (figure 8.3). But most important, Maruoka argued, it was an act of self-identification as a minority group, as an outsider, as different. In this act of conformity, these young women

Figure 8.3. *Source:* © Rizwan Saeed/Reuters/Corbis.

sought to differentiate themselves from their classmates, forging an oppositional identity. (On the other hand, many of these young women's parents had immigrated from
countries like Malaysia and Indonesia, where veils are virtually unheard of. Their view
of a global Islamic practice was likely the result of watching Al-Jazeera, the Saudi-
financed global Muslim television channel that promotes such a unified vision, rather
than any genuine act of solidarity with some mythic Islamic world.)[18]

Perhaps, as psychologist Rosine Perelberg writes, these multiple meanings attached to the same activity suggest how "power can be exercised from a subordinate
position" and that such fluidity "is fundamental to both the way in which gender roles
are constructed in different societies and the respective positions from which men and
women perceive themselves."[19]

Of course, it is the body and its pleasures that especially elicit religious passions.
I suspect that all religions require the suppression of sex for the glory of God. Yet even
here, there are many interpretations. Among Orthodox Jews, for example, women
and men are both entitled—indeed, *encouraged*—to experience sexual fulfillment in
marriage.

One of Christianity's innovations over Judaism was a strict repression of
sexuality. Sex was to be avoided and engaged in only for procreation. According
to St. Augustine, sex was the vehicle by which **original sin** was transmitted from
one generation to the next. **Celibacy** was promoted as a higher moral and spiritual
position. Lust is listed as among the seven deadly sins, and women (of course) are
the repositories of lust. As the infamous *Malleus Maleficarum* put it (this was the
church manual for witch hunting): "All witchcraft comes from carnal lust, which
is in women insatiable."[20]

At the same time, Christian writers have penned best-selling Christian sex
manuals that basically say that God wants you to have great sex—as long as you are
married, heterosexual, and faithful to your spouse. This has naturally led to a certain amount of confusion among contemporary Christians. As one young man in
Lubbock, Texas, put it,

> Life in Lubbock, Texas taught me two things:
> One is that God loves you and you are going to hell;
> The other is that sex is the most awful, filthy thing on Earth and you
> should save it for someone you love.[21]

Generally, that "someone you love" has to be someone of a gender different from yours.
Another of religion's hallmark elements of maintaining gender difference is to require us
to love only those of a different gender. Many religions either discourage or prohibit
homosexuality—and this is particularly true of monotheistic religions. While 60 percent
of all Americans believe that homosexuality should be accepted by society, three-quarters
of Jehovah's Witnesses (76 percent), about six in ten Muslims (61 percent), and roughly
two-thirds of Mormons (68 percent) and members of evangelical churches (64 percent)
say homosexuality ought to be discouraged.

The majority of other religious groups say homosexuality should be accepted
by society. This includes Catholics (64 percent), members of mainline churches
(65 percent), Jews (79 percent), Buddhists (82 percent), and the unaffiliated (79 percent).

OH? REALLY • Christians Have Better Sex

According to Pat Fagan of the conservative Christian Marriage and Religion Research Institute, Christians have more and better sex. "We've got it more orgasmic, more enjoyable, more frequent!" Taunting nonbelievers, he added, "We know how to have sex much better than you do!"

His evidence for this? According to the 1992 National Health and Social Life Survey, 88 percent of always-married people enjoy having intercourse with their current partner extremely or very much—compared to 72 percent of divorced or separated people and 66 percent of single people. And 84 percent of people who attend church regularly are very happy with their sex lives, compared to 79 percent of people who never go to church. (The people who rated their sex lives the worst, though, were the ones who went to church occasionally.)

But is that because Christians are more proficient at achieving sexual ecstasy? Or is it really simply a matter of the ability to compare? Always-married churchgoers are likely to have had only one sex partner in their lives, so they have little grounds for comparison, and they likely add lots of religious meaning to it, so even if the sex itself isn't so ecstatic, they might feel more spiritually satisfied. "Those who are monogamous have the best sex they'll ever know, because they don't know anything else," Fagan says, admiringly.

As for the orgasm gap between the churchgoers and nonchurchgoers—well, it doesn't hold for men, but it does for women. Perhaps that's really more about the relationship between monogamy and trust, since women often report higher frequency of orgasm when they know and trust their partner.

Source: Amanda Hess, "Do Christians Have Better Sex?" in *Slate*, July 19, 2013, http://www.slate.com/blogs/xx_factor/2013/07/19/the_family_research_council_argues_that_christians_have_more_orgasmic_frequent.html.

By contrast, members of historically black churches, Orthodox Christians, and Hindus are more divided over the issue of homosexuality. For example, four in ten members of historically black churches say homosexuality should be accepted, while 46 percent say it should be discouraged.[22]

Religiosity also tends to be associated with more negative views on gay marriage. According to a 2011 survey by the Pew Forum on Religion and Public Life and the Pew Research Center for the People and the Press, 46 percent of Americans support gay marriage, while 44 percent oppose it. But those with a high frequency of church attendance oppose it by a substantially wider margin (68 percent in opposition vs. 24 percent in favor) (from Pew 2010 data). Opposition among white evangelicals, regardless of frequency of church attendance, is even higher—at 74 percent. A majority of black Protestants (62 percent) oppose gay marriage, as do an equal percentage of Latino Catholics (42 percent). However, there has been a dramatic shift in support among certain sects (a 5 to 10 percentage point increase in support). For example, in 2007, while only Americans without a religious affiliation had majority support for gay marriage, today you find that those without religious affiliation (72 percent) are joined by white, mainline Protestants (54 percent) and white, non-Hispanic Catholics (57 percent).

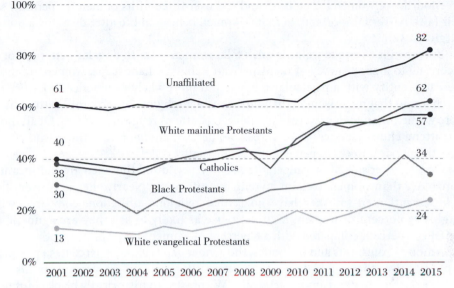

Figure 8.4. Percent of people who favor same-sex marriage.

Source: "Changing Attitudes on Gay Marriage," Pew Research Center, Washington, DC (July, 2015)

http://www.pewforum.org/2015/07/29/graphics-slideshow-changing-attitudes-on-gay-marriage/.

THE GENDER OF RELIGIOSITY

Both in doctrine and in practice, most mainstream monotheistic religions proclaim divinely inspired gender difference and thus legitimate gender inequality. Every morning, the Orthodox Jew thanks God he was not born a woman. The Catholic declares obedience to the Father, the Son, and the Holy Spirit. Muslims read in the Qur'an, "Men are in charge of women because God has made one to excel over the other." The Hindu Code of Manu, V, declares that "a woman must never be free of subjugation."[23] Where, you might ask, are the women?

In the pews. One of the great paradoxes of religion is that deities, doctrines, and institutional practices promote the naturalness of both gender difference and male domination, and yet the majority of the faithful are female.

Logically, you might imagine that it would be otherwise: that God imagined as male, the word of God has historically been the touchstone for assertions of gender difference, and, perhaps even more importantly, the basic justification for gender inequality; that religion would be a man's domain; that far more men would be religious—since it reaffirms natural differences and props up men's domination of women. Right?

Not so fast. In fact, women are far more religious than men. Here in the United States, which is the most religious nation in the industrial world, virtually everyone professes some religious belief. (The United States is the fifth most religious nation in the world, falling behind only Nigeria, Poland, India, and Turkey.) Over 95 percent of Americans say they believe in God or some universal spirit. More than three-fourths of women (77 percent) and just over three-fifths of men (63 percent) say their faith is "very important" to them. Women believe in life after death by a 60–40 margin as well.[24]

But when it comes to walking one's talk, women seem to do a far better job of it. According to a 2008 survey of the American Religious Landscape, women are more likely to identify with a particular religion and more likely to practice it. Earlier research found that more women than men consider religion "important" in their lives. More women than men pray, read the Bible, and attend religious services. Of all those who attend church services once a week, 60 percent are female; of those who attend more than once a week, 70 percent are female (figure 8.5).[25]

On the other side of the ledger, the 2008 survey found that men are significantly more likely than women to claim no religious affiliation. Nearly one out of every five (19.6 percent) men say they have no formal religious affiliation, compared with roughly 13 percent of women. Men are twice as likely to say they are agnostic or atheist (5.5 percent compared with 2.6 percent of women).

Among Protestants and Catholics, the gender gap is about 8 percent, 54 percent–46 percent. But that gap balloons to 20 percent (60 percent–40 percent) in historically black churches and among Jehovah's Witnesses. In historically black churches, women often make up from 70 to 90 percent of the congregation. Turns out that black women are the most religious of all. (Among Jews, Muslims, Buddhists, and

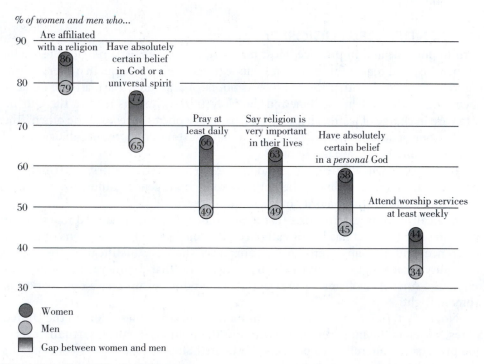

Figure 8.5. The spiritual gender gap.

Source: "The Stronger Sex—Spiritually Speaking," Pew Research Center, Washington, DC (February, 2009) http://www.pewforum.org/2009/02/26/the-stronger-sex-spiritually-speaking/.

Hindu Americans the gender gap goes the other way, ranging from a modest 4 percent [52 percent–48 percent] among Jews to a significantly larger 22 percent [61 percent– 39 percent] among Hindus.)[26]

There is some evidence in recent years that the gender gap in religion is narrowing somewhat. This does not appear to be because men's religious participation is increasing, but rather because women's is declining. Perhaps the demands of full-time work outside the home and performing virtually all the second shift tasks of housework and child care leave women little time to attend to the spiritual side of things. In one recent study of former White House Fellows, researchers found that the female alumnae were somewhat less religious than the men. The authors conclude that high-achieving women may not benefit from religion the same way men do, or that they don't get the same sorts of moral support as men. But these findings are pretty unpersuasive. After all, White House Fellows are predominately male (their survey had 362 male and 107 female respondents) and are appointed by political criteria, so the alumnae interviewed were more likely to be Republicans than Democrats, and the males who were selected might have been more likely to have been screened for religious affiliation. (After all, many aspire to political office, and proclamations of faith are required of all political candidates these days.) In short, so many other factors may explain the small differences between male and female White House Fellows that we really can't say for sure that elite status exerts such a disparate effect on religious preference.[27]

However, we should not mistake small swells in the ocean for massive changes in the natures of the tides. The level of enforcement of gender inequality varies historically. During periods of prosperity, religious structures may relax: Women may make great strides in the public arena without religious interference, and they also may successfully challenge doctrinal proscriptions on their religious participation. Periods of secular crisis, though, are often accompanied by fundamentalist calls to return to basic texts, to repurify the religion from contamination by secularizing forces. That is, during periods of prosperity, religions can turn outward and embrace others; during crises, they turn inward and demand increasing illustrations of faithful adherence.

The fundamentalist impulse is a sort of back to basics, a return to the tried and true. It redraws boundaries between in-group and out-group more firmly. One hardly "needs" **fundamentalism** when the old doctrines are firmly in place and unchallenged. During those moments, fundamentalists seek to return women to their "rightful" place as one method of solving massive confusion caused by social and economic upheavals. Just as women and men are becoming more and more equal throughout the world—in education, family life, the professions, or the workplace— fundamentalists seek to remind us that the differences between women and men, which are everywhere disappearing, are in fact indelible and fixed.[28]

RELIGION AS A GENDERED INSTITUTION

To a sociologist, religion is more than the codification of an ethical way of life, a set of beliefs about the meaning of life, its purpose and its creator, or a set of spiritual practices designed to express those beliefs. It's also a social institution, an institution that employs people, in which people have careers, earn livings, and make a most secular life for themselves. While there may be much mystery in the actual ideas of a religion, in a social sense, religious institutions may look like virtually any other institution.

There is significant symmetry between religious doctrine and institutional practices. Since monotheistic religions posit intractable divinely ordained gender differences, and thus justify gender inequality, their institutional arrangements often reflect these beliefs. Because the United States accords religious institutions the freedom to profess their beliefs and institutionalize practices based on them—within limits, of course—our government allows religious institutions to develop their own hiring and firing policies and to determine their own criteria for selection, hiring, and membership. Thus, even though the law prohibits gender as a criterion for hiring or promotion, we permit religious institutions to use gender as a criterion. However, this is not carte blanche to practice your religion in whatever way you might want. For example, even if your religious beliefs require that you stone adulterers or moneylenders to death, the U.S. penal code prohibits such behavior. (So bankers can breathe a sigh of relief, not to mention those who might be tempted to cheat on their spouse!)

Given the doctrinal beliefs of the three major monotheistic religions, then, it is not surprising to see dramatic sex segregation in the institutional positions that women and men occupy. (In chapter 9 on the workplace, we will discuss how sex segregation is the primary mechanism by which gender inequality is rendered to appear as "natural" when it is anything but.) Sex segregation is both an expression of gender inequality and one of its chief props.

Historically, women were simply prohibited from serving as ministers, imams, rabbis, or priests. The first female minister ordained in the United States was Antoinette Brown, a Congregationalist, in 1853. (Antoinette Brown soon married Samuel Blackwell, whose sister, Elizabeth, was the first woman to graduate from medical school in the United States. Quite a family!)

Yet in recent decades, there has been significant progress in enabling women to assume a position of greater equality. The Association of Theological Schools reports that the percentage of women seeking master of divinity degrees in member seminaries has increased by more than 700 percent in thirty years and that female seminarians constituted 32 percent in 2002. For example, while Reform and Conservative Judaism permit both women and gays and lesbians to be rabbis, Orthodox Judaism prohibits both. Reform Judaism began ordaining rabbis in 1972, and there are currently over four hundred female rabbis. Different Protestant denominations permit women to minister, and some permit gays and lesbians; other denominations proscribe either women or gays and lesbians or both. The Evangelical Lutheran Church in America says the percentage of its ordained clergy who are women doubled from 1991 to 2003, to 16 percent. The Episcopal Church began ordaining women in 1973; today, women constitute nearly 14 percent of all priests. And among Lutherans, nearly one in five ministers is a woman.[29]

Within the black church in America, only about 5 percent have female pastors, and these are often in small, remote, or troubled congregations. And only 5 percent of all seminary students are black women. (Two percent of all seminarians are Asian women, and 1 percent are Hispanic women.)

By contrast, the Catholic Church has remained steadfastly opposed to the ordination of women and of gay men and lesbians. Since priests are believed to act in the name of Jesus, they must resemble him physically: that is, they must be male. In the mid-1990s, then-Cardinal Ratzinger (who became Pope Benedict XVI) claimed that the pope's **prohibition** of women's ordination was to be considered "infallible" teaching, which means that it must be upheld without any debate or question as the word of God.

The Southern Baptist Convention reversed its long-standing position in 2000 and refused to ordain female ministers, despite the hundreds who had already been ordained since the practice was permitted in 1964.

Catholic clergy must also remain celibate, a vow that is not required of other monotheistic clergy. Celibacy extends traditional Catholic teachings that sex is the route by which original sin is transmitted from one generation to the next, so that those who seek to represent God's will on earth must themselves renounce not their own original sin (for all who are born are born with it), but must not transmit it to the next generation.

Partly because of these strictures, and the devastating and embarrassing pedophile priest scandal that has rocked the Catholic Church in the past decade, the number of men becoming priests worldwide has declined significantly, from 419,728 in 1970 to 412,236 in 2013—while the number of Catholics has nearly doubled, from 653 million to 1.2 billion over the same period. Thousands of parishes have closed, and nearly fifty thousand existing parishes have no priest. As a result, various Catholic organizations have tried to re-masculinize the priesthood, suggesting that only "real men"—and decidedly not gay men—are strong enough to be priests.

Intransigent resistance to the movements for gender equality and the recognition of a diversity of sexuality puts the Catholic Church increasingly at odds with many of its parishioners. A commission of biblical scholars appointed by the pope in the 1970s found no scriptural foundation for the prohibition of women from the priesthood, and a 2005 Associated Press poll found that nearly two-thirds (64 percent) of all American Catholics believed that women should be ordained.[30]

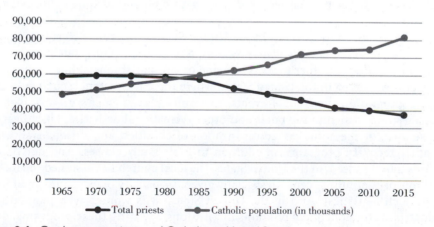

Figure 8.6. Gap between priests and Catholics in United States.

Source: "Frequently Requested Church Statistics" accessed on September 24, 2015 from cara.georgetown.edu Center for Applied Research in the Apostolate (CARA), Georgetown University, Washington, DC 20007.

Despite this, when Father Roy Bourgeois participated in the ordination of Janice Sevre-Duszynska in Lexington, Kentucky, in August 2008, he was threatened with excommunication. "Deeper than the hurt, the sadness, there's a peace that comes from knowing I followed my conscience in addressing this great injustice," he said.[31]

Women's progress toward the altar has been slow but steady. The National Congregations Study found that 10 percent of congregations had senior women pastors in 1998, while the 2001 Pulpit and Pew survey of American pastors found that 12 percent were female. By 2010, one national survey found that 12 percent of all U.S. congregations had a woman senior pastor or sole ordained leader. In mainline Protestant congregations the figure was 24 percent, while for evangelical congregations the number dropped to 9 percent.[32] Despite the proscriptions against women's ordination, those who work in religious institutions almost exactly parallel church membership. At the turn of the twenty-first century, more than three out of every five people (62 percent) who worked in religious settings—everyone from clergy to managerial and secretarial and even janitorial positions—were women. Women also compose more than half of all students studying for the clergy and more than a quarter of all students studying for advanced degrees in theology.[33]

What's more, in practice, even the Catholic Church's ban on female clerics breaks down. Given the worldwide crisis in recruitment of Catholic clergy—there are currently half the number of priests in the United States that there were in the 1960s, and there are more Catholic priests over ninety years old than under thirty—laypeople have begun to take over ministerial functions out of expedience or necessity. There are more than thirty thousand lay ministers who are serving as substitutes in parishes that do not have regular priests—and more than four out of five of these lay church people (82 percent) are women.[34] (There are some things that the women are not permitted to do, like administer last rites, but they can and do perform other rituals, like communion, baptism, confirmation, and marriage.) If present trends continue, women will probably eventually be ordained in the Catholic Church not because of a sudden change of heart from the Vatican, but because the church will simply have run out of men who are willing to embrace lifelong celibacy in the priesthood.[35]

Finally, religious institutions in the United States serve many civic functions as well as spiritual ones. On any given weekday, a tourist in a European church might encounter a few dozen other tourists and one or two parishioners. But the church is largely empty. Not so in the United States, where there is constant secular activity—day-care programs, after-school events, maternity classes, men's groups, women's groups, gyms and swimming pools and other recreational activities, Little Leagues, meal service for the homeless, administration of charities, and various twelve-step and other recovery programs, in addition to Bible study classes. And don't forget Sunday school! Indeed, in the United States, the local church has assumed the institutional role of community center (especially given the paucity of local municipal funding for such activities). And in the United States, it is women who maintain the nondoctrinal components of religious institutions, running these programs, organizing all the secular functions, and arranging for the institution's upkeep and maintenance.

PUMPING UP THE PROPHETS: RE-ENGAGING MEN IN RELIGION

The gender of religiosity poses two parallel problems. One is how to increase men's religiosity and the other might be characterized as how to *decrease* women's. Well, if not to decrease it, at least to transfer it to a domain in which women are at least the equals of men.

One of the reasons that women are more religious than men has to do with the fact that being observant itself is gender-coded. Stated most simply: Real men don't pray. They don't need to. They can take care of things on their own. There is an implied contradiction between masculinity—being in control, powerful, and king of the hill—and religiosity, which implies service, subservience, and acknowledging that you are *not* in control. Indeed, ministers have long been plagued by the question of how to reconnect men to religious institutions. What will attract men back to the pews?

This isn't a new question. In the middle of the last century, one observer commented he had never seen a country "where religion had so strong a hold upon the women or a slighter hold upon the men" than the United States. By the turn of the last century, Protestant ministers worried that religion had become a women's domain, that the sentimental piety and sanctimonious moralism—churches were the springboards for Prohibition, after all—were well-suited for female churchgoers, but hardly enticing to men, who needed to steel themselves for the rigors of competition in the urban jungle. The typical Protestant minister "moved in a world of women." Henry James Sr., father of the great novelist, lamented that the old "virile" religion had disappeared and been "replaced by a feeble Unitarian sentimentality."[36]

Images of Jesus himself reinforced this perceived feminization of religion. In paintings and drawings of the late nineteenth and early twentieth centuries, Jesus was imaged as a thin, reedy man, with long, bony fingers and soft, doelike eyes, a man who could easily counsel you to turn the other cheek and love your enemies. Such an image was actually thought to be transformative to American men; one Methodist minister described that transformation:

> It is wonderful to see a great burly man, mostly animal, who has lived under the dominion of his lower nature and given rein to his natural tendencies, when he is born of God and begins to grow in an upward and better direction. His affections begin to tap over his passion . . . The strong man becomes patient as a lamb, gentle as the mother, artless as the little child.

That is, he ceases to be a "real man." "Have we a Religion for men?" asked one disgruntled guy.[37]

His prayers were quickly answered. A new movement was born: Muscular Christianity, a movement "to bring manliness in its various manifestations to church and to keep it awake when it got there." Its goal was to revirilize the image of Jesus and thus to masculinize the church. Jesus was "no doughfaced, lick-spittle proposition," proclaimed evangelist Billy Sunday, but "the greatest scrapper who ever lived." Books such as *The Manhood of the Master* (1913), *The Manliness of Christ* (1900), and *The Manly Christ* (1904) all sought to refashion Jesus as more Hans and Frans than girly man.

Billy Sunday was perhaps the most celebrated of these Muscular Christians. Sunday abandoned his lucrative career as a professional baseball player to become an evangelical preacher (he was the model for Elmer Gantry) who organized **tent revivals** all across the Midwest and South (figure 8.7). These tent meetings were for men only, and they drew effusive praise from journalists and new followers:

> He stands up like a man in the pulpit and out of it. He speaks like a man. He works like a man . . . He is manly with God and with everyone who comes to hear him. No matter how much you disagree with him, he treats you after a manly fashion. He is not an imitation, but a manly man giving all a square deal.[38]

These all-male revivals celebrated Jesus as he-man with colorful language and spirited services. Sunday proclaimed that mainstream ministers had become "pretentious, pliable mental perverts" who were egged on by their cronies, intellectuals, who were "fudge eating mollycoddles," and big-city fat cat capitalists ("big, fat, hog-jowled, weasel-eyed, pussy-lobsters"). "Lord save us from off-handed, flabby cheeked, brittle boned, weak-kneed, thin-skinned, pliable, plastic, spineless, effeminate, ossified three-karat Christianity!" he thundered in "The Fighting Saint," his most famous sermon. "Don't tell me about the peaceful gentle Jesus! Jesus Christ could go like a six cylinder engine . . . I'd like to put my fist on the nose of the man who hasn't got grit enough to be a Christian."[39]

Such gendered evangelical fervor was part of the birth of modern society at the turn of the last century, true, but it is revived every so often as the gender differences in religiosity become an organizing vehicle for renewed religiosity among men. In the 1990s, several evangelical preachers made the manhood of Jesus a central element in their ministry. "Christ wasn't effeminate," grumped Jerry Falwell. "The man who lived on this earth was a man with muscles . . . Christ was a he-man!"[40]

Figure 8.7. Billy Sunday preaching to an all-male audience. From the archives of the Billy Graham Center, Wheaton, Illinois.

The most visible of these renewed revirilization efforts has been the **Promise Keepers**, who held massive fifty-thousand- to seventy-five-thousand-men-only rallies in sports stadiums (because it was where men felt comfortable gathering), where ministers (called coaches) and their assistants (dressed in zebra-striped shirts as if they were football referees) sought to return men to the church. Founded in 1990 by Bill McCartney, former football coach at the University of Colorado, the Promise Keepers are an evangelical Christian movement that seeks to bring men back to Jesus. They heralded a more "feminine" notion of evangelical Christianity—ideals of service, healing, and racial reconciliation—with a renewed assertion of men's God-ordained position as head of the family and master of women. In return for men keeping their promises to be faithful husbands, devoted fathers, and general all-around good men, the movement's "bible," *The Seven Promises of a Promise Keeper*, suggests that men deal with women this way:

> Sit down with your wife and say "Honey I've made a terrible mistake. I've given you my role in leading this family and I forced you to take my place. Now I must reclaim that role" . . . I'm not suggesting that you ask for your role back . . . I'm urging you to take it back . . . There can be no compromise here. If you're going to lead you must lead.[41]

Others have followed suit. Bodybuilder John Jacobs founded the "Power Team," a group of massively muscled zealots who used a pumped-up theology as the basis for motivational speaking. "Jesus Christ was no skinny little man," Jacobs claimed. "Jesus Christ was a man's man." He and his acolytes performed circus feats of masculine strength, like breaking stacks of bricks or large blocks of ice with their bare hands, to illustrate Christ's power.[42] And then there are the "JBC Men," who promised to deliver the "shock and awe" gospel to manly men. JBC stands for "Jesus–Beer–Chips"—and the organization provides the beer and chips! With film clips from *Gladiator, Braveheart,* and *The Matrix,* these religious Rambos expound a "manly gospel," saturated with images of redemptive violence. They promise a "shock and awe" gospel and sermons about how "Jesus is no Mr. Rogers." (Even their website, linked military masculinity, 9–11, and evangelical Christianity.) And Seattle evangelical minister Mark Driscoll rehearses Billy Sunday's fulminations almost verbatim. The mainstream church has transformed Jesus into "a Richard Simmons, hippie, queer Christ," a "neutered and limp-wristed popular Sky Fairy of pop culture that . . . would never talk about sin or send anyone to hell."[43] And to Driscoll, reasserting traditional gender roles—women as utterly subservient to men—is part of God's divine plan.

And then there's Tim Tebow, the former backup quarterback for the New York Jets (figure 8.8). A fervent evangelical Christian, Tebow became famous for kneeling in prayer. In fact, it's called "Tebowing." One theologian suggested that Tebow had become a cipher for both ardent evangelicals—who saw in him a charismatic leader, the sublimely gifted athlete who was still a humble supplicant—and equally fervent atheists, who saw in him the smug sanctimoniousness of those who are "too sure" of their faith. Both sides watched him with growing fascination; half wanted him to succeed, the other to fail.

Of course, these efforts to re-masculinize Jesus are only partly about men and masculinity. They suggest just how malleable are portrayals of religious prophets.

Figure 8.8. Tim Tebow "Tebows." From Donovan Schaefer, "Tebow and the Religious Body (Politic)" in *Religious Bulletin*, available at www.equinoxjournals.com/blog/2012/01/tebow-and-the-religious-body-politic.

Source: Courtesy AP Images.

Don't forget that Jesus has also been portrayed as a socialist (the working-class man, a carpenter, who organizes the working masses to rise up against their ruling-class oppressors) and a capitalist (Jesus was a "turnaround specialist" who motivated workers to be a "lean, mean, marketing machine" according to the book *Jesus, CEO*). He's been imagined as a white racist (the resurgent Ku Klux Klan invokes a "red blooded and virile" man who "purged the temple with a whip" and wrestled "the continent from savages") and a passionate advocate of civil rights and racial equality (as in the black church).[44]

And while Jesus's gender identity has long been a major theme among American Protestants, it is interesting that while the gender gap in religiosity is greater in Europe, there have been no comparable movements to "masculinize" religion there.

Most of all, these movements and groups are responses to women—or, more accurately, to women's increased equality. Katie Ladd, a liberal Methodist, offered a bit of a historial perspective when she observed that "it's only since women have been in church leadership that this backlash has come."

A revirilized Jesus seems necessary to re-establish the divinely ordained hierarchy of men over women, but only by those who feel threatened by women's equality.[45] One might even say, the more equal women get, the more masculine God becomes in the eyes of His earthly stewards.

"First, I'd like to blame the Lord for causing us to lose today."

Figure 8.9. David Sipress/The New Yorker Collection/The Cartoon Bank.

READ ALL ABOUT IT!

Stereotypes hold that gay men aren't "real" men, but are somehow more effeminate. And similarly, stereotypes hold that religious men are not "real" men, since they are committed to peace, turning the other cheek, and loving their neighbors instead of killing them. (As we've seen, the entire "Muscular Christianity" movement was an effort to masculinize religion and make Jesus more "butch.") So how do men compensate for this slander on their manhood? And how do gay Christian men reaffirm masculinity? Sociologist Ed Sumerau explores the compensatory behaviors that rescue these men's sense of themselves as men.

A WOMAN-CENTERED SPIRITUALITY

There has also been significant opposition to these efforts to masculinize Jesus. Parallel to this movement has been a feminist-inspired effort to challenge the implicit or explicit subordination of women by citing alternative contemporaneous texts or by reinterpreting texts or images in different ways. Throughout American history, female-dominated Protestant sects have emerged, such as the Shakers and Christian Scientists. For example, in the early 1970s, theologian Leonard Swidler argued that

Jesus was a "feminist" who "vigorously promoted the dignity and equality of women in the midst of a very male-dominated society."[46]

Back in the era of Billy Sunday, feminist sociologist Charlotte Perkins Gilman turned Muscular Christianity on its head. In an indictment of mainstream Protestantism, *His Religion and Hers* (1923), Gilman asks a simple question: Why is it that "neither religion, morality, nor ethics has made us 'good'"?[47] Typically, theologians would point to human fallibility: No matter how the clergy had tried to steer us toward the path of God, we humans always seemed to manage to fall off the path. That is, it's our fault for being so imperfect.

Gilman stands this on its head. It's not that we are imperfect, but that the religion that has been foisted upon us has led us astray. Religion has focused on the wrong thing—life after death instead of life before death—because, stated most simply, men have been in charge of it. "Religion, our greatest help in conscious progress, has been injured by coming through the minds of men alone." This is, she is quick to point out, "not in any essential fault of the male of our races."[48] It's not that men have done this deliberately, but that this distortion of what religion *could* be, *should* be, is the inevitable by-product of the great tragedy of our species—the subjugation of the female."[49] Much of the book is spent detailing the calamitous consequences of what she believes is our original sin: "Making a private servant of the mother of the race.[50]

Just as the sociologist Jessie Bernard had argued that there were two marriages, "his" and "hers," so, too, did Gilman argue that there were two religions. "His" religion is preoccupied with death. Because men in prehistory were concerned with war and hunting and competition among men, they developed a religion that revolves around the question "What is going to happen to me after I am dead?"[51] Heaven, in this scheme, is a hypermasculine paradise. "Never a feminine paradise among them. Happy Hunting Grounds—no Happy Nursing grounds."[52] All of this justifies war, which enables death-based religions to carry out wars with moral righteousness. "No peace can ever be maintained in a wholly male world," she writes. "No war could ever endure for long in a world of equal men and women."[53]

Against this, Gilman proposes "her" religion. Because women experience childbirth and nurturing of life, so their religion would be life-affirming. Such a "birth-based religion" would pose a different framing question: "What must be done for the child who is born?" It is the Great Mother—a somewhat mythic creation that stands as a foil to the cavalcade of priests and saints and superordinate males who have constructed "his" religious edifice—who is the real source of life, the origin of humanity. And the mother, Gilman writes, is, by virtue of her experience, altruistic: "She works, not to get but to give." And God? God is "within us," not "above us."[54]

And just as the Muscular Christianity of Billy Sunday echoed through the late twentieth and early twenty-first centuries, so, too, has Gilman's anchoring of spirituality in women's concrete embodied experience as mother. In the early years of the contemporary feminist movement, feminist theologians undertook a struggle to emancipate women's spirituality. This endeavor had several fronts.

First, there were efforts to reinterpret traditional texts in a more favorable light. After all, as feminist theologian Mary Daly argued in her first book, the authors of the Bible were men of their times, "and it would be naïve to think that they were free of the prejudices of their epochs."[55] Extracting the original intentions of various prophets from the layers of interpretation by more fallible human interpreters is always tricky, but so, too, is finding the actual textual references that point to the marked inequality that has been imposed on those same prophets' words. And those texts often do seem more egalitarian than some of those fallible interpretations. For example, Paul makes a pretty radical and egalitarian case when he cautions that "there is neither Jew nor Greek, there is neither bond nor free, there is neither male nor female; for ye are all one in Christ Jesus" (Galatians 3:28). (And you wonder how slave owners also used the Bible to justify slavery!) If there are no distinctions, then there can be no inequality, for the claims of inequality, as we've seen, have always rested on difference, whether biologically derived or divinely ordained.[56]

Second, there were efforts to retrieve from obscurity females who had been religious leaders—prophetesses and priests, goddesses and theologians—and to retrieve lost or suppressed texts and restore them to the central canonical doctrines. Important texts, such as the Gnostic Gospels, as well as female prophets and priests have been restored to prominence. Yet even this restorative move, while important historically, often fails to fully resonate with the faithful, in part because the teachings of these women, while laudable, do not approach the rhetorical power or spiritual depth of the original prophets.

And besides, discovering such worthies may actually distract us from the more pressing historical questions. (This is analogous to searching for great female artists or composers during the Renaissance and Baroque periods who were the equals of Michelangelo and Rembrandt or Bach and Handel. Elevating Christine de Pisan or Hildegard von Bingen does not solve the problem; indeed, it only begs the question: What were the historical circumstances that *prevented* truly talented women from becoming great composers or artists?)[57]

Part of this tradition has been to look less at official doctrine or at organized religious institutions and more at the way people actually *use* religion, or experience the sacred, in daily life. To take one impressive example, anthropologist Laurel Kendall has shown how in small Korean villages, it is women who are the local shamans, blessing families, offering prayers for propitious events, helping them choose auspicious days for weddings and the like, offering potions for illness, smoothing over family problems, and scaring away evil spirits. "The job of the Korean shaman is to seek out the gods, lure them into houses, and bargain with them." She's part nurse-practitioner, part family therapist, and part itinerant priest. Thus, despite a patriarchal official culture in which women are relegated to the home and official religions like Christianity, Confucianism, and Buddhism that are male-dominated, at the daily practical level, **shamanism** is the dominant religion in the country, and it is carried out entirely by women. Here Kendall finds that shamans offer a vision of women's empowerment and engage women in a spiritual life from which they are officially barred.[58]

Third have been efforts to re-envision female spirituality in more experiential ways, to anchor a spiritual vision within the lived experience of women. Like Gilman at the turn of the twentieth century, it is women's presumed connection to life—as mothers—and to the Earth ("Mother Earth") that enables women to have a different, and presumably superior, spirituality to that of men. Ecofeminism is a spiritual branch of feminism that celebrates women's intimate connection to life—as mother—as the potential salvation of an Earth that seems hell-bent on destroying itself. Women are closer to the Earth, to its natural balances, its rhythms and forces, and thus better able to realign Mother Earth with its core principles of harmony. Here is Charlene Spretnak, one of the pioneering ecofeminists, explaining the core of the movement's beliefs:

> Earth is a bountiful female, the ever-giving Mother, Who sends forth food on Her surface in cyclical rhythms and receives our dead back into Her womb. Rituals in Her honor took place in womb-like caves, often with vulva-like entrances, and long slippery corridors. The elemental power of the female was the cultural focus as far back as we can trace. At the moment this awe turned to envy, resentment, and fear, patriarchy was born. Why or how we do not know . . . The objective of patriarchy was and is to prevent women from achieving, or even supposing, our potential . . . They [patriarchy] almost succeeded.[59]

It may also involve a more direct and literal (or mythic) retrieval of the past. Mary Daly, for example, espouses what she calls "Gyn/Ecology"—an essentially feminine spirituality that invokes "the Witch within ourSelves, who spins and weaves the tapestries of Elemental creation."[60] The revival of **Wicca** is one such example. Wicca represents a retrieval of ancient polytheistic and naturalist theologies by women who proudly declare themselves to be witches; they worship a Mother Goddess and focus on the intimate connections among all living creatures.[61]

Feminist spirituality is more than simply a critique of a male-dominated religion or a religious institution that justifies and legitimates male domination. It is also a powerful testament to the human yearnings for the sacred—a realm in which all are equal on earth and in heaven.

CONCLUSION

It's one of the great ironies of American religion that an institution that is among the central pillars of gender inequality and male domination—whether in theological doctrine that places men above women and demands that women remain subservient to men, institutional arrangements that enshrine sex segregation and gender discrimination, placing a permanent glass ceiling on women's occupational mobility, or the representations of God and "his" prophets themselves—actually finds more adherents among women than among men. Perhaps it's so "naturalized," so taken for granted, that men feel they needn't participate to sustain their dominance. Perhaps men aren't religious for the same reason men don't do housework: Because they don't have to.

Feminist theologian Mary Daly explained the connection between gendered religion and our gendered society.

> The symbol of the father God spawned in the human imagination and sustained as plausible by patriarchy, has in turn rendered service to this type of society by making its mechanisms for the oppression of women appear right and fitting. If God in "his" heaven is a father ruling "his" people, then it is in the "nature" of things and according to divine plan and the order of the universe that society be male-dominated.[62]

In the middle of the nineteenth century, as women began their long march for equality, the pioneering women's rights advocate Elizabeth Cady Stanton reminded women that "the first step in the elevation of women under all systems of religion is to convince them that the great Spirit of the Universe is in no way responsible for any of these absurdities."[63] Religion, she insisted, is always political, because it deals with secular arrangements such as power, obligation, and inequality between women and men, inequalities she called "absurdities." God, the omnipotent and infallible, may have created the heavens and the Earth, but men are frail, fallible, and easily given to temptation. Gender inequality is the work of men, not God.

KEY TERMS

Celibacy	Original Sin	Tent Revivals
Burka	Prohibition	Wicca
Fundamentalism	Promise Keepers	Witchcraft
Goddess Traditions	Religiosity	Women's Spirituality
Hijab	Ritual Purification	
Monotheism	Shamanism	

SEPARATE *and* UNEQUAL

The Gendered World of Work

Well, Son, I'll tell you:
Life for me ain't been no crystal stair.
It had tacks in it,
And splinters,
And boards all torn up,
And places with no carpet on the floor—
Bare.

—Langston Hughes, "Mother to Son"

Freud once wrote that the two great tasks for all human beings are "to work and to love." And it is certainly true that people have always worked—to satisfy their basic material needs for food, clothing, and shelter; to provide for children and loved ones; to participate in community life; as well as to satisfy more culturally and historically specific desires to leave a mark on the world and to move up the social ladder. So it shouldn't surprise us that virtually every society has developed a division of labor, a way of dividing the tasks that must be done in order for the society as a whole to survive. And because gender, as we have seen, is a system of both classification and identity and a structure of power relations, it shouldn't surprise us that virtually every society has a **gendered division of labor**. There are very few tasks, in very few societies, that are not allocated by gender. This doesn't necessarily imply that the tasks assigned to one gender are less or more significant to the life of the community than the tasks assigned to the other. One might use a variety of criteria to assign tasks, and one might determine the relative values of each in a variety of ways. Valuing women's work over men's work, or vice versa, is not inevitable; it is an artifact of cultural relationships.

All this hardly comes as a surprise. But what might surprise contemporary American readers is that the gendered division of labor that many have called "traditional," the separation of the world into two distinct spheres—the public sphere of work, business, politics, and culture and the private sphere of the home, domestic life, and child care—is a relatively new phenomenon in American society. The doctrine of separate spheres was not firmly established until the decades just before the Civil War, and even then it was honored as much in the breach as in its fulfillment. Women have always worked outside the home for both economic and personal reasons—though they have had to fight to do so. The so-called traditional system of dads who head out to work every morning, leaving moms to stay at home with the children as full-time housewives and mothers, was an invention of the 1950s—and part of a larger ideological effort to facilitate the reentry of American men back into the workplace and domestic life after World War II and to legitimate the return of women from the workplace and back into the home.

OH? REALLY. Men work longer and harder than women.

That's wrong, both globally and in the United States. Just as poor people probably work harder and longer hours than rich people, so too do women work longer hours than men.

Globally, the Organization for Economic Cooperation and Development (OECD) estimates that between one-third and one-half of all "valuable economic activity" in its twenty-six member countries is not accounted for by measures of wages and hours. And since women do far more of that work than men, their contribution to the economy is seriously underestimated.

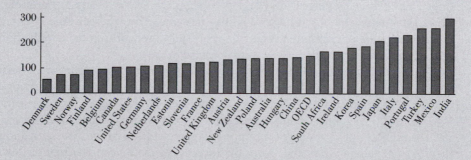

Female less male unpaid working time in minutes per day, for the population aged 15–64 over the period 1998–2009.

Source: OECD, Miranda, V. (2011), "Cooking, Caring, and Volunteering: Unpaid Work Around the World," OECD Social, Employment and Migration Working Papers, No. 116, OECD Publishing, Paris. http://dx.doi.org/10.1787/5kghrjm8s142-en.

And what also might surprise us is that this universal gendered division of labor tells us virtually nothing about the relative values given to the work women and men do. And, interestingly, it turns out that in societies in which women's work is less valued—that is, in more traditional societies in which women's legal status is lower—women do *more* work than the men do, up to 35 percent more in terms of time.

THE CHANGING GENDER COMPOSITION OF THE LABOR FORCE

Perhaps the most significant change in the relationship of gender and work is numerical—the enormous shift in the gender composition of the labor force. In the twentieth century, women entered every area of the labor force and in unprecedented numbers. The impact has been enormous. In my classes I often illustrate this phenomenon by asking the women who intend to have full-time careers or jobs outside the home to raise their hands. Without exception, all two hundred or so women do. Then I ask them to keep their hands raised if their mothers have or had a full-time job or career outside the home for at least eight years without interruption. About one-third put their hands down. Then I ask them to keep their hands raised if their grandmothers had a full-time job or career outside the home for at least eight uninterrupted years. Perhaps now four or five hands remain raised. In the class, one can clearly see the differences in women's working lives over just three generations.

What would happen if I posed the same question to the men in the class? "How many men expect to have full-time careers, outside the home, when they graduate from college?" The very question sounds ridiculous. *Of course* they expect to have careers, as did their fathers, grandfathers, and great-grandfathers. They'd never put their hands down, unless a distant relative was unemployed or we reach back to the 1930s Great Depression.

This experiment illustrates in miniature the dramatic change in the composition of the labor force. The percentage of both women and men entering the labor force increased throughout the last century, but women's rate of increase far outpaced men's. The percent of women working rose from 20.6 percent in 1900 to 57.2 percent in 2013 (men's rates were 85 percent and 69.7 percent, respectively). Marriage and children slowed that entry, but the trajectory is still the same. And whereas only 12 percent of married women with children under six years old were working outside the home as recently as 1950, nearly 64 percent were doing so in 2013.[1]

This dramatic increase in **labor force participation** has been true for all races and ethnicities. In 2013 black women's rates (59.2 percent) were slightly higher than white women's (56.9 percent), and Hispanic women's were slightly lower (55.7 percent) than those of both black and white women. Among men in 2013, however, Hispanic men had the highest rates (76.3 percent), compared with white men (70.5 percent) and black men (63.5 percent).[2] Even since 1970, the increase in women's participation has been dramatic (figure 9.2). In the next decade, 80 percent of all new entrants into the labor force will be women, minorities, and immigrants. Among married women, the data are actually more startling. In 1900, only 4 percent of married women were working, and by 1960, only 18.6 percent of married women with young children were working. This number has tripled since 1960, so that today, over 64 percent of all married women with children under six years old are in the labor force.[3]

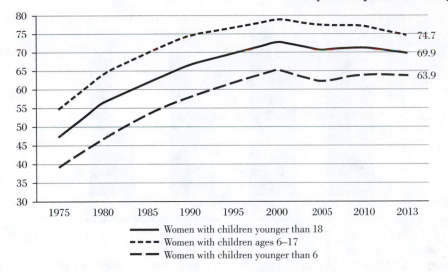

Figure 9.1a. Labor force participation rate of mothers, 1975–2013 percentages of women in the labor force.

Source: U.S. Bureau of Labor Statistics, Women in the Labor Force.

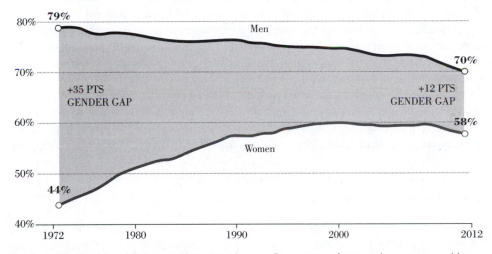

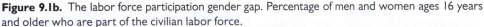

Figure 9.1b. The labor force participation gender gap. Percentage of men and women ages 16 years and older who are part of the civilian labor force.

Source: "The disappearing male worker," Pew Research Center, Washington, DC (September, 2013) http://www .pewresearch.org/fact-tank/2013/09/03/the-disappearing-male-worker/.

Women's entry into the labor force has taken place at every level, from low-paid clerical and sales work through all the major professions. In 1962, women represented less than 1 percent of all engineers, 6 percent of all doctors, and 19 percent of all university professors. By 1990, women made up over 7 percent of all engineers, 20 percent of all doctors, and almost 40 percent of all university professors, and by 2013, they made up 10.8 percent of all architects and engineers, 36.1 percent of doctors, and 47.5 percent

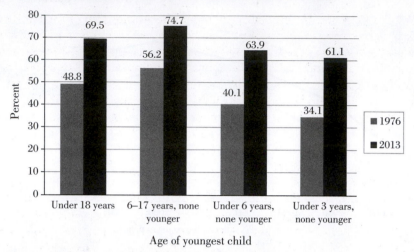

Figure 9.2. Labor force participation rates have increased dramatically among mothers over the past thirty-seven years.

Source: Bureau of Labor Statistics.

of university professors.[4] From 1970 to 1995, women's shares of doctoral degrees jumped from 25 percent to 44 percent among whites and from 39 percent to 55 percent among blacks. "The increasing representation of women among the ranks of managers in organizations," writes sociologist Jerry Jacobs, "is perhaps the most dramatic shift in the sex composition of an occupation since clerical work became a female dominated field in the late 19th century."[5]

We've come a long way, indeed, from the mid-nineteenth century, when a young Mary Taylor wrote to her friend Charlotte Brontë that "there are no means for a woman to live in England, but by teaching, sewing, or washing. The last is the best, the best paid, the least unhealthy and the most free." These changes have rippled

Try This at Home: Economic Shift

Interview your parents, grandparents, and other relatives to find out what jobs your ancestors had. Go back as far as you can. If your grandparents were born in this country, odds are that most will have been farmers in 1820 and factory workers in 1920, as the agricultural economy was replaced by the industrial economy. If your grandparents or parents were immigrants, odds are that the people who immigrated were the agricultural workers. If not, it's a good bet they were small shopkeepers or craft workers, and when they came here they began their careers as factory workers or peddlers (sales) of some sort.

And what about the men and the women? Odds are that both women and men worked on those farms or that those first immigrant relatives, both male and female, were working to try to support their families. If there are stay-at-home moms in your family history, in what generation did the women *stop* working? Where was the family living? Odds are that the women stopped working when the family moved to the suburbs or small towns: Among farmers and the urban poor, everyone worked.

through the rest of society, gradually changing the relationship of the family to the workplace. Gone forever is the male breadwinner who supports a family on his income alone. What was the norm at the turn of the twentieth century now constitutes less than 5 percent of all families. Forget the Cleavers, the Andersons, and the Nelsons. Forget the Cramdens and the Nortons. And forget even Lucy, whose every scheme to enter the work world, from the bakery to Ricky's nightclub act, ended in disaster. Today, the norm is the dual-earner couple. And yet we don't seem to get it. The *Workplace 2000* forecast report issued during the Reagan administration, for example, admitted that "most current policies were designed for a society in which men worked and women stayed home."[6]

THE PERSISTENCE OF GENDER IDEOLOGIES

Such statements acknowledge that whereas the realities of home and workplace have changed, our ideas about them have lagged far behind. Many Americans still believe in the "traditional" male breadwinner/female housewife model even if our own lives no longer reflect it—much like the way we say we believe in the individual small shopkeeper, the mom-and-pop grocery on Main Street, as the cornerstone of American business—even as we shop almost exclusively at Walmart, the Gap, Sam's Club, and shopping malls. Our adherence to gender ideologies that no longer fit the world we live in has dramatic consequences for women and men, both at work and at home.

Since the early nineteenth century, the workplace has been seen as a masculine arena where men could test and prove their manhood against other men in the dog-eat-dog marketplace. Working enabled men to confirm their manhood as breadwinners and family providers. The workplace was a site of "homosocial reproduction"—a place where men created themselves as men. As psychiatrist Willard Gaylin writes:

> Nothing is more important to a man's pride, self-respect, status, and manhood than work. Nothing. Sexual impotence, like sudden loss of ambulation or physical strength, may shatter his self-confidence. But . . . pride is built on work and achievement, and the success that accrues from that work. Yet today men often seem confused and contradictory in their attitudes about work.[7]

Gaylin captures a contradiction at the heart of men's relationship to the workplace: On the one hand, it is the most significant place where men prove manhood and confirm identity, but, on the other hand, all that breadwinning and providing do not necessarily make men happy. "I have never met a man—among my patients or friends," Gaylin writes, "who in his heart of hearts considers himself a success."[8]

The nineteenth-century ideal of the self-made man and the prospect of unlimited upward mobility for those who worked hard enough placed men on a treadmill of work, sacrifice, and responsibility. If a man could rise as high as his dreams and discipline could take him, he could also fall just as far. A 1974 Yankelovitch survey found that about 80 percent of American men were unhappy in their jobs. Another study found that 74 percent of men said they would choose a slower career track to spend more time with their families. "No man on his deathbed ever said he wished he had spent less time with his family and more time at the office," as the familiar cliché has it.

Yet why would men be unhappy in an arena whose homosociality they struggle so hard to maintain? Part of the reason has to do with what women and men carry with them into the workplace. Though most married couples are now dual-earner couples, when the wife outearns the husband all sorts of assumptions might bubble up to the surface: His masculinity may no longer be tied to being the only worker, but rather it may be tied to making the most money to support the family. The gender ideologies about who earns more are currently in much flux: A *Newsweek* poll found 25 percent of respondents thought it unacceptable for a wife to earn more than her husband, but 35 percent of men said they'd quit their jobs or reduce their hours if their wives earned more money. And though traditional gender stereotypes would have us believe that women would be content to marry less attractive but financially stable men (whereas men would be happier marrying very attractive women, without regard to finances), 50 percent of women now say that earning potential is "not at all important" in their mate choice. Men, alas, are still drawn to the gorgeous bombshell with no earning capacity.[9]

Another part of the reason has to do with what happens in the workplace. Given the demands of corporate or factory life, men rarely, if ever, experience any ability to discuss their inner lives, their feelings, their needs. The workplace becomes a treadmill, a place to fit in, not to stand out. It is a place where a man sacrifices himself on the altar of family responsibility. Many men say they lose sight of what they're working for. Men often feel that they are supposed to be tough, aggressive, competitive—the "king of the hill," the boss, their "own man," on "top of the heap." We measure masculinity by the size of a man's paycheck. Asked why he worked so hard, one man told an interviewer:

> I don't know . . . I really hate to be a failure. I always wanted to be on top of whatever I was doing. It depends on the particular picture but I like to be on top, either chairman of the committee or president of an association or whatever.[10]

Most men, of course, are neither at the top of the hierarchy nor likely to get there. Raised to believe that there are no limits, they bump constantly into those limits and have no one to blame except themselves. And because men conflate masculinity with workplace success, they remain unaware that the work they are doing is also producing and reproducing gender dynamics; they see it as just "work."[11] Men, as the saying goes, are "unsexed by failure": They cease to be seen as real men.

Women, on the other hand, are "unsexed by success." To be competent, aggressive, and ambitious in the workplace may be both gender confirming and gender conforming for men, but those traits are gender *non*conforming and thus gender disconfirming for women, undermining women's sense of themselves as feminine. Geri Richmond, a chemist, describes how she constantly battled between being "feminine" and being a scientist. A high school cheerleader and chemistry whiz, she gradually shed all the trappings of traditional femininity in graduate school in order to fit in—she threw out her dresses, nail polish, makeup, high-heeled shoes. She even tossed out her hand lotion, out of fear that its scent would evoke femininity.[12]

In the all-male workplace, women's role was to "lubricate" the male-male interactions. Women performed what sociologist Arlie Hochschild calls "**emotion work**," making sure that the all-male arena was well-oiled and functioning smoothly. So, for

OH? REALLY.

We like successful men better than successful women.

"As a man gets more successful, he is better liked by men and women, and as a woman gets more successful, she is less liked by men and women." So wrote Sheryl Sandberg, COO of Facebook and author of the best-seller *Lean In*.

And on the surface, this seems to be true. In one famous experiment in 2003, business school professors Frank Flynn and Cameron Anderson recruited students to evaluate the résumés of a real-life successful Silicon Valley venture capitalist named Heidi Roizen. But for half of the students, Heidi's name was changed to Howard; everything else remained the same. Students rated Heidi and Howard as equally competent, but they liked Howard more. They found Heidi more "selfish."

This would seem to demonstrate the persistence of gender stereotypes in our evaluation of success. But does it? After all, these were students, looking at résumés. What about in the actual business case?

Well, maybe not. A 2011 study of sixty thousand workers found something interesting. When asked whom they would rather have as a boss, 54 percent had no preference; of those who did have a preference, 72 percent wanted the male boss. But those who had female managers did not rate them less favorably than did those with male supervisors. In other words, the preferences may exist in the abstract, where stereotypes reign, but not in real life, where real people interact with other real people and those stereotypes break down.

In a recent CNN segment, ten years after the original one, Anderson Cooper had NYU replicate the Heidi–Howard study. This time students rated the female entrepreneur more likable and desirable as a boss. (And Frank Flynn no longer posts the original study on his website.)

Sources: Kim Elsesser and Janety Lever, "Does Gender Bias Against Female Leaders Persist? Quantitative and Qualitative Data from a Large Scale Survey," in *Human Relations*, 64(12), pp. 1555–1578; Eleanor Barkhorn, "Are Successful Women Really Less Likable than Successful Men?" in *Atlantic*, 2014; www.frankflynn.com.

---

example, women performed jobs like stewardess, office manager, cocktail waitress, and cheerleader to make sure the male-male interactions went smoothly—and remained unmistakably heterosexual.[13]

If women had no "real" role in the workplace, what did they do there? The traditional idea was that women worked either because they *had* to—because they were single, working class, and/or the sole economic support for their children or themselves—or because they wanted to earn the extra pocket money ("play money") that they, as middle-class consumers, wanted for their trifles. This often made working women apologetic for working at all. "If the world were perfect," it pushed them to say, "we would stay home with our children, which is, after all, where we belong and where we would rather be." But such a position belies women's actual experience. Women work, the political columnist Katha Pollitt writes, "because we enjoy our jobs, our salaries, the prospect of a more interesting and secure future than we would have with rusted skills, less seniority, less experience."[14]

Of course, these traditional gender ideologies have undergone significant change as well. It's not the 1950s—even in our heads. (Actually, even the 1950s weren't the 1950s—that is, the reality, as we saw in the chapter on the family, hardly resembled the sanitized image of nostalgic conservatives that has been romanticized by Hollywood.)

Take, for example, *Mad Men*, among the most popular television shows of the past few years. *Mad Men* depicts a group of ambitious advertising executives at the very beginning of the 1960s. The world is perfectly gender segregated: All the executives are male; all the secretaries are female. (Incidentally, almost every single character is white, and no one—either "then" or now—seems to make much of a fuss about that.) The world of male entitlement is fully intact, and the men's sexual predation isn't considered sexual harassment; it's just how things are. The show elicits a sort of self-congratulatory feeling from a contemporary viewer—back in the day, we say to ourselves, they did all sorts of things we now know to be wrong: Everyone smoked everywhere; the men drank pretty much all day in their offices and preyed on female support staff as if in a brothel. (One secretary's ambition to become an account executive provides a tension-filled plotline for an entire season.) How benighted their views! How archaic! We know better *now*!

But the transparently anachronistic themes only mask how today those archaic attitudes still hold sway and how they continue to clash with the changing realities of the work world. And that clash makes the workplace a particularly contentious arena for gender issues. On the one hand, women face persistent discrimination based on their gender: They are paid less, promoted less, and assigned to specific jobs despite their qualifications and motivations; and they are made to feel unwelcome, like intruders in an all-male preserve. On the other hand, men say they are bewildered and angered by the changes in workplace policy that make them feel like they are "walking on eggshells," fearful of making any kind of remark to a woman lest they be hauled into court for sexual harassment.

The structural backdrop to this current workplace wariness and corporate confusion is one of the highest levels of workplace gender inequality in the industrial world. That the United States manifests this gender inequality may contradict American assumptions about freedom and equality of opportunity, but it is not so terribly surprising because we also have among the highest levels of income inequality in general in the industrial world. According to a study commissioned by the Organization for Economic Cooperation and Development, the difference between the best-paid 10 percent and the lowest-paid 10 percent of all working Americans is

COMPARED *to* WHAT?

While the self-congratulatory nostalgia of *Mad Men* invites us to compare the progress made in the American workplace since the 1960s, a glance at other countries can be both sobering and edifying. In China, for example, old stereotypes about gender persist and hamper individual women's ability to pursue the careers they want. One young woman, for example, is a twenty-six-year-old business school graduate, fluent in English, Chinese, French, and Japanese. Yet in interviews she was asked only about when she was planning to have a baby, and even though she said she was planning to wait for at least five years, the interviewers didn't believe her. She was rejected countless times and eventually took a lower-paying job in the state sector.

Source: Didi Kirsten Tatlow, "Old Biases Hamper Women in China's New Economy" in *New York Times*, November 30, 2010, p. A-18.

Subtle Sexism

Gender discrimination is both structural and attitudinal; it's embedded both in social institutions and structural arrangements and in our heads. Of course, the blatant forms of sexism of the 1950s workplace are no longer acceptable. Gone, largely, is Don Draper's (of *Mad Men*) patronizing pat on his secretary's butt. But in its place has come a myriad assortment of subtle attitudes and behaviors that reproduce workplace inequality. In a marvelously clever analysis, sociologist Nicole Benokraitis outlines several forms of "subtle sexism," behaviors that may even be invisible to those who enact them.

Condescending chivalry: A supervisor withholds useful criticism from a female employee to "protect" her.

Supportive discouragement: Discouraging a woman from competing for a challenging opportunity because she might not succeed.

Friendly harassment: Kidding a woman in public about her appearance.

Subjective objectification: Believing that all women fit some particular stereotype.

Radiant devaluation: Offering exaggerated praise for an accomplishment that might otherwise be seen as routine.

Liberated sexism: Inviting a woman for a drink after work, just like one of the boys, but then refusing to let her pay for a round.

Benevolent exploitation: Giving a woman the opportunity to work on a project to get experience, but then taking all credit for the final product.

Considerate domination: Making decisions for women about what they can and cannot handle (as, for example, a new mother) without letting her decide how best to manage her time.

Collegial exclusion: Scheduling meetings at times when parents have family responsibilities that might conflict, such as 7 a.m. breakfast "networking" or "team building" meetings.

Source: Nicole Benokraitis, *Subtle Sexism: Current Practices and Prospects for Change* (Thousand Oaks, CA: Sage, 1997).

wider than that in any other industrial nation. During the economic boom of the 1980s, the top 1 percent of the income pyramid received about 60 percent of all the economic gains of the decade. The next 19 percent received another 25 percent, so that, in all, 85 percent of all economic gains of the decade went to the top 20 percent of the economic hierarchy. The bottom 20 percent of Americans actually lost 9 percent, and the next 20 percent above them lost 1 percent. So much for "trickle down" economics! For the bottom 80 percent of Americans, the peak earning year in the past decades was 1973—that is, their annual incomes have since then either remained flat or declined. According to the Congressional Budget Office, median family income, in fact, has remained absolutely flat. Measured in 2012 dollars, median family income in 1973 was $62,261; in 1990 it was $52,533; in 2010, it was $52,015; and in 2014, it was $51,939.[15]

Remember, also, this is average *family* income—and the greatest single change in the labor force is the increasing presence of women. So this means that men's incomes have actually declined over the past quarter-century. A thirty-year-old man in 1949 saw his real earnings rise by 63 percent by the time he turned forty. In 1973, that same thirty-year-old man would have seen his real income *fall* by 1 percent by his fortieth birthday. These economic indicators are particularly important as the general context for gender inequality, because they suggest that the majority of male workers have felt increasingly squeezed in the past two decades, working longer and harder to make ends meet while experiencing a decline in income. This increased economic pressure, coupled with increased economic precariousness caused by downsizing, corporate layoffs, and market volatility, has kept American men anxious about their previously unchallenged position as providers and breadwinners. Indeed, male workers account for more than four out of every five jobs lost in the current recession (since June 2008).[16]

READ ALL ABOUT IT!

The dynamics of workplace inequality—wage discrimination, sex segregation, sexual harassment—have been shifting dramatically in recent years. Women have "leaned in," and the glass ceiling has been pushed higher. But from a bird's eye view, as sociologist Paula England writes, progress has been "uneven" and the gender transformation of the workplace has "stalled." This is clearly a case of "both/and" and not "either/or"—to a sociologist, what is interesting is where things have gotten better, where progress has been frustrated, and what dynamics have led to these arrangements.

THE PERSISTENCE OF GENDER DISCRIMINATION IN THE WORKPLACE

For many years, the chief obstacle facing women who sought to enter the labor force was sex discrimination. Discrimination occurs when we treat people who are similar in different ways or when we treat people who are different in similar ways. For example, women and African Americans are seen, legally, as "similar" in all functionally relevant aspects relating to employment, housing, and education. Therefore, to exclude one race or gender from housing, educational opportunities, or employment would be a form of discrimination. On the other hand, people with certain physical disabilities are seen as legally *different* and thus deserving of antidiscrimination protection. Treating them "the same" as able-bodied people—failing to provide wheelchair-accessible facilities, for example—is therefore also a form of discrimination.

In **gender discrimination** in the workplace, employers have historically referred to a variety of characteristics about women in order to exclude them, for example, women don't really want to work; they don't need the money; they have different aptitudes and interests. It was assumed that women either couldn't do a job or, if they could, would neither want to nor need to do it. What these arguments share is a belief that the differences between women and men are decisive and that these differences are the source of women's and men's different experiences. Such arguments also provided the pretense for justifying race discrimination in employment and education, at least until 1954, when the Supreme Court ruled in *Brown v. Board of Education of Topeka* that there were no compelling differences between blacks and whites that could serve as a qualification for equal access to employment or education. Today, the Court holds race cases to what it calls "strict scrutiny," meaning that discrimination on the basis of race is always legally suspect and that there are no legal grounds for racial discrimination. It is discrimination to treat those who are alike—blacks and whites—as if they were different.

This is not completely true, however, when it comes to gender. In its cases involving gender discrimination, the Supreme Court has granted only "intermediate scrutiny." Discrimination on the basis of gender is permissible, but only under the most exceptional of circumstances. The basis for the discrimination may not rely on any stereotypic ideas about the differences between women and men, and there must be a "bona fide occupational qualification"—that is, the discrimination must be based on some occupational requirement that either only men or only women could meet. In federal cases, the discrimination must also be "substantially related to an important governmental interest"—that is, it must serve some larger goal of the government.

Consider, for example, the case of a nine-year-old girl who applies to work as a lifeguard at the beach. Denying her the job would not be a case of either gender or age discrimination because one would equally deny the job to a nine-year-old boy, as age is a functionally relevant category for the performance of the job. But it is extraordinarily difficult to demonstrate in court that the requirements of any particular job are such that only women or only men could possibly perform that job.

One such case involved a woman who applied for a job with Trans World Airlines. During her interview, she was asked about her marital status, her plans regarding pregnancy, her relationship with another TWA employee, the number of children she had, whether they were legitimate, and her child-care arrangements. In fact, that was *all* she was asked at her first interview. She was not hired. The courts found that she had been treated differently based on gender and thus had been discriminated against. Can we even imagine the interviewers asking a male applicant those kinds of questions?

Most legal cases of workplace discrimination have involved women bringing suit to enter formerly all-male workplaces. One interesting recent case, however, explored the other side of the coin. The Hooters restaurant chain was sued by several men who sought employment as waiters in restaurants in Illinois and Maryland. Historically, Hooters hired only "voluptuous" women to work as their "scantily clad" bartenders and food servers. The male plaintiffs, and their lawyers, argued that such a policy violates equal employment statutes. Hooters countered that its restaurants provide "vicarious sexual recreation" and that "female sexuality is a bona fide occupation," citing other all-female occupations like Playboy Bunnies and the Rockettes. Hooters waitresses "serve Buffalo wings with a side order of sex appeal" was the way one newspaper columnist put it. Company spokesman Mike McNeil claimed that Hooters doesn't sell food; it sells sex appeal—and "to have female sex appeal, you have to be female." The Equal Employment Opportunity Commission (EEOC) quietly dropped its own investigation, saying it had better cases to pursue. Eventually, the case was settled out of court, with Hooters paying $3.75 million to the men and their attorneys and adding a few men to its staffs as bartenders—but not as waiters.[17]

Gender discrimination is often compounded by discrimination based on other factors, such as race or sexual orientation. While men have higher incomes than women in all categories—white or black, gay or straight—how these different categories of identity work themselves out is far from obvious. In a fascinating study, sociologist David Pedulla found that stereotypes about gay men being effeminate and weak will result in discrimination against white gay men, but that these same stereotypes might cancel out the negative stereotypes about black men being threatening and criminal. In this way, racial stereotypes conflict with homophobic stereotypes, and actually may provide a small advantage to black gay men over either white gay men or black heterosexual men.[18]

SEX SEGREGATION

Outright gender discrimination is extremely difficult to justify. But far more subtle and pervasive mechanisms maintain gender inequality. Perhaps the most ubiquitous of these is sex segregation. Sex segregation, writes sociologist Barbara Reskin, "refers to women's and men's concentration in different occupations, industries, jobs, and levels in workplace hierarchies." Thus sex segregation becomes, itself, a "sexual division of paid labor in which men and women do different tasks, or the same tasks under different names or at different times and places." Different occupations are seen as more appropriate for one gender or the other, and thus women and men are guided, pushed, or occasionally shoved into specific positions.[19]

In fact, sex segregation in the workplace is so pervasive that it appears to be the natural order of things, the simple expression of women's and men's natural predispositions. In that sense, it's more subtle than some garment factories in Bangladesh, where male and female workers actually work on different floors to ensure no contact between them. In the United States, it *appears* to be the result of our "natural" differences; but, as we have seen before, these differences are themselves the consequence of segregation. Today, fewer than 10 percent of all Americans have a coworker or a colleague of the other sex who does the same job, for the same employer, in the same location, on the same shift. Though almost equal numbers of women and men go off to work every morning, we do not go together to the same place, nor do we have the same jobs. In fact, of the nearly sixty-six million women in the labor force in the United States, 30 percent worked in just 10 of the 503 "occupations" listed by the U.S. Census. Or, to put it another way, more than 52 percent of all women or of all men would have to change their jobs for the occupational distribution to be completely integrated.[20]

Sex segregation starts early and continues throughout our work lives. And it has significant consequences for incomes and experiences. I frequently ask my students how many of them have worked as babysitters. Typically, at least two-thirds of the women say they have, and occasionally one or two men say they have. How much do they earn? They average about $4 to $5 an hour, typically earning $20 for an afternoon or evening. When I ask how many of them have earned extra money by mowing lawns or shoveling snow, though, the gender division is reversed. Most of the men, but only an occasional woman, say they had those jobs and typically earned about $20–$25 per house—or about $100 a day. And although it is true that shoveling snow or mowing lawns requires far more physical exertion than babysitting, babysitting also requires specific social, mental, and nurturing skills, caring and feeding, and the ability to respond quickly in a crisis. And in most societies, ours included, it is hardly the menial physical laborers who are paid the most (think of the difference between corporate executives and professional lawn mowers). In fact, when grown-ups do these jobs—professional baby nursing or lawn maintenance—their incomes are roughly similar. What determines the differences in wages for these two after-school jobs has far less to do with the intrinsic properties of the jobs and far more to do with the gender of who performs them. That we see the disparities as having to do with something other than gender is exactly the way in which **occupational sex segregation** obscures gender discrimination.

The impact of sex segregation on income remains just as profound as the differences between babysitting and snow-shoveling for the rest of our lives. Job segregation by sex is the single largest cause of the pay gap between the sexes (tables 9.1 and 9.2). Consider that in 2013, while women represented just over 44 percent of all workers in the civilian labor force, they were 32.7 percent of all dentists; 34.8 percent of all lawyers and 38.8 percent of all judges; 13 percent of all police officers; 3.1 percent of all firefighters; 4.2 percent of all workers in natural resources, construction, and maintenance occupations; and 36.1 percent of all physicians and surgeons. On the other hand, women were also 94.7 percent of all secretaries, 91 percent of all nurses, 93 percent of all child-care workers, 75.3 percent of all teachers (excluding college and university), and 80.4 percent of all data entry keyboard operators.[21] Almost half of all female employees today work in occupations that are more than 75 percent female. And yet all of these represent significant *improvements* since 1990.[22]

Explanations of sex segregation often rely on the qualities of male and female job seekers. Because of differential socialization, women and men are likely to seek different kinds of jobs for different reasons. However, socialization alone is not sufficient as an explanation. "Socialization cannot explain why a sex-segregated labor market emerged, why each sex is allocated to particular types of occupations, and why the sex typing of occupations changes in particular ways over time." Instead, we need to think of sex segregation as the outcome of several factors—"on the differential socialization of young men and women, sex-typed tracking in the educational system, and sex-linked social control at the workplace, at the hiring stage and beyond."[23]

If sex segregation were simply the product of socialized differences between women and men, we should expect that professions would have roughly comparable gender distributions in other cities or countries. But they do not. For example, in New York City, there are only 44 women out of 10,500 firefighters, or .4 percent of the force. In Minneapolis, 17 percent of the firefighters are women. New York lags behind San Francisco (15 percent) and Seattle (8 percent) and is actually less than one-tenth the national average of 4.5 percent. (Minorities don't fare that much better: The national averages for Latinos [9.3 percent], African Americans [7.1 percent] and Asian Americans [.7 percent] remain markedly low.)[24]

Or take dentists. In the United States, dentistry is a male-dominated profession (figure 9.3); in Europe, most dentists are female. In Russia, about half of all doctors are women and have been for some time. Assuming that European and Russian women and men are roughly similar to North American women and men, you would expect the gender composition of dentistry or medicine to be similar.

This leads to another consequence of sex segregation: wage differentials. Professions that are male dominated tend to have higher wages; professions that are female dominated tend to have lower wages. And though one might be tempted to explain this by the characteristics of the job, it turns out that the gender composition of the position is actually a better predictor. Again, take dentists. In the United States, dentistry sits near the top of the income pyramid. In Europe, the income level of dentists is about average. This difference has nothing to do with the practice of dentistry, which is,

Table 9.1. The Ten Most Common Occupations for Women (Highest Percentage of Workers Who Are Female, Full-time Workers Only), 2013

	Men's median weekly earning	Women's median weekly earning	Women's earning as percent of men's	Share of female workers in occupation	Share of male workers in occupation as percent of all male workers	Share of female workers in occupation as percent of all female workers
	$860	$706	82.1%	44.4%	100%	100%
All female workers (46,268,000)						
Elementary and middle school teachers	$1,025	$937	91.4%	80.1%	0.9%	4.6%
Secretaries and administrative assistants	$772	$677	87.7%	94.6%	0.2%	4.6%
Registered nurses	$1,236	$1,086	87.9%	88.8%	0.4%	4.4%
Nursing, psychiatric, and home health aides	$499	$450	90.2%	86.6%	0.3%	2.6%
Customer service representatives	$639	$616	96.4%	66.1%	0.9%	2.3%
First-line supervisors of retail sales workers	$778	$612	78.7%	42.3%	2.3%	2.1%
Accountants and auditors	$1,268	$1,029	81.2%	62.3%	1.0%	2.0%
Cashiers	$426	$379	89.0%	69.0%	0.7%	2.0%
First-line supervisors of offices and administrative support workers	$846	$748	88.4%	67.7%	0.7%	1.8%
Receptionists and information clerks	$600	$527	87.8%	91.9%	0.1%	1.8%
Sum					7.6%	28.2%

Source: U.S. Department of Labor, Bureau of Labor Statistics. 2013. "Household Data Annual Average. Table 39." http://www.bls.gov/cps/cpsaat39.htm (retrieved November 2014).

Table 9.2. The Ten Most Common Occupations for Men (Highest Percentage of Workers Who Are Male, Full-time Workers Only), 2013

	Men's median weekly earning	Women's median weekly earning	Women's earning as percent of men's	Share of female workers in occupation	Share of male workers in occupation as percent of all male workers	Share of female workers in occupation as percent of all female workers
	$860	$706	82.1%	44.4%	100%	100%
All male workers (57,994,000)						
Driver/sales workers and truck drivers	$738	$583	79.0%	4.1%	4.3%	0.2%
First-line supervisors of retail sales workers	$778	$612	78.7%	42.3%	2.3%	2.1%
Janitors and building cleaners	$517	$418	80.9%	27.4%	1.9%	0.9%
Retail salespersons	$719	$485	67.5%	40.3%	1.9%	1.6%
Construction laborers	$592	—	—	2.7%	1.8%	0.1%
Laborers and freight, stock, and material movers, hand	$524	$421	80.3%	17.3%	1.8%	0.5%
Software developers, applications and systems software	$1,737	$1,370	78.9%	19.8%	1.5%	0.5%
Sales representatives, wholesale and manufacturing	$1,131	$859	76.0%	22.8%	1.4%	0.5%
Cooks	$411	$382	92.9%	34.6%	1.4%	0.9%
Grounds maintenance workers	$441	—	—	3.9%	1.3%	0.1%
Sum					19.6%	7.3%

Note: Dash indicates no data or data that do not meet publication criteria (values not shown where base is less than 50,000).

Source: U.S. Department of Labor, Bureau of Labor Statistics. 2013. "Household Data Annual Average. Table 39." http://www.bls.gov/cps/cpsaat39.htm (retrieved November 2014).

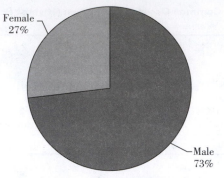

Figure 9.3. Percentage distribution of all professionally active dentists in the United States by gender, 2013.

Source: American Dental Association, Health Policy Institute analysis of ADA masterfile. Copyright © 2015 American Dental Association. Reprinted by permission.

Case in Point: The Case of Nurses

Nursing is one of the most gender-segregated professions. Close to nineteen out of twenty nurses are female. It's a profession that requires patience, empathy, emotional engagement, and a desire to help others—all qualities generally coded as feminine. At the same time, there is a worldwide nursing shortage, which is only expected to become more intense as an aging population requires more medical care. What's a profession to do?

Well, legislate, for one thing. In 2013, Senator Barbara Boxer (D-CA) introduced Senate Bill 739, the National Nursing Shortage Reform and Patient Advocacy Act. (It's in committee at this writing.)

And, of course, recruit men. Make nursing masculine! Sociologist Marci Cottingham examined various recruitment strategies to engage men to become nurses, including this advertisement from Central Florida (with many others that have copied it):

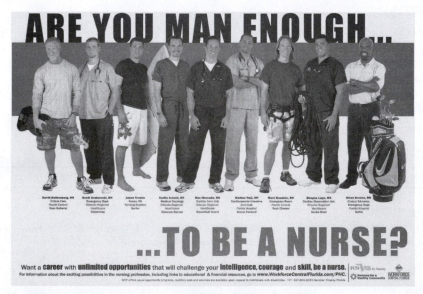

Source: Partners for a Healthy Community, Workforce Central Florida.

Of course, when men enter the field, the old rules apply. At every level, male nurses out-earn female nurses. According to the U.S. Department of Labor, male nurses earn about $5,100 more per year than female nurses. Among the highly specialized nurse anesthetists, the gap was a whopping $17,290!

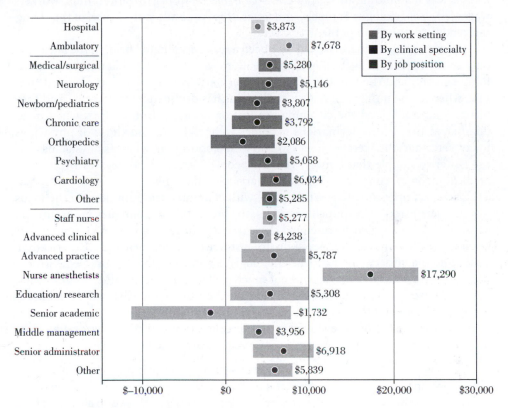

Salary gaps between male and female registered nurses.

Notes: Figures are in 2013 dollars. Lighter bars indicate margin of error (at a 95 percent confidence interval).

Source: Analysis of data from the National Sample Survey of Registered Nurses (1988–2008) by Dr. Ulrike Muench, et al. Published in the *Journal of the American Medical Association.* Credit: Alyson Hurt/NPR.

Sources: Marci Cottingham, "Recruiting Men, Constructing Manhood: How Health Care Organizations Mobilize Masculinities as Nursing Recruitment Strategy" in *Gender & Society*, 28(1), February 2014, pp. 133–156; Catherine Saint Louis, "Stubborn Pay Gap Is Found in Nursing" in *New York Times*, March 24, 2015, http://well.blogs.nytimes.com/2015/03/24/stubborn-pay-gap-is-found-in-nursing/?_r=2.

one assumes, fairly comparable. The wage difference is entirely the result of the gender of the person who does the job. There is nothing inherent in the job that makes it more "suitable" for women or for men.

One of the easiest ways to see the impact of sex segregation on wages is to watch what happens when a particular occupation begins to change its gender composition. For example, clerical work was once considered a highly skilled occupation, in which a virtually all-male labor force was paid reasonably well. (One is reminded, of course, of the exception to this rule, the innocent and virtuous Bob Cratchit in Charles Dickens's

A Christmas Carol.) In the early part of the twentieth century, in both Britain and the United States, though, the gender distribution began to change, and by the middle of the century, most clerical workers were female. As a result, clerical work was reevaluated as less demanding of skill and less valuable to an organization; thus, workers' wages fell. As sociologist Samuel Cohn notes, this is a result, not a cause, of the changing gender composition of the workforce.[25]

Veterinary medicine, also, had long been a male-dominated field. In the late 1960s, only about 5 percent of veterinary students were women. Today that number is closer to 60 percent, and the number of female veterinarians has more than doubled since 1991, whereas the number of male veterinarians has declined by 15 percent. And their incomes have followed the changing gender composition. In the 1970s, when males dominated the field, veterinarians' incomes were right behind those of physicians; today, veterinarians average about $70,000 to $80,000 a year, whereas physicians average closer to double that figure. "Vets are people with medical degrees without the medical income," commented one veterinary epidemiologist.[26]

The exact opposite process took place with computer programmers. In the 1940s, women were hired as keypunch operators, the precursors to computer programmers, because the job seemed to resemble clerical work. In fact, however, computer programming "demanded complex skills in abstract logic, mathematics, electrical circuitry and machinery, all of which," sociologist Katharine Donato observed, "women used to perform in their work" without much problem. However, after programming was recognized as "intellectually demanding," it became attractive to men, who began to enter the field and thus drove wages up considerably.[27]

The relationship between gender composition and prestige (and wages) has long been in evidence. In the 1920s, the feminist writer Charlotte Perkins Gilman found it

> amusing to see how rapidly the attitude toward a given occupation changed as it changed hands. For instance, two of the oldest occupations of women, the world over, were that of helping other women to bring babies into the world and that of laying out the dead. Women sat at the gates of life, at both ends, for countless generations. Yet as soon as the obstetrician found one large source of income in his highly specialized services, and the undertaker found another in his, these occupations became "man's work"; a "woman doctor" was shrunk from even by women, and a "woman undertaker" seemed ridiculous.[28]

(It is interesting that women have returned to obstetrics, but undertaking remains virtually all male.)

The effects of sex segregation may be "geographic" in everyday life—both in the workplace and in leisure. In a 2008 study, Michelle Arthur, Robert del Campo, and Harry Van Buren, three business professors at the University of New Mexico, studied golf courses. Well, what they actually studied were the placement of the tees at the beginning of each hole at 455 courses in all fifty states. Typically, women tee off from a tee placed somewhat in front of the men's tee (part of an understanding that equality doesn't mean treating people exactly the same, since the only place where women's and men's different upper body strength actually makes a difference is on the first shot). What Arthur, Del Campo, and Van Buren found was a correlation between the distance between the men's and women's tee and the **wage gap** in that immediate locale.

That's right: The farther apart were the tees, the lower were women's wages! The closer the tees were, the higher were women's wages.

How is this to be explained? The obvious answer is that those locales where golf course administrators believed women needed increased assistance were those characterized by a patronizing view of women's abilities in general. And those attitudes would have seeped into local workplaces, where women's abilities would have been undervalued. Seems plausible. But the authors also suggested a less attitudinal explanation as well. Where the tees were closer together, women and men were more likely to ride in the same golf carts; where the tees were far apart, women were more likely to ride only with other women. And it's in those golf carts, in the informal conversations and networking that accompany our "leisure time," that one hears of opportunities, connections, and contacts that can advance a career.[29]

The sex of the worker is also vitally important in determining wages. Women and men are paid to do not the same work, but rather different work, and they are evaluated on different standards. As William Bielby and James Baron write, "Men's jobs are rewarded according to their standing within the hierarchy of men's work, and

OH? REALLY•

Men take all the dangerous jobs, so they should be paid more. You've heard this, right? The most dangerous jobs are all heavily male dominated, and since men are willing to take those risks, they should be compensated for it. Here's the list:

Top Ten Most Dangerous U.S. Occupations and Percent Male, 2013

Rank	Occupation	Fatal injury rate per 100,000 workers	Percent male
1	Logging workers	91.3	97.9%
2	Fishers	75.0	100.0%
3	Aircraft pilots	50.6	94.5%
4	Extraction workers	46.9	97.9%
5	Roofers	38.7	99.3%
6	Refuse collectors	33.0	95.2%
7	Mining machine operators	26.9	95.0%
8	Truck drivers	22.0	94.8%
9	Farmers and ranchers	21.8	74.7%
10	Electrical power-line workers	21.5	98.9%

Source: Bureau of Labor Statistics, Census of Fatal Occupational Injuries.

Well, that would be true—if we paid those who do those jobs the most money. I mean, it's a lot more "dangerous" to be a roofer or a logger or a fisherman than it is to be an investment banker or a corporate lawyer—but we don't pay them commensurately to the dangers they face.

But it would also make more sense if the resistance to women's entry into those fields wasn't so fierce. Women who try to become loggers or roofers or mining machine operators face a steady barrage of physical and sexual harassment by the very men who complain that men take all the dangerous jobs. Perhaps that is because when men take those jobs, they are also doing so to prove that they are "real men"—and women's entry, they believe, would dilute that.

women's jobs are rewarded according to their standing within the hierarchy of women's work. The legitimacy of this system is easy to sustain in a segregated workplace." Stated simply, "Women's occupations pay less at least partly *because* women do them."[30]

Here's a novel way to consider the impact of sex segregation on wages. As we just saw, when a particular occupation shifts its gender composition, wages shift too. The more "masculine," the higher the wages; the more "feminine," the lower the wages. But what happens when the gender of the worker changes? I'm not talking about the gender of a category of workers. Rather, the actual gender of the actual individual worker: Then what happens? In their research sociologist Kristen Schilt and economist Matthew Wiswall tracked the wages of transgender people—before and after their transitions. Female-to-male transgender people's wages went up slightly following their transitions, while average wages for male-to-female transgender workers fell by nearly one-third. What's more, male-to-female workers saw a loss of authority, greater levels of harassment, and possible termination compared with female-to-male transgender people, who often saw an *increase* in respect and authority. Remember—these were the same human beings. Only their gender had changed. And that mattered a lot.[31]

Legal remedies for sex stereotyping of occupations have yielded mixed results. In a 1971 case, *Diaz v. Pan American World Airways*, the U.S. Court of Appeals for the Fifth Circuit ruled that men could not be denied employment as flight attendants on the grounds that passengers expected and preferred women in this position. In 1996, you will recall from the last chapter, the Supreme Court ruled that women could not be denied the educational opportunity offered to men at the Virginia Military Institute, despite the school's arguments that women would not want such an "adversative" education, nor would they be able to withstand the physical rigors of the program.

Perhaps the most widely cited case in sex segregation is the case of *EEOC v. Sears*, a case brought by the Equal Employment Opportunity Commission against the giant chain of retail stores. The EEOC had found that Sears had routinely shuttled women and men into different sales positions, resulting in massive wage disparities between the two. Women were pushed into over-the-counter retail positions, largely in clothing, jewelry, and household goods, where commissions tended to be low and where workers received a straight salary for their work. Men, on the other hand, tended to be concentrated in sales of high-end consumer goods, such as refrigerators and televisions, which offered high commissions.

Sears argued that this sex-based division of retail sales resulted from individual choice on the part of its male and female labor forces. Differential socialization, Sears suggested, led women and men to pursue different career paths. Women, Sears claimed, were less interested in the more demanding, intensely competitive, and time-consuming higher-end commission sales positions and were more interested in those that offered them more flexibility, whereas the men were more interested in those pressure-filled, high-paying positions. Women, Sears argued, were more relationship-centered and less competitive.

The EEOC, by contrast, argued that although Sears did not intend to discriminate, such outcomes were the result of gender-based discrimination. The case did not pit the interests or motivations of all men against those of all women, but rather included only those women who were already in the labor force, who, one assumed, had similar motivations to those of men in the labor force. Just because it is true, argues historian Alice Kessler-Harris, who was an expert witness for the EEOC, that there are average differences between women and men in their motivations does not mean that every single member of the group "men" or "women" is identical and that some would not seek the opportunities afforded to the other group. To discriminate against individuals on the basis of average between-group differences ignores the differences *within* each group, differences that often turn out to be greater than the differences between the groups.

Such behavior, of course, relies on stereotypes and should be prohibited under the law. Stereotypes assume that all members of a group share characteristics that, possibly, some members of the group share—and even, occasionally, most members share. Logically, stereotypes fall into a compositional fallacy—assuming that what is true of some is true of all. So it would be illogical to assert that just because all members of category A are also members of category B, all members of category B are members of category A. You know nothing, for example, about the relative size of these categories: All A's may be B's, and yet all B's may not be A's. Thus in the classic formulation of the compositional fallacy one might say, "All members of the Mafia are Italian, but all Italians are not members of the Mafia" or "All humans are animals, but not all animals are human."

In the Sears case, the U.S. Supreme Court upheld Sears's acquittal on sex discrimination charges, in part because the Court said that no single individual woman had stepped forward and declared that she had sought to enter high-commission sales or had been refused because of these stereotypes. (Often legal cases seem to need a concrete plaintiff because the courts are less convinced by aggregate statistical disparities if no individual has been harmed.) And the Court found that gender differences did play a role, that "since difference was real and fundamental, it could explain statistical variations in Sears hiring." Yes. And it probably also explains the differences in salary.[32]

INCOME DISCRIMINATION—THE WAGE GAP

Another major consequence of the combination of sex segregation and the persistence of archaic gender ideologies is income discrimination. At both the aggregate level and the individual level—whether we average all incomes or look at specific individuals' wages for the jobs they do—women earn less than men. This wage difference begins early in our lives—even before we begin working. A 1995 *Wall Street Journal* report observed that elementary school girls receive smaller allowances and are asked to do more chores than boys are.[33]

Income inequality often remains invisible precisely because of sex segregation—what appears to us simply as paying people doing different *jobs* is actually a way of paying different *genders* differently for doing roughly the same jobs with the same skill levels. As long as it appears that pay is the attribute of the job, and not of the gender of the person doing the job, income inequality remains invisible to us (figures 9.4 a and b). In 1999, the median annual income for men working full time was $37,057. For women it was $27,194, about 73 percent of men's annual income. By 2013, that gap had shrunk—women's wages were about 78.3 percent of men's wages (77.4 percent for whites, 84.1 percent for blacks and Hispanics). Actually, that is due, in large part, not to the massive increases in women's wages, but rather to the decline in men's wages—the

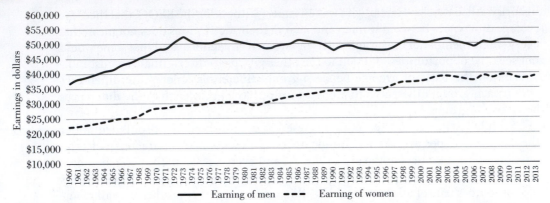

Figure 9.4a. Full-time, year-round workers by median earnings and gender, 1960–2013.

Source: U.S. Census Bureau, Historical Income Tables: People, https://www.census.gov/hhes/www/income/data/historical/people/ (retrieved November 2014).

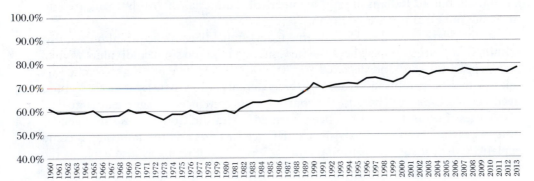

Figure 9.4b. Women's-to-men's earnings as a percentage of men's earnings, 1960–2013.

Source: U.S. Census Bureau, Historical Income Tables: People, https://www.census.gov/hhes/www/income/data/historical/people/ (retrieved November 2014).

decline, especially, in the high-wage skilled manufacturing sector of the economy, where jobs have been exported overseas to workers who receive decidedly lower wages.

On average, working women still bring home $154 a week less than men. To illustrate the extent of this wage inequality, every year the president proclaims a date in early April "National Pay Inequity Awareness Day." Why then? Because the average woman in a full-time job would need to work for a full year and then until early April of the next year to match what the average man earned the year before.[34]

The National Committee on Pay Equity estimated that in 1996 alone working women lost almost $100 million due to wage inequality. Over the course of her lifetime, the average working woman will lose about $420,000. And the gender gap in income is made more complex by both race and educational level. Black and Hispanic men earn less than white men, and black men earn only slightly more than white women. Black and Hispanic women earn significantly less than white men or white women, and black women earn slightly more than Hispanic men (figure 9.6).

Figure 9.5 The gender wage gap explained.

Source: B. Deutsch, leftycartoons.com.

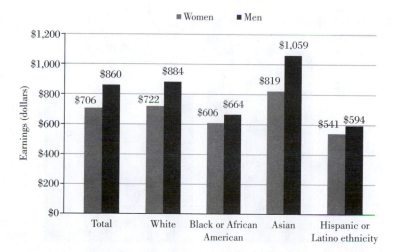

Figure 9.6. Median weekly earnings of workers sixteen years of age and over in 2013, by gender and race and Hispanic or Latino ethnicity.

Source: Data from the Bureau of Labor Statistics—Labor Force Statistics from the Current Population Survey (2013 annual averages), http://bls.gov/cps/cpsaat37.htm.

What is perhaps most astonishing is how consistent this wage gap has been. In biblical times, female workers were valued at thirty pieces of silver, whereas men were valued at fifty, in other words, women were valued at 60 percent. In the United States, this wage difference has remained relatively constant for the past 150 years! Since the Civil War, women's wages have fluctuated between one-half and two-thirds of men's wages.

The wage gap varies with the level of education. College-educated women earn 29 percent less than college-educated men; in fact, college-educated women earn about the same as non-college-educated men. And the gap varies with age. The reason for this is simple: Women and men enter the labor force at more comparable starting salaries; women aged fifteen to twenty-four earn 93 percent as much as their male counterparts. But as women continue their careers, gender discrimination in promotion and raises adds to the differences in income. Age also affects the wage gap. Before age thirty-five, women's wages are slightly lower than men's, but they drop precipitously between the ages of thirty-five and sixty-four—which just happen to be the prime child-raising and family-centric years of our lives. (Men's wages tend to skyrocket during those years, which exacerbates the gender gap.) Once the children are launched and retirements begin, women's wages go back up relative to men's (figure 9.7). A report from the General Accounting Office found that the difference in salaries between male and female managers actually grew by as much as twenty-one cents for every dollar earned between 1995 and 2000.[35]

Lawyers fare no better. A 2004 study, "Gender Penalties Revisited," found that despite their increasing numbers, female attorneys had not reached the top positions in the field. Between four and ten years after law school, women attorneys were making about 96 percent of their male counterparts' salaries; but after the ten-year mark, women's salaries dipped to only 74 percent of men's.[36]

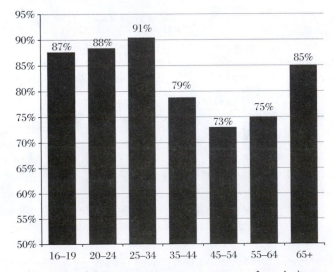

Figure 9.7. Women's median full-time earnings, as percentage of men's, by age, second quarter of 2012.

Source: BLS News Release, July 18, 2012.

OH? REALLY • Have you heard the gender wage gap is a myth, a "feminist fiction"? Some have argued that the wage gap is the natural outcome of differences in education, years working, and especially the different motivations that women and men bring to the workplace.

Don't believe it. Sure, people have different motivations when they enter the workplace. Unfortunately, these different motivations account for only a small amount of the differences in women's and men's wages. The wage gap persists because it combines structural inequalities, the attitudes and assumptions that both men and women carry around in our heads, and the choices we all have to make about balancing work and family.

Source: Arrah Nielsen, "Gender Wage Gap Is Feminist Fiction," Washington, D.C. Independent Women's Forum, April 15, 2005.

Such a gap is probably better explained by women's and men's different experiences than by any conspiracy by men at the top to "permit" women to rise only so far, and no further, in their chosen fields. It's far more subtle and thus far more difficult a problem to tease apart. When men enter the labor force, they enter for good, whereas women occasionally take time out for childbearing and parental leave. This has a calamitous effect on women's wages and fuels the growing gap across the life span. In fact, women who drop out of the labor force have lower real wages when they come back to work than they had when they left. Two sociologists recently calculated that each child costs a woman 7 percent in wages.[37]

Actually, there's a wage gap among men also that is especially instructive about gender relations. Psychologists Timothy Judge and Beth Livingston divided male and female workers into two groups based on their gender attitudes. After they controlled for other variables—hours worked, education, occupational segregation, and the like—they found that men with "traditional" gender role attitudes—such as believing that women's place was in the home—translated into a whopping $8,549 increase over men who held more egalitarian values. "If you are a man and you become more egalitarian, it really has a detrimental effect on your earnings," says Judge.[38]

Within any occupation, women tend to be concentrated at the bottom of the pay scale. Across all industries, women make up nearly 50 percent of the workers but only 12 percent of the managers. Sociologist Judith Lorber described the reason why female physicians earn less than male physicians. "The fault may not lie in their psyches or female roles, but in the system of professional patronage and sponsorship which tracked them out of their prestigious specialties and 'inner fraternities' of American medical institutions by not recommending them for the better internships, residencies, and hospital staff positions, and by not referring patients," she writes.[39]

As you might expect, the wage gap is complicated by other parts of our identities, like race, class, age, and sexuality (Table 9.3). Take, for example, age. While one can see the wage gap decreasing over time between women and men, younger women continue to fare much better than older women. On the other hand, in the past few years, even younger women have slipped back, from a gap of 7.7 percent in 2011 to 10.6 percent in 2013.[40]

Table 9.3. Annual Median Income for Different Groups

2013 person income, 18 to 64 years	Median income (dollars)	2013 person income, 18 to 64 years	Median income (dollars)
Male white alone, not Hispanic	42,520	Female white alone, not Hispanic	28,184
Male black alone	26,187	Female black alone	21,663
Male Asian alone	42,344	Female Asian alone	27,223
Male Hispanic (any race)	26,261	Female Hispanic (any race)	19,765

Source: CPS 2014 Annual Social and Economic Supplement.

And while women of color consistently make less than white women—as well as less than men of color—there are some variations, as you can see from the accompanying maps (figures 9.8a–d on pages 288–289).

How have women coped with this income inequality? In the 1860s, one woman came up with a rather novel solution:

> I was almost at the end of my rope. I had no money and a woman's wages were not enough to keep me alive. I looked around and saw men getting more money, and more work, and more money for the same kind of work. I decided to become a man. It was simple. I just put on men's clothing and applied for a man's job. I got good money for those times, so I stuck to it.[41]

Novel, yes, but not exactly practical for an entire gender! So women have pressed for equal wages—in their unions, professional associations, and every arena in which they have worked. In 1963, Congress passed the Equal Pay Act and established the Equal Employment Opportunity Commission to monitor discrimination by race and by gender. To date, the EEOC has heard thousands of cases, among them a 1986 case in which the Bethlehem Steel Corporation was found to be paying women workers about $200 a month less than men doing the same clerical work. (In a settlement out of court, the company paid each of the 104 female plaintiffs $3,000.) In a widely discussed 1992 case, a female assistant metropolitan editor at the *New York Times* earned between $6,675 and $12,511 less than male coworkers doing the same job. What's more, she earned $2,435 less than the male editor she replaced and $7,126 less than the man who replaced her when she quit in disgust.

Women thus face a **double bind** in their efforts to achieve workplace equality. On the one hand, traditional gender ideologies prevent them from entering those occupations that pay well; they are pushed into less-paying sectors of the economy. On the other hand, when they enter those well-paying fields, they are prevented from moving up. This is what is known as the "**glass ceiling.**"

THE "GLASS CEILING"

One consequence of sex segregation is discrimination against women in promotion. Women face the twin barriers of the "glass ceiling" and the "sticky floor," which combine to keep them stuck at the bottom and unable to reach the top. The sticky floor keeps women trapped in low-wage positions, with little opportunity for upward mobility. The glass ceiling consists of "those artificial barriers, based on attitudinal or organizational bias, that prevent qualified individuals from advancing upward within their organization into management level positions."[42]

In 1995, the U.S. government's Glass Ceiling Commission found that the glass ceiling continued "to deny untold numbers of qualified people the opportunity to compete for and hold executive level positions in the private sector." Although women held 45.7 percent of all jobs and more than 50 percent of all master's degrees, 95 percent of senior managers were men, and female managers' earnings were 68 percent of those of their male counterparts. Ten years later, women held 46.5 percent of all jobs but continued to hold less than 8 percent of top managerships, and their earnings were about 72 percent of those of their male colleagues. Absent some government-sponsored policy initiatives, these numbers are likely to remain low.[43]

A recent court case provides examples of both phenomena and a graphic illustration of how traditional gender stereotypes continue to work against women. Eight women brought suit against the Publix Super Markets, Inc., a chain of groceries with over nine hundred stores throughout the South. One of the plaintiffs said that she was stuck in a cashier's job and was denied a transfer or promotion to stocking shelves because, as a male supervisor told her, women were not capable of holding supervisory positions. Another woman employee was denied a promotion on the grounds that she was not the head of her household—despite the fact that she was raising her three children alone! In February 1997, Publix agreed to pay $81.5 million to settle the case.

The glass ceiling keeps women from being promoted equally with men. Women hold only 15.7 percent of all corporate board seats. There are only seventeen women CEOs in the *Fortune* 500 (about 3.4 percent) and only another nineteen in the next five hundred. And the glass ceiling's effects are multiplied when race is brought into the equation. In 1970, between 1 and 3 percent of all senior management positions in all *Fortune* 500 companies were held by women and minorities; in 1990, only 5 percent were held by women and minorities. In 1988, 72 percent of all managers in companies with more than one hundred employees were white men; 23 percent were white women; 3 percent were black men; and 2 percent were black women (figure 9.9).

In 2004, white men held 71.2 percent of board seats associated with the nation's *Fortune* 100 companies. By 2010, that figure had decreased slightly to 69.9 percent. During that same period, women gained sixteen board seats—with five occupied by minority women. But that growth represented just a 1.1 percentage point increase for women on corporate boards over six years. When including *Fortune* 500 companies, there was not a single Latino female board chair of a *Fortune* 500 company in 2010. Also, just twenty-six of the nation's *Fortune* 500 boards include at least one member of each of the major ethnic groups tracked by the U.S. Census. Right now, there are nearly nine hundred *Fortune* 1000 companies that do not have a single Latino member of their board. Among *Fortune* 100 companies, only half have a Latino board member.

Business Week surveyed 3,664 business school graduates in 1990 and found that a woman with an MBA from one of the top business schools earned an average of $54,749 in her first year after graduation, whereas a man from a similar program earned

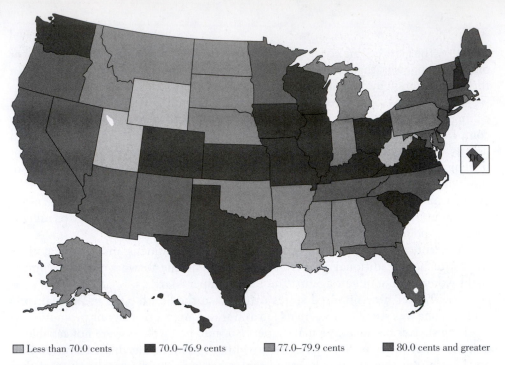

Less than 70.0 cents 70.0–76.9 cents 77.0–79.9 cents 80.0 cents and greater

Figure 9.8a. What women make for every dollar men make.

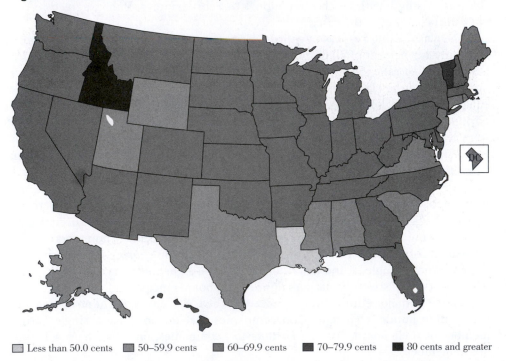

Less than 50.0 cents 50–59.9 cents 60–69.9 cents 70–79.9 cents 80 cents and greater

Figure 9.8b. What African-American women make for every dollar white, non-Hispanic men make.

Source note: "What a woman makes for every dollar a man makes" is the ratio of female and male annual median earnings for full-time, year-round workers. The "wage gap" is the additional money a woman would have to make for every dollar made by a man in order to have equal annual earnings. Overall figures calculated by the NWLC are based on 2013 American Community Survey data. Figures for African-American women, Latinas, and Asian-American women calculated by the NWLC are based on

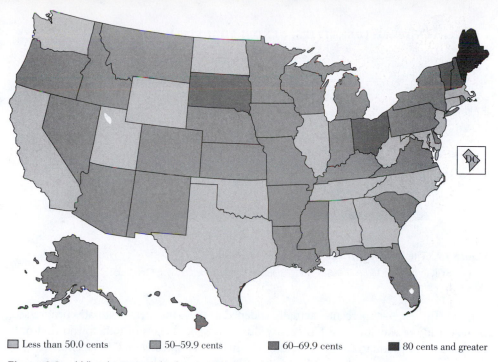

| ☐ Less than 50.0 cents | ☐ 50–59.9 cents | ☐ 60–69.9 cents | ■ 80 cents and greater |

Figure 9.8c. What Latinas make for every dollar white, non-Hispanic men make.

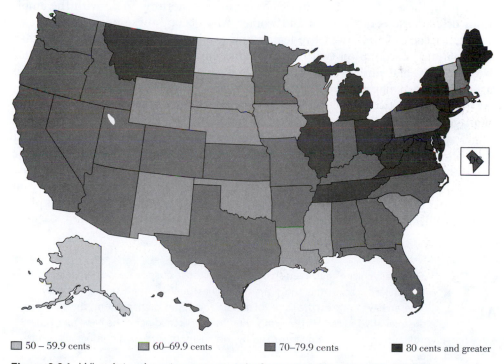

| ☐ 50 – 59.9 cents | ☐ 60–69.9 cents | ☐ 70–79.9 cents | ■ 80 cents and greater |

Figure 9.8d. What Asian-American women make for every dollar white, non-Hispanic men make.

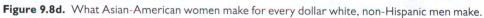

2011–2013 American Community Survey three-year estimates. State minimum wages from Department of Labor, Wage and Hour Division, "Minimum Wage Laws in the States—September 1, 2014." Minimum wages for tipped workers are often lower.

Images used with permission of the National Women's Law Center, *source:* http://www.nwlc.org/wage-gap-state-by-state.

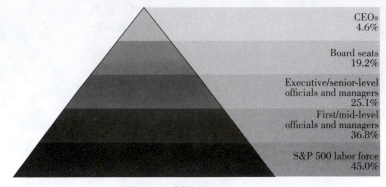

Women in S&P 500 companies

Figure 9.9. The Catalyst Pyramid: U.S. women in business.

Source: Catalyst. Pyramid: Women in S&P 500 Companies. New York: Catalyst, October 13, 2015.

$61,400. This gap—12 percent—actually widened as these business graduates progressed. A 1993 study of the Stanford University Business School class of 1982 found that only ten years after graduation, 16 percent of the male graduates were CEOs, chairmen, or presidents of companies, compared with only 2 percent of the female graduates.

Again, these different trajectories have virtually nothing to do with the ambitions or aspirations of the men and women who occupy these positions. For two years, an economist followed five female and five male trainees in a large Swedish multinational corporation (with six thousand employees). All came from similar backgrounds, had similar education, and had similar goals and ambitions. All ten aspired to top management positions. After their training, they all still were similar. At the end of the two years, all the men and none of the women had entered the top management group.

The glass ceiling occurs under a variety of circumstances. Corporate management may be either unable or unwilling to establish policies and practices that are effective mechanisms to promote workplace diversity. The company may not have adequate job evaluation criteria that allow for comparable-worth criteria, or it may rely on traditional gender stereotypes in evaluation. Limited **family-friendly workplace policies** will also inhibit women's ability to rise.

OH? REALLY •

The "glass ceiling" has been shattered by all those corporate women leaning in. While it's true that the glass ceiling has been pushed up significantly, as women have entered the ranks of middle and upper management, the doors to the executive suites remain firmly shut. In fact, according to the *New York Times*, there are more companies in the United States run by men named John than companies run by women. David, too.

Source: Justin Wolfers, "Fewer Women Run Big Companies Than Men Named John" in *New York Times*, March 2, 2015, http://www.nytimes.com/2015/03/03/upshot/fewer-women-run-big-companies-than-men-named-john .html.

COMPARED *to* WHAT?

A 2010 study by the consulting and accounting firm Deloitte compared the percentage of women serving on corporate boards. (An asterisk indicates that the country has legislative quotas for women serving on boards.)

Norway	34.3%*
Canada	12.5%
United States	12.2%
New Zealand	12.1%
France	9.5%* (pending)
United Kingdom	8.5%
Australia	8.3%
Germany	8.2%
Spain	8.0%*
Belgium	6.8%* (pending)
Netherlands	4.0%* (pending)
Italy	3.4%* (pending)

Source: Deloitte Global Center for Corporate Governance, "Women in the Boardroom: A Global Perspective," January 2011.

Perhaps the most important element that reinforces the glass ceiling is the informal effort by men to restore or retain the all-male atmosphere of the corporate hierarchy. Equal opportunities for advancement would disrupt the casual friendliness and informality of the homosocial world at the top—the fact that those with whom one interacts share similar basic values and assumptions. "What's important is comfort, chemistry, relationships and collaborations," one manager explained. "That's what makes a shop work. When we find minorities and women who think like we do, we snatch them up." One British study of female MBAs, for example, found that by far the "most significant" and "most resistant" barrier to women's advancement was the "'men's club' network."[44]

The most celebrated decision involving a corporate glass ceiling was the 1989 Supreme Court decision in *Hopkins v. Price Waterhouse.* A woman, Ann Hopkins, was denied promotion to partnership in one of the nation's largest and most prestigious accounting firms. Although she had brought more business into the company than any of the men who were promoted, she was perceived as abrasive and demanding. Opponents of her promotion said she was "macho" and that she "overcompensated for being a woman" and that she would benefit from "a course at charm school." One of her supporters told her that she might make partner if she could learn to "walk more femininely, talk more femininely, dress more femininely, wear makeup, have her hair styled, and wear jewelry." The court awarded her $400,000 in back pay and fees and required that she be promoted to partner.

The Hopkins case provides a perfect illustration of the ways in which traditional gender stereotypes also impede women's progress. Had Ms. Hopkins *been* more traditionally feminine, she would never have been the aggressive and ambitious success that she became. Thus, either way, women lose. Either they are too aggressive, in which case they are seen as mannish, "ball-busting bitches," or they are too ladylike and as a result are passed over as being too passive, sweet, and not ambitious enough.

In 1991, Congress passed the Civil Rights Act, which established the Glass Ceiling Commission to eliminate "artificial barriers based on attitudinal or organizational bias." These barriers included management relying on word of mouth to fill upper-level positions (the "old boys' network"). The commission suggested that a system of monetary compensations be instituted for word-of-mouth referrals of qualified women and minorities. Some companies have already instituted their own policies designed to enable women to break through the glass ceiling in all three areas where women experience it—hiring, promotion, and retention. These companies tend to be among the more forward-looking companies. For example, in 1992, Reebok International initiated a diversity program in hiring practices by developing effective college recruitment policies and internships for women and minorities. In two years, the company tripled its minority employment to 15 percent of its U.S. workforce and increased the number of women to more than 50 percent. The Bank of Montreal targeted promotion and between 1991 and 1993 increased the percentage of women at the executive level from 29 percent to 54 percent. The bank also initiated a program that specified targets for promoting and retaining women and minorities and developed a series of gender-awareness workshops for senior management. Finally, in 1993–1994, Lotus, the international software company, tried to increase retention of capable women and minorities who were leaving the company because they felt they did not get either the information they needed to be effective or the opportunities they expected. The company offered incentives to managers who reduced turnover and initiated disincentives for managers whose staff showed higher turnover rates. Turnover of women fell from 21 percent to 16 percent and among African Americans from 25.5 percent to 20.5 percent.

READ ALL ABOUT IT!

Women's entry into and rise across the entire economic spectrum has been one of the most notable achievements of the women's movement. But at what cost? And does it mean we've "arrived" at some gender equality? Hardly. As Harvard Business School professor Robin Ely and her colleagues note, no matter how hard women strive, and how many sacrifices they make, they never achieve the same level of professional success that their male colleagues do. And this is true even when you match them from the same class of MBAs, over the course of their lives. Structural and interactional constraints keep women from achieving all they want to achieve. Even when they lean in as hard as they can, sometimes the walls of the organizations are just too inflexible.

The glass ceiling has different impacts on men, depending upon your political persuasion. Writer Warren Farrell argues that all the attention paid to the ways

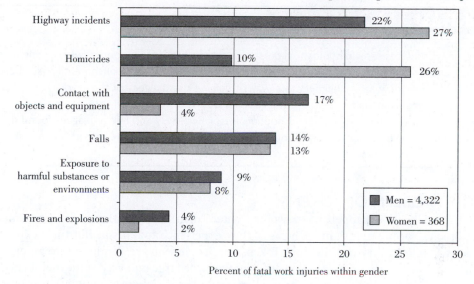

Figure 9.10. Distribution of fatal injury events, by gender of worker, 2010.

Source: U.S. Bureau of Labor Statistics, U.S. Department of Labor, 2012.

women are held back from promotion by the glass ceiling hides the fact that it is *men* who are the victims of sex discrimination in the workplace. Men, Farrell argues, are the victims of the **"glass cellar"**—stuck in the most hazardous and dangerous occupations. In fact, Farrell argues, of the 250 occupations ranked by the *Jobs Related Almanac*, the twenty-five worst jobs (such as truck driver, roofer, boilermaker, construction worker, welder, and football player) were almost all male. Over 90 percent of all occupational deaths happen to men (figure 9.10). All the hazardous occupations are virtually all male—including firefighting (99 percent), logging (98 percent), trucking (98 percent), and construction (97 percent)—whereas the "safest" occupations are those held by women, including secretary (99 percent female) and receptionist (97 percent).[45]

Farrell has a point: Many of the jobs that men take *are* hazardous—and made more so unnecessarily by an ideology of masculinity that demands that men remain stoic and uncomplaining in the face of danger. Thus on dangerous construction sites or offshore oil rigs, men frequently shun safety precautions, such as safety helmets, as suitable, perhaps, for sissies or wimps, but not for "real" men. But the conclusion that men, not women, are discriminated against flies in the face of both evidence and reason. Because the jobs that are the most exclusively male are also those whose workers have fought most fiercely against the entry of women in the first place. And they're far better paying than the jobs that are almost exclusively female. For example, the nation's fire departments have been especially resistant to women joining their "fraternal order," doing so only under court order and often admitting women with a significant amount of harassment. It would be odd to propose that this is the result of discrimination against men or to blame women for not entering those occupations from which they have been excluded by men's resistance.

READ ALL ABOUT IT!

Some workplaces remain homosocial preserves, workplace "locker rooms" where male bravado and risk-taking are the norm. They don't get more "macho" than offshore oil rigs, where men often eschew safety helmets as a way of defying the dangers of the work. Turns out, though, that all that male posturing is not good for business. After nearly two years of working with these men, Harvard Business School professor Robin Ely and her colleagues found that hypermasculine behavior is actually counterproductive, and that, as they put it, "extinguishing macho behavior is vital to achieving top performance."

THE PROBLEM OF TOKENS

What really does happen when women enter "men's" occupations and men enter "women's" occupations? In both cases, they experience **tokenism**. But their experiences as tokens vary considerably. Tokens are people who are admitted into an organization but who are recognizably different from the large majority of the members of the organization. But tokens are more than simply the members of a numerical minority: Tokens are accepted not *despite* their minority status but rather *because* of it. They are actively discouraged from recruiting others like themselves and become eager to fit in and become part of the organizational mainstream. Typically, tokens may even become more strongly wedded to organizational norms than do members of the numerical majority.

According to Rosabeth Moss Kanter, whose pioneering work *Men and Women of the Corporation* first analyzed the problem, tokenism widens the contrasts between groups rather than narrowing them, as the contrasts between the token and the majority are exaggerated to become the sole difference. Tokens, Kanter writes, are thus "often treated as representative of their category, as symbols rather than as individuals."[46] The token is always in the spotlight—everyone notices him or her, but only because he or she is different. Tokens are rarely seen as similar to others in the group. Thus tokens have a double experience of visibility—they are *hyper*visible as members of their "category," but they are completely *invisible* as individuals.

Think about a situation where you were virtually the only "something" in a group. It could be that you were the only man or woman, the only white person or person of color, the only gay or straight person in a group. How did you feel when someone would turn to you and say, "So, how do white people feel about this issue?" or "What do women say about this?" At that moment you cease to be an individual and are seen only as a representative of the group. Chances are you responded by saying something like, "I don't know. I'm not all women or all white people. You'd have to take a survey." If you can imagine that experience of hypervisibility and invisibility all the time in your workplace, you'll begin to have an idea of what tokenism feels like.

Simultaneous hypervisibility and invisibility have serious consequences. "The token does not have to work hard to have her presence noticed, but she does have to work hard to have her achievements noticed," Kanter writes. The token is often forced to choose between the two—"trying to limit visibility—and being overlooked—or taking advantage of the publicity—and being labeled a 'troublemaker.'" This can inflict an enormous emotional and psychological toll:

Tokenism is stressful; the burdens carried by tokens in the management of social relations take a toll in psychological stress, even if the token succeeds in work performance. Unsatisfactory social relationships, miserable self-imagery, frustrations from contradictory demands, inhibition of self-expression, feelings of inadequacy and self-hatred, all have been suggested as consequences of tokenism.[47]

Kanter argues that her theory of tokenism holds regardless of whether the tokens are male or female. Subsequent research has suggested dramatically different experiences when women are the tokens in a largely male work world and when men are the tokens in a largely female occupation.[48] Men entering mostly female occupations have the opposite experience from women. They don't bump up against a glass ceiling; instead, they ride on what sociologist Christine Williams calls the "**glass escalator**," having a much easier time being promoted than even women do. Williams conducted interviews with seventy-six men and twenty-three women in four fields—nursing, librarianship, elementary education, and social work. She found that men experienced positive discrimination when entering those fields; several people noted a clear preference for hiring men. And men were promoted to managerial positions more rapidly and frequently, thus making men overrepresented in the managerial ranks. Men who do women's work, it appears, may earn less than men who work in predominantly male occupations, but they earn more and are promoted faster than women in the same occupation.[49]

READ ALL ABOUT IT!

Women who seek to rise in "male" occupations bump into the glass ceiling, while men who seek to rise in "female" occupations—say, librarian or nurse—seem to ride a "glass escalator" to the administrative tops of their professions, as sociologist Christine Williams once put it. Not so fast, says sociologist Adia Harvey Winfield. That glass escalator may work well for white men, but it's not nearly as easy a path for men of color.

Men did experience some negative effects, especially in their dealings with the public. For example, male nurses faced a common stereotype that they were gay. Male librarians faced images of themselves as "wimpy" and asexual; male social workers were seen as "feminine" or "passive." One male librarian found that he had difficulty

OH? REALLY. Men don't like working for a female boss—and their productivity shows it.
Not true! University of Cincinnati sociologist David Maume used national data from the National Study of the Changing Workforce and found that men received more job-related support and were more optimistic about their careers when they reported to a female supervisor. He suggests that female supervisors are both encouraged to, and also want to, promote the careers of male subordinates so it doesn't appear they are playing favorites.

Source: David Maume, "Meet the New Boss . . . Same as the Old Boss?: Female Supervisors and Subordinate Career Prospects" in *Social Science Research*, January 2011, pp. 287–298.

establishing enough credibility so that the public would accept him as the children's "storyteller." Ironically, though, Williams found that these negative stereotypes of men doing "women's work" actually added to the glass escalator effect "by pressuring men to move *out* of the most female-identified areas, and *up* to those regarded as more legitimate and prestigious for men."[50]

Williams concluded that men "take their gender privilege with them when they enter predominantly female occupations: this translates as an advantage in spite of their numerical rarity." Men, it seems, win either way. When women are tokens, men retain their numerical superiority and are able to maintain their gender privilege by restricting a woman's entry, promotion, and experiences in the workplace. When men are tokens, they are welcomed into the profession and use their gender privilege to rise quickly in the hierarchy. "Regardless of the problems that might exist," writes Alfred Kadushin, "it is clear and undeniable that there is a considerable advantage in being a member of the male minority in any female profession."[51]

Such a statement goes a long way toward explaining why men continue to resist workplace equality. After all, men have a pretty good deal with things as they are; as economist Heidi Hartmann writes:

> Low wages keep women dependent on men because they encourage women to marry. Married women must perform domestic chores for their husbands. Men benefit, then, from both higher wages and the domestic division of labor. This domestic division of labor, in turn, acts to weaken women's position in the labor market. Thus, the hierarchical domestic division of labor is perpetuated by the labor market, and vice versa.[52]

Workplace inequality is not only a good deal for men, but also often invisible to them. Inequality is almost always invisible to those who benefit from it—in fact, that's one of the chief benefits! What is certainly not a level playing field is *experienced* as level, which leads men to feel entitled to keep things just as they are. Let me give you one example. I recently appeared on a television talk show opposite three "angry white males" who felt that they had been the victims of workplace discrimination. The show's title, no doubt to entice a large potential audience, was "A Black Woman Stole My Job." These men all complained that they had been the victims of "reverse discrimination," because, they believed, they had lost a job possibility to a woman who was less qualified than they.

In my comments to these "angry white males," I invited them to consider one word in the show's title—the word "My." What did that word mean? Did they feel that those jobs were actually "theirs," that they were entitled to them, and that when some "other" person—black, female—got the job, that person was really taking "their" job? But by what right is that their job? By convention, perhaps, by a historical legacy of discrimination, certainly. Of course, a more accurate title for the show should have been "A Black Woman Got *a* Job" or ". . . Got *the* Job." But "my" job? Competing equally for rewards that we used to receive simply by virtue of our race or our sex actually feels like discrimination. Equality will always feel uncomfortable for those who once benefited from inequality.

Another reason why men resist the gender-integrated workplace is that men say they would be distracted by women. A headline in the *Wall Street Journal* in 1991 announced, "Women as Colleagues Can Turn Men Off." The 1995 report of the Department of Labor's Glass Ceiling Commission quoted one male executive who said, "What's important is comfort, chemistry, . . . and collaborations." Many white men, he continued, "don't like the competition and they don't like the tension" of working alongside female colleagues. That the presence of women would distract men from the tasks at hand or disturb the fragile yet necessary bonding among males was also the argument made by men in the military and at military schools like VMI and the Citadel.[53]

Except, as we've seen, it's not necessarily true. There are many situations in which women and men work side by side without there being any "distractions." Doctors and nurses, managers and secretaries don't seem to have much problem with distraction. And all the women at VMI and the Citadel (before co-education)—all those professors, service workers, staff, maids, and kitchen workers—didn't seem to upset the cadets very much. It's not the presence or absence of women that seems to be distracting—it's the presence of women *as equals* that men are really worrying about.

SEXUAL HARASSMENT

Sexual harassment is one of the chief ways by which men resist gender equality in the workplace. The nation's current preoccupation with sexual harassment is fueled by several different trends—the increased reporting by women of their experiences at work or in school, the relabeling of behaviors that men used to take for granted, the increasing pressure that men face in the workplace, and the increasing willingness of the legal system to assign blame—costly blame—for this practice. Sexual harassment was first identified as a form of sex discrimination and litigated in the late 1970s. Feminist lawyer Catharine MacKinnon argued that sexual harassment is a violation of Title VII of the 1964 Civil Rights Act, which makes it "an unlawful employment practice for an employer . . . to discriminate against any individual with respect to his compensation, terms, conditions, or privileges of employment, because of such individual's race, color, religion, sex, or national origin." Sexual harassment, MacKinnon argued, violates this law because it discriminates against women on the basis of their sex, and, what's more, sexual harassment creates a hostile environment for working women.[54] By 1982, the U.S. Court of Appeals for the Eleventh Circuit declared:

> Sexual harassment which creates a hostile or offensive environment for members of one sex is every bit the arbitrary barrier to sexual equality at the workplace that racial harassment is to racial equality. Sure, a requirement that a man or woman run a gauntlet of sexual abuse in return for the privilege of being allowed to work and make a living can be as demeaning and disconcerting as the harshest of racial epithets.[55]

But it was not until 1991 that the extent of the problem and its effects on women in the workplace began to be fully recognized. In October of that year, Anita Hill declared that she had been sexually harassed by Clarence Thomas when she worked for him at the EEOC, and suddenly the entire nation sat transfixed before its television sets as Thomas's confirmation hearings for the U.S. Supreme Court took a dramatically different turn. Hill alleged that she had been subjected to unwanted sexual advances, vile pornographic attempts at humor, and constant descriptions of Thomas's sexual prowess—even after she had made it clear that she was not interested in dating her boss.

At the time, the Senate Judiciary Committee treated Hill as if she were the criminal, accusing her of harboring desires for Thomas, insinuating that she was "a woman scorned," and implying that she was being duped by liberals who sought to derail the nomination. And, at the time, the nation split about evenly on the question of whom they believed, Thomas or Hill. The media declared in unison that the committee's harsh and suspicious treatment of Hill would have a "chilling effect" on American women, who would be less likely to come forward and describe the harassment that they had experienced.

A chilling effect? Have the media ever been more wrong? In the ensuing decade there was more of a national thaw—as thousands of women came forward to describe what they had earlier kept as shameful personal secrets. The number of sexual harassment cases has more than doubled since 1991. Suddenly the nation had a name for what had been happening for decades to women in the workplace. In homes across the nation women were telling their husbands, their children, their parents, their friends of what had happened to them. By 1997, well over 80 percent of Americans had come to realize that Anita Hill had been telling the truth all along.

Since that time, sexual harassment has become a major issue in America. Between 50 and 85 percent of working women will experience some form of sexual harassment during their career. In a 1981 study of female federal employees, 12 percent reported mild harassment (suggestive gestures or remarks, pressure for dates), 29 percent reported severe harassment (touching, fondling, pressure for sex, menacing letters or phone calls), and 1 percent were raped on the job. Nearly thirty years later, in December 2008, a Harris poll found that 31 percent of female workers had been harassed at work, as had 7 percent of male workers. (All of the women reported that their harasser was a man, as did 41 percent of the males who reported harassment.)[56]

A 1989 study of almost a thousand female attorneys found that 60 percent had experienced sexual harassment; 13 percent had been the victim of rape, attempted rape, or assault. Only 7 percent of those attorneys reported the incident to the firm. A 1997 study of two thousand attorneys at twelve of the largest law firms found that 43 percent had experienced sexual teasing, jokes, remarks, or questions; 29 percent had experienced suggestive looks or gestures, and 26 percent had experienced deliberate touching, pinching, leaning over, or cornering—all within the past year alone.[57]

And it's not just lawyers and other professionals. In fact, the number of cases filed with the EEOC doubled between 1990 and 1995 and has leveled off at between twelve thousand and fifteen thousand per year ever since—and the majority of those cases were from women in blue-collar jobs. Women were far more likely to experience sexual harassment in traditionally male-only jobs like mining, construction, transportation, or manufacturing than they were in professional and white-collar jobs. Clearly, when women try to "cross over" into male-dominated jobs, they are seen as invaders, and sexual harassment is a way to keep them out.[58]

Sexual harassment takes many forms, from sexual assault to mocking innuendo. Typically, it takes one of two forms. In the most obvious, quid pro quo form, a trade

North Country

The 2005 film *North Country*, starring Charlize Theron, recounted the story of Lois Jenson, a mineworker in Eveleth, Minnesota. Like the few other women mineworkers, Jenson, a single mother and daughter of a mineworker, was repeatedly threatened, humiliated, groped, stalked, and assaulted until she and twenty other women miners went to court in 1984 and eventually won a landmark sexual discrimination lawsuit—the first class-action sexual harassment case in U.S. history. "It really was about getting a better paying job with benefits. I didn't go there to bring up issues. I just wanted to make a decent life for my family," Jenson said in an interview.

of sexual contact is offered for a reward or the avoidance of punishment. This is the sex-for-grades model of teacher-student interaction, or the "sleep with me and you'll get promoted" or "don't sleep with me and you'll get fired" workplace scenario. Thus, for example, did U.S. Senator Robert Packwood end his congressional career—after nearly a dozen former female staffers accused him of unwanted kissing, fondling, attempts at sexual contact, and inappropriate remarks during his otherwise distinguished twenty-seven-year career.

The second form is far murkier and is understood as the creation of a "hostile environment," one in which women feel compromised, threatened, or unsafe. Women in medical schools, for example, described sexual harassment as taking several different forms, including being ignored, left behind during rounds, and not invited to assist during medical procedures. Consistently, female medical students reported being subjected to jokes or pranks, hearing women's bodies being mocked during anatomy classes, and finding pornography shuffled into anatomy slides during lectures. Some law students recalled "ladies' days," when women were actually called on in class.

One of the more interesting sexual harassment cases involved the Mitsubishi Motor Corporation. In December 1994, twenty-nine women working at the car company's plant in Normal, Illinois, filed a lawsuit alleging sexual harassment, claiming that their male coworkers routinely groped and grabbed at them. Some women had to agree to have sex in order to obtain jobs. Drawings of breasts, genitals, and sex acts were labeled with the names of women workers and attached to the cars' fenders as they passed down the assembly line. After an investigation, the EEOC filed its own suit against the company in April 1996 on behalf of more than 280 women employees. A little over a year later, after a critical review of the company's policies and procedures by former labor secretary Lynn Martin, the company settled its suit with twenty-seven of the twenty-nine original plaintiffs for $9.5 million and began to implement broad changes in its corporate management.[59]

Whether sexual harassment is manifest as quid pro quo or a hostile environment, it is rarely about sexual attraction between employees. Men accused of harassment are seldom men who are simply awkward at asking women out for dates or men who are unusually lustful. Sexual harassment is, in fact, just the opposite. It is about making workers feel unwelcome in the workplace, about reminding them that they do not belong because the workplace is men's space. As legal scholar Deborah Rhode writes, it is a "strategy of dominance and exclusion—a way of keeping women in their places and out of men's."[60]

Think, for example, of sexual harassment on the street. Imagine a man making a rude, offensive comment to a woman as she walks by. "Hey, baby," he shouts, "nice tits!" or, "You look good enough to eat!" If you were to ask this man about his comment, he might shrug off the issue by saying he was just trying to meet women or to indicate sexual interest. But what if we were to take these men at their word? Imagine what would happen if that woman who was being harassed were to turn around and say, "Who me? Great. Dinner at eight?" Or if she had met his crude remarks with some crudeness of her own. What would that man do now?

It's clear that these remarks are not meant to attract women, but rather to repel them and send them scurrying away, reminded that the streets belong to men and that women who dare to walk on them alone, or who show up in bars alone, are defying an unwritten ordinance. Such remarks are rude reminders of male entitlement, an unwritten and often unconscious sense that the public arena belongs to "us" and that interlopers, female invaders, will be reminded that they don't really belong.

Until recently, the workplace has been such a male space, a homosocial preserve. But that world has vanished forever. It is now virtually impossible for a man to go through his entire working life without having a female colleague, coworker, or boss. Women have entered the former boys' clubs—the streets, the corporate boardrooms, the hallowed halls of learning—and they are not going away, as much as some men might wish them to. Just when men's breadwinner status is threatened by economic downsizing and corporate restructuring, women appear on the scene and become easy targets for men's anger. *This* is the context in which we must consider the question of sexual harassment, its gendered political economy, so to speak. Sexual harassment in the workplace is a distorted effort to put women back in their place, to remind them that they are not equal to men in the workplace, that they are, still, after all their gains, just women, even if they are in the workplace. "Harassment is a way for a man to make a woman vulnerable," says Dr. John Gottman, a psychologist at the University of Washington.

And it works. Harassed women report increased stress, irritability, eating and sleeping disorders, and absenteeism. Often, as one researcher writes, they feel humiliated and helpless and describe the "daily barrage of sexual interplay in the office as psychological rape." Harassment occurs most frequently in the most recently integrated workplaces, like the surgical operating theater, firefighting, and investment banking, where women are new and in the minority. "Men see women as invading a masculine environment," says Dr. Louise Fitzgerald, a University of Illinois psychologist. "These are guys whose sexual harassment has nothing whatever to do with sex. They're trying to scare women off a male preserve."[61]

One other thing that sexual harassment is typically *not* about is one person telling the truth and the other person lying. Sexual harassment cases are difficult and confusing precisely because there are often many truths. "His" truth might be what appears to him as an innocent indication of sexual interest or harmless joking with the "boys in the office" (even if those "boys" happen to include women). He may experience sexual innuendo or references to pornography as harmless fun, as what the workplace is supposed to be like for men. He works there, therefore he's entitled to treat the workplace as an extension of the locker room. "Her" truth may be that his seemingly innocent remarks cause stress, anxiety about promotion, firing, and sexual pressure.

The law about sexual harassment has reflected these two truths. The legal standard of harassment has been whether a "reasonable person" would see the behavior as harassment. A 1991 Ninth Circuit Court case, *Ellison v. Brady*, nearly changed all that. For the first time, the court "saw" the invisibility of gender—and ruled that the "reasonable *person*" actually meant a reasonable *man* and that men and women might well see the situation differently. Harassers often "do not realize that their conduct creates a hostile working environment," the court found, but "the victim of sexual harassment should not be punished for the conduct of the harasser." Thus the court established a "reasonable *woman* standard," because, as the court opinion stated, "a sex-blind reasonable person standard tends to be male-biased and tends to systematically ignore the experiences of women."

Unfortunately, this reasoning didn't hold for too long, as cases became so complex and convoluted that the Supreme Court stepped in two years later and ruled in *Harris v. Forklift* again that the "reasonable person" standard is sufficient. However, the effect was noticeable: Now, no longer is the intention of the harasser the standard against which the crime is measured—it's the perceived effect on the victim by a "reasonable person."[62]

And this change has predictably caused a significant amount of defensiveness and confusion among American men. After all, the rules have been changed. What used to be routine behavior for men in the workplace may now be called "sexual harassment." "Clarence Thomas didn't do anything wrong, that any American male hasn't done," commented Dale Whitcomb, a thirty-two-year-old machinist during the Thomas confirmation hearings. Two-thirds of the men surveyed said they would feel complimented if they were propositioned by a woman at work, giving some idea about how men have misperceived the problem.

At the societal level, sexual harassment stymies women's equality. And it is costly. Both private and public sectors lose millions because of absenteeism, reduced productivity, and high turnover of female employees. One study by *Working Woman* magazine indicated that the top 150 of the *Fortune* 500 companies lose $6.7 million *per year* due to sexual harassment. The U.S. Merit Systems Protection Board reports that absenteeism, job turnover, and lost productivity because of sexual harassment cost the government an estimated minimum of $189 million a year. Corporate executives and partners in large law firms say they are terrified about massive lawsuits from charges of sexual harassment.[63]

Men are also harmed by sexual harassment. Male supervisors and employers are hurt when sexual harassment makes women less productive. With increased absenteeism, higher rates of turnover, and greater job-related stress, women will not perform to the best of their abilities. Some men may find such compromised performance a relief—competing with women as equals and losing may be too great a blow to fragile male egos—but supervisors cannot afford to have women working at less than their best without it eventually also affecting their own performance evaluations. Supervisors and

The Great Recession of 2008 was the most gendered economic downturn in our history. Between December 2007 and June 2009, 70 percent of all the jobs lost were jobs that had been held by men.

This is half true. What's true, of course, are the percentages. Seven out of every ten jobs lost were jobs held by men.

But the "most" gendered? Unlikely. After all, during the Great Depression of 1929–1930s, virtually all the jobs lost were jobs held by men—because they were disproportionately represented in the labor force to begin with.

The Recession of 2008 was so visibly gendered that it was also known as the "he-cession" or "Mancession." Less well known, though, is that the recovery has been just as gendered—in the other direction. After all, in all those shovel-ready programs that were awaiting bailout funding, what gender did you imagine was holding the shovel?

Since January 2010, job growth for men has been significantly greater than job growth for women. Women lost 222,000 jobs and men gained 640,000 jobs between July 2009 and December 2010.

This isn't exactly a "she-covery." Part of the explanation has not been whose jobs were lost or gained, but where the losses and gains were. The private sector has added jobs every single month since 2009, largely due to the stimulus package that spurred private sector growth. The way we have "paid" for the stimulus has been to slash public sector jobs at the state and local levels. Jobs in teaching, administrative support, and secretarial areas are mostly held by women. Women lost a whopping 99.6 percent of the 257,000 jobs cut from the public sector.

The American response to the Mancession was a massive transfer of wealth and jobs to the private sector and away from state and local governments. In a sense, we gave to "him"—at her expense.

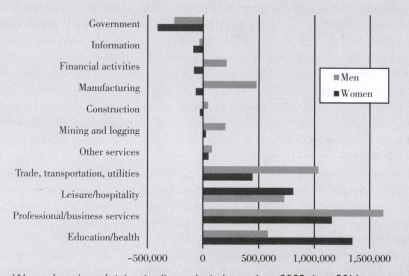

Women's and men's job gains/losses by industry, June 2009–June 2014.

Source: IWPR analysis of U.S. Department of Labor Bureau of Statistics, Current Employment Statistics (September 5, 2014).

Source: Heather Boushey, "The End of the Mancession" in *Slate*, January 25, 2011. National Women's Law Center, www.nwlc.org.

employers should want *all* their employees to feel safe and comfortable so that they may perform to the maximum of their abilities. Men's ability to form positive and productive relationships with equal colleagues in the workplace is undermined by sexual harassment. So long as sexual harassment is a daily occurrence and women are afraid of their superiors in the workplace, innocent men's cordial and courteous behaviors may also be misinterpreted.

And finally, men can be harmed by sexual harassment from other men. In March 1998, the U.S. Supreme Court ruled that men can be the victims of sexual harassment from other men, even when all the men involved are heterosexual. Slightly more than 10 percent of all cases filed with the EEOC in 1997 were by men, but that percentage has steadily climbed to over 17 percent today.[64] Although the majority of the harassers in such cases are also male, there are some cases in which a female supervisor has harassed a male subordinate. Sexual harassment, then, has been expanded to include men who are not traditionally "masculine" and are therefore punished for it by other men, as well as women who are harassed when they act "too" masculine or when they don't act masculine "enough." And people still believe that the workplace isn't gendered!

REMEDIES FOR WORKPLACE INEQUALITY

Despite all the arguments about gender difference that presume that men and women are from different planets, the fact is that comparable percentages of women and men are in the workplace and for the same reasons. Yet the workplace remains a decidedly unequal arena, plagued by persistent sex segregation, wage inequality, sex discrimination, and sexual harassment. These inequalities exaggerate and even create the differences we think we observe. How can the workplace become a more equal arena, a place in which women *and* men can earn a living to support themselves and their families and experience the satisfaction of efficacy and competence?

Well, women can just "lean in." *Lean In* was more than the title of Sheryl Sandberg's 2013 mega-best-selling book. Like Nike's slogan "Just Do It," it became a mantra for working women who were frustrated by continuing gender disparities in the workplace. Women were holding themselves back from promotion and raises by the strictures of traditional femininity; women had to "lean in" to smash through the glass ceiling.

Critics were quick to point out that "leaning in" shifts the entire burden away from structural barriers (sex segregation, discrimination, archaic stereotypes held by managers and supervisors) and onto women themselves. While leaning in might enable a woman to get a raise, or be noticed for a promotion, it wouldn't change the social and institutional arrangements that sustain a gender-unequal workplace.

In Japan, women are resisting leaning in, resisting entering the workforce at all, because, as they explain, they are still expected to be the sole child-care providers to their children, maintain the household, and care for aging relatives. To add a full-time job would be overwhelming and lead, they fear, to "karoshi"—death by overwork. Unless . . .

Unless *men* change. Leaning in asks nothing of men. It doesn't require a shift in men's attitudes or behaviors around housework and child care. Which is why Sheryl Sandberg launched a new campaign, "Lean In Together," to engage men to support gender equality, both at work and at home (www.leanin.org/together). Obviously, such personal change needs to be accompanied by policy initiatives as well.

One arena of change is the application of existing law. A good beginning might be full compliance with the 1963 Pay Equity Act, which prohibits employers from paying different wages to men and women who are doing the same or essentially the same work, or Title VII of the 1964 Civil Rights Act, which guarantees the absence of discrimination based on race, sex, or national origin. To date, thirty states have undertaken some form of pay equity reform, and about $527 million has been disbursed by twenty state governments to correct wage discrimination.

The Equal Employment Opportunity Commission is charged with prosecuting cases of discrimination and harassment based on race, gender, national origin, and pregnancy. And since the EEOC was established, lawsuits have spiraled upward every year. Between 1992 and 2001, sexual harassment charges increased 146 percent, pregnancy discrimination 126 percent, and sex discrimination 112 percent. Since 1980, sexual harassment charges have increased 150,000 percent—thanks to that one brave woman, Anita Hill, who had the courage to name what had happened to her while working for now–Supreme Court Justice Clarence Thomas—at the EEOC![65]

But a simple strategy of pay equity would be unlikely to make wages more equal, because, as we have seen, wage inequality depends on sex segregation for its legitimacy (and its invisibility). Comparable-worth programs require that "dissimilar work of equivalent value to the employer be paid the same wages." Thus comparable-worth programs require a systematic review of jobs, ordering them on criteria of complexity and skills required so that they can be compared and thus wages allocated on a more gender-equal basis. Some social scientists have devised the Gender Neutral Job Comparison System to measure jobs more accurately; the system also factors into its equations such traditionally invisible (and traditionally "female") skills as emotional labor or undesirable working conditions.[66]

Comparable-worth programs have become necessary because sex segregation is so intimately tied to wage inequality. But such programs have generated significant opposition, largely based on misperceptions of what the idea entails. For example, some argue that it is impossible to determine the worth of jobs, despite the fact that nearly two-thirds of all companies already utilize job evaluations. Others say such programs will interfere with the normal operations of the labor market—as if the labor market set wages to begin with, and not bureaucracies, union officials, and managers relying on gender stereotypes. (If the labor market operated perfectly, there would be no wage discrimination, would there?) Others argue that such programs open a door for a paternalist government to set wage levels or that they would bankrupt employers forced to pay women higher wages. But each firm could set its wage levels based on skill, not sex. And besides, women earning higher wages would increase consumer purchasing power, which would help the economy, not hurt it.[67]

Comparable-worth and pay-equity schemes are not, of course, without their problems. They might have a remedial effect of evening out women's and men's wages at lower levels, for example, but they would also preserve the gap between lower-level jobs and upper-level management jobs, because both pay equity and comparable worth preserve "the idea that some jobs are worth more than others." What's more, they mute the effect of persistent gender stereotypes in the evaluation of positions, so that some men would be able to continue to resist gender equality by embedding it in performance evaluations.[68]

Workplace equality also requires interventionist strategies in hiring and promotion. Although in recent years the trend has been for the United States to abandon **affirmative action** policies, such policies have been enormously effective in leveling the playing field, even a little bit. (Could that be why there's so much opposition? After all, as political commentator Michael Kinsley notes, affirmative action is one of the few policies that "gives white men whining rights in the victimization bazaar, just like minorities and women.") One reason why well-meaning Americans say they oppose affirmative action is that members of minority groups would find it demeaning to accept positions strictly on the ground that they are members of an underrepresented group, despite the fact that few women or minorities actually are hired or promoted for that reason alone. Anyway, it's probably more demeaning to be *denied* a position or a promotion because of membership in that group. When Barbara Allen Babcock, an assistant attorney general in the Carter administration, was asked how she felt about getting her position because she was a woman, she replied, "It's better than not getting your job because you're a woman."[69]

Another remedy will be the elimination of the "**mommy track**"—a subtle way that workplace gender inequality is reproduced. The mommy track refers to the ways in which workplace discrimination transmutes itself into discrimination against those workers who happen to take time off to get pregnant, bear children, and raise them. Though it is illegal to discriminate against women because of pregnancy, women are often forced off the fast track onto the mommy track because of what appear to be the demands of the positions they occupy. Young attorneys, for example, must bill a certain number of hours per week; failing to do so will result in their being denied partnerships. A woman thus faces a double bind: To the extent that she is a good mother, she cannot rise in the corporate world; to the extent that she rises in the corporate world, she is seen as a bad mother.[70]

The **Pregnancy Discrimination Act**, passed in 1978, makes it illegal for employers to use pregnancy (or the likelihood that an employee will become pregnant) as the basis for decisions concerning hiring or promotion. The **Family and Medical Leave**

OH? REALLY.

In the United States, our commitment to "family values" enables working women to opt out of working to take care of their families.

Such myths abound today. But let's look a little closer. First, the only women who seem to be "opting out" are women at the very top of the economic pyramid, since virtually all young people want to work—and have families. And those very few women who do opt out do so largely because their husbands do virtually no housework or child care. And who can balance work and family all by themselves? Did you know that in one survey of 173 countries, only 5 offered no paid leave for either parent in any segment of the labor force: Lesotho, Liberia, Papua New Guinea, Swaziland, and the United States. "Family values" encompasses the workplace as well as the family, and it requires placing the recourses of the state at the service of families. That is, family values requires that we actually, in our policies, value families.

Source: Jody Heymann, Alison Earle, and Jeffrey Hayes, *The Work, Family, and Equity Index* (Boston: Project on Global Working Families, 2006).

Act of 1993 provides up to twelve weeks of unpaid leave to care for a child, an adoptive child, or an ill child or relative. Compare this with the policies in the Nordic countries, where couples receive from twelve to fifteen months of *paid* parental leave to care for their newborn babies and in which both mothers and fathers are encouraged to take some portion of it.

Policies to remove the glass ceiling, especially on corporate boards, will likely have to come from governments that are brave enough to wade into intervention in corporate governance. Some governments have issued targets—the percentages of women they want on corporate boards. The European Union, as a whole, has begun to set such targets. Norway recently established a quota, mandating that the board of each company listed on its stock exchange be 40 percent female by 2008; France followed by mandating 20 percent for its boards by 2009.[71]

While quotas are controversial, we must also keep them in perspective. "We've excluded women for a thousand years," said Hilde Tonne, a Norwegian executive VP for a global telecommunications company. "So we have already had quotas—it's just that they were for men."[72]

The most obvious set of remedies falls under the general heading of "family-friendly workplace policies"—that collection of reforms, including on-site child care, flexible working hours, and parental leave, that allows parents some flexibility in balancing work and family life. *The National Report on Work and Family* reported in December 1997 that these were among the most significant criteria in helping companies to retain qualified and well-trained personnel.

Turns out it's good business strategy as well. Roy Douglas Adler, a marketing professor at Pepperdine University, has looked at data from the *Fortune* 500 for the past thirty years. Consistently, the companies that most aggressively promoted women outperformed the industry medians, with overall revenue profits about 34 pecent higher (equity profits were more than double that, or 69 percent higher). The top ten firms with the best record of promoting women showed even greater increases than those that were "merely" good. (Of course, one needs to be careful with such correlations. It might simply be that those companies that are more profitable may feel freer to experiment with promoting women. But when you find such results coming from other countries as well, as we do in Britain, Sweden, and Norway, then perhaps there is something to the other explanation: that promoting women is good for the company's bottom line.[73])

In the end, workplace equality will require significant ideological and structural change—both in the way we work and in the way we live. We still inherit such outmoded ideas about what motivates us to work and what skills we bring when we get to work. John Gray's book *Mars and Venus in the Workplace* rehashed his stereotypes about how men and women approach situations differently. According to Gray, in the workplace men "retreat to a cave" when they have a problem to work out by themselves, whereas women "demonstrate sharing, cooperation, and collaboration." Except that such interplanetary styles depend at least as much on the problem to be solved as on the gender of the person solving it. To make men feel more comfortable, Gray recommends that we take photos of male workers alongside their achievements and ask about their favorite football teams—ideas that Lucy Kellaway, a writer for the *Financial Times*, found "ill conceived, outdated and bizarre."[74]

Another sociologist, Karen Oppenheim Mason, writes that gender inequality in the workplace is likely to remain "unless major revisions occur in our ideology of gender and the division of labor between the sexes . . . Ultimately," she concludes, "job segregation is just a part of the generally separate (and unequal) lives that women and men in our society lead, and, unless the overall separateness is ended, the separateness within the occupational system is unlikely to end, either."[75]

But reform will be worth it. Workplace equality will enable both women *and* men to experience more fulfilling lives—both in the workplace and outside of it.

CONCLUSION: TOWARD A BALANCE OF WORK AND FAMILY

Despite enormous and persistent gender inequality in the workplace, women are there to stay. Women work for the same reasons that men work—to support themselves and their families, to experience the sense of accomplishment, efficacy, and competence that comes from succeeding in the workplace. Both men and women work because they want to and because they have to. The social and economic realities of most American families' lives these days are that both partners are working, which means that both are struggling to balance work and family life.

And a struggle it is, in part because our lives have changed faster than the institutions in which we find ourselves. "Our jobs don't make room for family obligations," writes Stephanie Coontz. "To correct this imbalance, we need to reorganize work to make it more compatible with family life." That is to say, we will never find

"O.K., now—on three, I'm going to toss a second job in there!"

Figure 9.11. *Source:* Danny Shanahan/The New Yorker Collection/The Cartoon Bank.

that balance if all we do is tinker with our family relationships, better organize our time, outsource family work, juggle, or opt out. It will be possible only when the workplace changes as well.[76]

Several different kinds of policy reforms have been proposed to make the workplace more "family friendly"—to enable working men and women to effect that balancing act. These reforms generally revolve around three issues: on-site child care, flexible working hours, and parental leave. By making the workplace more family friendly, by implementing these three policy reforms, the workplace would, we think, be transformed from Ebenezer Scrooge's accounting firm into the set from the hit film *9 to 5*. Suddenly, overnight, when the evil boss was gone, the workplace was transformed. Green plants were everywhere. The women's desks had photographs of their children, while their children played in playpens right behind them. And, of course, productivity shot up so high that the corporate CEO decided to maintain these changes permanently.

But in the United States, we continue to think of these reforms as *women's* issues. It is women who campaign for them and women who say they want them. One recent best-selling book put all the pressure on women to accommodate themselves to the virtual impossibility of balancing work and family. Sylvia Hewlett found startlingly high percentages of childlessness among high-achieving women and argued that "the brutal demands of ambitious careers, the asymmetries of male-female relationships and the difficulties of bearing children late in life conspire to crowd out the possibility of having children." Childlessness becomes, as she puts it, a "creeping non-choice," and she urges a woman to be "intentional" about family life—grabbing a husband and having babies in her twenties and putting the career on the back burner.[77]

Hewlett's solutions may appear overly voluntaristic, assuming that individual women need to make individual choices, rather than structural changes to the workplace itself, but they do have a ring of truth to them—because they are half right. The research does suggest that having children does stymie women's career ascendancy and that putting one's career first may hinder one's ability to have children.[78] But in both of these halves of the equation there is a variable missing: men. Women's career chances are stymied and their maternity is eclipsed *only if the men in their lives don't change.*

But on-site child care, flextime, and parental leave are not women's issues, they're *parents'* issues, and to the extent that men identify as parents, men ought to want these reforms as well. Politically, women probably cannot get the kinds of reforms they need without men's support; personally, men cannot have the lives they say they want without supporting these reforms. Women have already become what we might call "private careerists"—people who are willing to claim their workplace ambitions in the private domain of their homes and families, willing to reorganize the shape, the size, and the timing of their family lives to try to balance both. Now we need a "public fatherhood" to complement that—men who are publicly committed, in their workplaces, to reorganizing their career trajectories to accommodate their family responsibilities and commitments. Private careerism needs a public fatherhood.

Which was, you may recall, the trap that British prime minister Tony Blair fell into when he and his wife were expecting the birth of their son in 2000. Could he take the parental leave that he and his government had fought to institute? Did he dare? Of course, his wife, Cherie, a high-prestige lawyer who earned three times what Blair earned as prime minister and was the family breadwinner, took all of her allotted thirteen weeks of unpaid parental leave. Could Blair take a week off?

The answer was "almost." Public opinion was split: Overwhelmingly (72 percent) Britons supported the idea of men taking parental leave, but over half (57 percent) thought Blair shouldn't use it. His wife urged him to follow the example of the Finnish prime minister, who had just taken six whole days off when his daughter was born. In the end, Blair took two days off and worked from home.[79]

It's celebrated cases like this that make clear the problems we will continue to face in balancing work and family. These problems are both structural and attitudinal. Often the problem is that there are no policies in place that enable mothers and fathers to also be productive workers—that is, to balance their work and family commitments.

Take, for example, parental leave. Recall that the United States is one of only five countries in the world whose government offers no paid parental leave to either parent. And while some states (like Rhode Island and New Jersey) and some cities (like Washington, DC, and Boston) and many corporations have begun to fill the gap left by a federal government that is MIA in supporting working families, the obstacles to dual-career couples balancing work and family often feel insurmountable.

And when it comes to paternity leave, there's a real wasteland. Only 15 percent of American companies offer paid paternity leave. Companies have been slow to offer paternity leave, as much for cultural reasons as for financial ones. The ideal employee is "unencumbered," available to the company 24/7. An employee, especially a man, who is "distracted" by family obligations is not a reliable employee in that model. Even in Silicon Valley companies, where vegan entrees are served in the company cafeteriaand organized Frisbee games and regular massages are part of the "campus" amenities, companies struggle to enable employees to balance work and family. While Google offers men seven weeks of paid paternity leave, Yahoo offers eight, and Facebook and Reddit offer seventeen weeks, the companies still schedule all-night "hackathons," insist on early morning and late night work sessions, and require participation in weekend activities—all hardly conducive to those balancing work and family.

But the benefits of paid paternity leave are enormous—both to the companies and to the men and their families. Companies that offer parental leave tend to be more profitable and more flexible in responding to increasingly diverse economic landscapes. Men who take parental leave tend to remain more involved in their children's lives as their children grow up, and they share housework more equally also. And one Swedish study found that men who take paternity leave live longer than men who don't.[80]

The absence of a coherent national policy of family leave makes it very difficult for both women and men to balance work and family. We are increasingly a nation of dual-career/dual-carer couples, taking care of aging parents and young children, often at the same time.

And often the problem is that workers don't avail themselves of the policies. Men are afraid they'll be seen as less than fully committed to their careers, and their masculinity will be threatened; women fear they'll be forever pegged as "mommies" and not as employees. Both fear the mommy or the daddy track. "Young fathers need to feel very secure in their careers, and they believe that asking for flexibility is seen as a lack of commitment—which makes them more vulnerable," commented one British parental leave advocate. When Erika Kirby interviewed women and men about their experiences with parental leave policies she heard statements like this:

> "No one talked to me directly and said 'Gee, I resent the fact that you were on maternity leave,' but I know that people felt that way."
> "People don't understand that when I had six weeks off [for maternity leave] I needed six weeks off. I didn't sit there and play cards, you know what I mean, go shopping every day."
> "Someone wanted paternity leave, and everybody laughed. I mean, they thought that was funny."
> "I wanted to take two weeks [of paternity leave] and the supervisor was saying 'No, I don't think, you know, that's probably not a very good idea.'"

No wonder Kirby titled her article on the subject with another line she heard repeatedly: "The Policy Exists but You Can't Really Use It."[81]

Balancing work and family will enable women to live the lives they say they want to live. Working mothers are happier and more productive, both as mothers and as workers, than are full-time mothers, notes psychologist Faye Crosby. Another psychologist, Joan Peters, writes that "mothers *should* work outside the home. If they do not, they cannot preserve their identities or raise children to have both independent and family lives." But to do so will require a dramatic change in the lives of American men. Men will need to take on their share of housework and child care—not merely to "pitch in" or "help out." Balancing work and family will also enable American men to live the lives they say they want to live. As one man recently put it:

> It's amazing. I grew up thinking a man was someone who was gone most of the time, then showed up and ordered people around and, aside from that, never said a word. I don't want my sons to have to deal with that kind of situation or to think that's how the world is.[82]

With more men like him—and a generation of women whose members refuse to remain second-class citizens in the workplace—his sons and his daughters may come to know a very different world.

KEY TERMS

Affirmative Action
Double Bind
Emotion Work
Family and Medical Leave Act
Family-Friendly Workplace Policies
Gender Discrimination
Gendered Division of Labor
Glass Ceiling
Glass Cellar
Glass Escalator
Labor Force Participation
Mommy Track
Occupational Sex Segregation
Pregnancy Discrimination Act
Tokenism
Wage Gap

The GENDER *of* POLITICS *and* *the* POLITICS *of* GENDER

At a campaign stop early in the 2008 Democratic presidential primary season, New York Senator Hillary Clinton was addressing a crowd of supporters in New Hampshire. In the middle of her speech, a couple of young men held up a sign and began to chant "Iron My Shirt."

"Oh, the remnants of sexism are alive and well," Senator Clinton said. After everyone had settled down, she caught her breath and said, "As I think has just been abundantly demonstrated, I am also running to break through the highest and hardest glass ceiling."[1]

There are several items worth mentioning in this story. For one thing, I'd wager that very few of you actually even heard of it. (I'd even bet that most of your instructors didn't hear of it.) In 2009, just a year later, I asked my own students, and about 10 percent said they remembered that incident. It was barely covered in the media and disappeared without a trace.

Now recall that Clinton was running to be the first female president against Barack Obama, who was running to be the nation's first African-American president. Imagine, for a moment, that at an Obama rally some white people had held up a sign and started shouting something equally stereotypical and equally offensive, like, say, "Shine My Shoes."

Had that happened, I believe that every single front page of every newspaper in America would have carried a banner headline about racism; every television and radio news show would have led with the story; and every single candidate, Republican or Democrat, would have immediately denounced that behavior as racist and inappropriate.

But when the subject is a woman, and the sign expresses a sexist sentiment that a woman's place is only in the home? Well, that passes right under the radar of the media and the public. In a sense, it points out that, at this moment in history, sexism is far more permissible to be expressed than racism.

Clinton was right, of course, in another sense: In the United States, being elected to the highest office in the land has proved to be among the more enduring glass ceilings. No woman has been elected president in the United States—indeed, there have been only a handful of minor-party candidates since suffragist Victoria Woodhull ran (with Frederick Douglass as her vice presidential running mate) in 1872.

As we will see, it need not be that way: There have been plenty of women who have been elected to their country's highest political office, including several in countries that Americans routinely criticize as being "backward" or behind us on measures of gender equality. Yet a woman has twice been elected prime minister in India, where traditionally, women were such second-class citizens that widows were expected to throw themselves on their husband's funeral pyres and kill themselves; and twice in neighboring Pakistan, a Muslim country where we believe that women are far more oppressed than they are in the West. And that doesn't even count the European countries where women have been elected as heads of state: Great Britain, Norway, Germany, Iceland, Portugal, Denmark, Finland, and Ireland. Or Canada and Australia. Or these countries: Argentina, Bolivia, Senegal, Chile, Costa Rica, Jamaica, Brazil, South Korea, and Indonesia. Or these, where a woman's been elected more than once: Israel, Sri Lanka, New Zealand, Bangladesh, Lithuania, and the Philippines. It's no wonder that the United States has little credibility around the world when we proclaim our support for women's rights in such places as Bangladesh or Pakistan, since they've elected female heads of state twice each.[2]

Here's a list of current (January 2016) female heads of state:

- Angela Merkel, chancellor of Germany
- Ellen Johnson Sirleaf, president of Liberia
- Cristina Fernandez de Kirchner, president of Argentina
- Sheikh Hasina Wajed, prime minister of Bangladesh
- Dalia Grybauskaitė, president of Lithuania
- Kamla Persad-Bissessar, prime minister of Trinidad and Tobago
- Dilma Rousseff, president of Brazil
- Atifete Jahjaga, president of Kosovo
- Portia Simpson Miller, prime minister of Jamaica
- Park Geun-hye, president of South Korea
- Erna Solberg, prime minister of Norway
- Laimdota Straujuma, prime minister of Latvia
- Michelle Bachelet, president of Chile
- Marie Louise Coleiro Preca, president of Malta
- Beata Szydło prime minister of Poland
- Kolinda Grabar-Kitarović, president of Croatia
- Tsai Ing-wen, president of Taiwan

The United States lags woefully behind the rest of the world not only among heads of state, but also among legislators at every level. As of 2012, the United States ranked eighty-fourth in the world in percentage of female legislators—behind Bangladesh, Sudan, the United Arab Emirates, and Saudi Arabia—that is, behind countries we stereotypically think of as far less gender equal. Only 18.3 percent of the Senate and House of Representatives and 24 percent of state legislators are female. Of the hundred largest cities in the country, only nine have female mayors, and of the fifty governors, only six are women.

How are we to explain this dramatic gender gap? Generally, social scientists offer three possible explanations (figure 10.1).

First, simple prejudice. What holds women back is the attitudes of other people. Some people believe that women are just not suited for positions of political power. Women, they believe, are too emotional and too weak to be responsible leaders. Or their physiology gets in the way. For example, in 1995, arguing against women's participation in the military, former House Speaker Newt Gingrich commented that women shouldn't be soldiers because they "get infections," while males are "biologically driven to go out and hunt giraffes" (address at Reinhart College, January 5, 1995).

Although such overt prejudice has been declining in recent years, it still remains a significant barrier to women's full electoral success. In 1971, two-thirds of Americans said they would vote for a woman if she were nominated—which was nearly double the percentage just thirty-five years earlier. That is, even by 1971, fully one-third of Americans would not vote for a woman for elected office simply because she was a woman. Today nearly nine out of ten Americans say they would vote for a woman. Even though more than three times as many Americans believe that men make better leaders (21 percent) than women do (6 percent), nearly seven out of ten (69 percent) believe that it makes no difference at all. It is still the case that many people believe that, all things being equal, men are more suited for political leadership positions than women are.[3]

Some of those who believe that women are less qualified are women themselves. A second explanation puts more of the responsibility on women. Some psychologists of sex roles argue that differential socialization of men and women leads women to be

What is the greatest obstacle preventing more women around the world from entering politics?
(Average rank, greatest to smallest obstacle)

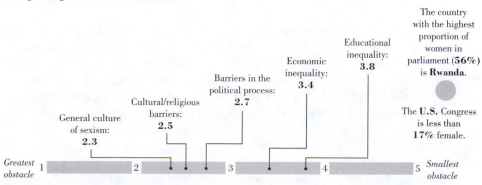

Figure 10.1. Survey regarding women leaders.

Source: From *Foreign Policy,* April 2012.

more reticent about taking leadership positions. Just as men are more likely to ask for raises at work than are women, so, too, are women less likely to put themselves forward for local office, which is the first step toward being elected to higher office.

And there is some truth to this explanation as well. Women are socialized to be more demure and self-effacing, but the many programs on campuses and in corporations to promote women's leadership have certainly identified large numbers of women willing and able to assume political responsibility.

A third explanation is more structural and has less to do with women's abilities or temperaments. The structure of politics—the requirement that one be so completely devoted to the job, constantly working either to be an effective legislator or campaigning for re-election—is like any other high-pressure profession. And just as we saw that differential socialization alone could not explain the historical shortage of qualified female lawyers or doctors or corporate board members, so too can it not alone explain the shortage of female legislators. Trying to balance work and family, and being a good parent requires significant effort and support. The lack of adequate child-care support is a major barrier to women's entry into politics—as it is in any other field.

A story told by former Colorado congresswoman Pat Schroeder is illustrative here. After her first election to office, her husband was asked how it felt to be the husband of a congresswoman. He replied that in the future, it would be he who would be taking the children to the pediatrician. When Schroeder heard this, she immediately called her husband on the telephone and said, "For $500, what is the name of our children's pediatrician?" He replied, somewhat sheepishly, that what he had *meant* to say was that he would be *willing* to take them if she asked him to.[4]

Is it any wonder that 86 percent of all female legislators do not have school-aged children at home when they are elected to office? It's a kind of double whammy for women: If they have children, they're scolded for neglecting them; if they don't have children, people wonder what's wrong with them. Ruth Mandel, director of the Eagleton Institute of Politics at Rutgers University, recalled one married female legislator who told her that "she was portrayed during the election as about to have children (thereby neglecting her constituents) and another said she was asked, 'Who is going to watch the baby?' . . . The female young elected leaders who were single said they faced gossip, even slanderous comments, about their sexual habits. Male candidates did not mention this as a problem for them."[5]

Politics is similar to other professions in another way: Getting ahead depends not only on what you know, but whom you know. Networks are essential: Party leaders (typically men) have to "notice" your talents and leadership abilities, groom you for the grueling process of elections, and promote you within the ranks of your political party. These networks are like supply chains for information, talents, and opportunities, and they are essential for a successful career. At the local level, then, formal criteria are accompanied by less formal (but no less institutional) factors such as networks. And women tend to have less developed institutional networks, fewer mentors, and worse access to information.

Finally, there's money. Female candidates often have a harder time raising money for campaigns than men do, as larger corporate donors tend to favor the people they already know and trust. The enormous initial cost of entering the political arena sets

READ ALL ABOUT IT!

Men spend a lot more time talking than women do, and men in power tend to take up an inordinate amount of airtime. But what about women in power, in, say, the U.S. Senate? According to organizational psychologist Victoria Brescoll, in her article "Who Takes the Floor and Why?," powerful male senators tend to speak a lot more than less powerful male senators. But this doesn't seem to be true of women. Since this could be an artifact of how long the senators have been in the Senate, she conducted an experiment in which women and men were "allotted" a certain amount of power in a group setting. Sure enough, the more powerful men tended to talk a lot more than the less powerful men, while the women tended to be more democratic. In fact, as Brescoll found out in a subsequent experiment, those women who did use up a lot of airtime tended to be more negatively viewed by others. That suggests that the gender difference is not because women "naturally" tend to be kinder and cede the floor, but because those women who don't yield are not listened to anyway.

a high bar for female candidates, which discourages many qualified candidates. To counter this initial barrier to entry, a group of wealthy women founded Emily's List in 1985 to raise money for women's election campaigns. (Emily is not a person; the name is an acronym for "Early Money Is Like Yeast.")

THE GENDER GAP IN VOTING

Not only is gender a key factor in who gets elected, but it is also a critical determinant of who does the electing. For some time, there has been a significant gender gap among the electorate. Women are more likely to vote Democratic, while men are more likely to vote Republican.

The gender gap is found when people are asked about their party affiliations as well (figure 10.2); not only are women more likely to vote Democratic, they are more likely to register as Democrats.

This gender gap in both voting and party affiliation is typically explained by two things. First, it reflects the increased independence of women, especially married women. Not that long ago, it was assumed that married women would vote the same way their husbands voted—that is, that they would vote the way their husbands told them to vote. In fact, one of the most popular arguments against woman suffrage in the first decades of the twentieth century was that it would violate the fundamental constitutional principle of "one man, one vote." Anti-suffragists argued, giving women the vote was akin to discriminating against single men by giving them only one vote while in effect giving married men two votes. It was inconceivable at the time that a woman might have a political opinion of her own.

Second, in general, women tend to hold more liberal attitudes than do men. For example, attitudes about same-sex marriage, alleviating poverty, racial equality, discrimination against LGBT people, the environment, women's rights, and the like all show some significant differences by gender, with women holding what would be called the more "progressive" position, supporting greater state intervention to remedy

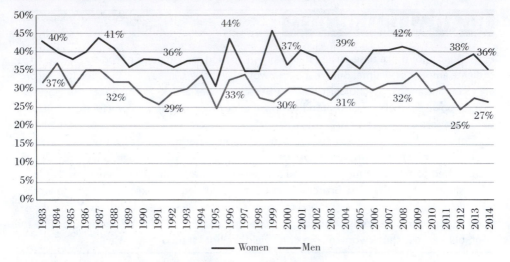

Figure 10.2. Percent identifying as Democrats or leaning Democratic by gender.

Source: "The Gender Gap: Party Identification and Presidential Performance Ratings," based on data from CBS/ *New York Times* and ABC News/*Washington Post* polls, Center for American Women and Politics, Rutgers University, http://www.cawp.rutgers.edu/sites/default/files/resources/ggprtyid.pdf.

inequalities. Since the Republican Party is understood to be more right wing and to support fewer government programs to address inequality, this gender gap in party affiliation and voting behavior provides an accurate picture of gender and political attitudes.

That the gender gap has increased in recent decades, however, is usually explained by the increasingly liberal political attitudes held by women or by the failure of the Republican Party to appeal to women's interests. However, women's voting patterns are only part of the picture. As Everett C. Ladd of the Roper Center explained, "Women are not really more Democratic than they were fifteen years ago." The real story is that "men have become more Republican."[6]

The gender gap in voting has become a staple of political analysis. But it's important to see that it changes dramatically when race is factored in (figure 10.3). White

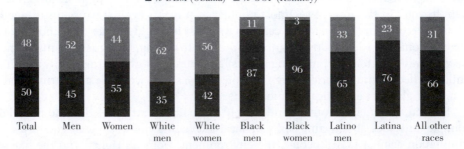

Figure 10.3. 2012 election: exit poll data by gender and race/ethnicity.

Source: Christina Bejarano, 2014. The Latino Gender Gap in U.S. Politics. Latino Decisions. http://www.latinodecisions .com/blog/2014/02/19/the-latino-gender-gap-in-u-s-politics/ (retrieved November 2014).

people—both women *and* men—are more likely to vote Republican, while African American and Hispanic voters—also both women *and* men—are more likely to vote Democratic. Yes, it's true that a higher percentage of African American or Hispanic women vote Democratic than African American or Hispanic men; in fact, the race and ethnic voting gap is actually larger than the gender gap.

POLITICS IS FOR "REAL MEN," NOT "GIRLIE MEN": THE MASCULINITY OF POLITICS

The flip side of believing that women's "natural" femininity disqualifies them for political office is the equally pervasive stereotype that only the manliest of men are qualified to hold such office. Elections are always meditations on masculinity: Is he man enough to push the button, stare down the nation's enemies, and, if necessary, be the commander in chief and lead them into battle? (Of course, political leaders must also exhort us to care for those less fortunate, insist that everyone share, and make sure that people are kind and respectful of the rights of others [i.e., traditionally feminine traits], but this recedes to the background when we contemplate that the business of politics is the capacity for war.)

Nowhere is this more evident than in presidential elections. Often, different parts of masculinity are embodied by different candidates, and the electorate often debates which particular version will triumph. Will it be the paternal, rational, and balanced masculinity of Washington (the "father" of our country), Jefferson, FDR, or Lincoln—calming stormy seas during turbulent times—or the saber-rattling, bellicose fulminations of Jackson, Teddy Roosevelt, or George W. Bush? (Once, it was literally the actual paternalistic father and vengeful son, as the nation elected first the "kinder, gentler" George H. W. Bush, with his "thousand points of light," and the militaristic George W. Bush, who went looking for weapons of mass destruction in all the wrong places and led the country into its longest and least successful war in history.)

Perhaps no campaign was more gendered than the presidential election of 1840. Then-president Martin Van Buren was an able if lackluster administrator. But his opponent, William Henry Harrison, a military hero fresh from victorious campaigns against the Seminoles in Florida, ran a relentless campaign questioning Van Buren's masculinity. Van Buren was ridiculed as a wimp whose administration was composed of "eastern officeholder pimps." Campaign songs chastised "Little Van," the "used up man," who "wore corsets, put cologne on his whiskers, slept on French beds, and rode in a British coach." One Harrison supporter declared Van Buren's White House to be staffed by "French cooks" who furnished the president's table with "massive gold plate and French sterling silver services." (It is true that Van Buren presided over the installation of indoor plumbing in the White House.) Davy Crockett, he of unimpeachable masculinity, declared that "it would be difficult to say," from Van Buren's appearance, "whether he was man or woman." And it was rumored that when Van Buren read about these scandalous attacks, "he burst his corset." Campaign posters depicted Harrison, his sleeves rolled up, spade in hand, in front of his log cabin.

Harrison's supporters chanted:

Old Tip he wore a homespun coat, he had no ruffled shirt
But Matt he has the golden plate, and he's a little squirt!

In fact, none of it was true. Van Buren was a capable administrator, the son of an upstate New York innkeeper; Harrison was an aristocratic scion, bred in a three-story manor on a Virginia plantation. But the campaign worked: Over 80 percent of the eligible white male voters turned out for the election, and Harrison won in a landslide.

Alas, the story has a sad coda. Harrison apparently believed his own hype. Taking the oath of office on one of the most bitterly cold days on record in Washington, Harrison refused to wear a topcoat, lest he appear weak and unmanly. He caught pneumonia as a result, was immediately bedridden, and died thirty-two days later—the shortest term in office in our nation's history.

It's not just the leaders, of course, but the political ideas they espouse and the parties they represent that are seen as gendered. The Democrats generally support higher taxes in order to develop programs for education, social services, and health care for those less fortunate. Republicans, by contrast, advocate both higher levels of military spending and dramatic cutting of taxes, offsetting those costs by cutting the very social programs the Democrats advocate. Thus, to the Republicans, the Democrats advocate a feminine government, a "Nanny State," more along the lines of the European social democracies, while, to the Democrats, the Republicans are the "Daddy Party," proposing a lean, mean fighting machine that operates as a reverse Robin Hood, taking from the poor and giving to the rich. Democrats, then, have to show they are manly; Republicans have to show they have at least a modicum of compassion.

Take a look at some fairly recent presidential contests.[7] Bill Clinton's manhood was always in doubt and always on display. He didn't serve in the military; his wife was hardly the subservient but gracious hostess we had come to expect from First Ladies; he expressed his feelings and felt our pain. Depicted by his enemies as alternately conniving and gay (in both cases, Hillary was depicted as a demonically masculinized hydra), he was also beloved by his admirers as deeply compassionate and politically astute. The revelations of a sexual liaison with Monica Lewinsky, a White House intern, seem to have confirmed rumors of his habitual skirt-chasing, and his subsequent impeachment trial was discrediting if not dethroning.[8]

The hotly contested election of 2000 featured two literal as well as symbolic sons. George W. Bush and Al Gore were both the namesake sons of venerated political fathers and had been carefully groomed for elective office. Yet Gore could not shake his image as a ruling-class wimp when compared to the equally preppy, equally Ivy League, and equally entitled Bush. No matter how Gore tried to "butch" it up and present the male toughness of an alpha male, as he was advised by feminist writer Naomi Wolf, he seemed officious, stiff, effete (figure 10.4). It was as if Gore presented the image of the man who had never been a boy; Bush, by contrast, appeared to be a boy who had never grown up, a good-time frat-boy Peter Pan. And, as we've seen, the gender gap was in full evidence, as white men voted overwhelmingly for Bush.

The election illustrated the deep **gendered political divide**. Red and blue states were seen as "masculine" or "feminine" states: gun owners versus gun controllers, aggressively military versus conciliatory and diplomatic, environmentally rapacious versus environmental stewardship, tax-cutting free-marketeers who run up the debt versus fiscal prudence in both taxation and spending.

Not since 1840 had a national election been more saturated with contested images of masculinity than the presidential election of 2004. As then, an aristocratic blue

Figure 10.4. The Kiss. Al Gore delivered a very long kiss with his then-wife Tipper Gore at the 2000 Democratic National Convention, no doubt as a way to butch up his image. And it worked, for a time. He got a short bump in the polls and went on to win the popular vote in the election.

Source: AP Photo/David J. Phillip.

blood—prep school, Ivy League, summering in Kennebunkport—cast himself as a virtual log-cabin-born everyman who pulled himself by his bootstraps. And he cast his opponent, a sage and sober bureaucrat, as a soft and sensitive Francophile, under the thumb of an emasculating wife. Bush snickered as Kerry windsurfed and waffled. Arnold Schwarzenegger, our own contemporary Davy Crockett, called Kerry a "girlie man." What might have been seen as "manly reticence" was sneered at as "patrician aloofness." Kerry, we heard, "looks French." Kerry and John Edwards, his running mate, were called "the first metrosexual presidential hopefuls." Edwards's styled hair brought him the label "the Breck Girl."[9]

Yet Kerry had fought bravely in a war and, following his experience in Vietnam, did the unthinkable for a man—he changed his mind. He then fought bravely against it. This was, of course, used against him, proof that he waffled and flip-flopped in a feminine way. (Rarely has an election so denigrated femininity as a liability.) On Memorial Day weekend, one New York tabloid published the fictitious menus of the two candidates. For Bush it was sausages and beer (nonalcoholic, of course), and for Kerry it was frogs' legs, Chardonnay, and crème brûlée. It was parodies like these, and not his meritorious service or economic policies, that seemed to resonate with white male voters, who turned out overwhelmingly for Bush. Former president Bill Clinton summed up this new

OH? REALLY• One particularly telling sign of the importance of masculinity in politics and elections is the fact that voters are more likely to elect candidates with deeper voices regardless of the speaker's gender!

Duke University researchers found that both male and female participants consistently preferred the lower-pitched voice of two potential candidates, even among two women. They also found that both men and women felt like lower-pitched female voices seemed stronger and more trustworthy and competent, but only male participants perceived lower-pitched male voices to be stronger and more competent. Researchers explain that male participants may have been more tuned in to the voice pitch to gauge the speaker's competitiveness and social aggressiveness, compared to female participants, who may not discriminate strength and competence based on male voices because they are focusing on other cues, not pitch, to evaluate those traits. No matter, the female participants ultimately chose potential candidates with deeper voices.

Source: Christine Hsu, "Voters Consistently Elect Candidates with Deeper Voices" in *Medical News Daily*, March 14, 2012, http://www.medicaldaily.com/voters-consistently-elect-candidates-deeper-voices-239941.

collective gendered psychology when he observed that when people feel uncertain or afraid, "they'd rather have somebody who's strong and wrong than somebody who's weak and right."[10]

THE ELECTIONS OF 2008 AND 2012

The election of 2008 was a "game changer" in many respects. On the one hand, it was the first national presidential campaign that featured two women vying for the presidency and vice presidency. And just as there surely was a choice of different masculinities in the candidacies of Barack Obama and John McCain, so too did Hillary Clinton and Sarah Palin offer a choice of femininities. On one side was Clinton, the brainy former First Lady who was as adroit an administrator and adept at policy analysis as her celebrated wonkish husband, but came across as coldly efficient and "masculine." Right-wing satires of Clinton even managed to transform her as the hapless victim of her husband's notorious philandering into a raving, crypto-lesbian "nutcracker," as one novelty item put it—thus fusing antifeminism, homophobia, and gender traditionalism in one swoop (figure 10.5).

If Hillary Clinton was the "bitch," then Sarah Palin's folksy, ditzy lack of command of any meaningful policy analysis managed to render her the "babe." Palin's handlers tried to massage her lack of experience and her laughably tenuous grasp of policy into an asset, so as to seduce white male voters to vote for the "brainless babe." Her attempts to bridge the divide between brainless babe and "ball-busting bitch" included one of her most oft-quoted lines from the campaign, "The heels are on, the gloves are off."[11]

This pairing of femininities captured in miniature the dilemmas of the contemporary American working woman—she must be competent, but not sacrifice her quaintly ladylike demeanor. She must be a good mother and devoted to her family, but also be sexually alluring to men. Warm *and* hot, competent and comely. While

Figure 10.5. Hillary Clinton is shown a "Hillary nutcracker," a novelty item that imagined this female presidential candidate as unfeminine.

Source: AP Photo/Elise Amendola.

contemporary American women want to "have it all," they often seem to feel they need to *be* everything to everyone.

Between Obama and McCain, the gendered choice was equally stark. "Now that the actual presidential campaign is under way, we have the traditionally 'masculine' style, embodied by John McCain, emphasizing experience, toughness, feistiness, stubbornness, grit, exclusivity, etc., and the newly emergent 'feminine' managerial style practiced by Obama and emphasizing communication, consensus, collegiality and inclusiveness."[12]

McCain reached for the mantle of heroic masculinity, playing on his heroic captivity as a POW during the Vietnam War. His campaign videos referred to his faith in the "fathers," his having been "tested in hard and cruel ways," and his "will to fight and survive" the brutality of his captivity.[13]

That Barack Obama was African American underscored the racial elements of the debate about masculinity and tinged it with a 250-year-old history of seeing race as a gender issue. Obama's masculinity was entirely tied up in racial stereotypes. His oratorical style was inspiring, but his demeanor was always measured, tempered, as if aware that any flash of anger might propel him backwards to those older stereotypes about out-of-control, hypermasculine black men. Filmmaker Byron Hurt's short campaign video "Barack and Curtis" contrasted Obama with the gangsta rapper

50 Cent, who, Hurt asserted, embodied every negative stereotype of the black man—an angry, inarticulate, money-grubbing sexual predator—that had fueled centuries of racist demonization. Obama may have been a "black man," but the emphasis was on the "man."[14]

And thus efforts to taint him as an effete Harvard-educated elitist fell equally flat. No amount of massaging his anemic attempts at bowling could offset his genuine prowess at basketball; and there were no photographs of him windsurfing off Nantucket Island or snowboarding in Sun Valley, as there had been of John Kerry.

Not that pundits and opponents didn't try. Media pundits declared Obama "kind of a wuss" (Tucker Carlson), "prissy" (Joe Scarborough), and "a sissy boy" (Don Imus). "Americans want their president, if it's a man, to be a real man," said Scarborough—ignoring the fact that they also sort of want a female president to be a "real man" *and* a real lady.[15]

Yet Obama not only weathered that emasculating storm, he transcended it. His even-tempered affability coupled with his sharp intelligence enhanced his status as a brilliant orator, a skilled politician, a devoted husband and father, and a decent man. Barack Obama became a sex symbol. "President Barack Obama is the personification of contemporary masculinity," cooed one blogger with an obvious man crush. Another called him "the embodiment of cool." "Smart, sexy, dashingly handsome and cool, he is the embodiment of the type of twenty-first-century contemporary man."[16]

Perhaps Obama, more than any other president before him, has been able to limn the boundaries of gender, embracing qualities that had been previously coded as either masculine or feminine. Legal scholar Frank Rudy Cooper called Obama the nation's first "unisex" president; others called him androgynous.[17]

The campaign of 2012 pitted a seasoned, but far more subdued, President Obama against a very different sort of masculine icon: the handsome ultra-rich elite in the person of Mitt Romney. Throughout the campaign Romney battled the perception that he was not in touch with everyday Americans, much the way George H. W. Bush lost votes in 1992 when he was asked the price of a gallon of milk in the presidential debate (because he hadn't actually shopped in decades, or, more likely, because his aides were so elite themselves that they never thought to find out to tell him). Both the elder President Bush and Romney (Figure 10.6) had an aristocratic bearing that was a throwback to an earlier era, when Americans preferred having native aristocrats as their leaders, endowing them with virtues that were different from those of the common man.

As we await the results of the presidential campaign of 2016, one thing is certain: There will be many masculinities on display, each trying to strike the balance between a virile decisiveness and unbendable strength with compassion for the struggles of everyday folk just trying to get by. And also, at least one iteration of femininity, trying to strike pretty much the same balance. Just how much empathy can a candidate show before we whip out the "w" word?

THE POLITICS OF GENDER

We've been discussing what could only be called "the gender of politics"—the way that we can see gender differences in political behavior, or in public perceptions of different candidates, or the ways that gender is used to both praise and criticize

Figure 10.6. *Newsweek*, October 19, 1987 (left); *Newsweek*, July 29, 2012 (right).

elected officials. But what about the other side, about the ways that various gender issues play out in the political arena? How did it happen that questions that raise gender issues—sexuality, work-family balance, women's reproductive rights—became "political"? Why should the government even care with whom you have sex, whether or not you use birth control, or how you decide to raise your child? Are these any of your neighbor's business?

But governments do care about gender issues, very much. For one thing, as we've seen, gender issues emerge in every arena, so other social institutions such as the family, education, and the workplace are all filled with gender issues. And gender also structures our intimate lives—our relationships with our friends, our lovers, our partners—and these, too, come constantly under the scrutiny of the political realm.

Take fertility, for example. How many children you might individually decide to have has enormous political and economic implications—it will affect the educational system and the number of people entering the workplace, which also affects the money that people leaving the workforce due to retirement will be able to have. It affects the health care system. "Too many" children will put a burden on the education and health care system, but will eventually help raise the money needed to fund Social Security and Medicare. "Too few" children eases the burden on the education and health care system, but will eventually dry up the funds that feed Social Security and Medicare. Clearly, these personal individual decisions have political implications. (And it's ironic, isn't it, that much of the debate about them is framed not in economic or political terms, but instead as questions of morality and religion?)

Here's a good illustration:

This is a photo of a panel of "experts" assembled to testify in Congress on the health care measure's coverage of birth control for women. Should birth control be covered by the health care law—that is, should women be able to have their insurance cover their expenses for birth control? Notice anything odd about this panel of experts testifying about women's sexuality and women's reproductive choices?

When this hearing took place in the early spring of 2012, there was a national outcry. In 2012, was it really impossible to find *any* qualified women—physicians, epidemiologists, public health experts, let alone actual women who felt they might have a stake in the outcome of such hearings—who might have been able to comment more authoritatively on women's sexual and reproductive needs?

Actually, the photograph presents a somewhat false picture, because there actually *were* some women who wanted to offer some expert testimony. But they were excluded from this blue-ribbon panel. You may remember the story of Sandra Fluke, a Georgetown University law student who asked to be heard and was denied. Fluke argued that her health care coverage should include birth control—because, in her view, her health depended on her ability to make safe choices about her sexuality. (Of course, birth control is far more cost-effective: birth control by private insurers costs the taxpayer nothing, while unwanted pregnancies are very expensive.)

In response, right-wing commentator Rush Limbaugh leapt into the fray, trying to shame Fluke for having the temerity to suggest that birth control might be part of her health care package:

> What does it say about the college co-ed Sandra Fluke, who goes before a congressional committee and essentially says that she must be paid to have sex, what does that make her? It makes her a slut, right? It makes her a prostitute. She wants to be paid to have sex. She's having so much sex she can't afford the contraception. She wants you and me and the taxpayers to pay her to have sex.

The next day, the unapologetic radio host went even further:

> If we're going to pay for your contraceptives and thus pay for you to have sex, we want something for it. We want you to post the videos online so we can all watch.

Reaction was swift and entirely negative. Sponsors of his show withdrew their ads and stations dropped the show, because they felt that Limbaugh's comments were offensive. But his comments were not only offensive; they were also incorrect. After all, it's not taxpayers who would be paying this woman to have sex, but a private health insurance company, into which she pays a monthly enrollment fee to be able to have sex *and not get pregnant unless she wants to*. What's more, if Rush Limbaugh has erectile dysfunction, as he has admitted in the past, he can get a prescription for Viagra or another erectile dysfunction medication. (He's said he uses Viagra.) His prescription will likely be covered by his insurance policy so that he pays only a modest copay. That is, by his logic, you, the reader of this book, will be paying for him to have sex. By his criteria, then, he will also be a prostitute. (About the videos? Maybe we shouldn't push it. I think I'd prefer that he demand for women the same privacy he'd expect for himself.)[18]

Take something a little less controversial. How about family-friendly workplaces? That's a gendered policy issue. As you may recall, currently the United States is one of only five countries in the world that offers no paid parental leave to either parent when they have a kid.[19] (The other four are Swaziland, Papua New Guinea, Lesotho, and Liberia.) We offer virtually no public, free child care prior to when the child enters public school at pre-K or nursery school, and many states and communities don't even offer that. Few workplaces offer on-site child care for their employees, and few offer flextime so that parents can balance their child care commitments. All these policy initiatives to bridge the gap between the public and the private arenas are gendered, as they dramatically affect women's economic participation.

On the other hand, declaring family-friendly policies such as child care and parental leave "women's issues" actually misses the point. Yes, of course, they are issues for women—those who seek to balance work and family commitments. But in that sense, they are also issues for *men* who want to balance their work and family lives. That is, they are *parents'* issues: issues that are really not about women and men, but about women and men who are parents. It's *parents* who want and need family-friendly workplace policies so that they can balance the two sides of their lives. Seeing them as women's issues equates women with mothers and thus leaves out all those women who are not mothers. But it also lets men entirely off the hook, assuming that men are "free" from family responsibilities and wouldn't want to try to balance work and family in the first place.

Obviously, then, the state takes an interest in our private lives, our gendered intimate lives. There are all sorts of laws regulating birth control, abortion, marriage, and divorce. There are laws prohibiting discrimination based on gender in employment, housing, and education. There are laws that protect women from unwanted sexual attention at work (or in school) that might interfere with their ability to perform their workplace duties. All of these are examples of how the realm of the political intersects with gender difference and gender inequality.

For example, the U.S. government believes that there are few functionally relevant gender differences on which you can develop a workplace or educational policy that would favor one gender over another. The key words there are, of course, "functionally relevant." Obviously the government takes no position on whether or not there are actual biological differences between women and men. Of course there are biological differences!

The question is what difference those differences make. What difference do our different physiologies, brain chemistries, hormone secretions have on our ability to do our jobs, go to school, be effective citizens? Here, the courts have advanced a somewhat equivocating position. Unlike race, which receives what the courts call "strict scrutiny"—the courts recognize no functionally relevant differences among people based on race, and so there can be no policies in education or housing or employment that would promote discrimination based on race—gender is slightly different. Gender receives what the courts have labeled "intermediate scrutiny." That means that under most circumstances, gender discrimination would be impermissible. There are some situations in which gender discrimination might be allowed, but the courts have set the bar fairly high.

Gender discrimination is permitted if—and only if—these criteria are met. First, the discrimination has to be based on "real differences" between women and men, not based on stereotypes. That means you can't argue that women are less aggressive than men and that therefore you won't allow them to enlist in the military. Why is that a stereotype? Because even if women as a group are less aggressive than men as a group, that doesn't mean that any particular woman is less aggressive than any particular man. We all know some pretty aggressive women and some pretty nonaggressive men. What we might want in the military is aggressive *people,* and such people come in all genders.

Second, the discrimination has to be actually relevant to the task at hand. That means that even if men are less empathic listeners than women are, again as groups, you can't therefore hire only women as nurses in hospitals. How, exactly, is being an empathic listener a qualification for the job? Finally, the third hurdle that a potential "discriminator" must pass is that there has to be a compelling state interest in the discrimination, a reason the state should set aside its general opinion that discrimination is wrong and inappropriate. That's pretty difficult to demonstrate, so the fallback position is that in virtually all circumstances, discrimination on the basis of gender is illegal.

However, the scrutiny afforded to people of color (strict scrutiny) and to women (intermediate scrutiny) is not offered at all to LGBT people. They get no scrutiny: LGBT people are not considered members of a protected class, in which the courts would intervene. Thus, in some people's eyes, there is no legal argument for same-sex marriage: LGBT people have no protected right to marry. But consider the issue of same-sex marriage through a gender perspective. The law regarding gender discrimination includes a clause "but for sex." Since the Fourteenth Amendment of the U.S. Constitution guarantees "equal protection under the law," that means that any form of discrimination would violate that equal protection (unless, as we've seen, the laws are based on real differences, are relevant to the position, and serve a legitimate state interest). So that notion—that were it not for your biological sex, such a right would be granted to you—is understood by the courts as grounds to declare the form of discrimination unconstitutional. Women's exclusion from various arenas was successfully challenged because the women could have been admitted, "but for sex" they were not.

So consider same-sex marriage through such a lens. If two people, let's call them David and Barbara, want to marry, there is nothing stopping them. But if David and *Bob* want to marry, there is something stopping them. That is, "but for sex" (in this case, Bob's biological sex), they would be permitted to marry. The only thing preventing them from marrying is Bob's biological sex. And that is clearly unconstitutional. In this way, it appears inevitable that same-sex marriage will become legal throughout the United States: Prohibiting it is clearly a case of sex discrimination.

But these issues do raise important questions. What about someone who was born female but has now transitioned and become a man? How shall we understand discrimination in this case? What if you could demonstrate that some type of gender discrimination met all three criteria the courts had set: it was free of stereotypes and based on real difference; it was based on actual criteria for the job; and the government had a compelling state interest in promoting it?

TRANSGENDER LAW AS GENDER POLITICS

Transgender individuals are subject to a host of gender-based discrimination. Here's an instance where the law has failed to keep pace with the changes in people's lives. Transgender people reveal that what we thought was a binary set of two categories— "men" and "women"—and that the entire task of society was to make sure all the biological males ended up in the "men" box and that all the biological females ended up in the "women" box—was actually a series of cross-cutting intersecting continua— biological sex at birth, social presentation of gender, performance of gender, and biological sex as an adult, among others. Identities such as transgender, gender queer, and "gender-fuck" are so new and culturally jarring to our previously held cultural understandings that we simply don't know how to understand this dizzying array of identities, bodies, and performances.

What about someone who was born a male, but who transitions and is now biologically a female? What should her birth certificate say? What about her passport, or driver's license? Or what about someone who is biologically female, but dresses like a man and acts "masculine" and calls herself Mick instead of Michelle? Now imagine that she goes to an all-female college. And what about someone whose "sex" we aren't really sure about, who dresses in neither a "masculine" nor "feminine" way in, for example, jeans and a sweatshirt? What public restroom should this person use? And what of someone who changes as the mood suits, one day dressing and acting as a very "masculine" man and another day as a very "feminine" woman? (One of the things about these new identities and behaviors is that they require the writer to put virtually everything in quotation marks. Such new identities reveal that nothing is fixed, nothing can be taken for granted; all these categories are such by convention and habit, not necessarily because they are found in nature.)

Consider just a few examples. The 2011 National Transgender Discrimination Survey found that one in five people who identified as transgender were the victim of housing discrimination at some point in their lives, and more than one in ten had actually been evicted because of their identity. At school, transgender students face serious discrimination and harassment. Nearly nine out of ten (89.5 percent) transgender students reported feeling unsafe in school. Transgender students are at significantly higher risk of dropping out of school and of suicide. Those who expressed a transgender identity or gender nonconformity in grades K–12 reported high rates of harassment (78 percent), physical assault (35 percent), and sexual violence (12 percent); harassment was so severe that it led almost one-sixth (15 percent) to leave a school in K–12 settings or in higher education.

The survey also found that transgender people experienced widespread abuse in the public sector: 22 percent reported being denied equal treatment by a government agency or official; 29 percent reported police harassment or disrespect; and 12 percent reported being denied equal treatment or harassed by judges or court officials. More-over, one-fifth (22 percent) of respondents who have interacted with police reported harassment by police, with much higher rates reported by people of color. Military regulations deny transgender Americans the right to serve openly, and transgender veterans face significant discrimination in the Veterans Affairs medical system.

Finally, nearly all—a startling 97 percent—had experienced harassment or other negative experiences at work, and more than a quarter (26 percent) reported losing their jobs because of their gender identity. In most states, it's still legal to fire someone simply for being transgender. And despite increasing protections, transgender people experience unemployment at roughly twice the rate of the general population, and rates for transgender people of color are nearly four times the national unemployment rate.[20]

You might say that such discrimination is legitimate because transgender people make the other employees uncomfortable, and when you're uncomfortable, you're dis-tracted and don't perform as well. Reasonable. But you'll also recall, of course, the case of *Pan Am v. Diaz*, where a man sued because he wanted to be a flight attendant, but the company said that a male flight attendant would make the passengers uncomfortable while serving drinks, might arouse feelings in him he would rather not have aroused."[21] The courts struck down Pan Am's policy and ruled that the "comfort" of the passengers was not a legitimate grounds for discrimination. Today you see plenty of male flight attendants. (And we'll probably get used to transgender coworkers just as easily.)

And then, of course, there is the problem of bathrooms. (Bathroom discrimination is actually housed under gender discrimination for housing and employment.) Where do transgender people go to, well, go? It's tricky. They don't say "male" and "female" but "men" and "women." So the bathrooms don't necessarily require anatomical maleness or femaleness, just gendered people who are *socially* men and women—that is, who look like they belong in that bathroom until they unfasten their clothes.

There are, of course, signs of change. In 2009, gender identity was added to federal hate crimes law, explicitly protecting transgender people under federal civil rights law for the first time. An increasing number of college campuses are adopting transgender nondiscrimination protections. Many colleges and universities now offer gender-neutral housing options for students living on campus. Even bathrooms are no longer so fraught with peril. Some institutions offer gender-neutral bathrooms, and others offer them as a third option, with a more traditional "men" and "women." And re-cently, a transgender woman was allowed to compete in the Miss Universe pageant (figure 10.7). Personally, I like the signs on the two bathrooms at my favorite coffee shop in Santa Cruz, California. No "men" or "women" here. Their signs? "Us" and "Them." You can decide for yourself where you belong (figure 10.8).

Figure 10.7. Jenna Talackova, born Walter Page Talackova, was prohibited and then permitted to compete as the Canadian contestant for Miss Universe in 2012.

Source: AP Photo/The Canadian Press, Aaron Vincent Elkaim.

THE STATE AS A GENDERED INSTITUTION

Not only do gender issues show up constantly on the political agenda, but the political arena is, itself, a gendered, and a gendering, institution. And that gender is masculine.

You'll recall from the discussion of the timing of the career clock in chapter 9—that the most intense work time is "front-loaded" so you'll have to work hardest during your first decade on the job, which is, coincidentally, the peak childbearing years—managable for a male worker whose children are being looked after by others (either their mother or a mother-substitute). That a career in medicine or law or as a professor requires the most time from the end of your training (late twenties) through your becoming "tenured" or a partner, or having an established practice, means that you won't be really able to devote much time to raising children until your mid-thirties. Suddenly, people have what you might call a "V-8 moment"—hitting yourself on the forehead as if to say, "Oh, wow, I forgot to have children!"

Figure 10.8. *Source:* Stopstreetharassment.com.

Gender is not only a facet of your identity—something you *have*—but also a set of processes, deeply embedded in the institutions, and the institutional logics, of our society. The dynamics of these institutions, their organizing principles, presuppose a gendered actor—whether the actor is a worker or a citizen. In a modern democratic society, the "citizen" is a man.

That's not because the founding fathers wrote that "all men are created equal." If only it were that easy to fix—a simple grammatical revision to say "All people are created equal." But, alas, just as it has proved incredibly difficult to envision the "citizen" as anything but a white person, so, too, is it incredibly difficult to envision the citizen as anything but a man.

Even when we venture outside the United States, though, the institutional arrangements of global society are gendered. The marketplace, multinational corporations, and transnational geopolitical institutions (World Court, United Nations, European Union) and their attendant ideological principles (economic rationality, liberal individualism) express a gendered logic. Imagine if the "ideal" worker was not an "unencumbered worker" about to devote *him*self to the job 24/7, but instead an "embedded" worker, who is anchored in a set of relationships that inform his or her life, inspire and motivate workplace activity, and who brings to the workplace skills honed in those relationships? Imagine if the conversation about the European debt crisis was about what is best for our children or our families or our elderly parents, rather than about what is best for the banks?

Globalization is gendered as well, as economic integration has differential impacts on women and men. At the national and global levels, the world gender order privileges men in a variety of ways, such as unequal wages, unequal labor force participation, unequal structures of ownership and control of property, unequal control over one's body, and cultural and sexual privileges. On the other hand, traditional notions of male breadwinners and female homemakers have created two large migrant populations—one of mothers who leave their children behind to care for other people's children and one of fathers who leave their families behind to seek manual work in other countries, often living in squatter camps and all-male dormitories on factory grounds.

It's equally true that the very definition of masculinity and femininity is shifting as a result of globalization. Increasingly, there is emerging a single dominant global model of corporate masculinity. Such a definition flattens and mutes traditional regional and local iterations of masculinity and replaces them with a version that looks and acts similarly regardless of the context. You can envision this dominant global "masculinity": he's white, middle-aged, sitting in the business-class lounge in any international hub airport. He's utterly connected by electronic gadgets to the Internet and his clients, with adapters for every conceivable electric outlet around the world. Regardless of his national origin, he speaks English fluently. Regardless of his traditional manner of dress, he wears a business suit, expertly tailored. He is cosmopolitan in his cultural style: He loves continental cuisine and good wines. His social and sexual preferences are very liberal, but his economic and political sympathies are very conservative. He is the global 1 percent. (He is so ubiquitous in our newspapers, magazines, and TV shows that it's often hard to remember that there are very few people in the world like him!)

READ ALL ABOUT IT!

Women's political participation varies enormously across nations. But according to sociologists Richard York and Shannon Elizabeth Bell, women's political participation is closely associated with other measures of life satisfaction. In their article "Life Satisfaction Across Nations," York and Bell show that life satisfaction—people's sense of well-being—is correlated with three other variables: high level of political participation by women, low military spending, and high levels of health care spending. Of course, this doesn't just mean that the women are happier—the men are, too.

If this is one of the gendered faces of the new globalized world, it also means that resistance to globalization often reveals a gendered face as well. Historically, movements against colonialism have often used gender as a way to mobilize nationalist resistance. For example, in late nineteenth-century Bengal, British colonialists justified their imperial domination by constantly humiliating Bengali men as both effeminate and rapacious predatory sexual animals, incapable of self-control. (Historically, marginalized groups are often subject to this twin depiction of the men of the subordinated group: They are hypermasculine and hypo-masculine, both out-of-control, predatory animals and irresponsible, lazy, and incapable of supporting a "normal" family.) So, on the one hand, Bengali men were seen as uncontrolled predators, and the British passed the Age of Consent Act in 1891, outlawing the marriage of young girls to grown men. As a Bengali newspaper put it, angrily:

> The Government wishes to civilize us for it seems we are a people who are extremely uncivilized and barbarous, and steeped in superstition . . . who subject their women to gross ill usage, nay commit bestial oppression on their girls.[22]

And, on the other hand, such predation was actually the result of "effeminacy, mental imperfection and moral debility" that was endemic to Bengali culture, as the *Indian Medical Gazette* put it.

Colonial powers nearly always used gender—both the inadequate masculinity of the colonized men and the helpless innocence of the colonized women, who were in dire need of rescue. So it is hardly a surprise that as they revolted against their imperial oppressors, they also used a gendered rhetoric for political mobilization. It's as if the men said: "It is *they*, not us, who abuse our women, and we, real men, manly men who are natives, must rise up and throw them out!"

You needn't look far to see this. Virtually every movement for national liberation during the nineteenth and twentieth centuries used a gendered language of emasculation to describe the impact of colonialism on native peoples. Theorists like Frantz Fanon argued that colonial powers had created a black "other" that was simultaneously emasculated and a projection of the repressed white desire. Grafting a Freudian analysis onto the situation of colonialism, Fanon argues that the white colonialist projects onto the black man all the repressed sexuality that is required for civilization. (One of the central tenets of Freud's theory is that civilization requires sexual sublimation: You take all that sexual energy and channel it toward more "productive" pursuits.) Here's Fanon in his explosive book *Black Skin, White Masks* (1952):

> Every intellectual gain requires a loss in sexual potential. The civilised white man retains an irrational longing for unusual eras of sexual license, of orgiastic scenes, of unpunished rapes, of unrepressed incest . . . Projecting his own desires onto the Negro, the white man behaves "as if" the Negro really had them . . . the Negro is fixated at the genital; or at any rate he has been fixated there.[23]

Racism is, by definition, sexual—that is, it is gendered. Fanon argues that the white man projects onto the black man all the untamed sexual desires that he, the white man, has had to repress and then assumes the black man is consumed by that very same uncontrolled lust. Thus, the white man becomes fascinated with black male sexuality; this is why fears of black men raping white women animated racists for centuries and why lynching often included the genital mutilation of the black man.

If the institutional forces of racist oppression and colonial subordination used gender as a justification for intervention, as well as a consequence or outcome of that intervention, it is no surprise that resistance movements are equally saturated with gendered ambitions (reclaiming manhood) and gendered strategies. In some cases, as with the Black Panther leader Eldridge Cleaver, it meant using the white man's fears of black sexuality against white people. Cleaver infamously (and reprehensibly politically, in my view) argued that for a black man to rape a white woman was a revolutionary act of resistance to racism.

But one can find elements of this gendered language in just about every social movement in the world today—whether progressive movements that seek to reclaim the nation for the people themselves (and therefore to kick out the colonizers) or movements against globalization that seek to "restore" the nation to its traditional, and often religious, foundations. Each social movement is a meditation on the appropriate roles for women and men and a debate about the manhood of each group of men.

In some cases, women have been imprisoned within the traditional society's constraints and then further subordinated by the colonial intervention. So, in movements such as the Iranian uprising of 2009 or the Arab Spring of 2010, women were very much in evidence demanding to be permitted to join the global public arena as the equals of men. "If you ask someone if they want gender equality, that's a loaded term here," explained one Egyptian woman. "Do you mean all women should be like men?

Figure 10.9. Despite women's active participation in the protest movements in the Middle East (illustrated by these women gathered in Tahrir Square in Cairo, Egypt, in 2011), there has been little progress in ending sexual assault and violence against them.

Source: AP Photo/Khalil Hamra, File.

Figure 10.10. Women demonstrate in Yemen, 2011.

Source: AP Photo/Muhammed Muheisen.

Most would say no. If you mean women have choice and equal protection under the law, most would say yes." And their participation does seem to be having some effect on the direction of the movements and their acceptance by the male leaders. "Our demands are somehow similar to men, starting with freedom, equal citizenship, and giving women a greater role in society," says Faizah Sulimani, twenty-nine, a protest leader in Yemen (figure 10.10). "Women smell freedom at Change Square where they feel more welcomed than ever before. Their fellow [male] freedom fighters are showing unconventional acceptance to their participation and they are actually for the first time letting women be, and say, what they really want."[24]

On the other side of the political spectrum, conservative and fundamentalist movements that seek to restore the society to its traditional foundations also seek to transform gender relations, but in exactly the opposite direction. Women, they may argue, have been "masculinized"—forced by market conditions to work outside the home, to refuse to be mothers, to seek to claim the rights and privileges in the public sphere that had been previously reserved for men. For example, the Taliban in Afghanistan, formed as both an anti-imperialist movement against the Soviet occupation in the 1980s and a fundamentalist religious movement, sought to remove women from all public life and return them to the home, where, they argued, women belong. All across the Islamic world, but particularly in Iran and Iraq, women had made enormous strides towards equality, asserting rights to go to school and even universities, to enter professions, to choose their husbands. Even in Saudi Arabia, women were insisting that they be allowed to open bank accounts and drive cars. They sought entry into the public realm, just as the country was entering the global political and economic arena.

Traditional movements have tried to put a stop to this, pushing women out of the labor force and closing girls' and women's schools. At the same time, these movements reassert men's dominance in the home, insisting that women obey their fathers and husbands, and punishing them, often brutally or even lethally, when they resist. "We will take action against women who go out shopping in the markets, and any shop-keeper seen dealing with women shoppers will be dealt with severely," is how one poster put it in Peshawar, Pakistan.[25]

While these efforts have been most visible in Muslim countries, there are many other examples. In Israel, for example, the ultra-Orthodox backlash against the secular Israeli state has punished women for sitting in whatever seat on the bus they choose (as opposed to sitting in the back) or thrown rocks at schoolgirls wearing their school uniforms (since these were deemed immodest by these self-proclaimed arbiters of fashion). Given this, it's no wonder that some of the leaders of the movements that made up the Arab Spring in 2010 were women. Women spearheaded the movements in Egypt and Iran and were also in evidence in the movements that toppled tradition-alist and authoritarian leaders in Tunisia, Libya, and Yemen.

Less visible, but equally gendered, have been the efforts to re-masculinize men (figure 10.11). If women had strayed into the "male" sphere of public life, men's un-questioned authority in that arena, as well as at home, had been steadily eroding. Men, these fundamentalist leaders argued, must return to being real men. For example, one group targeted by the Taliban in Afghanistan were the barbers, since not shaving one's beard is a symbol of virility commanded by the Prophet. (This is also true among the Haredi—the ultra-Orthodox—in Israel, who do not shave their sideburns

Figure 10.11. A barber stands by his window in Buner, Pakistan, where the Taliban has warned "Do Not Shave."

Source: Tariq Mahmood/AFP/Getty Images.

or their beards.) Afghani barbers who shaved men were in danger of having their hands cut off. In one well-known case, twenty-eight Afghani barbers were imprisoned for giving men haircuts that resembled Leonardo DiCaprio's in *Titanic*. "Beatles cut" hairstyles were legally banned as "dangerous."

Closer to home, in October 2011, three members of a breakaway Amish cult in Ohio were arrested for forcibly shaving the beards of several Amish men, an act of terrible humiliation to a religious group that does not permit shaving and denounces the use of electricity (as in electric shavers, which were used). Cult leader Sam Mullet (figure 10.12) explained the shavings as retaliation for marginalizing him. So, whether it's the Taliban prohibiting shaving or Sam Mullet forcibly shaving, it's clear that men's beards are more than simply a fashion statement: They're the proof of a divinely sanctioned masculinity.[26]

Even Osama bin Laden used gendered language to exhort the men of Al Qaeda to their suicidal terrorist sacrifice, first by claiming that Americans were weak and effeminate (since we allow women to join the military) and then by exhorting his followers to show that they are "real men":

> Our brothers who fought in Somalia saw wonders about the weakness, feebleness, and cowardliness of the U.S. soldier . . . We believe that we are men, Muslim men who must have the honor of defending [Mecca]—We do not want American women soldiers defending [it] . . . The rulers in that region have been deprived of their manhood . . . and they think that the people are women. By God, Muslim women refuse to be defended by these American and Jewish prostitutes.

Such statements provide ample evidence that the call to arms is almost always a call to reclaim, if not to prove, one's manhood. And, sadly, it will not be the last time we hear such calls.

REDRESSING THE GENDERED POLITICAL REALM

One of the great rallying cries of the feminist movement since the 1960s has been "the personal is political," by which people meant that the daily routines of personal life—housework, raising children, negotiating activities with your partners and your friends, what TV and movies you watched, what music you listened to, even sex—were "political," utterly intertwined with the political realities of gender inequality. How you lived your life, every single day, reflected and reproduced both gender difference and gender inequality.

It's equally true that "the political is personal"—the arena of the political, from policy decisions to the choices you have about voting in elections—all reflect the gender differences we assume are "natural" and the gender inequalities we often believe flow inevitably from those natural differences.

Since its origins in the mid-nineteenth century, the women's movement has sought to redress both elements of gender inequality. In the nineteenth century, women's campaigns for political inclusion were based on the moral and theological assumptions that since both women and men were equal souls in the eyes of God, there could be no justification for prohibiting women from participating in the fruits of democratic political life. From the first Woman's Convention at Seneca Falls, New York, in 1848, women sought political inclusion as a way to become equal citizens.

Figure 10.12. Sam Mullet led a breakaway Amish cult in Ohio that forcibly shaved his male rivals, an act of humiliation that also led to his arrest.

Source: AP Photo/Amy Sancetta, file.

The modern women's movement was born to remove obstacles to women's full participation in modern life. In the nineteenth century, the "**first wave**" of the women's movement was concerned with women's *entry* into the public sphere. Campaigns to allow women to vote (suffrage), to go to college, to serve on juries, to go to law school or medical school, or to join a profession or a union all had largely succeeded by the middle of the twentieth century. The motto of the National Woman Suffrage Association was "Women, their rights and nothing less! Men, their rights and nothing more!" Around the world, women began to challenge restrictive definitions of femininity and the barriers that prevented their full participation in society. From its origins, the women's movement has been a global movement, yet each national and cultural expression has sought changes tailored to its specific context. In the first decades of the twentieth century, women in Europe and North America obtained basic rights to enter the public arena. In the past few decades, some of the most active developments in global feminism have been generated outside the United States.

Once they had achieved the right to vote, serve in the military, and become doctors, lawyers, architects, and every other kind of professional, then the next step was to ensure that those women who did enter the public arena were able to live full lives in doing so: safe from harassment and discrimination in their public arenas and also able to have the sorts of family arrangements they wanted, to balance work and family. Beginning in the 1960s, a "**second wave**" of the women's movement appeared, determined to continue the struggle to eliminate obstacles to women's advancement but also equally determined to investigate the ways that gender inequality is also part of personal life, which includes women's relationships with men. In the industrialized world, the second wave focused on public participation—equality in the working world, election to political office—as well as beginning to focus on men's violence against women, rape, the denigration of women in the media, and women's sexuality and lesbian rights.

This required, of course, influencing the political arena that shaped how people live their personal lives. Women have campaigned, as women, for health care, reproductive rights, freedom to control their own bodies, and policies that would keep women safe when they left their homes from assault, violence, and rape, as well as safe from those same problems when they returned to their homes.

Think about all the rights that any contemporary American woman might take for granted: the right to vote, to drive a car, to serve on a jury, to play sports, to work in her chosen profession, to be able to work free of unwanted harassment and earn wages equal to the wages that men earn, to be safe on the streets and in her home, to be able to open a checking account in her own name, to run for office, to serve in the military, to put her own name on the mailbox of her own home, to have an orgasm. Contemporary women can take these rights for granted because other women, thousands of them, devoted their entire lives to fighting in the political arena just so contemporary women could be lucky enough to eventually take them for granted.

Today, a "**third wave**" of the women's movement has emerged among younger women. While third-wave feminists share the outrage at institutional discrimination and interpersonal violence, they also have a more playful relationship with mass media and consumerism. While they support the rights of lesbians, many third-wavers are also energetically heterosexual and insist on the ability to be friends and lovers with men. They are also decidedly more multicultural and seek to explore and challenge the "intersections" of gender inequality with other forms of inequality, such as class, race, ethnicity, and sexuality. They are equally concerned with racial inequalities or sexual inequalities and see the ways in which these other differences construct our experiences of gender. Third-wave feminists also feel more personally empowered than their foremothers; they often feel there is no need for feminism because they can now do almost anything they want.

The political position of many young women today is often "I'm not a feminist, but . . . " Most young women subscribe to virtually all the tenets of feminism—equal pay for equal work, the right to control their bodies and sexuality—but they believe that they are already equal to men and therefore don't need a political movement to liberate them and that the term *feminist* carries too many negative connotations.

Feminism is a catch-all term that describes the wide variety of theories that guide and shape women's efforts to transform the political arena. There are, of course, as many feminisms as there are feminists, but the general outlines of different strands of feminism also enable us to discern the different ways in which the women's movement has sought to politically mobilize people to redress gender inequality. Feminists believe that women should have the same political, social, sexual, economic, and intellectual rights that men enjoy. Feminists insist on women's equality in all arenas—in the public sphere, in interpersonal relations, at home and at work, in the bedroom and the boardroom. One can, of course, be a feminist and like men, want to look attractive, and shave one's underarms and wear mascara. Or not. Feminism is about women's choices and the ability to choose to do what they want to do with no greater obstacles than the limits of their abilities.

Feminism is also a global political movement—with local, regional, and transnational expressions. The United Nations Declaration of 1985 made it clear that women's rights were universal human rights—and that women's bodily integrity, her sexual autonomy, and her rights to public participation knew no national boundaries. There are several major strands of feminism. Each emphasizes a different aspect of gender inequality and prescribes a different political formula for equality.

Different strands of feminism focus on different political issues. For example, **liberal feminism** emphasizes removing the obstacles to individual women's entry into the public sphere. Liberal feminists have been at the forefront of campaigns for equal wages and comparable worth, as well as reproductive choice. The Equal Rights Amendment, which did not pass as a constitutional amendment in the 1970s, is an example of a liberal feminist political agenda. The amendment states simply that "equality of rights under the law shall not be denied or abridged by the United States or by any State on account of sex." Critics of liberal feminism claim that the focus on removing barriers to individual rights ignores the root causes of gender inequality; liberal feminists tend to be largely white and middle class, and their focus on career mobility reflects their class and race.

By contrast, **radical feminists** emphasize not so much the constraints on individual women's mobility and choices, but the systematic oppression of women—because they are women. Many radical feminists believe that women are oppressed and subordinated by men directly, personally, and most often through sexual relations. Radical feminists often believe that patriarchy is the original form of domination and that all other forms of inequality derive from it. To radical feminists, it is through sex that men appropriate women's bodies. Radical feminists have been active in campaigns to end prostitution, pornography, rape, and violence against women. Many argue that it is through "trafficking" in women's bodies—selling their bodies as prostitutes or making images of that trafficking in pornography—that gender inequality is reproduced. Pornography provides a rare window into the male psyche: This is how men see women, they argue. "Pornography is the theory, rape is the practice," is a slogan coined by radical feminist writer Robin Morgan (1976). Radical feminists have also been successful in bringing issues of domestic violence and rape to international attention. They have created a growing worldwide concern for the new and revived sex slave marketplace.

However, radical feminism relies too much on unconvincing blanket statements about all men and all women, without taking into account differences among men and among women. Thus, it's often "essentialist," claiming that the single dividing line in society is between men and women. That is, of all feminisms, it may be the radical variety that believes men are from Mars and women from Venus. Their claims about universal sisterhood have not been convincing to black feminists, who feel that when radical feminists say "women," they really mean "white women."

In response to the perceived whiteness of both liberal feminism and radical feminism, some women have tried to both broaden and deepen the reach of feminist analysis. Liberal feminists believe all women are individuals and therefore entitled to rights; radical feminists claim that each woman is "all women," which is to say that every woman faces a common oppression as a woman. They thus try to extend feminism to other women. But **multicultural feminism** begins where liberal and radical feminism end: acknowledging that the word "woman" means many different things, depending on class, race, ethnicity, region, religion, sexuality, age, or any other status. That is, multicultural feminism understands that each woman does not experience her oppression in quite the same way as every other. An older black lesbian in the countryside might relate differently, for example, to lesbian pornography than a young urban white heterosexual woman. (Or maybe not; the point is that one cannot claim that all women react the same way.) To multiculturalists, liberal feminism disaggregates the category "women" so profoundly that all commonalities are lost; radical feminism, by contrast, lumps all women into one master category, "woman," blurring any other distinctions among women.

Multicultural feminists tend to be third-wavers—younger, better educated, and of many different races and sexualities. They take an "intersectional approach" to the gender of politics, understanding the ways in which different facets of identity—race, or class, or ethnicity, or sexuality and the like—shape women's experiences as women. Multicultural feminists also sometimes clash with other types of feminism. For example, some feminist women denounce the burqa—the full covering required of Islamic women in some (but not all) Muslim countries—as oppressive to women, suppressing their ability to be full citizens. But some Islamic women defend the practice as their expression of their autonomy and their choice to express themselves as women. Such a debate cannot be resolved as an either/or. Both sides are right, for entirely different reasons. Multicultural feminism expresses and embraces those differences among women and thus must encompass differing, even conflicting, perspectives.

Multicultural feminists make another critical point: Feminism is a global movement, encompassing women around the world engaged in their own struggles for political power, public access, and an end to discrimination. Global feminist movements and organizations engage with gender inequality in every political arena—from transnational labor organizing to campaigns to increase political participation and those to decrease violence and trafficking.

MEN AND GENDER POLITICS

Feminism is a movement *for* women's equality, but that doesn't mean it's only *about* women. After all, women's equality would require not only the entry of women into the public sphere—a process by which men might simply move over to give women a seat at the table—but also the transformation of the most intimate and personal elements of relations between women and men. So since the beginning of the women's movement, there have been efforts to mobilize men—from ferocious denunciation of and resistance to women's equality to ardent support.

In the early days of the woman suffrage movement, there were visible and vocal male allies. In fact, at the first women's rights meeting at Seneca Falls in 1848, it was only after the great African-American former slave Frederick Douglass made an impassioned speech in favor of granting women the vote that the woman suffrage plank passed and was included in the "Declaration of Sentiments," the American women's movement's founding document.

Of course, a large number of men—from the mid-nineteenth century to the present—found in feminism such a dramatic challenge to traditional, unquestioned male authority that they opposed gender equality. Some **antifeminists** actively resisted women's entry into the public arena, often because they believed that women, as the inferior sex, were simply physically incapable of handling the stress and difficulty that such public participation might entail. Some went further, arguing that women's entry would degrade the public sphere, disrupting the male camaraderie that was necessary for workers, soldiers, doctors, lawyers, corporate executives, athletes, or even students. Thus did Josiah Bunting III, a VMI graduate and former military officer, claim that women's entry into the Virginia Military Institute would represent "a toxic kind of virus" that would pollute the pristine homosocial world of that all-male military school. (The Supreme Court rejected that argument in 1996, and women have been cadets at VMI ever since. No epidemics of viruses have been reported.)

Antifeminist men went further, arguing that women's entry would also destroy the traditional family, as women renounced their God-ordained and natural position as homemaker and mother. They predicted that divorce and promiscuity would both increase, while faith in tradition and religion would decrease. (Their predictions were true, but obviously not for the reasons they thought. Divorce rose because *men*, not women, did not rise to meet the challenge of balancing work and family life, and so women became predictably frustrated in their marriages.)

Today's antifeminists have largely abandoned physical ability as the grounds to exclude women from the public arena, except, of course, when women seek entry into occupations for which men have decided they are unfit, such as firefighting, the military, or construction. Most of the time, contemporary antifeminists argue only that women's liberation has gone too far and has now resulted in reverse discrimination against men. According to the men's rights activists, women now run virtually every show in town, and men have become the "second sex." Some antifeminist groups seek to return to a golden era of unquestioned male authority in the home. For example, the evangelical Christian group Promise Keepers embraces a traditional nineteenth-century vision of masculinity in which men are responsible fathers and providers—as long as their wives also return to a traditional nineteenth-century definition of femininity, staying home and taking care of the children.

The global struggle against gender inequality also engages men as allies. These "pro-feminist" men believe not only that gender equality is a good thing for women but that it would also transform masculinity in ways that would be positive for men, enabling them to be more involved fathers, better friends, more emotionally responsive partners and husbands—fuller individuals and human beings. They work with women to end men's violence against women and sexual harassment in the workplace and guarantee equality in the workplace and at home. Global organizations like the White Ribbon Campaign, begun in Canada in 1991, have groups in more than fifty countries working to end men's violence against women. In the United States, organizations such as the National Organization for Men Against Sexism (NOMAS), Men Can Stop Rape (MCSR), and A Call to Men seek to bring men together to promote gender equality.

Such groups are particularly visible on campuses—perhaps even your own. On campuses around the country, there are men's organizations working to support the campus women's groups. Groups such as Harvard Men Against Rape, Montana Men Against Rape, and Tulane Men Against Violence actively work to engage men in campus-based activities such as supporting "Take Back the Night" marches or *Vagina Monologues* productions or "Walk a Mile in Her Shoes" campaigns to raise men's awareness.

KEY TERMS

Antifeminists	Globalization	Radical Feminism
First-Wave Feminism	Liberal Feminism	Second-Wave Feminism
Gendered Political Divide	Multicultural Feminism	Third-Wave Feminism

The GENDERED MEDIA

In Saudi Arabia, women cannot drive cars, but they can get rides on Uber. Speech is heavily censored, but Saudi youth carry on debates via Twitter. Flirting is prohibited, but they use Snapchat and WhatsApp. Just before shops close for prayers, they can check their smartphones to find the nearest Dunkin' Donuts before it closes. One Saudi woman, dressed entirely in black from head to toe, is a medical student who likes Jimmy Kimmel and *Game of Thrones*, and has a half-million followers on Instagram. When asked what changes she would like to see in Saudi society, does she answer: woman suffrage, free speech, an end to brutal gender discrimination? No. "We need movies," she said. "I think if we could just achieve that, I mean, that's all we need."[1] Oppressed? There's probably an app for that.

Here in the United States, Americans have a love/hate relationship with the media. On the one hand, we're an utterly media-saturated society. As you've read this book, I'll bet you've also checked your Facebook page, texted several of your friends about what you are having for dinner, followed some inane celebrity's tweet, watched a movie on Netflix and a video of adorable kittens or cute babies on YouTube, played a video game (or several), and watched an episode of *The Big Bang Theory* on Hulu, your smartphone, your iPad, through a game console—or on an actual television set. We're weighed down by laptops, desktops, smartphones, tablets—each of which is supposed to make our workloads lighter and easier.

Our images of ourselves—how we are supposed to look, what we should wear, and how we should behave—are constructed by using the materials we get from the media—magazines, newspapers, television, Internet. We're bombarded with media images and representations, and we creatively construct identities and styles based on the images that appeal to us and our social circle.

Okay, you get the point. We rely on media, we love media, we couldn't live without media. So how come when something goes wrong, we instantly blame the media? When someone walks into his school armed to the teeth and opens fire, it must be because he watched violent video games! Lonely? It must be because we only know how to use the word "friend" as a verb. Sexual assault on campus? Must be because the guys all watch gonzo porn on the Internet. Disobedient children? Has their attention span become truncated and their diet of rebellious images become engorged?

Only when things go wrong, though. Consider the corollary: How come when something goes right, we don't credit the media? You met the love of your life on Match.com? Must be the media! Victorious in battle? Must be those military video games! Win the Nobel Prize in Medicine? Must be because you watched *House*.

Try this experiment. The next time there is a random school shooter who opens fire on his classmates—I choose my pronoun carefully; nearly 100 percent of random school shooters are boys—watch as the media-bashers come out to play.

"Common sense tells you that if these kids are playing video games, where they're on a mass killing spree in a video game, it's glamorized on the big screen," television therapist Dr. Phil told Larry King in the aftermath of Seung-Hui Cho's massacre of thirty-two classmates and professors at Virginia Tech in 2007. "You take that and mix it with a psychopath, a sociopath or someone suffering from mental illness and add in a dose of rage, the susceptibility is too high."

One Florida attorney, Jack Thompson, popped up all over the news, decrying the violent video games that caused the massacre. Cho, he claimed was an avid gamer, and his game of choice was CounterStrike. He threatened to sue Bill Gates because Microsoft manufactures video games. "This is not rocket science. When a kid who has never killed anyone in his life goes on a rampage and looks like the Terminator, he's a video gamer," Thompson said.[2]

Unfortunately for these instant experts on the relationship between video games and violence, the search of Cho's dorm room turned up no video games. Not one. (How many would they turn up in *your* dorm room?) His roommate said he never saw Cho playing any video games. Apparently, they played no part in his life. (This did not, however, lead to some other instant expert proclaiming that *if only* Cho had played violent video games he would have had a constructive outlet for all that pent-up aggression.)

As a society, we keep having this debate: Do the media *cause* violence, or do the media simply reflect the violence that already exists in our society?

Think of how many times we have heard variations of it. Do gangsta rap or violent video games or violent movies or violent heavy metal music lead to increased violence? Does violent pornography lead men to commit rape? Or do these media merely remind us of how violent our society already is?

Surely, the media play an enormous role in our lives. And, just as surely, the media are major building blocks in the construction of our identities as women and men. How do the various media contribute to our understanding of gender? What role do the various media play in the maintenance of gender difference or gender inequality?

THE MEDIA AS A GENDERED INSTITUTION

To say that the media are a gendered institution is to say simply that they are an institution, like all other institutions (schools, churches, families, corporations, or states, for example), that (1) reflects existing gender differences and gender inequalities, (2) constructs those very gender differences, and (3) reproduces gender inequality by making those differences seem "natural" and not socially produced in the first place. Part of an institution's function of maintaining inequality is to first create the differences and then to attempt to conceal its authorship so that those differences seem to flow from the nature of things.

Media reflect existing gender differences and inequalities by targeting different groups of consumers with different messages that assume prior existing differences. In a sense, women and men don't use or consume the same media—there are women's magazines and men's magazines, chick flicks and action movies, chick lit and lad lit, pornography and romance novels, soap operas and crime procedurals, guy video games and girl video games, blogs and 'zines—and, of course, advertising that is intricately connected to each of these different formats (figures 11.1a, b).

Adopting Jessie Bernard's famous phrase about marriage, to which we referred in chapter 6, there are also at least two medias—"his" and "hers." There are also multiple medias based on race—BET and WWE or "urban" and "country" radio, for example—class, ethnicity, and age (think of the complex rating system that says what age level is appropriate for some media content). And although, thinking of marriage, Bernard was right to say that "his" is better than "hers," such a statement may be less true when it comes to the media. Both media are part of a gigantic cultural apparatus designed to reproduce gender inequality by making it appear that such inequality is the natural result of existing gender differences. First, the media create the differences; then the media tell us that the inequality is the natural result of those differences.

The problem is that no matter how pervasive the avalanche of media might be, the ruse never completely works. The media are fabulously effective, and yet there are so many fissures in the walls they collectively construct that efforts to shore it up feel almost frenzied, an almost blind obsession with overkill, just to make sure that everyone gets the message. And still, we get several messages and do different things with them.

One reason for this is that many of the debates about the effects of the media present the media as the sole actor in the drama—and the consumer, namely us, as passive consumers, as sponges who uncritically soak up all the messages we're fed. To the social scientist, of course, nothing could be further from the truth. It is not the media itself, but rather the interaction of consumers and media that remains the constitutive force in gender relations. We bring our selves—our identities, our differences—to our encounters with various media; and we can take from them a large variety of messages. We need to also consider the way we act on the media, the way we consume it, actively, creatively, and often even rebelliously. The question is never whether or not the media do such and such, but rather *how* the media and its consumers interact to create the varying meanings that derive from our interactions with those media. We need to think differently about the media, to treat them as another central institution in our lives, not some outside influence that tells us what to do. The media are a

Figure 11.1a. *Source:* © Robert W. Ginn/Photo Edit.

Figure 11.1b. *Source:* © Michael Newman/Photo Edit.

primary institution of socialization. And like all the institutions whose mission is our socialization, the media are deeply gendered.

THE MEDIA AS A GENDERING INSTITUTION

That sentence—that the media are a primary institution of socialization—is an essential starting point in our analysis. And such a perspective takes us far beyond the traditional sociological canon. If you were to pick up an introductory sociology textbook from, say, the 1950s or even the 1970s, you would find that there were three major institutions tasked with the socialization of children: family, education, and religion (which are, not coincidentally, the first three chapters of this part of the book). Their sole purpose was the gradual and complete inculcation of a society's values, an acceptance of the legitimacy of established norms to express those values, and a belief in the institutional apparatuses designed to maintain social cohesion and stability. And you would read that the agents—the people—charged with those socializing tasks were, naturally, parents (family), teachers (education), and religious figures (clergy).

All well and good, and, of course, largely true. But to a child, the earlier list above—parents, teachers, and clergy—sounds more like "grown-ups, grown-ups, and grown-ups." And any child could tell you that the primary agents of socialization are also their friends, their peers, and the images of themselves they see represented in the media. We must now revise all those old textbooks to include the *six* primary institutions of socialization: family, schools, and religious institutions, to be sure—and also peer groups, the workplace, and the media.

The dynamics of socialization are also different than we earlier believed: We are not blank slates upon which these institutions imprint a uniform cultural code. Were that true, how could we explain the massive diversity we observe around us? In every arena—some more, some less, of course—we are active agents of our own socialization, active participants in this process.

The relationship between media and consumers is complex. Do we absorb all the images and then construct our identities from them, or do the media simply tell us what we already know? Neither—or, rather, a little of both. It is not simply that the media are part of the mechanism by which we construct our gendered identities. The media as an institution are gendered as well. The media, like all other social institutions, provide the materials for the construction of gendered identities, maintain and reproduce gendered inequality, and naturalize that inequality to appear as though it is the natural outcome of gender difference. The media are so saturated with images of gender—from normative depictions of appropriate or inappropriate behaviors to images that capture our aspirations and imaginations—that it is sometimes barely noticeable. Sometimes, in fact, that seems to be the chief function of many media—to entertain us by presenting various images of men and women and enabling us to identify with, aspire to, or laugh at them.

And as the media is saturated with gender, we are saturated with media. The average American home today has 3.8 television sets, 2.8 DVD/VCRs, 2.5 radios, 2.2 CD players, 2.3 video game consoles, 2 computers, and one TiVo/other DVR.[3]

Television is omnipresent: 63 percent of families with children have the TV on during dinner, and 51 percent are "constant television households"—that is, they have a TV on virtually all day, whether or not anyone is actually watching it.[4] More than two-thirds of American kids eight to eighteen have a TV in their bedroom. (Kids with TVs in their bedrooms spend, on average, 1.5 hours more per week watching TVs than kids who don't.) And while once restaurants and bars were a way to escape the isolation of being in front of the tube, now those restaurants and bars are as likely to have TVs mounted on the walls so you don't have to miss a second.

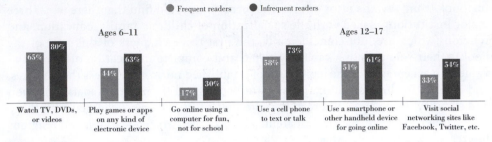

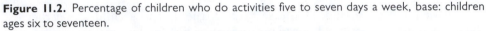

Figure 11.2. Percentage of children who do activities five to seven days a week, base: children ages six to seventeen.

Source: Kids & Family Reading Report™: Fifth Edition from Scholastic Inc. and managed by YouGov. 2015.

Maybe this is why 40 percent of eight- to thirteen-year-olds said they did not read any part of a book on the previous day, a figure that shoots up to 70 percent of kids fourteen to eighteen. In fact, the one medium people do *not* seem to interact with is books. In 2004, the U.S. Department of Education asked seventeen-year-olds, "How often do you read for fun on your own time?" Nearly one in five (19 percent) said "never"—double the rate from twenty years earlier. And four-fifths of American families say they did not buy a book last year.[5]

These media seem to reflect gender differences that are already there—that is, they appeal to different audiences who use them differently. These different ways of using "his" and "her" media are one of the primary ways in which we construct our gendered identities—and this, then, becomes one of the chief ways in which we naturalize gender inequality.

WHAT CHILDREN SEE

It starts so early. Early in the school years, children learn to read, thus opening a new source of influence. And they begin to observe the content of other media—television, films, or cartoons. Do these materials counter sex typing, or do they reinforce it? As we explore gender and mass media, it is important to discuss the ways in which the school-based curriculum reinforces gender stereotypes and makes those stereotypes feel as though they were based on something "natural."

Until recently, studies of children's books and anthologies have consistently reported traditional sex differences and pro-male biases. Females have been vastly underrepresented, and often absent, in pictures, in titles, and as main characters. In addition, female characters have usually been cast in insignificant or secondary roles. Their activities have been limited to loving, watching, or helping, whereas males have engaged in adventuring and solving problems. Women have not been given jobs or professions; motherhood has been presented as a full-time, lifetime job. The son in the family has worn trousers, and the daughter has worn a skirt; he has been active, she has been passive. In biographies, women have often been portrayed as dependent. For example, Marie Curie has been depicted as a helpmate to her husband, rather than as the brilliant scientist and Nobel Prize–winner that she was.[6]

In preschool school books, the gender bias has been consistent. In 1972, Leonore Weitzman and her colleagues surveyed winners of the Caldecott Award for the best

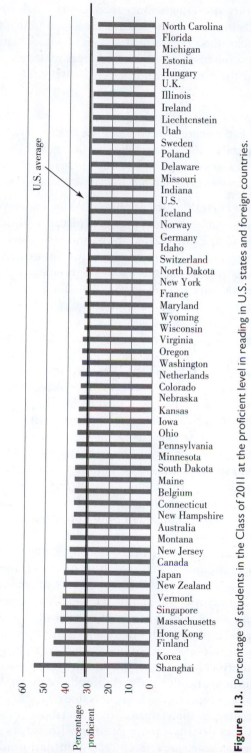

Figure 11.3. Percentage of students in the Class of 2011 at the proficient level in reading in U.S. states and foreign countries.

Source: Figure 2, p. 12 of *Globally Challenged: Are U.S. Students Ready to Compete?*. August 2011. The Program on Education Policy and Governance, Harvard Kennedy School.

children's books for the years 1967 to 1971. Since then, the research has been updated several times, most recently in 2011, and the researchers now find that though females are more visible in the books, their portrayal still reveals gender biases. Females are still depicted in passive and submissive positions, whereas males are shown as active and independent. Even in these more recent books, Weitzman and her colleagues conclude:

> Not only does Jane express no career goals, but there is no model to provide any ambition. One woman in the entire twenty books has an occupation outside the home and she works at the Blue Tile Diner. How can we expect Dick to express tender emotions without shame when only two adult males in this collection have anything resembling tender emotions and one of them is a mouse?[7]

In 1975, the U.S. Department of Health, Education, and Welfare surveyed 134 texts and readers from sixteen different publishers, looking at the pictures, stories, and language used to describe male and female characters. **"Boy-centered" stories** outnumbered **"girl-centered" stories** by a 5:2 ratio; there were three times as many adult male characters as adult female characters; six times as many biographies of men as of women; and four times as many male fairy tales as female. Recalling her American history classes, one scholar recently remembered a strange biological anomaly—"a nation with only founding fathers."[8]

Of course, some changes have occurred over the past forty years. In children's books today, girls and women are far more likely than before to be depicted as the main character and far less likely to be depicted as passive, without ambition or career goals. But gender stereotypes still prevail: Girls are still depicted as more interested in domestic life than boys are. In fact, the major change in all media images—books, television, and movies—has been that women are no longer cast as helpless domestic helpmates. There has been no comparable change in the depiction of men or boys in children's books, no movement of men toward more nurturing and caring behaviors. As in real life, women in our storybooks have left home and gone off to work, but men still have enormous trouble coming back home.[9]

As in children's books, so, too, in the other media that enter our lives. What children learn in school is reinforced at home, not only in our families, but also in our entertainment. Television programs, movies, music videos—all reiterate gender stereotypes. Television takes vast chunks of its time to deliver entertainment and commercial messages to younger children as well as to those in school. There are programs for preschoolers in the morning, for schoolchildren in the afternoon, and for all children every Saturday morning. For many children, this is one of their largest commitments of waking time; for parents, it often serves as a built-in baby sitter.

The presentation of gender roles on children's television shows has been, at least until recently, quite similar to that of children's readers, the playground, and the schools. Boys are the centerpiece of a story; they do things and occupy the valued roles. Girls serve as backdrop, are helpful and caring, and occupy the less valued roles. Even *Sesame Street*, hailed as a breakthrough in enjoyable educational programming, presented far more male characters than female. Commercials for children on Saturday morning usually depict boys driving cars or playing with trucks and depict girls playing with dolls. There has been some pressure to eliminate gender stereotyping in both commercials and show content, but television shows are linked to a gender-stereotyped system. Toy manufacturers sell gender-linked toys, parents buy them, and writers often take their stories from existing materials (including the toys that are for sale, such as G.I. Joe and the Ninja Turtles) for children.

Television commercials are especially powerful, perhaps even more powerful than the shows themselves, because they are expressly designed to persuade. Commercials also link gender roles to the significant adult roles that the young will be playing in the future. The authoritative voices advising you what to buy are nearly all men's voices, which indicates to children who the experts are. Similarly, gender stereotypes are attached to consumption, one of the most valued activities in U.S. society. By linking material benefits to gender roles, the commercials teach a powerful lesson—if you consume this product, this is the kind of man or woman you can be.

Television, films, and other media also habituate viewers, young and old, to a culture that accepts and expects violence. In the nation's most thorough investigation of violence on television, the National Television Violence Study, four teams of researchers systematically examined TV violence. They found that violence is ubiquitous (61 percent of all shows contained some violence) and that typically it is perpetuated by a white male, who goes unpunished and shows little remorse. The violence is typically justified, although nearly one-half (43 percent) of shows presented it in a humorous way. Consistently, "the serious and long-lasting consequences of violence are frequently ignored."[10]

On broadcast television a bladed weapon or gun appeared on screen every three minutes. These calculations represent only when a new weapon entered the scene. The numbers do not account for the length of time a weapon remained on screen. The most violent shows on broadcast TV have essentially similar levels of violence as the most violent cable TV shows, rendering untrue the popular assumption that broadcast TV is a "safer" media environment for children.[11]

Violence against women and teenage girls on television is increasing at rates that far exceed the overall increases in violence on television. Violence, irrespective of gender, on television increased during the study period only 2 percent from 2004 (3,840 storylines that included violence) to 2009 (3,929 storylines). During that same period instances of violence against women increased 120 percent (from 195 storylines that included female victims of violence in 2004 to 429 storylines in 2009). Although female victims appeared to be primarily of adult age, collectively, there was a 400 percent increase in the depiction of teen girls as victims across all networks from 2004 to 2009.[12]

Media presentations do not have immediate effects on the gender behavior of children. Although media influence the ideas about gender that children have, children also negotiate a real world of people who do not fit these stereotypes. Media representations become just one more element in a child's process of organizing his or her own ideas of gender, part of his or her "concept formation" about gender. Nor do these media representations have the dramatic and immediate effects that media critics often ascribe to them, because most of human learning is a steady accumulation of information, attitudes, and ways of responding rather than a sudden revelation or recognition. The media simply provide another push toward accepting current arrangements as if they were natural, right, and preordained.

Let's look next at gender differences—both in media use and in media content. What we use, what we watch, what we consume—these are clearly marked by gender. There are his and her magazines, books, TV shows, radio shows, satellite radio, movies, video games. He has *Maxim* and *FHM* and *Sports Illustrated* and *Playboy* and *Penthouse*; she has *Vogue, Glamour, Modern Bride,* and *Cosmopolitan.* She has novels and short stories, and he has books about business. He has Spike TV and dozens of sports-related channels; she has WE, Oxygen, OWN, and Lifetime. He has action flicks and horror movies, 007 and Freddy; she has chick flicks like *Bridget Jones's Diary* and *Pride and Prejudice.* He has *The Americans, Better Call Saul, Game of Thrones, The Walking Dead,* and *Brooklyn Nine-Nine.* She has *Against the Wall, Covert Affairs, Army Wives, New Girl,* and *Switched at Birth.* He has online pornography and poker; she has online shopping and e-mail contact with family and friends. He has Eminem, 50 Cent, and Nickelback; she has Ani diFranco, Nelly Furtado, and "grrl power" music. He has G.I. Joe; she has Barbie and Bratz.

By now I suspect that many of the male readers of this book are nodding their heads in agreement. "Yeah, that's true, that's the stuff I watch and I would never watch or listen to what *she* likes. Yuck." And I suspect that many women are saying, "Huh? I like some of that stuff Kimmel says are 'his' media! And I definitely do not like some of the stuff he says are 'her' media. He's completely wrong."

And you'd both be right. One way to look at it is that he has "his" media, but she can also share "his" media—that she seems to have more choices than he does. Or you could say that he wouldn't be caught dead consuming her media, whereas the penalties when she crosses over into his media are far less severe. It is not simply that the gendered world of media production and consumption is neatly divided into his and her realms. It is also useful to remember what Jessie Bernard said about marriage. Not only is there "his" and "hers," she wrote, but also "his is better than hers."

So, too, with media. And that's because his and her media are not simply equivalent, satisfying the different needs that derive naturally from preordained gender differences. It's that his and her media exist in a world of gender inequality—and his media *are* better than hers; in fact, his are often *the* media, and she fits herself in around the margins. And she crosses over because, well, what are her choices? Recall, for example, Barrie Thorne's important research about the elementary school playground. Girls can try to cross over into the boy zones, but boys must never cross over into the girl zones. Separate is never equal.

There are far more women who like sports TV, Tool, gangsta rap, online pornography, and Grand Theft Auto than there are guys who like *General Hospital, Bridget Jones,* and romance novels. That's not just a reflection of difference: It's the production of inequality.

"HIS" AND "HERS" MEDIA: SEPARATE AND UNEQUAL

Take, for example, the new "crisis" in television—a perfect illustration of the dynamics I'm describing. For years, television neatly divided up its audience into its targeted demographic niches to better enable advertisers to reach the consumers they most wanted to reach. Guy TV was weekend sports, crime dramas, and westerns—in the 1950s it was shows like *Dragnet* and *Bonanza* (a delightful "family" drama, in which there were no women!). Gal TV was soap operas and game shows during the day and sitcoms and variety shows in prime time. That is, "her" TV invited him to watch (men watched *Ed Sullivan* as much as women did)—but his shows were pretty much his alone.

All gender stereotypes were fully in place. Back then, male characters were more courageous and active, fighting crime and solving mysteries. Female characters were caring but befuddled housewives who occasionally ventured outside the home only to realize that they really loved baking cookies. (Lucy is the standard-bearer of the genre, constantly coming up with hare-brained ideas to work outside the home and just as constantly screwing them up and returning to Ricky's admonishingly forgiving domestic embrace.)[13]

These differences are important, especially because increased exposure to images of inequality often can contribute to more stereotypical ideas. For example, the more television you watch, the more gender-stereotypic are your gender attitudes likely to be.[14]

But something happened to television in the 1970s and 1980s—in the wake of the civil rights and feminist movements. Feminist and minority media critics began to point out just how separate and unequal the world of the small screen actually was. Women and men watched different shows at different times of day, and the characters fully reproduced gender and racial stereotypes. Hollywood's response? Those shows that targeted women or minorities became increasingly "ghettoized"—attracting fewer men and white audiences. Men rarely watched *Alice* or *Rhoda* whites almost never watched *Sanford and Son* or *Good Times*. But the shows for men began to attract more female viewers, so that by the mid-1980s, from *Hill Street Blues* to *L.A. Law*, the "ensemble" cast, including several female and minority characters, became a new Hollywood norm.

The ensemble prime-time drama (like *L.A. Law* in the 1980s and *ER* and *NYPD Blue* in the 1990s and *Grey's Anatomy* and *Lost* recently) has far more racial and gender diversity than any other TV shows in our history. Even standard formats like crime procedurals and detective stories were refashioned with more diverse casts, as in the *CSI* and *Law and Order* franchises. Women have entered the formerly all-male workplace—the police station, court house, hospital operating theater—in both real life and prime-time drama. (Even the hit show *Desperate Housewives* was a clever throwback that presumes a certain new equality of desire—and boredom—in domestic life!)

And what has been the result? For one thing, women have been abandoning the traditionally "female" TV world of daytime soap opera, a decline of nearly 10 percent in 2005 alone. Women cross over far more readily than men do, and they're leaving the all-female ghetto. "I think women have broad tastes and are more likely to watch a show their husband or boyfriend wants to watch than the reverse," noted Susanne Daniels, president of entertainment at Lifetime Television.[15]

READ ALL ABOUT IT!

Nearly everyone watches reality television, and we especially love those makeover shows like *The Biggest Loser*. An increasing number of men are contestants on reality makeover TV shows, and this enables sociologists Alexander Davis, Laura Rogers, and Bethany Bryson to examine the ways that reality makeover shows try to enable men to "achieve" a greater sense of themselves as men. By engaging in "manhood acts," they assert themselves and remake themselves as men. In the zero-sum world of makeover television, the more the man enhances his masculinity, the more he seems to expect deference from women and to benefit from gender inequality. After all, from his perspective, he's "earned" it.

Meanwhile, male viewers have been leaving *network* television in droves—network viewing by males in the eighteen to thirty-four age range has declined precipitously. Just as women have been entering, men have been leaving. Executives now worry about the "feminization of prime time" because the network fare no longer appeals to the "elusive" and "disappearing" male viewer. "Men want shows with action and explosives. Women want to watch programs about relationships. Some shows try to mix the two," noted Tim Brooks, executive vice president of research for Lifetime. But the reality is that men can't bear any pollution of their media. Women watch the action shows; men run away—and the men are supposed to be the driving engine of American consumerism, the consumers everyone wants to land. (This is, by the way, a myth, because women either influence or make about 85 percent of all consumer purchases, including those of cars and stereo equipment. It shows how ideology—men buy stuff and women use it—trumps even the market research the networks pay so handsomely for.) Network executives are trying desperately to recapture these guys, who are bailing out for the Internet, cable, video games, and other media. Some networks are even gobbling up small video and Internet games to add content to lure those guys back.[16]

And it's not just gender equality that seems to frighten men away and back into the cozy comfort of all-action hero and sexy babe TV. It's racial equality as well. White men seem to turn off shows that have African Americans in leading roles—or even ensemble casts that have minority actors alongside females, even if the majority of the cast remains white and male.[17]

Fortunately for these men, there's sports: sports TV, sports radio, sports magazines and newspapers, and the sports section of the daily newspaper. There are dozens of sports on television every single day and dozens of shows about sports in between. And if you don't want to watch sports, talk about sports on sports radio, or read about sports in sports magazines or daily newspapers, perhaps you'll want to watch nonsports TV or listen to nonsports radio. On talk radio or TV talk shows, male emcees outnumber females; they talk differently and listen differently. Talk show hosts like Howard Stern, Mike Savage, and Rush Limbaugh yell at each other about everything; they and their legions of fans alternate between fuming at lost privileges, whining about how "they"—minorities, women, gays—are taking over, and seething that they are now society's victims. Meanwhile, Oprah—and her many imitators—cocks her head to the side and nods empathically, really listening to your heartache. (Among the more notable exceptions are Dr. Phil, who embodies tough love, empathic but stern, and Ann Coulter, who loves being tough.) Late at night, it's a steady parade of men: Colbert, Meyers, Kimmel (no relation!), Conan, Fallon, and all the rest. This is the new male media, the "den" of television, the garage, the barbecue pit—the "man's zone." It's like the clubhouse when they were seven-year-olds, with the sign that read "He-Man Woman Haters Club." At least here, in this virtual "room of his own," a man can finally be alone—with other guys.

"When did men become women?"

Figure 11.4. *Source:* William Haefeli/The New Yorker Collection/The Cartoon Bank.

"HIS" AND "HER" PRINT MEDIA

As with TV, so, too, with those older, more established media, like books and magazines. Women and men buy and read different sorts of books and magazines and read them differently. In the literary world, women outnumber men in the purchase of every single genre (except war and sports stories), and they also buy 80 percent of all fiction sold in the United States and Europe. That's right—four out of every five novels are bought by women—and that includes guy writers like Tom Clancy, Michael Crichton, and J. R. R. Tolkien.

Is the novel a "feminine" form? Generations of hardy American men have suggested as much. Even, ironically, in our nation's first novels was this anti-intellectualism evident. In James Fenimore Cooper's *The Last of the Mohicans*, Natty Bumppo, the first in a long literary series of "the last real man in America," lashes out against the whole enterprise: "'Book!' repeated Hawk-eye, with singular and ill-concealed disdain. 'Do you take me for a whimpering boy at the apron string of one of your old gals . . . Book! What have such as I, who am a warrior of the wilderness . . . to do with books?'" Real men act; they don't read. (Apparently they don't write, either; recall Nathaniel Hawthorne's tirade against all those "scribbling women" and Hemingway's near-obsessive concern with trying to write a masculine sentence.) Recall the words of the boys in the chapter on education—how they saw English as a subject fit only for "sissies." (Of course, Cooper wrote this hoping to entice men to do exactly that—and

OH? REALLY ●

Sexism in the movies and on TV is a thing of the past. Why, today, there are female characters in every single movie and TV show. Gender inequality in the media is an old story.

Not so fast. In the early 1990s, journalist Katha Pollitt coined what she called "the Smurfette Principle." That's the tendency to "achieve" gender equality by adding one—and only one—female character to any TV show or movie and declaring gender equality to have been achieved. In case you've forgotten those cute little blue cherubs, here's the Smurfette Principle in action (well, the males are acting; she's standing there offering a flower).

Go ahead and try it out: Miss Piggy. Princess Leia. Penny (*The Big Bang Theory*). Kanga. Hermione. Jessie. Katniss Everdeen. (Well, okay, if you count Rue it's two, but that's stretching it.) One female among many equals gender equality!

But it's more than just how many female characters there are. It's what they do. Alison Bechdel, a feminist cartoonist, came up with a test to see just how equal the characters actually are. Say you are watching a movie or TV show and you want to know how gender equal it is. Answer three questions:

1. Are there two or more female characters with names?
2. Do they talk to each other?
3. Do they talk about something other than men?

Source: Katha Pollitt, "The Smurfette Principle" in *New York Times*, April 7, 1991.

in rather precious prose.)[18] A decade or so later, General Robert E. Lee chimed in, declaring that fiction "weakens the mind."

Think for a moment of the meteoric rise of "chick lit"—the most successful new genre of fiction in the past quarter-century. Chick lit, like Helen Fielding's *Bridget Jones's Diary* in 1998, which sold two million copies, spawned two sequels, two films, and countless imitators, centers around affably befuddled modern urban women who struggle mightily to sustain careers that don't consume them and develop intimate relationships with men who do. It's the literary version of Ally McBeal and the gal pals on *Sex and the City*.

Now consider the sad fate of "lad lit"—the male riposte to chick lit. It was ostensibly heralded by Nick Hornby's *High Fidelity*, in which Rob, a thirty-five-year-old London slacker, works at a record store and organizes his life by top five lists; or *About a Boy*, in which the well-named Will Lightman drifts along on inherited family money (his father composed a truly horrific and massively successful Christmas jingle). Worldly wise and wisecracking, both men are temperamentally unable to commit to relationships or even to a sense of purpose in their own lives. But then something happens—and they actually do get a life, commit, and live, if not happily, then at least in a relationship, ever after.

But contemporary American purveyors of lad lit present a sort of anti-bildungsroman, in which a wry, clever, unapologetic slacker refuses to grow up, get a meaningful job, commit to relationships, or find some meaning in life. Works such as *Booty Nomad, Love Monkey,* and *Indecision* have tanked at the bookstore and failed miserably as TV adaptations. And they failed precisely because their protagonists refuse to be transformed in the course of the novel by their relationship with women. They failed because *women* won't read them unless there is some hope of redemption, and men won't read them because men don't read fiction.[19]

One more example should suffice. It has become virtually axiomatic in feminist literature that women's magazines are a prime example of women's oppression—that the magazines construct unattainable ideals of femininity, lock women into never-ending struggles to be skinny enough, sexy enough, and gorgeous enough, and thus contribute to women's second-class status. Dozens of class projects in women's studies have found countless students clipping ads and showing how the media representations of women in magazines are a prime agent of their subordinate status.

Actually, this critique is the well from which Betty Friedan poured the second wave of feminism itself with her incendiary call to women, *The Feminine Mystique* (1963). Friedan argued that women's magazines constructed "a weak, passive, vacuous woman who is dependent on her husband for happiness and status, who is devoid of ambition beyond mothering and home decoration, and who lacks a voice to express the emptiness, the incompleteness, of her gender-delimited life," writes media critic Amy Aronson.[20] (Never mind that Friedan's book was first serialized in *Mademoiselle* and later in *Ladies' Home Journal* and *McCall's*, where Friedan herself worked as an editor and writer!)

To Friedan, magazines were part of a full-scale cultural onslaught that constructed the feminine mystique: "This image," she wrote, "created by the women's magazines, by advertisements, television, movies, novels, columns and books by experts on marriage and the family, child psychology, sexual adjustment and by the popularizers of sociology and psycho-analysis . . . is young and frivolous, fluffy and feminine; passive; gaily content in a world of bedroom and kitchen, sex, babies and the home."[21]

This argument became the prevailing feminist orthodoxy about the impact of women's magazines; they were accused of "debilitating women, making them dependent on men" (and on the magazines themselves), preventing self-realization, promoting self-denial, and treating the reader as little more than ornament, object, euphemism, maid, or mom machine. Most scholarship has seen the women's magazine as capable of perfect domination and its popular women readers as utterly "feminine": passive, dependent, and witless in the extreme.[22] "What makes women's magazines particularly interesting," writes another feminist critic, Marjorie Ferguson, "is that their instructional and directional nostrums are concerned with more than the technology of knitting or contraception of cooking. They tell women what to think and do about themselves, their lovers, husbands, parents, children, colleagues, neighbors or bosses . . . Here is a very potent formula indeed," she concludes, "for steering female attitudes, behavior and moving along a particular path of femininity."[23]

Others have fully embraced this critique, from sociologist Gaye Tuchman in her 1977 co-edited volume *The Symbolic Annihilation of Women by the Mass Media*, to media critic Jean Kilbourne in her trenchant critique of advertising images of women "Killing Us Softly," to, finally, Naomi Wolf in her debut work, *The Beauty Myth*.[24]

Recently, though, commentators have assailed the American women's magazine for having exactly the opposite impact on women: rendering them dissatisfied by instilling ideals of careers, consumerism, and independence. Just as feminists saw a conspiracy to keep women in their place, these antifeminist critics see a conspiracy to enrage women and cause their rebellion. The Media Research Center in Alexandria, Virginia, a conservative watchdog group, studied thirteen popular women's magazines over a twelve-month period and reported in late 1996 that all are "left-wing political weapon[s]" that "hammer home a pro-big government message and urge liberal activism."[25] Christina Hoff Sommers accused such magazines as *Redbook, Mademoiselle, Good Housekeeping*, and *Parenting* of advancing "Ms.-information" that "gives the Democrats a clear advantage."[26] As Danielle Crittenden writes:

> The women who buy these magazines today have heeded their mothers' advice: *Do something with your life; don't depend on a man to take care of you; don't make the same mistakes I did* . . . So they are the women who postponed marriage and childbirth to pursue their careers only to find themselves at thirty-five still single and baby-crazy, with no husband in sight . . . They are the female partners at law firms who thought they'd made provisions for everything about their careers—except for that sudden, unexpected moment when they find their insides shredding the first day they return from maternity leave, having placed their infants in a stranger's arms.[27]

So one side says women's magazines enslave women to household drudgery, and the other side says such magazines offer them false freedoms. Who's right?

Each polarized position focuses on only one element and is therefore wrong. Women's magazines do both. Pick up a copy of *Cosmopolitan* or *O* or *Glamour* or *Latina* sometime. Try minority-themed magazines like *Essence* or *Latina*. Sure, there are several articles instructing readers on how to lose ten pounds in a week or keep their boyfriends sexually delighted and photo spreads of the sexiest new bikinis and lipsticks. *And* there is also an article about how the right wing is trying to take away your right to choose and about how global warming might impact more than your shopping for next year's Uggs. In other words, women's magazines offer *polyvocality*—multiple voices, differing perspectives.

And it's always been that way. Since the first women's magazines appeared, Amy Aronson found, this polyvocality has been one of the hallmarks of women's magazines—which makes them, in a sense, so democratic. (The earliest women's magazines were largely composed of letters to the editor and articles cribbed from other magazines.) Women's magazines are so polyvocal because women cross over into men's arenas (like the workplace or sexual agency). Women are not duped into being household drudges or glamorous objects or liberal harpies because women are so diverse.[28]

Men's magazines, by contrast, are as monotonal as you can get. Pick up *Maxim* or *FHM*. On the front cover of virtually every issue are bikini-clad buxom babes, usually drenched in sweat or water. Inside, along with articles about muscles and sexual prowess, are nearly naked starlets, models, and other assorted hotties, all suggestively posed. "All babes all the time" is, apparently, the only way to successfully launch a new magazine geared exclusively to this demographic segment. The two magazines boast 2.5 million and 1 million subscribers, respectively. According to its editors, *Maxim's* readers are overwhelmingly male (76 percent), unmarried (71 percent), and young (median age is twenty-six).[29]

Maxim is but one of a spate of "new lad" magazines that began in Britain, in part as an antifeminist backlash, a way to help men "regain their self-esteem," having been "diminished by the women's movement."[30] Here in the States, Madison Avenue advertisers have tried for years to figure out how to market cosmetics—shaving para-phernalia, colognes, skin-care products—to straight white men. (Only gay men and black men were fashion-conscious enough to read *GQ* or *M*, and these magazines morphed into a kind of *Queer Eye for the Straight Guy* a decade before the hit TV show.) But *Maxim* figured it out by being brazen enough to make every magazine cover a wet T-shirt contest. And it's been wildly successful.[31]

As has *Men's Health*, the most successful magazine launched in the 1980s and 1990s. Once devoted to organic foods and herbal medicines for various men's illnesses, *Men's Health* reconfigured itself into a magazine that caters to men's sexual anxiety by assuring them that they can be the sexual acrobats they had only dreamed of becom-ing before. Next to the articles that suggest some pointers on how to have abs of steel, buns of iron, and other body parts turned into resilient metals flows a steady stream of articles about how to drive her wild in bed, how to be bigger, thicker, harder, and how to have more sexual endurance. *Men's Health* panders to sexual anxiety by suggesting one can never be potent enough or enough of a sexual athlete.

And the best-selling single issue of men's magazines in America? The "Swimsuit" issue of *Sports Illustrated*, which depicts women who could not possibly swim in the skimpy bikinis they almost wear, and the "Back to School" issue of *Playboy*, which features a dozen or so "coeds" from some collegiate athletic conference playfully disrobed. (They don't bother with the swimsuits.) "Women of the ACC!" "Women of the Southeast Conference!" Even "Women of the Ivy League!" These magazines are so popular because men are eager to know that those college girls, the ones who are at least their equals in chemistry class, on the debating team, or even on the soccer field, are really, underneath it all, "just girls" who are happy to bare their breasts and let men look. Everywhere, even on campus, the magazines tell us, men are entitled to look at naked women—and the women volunteer to do it. Even those brainy Yalies are, well, just girls who like to take their clothes off for men.

Yet efforts to retain these male readers as they age out of laddism have failed. "What we discovered pretty quickly," publisher Phil Hilton told a journalist, "is that there is not an age any more when men suddenly grow up and start getting interested in IRAs and bathroom tiles. They are never interested in those things. For better or worse, most men stay interested in looking at girls and knowing about cars and talk-ing about football."[32]

Why are women's magazines so diverse and men's magazines so monochromatic? Why is it that as prime-time TV shows inch toward gender equality, men seem to be leaving? Are men so frightened of equality that when the going gets tough, the tough run away to Spike TV and Howard Stern?

The only way to understand these dynamics, I've suggested, is to understand that the worlds of women and men may be separate, but they are not equal. She can enter his world—whether it's the military or science or business—and in both reality and media representation. Magazines that appear to be "gender-neutral" illustrate this issue. For example, when *Forbes* or *Fortune* has an article about a female CEO, it's always the "women's issue," and the female gender is played to attract female readers. That is, readers of these mainstream magazines about money and finance have two groups of consumers: "female readers" (a specialized niche) and "readers" (the general public, meaning, of course, *men*).

Girls can play with boys' toys (sports equipment, action heroes, science games), but boys dare not play with girls' toys. Girls can play sports; boys dare not be uninterested in sports. Women can balance family and career; men must stay focused on their careers at all costs.

Thus far in our history, gender equality has come almost entirely from women entering "male" spheres formerly closed to them. Men have retreated into smaller and smaller pristine preserves of "pure" masculinity that become increasingly hyperbolic in their assertions of the one "true" way to be a "real man"—and as the men themselves become increasingly anxious and defensive.

WE GOT GAME(S)

Video games began innocently enough with *Pong*, a computer-generated Ping-Pong game in 1972; Centipede was introduced later that same year. Who would have predicted then that video games would today be the fastest-growing segment of the entertainment industry? Worldwide, more than 1.2 billion people play video games. Video games made about $76 billion in revenues in 2014. In the United States, video games earned about $24 billion in 2014 on sales and rentals. (Sales of hardware and game software topped $10 billion in 2003, 2004, and 2005 and $9.5 billion in 2010.) That's nearly two games purchased *per household* every year since 2000. Nearly 75 percent of Americans age six and older play video games regularly.

The most popular game of 2014 was *Titanfall*, a new futuristic game developed by the creators of the *Call of Duty* franchise (*Call of Duty: Ghosts* was the second-best seller). It's a violent, militaristic game of futuristic soldiers, massive weapons and robots, and terrifying machines bent on destroying the world.[33]

Although the age range of gamers is wide—the average age is thirty-one—games tend to appeal most to guys in their teens and twenties. However, women age eighteen or older represent a significantly greater portion of the game-playing population (37 percent) than boys age seventeen or younger (13 percent). The average teenage boy plays video games for about ten and a half hours a week; girls play about six hours a week. (Both boys and girls watch TV about thirty-one hours a week.) One-third of Americans rank computer and video games as their "favorite entertainment activity."[34]

The games vary a lot—by type, by format, and, of course, by gender. Some games are played by one or two (or a few more) players on a console box, hooked up to the TV. Others are played online, on a computer. And some, called "massively multiplayer online role-playing games" (or MMORPG), are played live, with thousands of people all over the world playing simultaneously.

Of video games, sports games—like *Madden NFL* or the various baseball and basketball games—command a large share of the market. Adventure and action games, like *GTA* and *Halo*, are by far the most popular genre. And strategy games, like Sims, involve players in real-life decision making and strategic thinking, not simply adventures in the land of blood and guts. There's even a game called *Bully* that revolves around elite prep school "pranks."

Although the majority of players of every game format and genre are male, the percentages vary enormously.[35] At a recent World Cyber Games competition in Singapore, seven hundred boys and men—and one woman!—crossed cyber-swords in

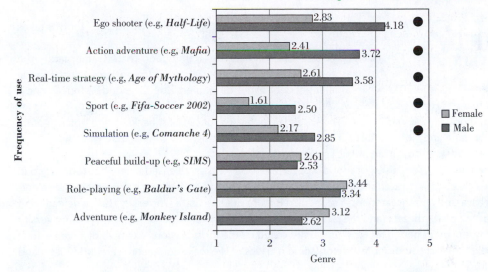

Figure 11.5. Gender preference for different types of video games.

Source: T. Hartmann and C. Klimmt. "Gender and Computer Games: Exploring Females' Dislikes." *Journal of Computer-Mediated Communication*, 11(4), 2006, article 2, available at: http://jmcm.indiana.edu/vol11/issue4/hartmann .html. © 2006 International Communication Association, published by John Wiley and Sons.

online game competition.[36] But female gamers are catching up. Today, only 52 percent of all gamers are male. From 2012 to 2013, the number of female gamers increased by 32 percent. Perhaps this rapid influx of female gamers is what has made so many young male gamers so anxiously, angrily defensive about what they might perceive as the last homosocially pure locker room in the world.[37] Sports and adventure games come close to 95 percent male players; whereas strategy games, like *Sims*, are the only genre where female players have made any inroads. In *Sims*, the "action," such as it is, has to do with real-life situations in the home. People get jobs, get married, have kids, and even clean the house. "All the men in my class HATED that game," comments sociologist William Lugo, who studies video games and teaches a college course on them (figure 11.5). "It was a little too realistic for them."[38]

READ ALL ABOUT IT!

Video games are a central site for gender expression and construction. In fantasy and play, we temporarily try on new identities, test ourselves, and release tension. As more and more girls play video games, the gaming world has become more gender-integrated than ever. But the images of women in these games have not kept pace at all with the change in the compositions of the gamer community. Actually, it seems to be getting worse. Alicia Summers and Monica Miller examined video game magazines over the last twenty years, and found that images of women went from more benign "damsels in distress" to more actively hostile portrayals of women as "sexy superheroes."

C'mon dude, lighten up. Games are just a way to blow off steam. Nobody takes them that seriously.

Oh really? What about Gamergate? Remember that? Gamergate—the name that was given to a very nasty social media campaign against several women—began in 2013 when an independent game developer, Zoe Quinn, developed a new game that got really good reviews. A bunch of gamer guys objected that she was only getting attention because she was female. The hate mail, public denunciations, hacking, and doxing got so bad, the rape and violence threats so persistent and menacing, that she had to change her phone number and withdraw from public space.

Then, in 2014, feminist writer and blogger Anita Sarkeesian released a new YouTube video in a series that had illustrated the depiction of women in the media. She was immediately and relentlessly harassed and threatened. A scheduled lecture at Utah State University had to be canceled because of death threats (and the fact that the state's "open-carry" laws meant that the university could not protect her). The *New York Times* called it "the most noxious example of a weeks long campaign to discredit or intimidate outspoken critics of the male-dominated gaming industry and its culture."

Whether in fantasy games or in reality, men often feel threatened by women's entry into an arena they perceive as their own. As women have entered every arena of the public sphere, some men, insecure and terrified that the purity of the homosocial arena is forever tainted, will defensively circle the wagons.

Death threats for critiquing media images? Sound familiar? It should: It's what these same guys probably condemned when terrorists murdered twelve of the staff and others of *Charlie Hebdo* in France.

So, c'mon dudes. Lighten up. It's only a game.

Sources: Nick Wingfield, "Feminist Critics of Video Games Facing Threats in 'GamerGate' Campaign" in *New York Times,* October 15, 2014; Anita Sarkeesian, "Tropes vs. Women in Video Games," available at https://www.youtube.com/watch?v=5i_RPr9DwMA.

Nina Huntemann, communications professor and avid gamer, is a keen observer and has researched games and created the documentary *Game Over* for the Media Education Foundation. "I constantly got the message that gaming was for guys," she told me. The computer labs in college were "completely dominated by guys," she says now, "and the fact that I liked games, and liked them for the same reasons that they did, made more than a few somewhat uncomfortable."[39]

Sex segregation of the game console is only one element of video games' obvious gendered element. The characters are almost always massively exaggerated gender stereotypes: The male characters in their torn T-shirts and Army fatigues have biceps that would make G.I. Joe look puny; indeed, their upper torsos are so massive, their waists so small, and their thighs so powerfully bulging that there is no way that most of these characters could stand up.[40]

Even if they resemble contemporary gay male stereotypes of pumped bodies, avatars in gameland are all straight. And so are the women—powerful and strong enough to be threatening, but always straight, with blond, disheveled, "bedroom" hair—a sort of recently sexually ravaged look—with breasts so large and a waist so small they make Barbie look like a waif.[41] And they're eternally grateful to their hypermasculine muscle-bound rescuers. In one game, Duke Nukem, the "Everyman American Hero," finds a landscape in which all the men have been killed, and only Duke can rescue a million "babes" who have been captured by aliens. The women are, of course, grateful. Even Lara Croft, the female action-game icon, is a hypersexualized "babe"—she just happens to know how to handle a grenade launcher.[42]

Some games blur the boundaries between militarized urban war zones and pornographic revenge fantasies. Take *Panty Raider*. "It's More Than Just Underwear," the ads for this popular game read, "It's an Adventure!" The object of this adventure is to lure supermodels from their hiding places out into the open and then use X-ray goggles to see if they are wearing the lingerie that was prescribed by the aliens. If they are, then you try to shoot them, hit them with some cyber-goop to melt their clothes off, and snap a picture of them in their panties.

For some players, the fantasy world of video games doesn't offer a sufficient real-time dose of reality. Millions of players—overwhelmingly male—around the world log on to MMORPGs. These games, like *EverQuest* or *World of Warcraft*, are elaborate fantasy worlds, often quite Tolkienesque, where players battle each other or battle against monsters, live, online, in real time. *World of Warcraft* has five million subscribers. One needs to accumulate various props in the game—property, weapons, gold, various potions—and these enable the player to gain advantages over other players. These MMORPGs are so seductive because they are both virtual and real; the games utterly blur the boundaries between reality and fantasy, as commodities flow across the borders of cyberspace into the real marketplace. Edward Castronova worries that some players will experience a sort of "toxic immersion," in which their virtual lives become more real, and more pressing, than their real-world lives.[43]

PORN IN THE USA

Women's entry into a formerly all-male media environment is nowhere more evident than in the **pornography** industry. No, I'm not talking about the featured actors and actresses (who, in various gender combinations, are about equal numerically). Women are consuming far more pornography than ever, and, some of them say, they are even liking it more than they ever did—or than they feel they are "supposed" to, because it's so unfeminine. By contrast, there are very few men who are renting movies from Femme Productions. Again, women can enter men's space, but men dare not enter women's. And though I will deal with pornography as a mechanism in the construction of our sexualities in a later chapter, here I want to focus on pornography not only in its representation of sex, but also in its representation of gender.

Pornography is a massive industry in the United States, with gross sales of all pornographic media ranging between $10 billion and $14 billion annually for the whole industry—more than the NFL, the NBA, and Major League Baseball combined or, in media terms, with revenues greater than ABC, NBC, and CBS combined. Sales and rentals of videos and DVDs alone gross about $4 billion a year. More than two hundred pornographic videos are produced every week. Adult "entertainment" outnumbers McDonald's restaurants in the United States—by a margin of at least three to one. On the Internet, pornography has increased 1,800 percent, from 14 million webpages in 1998 to 420 million in 2008.[44]

OH? REALLY •

"Playing violent video games has no effect on the rest of my life. I know the difference between fantasy and reality. It just lets me let off steam."

That's the sort of defensive pushback from gamers that parents, educators, and cultural critics often hear when anyone dares to offer a critique of entertainment.

But it's only half right. Of course, there is no quasi-Pavlovian response pathway that is activated by repeated video game play, causing you to suddenly pick up an assault weapon and start murdering immigrants, women, terrorists, or anyone else who is demonized in your video game. But on the other hand, would you really want to claim that consumption of media images has no effect on our behaviors? That would be like saying that the entire advertising industry does not help to shape our consumer choices.

Of course media images affect our behaviors. The question isn't whether or not; it's how and how much.

The empirical evidence is revealing. Again, nothing Pavlovian, no monkey-see, monkey-do. But recent empirical studies by Yang Wang and his colleagues in the Radiology Department at Indiana University should give us pause. Dr. Wang performed MRIs on two groups of young adults. One group played violent video games for ten hours during one week and then none at all for the next week. The other group played no video games at all. MRIs of their brains were conducted before the gaming, at the end of the first week, and at the end of the second week.

After the first week, the video game group showed less activation in their brain functions, both in the areas of the brain that are linked to emotion and those involved in mathematical reasoning, than did the nongamers. After the second week, the first group's brain functions had returned to near-normal, but were not quite the same as the nongamers'.

Does this mean that playing violent video games makes you stupid and callously nonempathic? Not entirely. It does mean that it has an effect on your brain—that's the point, after all. But it doesn't transform you permanently into some game-zoned-out zombie. You'll have to work harder to achieve that.

Sources: Tom A. Hummer, Yang Wang, William G. Kronenberger, Kristine Mosier, Andrew Kalnin, David Dunn, and Vincent Mathews, "Short-Term Violent Video Game Play by Adolescents Alters Prefrontal Activity During Cognitive Inhibition" in *Media Psychology*, 13, 2010, pp. 136–154; "Short-Term Exposure to a Violent Video Game Induces Changes in Frontolimbic Circuitry in Adolescents" in *Brain Imaging and Behavior*, 3, 2009, pp. 38–50; "The Interacting Role of Media Violence Exposure and Aggressive-Disruptive Behavior in Adolescent Brain Activation During an Emotional Stroop Task" in *Psychiatry Research: Neuroimaging*, 192(1), 2011, pp. 12–19.

And it is hardly sleazy, clandestine back-alley production. "The adult film industry in Southern California is not being run by a bunch of dirty old men in the back room of some sleazy warehouse," wrote Larry Flynt in an op-ed article in the *Los Angeles Times* in 2004. "Today, in the state of California, XXX entertainment is a $9 billion to $14 billion business run with the same kind of thought and attention to detail that you'd find at GE, Mattel, or Tribune Co."[45]

As of 2012, 13 percent of all web searches on the Internet are for porn sites. More people access pornography than access Twitter, Netflix, and Amazon—combined. More than twenty-five thousand of us are watching porn every second. And two-thirds of those watchers are male. Indeed, nearly eight out of ten guys, age eighteen to twenty-four, visit a porn site in a typical month. And two-thirds of human resource professionals have found porn on employees' computers.[46]

But perhaps equally important is not simply the size of the pornographic market but its reach and its pervasiveness. It's everywhere, creeping into mainstream media as well as growing in the shadowlands to which it has historically been consigned. A large percentage of Americans use pornography "as daily entertainment fare." Of the one thousand most-visited sites on the Internet, one hundred are sex-oriented.[47] Our society has become, as journalist Pamela Paul titles her book, *Pornified*. As she puts it, pornography today "is so seamlessly integrated into popular culture that embarrassment or surreptitiousness is no longer part of the equation."[48]

The standard claim of pornography's defenders is that the women and men who participate in pornography are doing so out of free choice—they choose to do it—so it must be an accurate representation of *both* the women's and the men's sexual desires. And, in that framing, pornography depicts an egalitarian erotic paradise, where people always want sex, get what they want, and have a great time getting it. On the surface, it appears to be equal—both women and men are constantly on the prowl, looking for opportunities for sexual gratification.

But this equality of desire is a fiction. The typical porn scene finds a woman and a man immediately sexually aroused, penetration occurs immediately, and both are orgasmic within a matter of seconds. That is, the fantasy is one in which women's sexuality is not their own, but rather men's sexuality. In the erotic paradise of pornography, both women and men act, sexually, like men—always ready for it, always wanting it, and always having penetration and intercourse lead to an immediate orgasm. No wonder antipornography activist John Stoltenberg writes that pornography "tells lies about women" even though it "tells the truth about men."[49]

The lie about women is, of course, that women's sexuality is as predatory, depersonalized, and **phallocentric** as men's sexuality. Women's sexuality in real life, by contrast, usually requires some emotional connection. "For sex to really work for me, I need to feel an emotional *something*," commented one woman to sociologist Lillian Rubin. "Without that, it's just another athletic activity, only not as satisfying, because when I swim or run, I feel good afterward."[50]

I think pornography also tells lies about men—but they are lies men really want to hear. And the major lie is that every woman really, secretly, deep down, wants to have sex with you. It is a lie that is a revenge fantasy more than an erotic fantasy, revenge for the fact that most men don't feel they get as much sex as they think they are supposed

OH? REALLY •

Pornography is harmless entertainment. It doesn't affect our actual experiences at all.

Actually, pornography does influence our perceptions and attitudes about men, women, and sex. Of course there is no one-to-one correspondence, no monkey-see-monkey-do behaviorist response, but it does leave an impression. (If media images didn't work on our perceptions, the entire advertising industry would collapse!) In one recent psychological experiment, 154 undergraduates evaluated ads after some had seen sexually explicit materials featuring young girls (the "barely legal" porn category). Exposure to virtual child pornography led viewers to be "more likely to associate sex and sexuality to subsequent, non-sexual depictions of minors." That is, if you see it in pornography, you are more likely to see it in nonpornographic images.

to get. Pornography also provides hassle-free vicarious sex. "You don't have to buy them dinner, talk about what they like to talk about," says Seth, a twenty-four-year-old computer programmer in New York. "And even when you do, there's no guarantee that you're gonna get laid. I mean with pornography, no one ever says no."

And if they do say no, well, they really mean yes. In a sexual marketplace that men feel is completely dominated by women—from women's having the power to decide if you are going to get sex in the first place to all those dispiriting reminders that "no means no"—pornography gives you a world in which no one takes no for an answer.

I remember a performance piece by New York City performance artist Tom Cayler:

> I come home from work and I am tired. I wanna take a shower, see the kids, get something to eat and lie down, watch a little TV. Maybe if there's not a ballgame on, I'll read a book, okay? So, there I am, I'm reading this adventure novel and I get to the portion of the book where the hero has got this gorgeous dame writhing above him, biting her lips with pleasure. I mean, how do you even do that? That doesn't feel so good to me.
>
> But I am getting turned on by this. I am getting turned on by this imaginary, illicit, sexual liaison. And I say to myself, "Hey, there's the wife. She is lying right next to you. She is gorgeous, available, warm, loving, naked." But am I turned on by her? No, I am turned on by these little black dots marching across the page.
>
> Because, see, if I wanted to have sex with her, I would have to put down my book, I would have to roll over, I would have to ask her to put down her book, I would have to say . . . "How ya doin? Are the kids in bed, is the cat out, is the phone machine on, are the doors locked, maybe we should brush our teeth, is the birth control device handy?" Then I would have to turn on the sensitivity. I would have to ask her what's been goin' on with her, what she's been dealin' with, I mean with the kids and the house, and the budget, and her mom, and everything like that. I'd have to tell her what was happenin' with me. My problems, my worries. I'd have to hold her, I'd have to stroke her. I would have to tell her how important she is to me. I would have to commit myself to an act which these days I may or may not be able to consummate. You think that is easy? The little black dots, they are easy.[51]

The world of escape offered by guys' media is "easy." It makes few relationship demands; it asks so little of us morally, intellectually, politically and offers so much in return: the illusion of power and control.

The major reason why guys say they watch and play is escape, to "get away from reality." "They love to be able to win the Super Bowl, or travel to another planet," says sociologist William Lugo.[52] They want to escape to a world where men rule, where reality doesn't get in the way. "Where else can you get the chance to storm the beach of Normandy or duel with light sabers or even fight the system and go out for a pizza when you're done?" asks David, an avid gamer for over twenty years.

GENDER AND SOCIAL MEDIA

The gaming world is decreasingly gendered as more and more women are entering that world. The world of social media has been pretty gender-equal from the beginning. Of all Internet users, 72 percent of males and 76 percent of females use social networking sites. But like gaming, it's which social media they use that is gendered. Across different sites, men and women have varying degrees of engagement. Among Internet users, women are significantly more likely than men to use Facebook, Pinterest, and Instagram. A roughly equal proportion of men and women use Twitter and Tumblr. reddit is the only site in which men are significantly more likely than women to be users.[53]

But what do such differences tell us? Could it be that those sites that encourage networking, sustaining relationships, and sharing useful information are coded as "feminine," and are favored by women, and those where you complain, mouth off about others anonymously, or attack others are coded as "masculine" and are more likely to be favored by men? Perhaps. Men have long sought those all-male spaces to prove their masculinity in front of other men. Once, it was the frontier, the "Wild West," where a man could go test himself against the elements and other men. When the frontier era ended, American men kept reinventing it—in other countries through imperial expansion, in Alaska and other untamed wildernesses. In his inaugural address in 1961, President John F. Kennedy proclaimed a "new frontier." A few short years later, in 1966, *Star Trek* announced that space was "the final frontier." Perhaps in the twenty-first century, it's "cyberspace, the final frontier"—or so men might like to think.

This might explain both the sex segregation of social media, the "his" and "hers" of social media—and also the gender inequality of that gender difference. It may be that women use social media to stay connected, and men use social media to connect with other men—in order to keep women out. Once again, gender difference may actually be a mechanism by which gender inequality is maintained.

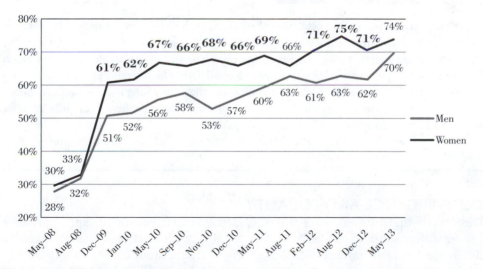

Figure 11.6. Women, men, and social networking over time. Among Internet users, the percent of men versus women who use social networking sites.

Note: Percentages in bold, larger font indicate statistical significance between men and women.

Source: "It's a woman's (social media) world," Pew Research Center, Washington, DC (September, 2013) http://www.pewresearch.org/fact-tank/2013/09/12/its-a-womans-social-media-world/.

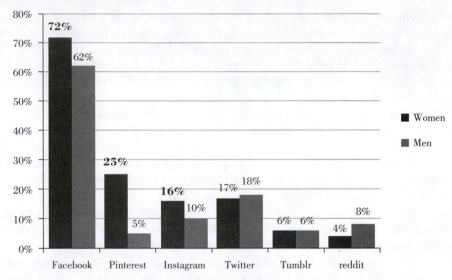

Figure 11.7. Men's versus women's site-specific social media use. Among Internet users, the percent of men versus women who use the following sites.

Note: Percentages in bold, indicate statistical significance between men and women.

Source: "It's a woman's (social media) world," Pew Research Center, Washington, DC (September, 2013) http://www.pewresearch.org/fact-tank/2013/09/12/its-a-womans-social-media-world/.

READ ALL ABOUT IT!

Jenna Mourey has one of the most subscribed channels on YouTube. As Jenna Marbles, she humorously explains the meaning of life, from the tiniest and least important of issues like "how Lady Gaga writes a song" to, well, slightly less tiny and slightly more important issues like, say, how to get everyone to think you're cool. That a woman dares to comment on contemporary life is enough to send a significant number of young men around the bend, and in "Performing Gender on YouTube," English and journalism professors Lindsey Wotanis and Laurie McMillan analyze the reactions to Jenna Marbles's YouTube channel. The good news is that Mourey seems relatively unfazed and continues to have more than fifteen million subscribers.

CONVERGENCE AND EQUALITY

Despite all the different ways that the media reflect, constitute, and reproduce gender differences and gender inequality, it's somewhat startling to see that gender differences are really rather small, though, as I've argued, quite consequential. Despite all the ways in which women have begun to enter formerly all-male domains and men have retreated in the face of this new media equality, the differences are shrinking. Despite all the efforts to keep women and men apart, so that men can stay men (even if women are changing), our media use is increasingly converging. And despite all the extraordinarily pervasive efforts of various media to convince us that we are Martians and Venusians, as different as night and day, we are increasingly Earthlings, using the same media, in roughly equal amounts, and for roughly the same reasons.

Nowhere is this more true than with newer media—like iPods, the Internet, and other digital technologies. Gender differences in the use of these media are actually far smaller than we assume they are. And on websites for younger people, like Instagram, Snapchat, and Facebook, the percentages are about even. Online, for example, women and men are roughly equal users of the Internet. Although men dominated the Internet in its earliest days, that gender gap has disappeared; 78 percent of men and women use the Internet.[54]

Women and men use the Internet for somewhat different purposes. For example, although women and men equally use the Internet to buy products and do their banking, men are more likely to pay bills, participate in auctions, trade stocks, and buy digital content (like Internet pornography). Men search for information more often than women; women use e-mail to maintain relationships and communicate with friends more than men do.[55]

But the biggest difference turns out to be not who uses it and why: The biggest difference turns out to be *what we think*. Although all available studies suggest that women are just as adept at navigating the Internet as men are, men think they're a lot better at it. In a study of one hundred Internet users in New Jersey, researchers never heard a woman say she was an expert and never heard a man say he was a complete novice. Yet when faced with increasingly complex tasks, both women and men did equally well. "It could be that women are underestimating their skills and men are overestimating their skills," commented the author of the study. "I can't say which." Well, maybe it's both.[56]

Even in some traditionally male bastions, like sports, the evidence of gender convergence is pretty hard to miss. Three-fourths of American adult men—and fully half of all adult women—say they are sports fans, according to a Gallup poll.[57] The Super Bowl still dwarfs all other single-event shows for sheer numbers of viewers, and weekend football games continue to attract huge audiences. But whereas some sports—like the spectacle of professional wrestling—skew almost entirely toward men, the other really popular sports—including NASCAR and golf—are approaching gender parity. Women currently comprise 40 percent of NASCAR's seventy-five million viewers—as well as a full 50 percent of the Super Bowl's 111.9 million viewers. Not content with a single "super" event, women also comprise 38 percent of the NFL's 120 million total annual viewers. Quick—how many men watch Oprah, let alone the WNBA?[58]

When women and men diverge, it's not in their enjoyment of watching or playing sports. It's when they watch "sports"—that is, when they're not watching the real thing, but watching the fake thing. Four and one-half million of them—virtually all male—are watching World Wrestling Entertainment; WWE's *Raw* is the number one weekly cable program among the male audience. And when they "play" sports—not on a field, but on a screen or on a computer—with video games or fantasy leagues, they've entered, again, a pristine homosocial preserve. The most popular video game of all is *John Madden NFL Football*, and the NBA and baseball video games are close behind. And thirty-two million Americans—92 percent of them men—are playing some version of fantasy sports. They're spending several hours a day, every day of the week, assembling their teams, trading players, assessing their opponents, and then poring over box scores online and in the newspapers to calculate how their players have fared in their fantasy game.[59]

Perhaps nowhere is the sports world more gendered than in sports *talk*. Guys talk constantly, endlessly, about sports. (At least straight guys do; perhaps it's one way that guys can hang out together and remind themselves that they're straight?) Every major media market boasts sports talk radio stations, and guys call in constantly to voice their opinions. Among young men, participating in sports talk has pretty much replaced playing sports as the line of demarcation between women and men. Girls may be running circles around guys on the soccer field, and women can be working out and toning up as much as the next guy, but the one thing women don't do is talk about sports. They don't pore over the box scores as if they were the Talmud. The woman you work with or the one sitting across from you in a chemistry lecture may be as athletic as you are, but she wouldn't be able to tell you how many saves Mariano Rivera has for his career, Tom Brady's total yards passing during the 2011 season, or who had the highest field goal percentage in the NBA during the 2011–2012 season. (For your information, the answers are 608, 5,235, and Joakim Noah, respectively. Bonus: Noah's field goal percentage was .731. I am a guy, after all.) Nor would she care. For women, sports are something you *do*, not something you are.

One of the best titles for any book I've read in recent years is Mariah Burton Nelson's *The Stronger Women Get, the More Men Love Football*. In her book, she shows how women's increasing equality on the sports field had led men to increasingly proclaim the superiority of football over all other sports—it's the one sport exempt from Title IX, and it's the one sport women don't play. Nelson's title perfectly illustrates the increasing anxiety men feel about women's equality. The more and more equal women get in the real world, the more men are retreating into mediated fantasy worlds of video games, pornography, online poker, and sports talk. Only there do they feel that they are still the masters of the universe, sexually omnipotent, kings of the world.

Yet women's increasing equality comes at a steep price in a world marked less and less by gender difference, but still marked by gender inequality. Women can enter men's fields, but then they are on men's turf and play by men's rules. Just as when women enter men's fields in the workplace, or in education, or in the professions, if they succeed too well, they can be seen as insufficiently feminine, have their sexuality called into question, and risk not being taken seriously as women. If they fail, they are seen as very feminine women, demonstrating that inequality is really the result of difference, not its cause. Gender equality in the virtual world of the media, just like the real world, will come not when gender difference disappears, but rather when gender inequality disappers, when Nelson's book could be titled *The Stronger Women Get, the More Men Like It*.

KEY TERMS

Boy-Centered Stories   Phallocentrism   Pornography
Girl-Centered Stories

Gendered Interactions

GENDERED INTIMACIES

Friendship and Love

"Man's love is of man's life a thing apart," wrote the legendary British Romantic poet George Gordon, Lord Byron, "'Tis woman's whole existence." Presumably, this is because men like Byron have other, far more important things to occupy their time—like poetry, politics, and sexual conquest. A few years later, a fellow English poet, Robert Browning, offered that "love is so different with us men." A century and a half later, novelist Doris Lessing commented that she'd never met a man who would destroy his work for a love affair—and she'd never met a woman who wouldn't.

Such sentiments underscore how unconsciously our most intimate emotional relationships are shaped by gender, how women and men have different experiences and different expectations in friendships, in love, and in sex. Like the family, sex and love are also organized by gender, which may not come as much of a surprise. After all, how often have we heard a woman complain that her husband or partner doesn't express his feelings? How often have we heard men wonder what their wives are doing talking on the phone all the time? And how often do we hear of men saying that their extramarital affair was "just sex," as if sex could be separated from emotions? How often do we hear women say that?

Part of the interplanetary theory of gender—that women and men come from different planets—emphasizes these differences between women and men. We hear that it is our celestial or biological natures that decree that women be the emotionally adept communications experts and that men be the clumsy unemotional clods. And yet the gender differences in intimate relationships often don't turn out to be the ones we expected; nor are the differences as great as commonsense assumptions predict. Although it is true that men and women often have different ways of liking, loving, and lusting, these differences neither are as great as predicted, nor always go in the directions that common sense would lead us to expect. Moreover, the differences we observe in the contemporary United States did not always exist, nor are they present in other cultures. In this and the next chapter, I'll explore the gender of intimacy by examining friendship, love, and sexuality. (I've already discussed the gender of marriage and the family, so I'll confine myself here to nonmarital relationships.) What we'll see is that the gendering of intimate life—of friendship, love, and sex—is the result of several historical and social developments.

READ ALL ABOUT IT!

Men like to look at women's bodies; it's just that simple. Or is it? When do they like to look at women? Why? Under what circumstances? What do they hope to achieve? Does it lead to anything else? In a thoughtful empirical study, "Sexual Harassment and Masculinity: The Power and Meaning of 'Girl-Watching,'" sociologist Beth Quinn addresses these questions. She suggests that the purpose of girl-watching is a form of male bonding—cementing relationships among men in the workplace that might otherwise be fraught with tension—and dominance bonding, which means that the foundation of male bonding is the various ways that men keep women in their place. In that sense, it's hardly benign. Sometimes, looking at someone can be the same as appreciating a work of art—even though that work of art doesn't have feelings. And sometimes looking can be a behavior, an action that makes you feel good by making someone else feel bad.

THE GENDER OF FRIENDSHIP

In fact, women were not always considered the emotional experts. As Byron's maxim suggests, historically, it was men's "way of loving" that was considered superior. From Greek and Roman myths to Renaissance balladry, men's friendships were celebrated as the highest expression of the noblest virtues—bravery, loyalty, heroism, duty—which only men were thought to possess. Think of Orestes and Pylades, Hercules and Hylas, David and Jonathan, Roland and Oliver, Achilles and Patroclus.

For the Greeks, friendship was even more noble than marital love or the eroticized idealization of the young boy by the older man. As described by Plato and Aristotle, friendship occurred only between peers and transcended sexuality. Only men could develop the emotional depth and connections that could cement a friendship. And our own literature affords us no shortage of such friendships—from Huck Finn and Tom Sawyer, Wyatt Earp and Doc Holliday, Butch Cassidy and the Sundance Kid, and the Lone Ranger and Tonto to Kirk and Spock and Murtaugh and Riggs. Walt Whitman constantly celebrated "the dear love of man for his comrade, the attraction of friend to friend."

A virtual parade of literary figures commented on men's capacity for friendships and women's inability to form deep and lasting friendships, attributed largely to women's lack of strong emotions about anything. The sixteenth-century French moralist Michel Montaigne's classic essay "On Friendship" described his relationship with his best friend in a language that most of us would use to describe our spouse (Montaigne wrote little about his wife and children). Friends, for instance, are "souls that mingle and blend with each other so completely that they efface the seam that joined them." In a 1960 essay on the topic, the great British man of letters C. S. Lewis treated friendship as if it were entirely a masculine domain. "Only men," wrote Jeremy Taylor in his *Discourse on Friendship,* are "capable of all those excellencies by which men can oblige the world."[1]

Many women agreed. For example, the great eighteenth-century British feminist and writer Mary Wollstonecraft believed that although "the most holy bond of society is friendship," it is men, not women, who are most adept at it. And Simone de Beauvoir, whose book **The Second Sex** is one of modern feminism's groundbreaking works, commented that "women's feelings rarely rise to genuine friendship."[2]

Why were men's friendships considered deep and lasting but women's fleetingly emotional? In a controversial study, anthropologist Lionel Tiger argued that the gender division of labor in hunting-and-gathering societies led to deeper and more durable friendships among men. Hunting and warfare, the domains of male activity, required deep and enduring bonds among men for survival, and thus close male friendships became a biologically based human adaptation. Women's friendships, however pleasant, were not "necessary" in an evolutionary sense.[3]

In the twentieth century, however, we witnessed a dramatic transformation in the gendered division of emotional labor. Since the early 1970s, studies of friendship have taken a decidedly different turn, fueled in part by two related events. On the one hand, feminism began to celebrate women's experiences not as a problem but rather as a source of solidarity among women. Women's greater experiences of intimacy and emotional expressiveness were seen not as a liability but rather as an asset in a culture that increasingly elevated the expression of feelings as a positive goal. And it was not just women who were suddenly celebrating exactly what Tiger and others had claimed women lack—the capacity for the deep and intimate bonds of friendship. A new generation of male psychologists and advocates of "**men's liberation**" were critical of the traditional male sex role as a debilitating barrier to **emotional intimacy**. It was *women's* experiences in friendships and women's virtues—emotional expressiveness, dependency, the ability to nurture, intimacy—that were now desirable.

And it was *men* who were said to be missing something—a capacity for intimacy, skills at nurturing. One psychologist derided "the inexpressive male," and sociologist Mirra Komorovsky explored men's "trained incapacity to share." Another psychologist claimed that men's routine avoidance of self-disclosure was dangerous to their emotional and even physical health, whereas another explored the very few social skills that men have developed to cement close intimate friendships. No wonder that psychologist Joseph Pleck spoke for many male liberationists when he observed that men's emotional relationships are "weak and often absent."[4]

Psychologist Robert Lewis examined four "barriers" to emotional intimacy among men: (1) competition, which inhibits the ability to form friendships and also minimizes the ability to share vulnerabilities and weaknesses; (2) the false need to be "in control," which forbids self-disclosure and openness; (3) homophobia, which inhibits displays of affection and tenderness toward other men; and (4) lack of skills and positive role models for male intimacy. Men, he argued, learn to avoid appearing weak and vulnerable in order to maintain a competitive edge.[5]

In contemporary society, we have reversed the historical notion of friendship. Most women, according to surveys, believe that women's friendships are decidedly better than men's because they involve personal concern, intimate sharing, and more emotional exchange, whereas men's friendships are seen (by the same women) as more likely to involve work, sports, business, and other impersonal activities. By contrast, men, when asked the same question about which gender's friendships are better, responded that they hadn't really given the matter much thought. In a widely cited study, psychologist Daniel Levinson concluded that for men, friendship is noticeable, largely, by its "absence"; as he writes:

> As a tentative generalization, we would say that close friendship with a man or woman is rarely experienced by American men. The distinction between a friend and acquaintance is often blurred. A man may have a wide social network in which he has amicable "friendly" relationships with many men and perhaps a few women. In general, however, most men do not have an intimate male friend of the kind that they recall fondly from boyhood or youth. Many men have had casual dating relationships with women, and perhaps a few complex love-sex relationships, but most men have not had an intimate non-sexual friendship with a woman.[6]

Before we continue, ask yourself how you felt as you read the preceding statement. Does it describe your experiences? Or does it reveal that the definitions of friendship, love, and intimacy have been transformed from glorifying the more "masculine" components at the expense of "feminine" ones to the reverse? One sociologist has criticized what she calls the "feminization of love," so that now intimacy is defined by "feminine" norms that favor gender differences over similarities, reinforce traditional gender stereotypes, and render invisible or problematic men's ways of creating and sustaining intimacy.[7]

While we may "friend" a lot of people, we seem to have fewer close friends. Yet friendship is extremely important. It even changes your perception of the world. In a clever experiment, four psychologists took a group of students at the University of Virginia to the base of a steep hill and fitted them with weighted backpacks. They were told they would climb the hill and they were then asked to estimate how steep the incline of the hill was. Some stood next to a close friend, some stood next to an acquaintance, and others stood alone. Those who stood with a close friend saw the steepness as significantly less than those who stood alone. In fact, the closer the friend who stood next to you, the less steep the hill seemed. The researchers concluded that this feeling of closeness acts as a material resource that enables people to see obstacles as less difficult.[8]

GENDER DIFFERENCES IN FRIENDSHIP: REAL AND IMAGINED

Most of the research on gender differences in friendship turns out to reinforce existing stereotypes of women as emotionally expressive and men as inexpressive and either incapable or uninterested in nurturing. There's even some evidence that brain differences account for friendship differences. A recent study found that whereas men respond to stress with the now-famous "fight-or-flight" response, women look to friends or allies as a source of emotional sustenance in a response labeled "tend and befriend." The researchers believe that this is because men respond to stress by releasing testosterone, which causes the fight-or-flight response, whereas women release oxytocin, which produces a calming effect and a desire for closeness. (I suspect men's response may have less to do with testosterone and more to do with norms of masculinity that turn every stressful encounter into a demonstration of masculine prowess; women's tending and befriending may also be a rational sizing-up of the situation and a need for allies to even the odds.)[9] In another psychological experiment, Sharon Brehm reversed the genders of two stereotypically gendered friendship events to reveal how different, and "odd," they would sound:

> Jim and Henry were good close friends. Often, they would stay up half the night talking about love and life and how they felt about everything and everyone. In times of trouble, each was always there for the other to lean on. When they experienced any conflicts in their romantic relationships with women, they'd immediately be on the phone to each other, asking advice and getting consolation. They felt they knew everything about each other.
>
> Sally and Betty were good close friends. Often, they would stay up half the night playing chess or tinkering with Sally's old car, which was constantly breaking down. In times of trouble, they'd always help each other out. Sally would loan Betty money, or Betty would give Sally a ride home from work whenever their best efforts had failed to revive Sally's beloved 1960 Chevy. They went everywhere together—to the bars, to play basketball, to the latest sci-fi movie. They felt they were the best of buddies.[10]

It does sound strange, of course. But does it mean that men have shallower, less emotionally demanding and rewarding friendships than women or that women and men achieve the same ends via different means?

Some psychologists have found few differences in what women and men say they desire in a friend. Mayta Caldwell and Letitia Peplau, for example, studied college students' friendships and found that although both women and men desire intimacy and closeness, have roughly the same number of close and casual friends, and spend about the same amount of time with their friends, they often have different ways of expressing and achieving intimacy with them. Men were almost twice as likely to say they preferred "doing some activity" with their best friend and looked for friends who liked "to do the same things" as they did. Women, by contrast, were more likely to choose someone "who feels the same way about things" as a friend and to favor "just talking" as their preferred mode of interaction. Sociologist Beth Hess found that women were twice as likely to talk about personal issues with their friends. And women and men are far more similar than different in both providing and responding to supportive communication from a friend during "trouble talk"—that is, when they are feeling some relationship distress.[11]

Other researchers don't believe the men's responses—no matter what they say. Men may "*perceive* that they are being open and trusting," write sociologists Lynne Davidson and Lucille Duberman, "even though they report little investment in the personal and relational levels of the friendship." Despite the findings that both women and men say they disclose equal amounts of personal information and that they are completely open with and trusting of their best friends, the authors conclude that women actually disclose more to their friends. For example, the authors describe one man who said of his best friend, "We are pretty open with each other, I guess. Mostly we talk about sex, horses, guns, and the army." From this, they conclude that these friends do not disclose their feelings. Yet the authors do not probe beneath this response to uncover, possibly, the way that talking about sex (like sexual fears, questions, or inadequacies) or the army (and the intense emotions of terror, exhilaration, and shame it evokes) requires just as deep a level of trust as women's friendships.[12]

Not all research that finds gender differences in friendship turns a deaf ear to the voices of half its informants. In a revealing portrait of the role of friendship in our lives, Lillian Rubin interviewed over three hundred women and men and found startling differences in both the number and the depth of friendships. "At every life stage between twenty-five and fifty-five, women have more friendships, as distinct from collegial relationships or workmates, than men," she writes, "and the differences in the content and quality of their friendships are marked and unmistakable." Generally, she writes, "women's friendships with each other rest on shared intimacies, self-revelation, nurturance, and emotional support." By contrast, she argues that men's friendships are characterized by shared activities and that conversations center on work, sports, or expertise—"whether about how to fix a leak in the roof or which of the new wine releases is worthy of celebrating." Three-fourths of the women Rubin interviewed could identify a best friend, whereas over two-thirds of the men could not. Even when a man could identify a best friend, Rubin found that "the two usually shared little about the interior of their lives and feelings." If we understand intimacy to be based on both verbal and nonverbal sharing of thoughts and feelings so that the intimate understands the inner life of the other, then men's friendships are, Rubin concludes, "emotionally impoverished."[13]

Other research corroborates some of her findings. Women were far more likely to share their feelings with their friends than were men, to engage in face-to-face interactions instead of men's preferred side-to-side style, and to discuss a wider array of issues than men did. Women's friendships seem to be more person oriented; men's more activity oriented. Women's friendships appear to be more "holistic" and men's more "segmented." Women may say they have fewer friends, one study found, but those they have are more intimate.[14]

These differences are reinforced by technological developments. Take, for example, the telephone. For women, the telephone serves as the chief form of relationship maintenance, making it possible to sustain friendships over long distances and with increased time pressures. However, for men, the telephone is a poor substitute for the shared activities that sustain men's friendships. Men tend to use the telephone far less to sustain intimacy. "I'm not friends the way she's friends," one man told sociologist Karen Walker. "I don't work on them. I don't pick the phone up and call people and say 'how are you?'" And another man compared his friendships with those of his partner:

> It's not like Lois, the woman I live with, and the women in her group. They're real buddies; they call each other up and talk for hours; they do things together all the time. We just never got that close, that's all.[15]

Even after a long day in a workplace where she talks on the phone constantly as a receptionist or secretary, a woman is far more likely to call her friends at night.

Without such relationship maintenance, men's friendships experience greater attrition than women's over time. "Over the years, the pain of men's loneliness, the weakening of their male ties, the gradually accumulating disillusionment with male friends, the guilt at their own betrayals of others, are just ignored. Partly it is a result of resignation. We lower our expectations. The older we get, the more we accept our essential friendlessness with men."[16]

In general, gender differences in friendships tend to be exactly what commonsense observation and talk-show pseudorevelations would suggest. Men are more reserved in their emotional patterns and less likely to disclose personal feelings, lest they risk being vulnerable to other men; women tend to be comparatively more open and disclosing. But that is part of the problem. These differences make it appear that men and women come from different planets, when often the differences have nothing whatever to do with gender and everything to do with *other* factors in our lives—like our workplace experiences, our marital status, our age, race, ethnicity, and sexual orientation. Those factors may tell us more about which gender differences are "real" and which are really symptomatic of something else.

Of course, at the same time, we should be careful not to overstate the case. As one psychologist warns:

> There is, of course, a danger here of "reifying" gender differences by underplaying the other factors which shape people's friendships . . . In order to analyse friendship satisfactorily it is necessary to examine the range of social and economic factors that pattern an individual's immediate social environment, rather than focusing solely on any particular one . . . Friendship is certainly influenced by gender, but exactly in what way depends on the interaction there is with the other factors that collectively shape the personal space for sociability that people have.[17]

In fact, it turns out that there is "much more similarity than dissimilarity in the manner in which women and men conduct their friendships," writes psychologist Paul Wright in a review of the existing literature of gender differences. Although it is true, he notes, that women are "somewhat more likely to emphasize personalism, self-disclosure, and supportiveness" and that men are "somewhat more likely to emphasize external interest and mutually involving activities," these differences "are not great, and in many cases, they are so obscure that they are hard to demonstrate." What's more, what differences there are tend to diminish markedly and virtually disappear "as the strength and duration of the friendship increases."[18]

For example, when women and men choose a best friend, they look for the same virtues—communication, intimacy, and trust. And the majority of us—75 percent of women and 65 percent of men—choose someone of the same sex as our best friend. Even when we're not looking for a "best friend," women and men tend to look for similar things in a potential friend. Both women and men select the same indicators of intimacy. In fact, Wall and her colleagues' study of fifty-eight middle-class men revealed a pattern—stressing confidentiality and trust over simply the pleasure of one's company—that was more consistent with middle-class British women than middle-class British men. This really isn't much of a surprise; we all—women and men—know what we are *supposed* to want and value in a friend.[19]

But apparently what we do in our friendships turns out to be not nearly as great as we might have thought. Differences in self-disclosure turn out to be very small. Men's friendships seem to be based on "continuity, perceived support and dependability, shared understandings, and perceived compatibility," qualities based on shared perceptions rather than constant, sustained interaction to maintain them. Yet men's friendships also center on "self-revelation and self-discovery, having fun together, intermingled lives, and assumed significance"—as do women's.[20]

In sum, most studies that measure interpersonal skills, friendship styles, or self-disclosure find few, if any, significant differences between women and men when it comes to friendship. What is more, because "feminine" expressions of intimacy now define the criteria for evaluation, men's styles of intimacy may become invisible. It is not that men do not express intimacy, but rather that they do it in different ways. Psychologist Scott Swain argues that men do express intimacy "by exchanging favors, engaging in competitive action, joking, touching, sharing accomplishments and including one another in activities." It's often covert, embedded in activities, rather than direct. One man Swain interviewed put it this way:

> I think that the men characteristics [sic] would be the whole thing, would be just the whole thing about being a man. You know, you go out and play sports with your brothers, and have a good time with them. You just . . . you're doing that. And there are some things that you can experience, as far as emotional, [with] your best friends that are men . . . you experience both. And that's what makes it do good is that. With most of the girls you're not going to go out and drink beer and have fun with them. Well, you can, but it's different. I mean it's like a different kind of emotion. It's like with the guys you can have all of it.[21]

Who Makes Better Friends?

"Who makes better friends, men or women? And why?"

I've asked this question in my classes on gender for the past twenty years. And I've noticed a significant change. Until about eight years ago, both women and men answered overwhelmingly that women made better friends than men. Some years the majority was as high as 80 percent. Why? Here is what the students said:

> "Women are more honest."
> "Women tell you what they really feel."
> "With a girl, you can really express your feelings."
> "It's just so much more intimate and connected."

In 2000 or so, that trend began to shift. Women and men pretty much split down the middle. And in 2007 and 2008, I recorded a slight majority of both women and men (54 percent) who said men make better friends. Why?

> "Guys don't judge you."
> "Two words: cat fight."
> "You can relax."
> "Girls always want you to talk about your feelings."

What do you make of this? Have guys become better friends, or have women become worse friends? Maybe neither. It appears more that the criteria by which we measure the quality of our friendships may have begun to shift. Instead of looking to our friends to tell us the truth, engage us emotionally, push us around, and invite us to explore our real feelings, we're looking to our friends to provide a vacation from that self-exploration, to simply chill without judgment.

And what about those "differences" in friendship styles, like using the telephone? Perhaps it is true that women use the telephone more to sustain friendships, but that may be because men see the telephone as impersonal, and they see friendship as a relief from having to do business over the phone. In other words, gender might not be the only variable in predicting phone use in friendships. Barbara Bank reports that men are just as likely to defend their friends, to ask for help when needed, and to go out of their way to help their friends as are the women she studied. What's more, women are just as capable of developing friendships that incorporate traditionally "masculine" friendship virtues—trust, loyalty, obligation—as are men, and it is these qualities that often lead women to value friendship highly in their social worlds.[22]

Harry: You realize of course that we could never be friends.

Sally: Why not?

Harry: What I'm saying is—and this is not a come-on in any way, shape or form—is that men and women can't be friends because the sex part always gets in the way.

Sally: That's not true. I have a number of men friends and there is no sex involved.

Harry: No you don't.

Sally: Yes I do.

Harry: No you don't.

Sally: Yes I do.

Harry: You only think you do.

Sally: You say I'm having sex with these men without my knowledge?

Harry: No, what I'm saying is they all want to have sex with you.

Sally: They do not.

Harry: Do too.

Sally: They do not.

Harry: Do too.

Sally: How do you know?

Harry: Because no man can be friends with a woman that he finds attractive. He always wants to have sex with her.

Sally: So you're saying that a man can be friends with a woman he finds unattractive?

Harry: No, you pretty much want to nail 'em too.

That's the dialogue between Harry and Sally early in the 1989 film *When Harry Met Sally*. (That scene takes place in the early 1970s.) By the 1980s, in the film, they've become friends—best friends, but "just friends," as they say, to make sure that sex doesn't get in the way. And, of course, by the end of the film they also discover that they're in love.

If they are anything like me, your parents are probably from the "When Harry Met Sally Generation," believing, like Harry, that women and men can't be friends. But how many of you actually do not have a good friend of the opposite sex? If you're like the students in my classes, no one. Nearly everyone has a good cross-sex friend. (When I started asking, twenty-five years ago, around the time of the film, about 20 percent of my students said they had a good cross-sex friend.) In fact, cross-sex friendship may be the single biggest change in our intimate lives in the past half-century. But try explaining that to your parents.

Perhaps it's the combination of gender with other factors that best predicts our friendship patterns. For example, some of the studies that found gender differences compared working men with homemakers. But surely whether one works outside the home or not dramatically affects both the quality and the quantity of one's friendships. "The combination of the inflexible demands of the workplace and the cultural expectations associated with familial roles are at least as powerful as determinants of the nature of men's social ties, as are whatever socially acquired capacities and preferences men might possess," writes sociologist Ted Cohen. Those who work outside the home satisfy their intimacy needs in the family and thus seek friendship to meet needs for sociability. This is true of both women *and* men who work outside the home. By contrast, those who stay at home with children need friends to fulfill intimacy needs as well, because children, no matter how much we love them, are not capable of sustaining intimate relationships of mutual self-disclosure with their parents (nor would we want them to). Because those who remain at home with children tend to be women, these people have "less space in their lives for leisure and less opportunity for engaging in sociable relationships than most men."[23]

READ ALL ABOUT IT!

One of the biggest changes in young people's friendships is the near-universality of cross-sex friendships. Nearly every one of you has a good friend of the opposite sex. What you might not know is how recent this is in our history. Just twenty-five years ago, Billy Crystal said to Meg Ryan in one of the iconic scenes in *When Harry Met Sally* that women and men can't be friends, because sex always gets in the way. Not anymore. Cross-sex friendships are so recent that often people feel that they are making up the rules as they go along. Which is why "Gender Rules" by sociologist Diane Felmlee and her colleagues is so useful in delineating the new emergent norms for cross-sex friendships.

WHAT ELSE AFFECTS OUR FRIENDSHIPS?

Sociologists who explore the impact of race, ethnicity, age, class, or sexuality on social life suggest that factors other than gender may complicate the convenient gendering of friendship. Men and women may be more alike in their emotional lives, but there may be big differences among, say, working-class white women and men, on the one hand, and middle-class Latinos on the other.

Racism, for example, directly affects black men's and women's experiences of friendships. For example, impassivity and inexpressiveness for men may be an adaptive strategy to "disguise painful emotions such as shame and sadness influenced by frustrations encountered with mainstream society." On the other hand, black men exhibit significant emotional expressiveness, often designed to release anger and resentment toward the existing social structure. (Thus the expressive styles of black men, which whites come to assume are part of black culture, are, in fact, adaptive strategies to deal with the outrage and injustice of racism and economic inequality.) "For Black men in this society," writes journalist Martin Simmons, "the world is a hostile, dangerous place—a jungle." Friendship is a survival strategy: "Me and him against the world."[24]

Class also shapes black men's emotional experiences. Working-class black male friendships are often self-disclosing and close, in part due to a shared political ideology. Yet upwardly mobile black men have fewer friends, and those they have are less intimate than those of their working-class counterparts, in part because they have accepted traditional definitions of masculinity. Although such celebration may be a useful rhetorical strategy of resistance to racism, it may have negative consequences for male-female relationships and for the men themselves. Shanette Harris suggests that the very strategies embraced by black men to "promote African American male empowerment and survival" may also lead to such maladaptive behaviors as gang membership and to fewer economic opportunities than might have accrued via adopting traditional masculine behaviors. She suggests that the definition of masculinity must be "redefined to exclude themes of domination and superiority."[25]

Age and marital status also affect friendship patterns. Unmarried men are more likely to maintain close and intimate friendships with both women and other men than are married men, for example. And the dynamics of the friendships themselves tend to erase gender differences. For example, when the duration and closeness of friendships are controlled, women do not exhibit the face-to-face style and men the side-by-side style that researchers found. Women and men are just as likely to be self-revealing in face-to-face interactions with close long-time friends.[26]

When we sift through the conflicting evidence, some gender differences in friendships do assert themselves with a certain insistence. And most of them concern sexuality—whether avoiding it with same-sex friends or confronting it with cross-sex friends. With cross-sex friends, sexual attraction almost always complicates matters.

Harry (see *Oh Really?*) was half right. Sex does show up in cross-sex friendship among heterosexual women and men. Inevitably. But men and women *can* still be friends. It's just more work. In one recent study, both men and women listed "attraction" as a cost in a friendship rather than a benefit.[27] Virtually all the men and women Lillian Rubin interviewed described sexual tension in their cross-sex friendships, which made stability and trust in the relationship more fragile. "Once a relationship becomes sexual, I'm inclined to give too much away," said one woman, explaining why she didn't want to confuse the two. Another woman explained the contradiction in her life:

> I'd like to have friendships with men, but I don't seem to be able to pull it off very well. If you get sexually involved, it ruins whatever friendship was possible, and if you don't, there's all that gaminess that goes on. In my experience, it's a problem whatever you do or . . . don't do.
>
> I used to be friends with this guy who never made any kind of a sexual overture, and I didn't exactly love that either. It made me feel unattractive and undesirable. It wasn't even so much that I wanted to go to bed with him, but I wanted him to want to.[28]

When we say someone is "just a friend," we're usually lowering that person on the cosmic hierarchy of importance. But it's equally true that we believe friendships to be purer and more lasting than sexual relationships. In our world, lovers may come and go, but friends are supposed to be there forever. That's why we also often find ourselves saying that we don't want to "ruin" the friendship by making it sexual. This contradiction—the ranking of lover over friend in the statement "just a friend" versus the ranking of friend over lover in our desire not to "ruin" the friendship—also may work itself out in gendered ways, though exactly the opposite of the ways we typically expect women and men to behave. After all, it is typically women, not men, who try to keep the love of a friend and the sexual attraction of a lover separate, and it's men who seek to connect sex and love.

Because emotional disclosure equals vulnerability and dependency, and those feelings accompany sexual relationships with women, most men report that they are less comfortable disclosing their true feelings to a close male friend than to a woman friend. To be emotionally open and vulnerable with another man raises the second significant gender difference in friendship—the impact of homophobia. Homophobia is one of the central organizing principles of same-sex friendships for men but virtually nonexistent for women. **Homophobia** is more than simply the irrational fear and hatred of gay people; it is also the fear that one might be misperceived as gay by others. Think of all the things that you do to make sure no one gets the "wrong idea" about you—from how you walk and talk to how you dress and act to how you interact with your friends.

READ ALL ABOUT IT!

Cross-sex friendships are relatively new on the historical stage; cross-gender-identity friendships are even more recent. In fact, they're so recent it sometimes feels like there are no rules yet. How do transgender individuals navigate the world of sexual orientation and gender identity in their friendship patterns? Do transmen tend to gravitate toward other men—heterosexual or gay—or women—heterosexual or lesbian? Or other trans people? Transmen? Transwomen? All? Some? In a large-scale survey of over five hundred transgender individuals, psychologist M. Paz Galupo and her colleagues found both similarities and differences in all these possible friendship permutations, and suggest some of the ways in which these more fluid gender identities can both disrupt and energize our friendship circles.

For men, friendship itself may be seen as a problem to be explained. Needing, caring about, being emotionally vulnerable and open to another man are acts of non-conformity to traditional notions of masculinity. As one sociologist puts it:

> The very basic assumption friends must make about one another is that each is going beyond a mere presentation of self in compliance with "social dictates." Inevitably, this makes friendship a somewhat deviant relationship because the surest test of personal disclosure is a violation of the rules of public propriety.[29]

Thus to even raise the question of male friendships is to raise the "spectre" of homosexuality. In the opening pages of his book on male friendships, Stuart Miller writes that the first person he sought to interview, a philosophy professor, said to him, "Male

OH? REALLY●

"Homophobia does not affect my friendships with my bros." I hear this line from guys all the time, how their friendships with their guy friends are as intimate as women's friendships. In fact, they often proclaim that their greatest emotional allegiances are to other guys: "Bros before hos." And what about "bromances"?

But studies of male friendships indicate that homophobia is among the dominant themes of male friendships. Fears that straight guys might appear to be gay constrain their physical expressiveness and compromise their ability to become emotionally vulnerable and disclose their feelings.

But heck, you don't have to believe all that social science literature. Just go to the movies. Watch two guys who come to the movies together. How many seats do they take up? Even if they are good friends, the usual answer is three. They use the seat between them for their jackets, or just to have more room. "You just don't want anyone to think you're there, like, 'together,'" commented one of my students.

How many seats do women take up?

friendship. You mean you're going to write about homosexuality?" The next interviewee, a science professor, brought up the same issues. "You must be careful. You know, of course, that people will think you're writing about homosexuality." "Everywhere I have gone," Miller reports, "there has been the same misconception. The bizarre necessity to explain, at the beginning, that my subject is not homosexuality." And Lillian Rubin found that "association of friendship with homosexuality is so common among men."[30]

Changes in men's friendships have become a Hollywood staple. Take "**bromance**" movies. It's as if young Hollywood directors read the older social psychological research that suggested men's friendships were deficient and have offered us a host of guys for whom friendship is a mainstay of their lives. Homophobia still creeps in, of course—all the characters are definitely straight—but they are also capable of that endearing knuckleheaded tenderness that is expected of a real male friend. From *The Hangover* to *Wedding Crashers*—indeed, just about any movie with Owen Wilson, Vince Vaughn, Seth Rogen, or Paul Rudd—revolves on the changing world of men's friendships.

The consequences are significant. In a lovely ethnography of urban boys, developmental psychologist Niobe Way observed deep and intimate friendships among young boys—and the language to express it:

> Regardless of what happens, he will be there. There is nothing we don't do or say, there is nothing I can do or say that would make us less close than we are . . . yes, he is the only person that I know that I am never going to NOT have a relationship with, understand? Yes, it's not ever going to change between us . . . we love each other, we agree how we feel.

So says a fifteen-year-old. But, alas, Way documents that something does change, and that by junior or senior year, most boys have lost that one true, deep friend.

They mourn the loss of intimacy, they know something is gone, and that it is likely irretrievable; one boy sadly notes that he no longer has a best friend:

> Not really . . . The friend I had, I lost it . . . That was the only person that I could trust and we talked about everything. When I was down, he used to help me feel better. The same I did to him. So I feel pretty lonely and sometimes depressed . . . because I don't have no one to go out with, no one to speak on the phone, no one to tell my secrets, no one for me to solve my problems.

And so, they become stoic, hardened, determined not to let anyone ever get that close again.

But it is *that* hardening, that manly stoicism that comes from a deep loss, which facile friendship researchers interpret as something inherent about men's friendships. They see the symptom, but they fail to see the process by which the symptom emerges and thus utterly misunderstand the deep, long-suppressed anguish of loss that preceded it. This gradual diminishment of male friendships is not due to some hormonal imbalance, brain chemistry, or evolutionary imperative. It's due to the persistence of homophobia in boys' and young men's lives—a fear of the misperception that somehow one is a sissy or gay. Having a dear, close, intimate friendship may be perceived as emasculating for teenage boys, and they would rather lose intimacy than lose face.[31]

Homophobia inhibits men's and women's experience of physical closeness. In one famous experiment from the early 1970s, high school girls behaved as close friends had behaved in the nineteenth century. They held hands, they hugged each other, sat with their arms around the other, and kissed on the cheek when they parted. They were instructed to make sure that they did not give any impression that such behavior was sexual. And yet, despite this, their peers interpreted their behavior as an indication that they were lesbian, and their friends ostracized them. For men, also, homophobia restricts expressions of intimacy. One man explained why he would feel weird if he hugged his best friend:

> The guys are more rugged and things, and it wouldn't be rugged to hug another man. That's not a masculine act, where it could be, you know, there's nothing unmasculine about it. But somebody might not see it as masculine and you don't want somebody else to think that you're not, you know—masculine or . . . but you still don't want to be outcast. Nobody I think wants to be outcast.[32]

For men or women who are, "you know, together"—that is, for lesbians and gay men—cross-sex and same-sex friendships often have different styles. In a 1994 survey, Peter Nardi and Drury Sherrod found significant similarities in the same-sex friendship patterns of gay men and lesbians. Both value close, intimate friendships, define intimacy in similar ways, and behave similarly with their friends. Two differences stood out to the researchers—how gay men and lesbians dealt with conflict and sexuality within their friendships. Gay men, for example, are far more likely to sexualize their same-sex friendships than are lesbians. "Like their straight sisters, lesbians can have intensely intimate and satisfying relationships with each other without any sexual involvement," writes Lillian Rubin. Although it may overstate the case to claim, as Rubin does, that asexual gay male friendships are "rare," such gender differences between lesbians and gay men underscore that gender, not sexual orientation, is often the key determinant of our intimate experiences. For gay men, it may be that sex is less significant, rather than that friendship is more significant.[33]

Gay men, after all, also report far more cross-sex friendships than do lesbians, who report few, if any, male friends. Yet lesbians have far more friendships with heterosexual women than gay men have with heterosexual men. Lesbians' friendships tend to be entirely among women—straight or gay. Gay men, by contrast, find their friends among straight women and other gay men. "Lesbians apparently feel they have more in common with straight women than with either gay or straight men," writes one commentator.[34]

Of course they do. Gender is one of the key determinants in their social lives. And yet gay men and lesbians also share one important theme in the construction of their friendships. Whereas heterosexuals clearly distinguish between friends and family, many gay men and lesbians fuse the two, both out of necessity (being exiled from their families when they come out) and by choice. "A person has so many close friends," comments a gay male character in Wendy Wasserstein's Pulitzer Prize–winning play *The Heidi Chronicles*. "And in our lives, our friends are our families."[35]

THE HISTORICAL "GENDERING" OF INTIMATE LIFE

These three major differences—the different experience of sexual tension in cross-sex friendships, the impact of homophobia, and the gendered differences in friendship patterns among gay men and lesbians—require some explanation. Lionel Tiger, for example, stressed evolutionary prehistoric demands of hunting and warfare as the reasons why men's friendships appeared to him to be so much deeper than women's. Contemporary research has no shortage of reasons why women's friendships are deeper and more intimate than men's. Many of these reasons, though, turn out to be tautologies in which gender is both the dependent and independent variable. Women's and men's friendship patterns differ because women and men are different. Men are more instrumental and task-oriented, women more expressive and empathic. And thus their friendships are described with the same language. Such explanations don't explain very much.

Some writers offer psychoanalytic explanations. For example, scholars like Lillian Rubin and Nancy Chodorow, who are both sociologists and psychologists, argue, as Rubin puts it, that "the traditional structure of parenting comes together with the developmental tasks of childhood and the cultural mandates about masculinity and femininity to create differences in the psychological structures of women and men." Our experiences of friendship, love, and intimacy are the result of the different developmental tasks of young boys and young girls as they struggle to achieve a sense of self and identity. The young boy must separate from his mother—the source of love, nurturance, and connection—and establish his independence. He learns to downplay the centrality of those experiences, because they will tend, he thinks, to emasculate him. Thus emotional intimacy often negates or diminishes sexual excitement for men. For girls, by contrast, continued connection with their mothers ensures a continuity of emotionality, love, and nurturance: In fact, it becomes the foundation for women's experience of sexual intimacy, rather than its negation. As a result, separation and individuation are more difficult for women; connection and intimacy more difficult for men. This constellation permits women "to be more closely in touch with both their attachment and dependency needs than men are."[36] (See chapter 4 for a fuller discussion of this process.)

Although such explanations seem right, they take little notice of the dramatic variations in gender development and friendship styles in other cultures. In some societies, for example, boys must still undergo rigorous ritual separation from their mothers; and yet they, and not women, are still seen as having the deeper interior emotional lives and the more intimate and expressive friendships. For example, anthropologist Robert Brain documents several societies in Africa, South America, and Oceania in which men develop very close male friendships, ritually binding themselves together as "lifetime comrades, blood brothers, or even symbolic 'spouses.'"[37]

Psychoanalytic explanations take us part of the way, but even they must be inserted into the larger-scale historical transformation of which they are a part. The notion that boys and girls have such dramatically different developmental tasks is, itself, a product of the social, economic, and cultural transformation of European and American societies at the turn of the twentieth century. That transformation had several components that transformed the meaning and experience of friendship, love, and sexuality. Both Rubin and Chodorow recognize this. "Society and personality live in a continuing reciprocal relationship with each other," Rubin writes. "The search for personal change without efforts to change the institutions within which we live and grow will, therefore, be met with only limited reward."[38]

Rapid industrialization severed the connection between home and work. Now, men left their homes and went to work in factories or offices, places where expressions of vulnerability or openness might give a potential competitor an economic advantage. Men "learned" to be instrumental in their relationships with other men; in their friendships, men have come to "seek not intimacy but companionship, not disclosure but commitment." The male romantic friendship, so celebrated in myths and legend, was, in America, a historical artifact.[39]

Simultaneously, the separation of spheres also left women as the domestic experts: Women became increasingly adept at emotional expression just as men were abandoning that expressive style. Separate spheres implied more than the spatial separation of home and workplace; it divided the mental and social world into two complementary halves. Men expressed the traits and emotions associated with the workplace—competitiveness, individual achievement, instrumental rationality—whereas women cultivated the softer domestic virtues of love, nurturance, and compassion.

The cultural equation of femininity with emotional intimacy exaggerated gender differences in friendships, love, and sexuality. These differences, then, were the *result* of the broad social and economic changes, not their cause; the exclusion of women from the workplace was the single most important differentiating experience. That is, again, a case where gender inequality produced the very differences that then legitimated the inequalities. And, ideologically, the triumph of autonomy as the highest goal of individual development, along with the ascendant ideal of companionate marriage—marriage based on the free choice of two people who devote themselves emotionally to each other— reinforced the growing gender gap in emotional expressiveness. When we began to marry for love, we fused sexual passion and deep friendship—for the first time in history. (Remember how the Greeks had kept those three completely separate.)

Finally, the birth of the modern homosexual had enormous implications for the construction of gendered ways of loving. French philosopher Michel Foucault argued that "the disappearance of friendship as a social institution, and the declaration of homosexuality as a social/political/medical problem, are the same process." Prior to the start of the twentieth century, the word "homosexual" described behaviors, not identity. But as the word changed from an adjective to a noun, homophobia became increasingly significant in men's lives. Homophobia increases the gender differences between women and men because "the possible imputation of homosexual interest to any bonds between men ensured that men had constantly to be aware of and assert their difference from both women and homosexuals," writes sociologist Lynne Segal.[40]

Industrialization, cultural ideals of companionate marriage and the separation of spheres, and the emergence of the modern homosexual—these simultaneous forces created the arena in which we have experienced intimacy and emotional life. Its division into two complementary gendered domains is part of the story of our gendered society.

LOVE AND GENDER

The separation of spheres also had a profound impact on our experiences of love. As with friendship, love has a history: Its meanings and expressions change over time. "Passionate attachments between young people can and do happen in any society," writes historian Lawrence Stone, "but the social acceptability of the emotion has varied enormously over time and class and space, determined primarily by cultural norms and property arrangements." As with friendship, women have come to be seen as the love experts—notice how all the advice columns on love and relationships are written for and by women—whereas men's attempts to express love are evaluated on what have become "feminine" criteria. "Part of the reason that men seem so much less loving than women," argues sociologist Francesca Cancian, "is that men's behavior is measured with a feminine ruler." This has devalued and displaced one type of loving and replaced it with another. "His" expressions of love included sexual passion, the practical aspects of providing and protecting, ensuring material survival and mutual aid. "Her" way of loving was sharing feelings, developing mutual emotional dependency, and nurturing through talk.[41]

It wasn't always this way. Troubadours of the eleventh to thirteenth centuries described undying passion as a hallmark of love for both women and men. But the romantic love they described was also seen as socially disruptive, a threat to the power of the church, the state, and the family. Thus by the sixteenth and seventeenth centuries, "every advice book, every medical treatise, every sermon and religious homily ... firmly rejected both romantic passion and lust as suitable bases for marriage." By the eighteenth century, attitudes had softened, and individuals were advised to make marital choices based on love and affection—provided, of course, that the two families approved and the individuals' social and economic statuses were roughly equal.[42]

It wasn't until the nineteenth century that love became the ordinary experience for couples, that it was "normal and indeed praiseworthy for young men and women to fall passionately in love, and that there must be something wrong with those who fail to have such an overwhelming experience sometime in late adolescence or early adulthood." But in the nineteenth-century marriage manuals, love is rarely mentioned

The "Rating-Dating-Mating Complex"

Based on his research at Penn State University, sociologist Willard Waller wrote his classic article "The Rating and Dating Complex" (1937), which suggested that dating among high school and college students was a competitive enterprise, organized among peers, with significant social consequences. People wanted to date someone of slightly higher social rank than they thought they were ranked—not too much higher, but certainly not too much lower, either. Both boys and girls wanted to be seen as good dates and also to date others who were seen as good dates.

Boys competed with other boys and girls competed with other girls to get the best dates, because the higher the ranking of their dating partner, the higher would be their ranking among their same-sex peers. Equally, boys and girls competed with each other over the meaning of being a "good" date. For girls, it meant preserving their reputation, so they wouldn't be seen as "easy." For boys, it often meant being seen as sexually sophisticated and experienced.

---

as a reason to get married. In fact, love "is presented more as a product of marriage than its prerequisite." By the end of the century, though, "love had won its battle along the whole line in the upper sections of the middle class. It has since been regarded as the most important prerequisite to marriage."[43]

So love as we know it—the basis for marriage, sexuality, and family—is relatively recent. Nor is it the foundation of marriage and/or sexual expression everywhere else in the world. As the basis for sexual activity, love turns out to be relatively rare. Love and sex turn out to be most highly associated in cultures where women and men are more unequal and where women are materially dependent upon men. Where women and men are mutually dependent and relatively equal, love and sex tend not to be equated. Even in our society, love may or may not accompany sexual activity or family life, and it may wax and wane in its intensity. In a classic article, sociologist William J. Goode noted that there was little evidence that the ideology of romantic love was widely or deeply believed by all strata of the American population.[44]

GENDERED LOVE, AMERICAN STYLE

Since the mid-nineteenth century, according to historians, love has come to mean tenderness, powerlessness, and emotional expression. And love has become increasingly a woman's business, the home its domain. The masculine workplace was rough and competitive, "a vast wilderness," a "rage of competitive battle," and demanded that men suppress their emotions; home was the place where a man "seeks refuge from the vexations and embarrassments of business, an enchanting repose from exertion, a relaxation from care by the interchange of affection," as one New England minister explained in 1827. Women, said to possess "all the milder virtues of humanity," became the ministers of love. (This separation of emotional spheres was neither intended nor experienced as a gain for women. Indeed, women's emotionality—women were "accustomed to feel, oftener than to reason," as one Unitarian minister put it—was the chief justification for excluding women from the workplace, colleges and universities, and the voting booth.)[45]

Like friendship, then, the separation of spheres **"feminized"** love, so that today love implies "an overemphasis on talking and feeling, a mystification of the material basis of attachment, and a tendency to ignore physical love and the practical aspects of nurturance and mutual assistance." Men's style of loving, focusing on "practical help, shared physical activities, spending time together, and sex," has been demoted to "less than" the feminine style. These different styles of loving are the products of the large-scale transformations that created the modern system of gender relations, and they are as much the cause of gender inequality as the result of preexisting gender differences. They are the result of gender inequality; these differences, as psychologist Carol Tavris tells us, emerged "because women are expected, allowed, and required to reveal certain emotions, and men are expected and required to deny or suppress them." They are the source of so much miscommunication between women and men that it often feels as though we are from different planets, or at least, in Lillian Rubin's phrase, "intimate strangers."[46]

Consider, for example, the classic "he said/she said" tussle about whether we really love our partner. Here's what one husband said to Lillian Rubin:

> What does she want? Proof? She's got it, hasn't she? Would I be knocking myself out to get things for her—like to keep up this house—if I didn't love her? Why does a man do things like that if not because he loves his wife and kids? I swear, I can't figure out what she wants.

His wife said something very different. "It is not enough that he supports us and takes care of us. I appreciate that, but I want him to share things with me. I need for him to tell me his feelings."

These two statements aptly illustrate the differences between "his" and "her" ways of loving.[47] Or do they? The empirical research on the gender of love reveals fewer differences, and of less significance, than we might otherwise expect. One recent review of the literature, for example, found that women's and men's experiences and attitudes are statistically similar on forty-nine of the sixty correlates of love. And a recent study found that generally women and men are pretty much equally emotionally expressive—although women are more likely to express those emotions associated with inequality (smoothing things over, unruffling feathers, and the like).[48]

And those differences that we do find are occasionally the opposite of what we might have expected. Take, for example, the received wisdom that women are the romantic sex, men the rational, practical sex. After all, women are the domesticated, emotional experts and the primary consumers of romance literature, emotional advice columns, and television talk-show platitudes.

Some research confirms these **gendered love** stereotypes. One study found that men are more likely to respond to ephemeral qualities such as physical appearance when they fall in love and are far more likely to say they are easily attracted to members of the opposite sex. Yet most studies have found *men* to be stronger believers in romantic love ideologies than are women. (On the other hand, men also tend to be more cynical about love at the same time.[49]) Men, it seems, are more likely to believe myths about love at first sight, tend to fall in love more quickly than women, are more likely to enter relationships out of a desire to fall in love, and yet also tend to fall out of love more quickly. Romantic love, to men, is an irrational, spontaneous, and compelling emotion that demands action. Who but a man, one might ask, could have said, as Casanova did, that "nothing is surer than that we will no longer desire them, for one does not desire what one possesses"?[50]

Women, on the other hand, show a more "pragmatic orientation" toward falling in and out of love and are more likely to also like the men they love. Once in love, women tend to experience the state more intensely. One experiment found that after only four dates, men were almost twice as likely as women to define the relationship as love (27 percent to 15 percent). But by the twenty-first date, 43 percent of the women said that they were in love, whereas only 30 percent of the men did. The researchers write:

> If by "more romantic" we refer to the speed of involvement and commitment, then the male appears to be more deserving of that label. If, on the other hand, we mean the experiencing of the emotional dimension of romantic love, then the female qualifies as candidate for "more romantic" behavior in a somewhat more judicious and rational fashion. She chooses and commits herself more slowly than the male but, once in love, she engages more extravagantly in the euphoric and idealizational dimensions of loving.[51]

Despite the fact that men report falling out of love more quickly, it's women who initiate the majority of breakups. And women, it seems, also have an easier time accepting their former romantic partners as friends than men do. After a breakup, men—supposedly the less emotional gender—report more loneliness, depression, and sleeplessness than women do. This is equally true after divorce: Married men live longer and emotionally healthier lives than divorced or single men; unmarried women live longer and are far happier than married women.[52]

Though some gender differences tend to both confirm and contradict traditional gender stereotypes, there is some evidence that these differences have narrowed considerably over the past few decades. In the late 1960s, William Kephart asked more than one thousand college students, "If a boy (girl) had all the other qualities you desired, would you marry this person if you were not in love with him (her)?" In the 1960s, Kephart found dramatic differences between men, who thought that marriage without love was out of the question, and women, who were more likely to admit that the absence of love wouldn't necessarily deter them from marriage. (Kephart attributed this to women's economic dependence, which allowed men the "luxury" of marrying for love.)[53]

Since the 1960s, sociologists have continued to ask this question, and each year fewer women and men say they are willing to marry for any reason but love. By the mid-1980s, 85 percent of both women and men considered such a marriage out of the question; and by 1991, 86 percent of the men and 91 percent of the women responded with an emphatic "no." A 2012 survey (Singles in America) found that 31 percent of adult men said they'd commit to a person they were not in love with—as long as she had all the other attributes they were looking for in a mate—and 21 percent said they'd commit under those same circumstances to somebody they weren't sexually attracted to. Women, meanwhile, were more likely than men to say they "must have" someone with a similar level of education, participating in the same religion, who has a successful career and a sense of humor. It would seem that women are now the "pickier" sex.[54]

But such studies yielded very different results in different countries, suggesting that our definitions of love may have more to do with cultural differences than they do with gender. When students in Japan and Russia were asked the same question in 1992, their answers differed dramatically from those of Americans. More Russian women (41 percent) and men (30 percent) answered yes than did either the Japanese (20 percent of the men and 19 percent of the women) or the Americans (13 percent of the men and 9 percent of the women). And whereas the American and Japanese women were slightly less likely than the men to say yes, Russian women were much more likely than Russian men to do so.[55]

Another study compared American men and women with Chinese men and women. The differences between women and men were small—as were the differences between the Chinese and American samples. Culture, not gender, was a far more salient variable in understanding these differences. In both cases, men were more likely to hold romantic and idealized notions about love but were slightly more likely to be willing to marry without love. American men held less erotic notions about love (that is, they were more likely to separate love and sex) and more "ludic" notions (love is about closeness and intimacy) than did women.[56]

And it may be that other factors enhance or diminish women's and men's ways of loving. Remember that man and woman cited earlier, whose statements about what they want from each other seemed to speak so loudly about intractable gender differences? These two statements may actually say more about the transformation of love in a marriage than they do about deep-seated personality differences between women and men. Some startling research was undertaken by sociologist Cathy Greenblat on this issue. Greenblat asked thirty women and thirty men two questions just before they were to get married: "How do you know you love this person?" "How do you know you are loved by this person?"[57]

Prior to marriage, the answers revealed significant gender differences that meshed in a happy symmetry. The men "knew" that they loved their future wives because they were willing to do so much for them, willing to sacrifice for them, eager to go out of their way to buy them flowers or demonstrate their love in some other visible way—willing, as one might say, to drop everything in the middle of the night and drive three hours in a blinding snowstorm because the women were upset. Happily, conveniently, their future wives "knew" that they were loved precisely because the men were willing to go to such extraordinary lengths to demonstrate it. The women "knew" that they loved their future husbands because they wanted to take care of them, to nurture and support them, to express their emotions of caring and tenderness. And, happily, the men "knew" they were loved because the women took care of them, nurtured them, and were emotionally caring.

So far, so good—and perfectly symmetrical. Greenblat then interviewed twenty-five couples who had been married at least ten years. She added a question asking whether the men and women questioned whether they loved their spouse or whether their spouse loved them. Overwhelmingly, women had no doubts that they still loved their husbands but had significant doubts about whether they were still loved by their husbands. By contrast, the husbands had no doubts that they were loved by their wives but had serious doubts about whether they loved their wives any longer.

It would be easy to interpret such data as revealing a gender difference: Men fall in love sooner but also fall out of love sooner than women. But such research may tell us more about the way that the structure of marriage transforms our ability to love and to be loved. After all, when you are married, you no longer have many opportunities to go well out of your way to do extraordinary things in order to demonstrate your love. You live together, come home from work to each other every day, and raise children together. Although that may, in my estimation or yours, be heroic enough in itself, it does not lead men to feel that they are expressing their love in the way they "know" they love someone. Hence, they may begin to doubt whether they truly love their wives. By contrast, the nuclear family in the suburban single-family home enhances women's expression of loving as domestic nurturing and care giving. Thus the wives were certain that they still loved their husbands but were unsure that their husbands still loved them.

To "read" such differences as revealing something essential about women and men would be to miss the structural impact of the modern family arrangement and the way that structural arrangements enhance some relational styles and inhibit others. Even if women and men are not from different planets, the modern, insular, nuclear family may be foreign territory for men's ways of expressing the love they feel. It may mean that we need to expand our capacities for loving in different ways in different situations.

Our current feminization of love, psychologist Carol Tavris argues, has detrimental effects on women's lives:

> The feminization of love in America, the glorification of women's ways of loving, is not about the love between autonomous individuals. It celebrates a romantic, emotional love that promotes the myth of basic, essential differences between women and men. It supports the opposition of women's love and men's work. In so doing, it derails women from thinking about their own talents and aspirations, rewarding instead a narrowed focus on finding and keeping Mr. Right.[58]

Fortunately, love need not be feminized, as Francesca Cancian argues. Men's way of loving—"the practical help and physical activities"—is, she notes, "as much a part of love as the expression of feelings." And the feminization of love as the expression of feelings, nurturing, and intimacy also obscures women's capacity for instrumental, activity-centered forms of love and thus, in effect, freezes men and women into patterns that mask some of their traits, as if right-handedness meant one could never even use one's left hand. Cancian poses an important question: "Who is more loving," she asks, "a couple who confide most of their experiences to each other but rarely cooperate or give each other practical help, or a couple who help each other through many crises and cooperate in running a household but rarely discuss their personal experiences?" Perhaps, Cancian suggests, what we need is a more embracingly universal definition of love that has as its purpose individual development, mutual support, and intimacy—and that women and men are equally capable of experiencing.[59]

CONCLUSION

Love and friendship are perhaps the major avenues of self-exploration and, along with sexuality (the subject of the next chapter), the chief routes we take in our society to know ourselves. "Love provides us with identities, virtues, roles through which we define ourselves, as well as partners to share our happiness, reinforce our values, support our best opinions of ourselves and compensate for the anonymity, impersonality or possibly frustration of public life," writes Robert Solomon. Our friends, Lillian Rubin writes, "are those who seem to us to call up the best parts of ourselves, even while they also accept our darker side."[60]

Yet friendship is so precarious. "Unlike a marriage," Rubin writes, friendship "is secured by an emotional bond alone. With no social compact, no ritual moment, no pledge of loyalty and constancy to hold a friendship in place, it becomes not only the most neglected social relationship of our time, but, all too often, our most fragile one as well." So, too, are love relationships, which require much care and nurturing in a world that seems to present an infinite number of distractions and subterfuges. Sexual encounters are more fragile still, holding at any particular moment only the most fleeting promise of sustained emotional connection.

To sustain our lives, to enable us to experience the full range of our pleasures, to achieve the deep emotional connections with lovers and friends, we must remember the ways that gender does *and does not* construct our emotional lives. To pretend that women and men are from different planets condemns us, at best, to occasional intergalactic travel, with interpreters and technical assistance. I'd prefer that the interpreters stay home and that we learn to reveal more of ourselves. Love and friendship are deeply human experiences—ones we should be able to manage on our own. As the great British novelist E. M. Forster once wrote of passionate human connection, "Men and women are capable of sustained relations, not mere opportunities for an electrical discharge."

KEY TERMS

Bromance	Gendered Love	*The Second Sex*
Emotional Intimacy	Homophobia	
Feminized Love	Men's Liberation	

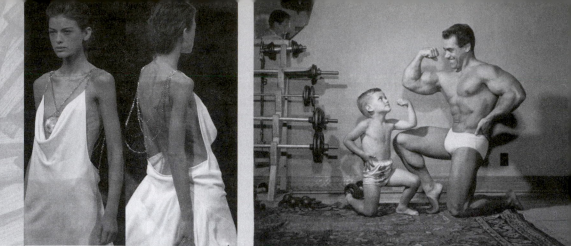

13

The GENDERED BODY

W e think of our bodies as either our own private possessions, over which we exercise complete control, or as collections of biological impulses over which we have virtually no control at all. And though our culture is saturated with sexual jokes and innuendo, and we talk about sex incessantly, for most of us sexuality remains a pretty private experience, rarely discussed honestly and openly. For centuries, the body has been shrouded in myth, taboo, and ignorance.

Yet nothing could be more gendered than these most individual, private experiences. We inscribe our bodies with a wide range of cultural signs and symbols, and our sexualities are intimate expressions of well-established social norms and practices. Our bodies become social texts that we construct to be "read" by others. And significant changes in the past few decades—new surgical procedures, over-the-counter emergency contraception, the Internet—have transformed this system of gendered signifying, making us more aware of our bodies than ever before and enabling new groups to claim their own embodied agency, a kind of embodied democracy that has also been met, characteristically, with increased backlash.[1]

GENDER AND THE BEAUTY MYTH

Our ideals of beauty and attractiveness themselves are deeply gendered. For one thing, we know a lot more about **standards of female beauty** in other cultures than we know about standards of male beauty—in part because it's men who created those standards in the first place, and their valuation derived from other things, like wealth and power. Specifically, sexual standards of beauty often vary depending on the status of women. In societies where women's status is higher, smaller breasts are considered more attractive, probably because smaller breasts minimize the anatomical differences between women and men and also because smaller breasts make it easier for women to move about quickly. In the United States, men's preferences for larger or smaller breasts on women tend to vary with economic trends—as do the hemlines on women's skirts. During periods of prosperity, when male breadwinners can afford to have their wives stay at home, larger breast sizes and shorter hemlines tend to be preferred, because these exaggerate the biological differences between women and men (and thus reinforce the social separation of spheres). During economic downturns, women's hemlines come down, and smaller breast sizes

OH? REALLY.

Florence Colgate was awarded the title "Britain's Most Beautiful Face" in 2012.

The competition was sponsored by a cosmetics company, and eight thousand women entered. The company used a mathematical algorithm to determine beauty "scientifically." Here's an extract of that algorithm:

> A woman's face is said to be most attractive when the space between her pupils is just under half the width of her face from ear to ear. Florence scores a 44 percent ratio. Experts also believe the relative distance between eyes and mouth should be just over a third of the measurement from hairline to chin. Florence's ratio is 32.8 percent.

Sounds pretty scientific, right? But then listen to how one psychologist unpacked that mathematical formula for "classical" beauty:

> Florence has all the classic signs of beauty. She has large eyes, high cheekbones, full lips and a fair complexion. Symmetry appears to be a very important cue to attractiveness.

Wait! "Fair complexion"? "Science of beauty"?

Can our diverse multicultural society come up with a "scientific" analysis of beauty that isn't based on racial codes? Beauty may be skin deep; racism goes a lot deeper and may be far more subtle.

Source: Lisa Wade, "Colorism and the 'Science' of Beauty" in *Society Pages*, May 12, 2012, http://thesocietypages.org/socimages/2012/05/12/colorism-and-the-science-of-beauty. Image courtesy of: ©SWNS.COM

tend to become the norm, as women and men both work to make ends meet, and the natural distinctions between women and men are minimized.

In many tropical cultures, women do not cover their breasts, but this doesn't mean that the men there are in a constant state of sexual frenzy. The breasts are simply not considered a sexual stimulus in those cultures, and attention may be focused elsewhere. And in some Islamic cultures, women are believed to be so sexually alluring (and men so unable to control themselves when confronted with temptation) that women practice purdah, which requires that they keep their entire bodies covered.

In the United States, women's beauty is placed at such a high premium and the standards of beauty are so narrow that many women feel trapped by what Naomi Wolf calls the "**beauty myth**"—a nearly unreachable cultural ideal of feminine beauty that "uses images of female beauty as a political weapon against women's advancement." Just as Max Weber decried the "iron cage" of consumption in modern society, so, too, does Wolf decry the "**Iron Maiden**" created by this beauty myth, which entraps women in an endless cycle of cosmetics, beauty aids, diets, and exercise fanaticism and makes women's bodies into "prisons their homes no longer were." Is this "tyranny of slenderness," as one writer called it, an ironic outcome of women's increased independence—a kind of backlash attempt to keep women in their place just as they are breaking free? It's unlikely that it is any more than a coincidence, but it is worth noting that the first Miss America pageant was held in 1920—the same year women obtained the right to vote.[2]

Women are particularly concerned with weight and breast size. Breasts are "the most visible signs of a woman's femininity," writes philosopher Iris Young, "the sign of her sexuality." Women are often trapped in what we might call the "**Goldilocks dilemma**," after the young girl of the fairy tale. As Goldilocks found the porridge "too hot" or "too cold" but never "just right," so, too, do women believe their breasts are either too large or too small—but never just right. In 2001, cosmetic surgeons performed nearly 220,000 breast augmentations and close to half as many breast reductions.

Women's weight often forces women to submit to the tyranny of slenderness. For example, the average weight of Miss America and *Playboy* pinups has decreased steadily since 1978, even though their average height and breast size have increased. In 1954, Miss America was five foot eight and weighed 132 pounds. Today, the average Miss America contestant still stands five foot eight but now weighs just 118 pounds. (An article in *Harper's Bazaar* in 1908 declared the normal weight for a healthy woman of five foot eight to be 155 pounds; 133 would have been normal for a woman of five foot three, and 117 would have been less than the prescribed weight of 120 pounds for a woman who stood five foot one.) In 1975, the average fashion model weighed about 8 percent less than the average American woman; by 1990, that difference had grown to 23 percent, and it remains about 20 percent today. And though the average American woman today is five foot four and weighs 162.9 pounds and wears a size 14 dress, the average model is five foot eleven and weighs 117 pounds and wears a size 2.[3] Marilyn Monroe, perhaps the twentieth century's most recognizable sex symbol, wore a size 12 dress; contemporary sex symbols are more likely to wear a size 4. For instance, Gisele Bundchen was *Vogue*'s model of the year in 2011, in part because, as the magazine states, she strays from the rail-thin image. Gisele is five foot eleven and weighs only 115 pounds. That is 25 percent below her ideal body weight. Even "plus-size" models have shrunk. A decade ago, plus-size models averaged between size 12 and size 18. Today, a model is considered "plus-size" starting at a size 6.[4] "Girls are terrified of being fat," writes Mary Pipher. "Being fat means being left out, scorned, and vilified . . . Almost all adolescent girls feel fat, worry about their weight, diet and feel guilty when they eat." Perhaps most telling is that 42 percent of girls in first through third grades say they want to be thinner, and 81 percent of ten-year-olds are afraid of being fat. Forty-six percent of nine- to eleven-year-olds are on diets; by college the percentage has nearly doubled.[5]

Current standards of beauty for women combine two images—dramatic thinness and muscularity and buxomness—that are virtually impossible to accomplish. Research on adolescents suggests that a large majority consciously trade off health concerns in their efforts to lose weight. As a result, increasing numbers of young women are diagnosed with either **anorexia nervosa** or **bulimia** every year. Anorexia involves chronic and dangerous starvation dieting and obsessive exercise; bulimia typically involves "binging and purging" (eating large quantities of food and then either vomiting or taking enemas to excrete the food). Although anorexia and bulimia are extreme and very serious problems that can, if untreated, threaten a girl's life, they represent only the furthest reaches of a continuum of preoccupation with the body that begins with such "normal" behaviors as compulsive exercise or dieting.

It is important to remember that rates of anorexia and bulimia are higher in the United States than in any other country—by far. Estimates in the United States range between 5 and 10 percent of all post-pubescent girls and women affected—that means about twenty million girls and women and ten million men. Anorexia is the third most common chronic illness among adolescents. Half of all American girls between the ages of eleven and thirteen see themselves as overweight.[6]

In Britain the number is more like 1 to 2 percent of young women, and across Europe only 14.5 of every 10,000 women suffer from bulimia or anorexia, according to the European Medical Association. That's just over one-tenth of 1 percent—and about fifty times less than in the United States.[7] By contrast, many non-Western societies value plumpness, and there is a correlation between body weight and social class, and throughout Europe and the United States, nonwhite girls are far less likely to exhibit eating disorders than are white and middle-class girls. (Ironically, in societies where food is plentiful, ideals of thinness are imposed constantly, while in societies where the food supply is erratic, plumpness is more often the feminine ideal.)[8] Recent dramatic increases have, however, been observed among young middle- and upper-class Japanese women.[9]

Combine this preoccupation with thinness with the equation of thin and sexy, and you have a cultural recipe for some very confused people. Clothing stores sell thongs sized for seven- to ten-year-olds. In early 2012, Abercrombie Kids was forced to remove a "push-up" bikini top from its stores and online sales site over public outrage. They issued a statement on their Facebook page, agreeing "with those who say it is best 'suited' for girls age 12 and older." (Abercrombie Kids markets its clothing for ages 7 to 14.)[10] The American Psychological Association was so alarmed at this trend that it convened a task force on the sexualization of young girls.[11]

Although some stereotypic understandings would have it that such dramatic emphasis on thinness afflicts only middle- and upper-class white girls and women, the evidence suggests that this emphasis also defines working-class and black ideals of the feminine body. Largeness "was once accepted—even revered—among Black folks," lamented an article in *Essence* magazine in 1994, but it "now carries the same unmistakable stigma as it does among Whites." And a study the following year found that black adolescent girls demonstrated a significantly higher drive for thinness than did white adolescent girls. The media coverage of Oprah's dramatic weight loss and the depiction of ultrathin African-American models and actresses may have increased black women's anxieties about their weight; indeed, it may be a perverse signal of assimilation and acceptance by the dominant culture that "their" ideal body type is now embraced by the formerly marginalized.[12]

Here's a good example. In March 1985, the *New York Times* ran a story with the big banner headline "Dislike of Own Body Found Common Among Women." The article went on to describe the growing concern about eating disorders and unhealthy body image. Not much new there now, right? But underneath that banner headline was a little box with what is called in journalism a "call out"—a short phrase that illustrates some big theme in the article. It said, "Men tend to see themselves as just about perfect."

How true is that today? Could it be that the biggest change in body image is not women's continued dislike of their bodies but the fact that men no longer "see themselves as just about perfect"? Over the past thirty years, men, too, have come to dislike their own bodies. Men haven't exactly caught up to women on the dislike-o-meter, but we're closing the gap considerably. Some progress, huh?

Men have become increasingly concerned with their bodies, especially in fitness and weight. Although men have long been concerned about appearing strong and fit— witness the enormous success of Charles Atlas bodybuilding apparatus since the turn of the twentieth century—the building of strong muscles seems to increase as a preoccupation and obsession during periods when men are least likely to actually have to use their muscles in their work. That is, we want to look stronger during periods when we actually don't need it, re-creating in our appearances what we no longer require in actuality. Today, successful new men's magazines like *Men's Health* encourage men to see their bodies as women have been taught to see theirs—as ongoing projects to be worked on. (The magazine's circulation grew from 250,000 to over 1.5 million in its first seven years—the most successful magazine launch in history.) In part, this

READ ALL ABOUT IT!

Almost daily, we read alarming studies about the obesity crisis in the United States—that Americans are getting fatter, and nearly half of all Americans have been classified as "obese" or "overweight" since the 1980s. Our remedies range from diets based on willpower, prepared foods, or drugs to healthy and unhealthy exercise regimes and a national anxiety about bodies and their vicissitudes. In "The Unequal Weight of Discrimination: Gender, Body Size and Income Inequality," sociologist Katherine Mason explores the social meanings of obesity and the ways that social consequences for obesity differ for men and women (men suffer some forms of discrimination, which disappear over time; discrimination against women tends to stick around).

What Mason shows is that the solution to this "crisis" of obesity is not a national diet, but a rethinking of our understanding of the body and gender identity.

coincides with general concerns about health and fitness, and in part it is about looking young in a society that does not value aging. But more than that, it also seems to
be about gender.

Men's bodily anxieties mirror those of women. Whereas women are concerned
with breast size and weight, men are concerned with muscularity—that is, both are
preoccupied with those aspects of the male and female body that suggest and exaggerate innate biological differences between the sexes. It would appear that the more
equal women and men become in the public sphere, the more standards of beauty
emphasize those aspects that are biologically different.

Standards of male muscularity have also increased dramatically. Many men experience what some researchers have labeled "**muscle dysmorphia**," a belief that one is
too small, insufficiently muscular. Harrison Pope calls it the "**Adonis Complex**"—the
belief that men must look like Greek gods, with perfect chins, thick hair, rippling
muscles, and washboard abdominals. The increasing packaging of men's bodies in the
media—it is now common to see men's bodies displayed in advertising in ways that
were conceivable only for women's bodies a generation ago—coupled with increased
economic anxiety (which leads us to focus on the things we *can* control, like how we
look) has led to a dramatic shift in men's ideas about their bodies.[13]

In 1999, Pope and his colleagues took G.I. Joe's proportions and translated them
into real-life proportions (parallel to the descriptions of Barbie's changes). In 1974,
G.I. Joe was five feet ten inches tall, had a thirty-one-inch waist, a forty-four-inch
chest, and twelve-inch biceps. Strong and muscular, it's true, but at least within the
realm of the possible. G.I. Joe in 2002 was a little bit different. He was still five feet ten
inches tall, but his waist had shrunk to twenty-eight inches, his chest had expanded to
fifty inches, and his biceps were now twenty-two inches—almost the size of his waist.
Such proportions would make one a circus freak, not a role model (figure 13.1).[14]

Such hypertrophied ectomorphs make many men feel utterly inadequate. Nearly
half of all men in one survey reported significant body image disturbance. A 1997
study reported in *Psychology Today* found that 43 percent of the men were dissatisfied
with their appearance, compared with only 15 percent twenty-five years earlier. And
now, a British study finds nearly double that rate (80.7 percent) talk in ways that suggest significant anxiety about their bodies. (Two of five would sacrifice a year of their
lives for a perfect body.)[15]

> When I look in the mirror, I see two things: what I want to be and what I'm not.
> I hate my abs. My chest will never be huge. My legs are too thin. My nose is an
> odd shape. I want what *Men's Health* pushes. I want to be the guy in the Gillette
> commercials.[16]

And increasing numbers of men are also exhibiting eating disorders. Pope and
his colleagues believe that over one million men suffer from some form of eating
disorder. Some experts believe that about 40 percent of binge eaters and one-fourth
of anorexia and bulimia sufferers are male—compared with only 10 percent a
decade ago—while the equivalent rates for women have not changed significantly.[17]
(According to one study, men are far less likely to seek treatment for eating disorders because they believe such disorders to be a woman's illness.) Although these
problems may be more prevalent among gay men, increases among heterosexual

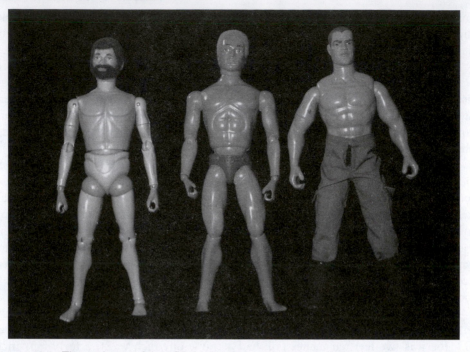

Figure 13.1. The evolution of the "G.I. Joe" action toy from 1964 (left) to 1975 (center) to 1992 (right), showing an increasing emphasis on muscularity through the years.

Source: For additional similar images and a detailed discussion, see Pope HG, et al. "Evolving ideals of male body image as seen through action toys," *International Journal of Eating Disorders* 1999; 26:65–72.

men are also pronounced. A 1994 study of football players at Cornell found that 40 percent engaged in dysfunctional eating patterns and 10 percent manifested diagnosable eating disorders. Two recent studies indicate that while virtually no male college athletes have been diagnosed with an eating disorder, about 16 to 20 percent are symptomatic. "Although the frequency of pathogenic behaviors was low," the authors write, "exercise (37 percent) and fasting/dieting (14.2 percent) were the primary and secondary means for controlling weight; fewer than 10 percent used vomiting, laxatives, or diuretics."[18] A 1997 survey of 1,425 active-duty naval men found that nearly 7 percent fit the criteria for bulimia, another 2.5 percent were anorexic, over 40 percent fit the criteria for eating disorder, and nearly 40 percent reported current binge eating. One in four reported compensatory behaviors such as fasting, vomiting, taking laxatives, and taking water pills—numbers that doubled when physical standards were being measured. And a recent survey of Australian college men found that one in five had used restrained eating, vomiting, laxative abuse, or cigarette smoking for weight control. About one in five also reported binge eating and weight control problems.[19]

And just as women have resorted to increasingly dangerous surgical and prosthetic procedures—such as having silicone-filled bags placed in their breasts or being given mild localized doses of botulism to paralyze facial muscles and thereby "remove" wrinkles—so, too, are men resorting to increasingly dramatic efforts to get large. The use of anabolic steroids has mushroomed, especially among college-aged men. Legal prescriptions for steroids have quadrupled since 1997, to more than 1.75 million in 2002 and 4.5 million in 2010, and countless more illegal sources provide less-regulated doses. One study found that more than 40 percent of middle school and high school boys exercised regularly with the goal of increasing muscle mass, 38 percent used protein supplements, and nearly 6 percent said they had experimented with steroids.[20] Steroids enable men to increase muscle mass quickly and dramatically, so that one looks incredibly big. Prolonged use also leads to dramatic mood changes, increased uncontrolled rage, and a significant shrinkage in the testicles.[21]

Eating disorders among women and muscular dysmorphia among men are parallel processes, extreme points on a continuum that begins with almost everyone. There are, for example, very few women who do not have a problematic relationship with food—virtually all women see food as something other than simple taste or nourishment but instead mentally count the calories, determine whether this indulgence is worth it, and calculate how much extra time they can spend in the gym to compensate and how much they weigh. And virtually all young men have a problematic relationship with violence. (As we'll see in the next chapter, violence is so closely equated with masculinity that it would be difficult to extricate the two.) And what signifies the capacity for violence but physical strength—or at least looking strong? One can hear this in the voices of the anorexics and the obsessive bodybuilders. The young women, literally starving to death, talk constantly about how fat they are and how if only they could lose weight they'd feel better about themselves, whereas their male counterparts, who are so muscle-bound that they cannot bend over to tie their shoes, talk about how "small" they are and how much they have to eat and work out to get larger. If a measure of successful femininity is being thin, and if a measure of masculinity is appearing strong and powerful, then anorexics and obsessive bodybuilders are not psychological misfits or deviants: They are overconformists to gender norms to which all of us, to some degree, are subject.[22]

READ ALL ABOUT IT!

How do we understand the changes in our bodies, and the relationship of those changes to gender, ethnicity, race, and other aspects of our identities? During puberty, our bodies go through some big changes, especially as hormones kick in and secondary sex characteristics emerge. But even if those bodies change in similar ways, certainly we would understand that the meanings attached to those changes vary enormously by race, ethnicity, region, and so on. How could we think otherwise? In "Do It All for Your Pubic Hairs," sociologist Richard Mora explores the meaning of puberty to young Latino males in the United States, finding that their associations among physical changes, emergent masculinity, and feelings of entitlement and dominance have a very specific constellation.

Just as there has been an increase in the gap between rich and poor—the gap between the top 20 percent and the bottom 20 percent of American society is currently the highest in our history—so, too, has there been an increased bifurcation between the embodied "haves" and "have-nots." Americans are both increasingly thin and increasingly overweight, obsessive exercisers or sedentary couch potatoes, eating tofu and organic raw vegetables or Big Macs and supersized fried foods. This growing divide reflects different class and racial cultures, but it also is deeply gendered.

CHANGING THE BODY

Virtually all of us spend some time and energy in some forms of bodily beautification, by wearing fashionable clothes and jewelry, for example. But until recently, only a few marginalized "out-groups," like motorcycle gangs, practiced any forms of permanent bodily transformation—running the gamut from simply piercing ears to piercing other body parts, getting tattoos, having cosmetic surgery, and even undergoing sex-change operations. Today, body piercing involves far more than the earlobes and can include the tongue, eyebrows, navel, nose, lips, nipples, and even the genitals. Increasing numbers of young people are also getting tattoos. Given their vaguely transgressive character in American society, tattoos and piercing denote a slight sexualized undertone—if only because they indicate that the bearer is aware of his or her body as an object of pleasure or desire.

About 45 million Americans—about 21 percent—have at least one tattoo, described by one psychiatrist as a "bumper sticker of the soul." And more than a third (36 percent) of Americans aged eighteen to twenty-five has one. And while gay men, lesbians, and bisexuals are more likely to have tattoos than heterosexuals, males and females are about evenly split.

Design and placement are highly sexually charged; we believe they say something about ourselves and our sexuality. Among Americans with tattoos, 31 percent said having a tattoo has made them feel sexier. Interestingly, more tattooed females (42 percent) feel this way than males (25 percent). Additionally, those with tattoos said that having a tattoo has made them feel more rebellious (25 percent), while others said a tattoo makes them feel more attractive (21 percent). The most recent fiftieth anniversary Barbie is—you guessed it—"Totally Stylin' Tattoos Barbie."[23]

Barbie's tattoos are removable; most are not, however, except with laser surgery. Although 86 percent of people do not regret getting tattoos, one 2006 survey of people seeking removal found that 44 percent of participants said they had chosen to have a tattoo to feel unique, 33 percent said to feel independent, and 28 percent said to make life experiences stand out. This stands in contrast to a 1996 study in which motivations for a tattoo were "to be part of a group," because a person "just wanted one," "sheer stupidity," and "love." Researchers of the 2008 study concluded that, unlike the 1996 study, "While the vast majority of individuals who are tattooed are pleased with their skin markings, the popularity and prevalence of tattoos often mean that dermatologists are increasingly hearing stories of regrets and requests for tattoo removal."[24]

Recently, though, laser surgeons report that women are having their tattoos removed because of "social stigma." In one recent survey, 93 percent of women seeking removal of their tattoo said that having to hide the tattoos on occasion was a factor in the removal, compared with only 20 percent of men. About 40 percent of women endured negative comments at work, in public, or in school, compared with 5 percent of men. "Societal support for women with tattoos may not be as strong as for men," said the authors of the study.[25]

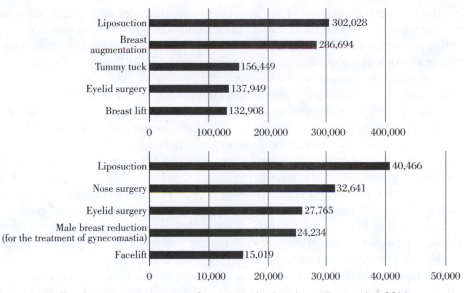

Figure 13.2. Top five cosmetic surgeries for women (top) and men (bottom) in 2014.

Source: The American Society for Aesthetic Plastic Surgery 2014 Cosmetic Surgery Statistics.

One of the fastest-growing methods of bodily transformation is cosmetic surgery (figure 13.2). According to one study by the American Society of Plastic and Reconstructive Surgeons, the total number of cosmetic procedures increased from 413,208 in 1992 to 15.1 million in 2013. And the most common procedures increased by almost 500 percent. In 2013, cosmetic surgeons performed over 290,000 **breast augmentations** (breast implants), but only 23,770 implant removals for women and 22,939 reductions for men.[26] In addition to breast augmentation and reduction, these included 199,817 liposuctions (compared with 47,212 in 1992) and 215,641 eyelid surgeries (59,461 in 1992).[27]

OH? REALLY.

No one is more preoccupied with body image than Americans.

While it often seems impossible to imagine a more beauty-obsessed culture than the United States, when it comes to cosmetic surgery, we're only number six. The number one slot belongs to South Korea—by a lot. It's estimated that between one-fifth and one-third of women in Seoul have had some cosmetic surgery; the BBC believes that the number is closer to 50 percent for women in their twenties. "We want to have surgeries while we are young so we can have our new faces for a long time," explained one college student to a journalist. While eyelid surgery remains by far the most popular (blepharoplasty, the insertion of a crease into the top of the eyelid to make them appear more "Western"), nose jobs and chin-thinning techniques are popular gifts for girls' high school graduation.

Source: Patricia Marx, "About Face" in *New Yorker,* March 23, 2015, pp. 50, 51.

Though women continue to be the primary consumers of such cosmetic surgery, male patients have gone from 54,845 in 1992 to 204,359 in 2007 and now make up more than 13 percent of all surgical procedures. "More men are viewing cosmetic surgery as a viable way of looking and feeling younger," observed ASPRS President Dennis Lynch, MD, "especially to compete in the workplace."

This comment raises what may be most interesting from our gender perspective: not which gender is *having* the surgery, but rather which gender is the one *for whom* the surgery is being performed. It may be that, as one writer explains, "the traditional image of women as sexual objects has simply expanded: everyone has become an object to be seen." The question remains: Seen by whom? Whom do we imagine seeing us in our newly reconstructed state?[28]

For women, the answer is usually men. Women's beauty—thinness, breast size, attractiveness—is valuable currency in the sexual marketplace, and given gender inequality, women have traded on their physical appearance to attract a mate. (Ironically, in one study, virtually all the male partners of women having plastic surgery thought the procedure was unnecessary.)[29]

For men, though, the answer is men. Men also are the object of the "male gaze" and feel a need to look big, strong, and virile in front of other men. Take one extreme example of this—**penile enlargement surgery**. This is a dramatic (and expensive) procedure—every year about fifteen thousand men pay about $6,000 to have it done— by which the penis can be lengthened by about two inches. (The average flaccid penis is about 3.5 inches long; erect it's about 5.1 inches long.) In one of the few studies that relies on data and not anecdotal evidence and thrilled testimonials, psychologist Randy Klein found that the average penile length before surgery was 2.6 inches (flaccid) and 5.4 inches (erect); after surgery, penile length was 3.8 inches (flaccid) and 5.7 inches (erect). That is, the only significant difference in length was when the penis was flaccid.[30]

One would think that men engage in this painful procedure to be "better" lovers or to please women more, and indeed many men say that is part of their motivation. But in many cases it has far less to do with women's potential pleasure than men's visual perception. Men who have this procedure more often experience what one physician called "locker room syndrome"—the fear of being judged as inadequately masculine *by other men*. Take, for example, the testimonial letter from a satisfied customer:

> I was always afraid to get into situations where I would have to shower with other men or be seen by anyone. I can remember avoiding many of the sports and activities I loved dearly, all because I was afraid that I would be seen and made fun of . . . I even avoided wearing shorts and tight clothes because of my fear that others would notice me.

"The thing I missed most was the changing room camaraderie and male bonding associated with these sports which was always something I enjoyed," writes another. "I felt ashamed to even go to the urinals in a public place and have made sure I never use these whilst other men are there too."[31]

Women, too, seem to undergo **genital "reconstruction" surgery** to please men. Plastic surgery can tighten the labia, the vaginal walls, or the skin around the vagina—all

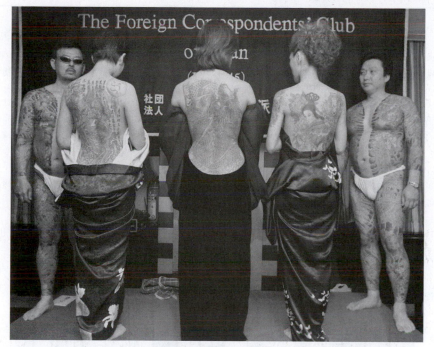

Figure 13.3. Models show off their tattoos.

Source: Kazuhiro Nogi/AFP/Getty Images.

in the name of looking like a nubile twenty-something centerfold. And plastic surgery can also physically reshape women so that they "appear" to be as virginal as those models as well. Hymenoplasty—the surgical reconstruction of the hymen, which is usually broken during first intercourse—was once used by panic-stricken parents of "deflowered" Muslim, Asian, or Latina girls whose value in the marriage market had suddenly plummeted to zero. Now it's increasingly popular among young women who want to keep their earlier sexual experience a secret and who want their new boyfriend to have the "thrill" of being their "first," or even among Christian women who violated the abstinence pledge. "You wouldn't want your boyfriend/future husband to feel ashamed because your hymen no longer existed" is the way Revirgination.net put it in their web-based advertising. "It's the ultimate gift for the man who has everything," says Jeannette Yarborough, a forty-year-old medical assistant from San Antonio.[32]

One Los Angeles plastic surgeon offers "laser vaginal rejuvenation" that will "completely re-sculpt and rejuvenate the vagina with a 1 hour laser procedure"; he promises "enhancement of sexual gratification."[33] Just whose sexual gratification might be enhanced by lasering the labia is not difficult to guess.

Nowhere is gender inequality better observed than in the motivations of both women and men in changing their bodies. It is the male gaze—whether of a potential sexual partner, a potential sexual rival, or a competitor in the marketplace or athletic field—that motivates such drastic measures, among both women and men.

Gender, Race, and Beauty

Standards of beauty may be culturally specific, but they also cross national borders. In Asia, for example, there is a steadily growing demand for eyelid surgery, to implant a second fold in the eyelid to make the eyes look more Western. It is also the most common cosmetic surgical procedure for Asian Americans (figure 13.4).

In recent years, Chinese women have also been undergoing a far more dramatic cosmetic surgical procedure: leg lengthening. The influence of very tall, leggy supermodels has led many Chinese women to undergo this painful procedure. The legs are broken and steel pins are pushed into the tibia. The legs are attached to an external brace that stretches them up to four inches over several months. (The patient turns the screws each day to increase the stretch. See figure 13.5.)

Source: Jonathan Watts, "China's Cosmetic Surgery Craze" in *Lancet*, 363, March 20, 2004, p. 958.

Figure 13.4. *Source:* Reuters/Nir Elias.

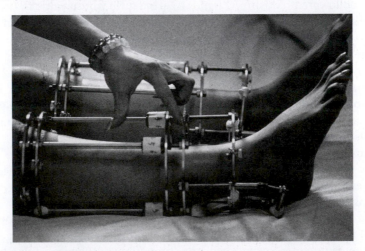

Figure 13.5. *Source:* AP Photo/Elizabeth Dalziel.

SEXUALITY

Nowhere in our intimate lives is there greater expression of gender difference than in our sexual relationships. Yet even here, as we shall see, there are signs of change and convergence. As friendship and love have become "feminized"—that is, as the model of appropriate behavior has come to resemble what we labeled as traditionally "feminine" models of intimacy—sexuality has become increasingly "masculinized." The "masculinization of sex"—including the pursuit of pleasure for its own sake, the increased attention to orgasm, the multiplication of sexual partners, the universal interest in sexual experimentation, and the separation of sexual behavior from love—is partly a result of the technological transformation of sexuality (from birth control to the Internet) and partly a result of the **sexual revolution**'s promise of greater sexual freedom with fewer emotional and physical consequences. In many respects, male and female sexuality are similar—and becoming more similar all the time. There are virtually no differences between males and females in the timing of their first sexual experience: The average age of first intercourse for both males and females is seventeen years old.

But not only are behaviors converging, but so too are motivations: Males and females seem to be having sex for similar reasons—adventure, pleasure, emotional expression. But the *interpretation* of that similar behavior for similar reasons by the wider society remains remarkably wedded to the sexual double standard, which remains in place—perhaps a bit less stable now, true, but still in place.

In fact, the sexual revolution was a rejection of both general social prudishness—social discomfort with and disapproval of sex in the first place—and the sexual double

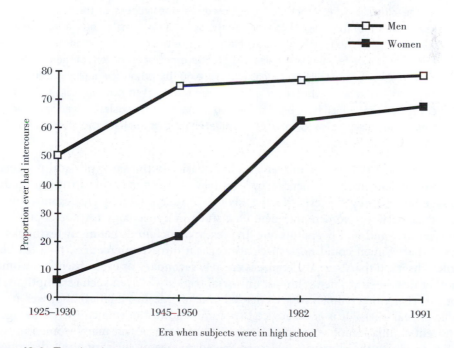

Figure 13.6. Trends in heterosexual experience among teens.

Source: From Pepper Schwartz and Virginia Rutter, *The Gender of Sexuality: Sexual Possibilities* (Altamira Press, 1998), p. 165. Republished with permission of Altamira Press; permission conveyed through Copyright Clearance Center, Inc.

standard that prescribed different sexual behaviors for women and men. That double standard was, after all, merely the nineteenth-century version of the interplanetary theory of gender. According to writers of the time, women and men were different species. As the celebrated French historian Jules Michelet put it in 1881:

> [Woman] does nothing as we [men] do. She thinks, speaks, and acts differently. Her tastes are different from our tastes. Her blood even does not flow in her veins as ours does, at times it rushes through them like a foaming mountain torrent . . . She does not eat like us—neither as much nor of the same dishes. Why? Chiefly, because she does not digest as we do. Her digestion is every moment troubled with one thing: She yearns with her very bowels. The deep cup of love (which is called the pelvis) is a sea of varying emotions, hindering the regularity of the nutritive function.[34]

Sex was invariably seen as bad for women—unhealthy and immoral—whereas it was tolerated or even encouraged for men. "The majority of women (happily for them) are not much troubled with sexual feelings of any kind," wrote one physician (obviously male) in the 1890s.[35]

Even when Alfred Kinsey undertook his pioneering studies of sexual behavior in the decade after World War II, this double standard was still firmly in place. As he wrote in 1953:

> We have not understood how nearly alike females and males may be in their **sexual responses**, and the extent to which they may differ. We have perpetuated the age-old traditions concerning the slower responsiveness of the female, the greater extent of the erogenous areas on the body of the female, the earlier sexual development of the female, the idea that there are basic differences in the nature of orgasm among females and males, the greater emotional content of the female's sexual response, and still other ideas which are not based on scientifically accumulated data—and all of which now appear to be incorrect. It now appears that the very techniques which have been suggested in marriage manuals, both ancient and modern, have given rise to some of the differences that we have thought inherent in females and males.[36]

Kinsey believed that males and females have basically the same physical responses, though men are more influenced by psychological factors. Note in the preceding passage how Kinsey suggests that the advice of experts actually *creates* much of the difference between women and men. One study of gynecology textbooks published between 1943 and 1972 bears this out. The researchers found that many textbooks asserted that women could not experience orgasm during intercourse. One textbook writer observed that "sexual pleasure is entirely secondary or even absent" in women; another described women's "almost universal frigidity." Given such assumptions, it's not surprising that women were counseled to fake orgasms; after all, they weren't capable of real ones. "It is good advice to recommend to the women the advantage of innocent simulation of sex responsiveness; as a matter of fact many women in their desire to please their husbands learned the advantage of such innocent deception," was the way one text counseled gynecologists to raise the issue with their patients.[37]

READ ALL ABOUT IT!

Even if women and men are not from different planets, there are some significant differences between us as we approach each other in adolescent sexual relationships. Even the ideologies of masculinity and femininity themselves serve as a touchstone for young men and women as they begin to navigate heterosexual attractions and activities. Psychologist Deborah Tolman and her colleagues found that the ideology of interplanetary gender is not the cause of adolescent male and female experiences in heterosexual couplings as much as it is the consequence. We learn to be sexual as we confirm that interplanetary theory; it comes to feel natural and right. But, Tolman and her colleagues insist, it needn't be this way, and a feminist critique of these first forays also challenges notions that sexual coercion is a "normal" part of the male psyche.

The double standard persists today—perhaps less in what we actually do and more in the way we think. Men still stand to gain status and women to lose status from sexual experience: He's a stud who scores; she's a slut who "gives it up." Boys are taught to try to get sex; girls are taught strategies to foil the boys' attempts. "The whole game was to get a girl to give out," one man told sociologist Lillian Rubin. "You expected her to resist; she had to if she wasn't going to ruin her reputation. But you kept pushing. Part of it was the thrill of touching and being touched, but I've got to admit, part of it was the conquest, too, and what you'd tell the guys at school the next day." "I felt as if I should want to get it as often as possible," recalled another. "I guess that's because if you're a guy, you're supposed to want it." "Women need a reason to have sex," commented comedian Billy Crystal. "Men just need a place."[38]

The **sexual double standard** is much more than a case of separate-but-equal sexual scripting, much more than a case of one sexuality for Martians and another for Venusians. The sexual double standard is itself a product of gender inequality, of sexism—the unequal distribution of power in our society based on gender. Gender inequality is reinforced by the ways we have come to assume that men are more sexual than women, that men will always try to escalate sexual encounters to prove their manhood, and that either women—or, rather, "ladies"—do not have strong sexual feelings or those they do have must be constantly controlled lest they fall into disrepute. With such a view, sex becomes a contest, not a means of connection; when sexual pleasure happens, it's often seen as his victory over her resistance. Sexuality becomes, in the words of feminist lawyer Catharine MacKinnon, "the linchpin of gender inequality."[39]

Women are raised to believe that to be sexually active or "promiscuous" is to transgress the rules of femininity. These rules are enforced not just by men, of course, but also by other women and institutionalized in church, state, and school. The pursuit of sex transforms good girls into bad girls, so most women accept the cultural standard of sexual minimalism—few partners, fewer positions, less pleasure, less sex without emotional commitment. Such an ideology keeps a woman waiting for her Prince Charming to liberate her, to arouse her with his tender kisses, and to release the passion smoldering beneath her cooler surface.[40]

The sexual double standard is far more rigidly enforced than any ideological difference in men's and women's patterns of friendship and love. As a result, we are far more likely to observe significant gender differences in sexuality. Examples of these different scripts abound—in what we think about, what we want, and what we actually do. For example, consider what "counts" as sex. When they say the word "sex," women and men often mean different things. In one study, monogamous heterosexual couples in their mid-forties were asked, "How many times did you make love last week?" Consistently, the researchers found, the men reported slightly higher numbers than the women. What could this indicate—better memories? Masculine braggadocio? Clandestine affairs? Solitary pleasures? When the researchers asked more questions, they found the difference was the result of women and men counting different experiences as "making love." The women would count one sexual encounter once, whereas the men tallied up the number of their orgasms. Thus, whereas a woman might say, "Hmm, we made love three times last week," her husband might say, "Hmm, let me see, we did it three times, but one of those times we did it twice [meaning that he had two orgasms], so I guess the answer is four."

The differences in counting criteria reveal deeper differences in the understanding of sexual expression. Women's understanding that sex equals the entire encounter gives women a somewhat broader range of sexual activities that count as sex. Men's focus on orgasm as the defining feature of sex parallels men's tendency to exclude all acts except intercourse from "having sex." Oral and manual stimulation are seen as "foreplay" for men, as "sex" for women. Men cannot tally the encounter on their mental scorecard unless intercourse also occurs. This often results in complex rules about what constitutes a "technical virgin." (The public seminar on what counts as "sexual relations" in the impeachment trial of President Clinton in the late 1990s bears this out. Because he and Monica Lewinsky did not have sexual intercourse and instead did what girls in my high school used to call "everything but," Clinton argued that he did not lie when he denied having sex with Lewinsky. In his mind, as one of my pals in the locker room explained it to me, "it only counts if you put it in." And some recent medical evidence bears this out; a recent article in the *Journal of the American Medical Association* reported that only intercourse "counted" as sex.)[41]

Intercourse and orgasm are more important forms of sexual expression for men than they are for women. This leads to a greater emphasis on the genitals as the single most important erogenous zone for men. If men's sexuality is "phallocentric"— revolving around the glorification and gratification of the penis—then it is not surprising that men often develop elaborate relationships with their genitals. Some men name their penis—"Willie," "John Thomas," or "Peter"—or give them cute nicknames taken from mass-produced goods like "Whopper" and "Big Mac." Men may come to believe that their penises have little personalities (or, perhaps, what feel like big personalities), threatening to refuse to behave the way they are supposed to behave. If men do not personify the penis, they objectify it; if it is not a little person, then it is supposed to act like a machine, an instrument, a "tool." A man projects "the coldness and hardness of metal" onto his flesh, writes the French philosopher Emmanuel Reynaud.[42]

Few women name their genitals; fewer still think of their genitals as machines. Can you imagine if they called their clitoris "Shirley" or their labia "Sally Ann"? In fact,

OH? REALLY ● Everybody knows that men think about sex more often than do women.

There's some evidence for this. When asked how often they think about sex, 54 percent of men and 19 percent of women said "very frequently"—but no one measured exactly how much "very frequently" means. Once an hour? Every ten minutes? Every five seconds? Some crazed pundits estimate that men think about sex eight thousand times in a typical sixteen-hour waking day.

When the amount was quantified, the gender gap largely disappeared. Men's nineteen thoughts about sex per day barely beat out thoughts about food, which reached eighteen. Most women, on the other hand, reported ten thoughts per day about sex and fifteen about food. Men and women thought about sleep eleven and eight times per day, respectively.

The study suggests men do think about sex more than women, but less than expected. "Males did think more about sex but they also thought more about food and sleep," said the author. "It's not clear whether they're just more focused on need-related states than females or whether they simply recall thoughts more often or are more willing to report them."

Source: Terri D. Fisher, Zachary T. Moore, and Mary-Jo Pittenger, "Sex on the Brain? An Examination of Frequency of Sexual Cognitions as a Function of Gender, Erotophilia, and Social Desirability" in *Journal of Sex Roles,* 49(1), 2012, pp. 69–77, available at http://www.ncbi.nlm.nih.gov/pubmed/21512948.

women rarely refer to their genitals by their proper names at all, generally describing vulva, labia, and clitoris with the generic "vagina" or even the more euphemistic "down there" or "private parts." And it would be rare indeed to see a woman having a conversation with her labia.[43] So when they think about sex, men and women are often thinking about different things.

Forty years earlier, Alfred Kinsey and his colleagues had found that 89 percent of men who masturbated fantasized, whereas only 64 percent of women did. And what men and women "use" for their fantasies differs. Today, nearly one-fourth (23 percent of men and 11 percent of women) use X-rated movies or videos; 16 percent of men and 4 percent of women use sexually explicit books or magazines.[44] And what they fantasize about differs dramatically. A research assistant and I have collected over one thousand sexual fantasies from students over the past decade. In those fantasies, definite gender patterns emerge. Men tend to fantasize about strangers, often more than one at a time, doing a variety of well-scripted sexual acts; women tend to fantasize about setting the right mood for lovemaking with their boyfriend or husband but rarely visualize specific behaviors. Consider, for example, these "typical" scenes, composites of fantasies we've collected. The following were reported by women:

> My boyfriend and I are on a deserted island. The palm trees flap in the soft breeze, the sand glistens. The sun is warm and we swim for a while in the cool blue water and then come back to the beach and lie there. We rub suntan oil on each other's bodies, and soon we are kissing passionately. Then we make love in the sand.

> My husband and I are at a ski resort, in a cabin and it's late at night. It's snowing outside, so we build a fire in the fireplace and lie down on the fur rug in front of it. We sip champagne by the roaring fire, and then he kisses me and takes my blouse off. Then we make love.

Compare them with this one, a composite of a typical man's fantasy:

> I'm walking down the street and these two unbelievably gorgeous blondes are walking towards me. Our eyes meet and we realize we have to have each other. One of them kneels in front of me and unzips my fly and begins to give me the best blow job I've ever had. The other pulls down her shorts and begins to play with herself. Then I do her while the first one gets eaten out by the one I'm fucking. We do it every way we can imagine, and then they get it on while I'm resting, but watching them turns me on, so we start up again. Then we all get up and walk away with these big smiles on our faces. We never see one another again.[45]

READ ALL ABOUT IT!

Heterosexual behavior may be a compromise between "his" sexuality and "hers." Each side feels like they compromise a little and achieve some sort of balance in the middle. Is this true? And if so, what do women and men "really" want their sexual behaviors to look like? Working with one of my colleagues, Rebecca Plante, we asked young women and men about their sexual fantasies, thinking that the realm of fantasy was a realm without compromise, a world in which you could have everything in just the way you like it. After analyzing college students' sexual fantasies, we saw two significant trends, which we discuss in "The Gender of Desire." First, we found that when we started the research, men and women had very different sexual fantasies: Hers were saturated with romance and emotional closeness with someone she loved, and his were explicitly detailed sexual acrobatics with strangers selected for certain physical characteristics. Second, we began to notice over time that women's fantasies began to change, and the direction of that change was increasingly toward the fantasies that men had. Men's fantasies didn't change at all. This "masculinization" of sexual fantasies was not universal, but it took up a greater and greater share of women's fantasies. Why do you think that is?

Men's fantasies are idealized renditions of masculine sexual scripts: genitally focused, orgasm centered, and explicit in the spatial and temporal sequencing of sexual behaviors. We know exactly who does what to whom in what precise order. Physical characteristics of the other participants are invariably highly detailed; these participants are most often strangers (or famous models or actresses) chosen for their physical attributes. Rarely do these fantasies include the physical setting for the encounter. Women's fantasies, on the other hand, are replete with descriptions that set the scene—geographic and temporal settings, with elaborate placement of props like candles, rugs, and wine glasses. They often involve present or past partners. Explicitly sexual description is minimal and usually involves vague references to lovemaking. One-third of women fantasize about meeting for a sexual rendezvous at the Eiffel Tower; about a third of men think about the White House.

Thus we might say that women's *sexual* imaginations are impoverished at the expense of highly developed *sensual* imaginations; by contrast, men's sensual imaginations are impoverished by their highly developed sexual imaginations. (These differences hold for both heterosexual and homosexual women and men, a further indication that the basic component in our sexual scripts is gender, not sexual orientation.) Although there has been some evidence of shifts in women's fantasies toward more sexually explicit scenes and increasing comfort with explicit language, these fantasies do reveal both what we think and what we think we are supposed to think about when we think about sex.[46]

Where do these dramatically different mental landscapes come from? One place, of course, is sexual representation. Pornography occupies a special place in the development of men's sexuality. Nearly all men confess to having some exposure to pornography, at least as adolescents; indeed, for many men the first naked women they see are in pornographic magazines. And pornography has been the site of significant political protest—from an erotophobic right wing that considers pornography to be as degrading to human dignity as birth control information, homosexuality, and abortion to radical feminist campaigns that see pornography as a vicious expression of misogyny, on a par with rape, spouse abuse, and genital mutilation.

Whereas the right wing's efforts rehearsed America's discomfort with all things sexual, the radical feminist critique of pornography transformed the political debate, arguing that when men look at pornographic images of naked women, they are actually participating in a culture-wide hatred of and contempt for women. Pornographic images are about the subordination of women; pornography "makes sexism sexy," in the words of one activist. These are not fictional representations of fantasy; these are documentaries of rape and torture, performed for men's sexual arousal. Here is one pornographic director and actor, commenting on his "craft":

> My whole reason for being in the [pornography] Industry is to satisfy the desire of the men in the world who basically don't much care for women and want to see the men in my Industry getting even with the women they couldn't have when they were growing up . . . So when we come on a woman's face or somewhat brutalize her sexually, we're getting even for their lost dreams. I believe this. I've heard audiences cheer me when I do something foul on screen. When I've strangled a person or sodomized a person or brutalized a person, the audience is cheering my action, and then when I've fulfilled my warped desire, the audience applauds.[47]

The claims of **antipornography feminists**—that pornography causes rape or that it numbs us to the real effect of real violence in women's lives—have been difficult to demonstrate empirically. Few studies have shown such an empirical relationship, though several have documented some modest changes in men's attitudes immediately after exposure to violent pornography. (These changes tend to dissipate in the weeks after exposure.) Yet whether or not there is *any* empirical evidence that pornography alone causes rape or violence, there remains the shocking difference between us: On any given day in the United States, there are men masturbating to images of women enduring sexual torture, genital mutilation, rape, and violence. Surely, this points to a dramatic difference between women's and men's sexualities—one can hardly imagine many women masturbating to reenactments of Lorena Bobbitt's ministrations to her husband. Violence is rarely sexualized for women; that such images can be such a routine and casual turn-on for many men should at least give us pause.[48]

Given men's and women's different sexual mentalities, it's not surprising that we develop different sexualities, as evidenced in our attitudes and behaviors. For one thing, women's inclusion of their boyfriend or husband in their fantasies indicates that women's sexuality often requires an emotional connection to be fully activated. "For sex to really work for me, I need to feel an emotional *something*," one woman told Lillian Rubin. "Without that, it's just another athletic activity, only not as satisfying, because when I swim or run, I feel good afterward." Women's first sexual experiences are more likely to occur in the context of a committed relationship.[49]

Because women tend to connect sex and emotion, it makes sense that they would be less interested in one-night stands and in affairs and nonmonogamy. In one survey, women were about 20 percent more likely to agree that one-night stands are degrading (47 percent of the men agreed, 68 percent of the women agreed). Men are more likely to be unfaithful to their spouse, though that gender gap has closed considerably in the past two decades. And, of course, the separation of sex and emotion means that men are more likely to have had more sexual partners than women. In figure 13.6, one can see these differences and also observe how this gender gap has also been narrowing over the past few decades.[50]

Men's wider sexual repertoire usually includes desiring oral sex, about which women report being far less enthusiastic. As one woman explained:

> I like going down on him. It makes him feel good, truly good. I don't find it unpleasant. I don't say I wish I could do it all the time. I don't equate it with a sale at Bloomingdale's. That I could do all the time. But it's not like going to the dentist either. It's between two extremes. Closer to Bloomingdale's than to the dentist.[51]

OH? REALLY ●

Men are more likely to be unfaithful to their spouse. According to evolutionary psychologists, men's evolutionary imperative propels men to attempt to spread their seed far and wide, while psychologists often argue that differential socialization leaves men far better able to separate love and sex.

Actually, the most recent study found only modest differences in infidelity between women and men: 32 percent to 19 percent, respectively.

The actual differences aren't in the rate, but in the motivation. For men, predictors of infidelity tended to be personality variables, including propensity for sexual excitation (becoming easily aroused by many triggers and situations) and concern about sexual performance failure. (This latter finding might seem counterintuitive, but other studies confirm this. "People might seek out high-risk situations to help them become aroused, or they might choose to have sex with a partner outside of their regular relationship because they feel they have an 'out' if the encounter doesn't go well—they don't have to see them again," says the study's author.)

For women, it's far less about their personality and far more a comment on their relationship. Women who are dissatisfied with their relationship are more than twice as likely to cheat; those who feel they are sexually incompatible with their partners are nearly three times as likely.

Source: Kristen P. Mark, Erick Janssen, and Robin R. Milhausen, "Infidelity in Heterosexual Couples: Demographic, Interpersonal, and Personality-Related Predictors of Extradyadic Sex" in *Archives of Sexual Behavior*, (40)2011, 971–982..

But perhaps this has less to do with the intrinsic meaning of the act and more to do with the gender of the actor. For example, when men describe their experiences with oral sex, it is nearly always from the position of power. Whether **fellatio**—"I feel so powerful when I see her kneeling in front of me"—or **cunnilingus**—"being able to get her off with my tongue makes me feel so powerful"—men experience the giving and receiving of oral sex as an expression of their power. By contrast, many women perceive both giving and receiving oral sex from the position of powerlessness—not necessarily because they are forced to do so, but rather because "it makes him happy" for them to either do it or to let him do it. So oral sex, like intercourse, allows him to feel "like a man," regardless of who does what to whom.

GENDERED SEXUAL SOCIALIZATION

Where does the sexual gender gap come from? Though we are constantly bombarded with sexual images in the media and receive lessons about sexual morality from our parents, our teachers, and our religious institutions, most of our sexual learning comes during adolescence, and most of our adolescent **sexual socialization** is provided by our peers. We teach ourselves and each other about what feels good and why, and then we practice performing those activities until they feel the way we're told they're supposed to feel.

Remember, for example, those junior high school "wrestling matches"—two adolescents trying to negotiate, usually without words, the extent of their sexual contact. Both the boy and the girl have goals, though the goals may be very different. "His" goal, of course, is to score—and toward that end he has a variety of maneuvers, arguments, and other strategies his friends have taught him. "Her" goal may be pleasure, but it is also to preserve and protect her reputation as a "good girl," which requires that she be seen as alluring but not "easy." "Young men come to sex with quite different expectations and desires than do young women," the NORC sex survey declared. "Young women often go along with intercourse the first time, finding little physical pleasure in it, and a substantial number report being forced to have intercourse."[52]

Let's follow one typical adolescent boy and girl as they negotiate their competing desires. If they have been dating for a while, he may decide it's time to escalate the sexual relationship, to move from kissing (first base) to touching her breast (second base). It is nearly universally "his" job to escalate and "her" job to decide if she will let him. So he moves his hand toward her breast, on top of her blouse. She lets him.

Is our hero now thinking, "Mmmm. This feels good. Her breast is so soft and warm. I think I'll keep my hand here for a while"? Unlikely. If he's typical, he's already strategizing how to get underneath her blouse. And she's thinking—what? "Mmmm. This feels good. I like this better than when that other guy tried this a few weeks ago." More likely she is thinking, "I know he's going to try to get underneath my blouse now. Do I want him to? How do I stop him without hurting his feelings?"

Each time he escalates, he barely has time to enjoy it before developing his strategy to get to the next stage. And each time, she has to decide whether and how to prevent him from doing so. Rarely is either of them fully experiencing the thrill and pleasure of exploring the other's body. Both are actually far ahead, in the future, plotting their next move. Much of our adolescent sexual socialization emphasizes the future over the present; it often takes place as much in the future tense as the present tense.

If they are not in the same "time zone," you'd think, at least, that they'd be on the same planet. (Of course, they might each be on Mars and Venus anyway!) But, even here, their attention is divided. He may be thinking, "Wow, I got to third base! I can't wait to tell the other guys!" whereas she is thinking, "Oh, my God, I let him go too far. I hope none of my friends finds out!" So he promises not to tell anyone (even though that may be a lie) in return for her allowing him to go a bit further. Spatially, too, they are in different places—each with same-sex peers, enhancing and preserving their reputations. As one feminist researcher put it, "Although their sexual interest is focused on the opposite sex, it is primarily to their same-sex peers that adolescents will look for validation of their sexual attitudes and accomplishments." Given this spatial and temporal separation—both in the future and with their same-sex peers—it's a wonder that pleasure and intimacy happen at all![53]

This dynamic helps to explain why there seems to be so much pressure on adolescents and why there are so many breakdowns in communication, including boys attempting to go further than girls want them to. That young boys and young girls have sexual experiences for reasons other than intimacy and pleasure has been a truism in sex research. Psychologist Charlene Muehlenhard, for example, has been studying adolescents' sexual encounters for more than a decade. She found that more men (57.4 percent) than women (38.7 percent) reported that they had engaged in unwanted sexual intercourse due to being enticed—that is, the other person made an advance that the person had difficulty refusing. More men (33.5 percent) than women (11.9 percent) had unwanted sexual intercourse because they wanted to get sexual experience, wanted something to talk about, or wanted to build up their confidence. And more men (18.4 percent) than women (4.5 percent) said they engaged in sexual intercourse because they did not want to appear to be homosexual, shy, afraid, or unmasculine or unfeminine. Peer pressure was a factor for 10.9 percent of the men but only 0.6 percent of the women.[54]

By the time we get to be adults, this socialized distance between women and men can ossify into the different experiences we are said to have. Each gender is seeking to express different feelings, for different reasons, with different repertoires, and so it may appear that we are originally from different planets. On an episode of *Friends*, the tactless Phoebe is making small talk with her new boyfriend's mother and mentions that "he is the most gentle lover I've ever had." His mother looks aghast at this inappropriate revelation, but Phoebe misunderstands the woman's shock and reassures her. "Oh—I don't mean in a sissy way. Believe me, when he gets going, he's all man!" In the British film *Sammy and Rosie Get Laid*, a lesbian character suggests that heterosexuals are to be pitied. "The women spend all their time trying to come, and they're unsuccessful, and the men spend all their time trying not to come, and they're unsuccessful also."

She has a point. Because many men believe that adequate sexual functioning is being able to delay ejaculation, some develop strategies to prevent what they consider to be premature ejaculation—strategies that exaggerate emotional distancing, phallocentrism, the focus on orgasm, and objectification. Here's how Woody Allen put it in a stand-up comedy routine from the mid-1960s. After describing himself as a "stud," Allen says:

> When making love, in an effort to [pause] to prolong [pause] the moment of ecstasy, I think of baseball players. All right, now you know. So the two of us are making love violently, and she's digging it, so I figure I'd better start thinking of

OH? REALLY.

The best sex is when you both experience simultaneous orgasm.

While there is no biological reason why simultaneous orgasm would be more pleasurable, most of us understand it as an elusive quarry, sort of like seeing Bigfoot.

Actually, come to think of it, nearly half of respondents (46 percent) in a recent survey believed that they were *more* likely to see Bigfoot than to "finish" at the same time.

On the other hand, just over one in ten Americans under twenty-five said that they would read a text message while having sex.

Source: http://www.marketwatch.com/story/durex-survey-reveals-what-americans-really-want-in-the-bedroom-2012-04-30 and *Harper's Index,* September, 2010, p. II.

baseball players pretty quickly. So I figure it's one out, and the Giants are up. Mays lines a single to right. He takes second on a wild pitch. Now she's digging her nails into my neck. I decide to pinch-hit for McCovey. [pause for laughter] Alou pops out. Haller singles, Mays takes third. Now I've got a first and third situation. Two outs and the Giants are behind one run. I don't know whether to squeeze or to steal. [pause for laughter] She's been in the shower for ten minutes already. [pause] I can't tell you anymore, this is too personal. [pause] The Giants won.

Readers may be struck by several things—the imputation of violence, how her pleasure leads to his decision to think of baseball players, the requirement of victory in the game, and the sexual innuendo contained in the sports language. The text also supplies a startling revelation of male sexual distancing. Here's a device that is so successful at delaying ejaculation (or any sexual connection) that the narrator is rendered utterly unaware of his partner's experience. "She's been in the shower for ten minutes already," Allen remarks, as if he's just noticed. Other men describe mentally scripting sports scenes, reciting multiplication tables, or, in the case of one of my students, a chemistry major, reciting, in order, the elements of the periodic table. No wonder women often wonder what men are thinking about during sex!

And that doesn't factor in the variety of creams and ointments that are advertised in the back of men's magazines, products men can apply to their penises before intercourse to enable them to delay ejaculation. Such products have been incorporated into new "endurance" condoms. But what are these creams and ointments that promise delayed ejaculation? Most use benzocaine, a mild anesthetic (similar to the novocaine your dentist uses). Is it possible that men experience themselves as better lovers when they feel *less* pleasure?[55]

When it goes "right," we clearly observe the gendered qualities of sex. Another illustration of the genderedness of sex comes from research on what happens when things go wrong. For example, when men seek therapeutic evaluation for sexual problems, they rarely describe not experiencing enough pleasure. One man who experienced premature ejaculation reported that he felt like he "isn't a real man" because he "can't satisfy a woman." Another, with erectile problems, told a therapist that "a real man never has to ask his wife for anything sexually" and that he "should be able to please her whenever he wants." Each of these men thus expressed a sexual problem in gender terms; each feared that his sexual problem damaged his masculinity, made him less of a real man. For them, sexuality was less about mutual pleasuring and more about hydraulic functioning. Is it any wonder that men use the language of the work-place (in addition to using metaphors from sports and war) to describe sexual experi-ences? We use the "tool" to "get the job done," which is, of course, to "achieve" orgasm, or else we experience "performance anxiety." Men with sexual problems are rarely gender nonconformists, unable or unwilling to follow the rules of masculine sexual adequacy. If anything, they are overconformists to norms that define sexual adequacy by the ability to function like a well-oiled machine.[56]

It's in this gendered context that we can also understand the enormous popularity of Viagra and other drugs that minister to men's sexual problems. Although most men who experience "**erectile dysfunction**" (the current term for what used to be called "impotence," a term that equates erections with power in the first place) also experience "morning erections"—which indicates that their problems are not physiological but rather psychological—Viagra and other drugs enable men to achieve and sustain erec-tions. Viagra was the most successful new drug ever launched in the United States; over thirty-five thousand prescriptions were filled within the first two weeks on the market. Many men crowed that they had found the "magic bullet," the fountain of sexual youth. "You just keep going all night," gushed one man. "The performance is unbelievable."[57]

Certainly believable, however, was how these men experienced the demands of male sexuality in mechanical terms and how relieved they were that the machine had been repaired. And no sooner did Viagra appear on the market than it was misunder-stood. Viagra enables erections when there is adequate sexual desire—that is, when the men want to have sex and are aroused. Viagra does not work as an aphrodisiac, creating the desire in the first place. And what therapists call "inhibited sexual desire," or "low sexual interest"—once, interestingly, called "frigidity" in women—is now the leading sexual problem among men. Unfortunately, medical knowledge has yet to find a pharmaceutical remedy for that.[58]

CLOSING THE SEXUAL GENDER GAP

Despite the persistence of gender differences in sexual attitudes and behaviors, the sexual gender gap has been closing in recent years, as women's and men's sexual ex-periences come to more closely resemble one another's. Or, rather, women's have come to resemble men's. As I argued earlier, our experience of love has been feminized, and our sexuality has been increasingly "masculinized." Whereas men's sexual behavior has hardly changed, women's sexual behavior has changed dramatically, moving increasingly closer to the behavior of men. (This change probably both thrills and terrifies men.)

Part of this transformation has been the result of the technological breakthroughs and ideological shifts that have come to be known as the "sexual revolution." Since the 1960s, the pursuit of sexual pleasure for its own sake has been increasingly avail-able to women, as adequate and relatively safe birth control and legal abortion have made it possible to separate fully sexual activity from reproduction. (Men, of course, always were able to pursue sexual pleasure for its own sake; thus, in this sense, women's sexuality has come to more closely resemble men's.) "I guess sex was originally to pro-duce another body; then I guess it was for love; nowadays it's just for feeling good," was the way one fifteen-year-old boy summed up the shift. In addition, widespread sex education has made people more sexually aware—but not necessarily more sexually active. In one recent review of fifty-three studies that examined the effects of sex education and HIV education on sexual activity, twenty-seven found no changes in rates of sexual activity, and twenty-two observed marked decreases, delayed onset of activity, and reduced number of sexual partners. Only three studies found any increase in sexual activity associated with sex education. It would appear that sex education enables people to make *better* sexual decisions and encourages more responsibility, not less.)[59]

Ideologically, feminism made the pursuit of sexual pleasure, the expression of women's sexual autonomy, a political goal. No longer would women believe that they were sexually disinterested, passive, and virtuous asexual angels. Women were as entitled to pleasure as men were. And, practically, they knew how to get it, after feminists exposed what one feminist called "the myth of the vaginal orgasm." Feminism was thus, in part, a political resistance to what we might call the "socialized asexuality" of feminine sexuality. "Part of my attraction to feminism involved the right to be a sexual person," recalls one woman. Another envisioned a feminism that "validates the right for a woman to say yes instead of no." In the past three decades, then, it's been women's sexuality that has been transformed, as women have sought to express their own **sexual agency**. Consider, for example, the transformation of the idea of sexual experience in the first place. Whereas it used to be that men were expected to have some sexual experience prior to marriage, many women and men placed a premium on women's virginity. Not anymore. As Lillian Rubin writes, "In the brief span of one generation—from the 1940s to the 1960s—we went from mothers who believed their virginity was their most prized possession to daughters for whom it was a burden." Virginity was no longer "a treasure to be safeguarded"; now, it was "a problem to be solved."[60]

Rates of and motivations for masturbation have also begun to converge. What, after all, is masturbation but self-pleasuring—surely an expression of sexual agency. One recent large-scale national sex survey found that men's and women's motivations for masturbation are roughly similar (figure 13.7). As are sexual attitudes. In the NORC sex survey, 36 percent of men and 53 percent of women born between 1933 and 1942 believed that premarital sex is almost always wrong. These numbers declined for both groups but declined far more sharply for women, so that for those born between 1963 and 1974, only 16 percent of men and 22 percent of women believed that premarital sex is almost always wrong.[61]

Sexual behaviors, too, have grown increasingly similar. Among teenage boys, sexual experience has remained virtually the same since the mid-1940s, with about 70 percent of all high school–aged boys having had sexual intercourse (the rates were about 50 percent for those who went to high school in the late 1920s). But the rates for high school girls have increased dramatically, up from 5 percent in the 1920s to 20 percent in the late 1940s, to 55 percent in 1982 and 60 percent in 1991. There has been a bit of a decline since the 1990s. About one in five teenagers has had sex before age fifteen.[62] And the age of first intercourse has steadily declined for both boys and girls. Similarly, although the rates of teenage virgins have declined for both girls and boys, they have declined more rapidly for girls. The number of teenagers who have had more than five different sexual partners by their eighteenth birthday has increased for both sexes; the rate of increase is greater for girls as well.[63]

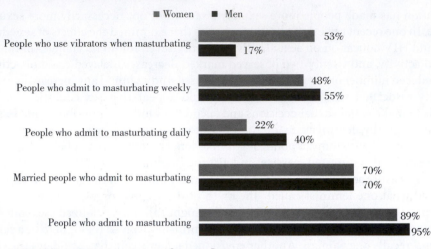

Figure 13.7. Masturbation statistics—Statistic Brain.

Source: 2014 Statistic Brain Research Institute, publishing as Statistic Brain. 7/7/2014. http://www.statisticbrain.com/masturbation-statistics/.

JUST SAYING NO

Just as adolescents' sexual experiences are becoming more similar, more "masculinized," a backlash political campaign has also been underway to stop adolescent sex in its tracks. Abstinence campaigns encourage young people to "just say no" to sex, to refrain from sexual intercourse until marriage. The campaigns were begun in the early 1990s in Southern Baptist churches and fueled in part by growing concern about **sexually transmitted diseases** (STDs), especially HIV. Teenagers are now encouraged to take a "**virginity pledge**" and avoid sexual intercourse until marriage. Abstinence has such political currency that it has now been celebrated as a dramatic success; a cover story in *Newsweek* magazine portrayed two white teenagers, happily hugging under the headline "The New Virginity: Why More Teens Are Choosing Not to Have Sex." Inside, the magazine offered data to show that the total percentage of high school students who say they've had sex had dropped from more than 50 percent in 1991 to slightly more than 45 percent in 2001. Teen birth rates had likewise dropped from 6 percent to about 5 percent of all births.[64] Proponents point to the success of abstinence-based sex education and elaborate publicity campaigns in a 10 percent drop in teen sexual activity.

Such efforts do appear to have *some* effect, but they are hardly a counterweight to the other messages teenagers are getting. Sociologist Peter Bearman analyzed data from over ninety thousand students and found that taking a virginity pledge does lead an average teenager to delay his or her first act of intercourse—by about eighteen months. And the pledges are effective only for students up to age seventeen. By the time students are twenty years old, over 90 percent of both boys and girls are sexually active. And the pledges were not effective at all if a significant proportion of students at the school were taking the pledges. That is, taking the pledges seems to be a way of creating a "deviant" subculture, a group of nonconformists, what Bearman called an "identity movement"—add "virgins" to the Goths, Deadheads, jocks, nerds, preppies, and rappers. Ironically, what that means is that in those schools where most kids take

Table 13.1. Percentage of Americans Performing Certain Sexual Behaviors in the Past Year, 2010 (N = 5,865)

	Age Groups																			
	14–15		16–17		18–19		20–24		25–29		30–39		40–49		50–59		60–69		70+	
Sexual Behaviors	Men	Women	Men	Women	Men	Women	Men	Women	Men	Women	Men	Women	Men	Women	Men	Women	Men	Women	Men	Women
Masturbated alone	62%	40%	75%	45%	81%	60%	83%	64%	84%	72%	80%	63%	76%	65%	72%	54%	61%	47%	46%	33%
Masturbated with partner	5%	8%	16%	19%	42%	36%	44%	36%	49%	48%	45%	43%	38%	35%	28%	18%	17%	13%	13%	5%
Received oral from women	12%	1%	31%	5%	54%	4%	63%	9%	77%	3%	78%	5%	62%	2%	49%	1%	38%	1%	19%	2%
Received oral from men	1%	10%	3%	24%	6%	58%	6%	70%	5%	72%	6%	59%	6%	52%	8%	34%	3%	25%	2%	8%
Gave oral to women	8%	2%	18%	7%	51%	2%	55%	9%	74%	3%	69%	4%	57%	3%	44%	1%	34%	1%	24%	2%
Gave oral to men	1%	12%	2%	22%	4%	59%	7%	74%	5%	76%	5%	59%	7%	53%	8%	36%	3%	23%	3%	7%
Vaginal intercourse	9%	11%	30%	30%	53%	62%	63%	80%	86%	87%	85%	74%	74%	70%	58%	51%	54%	42%	43%	22%
Received penis in anus	1%	4%	1%	5%	4%	18%	5%	23%	4%	21%	3%	22%	4%	12%	5%	6%	1%	4%	2%	1%
Inserted penis into anus	3%		6%		6%		11%		27%		24%		21%		11%		6%		2%	

Source: Tables 1 and 2 in Herbenick et al., "Sexual Behavior in the United States: Results from a National Probability Sample of Men and Women Ages 14–94," Journal of Sexual Medicine, 2010, 7(suppl. 5):255–265. ©2010 International Society for Sexual Medicine. Reprinted by permission of John Wiley and Sons via Copyright Clearance Center.

the pledges—in other words, in those very fundamentalist communities where such pledges are virtually mandated and have become normative—they don't delay sexual activity at all. And, what's worse, when the pledgers finally did have sex, they were *far less likely* to use contraception—and with no reduction in STDs, either.[65]

Not only don't virginity pledges seem to reduce the amount of teen sexual activity, but also they often lead to some strange understandings of sex itself. Because abstinence pledges are often bundled with religious resistance to sex education, kids seem not to know what abstinence actually means. In one study, 20 percent of teenagers who had taken an abstinence pledge believed that oral sex did not violate their pledge, and 10 percent believed that anal sex was still within the boundaries of abstinence. On the other hand, another 10 percent believed that kissing with tongues *did* violate their abstinence pledge.

It also appears that only boys' rates are declining, not girls' rates. Why would this be so? Partly, sociologists Barbara Risman and Pepper Schwartz argue, because girls are now presumed to be sexually active inside a romantic relationship, and so boys are more likely to begin their sexual lives with a girlfriend. (In the past, boys were more likely to begin their sexual careers furtively, with someone outside their social circle, a "bad girl.") The decline in boys' rates, then, "reflects girls' increasing negotiation power to restrict sex to relationships"; teen pregnancies are further testament to the increasing power of girls within romantic relationships because they are far more likely to insist on safer sex practices. If that's the case, feminism—the empowerment of women and girls—may actually have had a dampening effect on boys' sexual behaviors by empowering girls to insist on safer sex and relationship intimacy, whereas right-wing efforts to encourage students to "just say no" will actually increase teen pregnancy as fewer teenagers use contraception.[66]

CAMPUS CONVERGENCE: THE HOOK-UP CULTURE

One place where one can observe the political ramifications of the gender convergence in sexual behavior is the campus, where a culture of **hooking up** has virtually erased the older pattern of "rating-dating-mating" observed by sociologist Willard Waller decades ago. Waller saw a competitive marketplace, in which students evaluated their marketability in reference to both the opposite sex and the evaluations of their same-sex friends and sought to date appropriately—slightly up, but not too much.[67] But although the rest of the culture has embraced "dating"—singles go on blind dates or try speed dating, and even toddlers have "play dates"—colleges and universities have utterly abandoned the idea. No longer do students meet and mate with the intention of marrying. On campus, "hooking up" is the norm.

"Hooking up" is a deliberately vague blanket term; one set of researchers defines it as "a sexual encounter which may nor may not include sexual intercourse, usually occurring on only one occasion between two people who are strangers or brief acquaintances."[68] Although that seems to cover most cases, it fails to include those people who hook up more than once or twice or "sex buddies" (acquaintances who meet regularly for sex but rarely, if ever, associate otherwise) or "friends with benefits" (friends who do not care to become romantic partners but may include sex among the activities they enjoy together).

On many campuses, the sexual marketplace is organized around groups of same-sex peers who go out together and meet an opposite-sex peer group in a casual setting like a bar or a party. Party scenes feature hooking up as the standard mode of sexual interaction. In collaborative research I have undertaken with other sociologists at Stanford, Indiana, Ithaca, and Arizona among a dozen other schools surveying over twenty thousand students, we have found that hooking up covers a multitude of behaviors, including kissing and nongenital touching (34 percent), manual stimulation of the genitals (19 percent), oral sex (22 percent), and intercourse (23 percent). Almost all hooking up involves more alcohol than sex: Men averaged 4.7 drinks on their most recent hook-up, women 2.9 drinks. It would appear that Willard Waller's 1937 observation of "rating-dating-mating" has been, in some ways, reversed. Today, it is less about dating to find an appropriate mate and more, one might say, about mating to find an appropriate date!

There are two large gender differences in the hookup culture: pleasure and purpose. The Online College Social Life Survey found a significant "orgasm gap" between women and men. In their most recent hookup, only 19 percent of the women had an orgasm, compared with 44 percent of the men. When we asked if their partner had an orgasm in their last hookup, the women's estimations of their male partners' pleasure matched the men's self-reports pretty exactly. But the men seem to have dramatically overestimated their female partners' pleasure. For cunnilingus, the women reported an orgasm 40 percent of the time (the men estimated about 60 percent), and for intercourse, the women reported 34 percent (and the men estimated 58 percent).

Which means that either men aren't especially perceptive or that women are faking it. Or both. In interviews, women said that they sometimes faked it "to make them feel like they've done their job," or just basically "to end it." As Trish, a university senior, puts it:

> He was, like trying so hard to make me come. And there was like, no way it was going to happen. I felt so bad for him. I mean, I had gone down on him and he came already, and he was, like, trying to be a good sport about it, but really . . . So I just faked it, and he felt good and I felt relieved.[69]

Although hooking up is a mutual and consensual activity, it is up to the women to negotiate whether the hooking up proceeds to a deeper level of intimacy. And this is where the gender politics comes in. Women tend to be more ambivalent about the hookup culture; some report feeling sexy and desirable, while others feel it's cheap and rarely leads anywhere. On many campuses, women's initiative is typically to begin a conversation called the "DTR"—Define the Relationship, or, more simply, "the talk." "Are we a couple or not?" she asks. And, as one report worries, when she asks, "he decides."[70]

Antifeminist groups fret about women's lost modesty, chastity, or even their capitulation to male standards of sexual conduct. Women, they counsel, must remember the message that their grandmothers might once have told them: "Men want only one thing." And so women, if they yearn for commitment and marriage, have to relearn how to just say no. Such strategies, though, ignore the pleasure-seeking behaviors and intentions of both women *and* men and assume that women would be naturally chaste and virginal, were it not for those rapaciously predatory men. Such an image is probably insulting to women, who have shown themselves capable of **sexual entitlement** and agency themselves; and it is certainly insulting to men, because it assumes that men are, equally inevitably, violent, rapacious predators.

Perhaps the problem is not the sex, but rather the gender—that is, not the consensual sexual activity between two consenting near-adults, but rather the gender inequality that accompanies it. Mutually negotiated sexual contact—by which I mean mutually and *soberly* negotiated—with care for the integrity of the partner can be a pleasurable moment or form the basis of a longer-lasting connection. The question is who gets to decide.

ADULT SEXUAL CONVERGENCE

For adults, rates of premarital sex and the number of sex partners also seem to be moving closer. In another survey, 99 percent of male college graduates and 90 percent of female college graduates said that they had had sex before marriage. Researchers in one survey of sexual behavior from the 1970s found far greater sexual activity and greater variety among married women in the 1970s than Kinsey had found in the late 1940s. Ninety percent of all married women claimed to be happy with their sex lives; 75 percent were content with its frequency, whereas 25 percent wanted more. A study in the 1980s echoed this trend. Women and men displayed similar sexual desires—both wanted frequent sex, were happiest when initiating and refusing sex in equal amounts, and became discontent when sex was infrequent.[71]

What turns us on sexually is also similar. In the 1970s, psychologist Julia Heiman developed a way to measure women's sexual arousal. Samples of college women listened to two sorts of tapes—romantic and explicitly sexual—while wearing a tampon-like device that measured blood flow to the vagina. Like men, women were far more sexually aroused by explicit sex talk than they were by romance. And interest in sexual variety also appears to be converging. Experiences of oral sex have increased dramatically for both women and men. And, if one twenty-year-old college woman is to be believed, the meanings attached to oral sex seem to be shifting as well. "I was about 16 and I had this friend—not a boyfriend, a boy *friend*—and I didn't know what to give

OH? REALLY • Women are pressured into hooking up, even though they don't want to. And they don't enjoy it.

That's what you'd hear if you were to listen to some of the cultural critics of campus life. Campus life is wanton debauchery, where drug-addled and drunk students grope each other mindlessly. No wait, that was the 1960s. Actually, it's what people always have said about college life—even in the 1800s.

But it doesn't seem to be true any longer. Two recent studies of hooking up found the experience to be largely positive for both women and men (though slightly more positive for men), while another found no differences in reports of psychological problems among those college students who engaged in casual sex ("friends with benefits") compared to those who were in more committed relationships.

Sources: Jesse Own and Frank Fincham, "Young Adults' Emotional Reactions After Hooking Up Encounters" in *Archives of Sexual Behavior*, April 2011, pp. 321–330; Marla Eisenberg, Diann M. Ackard, Michael Resnick, and Dianne Neumark-Sztainer, "Casual Sex and Psychological Health Among Young Adults: Is Having 'Friends with Benefits' Emotionally Damaging?" in *Perspectives on Sexual and Reproductive Health*, 41(4), December 2009, pp. 231–237.

"If we're going to be friends with benefits, I want health and dental."

Figure 13.8. William Haefeli/The New Yorker Collection/The Cartoon Bank.

COMPARED *to* WHAT?

If conservatives in the United States are determined to reduce the rates of sexual activity among young Americans, cultural conservatives in Japan may be more concerned about how to *raise* it.

In a recent study by the Japan Family Planning Association, more than one-third (36 percent) of all males aged sixteen to nineteen described themselves as "indifferent or averse" toward having sex. That's nearly a 20 percent increase in just two years. But even if they were interested, they'd need to find a partner. Nearly three-fifths (59 percent) of Japanese females aged sixteen to nineteen said that they were uninterested or averse to sex.

Japanese politicians are seriously concerned about the declining birth rate, which has dipped below replacement levels.

him for his birthday, so I gave him a blow job. I wanted to know what it was like; it was just for kicks," is what she told an interviewer, who noticed she had not "a trace of embarrassment or self-consciousness."[72]

It would appear that women are having more sex and enjoying it more than ever in our history. And so women are far less likely, now, to fake orgasm. When Lillian

Rubin interviewed white working-class women in the mid-1970s for her study *Worlds of Pain,* she found that over 70 percent of the women said they faked orgasm at least some of the time. Now, she finds that the same percentage says that they never fake it. (Although the evidence from college students may actually begin to push that rate back upward.)[73]

The evidence of gender convergence does not mean that there are no differences between women and men in their sexual expression. It still means different things to be sexual, but the rules are not enforced with the ferocity and consistency that they were in the past. "It's different from what it used to be when women were supposed to hold out until they got married. There's pressure now on both men and women to lose their virginity," is how one twenty-nine-year-old man put it. "But for a man it's a sign of manhood, and for a woman there's still some loss of value."[74]

The current popular panic over the dramatic increases in oral sex among teenagers is a good indication of both gender convergence (what I've called the "masculinization of sex") and gender inequality. Recent articles express alarm and surprise that well over half of all teens ages fifteen to nineteen have had oral sex. By age nineteen, the number increases to about 60 percent. It's possible that parents' concern is fueled by the different meaning of oral sex to their generation—as a sexual behavior that was even more intimate than intercourse. Today, oral sex is viewed far more casually, as just a "kind of recreational activity that is separate from a close personal relationship." But a closer look at the sex research data indicates that a concern over "oral sex" among teenagers misses the real story. Whereas there has been

"By the way, what's your position on some-sex marriage?"

Figure 13.9. Robert Mankoff/The New Yorker Collection/The Cartoon Bank.

a small increase in cunnilingus among teens, there has been an epic rise in fellatio. The oral sex craze is not about mutual pleasuring, but rather about girls servicing boys. Teenage girls are often faced with a cruel dilemma: Because "guys rule" in teenland, guys get to set the rules for sexual engagement. If girls "hold out" on intercourse, they have to service the guys if they are going to be able to hang out with them, get invited to the right parties, and the like. Such a demand may lead to the undervaluing of oral sex as sexual intimacy, because it's a way for teenage girls to accommodate these new social demands. One teenager described this conversation at a party: "I was talking to this guy for like, I dunno, ten minutes, and he asked if I wanted to have sex, and I said no. So he said, 'OK, but could you, like, come into the bathroom and go down on me' and I was like, 'Huh?'"

In several other interviews, teenage girls described the "pressure" to perform oral sex on the popular boys. "They told me, like, it was like a ticket for admission or

OH? REALLY•

Men and women want different things out of sex. Evolutionary psychologists argued that women and men seek sex for diametrically opposed reasons: He wants immediate spontaneous pleasure with no strings attached; she wants romantic connection with someone with whom she is already emotionally intimate.

Not really. In a survey of undergraduates at the University of Texas, evolutionary psychologists Cindy Meston and David Buss found that women and men had sex for pretty much the same reasons. They argued they found significant gender differences. Oh really? Here are the top twelve reasons people (well, at least undergraduates at a large public university in Texas) had sex, along with the rankings:

Top Twelve Reasons Why Men and Women Had Sex

Men	Reason	Women
1	I was attracted to the person	1
2	It feels good	3
3	I wanted to experience the physical pleasure	2
4	It's fun	8
5	I wanted to show my affection to the person	4
6	I was sexually aroused and wanted the release	6
7	I was "horny"	7
8	I wanted to express my love for the person	5
9	I wanted to achieve an orgasm	14
10	I wanted to please my partner	11
17	I realized I was in love	9
13	I was in the heat of the moment	10

Source: Meston and Buss 2007:506. With kind permission from Springer Science + Business Medid.

Source: Cindy M. Meston and David M. Buss, "Why Humans Have Sex" in *Archives of Sexual Behavior*, 36, 2007, pp. 477–507.

"Over all, I liked it, but I have a couple of notes."

Figure 13.10. Alex Gregory/The New Yorker Collection/The Cartoon Bank.

something, like they wouldn't invite me to parties and stuff if I didn't do it. So I told myself, it's no big deal anyway, and it's not like I'm gonna get pregnant, so, like, whatever." Although today, both women and men feel entitled to pleasure, this is hardly a discourse of mutual pleasuring; rather, it is a discourse of gender inequality. This extends to other forms of entitlement and coercion. "I paid for a wonderful evening," commented one college man, "and I was entitled to sex for my effort." As a result of attitudes like these, cases of date rape and acquaintance rape continue to skyrocket on our campuses.[75]

About 15 percent of college women report having been sexually assaulted; more than half of these assaults were by a person the woman was dating. Some studies have estimated the rates to be significantly higher, nearly double (27 percent) that of the study undertaken by Mary Koss and her colleagues.[76] And, although some pundits have expressed outrage that feminists have transformed college-aged women into "victims," it is more accurate to express outrage that predatory males have turned college women into victims of **sexual assault**. Any number of rapes is unacceptable. But that significant numbers of college women are forced to change their behaviors because of the behaviors of these men—where they study, how late they stay in the library, which parties they go to, whom they date—is the outrage.

Among adults, women and men report quite different rates of forced sex. Although 96.1 percent of men and 77.2 percent of women say they have never been forced to have sex against their will, those who have been forced display dramatic differences. Just slightly more than 1 percent of men (1.3 percent), but more than 20 percent of women (21.6 percent) were forced to have sex by the opposite sex; only about 2 percent of men (1.9 percent) and just .3 percent of women were forced by someone of the same sex. Men continue to be the principal sexual predators. Several studies estimate the likelihood that a woman will be the victim of a completed rape to be about one in five. The figure for an attempted rape is nearly double that.[77]

Women's increase in sexual agency, revolutionary as it is, has not been accompanied by a decrease in male sexual entitlement or by a sharp increase in men's capacity for intimacy and emotional connectedness. Thus just as some feminist women have celebrated women's claim to sexual autonomy, others—therapists and activists—have deplored men's adherence to a "nonrelational" model of sexual behavior. As with friendship and with love, it's men who have the problem, and psychologists like Ronald Levant seek to replace "irresponsible, detached, compulsive, and alienated sexuality with a type of sexuality that is ethically responsible, compassionate for the well-being of participants, and sexually empowering of men."[78]

The notion of **nonrelational sex** means that sex is, to men, central to their lives, isolated from other aspects of life and relationships, often coupled with aggression, conceptualized socially within a framework of success and achievement, and pursued despite possible negative emotional and moral consequences. Sexual inexperience is viewed as stigmatizing. Examples of male nonrelational sexuality abound, report the critics. Men think about sex more often than do women; have more explicit sexual fantasies; masturbate more often than women; buy more porn; have more sex partners; and have more varied sexual experiences than women.[79]

In a recent edited volume on this problem, psychologist Gary Brooks pathologizes male sexual problems as a "**centerfold syndrome**." Symptoms include voyeurism, objectification, sex as a validation of masculinity, trophyism, and fear of intimacy. Ron Levant contributes a medical neologism, *alexithymia*, to describe the socially conditioned "inability to feel or express feelings." This problem must be serious: After all, it has a Greek name. Some authors also note the danger to women from men who have this type of "masculine" sex, who "deny the humanity of their partners, and . . . objectify and even violate the partner who is actually treated more as a prop." Others warn of "the damage ultimately done to men when they are socialized in a way that limits their ability to experience intimacy."[80]

Not all the studies of male nonrelationality are so critical. Psychologists Glenn Good and Nancy Sherrod argue that for many men nonrelational sex is a stage of development, not necessarily a way of being:

> Men progress through the NS [nonrelational sexuality] stage by mastering the developmental tasks associated with this stage . . . [which] include gaining experience as a sexual being, gaining experience with interpersonal aspects of sexuality, developing identity, and developing comfort with intimacy. Men following this route develop internally directed senses of their behavior that allow them to form and sustain intimate, caring relationships with others.

In fact, Good and Sherrod argue, experience with nonrelational sexuality may be a positive experience, allowing adolescents "to reduce sexual tensions," "gain sexual experiences, refine skills associated with sexual activities, and experience different partners and behaviors, thereby reducing curiosity about different partners in the future."[81]

The idea of nonrelational sex as a "problem" for men is relatively recent and is part of a general cultural discomfort with the excesses of the sexual revolution. In the 1970s, as Martin Levine and Richard Troiden point out, the significant sexual problems were problems that came from too little sexual experience—anorgasmia (the inability to achieve orgasm), especially for women, ejaculatory and erectile problems for men. Now the problems are sex "addiction," a relatively new term that makes having a lot of sex a problem, and "nonrelational sex," which makes pursuing sexual pleasure for its own sake also a problem. Although it may be true that nonrelational sexuality may be a problem for some men, especially for those for whom it is the only form of sexual expression, it is not necessarily the only way men express themselves sexually. Many men are capable of both relational and nonrelational sexuality. Some men don't ever practice nonrelational sexuality because they live in a subculture in which it is not normative; other men develop values that oppose it.[82] One possibly worthy goal might be to enlarge our sexual repertoires to enable both women and men to experience a wide variety of permutations and combinations of love and lust, without entirely reducing one to the other—as long as all these experiences are mutually negotiated, safe, and equal.

HOMOSEXUALITY AS GENDER CONFORMITY

Thus far, I've been describing the ways in which men and women are socialized toward "his" and "her" sexualities. I've deliberately avoided the obvious disclaimer that I was speaking about heterosexuality and not homosexuality, because this gendering of sexuality is as applicable to homosexuals as it is to heterosexuals. In fact, it may be even *more* obvious among gay men and lesbians, because in homosexual encounters there are two gendered men or two gendered women. That is, you have masculinity or femininity multiplied by two! Gender differences may even be exaggerated by sexual orientation.

This is, of course, contrary to our commonsense understandings of homosexuality, as well as those biological studies that suggest that gay men have some biological affinity with women, as opposed to with heterosexual men. Indeed, our commonsense assumption is that gay men and lesbians are gender *non*conformists—lesbians are "masculine" women; gay men are "feminine" men. But such commonsense thinking has one deep logical flaw—it assumes that the gender of your partner is more important, and more decisive in your life, than your own gender. But our own gender—the collections of behaviors, attitudes, attributes, and assumptions about what it means to be a man or a woman—is far more important than the gender of the people with whom we interact, sexually or otherwise. Sexual behavior, gay or straight, confirms gender identity.

That doesn't mean that these commonsense assumptions haven't completely saturated popular discussions of homosexuality, especially in those advice books designed to help parents make sure that their children do not turn out "wrong." For example, Peter and Barbara Wyden's book *Growing Up Straight: What Every Thoughtful Parent Should Know About Homosexuality* argued that "pre-homosexual" boys were identifiable by their lack of early childhood masculinity, which could be thwarted by an overly "masculine" mother, in other words, one who had a job outside the home and paid attention to feminist ideas![83]

A few empirical studies have also made such claims. For example, psychiatrist Richard Green tracked a small group of boys (about fifty-five) from preschool to young adulthood. All the boys were chosen for patterns of frequent cross-dressing at home. They liked to play with girls at school, enjoyed playing with dolls, and followed their mothers around the house doing housework. Their parents were supportive of this behavior. These "sissy boys," as Green called them, were four times more likely to have homosexual experiences than nonfeminine boys. But this research has also been widely criticized: Such gender nonconformity is extremely rare (there was great difficulty in finding even fifty-five boys) and thus cannot be the source of the great majority of homosexual behavior. Extreme patterns of nonconformity are not equivalent to milder patterns, such as not liking sports, preferring music or reading, and being indifferent to rough-and-tumble play. The homosexual experience may be a result of the social reactions to their conduct (persecution by other boys or the therapy to which they were often exposed), which thwarted their ability to establish conventional heterosocial patterns of behavior. It may have been the ostracism itself, and not the offending behavior, that led to the sexual experiences. When milder forms of gender nonconformity are examined, most boys who report such behavior turn out to be heterosexual. Finally, when studies by Green and his colleagues were extended to "tomboys," it was found that there was no difference in eventual sexual preference between girls who reported tomboy behavior and those who did not. (What Green and his colleagues seem to have found is that being a sissy is a far more serious offense to the gender order than is being a tomboy.)[84]

The evidence points overwhelmingly the other way: that homosexuality is deeply gendered and that gay men and lesbians are true gender conformists. To accept such a proposition leads to some unlikely alliances, with gay-affirmative writers and feminists lining up on the same side as an ultraconservative writer like George Gilder, who, in his unwavering critique of masculinity—both gay and straight—writes that lesbianism "has nothing whatever to do with male homosexuality. Just as male homosexuals, with their compulsive lust and promiscuous impulses, offer a kind of caricature of typical male sexuality, lesbians closely resemble other women in their desire for intimate and monogamous coupling."[85]

Since the birth of the **gay liberation movement** in the Stonewall riots of 1969—when gay men fought back against the police who were raiding a New York City gay bar—gay men have been particularly eager to demonstrate that they are not "failed" men, as earlier popular images portrayed them. In fact, many gay men became extremely successful as "real" men, enacting a hypermasculine code of anonymous sex, masculine clothing, and physical appearance, including bodybuilding. The "clone," as he was called, comprising about 35 percent of all gay men, was perhaps even more successful at masculinity than were straight men. By the early 1980s, this notion had produced some curious inversions of traditional stereotypes. In one popular song from 1983, Joe Jackson commented on this:

> See the nice boys, dancing in pairs
> Golden earring, golden tan, blow wave in their hair
> Sure they're all straight, straight as a line
> All the gays are macho, can't you see their leather shine?[86]

By contrast, the sexual lives of lesbians were quite different. For many lesbians, gay liberation did not mean sexual liberation. In the lesbian community, there was more discussion of "the tyranny of the relationship" than of various sexual practices; lesbian couples in therapy complained of "lesbian bed death," the virtual cessation of sexual activity for the couple after a few years. One woman told an interviewer:

> As women we have not been socialized to be initiators in the sexual act. Another factor is that we don't have to make excuses if we don't want to do it. We don't say we have a headache. We just say no. We also do a lot more cuddling and touching than heterosexuals, and we get fulfilled by that rather than just the act of inter-course . . . Another thing is that such a sisterly bond develops that the relationship almost seems incestuous after a while. The intimacy is so great. We know each other so well.[87]

Although some lesbians did embrace a sexual liberationist ethic and sought arenas for sexual variety, most remained gender conformists.

This was underscored by the fact that feminism also played a large role in the social organization of lesbian life. During the early waves of the women's movement, lesbianism was seen as a political alternative, a decision not to give aid and comfort to the enemy (men). How could a woman be truly feminist, some people asked, if she shared her life and bed with a man? The "political lesbian" represented a particular fusion of sexual and gender politics, an active choice that matched one's political com-mitment. "For a woman to be a lesbian in a male-supremacist, capitalist, misogynist, racist, homophobic, imperialist culture," wrote one woman, "is an act of resistance." Although, of course, not all lesbians are feminists, even this construct of political les-bianism is a form of gender conformity. If one resists gender inequality, political lesbi-ans argue, then one must opt out of sexual relationships with men and choose to be sexual only with women *because they are women*. Gender remains the organizing principle of sexuality—even a sexuality that is understood as a form of resistance to gender politics.[88]

The weight of evidence from research on homosexuality bears out this argument that gay men and lesbians are gender conformists. Take, for example, the number of sexual partners. In one study, sex researchers found that most lesbians reported having had fewer than ten sexual partners, and almost half said they had never had a one-night stand. A 1982 survey of unmarried women between the ages of twenty and twenty-nine found an average of 4.5 sexual partners over the course of their lives. But the average gay male in the same study had had hundreds of partners and many one-night stands, and more than a quarter of the men reported a thousand or more part-ners. Masters and Johnson found that 84 percent of males and 7 percent of females had had between fifty and one thousand or more sexual partners in their lifetimes and that 97 percent of men and 33 percent of women had had seven or more relationships that had lasted four months or less. Whereas 11 percent of husbands and 9 percent of wives in another study described themselves as promiscuous, 79 percent of gay men and 19 percent of lesbians made such a claim. (Among heterosexual cohabiters, though, 25 percent of the men and 22 percent of the women described themselves as promiscu-ous.) Gay men have the lowest rates of long-term committed relationships, whereas lesbians have the highest, and lesbians place much greater emphasis on emotional relationships than do gay men. Thus it appears that men—gay (or) straight—place sexuality at the center of their lives and that women—straight or lesbian—are more interested in affection and caring in the context of a love relationship.[89] New research also reports same-sex couples are actually happier than married heterosexual couples.[90]

Research on frequency of sexual activity bears this out. In one study among heterosexual married couples, 45 percent reported having sex three or more times per week during the first two years of their marriage, and 27 percent of those married between two and ten years reported such rates. By contrast, 67 percent of gay men together up to two years and 32 percent of those together two to ten years had sex three or more times per week. One-third of lesbians had sex three or more times per week in the first two years of their relationship, but only 7 percent did after two years. After ten years, the percentages of people reporting sex more than three times per week were 18 for married couples, 11 for gay men, and 1 for lesbians. Nearly half the lesbians (47 percent) reported having sex less than once a month after ten years together. One interviewer described a lesbian couple:

> She and her roommate were obviously very much in love. Like most people who have a good, stable, five year relationship, they seemed comfortable together, sort of part of one another, able to joke, obviously fulfilled in their relationship. They work together, have the same times off from work, do most of their leisure activities together. They sent me off with a plate of cookies, a good symbolic gesture of the kind of welcome and warmth I felt in their home.[91]

If heterosexuality and homosexuality are so similar, in that men and women express and confirm their gendered identities through sexual behavior, what, then, are the big differences between heterosexuals and homosexuals—aside, of course, from the gender of the partner? One difference is that gay relationships are more egalitarian. When we ask, for example, who initiates sex, gay men and lesbians report identical rates, which are far more egalitarian than the rates for married or cohabiting heterosexual couples.

And yet there are signs that this is changing. A recent study found some similarities to previous research, including an upward trend in monogamy among gay males, but not yet equal to the level of monogamy among lesbians. But gone were the large differences in, for example, initiating sex, which are now identical for gay and lesbian couples and heterosexual couples. And while the percentage of participants who have had sex with someone else during the time they have been a couple declined between 1975 and 2000 (we're becoming more monogamous), there were very small gender differences at all. And while gay men had the most sex outside the relationship, it too had declined, as had the number who had had a meaningful love affair outside their relationship.

Because homosexuals' identities are defined by their sexuality, and because their sexuality is not procreative, gay men and lesbians have also been more sexually experimental, especially with nonpenetrative sex. As one sex therapist writes, "Gay men have more ways of sexually relating than do heterosexual men." And Masters and Johnson found that gay couples have longer lovemaking sessions than heterosexual couples.[92]

*"What I was wondering is, Doctor, can you make me straight
during the week and gay on the weekends?"*

Figure 13.11. David Sipress/The New Yorker Collection/The Cartoon Bank.

One other way that heterosexuality and homosexuality are similar, actually, is in the impact of homophobia on sexual behavior. Obviously, for gay people homophobia saturates all their interactions. The systematic devaluation of homosexuality, the stigma attached to being homosexual, becomes a crucial element in one's identity. As sociologist Ken Plummer writes:

> The perceived hostility of the societal reactions that surround . . . homosexuality . . . renders the business of becoming a homosexual a process that is characterized by problems of access, problems of guilt, and problems of identity. It leads to the emergence of a subculture of homosexuality. It leads to a series of interaction problems involved with concealing the discreditable stigma. And it inhibits the development of stable relationships among homosexuals to a considerable degree.[93]

To understand more fully the experience of stigma, try this little thought experiment, which was developed by two social psychologists: Imagine for a moment that you are an anxious person and that being anxious is against the law. You must try to hide your anxiety from others. Your own home may be a safe place to feel anxious, but a public display of anxiety can lead to arrest or, at least, to social ostracism. At work one day, an associate looks at you and says, "That's funny, for a crazy moment there I thought you were anxious." "Heck, no," you exclaim a bit too loudly, *"not me!"* You begin to wonder if your fellow worker will report his suspicions to your boss. If he does, your boss may inform the police or will at least change your job to one that requires less contact with customers, especially those who have children.[94]

Whereas it is clear that homophobia constructs gay experience, we are less aware of the power of homophobia to structure the experiences and identities of heterosexuals. Although there is evidence that social attitudes toward homosexuality have become increasingly accepting in recent decades, homophobia is more than "acceptance" or the fear or hatred of homosexuals; it is also, for men, the fear of being perceived as unmanly, effeminate, or, worst of all, gay. This fear seems less keen among heterosexual women, though many worry about the dangers of homosexuals (nearly always men) to their children.[95]

READ ALL ABOUT IT!

But what of sexuality and gender identity? We know very little about the foundations on which transgender people construct their sexualities. If they've transitioned, do they tend toward the traditionally and stereotypically gendered behaviors of their "new" assigned sex, or do they hark back to previous behaviors? For those who have not transitioned or identify as genderqueer or nonbinary, do they "pick a side" or develop yet a third way of being sexual? Sociologist Raine Dozier gives us one potential answer: for transmen, a widely varied set of cognitive and behavioral mechanisms are used. Her article "Beards, Breasts, and Bodies" explains that when sex characteristics do not align with gender identity, sexual behavior becomes more important to confirming gender identity (e.g., transmen who are not yet ready, physically, as transmen tended toward more hypermasculine sexual behaviors); but when sex characteristics become more congruent with gender identity, sexual behavior becomes more fluid and varied. Definitively, we can say that we need more research on gender identity/expression—including voices from the diverse spectrum of identities—and sexuality.

Male heterosexuals often spend a significant amount of time and energy in masculine display so that no one could possibly get the "wrong" impression about them. In one study, many heterosexual men said they had sex in order to prove they weren't gay. Because our popular misperceptions about homosexuality usually center on gender inversion, compensatory behaviors by heterosexuals often involve exaggerated versions of gender stereotypic behaviors. In this way, homophobia reinforces the gender of sex, keeping men acting hypermasculine and women acting ultrafeminine. "Heterosexuality as currently construed and enacted (the erotic preference for the other gender) requires homophobia," write sex researchers John Gagnon and Stuart Michaels.[96]

WHAT ELSE AFFECTS SEXUALITY?

Although gender remains one of the organizing principles of sexuality, other aspects of our lives also profoundly influence our sexual behaviors and expectations. For one thing, sexual behavior, as we've seen, varies widely among different cultures. Margaret Mead found that in some cultures, the idea of spontaneous sex is not encouraged for either women or men. Among the Arapesh, she writes, the exceptions are believed to occur in women. "Parents warn their sons even more than they warn their daughters against permitting themselves to get into situations in which someone can make love to them." Another anthropologist reported that in one southwest Pacific society, sexual intercourse is seen as highly pleasurable and deprivation as harmful to both sexes. And Bronislaw Malinowski saw significant convergence between women and men in the Trobriand Islands, where women initiate sex as often as men and where couples avoid the "missionary" position because the woman's movements are hampered by the weight of the man so that she cannot be fully active.

In the contemporary United States, several variables other than gender affect sexuality, such as class, age, education, marital status, religion, race, and ethnicity. Take class, for example. Kinsey found that, contrary to the American ideology that holds that working-class people are more sensual because they are closer to their "animal natures," lower-class position does not mean hotter sex. In fact, he found that upper- and middle-class people were more sophisticated in the "arts of love," demonstrating wider variety of activities and greater emphasis on foreplay, whereas lower-class people dispensed with preliminaries and did not even kiss very much.

There is evidence that race and ethnicity also produce some variations in sexual behavior. For example, blacks seem to hold somewhat more sexually liberal attitudes than whites and have slightly more sex partners, but they also masturbate less frequently, have less oral sex, and are slightly more likely to have same-sex contacts. Hispanics are also more sexually liberal than whites and masturbate more frequently than

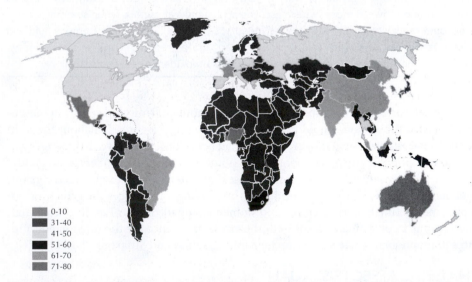

0-10
31-40
41-50
51-60
61-70
71-80

Figure 13.12a. Percent of people reporting "exciting" sex life by country. Where people have the best sex, the worst sex, and the most STIs.

Source: The data come from two surveys done by Durex, the condom folks. Their Sexual Wellbeing Survey (from 2007/2008) and Face of Global Sex (2012) are methodologically rigorous. Zack Beauchamp, "6 Maps and Charts That Explain Sex Around the World" in *Vox*, May 26, 2015, http://www.vox.com/2014/5/7/5662608/in-different-area-codes.

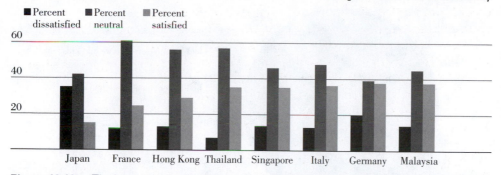

Figure 13.12b. The least sexually satisfied countries. Where people have the best sex, the worst sex, and the most STIs.

Source: The data come from two surveys done by Durex, the condom folks. Their Sexual Wellbeing Survey (from 2007/2008) and Face of Global Sex (2012) are methodologically rigorous. Zack Beauchamp, "6 Maps and Charts That Explain Sex Around the World" in *Vox*, May 26, 2015, http://www.vox.com/2014/5/7/5662608/in-different-area-codes.

blacks or whites, but they also have less oral sex than whites (yet more than blacks) and have fewer sex partners, either of the same or opposite sex, than do whites or blacks.[97]

Age also affects sexuality. What turns us on at fifty will probably not be what turned us on at fifteen. Not only are there significant physiological changes that augur a decline in sexual energy and interest, but also age is related to marital status and family obligations. As Lillian Rubin writes,

> On the most mundane level, the constant negotiation about everyday tasks leaves people harassed, weary, irritated, and feeling more like traffic cops than lovers. Who's going to do the shopping, pay the bills, take care of the laundry, wash the dishes, take out the garbage, clean the bathroom, get the washing machine fixed, decide what to eat for dinner, return the phone calls from friends and parents? When there are children, the demands, complications and exhaustion increase exponentially.[98]

Ah, children. By far one of the greatest **anaphrodisiacs**—sexual turn-offs—in our society is having children. Couples—gay and straight—with children report far less sexual activity than couples without children. There's less time, less freedom, less privacy—and less interest (figure 13.13).

You've probably heard reports that women hit their sexual peak in the late thirties and early forties, whereas men peak before they turn twenty, after which they are increasingly likely to appreciate softer, more sensual activities. And you've probably heard that such differences reveal biological differences in male and female sexual anatomy. But that ignores the ways in which women's and men's sexualities are related to each other. That "his" sexuality shifts toward the more sensual just as "her" sexuality takes a sharp turn toward the explicitly sexual indicates more than a simple divergence in biological patterns, especially because it is not the case in other cultures, where men and women biologically age "differently." What these reports suggest is that marriage has a pronounced effect on sexual expression, domesticating sex, bringing it into the domain historically reserved for women: the home. When men feel that

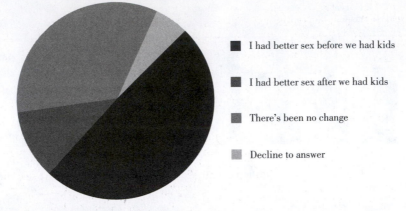

Figure 13.13. 2013 Married Sex Survey.

Source: iVillage.

sex is no longer dangerous and risky (which is, to them, exciting), their sexual repertoire may soften to include a wider range of sensual pleasures. When women feel that
sex is no longer dangerous and risky (which they interpret as threatening), they feel
safe enough to explore more explicitly sexual pleasures. Such an interpretation suggests, of course, that the differences we observe between women and men may have
more to do with the social organization of marriage than with any inherent differences between males and females.

In one recent study, researchers surveyed over one thousand older heterosexual
couples from five countries—the United States, Brazil, Germany, Spain, and Japan—
who had been together an average of twenty-five years and found something they
thought startling—and exactly the opposite of what they had expected. They found
that among the couples that had been together the longest, the women were the more
sexually satisfied but the men reported more relationship happiness. In fact, though, it
conforms entirely to the gendered sexualities argument we have been making. Each
gender offers its strength, so to speak, to the other. So, the men feel more emotionally
satisfied because the women are providing all the emotional nurturance they need. By
contrast, the women feel more sexually satisfied because their sexual needs are met by
men who are more interested in sex in the first place.[99]

Yet despite this, the longer-range historical trend over the past several centuries
has been to sexualize marriage, to link the emotions of love and nurturing to erotic
pleasure within the reproductive relationship. Thus sexual compatability and expression have become increasingly important in our married lives, as the increased amount
of time before marriage (prolonged adolescence), the availability of birth control and
divorce, and an ethic of individual self-fulfillment have combined to increase the importance of sexual expression throughout the course of our lives.

Here's one startling conclusion: Politics affects sex. Gender politics, that is. It
turns out that the more equal are women and men, the more satisfied women and men
are with their sex lives. In a recent survey of twenty-nine countries, sociologists found
that people in countries with higher levels of gender equality—Spain, Canada, Belgium,
and Austria—reported being much happier with their sex lives than those people in

OH? REALLY •

Electoral politics affects sex. The more liberal you are politically, the more "liberal" you are in your sexual behavior.

Actually, not true. While it is true that Democrats have more sex than Republicans, Republicans have more orgasms. In a recent survey, more than half of those who identified as conservative Republicans said they reached climax almost every time they had sex, compared to 40 percent of liberal Democrats.

Can you think why that might be the case? Remember, that's 50 percent of all survey respondents—male and female. So it's very possible that a high percentage of conservative Republican *men* had orgasms and a lower percentage of women, because the men were simply more concerned with their own pleasure than the pleasure of their partner. They do believe in freedom, after all. By contrast, those liberal Democrats don't have orgasms unless their partners do, since they believe in equality and all.

So the real finding is that there is a greater orgasm gap between Republican men and women than there is between Democratic men and women.

Source: Jessica Bennett, "Republicans Have More Orgasms, According to Match.com Sex Survey" in *Daily Beast*, February 2, 2012, http://www.thedailybeast.com/articles/2012/02/02/republicans-have-more-orgasms-according-to-match-com-sex-survey.html.

countries with lower levels of gender equality, like Japan. "Male-centered cultures where sexual behavior is more oriented toward procreation tend to discount the importance of sexual pleasure for women," said Ed Laumann of the University of Chicago, lead author of the study.[100]

What's more, within each country, the greater the level of equality between women and men, the happier women and men are with their sex lives. It turns out that those married couples who report the highest rates of marital satisfaction—and the highest rates of sexual activity in the first place—are those in which men do the highest amounts of housework and child care.[101] This led a recent article in *Men's Health* magazine to proclaim, "Housework Makes Her Horny"—but, I suspect, only when *he* does it. It makes intuitive sense: The more housework and child care the husband does, the more time and energy she has and the less resentful she feels about that inequality. That sounds like both opportunity and motive to me. Whether we compare countries or couples, gender equality turns out to be sexier than gender inequality. How's that for an incentive?

HEALTH, SEX, AND HIV-AIDS

With the onset of the **HIV-AIDS** epidemic, major changes occurred in the sexual patterns of gay men, including fewer partners, less anonymous sex, and increases in the practice of safe sex and the number of gay male couples. The emphasis on "safe sex" was seen by many as an effort to "feminize" sexuality, to return it to the context of emotional and monogamous relationships, thus abandoning the earlier gay liberationist ethic of sexual freedom. To men, the very phrase "safe sex" was experienced as an oxymoron: What's sexy—heat, passion, excitement, spontaneity—was the exact opposite of what's safe—soft, warm, cuddly. Many men feared that practicing safe sex would mean no longer having sex like men and that programs encouraging such gender nonconformity would be doomed to failure. (This is not simply an issue for gay men, of course. Heterosexual women have been trying to get heterosexual men to practice a form of safe sex for decades, finding that their own sexual expressivity is less encumbered when both partners take responsibility for birth control. Fear of pregnancy and fear of HIV transmission both require that one fuse sexual pleasure with sexual responsibility.)[102]

Critics needn't have worried. Much of the work to minimize the risk for HIV among gay men has been to reaffirm masculine sexuality, to develop ways that men could still have "manly" sex while they also practiced safe sex. Gay organizations promoted safe sex clubs, pornographic videos, and techniques. As a result, gay men did begin to practice safe sex, without disconfirming their masculinity, though there is some evidence of recent backsliding by younger gay men, especially because HIV treatments now seem to augur longer and healthier lives for HIV-positive people than previously.

Of course, the epicenter of the HIV epidemic has shifted dramatically since the disease was first diagnosed in 1984. Globally, more than twenty-one million men, women, and children have died from AIDS, and another thirty-four million are living with it—that's 1 out of every 162 people on Earth (figure 13.14). The global epicenter of AIDS has shifted dramatically since it was first diagnosed in the United States. Seven out of every ten people infected live in sub-Saharan Africa; adding South and Southeast Asia and Latin America brings the total up to 88 percent.[103]

It is noteworthy that rates of infection are roughly equally distributed between women and men throughout the underdeveloped world, where women's significantly lower status often renders them powerless to resist sexual advances, to insist on safe sex practices, or to have much access to health care. In sub-Saharan Africa, nearly three-fifths of all HIV-positive cases are women. Among African adolescents, girls outnumber boys among the infected by about five to one. Empowering women, affording women equal rights, will prove the major mechanism to reduce HIV. Dr. Pascoal Mocumbi, prime minister of Mozambique, challenged Africans to "break the silence regarding the sexual behaviour and gender inequalities that drive the epidemic."[104]

Such gender symmetry is true around the world—except in the United States and Western Europe and Australia and New Zealand. In North America and Western Europe, the percentage of HIV-positive women is less than 25 percent; in Australia and New Zealand (where women's status is the highest in the industrial world), only 7 percent.[105] In these places, AIDS remains a highly "gendered" disease. Although women and men are both able to contract the virus that causes AIDS—and, in fact, women are actually more likely to contract the disease from unprotected heterosexual intercourse than are men—and despite the fact that rates of new infection among women are increasing faster than among men, the overwhelming majority of all AIDS patients in the United States are men. (And rates of new infections are far higher among young black men than white men, an indication that class and race are also keys that drive the epidemic.)[106]

Seen in this way, AIDS is the most highly gendered disease in American history—a disease that both women and men can get but one that overwhelmingly disproportionately affects one gender and not the other. It would be useful to understand masculinity—risk taking, avoidance of responsibility, pursuit of sex above all other

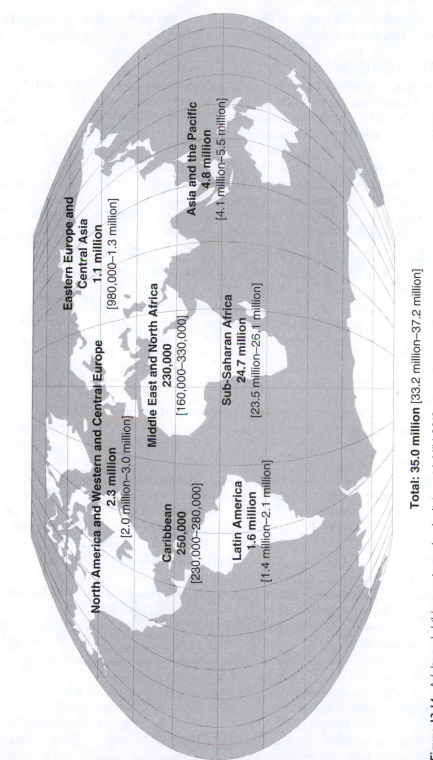

North America and Western and Central Europe
2.3 million
[2.0 million–3.0 million]

Caribbean
250,000
[230,000–280,000]

Latin America
1.6 million
[1.4 million–2.1 million]

Eastern Europe and Central Asia
1.1 million
[980,000–1.3 million]

Middle East and North Africa
230,000
[160,000–330,000]

Sub-Saharan Africa
24.7 million
[23.5 million–26.1 million]

Asia and the Pacific
4.8 million
[4.1 million–5.5 million]

Total: 35.0 million [33.2 million–37.2 million]

Figure 13.14. Adults and children estimated to be living with HIV, 2013.

Source: UNAIDS, http://www.aids.gov/federal-resources/around-the-world/global-aids-overview/.

ends—as a risk factor in the spread of the disease, in the same way as we understand masculinity to be a risk factor in drunk driving accidents.[107]

GENDERED HEALTH

Understanding gender to be a major risk factor in explaining drunk driving reminds us that health and illness are also deeply gendered. Historically, it was men who took all the health-related risks, both by engaging in behaviors like drinking and taking drugs and by considering it unmasculine to seek health care treatment. Ignoring health issues, "playing through pain," was, in fact, a symbol of masculinity. And it was women who took far fewer risks, took better care of their health, took vitamins, exercised, and saw doctors more regularly. An old adage among those who study gender and health is that "women get sicker, but men die quicker."[108]

Researchers have long understood gender to be a primary factor in health-related behavior. As men's health researcher and advocate Will H. Courtenay puts it:

> A man who does gender correctly would be relatively unconcerned about his health and well-being in general. He would see himself as stronger, both physically and emotionally, than most women. He would think of himself as independent, not needing to be nurtured by others. He would be unlikely to ask others for help. He would spend much time out in the world and away from home . . . He would face danger fearlessly, take risks frequently, and have little concern for his own safety.[109]

Howard Friedman, a psychologist at UC Riverside, found that "less manly" men lived longer than "masculine men."

Race, class, and ethnicity complicate the picture. Middle-aged black men, for example, have much lower longevity (up to seven years less) and much higher rates of stress- and lifestyle-related diseases (heart attack, stroke, diabetes) than their white counterparts (figure 13.15). A report by the Kellogg Foundation concluded that "from birth, a black male on average seems fated to a life so unhealthy that a white man can only imagine it." Although some part of this is attributable to age—young black males have astronomically higher health risks than do whites—and to class—working-class men of all races also have lower longevity and higher morbidity than middle-class men—this holds true even for middle-aged black men at every level of the class hierarchy. Whereas men, "overall, have a particular set of pressures to show strength and not reveal weakness," writes columnist Ellis Cose, "this feeling is intensified in black men." There is, he continues, "an ethic of toughness among black men, built up to protect yourself against racial slights and from the likelihood that society is going to challenge you or humiliate you in some way. This makes it hard to admit that you are in pain or need help." African-American and Latino men are significantly less likely to see a doctor—even when they are in poor health (figure 13.16).[110]

Yet even in health, there are signs of gender convergence. First, more women are disregarding traditional strictures of femininity and taking increased risks—in their sexual behaviors and elsewhere. Take drinking, for example. Of course, far more men drink to excess than women do, and drinking is heaviest among young,

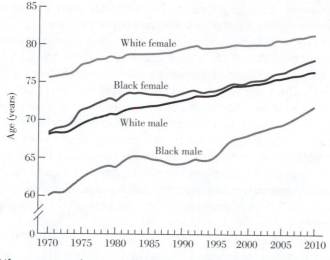

Figure 13.15. Life expectancy, by race and sex: United States, 1970–2010.

Source: S. L. Murphy, J. Q. Xu, and K. D. Kochanek, "Deaths: Final Data for 2010" in *National Vital Statistics Reports*, 61(4), 2013, pp. 1–118, http://www.cdc.gov/nchs/data/nvsr/nvsr61/nvsr61_04.pdf.

Figure 13.16. PSA road signs attempt to engage men in health-seeking behavior.

Source: Agency for Healthcare Research and Quality.

white, male students attending four-year institutions and often revolves around fraternities and sports events. But an increasing number of women are binge drinking as well, especially in sororities, where 80 percent of women are binge drinkers, compared with 30 percent outside sororities. "To be able to drink like a guy is kind of a badge of honor," commented one senior at Syracuse University. "For me, it's a feminism thing." Although few feminists would actually suggest that binge drinking is an index of women's liberation, many young women have come to feel that drinking, fighting, smoking, and other typically "masculine" behaviors are a sign of power—and therefore cool. "I don't think women gain any power in outdrinking a man," commented another Syracuse senior, "because it will always be a standard set by the man. In drinking and everywhere else, women need to start setting their own standards." As journalist Barbara Ehrenreich put it, "Gender equality wouldn't be worth fighting for if all it meant was the opportunity to be as stupid and self-destructive as men can be."[111]

And there are signs that more men are seeking health professionals, taking better care of their health—a domain that had been traditionally reserved for women. Efforts to develop men's health awareness have been especially successful in the underdeveloped world, where campaigns for reproductive health and family planning for women have branched out to include men in health planning. In such campaigns, it is clear that the health interests of women and men are hardly the conflicting interests of Martians and Venusians. There is no zero-sum game; rather, our interests are complementary. Both women's and men's health needs confront dominant ideas about gender that inhibit men's health-seeking behavior and often prohibit women's. Gender inequality is bad for both women's and men's health.[112]

Of course, predictably, just as there are increasing signs of gender convergence, there is a small backlash chorus that argues that the dramatic gains in women's health have come at the expense of men. After all, this chorus argues, the gender gap in life span has been slowly growing over the past century; whereas women outlived men by about one year in 1920, they now outlive men by almost six years. And men have a higher death rate for every one of the leading causes of death. And yet, this chorus claims, men are vastly underserved in the national health research budgets. Just as predictably, though, these critics rarely argue for *increased* funding for health care across the board. Rather, they see health care as a zero-sum game and urge decreases for women and increases for men.

But the **mortality gap** in the United States by which women outlive men is not found in the economic South, where men typically outlive women by the same six years—or more. Gender inequality—unequal access to health care, unequal nutrition, and men's control of reproduction—led the Nobel laureate economist Amartya Sen to estimate that worldwide there are one hundred million "missing women"—women whose deaths are directly attributable to gender inequality in health care.[113] Here in the United States several of the top ten causes of death are related to lifestyle—such as heart disease, injuries, diabetes, HIV, suicide, and homicide. The "enemy" of these misguided multitudes is not feminist-inspired efforts to promote health awareness for women but rather an ideology of masculinity that encourages us to "live fast and die young" and an indifferent federal government that makes the United States the only industrial nation without a national program of funded health care.[114] As usual, the solution to this problem is more gender equality—not less.

The women's health movement has made it abundantly clear that health is not a zero-sum game, in which one gender benefits at the expense of the other. Rather, efforts to promote women's health also invariably benefit men—from the decline in mortality of the women in our lives to the decline in mortality of fetuses and babies caused by poor prenatal treatment or illegal back-alley abortions to women's decreased dependence on men. And efforts to promote men's health also benefit women, both directly because they will increase the quality and longevity of the lives of the men women care about and indirectly because decreasing risk taking and drug and alcohol use will reduce the amount of violence that women endure from men.

Gender differences persist in our sexual expression and our sexual experiences, in our health experiences and our health seeking, but they are far less significant than they used to be, and the signs point to continued convergence. It may come as a relief to realize that our lovers are not from other planets but rather are capable of the same joys and pleasures that we are.

Yet one health issue remains—perhaps our nation's number one public health issue: violence. And it is here that the gender gap is as wide as it is deep. In fact, it is the only area in which the gender gap is increasing, where there are truly significant differences between women and men.

KEY TERMS

Adonis Complex
Anaphrodisiac
Anorexia Nervosa
Antiporn Feminism
Beauty Myth
Breast Augmentation Surgery
Bulimia
Centerfold Syndrome
Cunnilingus
Erectile Dysfunction
Fellatio

Gay Liberation Movement
Genital Reconstruction Surgery
Goldilocks Dilemma
HIV-AIDS
Hooking Up
Iron Maiden
Mortality Gap
Muscle Dysmorphia
Nonrelational Sex
Penile Enlargement Surgery
Sexual Agency

Sexual Assault
Sexual Double Standard
Sexual Entitlement
Sexual Response
Sexual Revolution
Sexual Socialization
Sexually Transmitted Diseases
Standards of Female Beauty
Virginity Pledge

The GENDER OF VIOLENCE

To be or not to be: that is the question:
Whether tis nobler in the mind to suffer
The slings and arrows of outrageous fortune,
Or to take arms against a sea of troubles,
And by opposing end them?

—WILLIAM SHAKESPEARE, *HAMLET*

I am not insane. I am angry. I killed because people like me are
mistreated every day. I did this to show society, "Push us and
we will push back."

—LUKE WOODHAM, 1997

Two sentiments—a question and an answer—separated by four centuries.
Does one suffer, or does one seek revenge? Get mad or get even? Each has an
unacceptably high price: Luke Woodham resolved the dilemma by stabbing his
mother to death and then killing two students in his Pearl, Mississippi, high
school in October 1997. Two months later, three students were killed in Paducah,
Kentucky. And four students and a teacher were killed in Jonesboro, Arkansas,
in March 1998. Both Woodham and the two boys who opened fire in Jonesboro
were said to be distraught after being snubbed by girls. Suffer a loss? Or make
someone pay?

As a nation, we are preoccupied by violence. We fret about "teen violence,"
complain about "inner-city crime," or fear "urban gangs." We express shock at

the violence in our nation's public schools, where metal detectors crowd the door-ways, and knives and guns crowd out pencils and erasers in students' backpacks. Those public school shootings left us speechless and sick at heart. Yet when we think about these wrenching events, do we ever consider that, whether white or black, inner city or suburban, these bands of marauding "youths" or these troubled teenagers are virtually all young men?

Nightly, we watch news reports of suicide bombings in the Middle East or terrorist attacks on the United States or on our (and our allies') outposts abroad or of racist attacks against Turks in Germany or Pakistanis in London or of homophobic gay-bashing murders or of Mexican drug lords and their legions of gun-toting thugs or of the well-armed right-wing militias. Do these reports ever mention that virtually every single one of these terrorists, suicide bombers, or racist gang members is male? Do they investigate how ideologies of masculinity may have contributed to the motivation for such heinous crimes?

Seldom do the news reports note that virtually all the violence in the world today is committed by men. Imagine, though, if the violence were perpetrated entirely by women. Would that not be *the* story, the only issue to be explained? Would not a gender analysis occupy the center of every single story? The fact that these are men seems so natural as to raise no questions, generate no analysis.

Let's look at how we understand youth violence. In 1993, *Youth and Violence*, the American Psychological Association's Commission on Violence and Youth report, at-tributed rising rates of violence to access to guns, involvement in gangs, mass media violence, physical punishment, parental neglect, substance abuse, poverty, prejudice, and absence of antiviolence programs. The next year, the Carnegie Corporation de-voted an entire issue of its quarterly journal to "Saving Youth from Violence" and came up with a list of factors that contribute to youth violence, including frustration, lack of social skills, being labeled as "dumb," poverty, abuse, neglect, drugs, alcohol, violent video games, and the availability of guns. Neither of these blue-ribbon panels' reports mentioned the word "masculinity."[1]

In 2013, more than 6.5 million men and about 2.5 million women were arrested in the United States. Nearly three-quarters (73.5 percent) of all arrestees were males. Males accounted for 79.9 percent of persons arrested for violent crimes and for 62.2 percent of persons arrested for property crimes. Men constituted 98.1 percent of all persons arrested for rape, 88.3 percent of those arrested for murder, 86.6 percent of those ar-rested for robbery, 77 percent of those arrested for aggravated assault, 72.2 percent of those arrested for other assaults, 73.3 percent of those arrested for all family violence, and 72.1 percent of those arrested for all disorderly conduct.[2]

From early childhood to old age, violence is the most obdurate, intractable behavioral gender difference. The National Academy of Sciences puts the case starkly: "The most consistent pattern with respect to gender is the extent to which male criminal participation in serious crimes at any age greatly exceeds that of fe-males, regardless of source of data, crime type, level of involvement, or measure of participation." "Men are always and everywhere more likely than women to commit criminal acts," write criminologists Michael Gottfredson and Travis Hirschi.[3] Yet how do we understand this obvious association between masculinity and violence? Is it a product of biology, a fact of nature, caused by something inherent in male anatomy? Is it universal? In the United States, what has been the historical association between gender and violence? Has that association become stronger or weaker over time? What can we, as a culture, do to prevent or at least ameliorate the problem of **male violence**?

There has surely been no shortage of explanations for male violence. Some researchers rely on biological differences between women and men, suggesting that "the durability, universality and generality of the relative aggressiveness of males" points definitively toward a genetic difference. So, for example, some scholars argue that androgens, male hormones, especially testosterone, are what drive male aggression. It is true that testosterone is highly correlated with aggressive behavior: Increased testosterone levels typically result in increased aggression. Other scholars have looked to more evolutionary explanations such as homosocial competition, in which male violence is the result of the evolutionary competition for sexual access to females. Men fight with each other to create dominance hierarchies; the winners of those fights have their choice of females.[4]

But, as we saw earlier, by itself the biological evidence is unconvincing. Although testosterone is associated with aggression, it does not cause the aggression but rather

---

OH? REALLY ●   Man Bites Dog

Did you know that a dog being walked by a man is four times more likely to attack another dog than one walked by a woman?

Researchers in the Czech Republic studied two thousand dog–dog interactions in different areas of the city where people walked their dogs. They found that dogs walked by men, who were on a leash, were the most aggressive.

How to explain this? First, the authors suggest a kind of cross-species male–male transfer of aggressive impulses. "Dogs are unusually skilled at reading human social and communicative behavior," wrote the researchers. So they pick up on the aggressiveness in their owners and project that outwards, perhaps with a "don't mess with me" swagger. And, of course, being on the leash is frustrating, especially when hot female dogs are nearby. That'll make any critter aggressive, right?

Can the explanation really be that there is an interspecies osmosis by which the dogs sense their human's innate virility and get all juiced on their own testosterone? Couldn't it be that male owners tend to have *male dogs*? And particular *breeds* of dogs? (If I'm a guy, and I'm walking a female miniature poodle, I wouldn't be worried about my dog attacking another dog!) Or that male owners handle their dogs on leashes more aggressively (all that greater upper-body strength and all)? And what about the owners' age? (Older men will have "family" dogs [i.e., less aggressive dogs]; younger single men will have "guy" dogs—think of the canine equivalent of minivans and muscle cars).

Alas, males—human and canine—may be more aggressive than females, but I somehow doubt that doggie aggression has much to do with the sex of the owner. Still, I'd be careful where you step.

Source: Petr Rezac, Petra Viziova, Michaela Dobesova, Zdenek Havlicek, and Dagmar Pospisilova, "Factors Affecting Dog–Dog Interactions on Walks with Their Owners" in *Applied Animal Behavior Science*, 134, 2011, pp. 170–176.

only facilitates an aggressiveness that is already present. (It does nothing for non-aggressive males, for example.) Nor does the causal arrow always point from hormone to behavior. Winners in athletic competitions experience increased testosterone levels *after* they win. Violence causes increased testosterone levels; hormonal increases cause violence. Nor does testosterone cause violence against those who are significantly higher on the dominance ladder. Increased testosterone will cause a midlevel male baboon, for example, to increase his aggression against the male just below him, but it will not embolden him to challenge the hierarchical order.[5]

In fact, there is also little evidence to support the evolutionary theory of homosocial competition. In some cultures, males are not in the least violent or competitive with each other. If "boys will be boys," as the saying goes, they will be so differently in different cultures. And, in some societies, including ours, males are especially violent against females—the very group they are supposedly competing for. (To murder or assault the person you are trying to inseminate is a particularly unwise reproductive strategy.) Sociologist Judith Lorber intelligently reframes the question:

> When little boys run around noisily, we say "Boys will be boys," meaning that physical assertiveness has to be in the Y chromosome because it is manifest so early and so commonly in boys. But are boys universally, the world over, in every social group, a vociferous, active presence? Or just where they are encouraged to use their bodies freely, to cover space, take risks, and play outdoors at all kinds of games and sports?[6]

Following Freud, some psychoanalysts have looked for an explanation of male violence in the Oedipal drama: The frustration of the young boy's sexual desires is translated into aggression (the frustration-aggression hypothesis). Stated more neutrally, the young boy must constantly and publicly demonstrate that he has successfully separated from his mother and transferred his identity to his father—that is, that he has become masculine. Male violence is a way to prove successful masculinity.

Or, at least, an adaptive strategy for males to avoid becoming prey themselves. In a fascinating study, Barbara Ehrenreich argues that the origins of war lie less in an innate propensity for aggression and a lust for predation than in the fear that we are slated to become someone else's dinner entree. The origins of society lie in defense—we became social not because we had some deep need for sociability, but rather because only together could we defend ourselves successfully. Thus, she argues, the near-universal association of masculinity and war is compensatory and defensive, a "substitute occupation for underemployed male hunter-defenders."[7]

Although not necessarily describing a cultural universal, these psychological models do help explain the particular association of masculinity with violence, especially among younger males. (There are, of course, many societies in which masculinity is not associated with violence.) In particular, psychologists have pointed out how violence is a form of masculine emotional expressiveness, as if the only legitimate emotion a man could express was rage. Hamlet's complex argument addressing the moral choices before him becomes Luke Woodham's self-justifying shrug.

Psychological explanations often assume universal generalizability. They take little account of either cross-cultural variation or the historical shifts in any culture over time. But such cultural and historical shifts are important if we are adequately to explain violence in the first place. In the 1980s, two social anthropologists reversed the question: What can we learn from those societies in which there is very little violence? They found that the definition of masculinity had a significant impact on the propensity toward violence. In societies in which men were permitted to acknowledge fear, levels of violence were low. But in societies in which **masculine bravado**—the posture of strength and the repression and denial of fear—was a defining feature of masculinity, violence was likely to be high. It turns out that those societies in which bravado is prescribed for men are also those in which the definitions of masculinity and femininity are very highly differentiated.[8]

So societies in which gender inequality is highest are those where masculinity and femininity are seen to be polar opposites, and thus they are societies that mandate "masculine bravado." For example, Joanna Overing tells us that in the Amazon jungle, the extremely violent Shavante define manhood as "sexual bellicosity," a state both superior to and opposed to femininity, whereas their peaceful neighboring Piaroas define manhood *and womanhood* as the ability to cooperate tranquilly with others in daily life. In sum, these are a few of the themes that anthropologists have isolated as leading toward both interpersonal violence and intersocietal violence:

1. The ideal for manhood is the fierce and handsome warrior.
2. Public leadership is associated with male dominance, both of men over other men and of men over women.
3. Women are prohibited from public and political participation.
4. Most public interaction is between men, not between men and women or among women.
5. Boys and girls are systematically separated from an early age.
6. Initiation of boys is focused on lengthy constraint of boys, during which time the boys are separated from women; taught male solidarity, bellicosity, and endurance; and trained to accept the dominance of older groups of men.
7. Emotional displays of male virility, ferocity, and sexuality are highly elaborated.
8. The ritual celebration of fertility focuses on male generative ability, not female ability.
9. Male economic activities and the products of male labor are prized over those of females.[9]

One of the most significant "causes" of male violence, then, is gender inequality. And the victims of this are not only women, but also men.[10] Taken together, these works provide some policy-oriented goals toward which we might look if we are to reduce the amount of **gendered violence** in society. First, it seems clear that the less gender differentiation between women and men, the less likely violence will be gendered. This means the more "like women" men can be seen—nurturing, caring, frightened—and the more "like men" women can be seen—capable, rational, competent in the public sphere—the more likely that aggression will take other routes besides gendered violence.[11]

Men's violence against women is the result of entitlement thwarted; men's violence against other men often derives from the same thwarted sense of entitlement. I imagine that there is a curvilinear relationship between male-to-male violence and male-to-female violence and the entitlement to patriarchal power. To find peaceful societies, we might want to look at societies in which entitlement to power is either not thwarted or not present. Societies with the least male-male gendered violence would be those in which patriarchy is either intact and unquestioned or else hardly present at all and hasn't been for some time.

READ ALL ABOUT IT!

Many Americans hold some stereotypic assumptions about gun ownership, especially that men who own guns—and the vast majority of handgun owners are men—are likely to be out to "prove" something. Feeling otherwise insecure about it, the gun is proof of masculinity. Whether it's inner-city gangs or suburban and rural guys, the handgun is the symbol of masculinity, an instant masculinity enhancer. But in a fascinating article, "Good Guys with Guns," sociologist Angela Stroud asks what about just regular guys, nice guys with guns? What about those guys who don't seem to have much to prove at all, who don't feel insecure about that manhood? How is gun ownership interwoven with other masculine virtues, like being a provider for and protector of his family and being a good father and husband? Making gun owners the problem, Stroud suggests, will get us nowhere in addressing the problem of gun violence in America.

THE GENDER OF CRIME

If we are to understand the association of masculinity and violence, we must, therefore, be specific. First, we must look at different groups of men. Surely, violence is not evenly distributed among all groups of men but rather varies by class, race, age, region, ethnicity, and sexuality. Second, we must explore the historical fluctuations of that association and compare the contemporary United States with other industrial countries.

When we do that, an astonishing picture emerges. Stated most baldly: *Young American men are the most violent group of people in the industrialized world.* Our homicide rate is between five and twenty times higher than that of any other industrial democracy, and we imprison five and twenty times more people than does any other country on Earth except Russia. (Some might say that our prison population is so much higher because our crime rate is higher; others argue the opposite case, that our crime rate is so high because our prison population is so high. I think that both are partly true but that the relationship between prison and crime is not what common sense would have us believe. Prisons not only deter crime, but also teach criminals how to commit crimes.) Nine out of ten male murder victims are killed by other men; and nine out of ten female murder victims are killed by men. The U.S. homicide rate declined by nearly half (49 percent), from 9.3 homicides per one hundred thousand U.S. residents in 1992 to 4.7 in 2011(figure 14.1), falling to the lowest level since 1963. From 2002 to 2011, the average homicide rate for males was 3.6 times higher than the rate for females. The average homicide rate for blacks was 6.3 times higher than the rate for whites.[12] This figure is about ten times higher than that of the next-closest industrialized country, Italy, and more than sixty times greater than that of the same age group in England.[13]

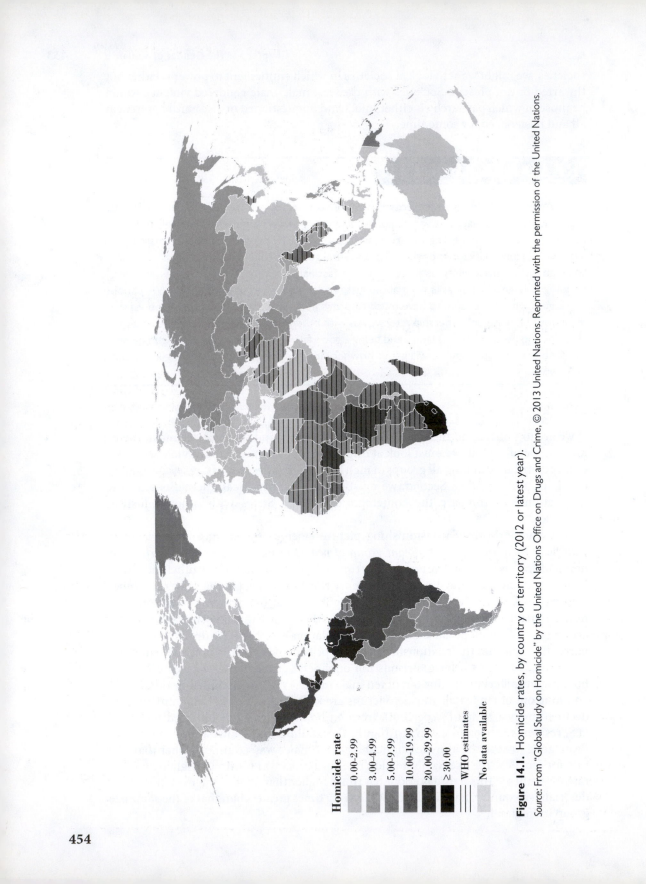

Figure 14.1. Homicide rates, by country or territory (2012 or latest year).

Source: From "Global Study on Homicide" by the United Nations Office on Drugs and Crime. © 2013 United Nations. Reprinted with the permission of the United Nations.

Homicide rate

- 0.00–2.99
- 3.00–4.99
- 5.00–9.99
- 10.00–19.99
- 20.00–29.99
- ≥ 30.00
- WHO estimates
- No data available

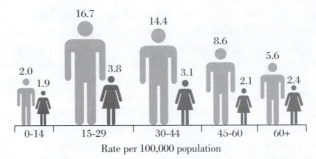

Figure 14.2. Global homicide rate, by sex and age group (2012 or latest year).

Source: From "Global Study on Homicide" by the United Nations Office on Drugs and Crime, © 2013 United Nations. Reprinted with the permission of the United Nations.

And it's getting worse. Between 1985 and 1994, the number of homicides by fourteen- to seventeen-year-old males more than tripled—as did the number of men in prison. In 1971, the American prison population was about two hundred thousand. Less than thirty years later it had mushroomed to more than 1.5 million convicted criminals incarcerated in the nation's fifteen hundred state and federal prisons, with another half-million sitting in the country's three thousand local jails. That's a rate of 645 per one hundred thousand Americans. On any given day, one out of every three African-American men in their twenties is either in prison, in jail, on probation, or on parole, compared with 17 percent of Hispanic males and 5.9 percent of white males.[14] In 2008, five states—Vermont, Michigan, Oregon, Connecticut, and Delaware—spent more on prisons than on higher education.[15]

According to the California Highway Patrol, nine out of ten of those arrested for drunk driving are men, 84 percent of those who are jailed for fatal accidents resulting from drunk driving are men, and 86 percent of arson crimes are committed by men.

The "Gender" of War and Peace

What do you think: Are war and peace somehow more masculine or feminine? If women were running things, do you think there would be less risk of violence and war?

Of course, if you subscribed to more biological arguments about brain chemistry or testosterone, you might agree with that idea: If you believe that males are programmed by evolution to be violent and competitive, or driven to aggression by testosterone, then you might also believe that you might well sleep more peacefully if tomorrow morning you awakened to a world in which every single political office—every local, national, and global institution—were staffed entirely by women.

But, you might say, what about those women who *are* in political office? They're no less bellicose than their male counterparts! What about Margaret Thatcher, Golda Meir, or Indira Gandhi?

And you'd be thinking sociologically. A sociological approach would consider the gender of the *person* occupying the office, as well as the gender of the *office* itself. Of course, it's true that if you raise one gender to be nonviolent empathic listeners who encourage children to "use their words," they might be less prone to use violence in public life. But it's just as true that certain offices require that one be willing, if one deems it necessary, to authorize violence.

Violence is the product of both gendered people and gendered institutional and political arrangements.

In fact, the classic profile of the arsonist is entirely gendered. "Look for a passive, unmarried man between the ages of 18 and 30 who lacks a capacity to confront people," according to Allan Hedberg, a California psychologist who studies arsonists. "Big forest fires with massive fire trucks and pandemonium are a way of making a masculine statement for an unstable young man who in the past has been wronged."[16]

On the other side of the police ledger, the statistics are also revealing. Although fewer than 5 percent of high-speed chases involve suspects wanted for violent felonies—most of the suspects are suspected of traffic violations—20 percent of all high-speed chases end in serious injury or death, most often of innocent bystanders. Why? Because it is almost always younger male officers who do the chasing. In one study in southern Florida, "winning a race" was cited by officers as the objective in a pursuit.[17]

Criminologist Marvin Wolfgang notes that violent crime rises any time there is an unusually high proportion of the population of young men between the ages of fifteen and twenty-four. Psychiatrist James Gilligan observes that the only two innate biological variables that are predictors of violence are youth and maleness. The relationship is immediately apparent if you look at a chart, as in figure 14.3a for mid-nineteenth-century Britain. And things aren't so different today, as you can see from a similar chart for Chicago between 1965 and 1990 (see figure 14.3b). Figure 14.3c shows the U.S. homicide rate in 2012 by age and sex.

Taken separately, gender and age are the two most powerful predictors of violence. Men are far more violent than women, and the likelihood of violence by either gender decreases as one ages. Consider, for example, the data from a survey of high school seniors in 1994. Nearly one-fifth of high school boys reported that they hurt

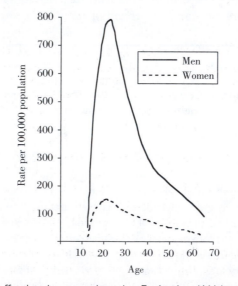

Figure 14.3a. Criminal offenders by age and gender, England and Wales, 1842–1844.

Source: Based on data from F. G. P. Neison, *Contributions to Vital Statistics*, 3rd ed. (London, 1857), pp. 303–304, as plotted by Travis Hirschi and Michael Gottfredson, "Age and the Explanation of Crime," *AJS*, 89, 1983, p. 556.

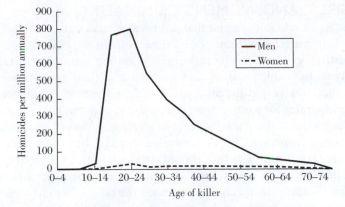

Figure 14.3b. Homicide rates in Chicago, 1965–1990, by age and gender.

Source: From "Darwinism and the Roots of Machismo," *Scientific American*, special issue, 2002.

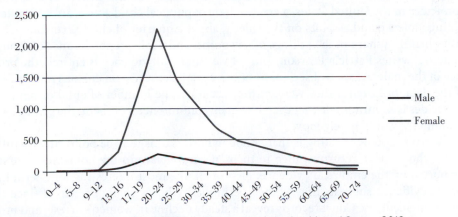

Figure 14.3c. Homicide rate by offender age group and gender, United States, 2012.

Source: Figure is based on Expanded Homicide Data Table 3 in the *FBI Crime in the United States 2012 Report*: https://www.fbi.gov/about-us/cjis/ucr/crime-in-the-u.s/2012/crime-in-the-u.s/2012/offenses-known-to-law-enforcement/expanded-homicide/expanded_homicide_data_table_3_murder_offenders_by_age_sex_and_race_2012.xls.

someone so badly that he or she needed to be bandaged or to see a doctor. One-twentieth of girls reported that level of violence.

In 2007, 5,764 young people ages ten to twenty-four were murdered—an average of sixteen each day (CDC 2010). Homicide was the second leading cause of death for young people ages ten to twenty-four years old. Among ten- to twenty-four-year-olds, 86 percent (4,973) of homicide victims were male and 14 percent (791) were female. In 2008, more than 656,000 young people ages ten to twenty-four were treated in emergency departments for injuries sustained from violence. Physical fighting was more reported by males (four in ten reported being in a physical fight in the preceding twelve months) than females (23 percent), but girls reported higher rates of bullying (21.2 percent) than males (18.7 percent).[18]

"MEAN GIRLS" AND WOMEN'S CRIMINALITY

Nonetheless, we should not pretend that just because males are overwhelmingly more likely to commit an act of violence or a crime, women never do so. In fact, there is some interesting evidence about criminality among women. Certainly, women commit crimes. But which crimes they commit and their reasons for committing them are sometimes very different from men's. In the mid-1970s, two sociologists noted that crime rates for women were increasing significantly. Freda Adler and Rita Simon each argued that there was evidence of increasing rates of **women's criminality**. And each blamed feminism. "Is it any wonder," asked Adler, "that once women were armed with male opportunities they should strive for status, criminal as well as civil, through established male hierarchical channels?" Simon nuanced her claims a bit more, arguing that feminism actually decreased the rates of female violent crime, because women were less subject to direct male control but that feminism increased the rates of property crimes.[19]

Some contemporary analysts blame feminism not for the increase in women's criminality, but rather for our ignorance of it. "Women commit the majority of child homicides in the United States, a greater share of physical child abuse, an equal rate of sibling violence and assaults on the elderly, about a quarter of child sexual abuse, an overwhelming share of the killings of newborns, and a fair preponderance of spousal assaults," writes Patricia Pearson, and yet we still think violence is entirely the province of the male. As we will see, many of these statistics hinge on curious misreadings of the data, but even if they were entirely accurate, the number of child or newborn homicides is so minuscule that even if women committed all of them, the gender ratio of homicide would barely move.[20]

What's more interesting is that although both claims may be politically useful to those who want to return women to their "natural" place in the home, they are not supported by the empirical evidence. First of all, the most interesting long-term historical evidence suggests that women's criminality has actually *decreased* since the eighteenth century. Court records reveal a steady decline in women's arrests and prosecutions since the eighteenth century, brought about, in part, by changes in the definition of femininity and the "**cult of domesticity**" that made women angels of their households:

> By the end of the nineteenth century, there was a clear separation of home and work, a firmer sexual division of labor, the exclusion of women from the public sphere and from productive work, and the confinement of women to reproductive and domestic work in the home ... There was also a decline in female criminal court involvement during this period.[21]

Despite the increases in crime rates for women over the past few decades, the base numbers were so small to begin with that *any* modest increase would appear to be a larger percentage increase than that among men. In fact, the sex differential in crime has remained roughly the same when seen as a number per one hundred thousand of population. Then it becomes clear that, as one criminologist put it simply, "relative to males, the profile of the female offender has not changed."[22]

Violent crimes by women actually seem to have decreased. Murder is the most prevalent form of violent crime committed by women, and nearly two-thirds of those women convicted of murder killed a relative, intimate, or someone else they knew (compared with less than one-third of the men). Over the past twenty years, the rate at which men have been killed by their wives has fallen by close to two-thirds, whereas the rate at which women have been killed by their intimate partners has fallen by one-third, which was the overall decline in the nation's homicide rate from 1981 to 1998.[23] (Although women convicted of murder receive, on average, a sentence more than three years shorter than that of men convicted of murder, this sentencing differential seems to have less to do with the gender of the murderer and more to do with the circumstances of the murder, the past criminal history of the murderer, and the murderer's relationship to the murdered—that is, men who murder an intimate partner tend to receive sentences roughly equal in length to those of the women.)[24] At least part of the explanation for this precipitous decline in the women's homicide rate must be the expansion of services for battered women, so that now women whose intimate partner batters and/or rapes them have alternatives that support their leaving the relationship.[25]

There have been some reported increases in women's property crime, especially fraud, forgery, and embezzlement, but most of those increases have been in petty theft—in other words, shoplifting, committing credit card fraud, passing bad checks. Crimes that seem to be most attractive to women are those that, like shoplifting, enable women to express their desires without taking responsibility for them. They want, they desire, they crave—but they know that femininity requires the suppression of desire. Shoplifting is "stealing beauty," as in the title of a recent film; stealing sexuality, adulthood, lust, and passion—without loss of reputation. As criminologist Jack Katz argues:

> The young girls seem especially seduced by items of makeup, jewelry, and clothes: things used to cover up the naked female self, to give the body the appearance of the mature female, and to make the self dazzlingly attractive to a world blinded to the blemishes underneath. Females take symbols of adult female identity—cosmetics, jewelry and sexy underwear.[26]

If, Katz argues, shoplifting is the prototypical "female" crime because it is about satisfying desire without taking responsibility, then the stickup is the prototypical "male" crime: fast, aggressive, dangerous, and violent. (Men outnumber women in arrests for robbery by about fifteen to one.) And directly personal. The "badass" stickup guy is phallic power—hard and tough, using his gun to threaten penetration. Street robbery may make little rational sense as a way of making money, but it is still enormously appealing to young males; it's a way of "doing gender":

> Unless it is given sense as a way of elaborating, perhaps celebrating, distinctively male forms of action and ways of being, such as collective drinking and gambling on street corners, interpersonal physical challenges and moral tests, cocky posturing and arrogant claims to back up "tough" fronts, stickup has almost no appeal at all.[27]

Yet the evidence on gender and violence does not lead to the conclusion that all men are violent, rapacious beasts and that all women are angelic and nonviolent little lambs. Societies that have high rates of male crime also tend to have high rates of female crime. We need to remember that the three most common arrest categories—for both women and men—are driving under the influence, larceny-theft, and "other except traffic" (a category that includes mostly criminal mischief, public disorder, and minor offenses). Taken together, these three offense categories account for 48 percent of all male arrests and 49 percent of all female arrests. It's when crime turns violent that the gender patterns emerge most starkly.[28]

There is evidence of female violence, of course—but it remains dramatically different from men's violence. For example, women's violence tends to be defensive, whereas men are more often the initiators of violent acts. And whereas men's violence may be instrumental—designed to accomplish some goal—or expressive of emotion, women's violence often is the outcome of feeling trapped and helpless. For example, the types of violent crimes that women are either as likely or more likely to commit than men—child homicide, child abuse, assault on the elderly, murder of newborns, as well as female-initiated spousal abuse or spousal murder—seem to stem from terror and helplessness.[29]

The gendered patterns of violence among children are also revealing. Among three-year-olds, for example, the most frequent acts of violence are boy-to-boy; girl-to-girl violence, by contrast, is the least frequent. Boy-to-girl violence is far more frequent than girl-to-boy. In one study, two Finnish psychologists contrasted physical, verbal, and "indirect" forms of aggression. They found that girls at all ages (except the youngest) were more likely to engage in indirect aggression (telling lies behind a person's back; trying to be someone's friend as revenge against another; saying to others, "Let's not be friends with him or her"). Boys at all ages were more likely to engage in direct aggression (kicking, hitting, tripping, shoving, arguing, swearing, and abusing) and verbal aggression. Girls at all ages were also more likely to use peaceful means (talking to clarify things, forgetting about it, telling a teacher or parent) to resolve problems and were also more likely to withdraw or sulk.[30]

We have some evidence that the gender gap in violence is decreasing. One study from Finland found that girls in the 1980s were much less violent than in the 1990s, both from self-reports and from reports of their peers. The study also found greater acceptance of violence among the girls. But in the late 1990s, the study found, violence had a more positive connotation for girls, "something that makes the girl feel powerful, strong, and makes her popular"—in short, doing for girls what violence and aggression have historically done for boys.[31]

A spate of recent books about girls' aggression throws new light on these issues.[32] Some writers, like Rachel Simmons, argue that such indirect aggression may have devastating effects on girls' development, self-esteem, and aspirations:

> Unlike boys, who tend to bully acquaintances or strangers, girls frequently attack within tightly knit friendship networks, making aggression harder to identify and intensifying the damage to the victims. Within the hidden culture of aggression, girls fight with body language and relationships instead of fists and knives. In this world, friendship is a weapon, and the sting of a shout pales in comparison to a day of someone's silence. There is no gesture more devastating than the back turning away.

But girls' indirect forms of aggression are not the expression of some innately devious feminine wiles, but rather the consequences of gender inequality. "Our culture refuses girls access to open conflict, and it forces their aggression into nonphysical, indirect, and covert forms. Girls use backbiting, exclusion, rumors, name-calling, and manipulation to inflict physical pain on targeted victims," Simmons writes. Indirect horizontal aggression is the safest and easiest way to express one's anger. Were girls permitted the kind of aggression that boys are, they would not express their anger in such backhanded ways.[33]

Evidence of women's increased violence—that is, of a decreasing gender gap—is still scant and spotty. In the United States, women constitute only 7 percent of the prison population (about 115,000 inmates). One-half of women prisoners are incarcerated in just four states—Florida, Texas, California, and New York. The female inmate population tends to mirror the male inmate population demographically (not in terms of offenses), including a disproportionate number of nonwhite, poor, and undereducated and unemployed women. Violence remains perhaps the most gendered behavior in our culture.[34]

GENDERED VIOLENCE: AN INSTITUTIONAL PROBLEM

After he had successfully tested a nuclear bomb in November 1952, creating a fusion explosion about one thousand times more powerful than the fission bomb that destroyed Hiroshima seven years earlier, Edward Teller, the Nobel Prize–winning nuclear physicist, wrote the following three-word telegram to his colleagues: "It's a boy." No one had to point out to Teller the equation of military might—the capacity for untold violence—with masculinity. Such a tragic connection remains fixed for both the military heroes of our masculine fantasies and the bespectacled scientists who create the technology that enables those Rambo-wannabes to conquer the world.

It would be easy to catalog all the phallic images and rhetoric in that vast historic parade of military heroes in decorated uniforms and scientists in white lab coats, suggesting that proving masculinity is a common currency for both warrior and wonk, gladiator and geek. Pop psychologists have yet to run out of sexually tinged phrases to describe this; one feminist calls masculine militarism a case of "missile envy"; another writes about how men "created civilization in the image of a perpetual erection: a pregnant phallus." But these images turn gender into a screen against which individuals project their psychological fears and problems, reducing war and the state's use of institutional violence to a simple aggregation of insecure men desperate to prove their masculinity. Although this argument is not entirely without merit, as we shall see, it leaves us without an understanding of the institutional violence that is implicit in the construction of the modern bureaucratic state. For that understanding we need to explore the link between the two realms, how "militarism perpetuates the equation between masculinity and violence" and how war "encodes violence into the notion of masculinity generation after generation."[35]

Though masculinity may be associated historically with war, the way we fight today would leave many men without the ability to test and prove their manhood in a conventional military way. After all, most soldiers today are not combatants. Most are in support services—transport, administration, technical support, maintenance. The increasingly technological sophistication of war has only sped up this process—nuclear weapons, "smart bombs," automatic weaponry, self-propelled military vehicles, and long-distance weapons all reduce the need for Rambo-type primitive warriors and increase the need for cool, rational button-pushers.[36]

Yet there is something powerful in the ways that our political leaders seek to prove an aggressive and assertive masculinity in the political arena. War and its technology confer upon men a "virile prestige," as French philosopher Simone de Beauvoir put it. Think of Andrew Jackson's man-making slaughter of the Seminoles or Theodore Roosevelt's thundering about the strenuous life as he charged up San Juan Hill. For much of our history, our political leaders have tried to balance manly restraint with equally manly belligerence. Military prowess and the willingness to go to war have been tests of manhood. Explaining why President Lyndon Johnson continued to escalate the war in Vietnam, a biographer writes,

> He wanted the respect of men who were tough, real men, and they would turn out to be hawks. He had unconsciously divided people around him between men and boys. Men were activists, doers, who conquered business empires, who acted instead of talked, who made it in the world of other men, and had the respect of other men. Boys were the talkers and the writers and the intellectuals, who sat around thinking and criticizing and doubting instead of doing.

(In case you find such sentiments strange, think about the cliché "Those who can do, and those who can't do, teach.") When opponents criticized the war effort, Johnson attacked their masculinity. When informed that one member of his administration was becoming a dove on Vietnam, Johnson scoffed, "Hell, he has to squat to piss!" And, as Johnson celebrated the bombings of North Vietnam, he declared proudly that he "didn't just screw Ho Chi Minh. I cut his pecker off."[37]

Such boasts continue to plague American politics. Jimmy Carter's reluctance to intervene in Iran led one security affairs analyst to comment that the United States was "spreading its legs for the Soviet Union" and led to the election of Ronald Reagan, who promised to rescue America from its post-Vietnam lethargy—which he accomplished, in part, by invading small countries like Grenada. As one political commentator put it, Reagan "made mincemeat of Mr. Carter and Mr. Mondale, casting them as girly-boys who lacked the swagger necessary to lead the world." George H. W. Bush inherited the right to that masculine mantle when he invaded Panama and the Persian Gulf for Operation Desert Storm. Bill Clinton's popularity ratings soared when, during his impeachment hearings in 1998, he threatened and eventually undertook air strikes against Iraq. And George W. Bush's invasion of Iraq proved popular enough to ensure Republican electoral victories and to knock the corporate scandals of his friends' companies, the failure of the war against terrorism, and an economic recession off the front page (figure 14.4).[38]

Such presidential sentiments both trickle down to those who are charged with creating and fighting those wars and bubble up to policymakers from the defense strategists who are trained to prosecute those wars and who are today calculating the megatonnage and kill ratios for future ones. "There is among some people a feeling of compulsion about the pursuit of advanced technologies—a sense that a man must be continually proving his virility by pioneering on the frontiers of what is only just possible." In an article about masculinity and the Vietnam War, journalist I. F. Stone illustrated this compulsive proving of masculinity among those who planned the war.

Figure 14.4. AP Photo/J. Scott Applewhite, File.

At a briefing about the escalation of the bombing of North Vietnam, one Pentagon official described the U.S. strategy as two boys fighting: "If one boy gets the other in an arm lock, he can probably get his adversary to say 'uncle' if he increases the pressure in sharp, painful jolts and gives every indication of willingness to break the boy's arm." And recently, when a German politician indicated he was concerned about popular opposition to Euromissile deployment, one American defense strategist opined, "Those Krauts are a bunch of limp-dicked wimps."[39]

Carol Cohn conducted an ethnographic analysis of defense intellectuals. She recalls that "lectures were filled with discussion of vertical erector launchers, thrust-to-weight ratios, soft lay-downs, deep penetration, and the comparative advantage of protracted versus spasm attacks—or what one military advisor to the National Security Council has called 'releasing 70 to 80 percent of our megatonnage in one orgasmic whump.' There was serious concern about the need to harden our missiles, and the need to 'face it, the Russians are a little harder than we are.' Disbelieving glances would occasionally pass between me and my ally—another woman—but no one else seemed to notice."[40]

It would be simplistic to reduce the complexities of military and political decisions to psychological "pissing contests," but it is equally important to include a discussion of gender in our investigations. From the top political leaders to military strategists and technological experts, issues of gender play themselves out in the formulation of military policy. And public opinion also plays an important role in these demonstrations of sexual potency. Recall, for example, how during the Gulf War, our enemy Saddam Hussein was constantly sexualized on bumper stickers that read "Saddam, Bend Over" and "U.S.A.—Up Saddam's Ass," insults that equated military conflict with homosexual rape. One widely reprinted cartoon showed Saddam Hussein bending over as if in Muslim prayer, with a huge U.S. missile approaching, about to penetrate him from behind. Thus was the sexual nature of military adventurism played out in sexual paraphernalia.

AMERICA: A HISTORY OF GENDERED VIOLENCE

Although we commonly think that all states require the use of violence—that the creation and maintenance of politics require both a police force and a military to subdue both ourselves and others—the equation of violence and masculinity remains a particularly strong one for Americans. The United States has a long and bloody history of specifically gendered violence, in which both individual men and Americans as a nation have demonstrated and proved manhood. It's not just our political and military leaders—although, as we have seen, they certainly have had their issues as well. One psychologist speaks of a "civic advocacy of violence as socially acceptable, appropriate and necessary." Our most venerated cultural heroes were soldiers—or, at least, the actors who played them in the movies.[41]

Historians suggest that this particularly American, and particularly tragic, code of violence arrived in the eighteenth century, imported and developed by Scottish and Irish immigrants to the American South, where brawling, dueling, fighting, hunting, and drinking became the means to express manhood. Andrew Jackson's mother told her son, arguably the most mean-tempered and violent president in our nation's history, that "the law affords no remedy that can satisfy the feelings of a true man." The American frontier—perhaps the single largest collection of younger males in the history of the industrialized world—provided a legacy of violence to American life. Violence has always been highest in those places where young men gather, especially away from the "civilizing" effect of women.[42]

In the aftermath of the Civil War, after the South had suffered a humiliating and emasculating defeat, young boys took to placing chips of wood on their shoulders, daring other boys to knock off the chips so the boys could legitimately fight with them. Only in America is "having a chip on one's shoulder" considered a badge of honor among boys. More than that, violence was seen as legitimate—as long as it was retaliatory. If someone else knocked that chip off, kicking his ass was a reasonable response. In her penetrating analysis of American violence, anthropologist Margaret Mead described the typically American refusal to initiate aggression but a willingness to retaliate far out of proportion to the original offense in "an aggression which can never be shown except when the other fellow starts it" and which is "so unsure of itself that it had to be proved." Remember these words the next time you watch two young boys square off in a playground. "You wanna start something?" one of them yells. "No, but if you start it, I'll finish it!" replies the other. No one wants to take responsibility for the initial act of aggression, but everyone wants to finish the fight.[43]

Violence has long been understood as the best way to ensure that others publicly recognize one's manhood. Fighting was once culturally prescribed for boys, who, the theory went, needed to demonstrate gender identity. In one of the best-selling advice manuals of the first part of the twentieth century, parents learned the following:

> There are times when every boy must defend his own rights if he is not to become a coward and lose the road to independence and true manhood...The strong willed boy needs no inspiration to combat, but often a good deal of guidance and restraint. If he fights more than, let us say, a half dozen times a week,—except, of course, during his first week at a new school—he is probably over-quarrelsome and needs to curb. The sensitive, retiring boy, on the other hand, needs encouragement to stand his ground and fight.

In this best-seller, boys were encouraged to fight once a day, except during the first week at a new school, when, presumably, they would fight more often![44]

Lurking beneath such advice was the fear that boys who were not violent would not grow up to be real men. The specter of the "sissy"—encompassing the fears of emasculation, humiliation, and effeminacy that American men carry with them—is responsible for a significant amount of masculine violence. Violence is proof of masculinity; one is a "real" man, because one is not afraid to be violent. Psychiatrist James Gilligan speaks of "the patriarchal code of honor and shame which generates and obligates male violence"—a code that sees violence as the chief demarcating line between women and men.[45]

The contemporary code of violence of the streets descended from old Southern notions of honor—a man had to be ready to fight to prove himself in the eyes of others. Southern whites called it "honor"; by the turn of the twentieth century it was called "reputation." By the 1950s Northern ghetto blacks spoke of "respect," which has now been transformed again into not showing "disrespect," or "dissing." It's the same code of violence, the same daring. Listen to one New York gang member describing the reasons that his gang requires random knife slashings as initiation rituals: "Society claims we are notorious thugs and killers but we are not," he says. "We're a family of survivors ... proud young black men living in the American ghetto. Harlem princes trying to rise up and refusing to be beaten down." Another man recalls his days in a juvenile detention facility where "you fought almost every day because everybody trying to be tougher than the next person." Another street hood gives a contemporary slant to the old "chip on the shoulder" when he describes what he calls the "accidental bump" when a male is walking around Spanish Harlem "with your chest out, bumping into people and hoping they'll give you a bad time so you can pounce on them and beat 'em into the goddamn concrete." Sociologist Vic Seidler writes that "as boys, we have to be constantly on the alert to either confront or avoid physical violence. We have to be alert to defend ourselves…Masculinity is never something we can feel at ease with. It's always something we have to be ready to prove and defend." And criminologist Hans Toch adds that "in cultures of masculinity, the demonstrated willingness to fight and the capacity for combat are measures of worth and self-worth."[46]

Masculinity is still often equated with the capacity for violence. From the locker room to the chat room, men of all ages learn that violence is a socially sanctioned form of expression. Male socialization is a socialization to the legitimacy of violence—from infantile circumcision to violence from parents and siblings to routine fights with other boys to the socially approved forms of violence in the military, sports, and prison (the United States is the only industrialized country that still employs capital punishment) to epigrams that remind us that we should get even, not mad, and that the working world is the Hobbesian war of each against all, a jungle where dogs eat dogs.

VIOLENCE AGAINST WOMEN

Men learn that violence is an accepted form of communication among men and between women and men. It's so commonplace, so deeply woven into the fabric of daily life, that we accept violence as a matter of course—within families, between friends, between lovers. Most victims of violence know their attackers; many know them

Not Just Whistlin' Dixie

What if I told you it's not just age and gender that are good predictors of violence, but also region? That young Southern white men are more prone to violence than young men in any other part of the country? Sound far-fetched?

In the early 1990s, two Michigan psychologists, Dov Cohen and Richard Nisbett, conducted an experiment to find out. They invited young men to fill out a questionnaire in a classroom building at the university and then to drop it off at the end of the hallway and then return to the classroom. Half the guys did just that. The other half, however, encountered another guy (a confederate of the experiment) in the narrow hallway, who opened a drawer in a filing cabinet as the "subject" walked by. The hallway was even narrower now, and the confederate looked up, annoyed, and slammed the filing cabinet drawer shut and muttered, in an audible voice, "Asshole."

Cohen and Nisbett then did a series of tests to see if the insult had any effect on the guys who experienced it. They watched and recorded their faces. They shook their hands to see if their grip changed. They took saliva samples to measure testosterone

levels. They asked the guys to read a short story and to supply an ending (to see if the insulted guys' ending was more violent).

For some of the guys, being insulted caused no changes at all. (They were like the control group who simply walked down the hall.) But for some of the guys, the insult changed a lot. And virtually all of them were from the South. (Northerners were more amused by it, and their reactions were unchanged.) Young white guys from the South, Cohen and Nisbett concluded, are driven by a strict code of honor; insult that honor and they are ready to fight.

Think of it this way. When the Canadian Neil Young wrote a song condemning racism in the South, some young white Southern boys took it as a slur on the South itself. That code of honor kicked into high gear and Lynyrd Skynyrd penned one of the angriest hymns to their home state of Alabama. Maybe white Southerners are, as Floridian Tom Petty put it, "born a rebel."

Source: Robert Nisbett and Dov Cohen, *Culture of Honor: The Psychology of Violence in the South* (Boulder: Westview, 1996).

intimately. Nearly one in five victims of violence treated in hospital emergency rooms was injured by a spouse, a former spouse, or a current or former boyfriend or girlfriend. Violence can be a private, personal, and intimate language, just as it can be a mode of public address between societies and social groups.

The gender imbalance of intimate violence provides insight into gender dynamics. According to the National Intimate Partner and Sexual Violence Survey prepared by the Centers for Disease Control, more than one out of three women (35.6 percent) and more than one out of four men (28.5 percent) have experienced rape, physical violence, and/or stalking by an intimate partner in their lifetime. For about one in four women (24.3 percent) and one in seven men (13.8 percent), that violence was severe. Just under half of both women and men have experienced psychological aggression. Between 30 percent and 40 percent of all women who are murdered are murdered by a husband or a boyfriend, according to the FBI (about 5 percent of males are murdered by wives or girlfriends) (Figure 14.5). Every six minutes a woman in the United States is raped; every eighteen seconds a woman is beaten; and every day four women are killed by their batterers.[47]

Interestingly, while rates of **intimate partner violence** have decreased over the past two decades, that decrease is almost entirely in the rates of *male* victims.

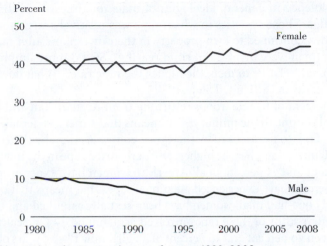

Figure 14.5. Homicides of intimates, by sex of victim, 1980–2008.

Note: Percentages are based on the 63.1 percent of homicides from 1980 through 2008 for which victim/offender relationships were known. Intimate includes spouses, ex-spouses, boyfriends, girlfriends, and same-sex relationships. Friend/acquaintance includes neighbors, employees, employers, and other known persons.

Source: U.S. Department of Justice Bureau of Justice Statistics: Homicide Trends in the United States, 1980–2008, http://www.bjs.gov/content/pub/pdf/htus8008.pdf, p. 18.

It doesn't have to be this way, of course. As we saw earlier, societies may be located on a continuum from rape-free to rape-prone. Anthropologist Peggy Reeves Sanday found that the best predictors of rape-proneness were levels of militarism,

OH? REALLY •

Remember Thornhill and Palmer, from chapter 2—the guys whose studies of fruit flies led them to claim that rape is an evolutionary strategy for guys who can't otherwise get a date?

Don't you wonder how they could explain rape as a strategy of war? Sure, they might say that the victorious soldiers might rape the women of the vanquished population so as to impregnate them with a new generation of "their" offspring. This seems to have been partially a motivation for the mass rapes of Bosnian Muslim women by Serbs or the half-million Tutsi women who were raped by Hutu men in the Rwandan genocide of 1994.

But it doesn't explain the **rape-as-recreation** model employed by the Soviet army in Germany after World War II (estimates vary between one hundred thousand and two million women raped), or the Bengali women raped by Indian soldiers in 1971, or the two hundred thousand Chinese sex slaves provided to the Japanese army during World War II. Let alone the Congo, where, at this writing, hundreds of thousands of women have been raped and murdered. A report by the Harvard Humanitarian Initiative and Oxfam examined rape survivors at one hospital in a northern province. Their ages ranged from three to eighty. Some were single, some married, some widowed. Three out of five had been gang raped. They were raped in front of husbands and children. Sons were forced to rape their mothers and killed if they refused.

There is nothing evolutionary or "natural" about this cruel sport.

Source: "War's Overlooked Victims" in *Economist*, January 15, 2011, pp. 63–65.

interpersonal violence in general, ideologies of male toughness, and distant father-child relationships. Those societies in which rape was relatively rare valued women's autonomy (women continued to own property in their own name after marriage) and valued children (men were involved in child rearing). Stated most simply, "the lower the status of women relative to men, the higher the rape rate." What does that tell us about women's status in the United States?[48]

Forty-five percent of female troops returning from Afghanistan and Iraq had experienced sexual trauma in the military. This means that American female soldiers are more likely—by far—to be attacked by their own comrades than by the enemy.[49]

In fact, the United States has the highest rate of reported rape in the industrial world. Between 12 percent and 25 percent of all American women have experienced rape, and another 12–20 percent have experienced attempted rape. That means that between one-fourth and nearly one-half of all women have been sexually assaulted and that between two-thirds and four-fifths of these rapes involved acquaintances. One calculation estimates that between 20 percent and 30 percent of all girls now twelve years old will suffer a violent sexual attack during their lives.[50]

What is perhaps more frightening is that of those twelve-year-old girls, more than 12 percent have *already* been raped. According to the National Intimate Partner and Sexual Violence Survey, 12.3 percent of rape victims were younger than age twelve when they were first raped, and 29.9 percent were between the ages of eleven and seventeen.[51]

Another study found that 96 percent of those female rape victims under twelve knew their attackers. In one of five cases, their rapist was also their father. Although there is some evidence that suggests that females under eighteen are also the most likely to file false reports of rape with the police (though virtually none of these allegations ever went to trial, and all the reports were retracted in the interview stage), these false reports seem to be the result of fears of pregnancy and the hope that declaring they were raped would permit the females to get an abortion, because in many states, abortion is legal only in cases of rape or a threat to the mother's health. But these cases of rape of young girls can hardly be subsumed under some vague and insulting heading of relationship "miscommunication."[52]

READ ALL ABOUT IT!

We all know that rape is less a crime of passion than a crime of violence. It is an assault, not a date-gone-wrong. So if we know that, how come so many of us get it "wrong"—that is, how come sexual assault remains one of the most painful aspects of campus life in twenty-first-century America? Maybe it's because we don't really understand what the assault is, what makes sexual assault "permissible" among large groups of us. Perhaps young men give themselves permission not to "understand" what "no" might mean—let alone what "yes" might mean. In a revealing study, psychologist Rachel O'Byrne and her colleagues found that men strategically don't hear that "no," or claim that it was "insufficient knowledge." As they put it, "If a girl doesn't say 'no' . . ." What might on the surface look like a miscommunication is actually far more strategic, and far less spontaneous, than we might have earlier thought.

OH? REALLY•

He said, she said?

Many of us believe that sexual assault is difficult to prosecute because it is a case of "he said, she said." But what he and she actually *say* is based on what they perceive. We may believe it when we see it, but in this case, see it only if we already believe it.

In perhaps the largest survey of sexual behavior ever undertaken in the United States, Edward Laumann and other researchers at the University of Chicago found that 96.1 percent of men had never been forced to do something sexual against their will. Over three-fourths of women (77.2 percent) had never been forced to do something sexual.

But that's not necessarily the most interesting part of the research findings. Here's what the researchers found:

Prevalence of Forced Sex, by Gender (percentages)

	Men	Women
Respondent ever forced a woman	2.8	.1
Respondent ever forced a man	.2	1.5
Never sexually forced	96.1	77.2
Forced by a woman	1.3	.3
Forced by a man	1.9	21.6
Forced by both men and women	.4	.5
Missing/no answer	.3	.5
N	1,409	1,749

Source: Laumann et al., *The Social Organization of Sexuality: Sexual Practices in the United States* (Chicago: University of Chicago Press, 1994), p. 336.

Sociologist Tristan Bridges notes that he asks students to reconcile the highlighted parts of the chart: 1.5 percent of women stated that they had forced sex on a man, which is a teeny-tiny bit higher than the percentage of men (1.3 percent) who said they'd ever had sex forced on them by a woman. In other words, the percentages match nearly perfectly. But 2.8 percent of men said they'd ever forced sex on a woman—which is close to eight times lower than the percentage of women who said they'd had sex forced on them by a man (21.6 percent).

How can we reconcile this? Women are overreporting? Men are lying? One can't tell by the data. What it means is that many men are unaware that they have sexually forced women in the first place. That is, what seemed "consensual" or "normal" was perceived by her as forcing. This is the result, Bridges puts it, of gender inequality "shaping the ways in which we experience desire in addition to the ways we fulfill those desires."

Sources: Edward Laumann, Robert Michels, John Gagnon, and Stuart Michaels, *The Social Organization of Sexuality: Sexual Practices in the United States* (Chicago: University of Chicago Press, 1994), p. 336; and Tristan Bridges, "Gendering Sex and Sexual Violence," available at http://inequalitybyinteriordesign. wordpress.com/2012/03/01/ gendering-sex-and-sexual-violence.htm.

The recent revelations of pervasive child sexual abuse by Catholic priests (and the church's subsequent efforts to cover up these crimes) remind us of how vulnerable boys are as well. Although these revelations have been shocking, pedophile sexual abuse should not be confused with homosexual rape; **pedophilia** is a "sexual orientation," not a variation of homosexuality. Pedophile priests are erotically attracted not to members of their own sex, but rather to children (some choose boys, others choose girls, and some are indiscriminant). The erotic charge comes from the presumed seductive innocence of the child, not the attraction of one's own gender. And boys are no more vulnerable to same-sex sexual assault by their peers (as opposed to adults) in the Catholic Church than they are in any other mostly single-sex and gender-unequal institutions.

As we saw in earlier chapters, different theoretical schools offer different explanations for all sorts of rape. Arguments that rape is simply the reproductive strategy for losers in the sexual arena are unconvincing. Equally unconvincing are psychological arguments that rape is an isolated, individual act, committed by sick individuals who experience uncontrollable sexual impulses. After all, almost 75 percent of all rapists plan their rapes. And only about 5 percent of rapists can be categorized as psychotic. Nor is it persuasive to blame alcohol or drugs as the cause of men losing control. Why, then, wouldn't women lose control of themselves in the same way?

An adequate explanation of rape has to recognize that it is men who rape women and ask the more frightening question: Why do so many "otherwise" typical, normal men commit rape? As sociologist Allan Johnson puts it, how can such a pervasive event be the work of a few lunatics? "It is difficult to believe that such widespread violence is the responsibility of a small lunatic fringe of psychopathic men," he writes. "That sexual violence is so pervasive supports the view that the focus of violence against women rests squarely in the middle of what our culture defines as 'normal' interaction between men and women." The reality is that rape is committed by all-American, regular guys. And, on campus, "college women are at greater risk of being raped or aggressed against by the men they know and date than they are by lunatics in the bushes."[53]

Surveys of college women reveal the prevalence of rape, and surveys of college men indicate how casually rape can be viewed. Mary Koss's research on campus date and **acquaintance rape**, although the subject of vicious backlash attacks, remains the most impressive and thorough research we have on rape's frequency and scope. She found that nearly half (44 percent) of all women surveyed experienced some forms of sexual activity when they didn't want to, 15 percent experienced attempted rape, 12 percent were coerced by drugs and alcohol, a full 25 percent had sexual intercourse when they didn't want to because they were "overwhelmed" by a man's overwhelming arguments and pressure, and 9 percent were forcibly raped. The National College Women Sexual Victimization Study, published in 2000, estimated that between 20 and 25 percent of college women experience completed or attempted rape during their college years.[54]

Further, a 2007 national-level study of drug-facilitated, incapacitated, and forcible rape, which included a sample of college women, found that approximately 673,000 of nearly six million current college women (11.5 percent) have been raped. In addition, another 2007 Department of Justice survey found 19 percent of the women reported experiencing completed or attempted sexual assault since entering college. Since entering college, slightly more women experienced completed sexual assault (13.7 percent) than attempted sexual assault (12.6 percent), with 7.2 percent of the women experiencing both completed sexual assault and attempted sexual assault during college.[55]

No wonder feminist writer Susan Griffin called rape "the all-American crime," engaged in by normal, all-American guys. Yet it is also equally true that most men do not commit rape. In several surveys, many men indicated that they would consider rape—provided the conditions were "right" and they knew that they would not get caught. In a survey of American college men, 28 percent indicated that they would be likely to commit rape and use force to get sex; 6 percent said they would commit rape but not use force, and 30 percent said they might use force but would not commit rape. Forty percent indicated that they would neither use force nor commit rape—less than half! In another survey, 37 percent indicated some likelihood of committing rape if they were certain they would not be caught.[56]

Something still holds men back—well, at least some men! Is it simply the fear of being caught? Or is it that they can't quite take demonstrating their masculinity to that next level? In a sense, what we see is not that rapists are nonconformists, psychologically unbalanced perverts who couldn't otherwise get sex but rather that rapists are actually *over*conformists—exceptionally committed to a set of norms about masculinity that makes every encounter with every woman potentially, even inevitably, about sexual conquest, that turns every date into a contest, and that turns a deaf ear to what a woman might want because, after all, women aren't men's equals to begin with. "The most striking characteristic of sex offenders," writes one researcher, "is their apparent normality." Bernard Lefkowitz, author of a chillingly detailed portrait of a gang rape of a mentally retarded girl by several high-status high school athletes in Glen Ridge, New Jersey, argues that "for a lot of boys, acting abusively toward women is regarded as a rite of passage. It's woven into our culture." So any discussion of rape has to take account of the ordinariness of the crime within the normative definition of masculinity and of the empirical reality that despite all that, most men do not and never will commit rape. If rape is normative, are nonrapists not real men?[57]

In a fascinating study of convicted rapists, sociologist Diana Scully develops these themes. Scully found that rape was used by men "to put women in their place," she writes. "Rape is a man's right," one convicted rapist told her. "If a woman doesn't want to give it, a man should take it. Women have no right to say no. Women are made to have sex. It's all they are good for. Some women would rather take a beating, but they always give in; it's what they are for." Men rape, Scully concludes, "not because they are idiosyncratic or irrational, but because they have learned that in this culture sexual violence is rewarding" and because "they never thought they would be punished for what they did."[58]

OH? REALLY •

Rapists are sick individuals who otherwise can't get sex.

Actually, that's not true at all. In her fascinating study of convicted rapists, sociologist Diana Scully found that rapists are just as likely to have regular sexual partners as nonrapists. In fact, they have higher rates (so much for being sexual "losers," as the evolutionary psychologists claimed). They're just as likely to be married and fathers as nonrapists. And most showed little evidence of mental illness.

Source: Diana Scully, *Understanding Sexual Vidence* (New York: Routledge, 1991).

Rape is a crime that combines sex and violence, that makes sex the weapon in an act of violence. It's less a crime of passion than a crime of power, less about love or lust than about conquest and contempt, less an expression of longing than an expression of entitlement. You might think that when men think about rape, then, they think about the power they feel.

You'd be wrong. Listen to the voice of one young man, a twenty-three-year-old stock boy named Jay in a San Francisco corporation, who was asked by author Tim Beneke to think about under what circumstances he might commit rape. Jay has never committed rape. He's simply an average guy trying to imagine the circumstances under which he would commit an act of violence against a woman. Here's what Jay says:

> Let's say I see a woman and she looks really pretty and really clean and sexy and she's giving off very feminine, sexy vibes. I think, wow I would love to make love to her, but I know she's not interested. It's a tease. A lot of times a woman knows that she's looking really good and she'll use that and flaunt it and it makes me feel like she's laughing at me and I feel degraded...If I were actually desperate enough to rape somebody it would be from wanting that person, but also it would be a very spiteful thing, just being able to say "I have power over you and I can do anything I want with you" because really I feel that they have power over me just by their presence. Just the fact that they can come up to me and just melt me makes me feel like a dummy, makes me want revenge. They have power over me so I want power over them.[59]

Jay speaks not from a feeling of power, but rather from a feeling of powerlessness. "They have power over me so I want power over them." In his mind, rape is not the initiation of aggression against a woman, but rather a form of revenge, a retaliation after an injury done to him. But by whom?

Beneke explores this apparent paradox by looking at language. Think of the terms we use in this culture to describe women's beauty and sexuality. We use a language of violence, of aggression. A woman is a "bombshell," a "knockout," a "femme fatale." She's "stunning," "ravishing," "dressed to kill." We're "blown away," "done in." Women's beauty is experienced by men as an act of aggression: It invades men's thoughts, elicits unwelcome feelings of desire and longing, makes men feel helpless, powerless, vulnerable. Then, having committed this invasive act of aggression, women reject men, say no to sex, turn them down. Rape is a way to get even, to exact revenge for rejection, to retaliate. These feelings of powerlessness, coupled with the sense of entitlement to women's bodies expressed by the rapists Diana Scully interviewed, combine in a potent mix—powerlessness and entitlement, impotence and a right to feel in control. The astonishing, shamefully high U.S. rape rate comes from that fusion.

Thus rape is less a problem of a small number of sick individuals and more a problem of social expectations of male behavior, expectations that stem from gender inequality (disrespect and contempt for women) and may push men toward sexual predation. A completed rape is only the end point on a continuum that includes sexual coercion as well as the premeditated use of alcohol or drugs to dissolve a woman's resistance. In the most famous study of college men's behaviors, Mary Koss and her colleagues found that one in thirteen men admitted to forcing (or attempting to force) a woman to have sex against her will, but 10 percent had engaged in unwanted sexual contact, and another 7.2 percent had been sexually coercive. In another study, Scott Boeringer found that more than 55 percent had engaged in sexual coercion, 8.6 percent had attempted rape, and 23.7 percent had provided drugs or alcohol to a woman in order to have sex with her when she became too intoxicated to consent or resist (which is legally considered rape in most jurisdictions). Such numbers belie arguments that rape is simply the crime of sick individuals.[60]

Men's feelings of both powerlessness and entitlement are also part of the backdrop to the problem of violence in the home. Though the family is supposed to be a refuge from the dangerous outside world, a "haven in a heartless world," it turns out that the home is, for women and children, the single most dangerous place they can be. Not even the legal "protection" of marriage keeps women safe from the threat of rape, and levels of violence against women in the home are terrifyingly high. Family violence researcher Murray Straus and his colleagues concluded that "the American family and the American home are perhaps as or more violent than any other American institution or setting (with the exception of the military, and only then in time of war)."[61]

Marriage certainly doesn't protect women from rape. In one study of 644 married women, 12 percent reported having been raped by their husbands. One researcher estimates that between 14 percent and 25 percent of women are forced by their husbands to have sexual intercourse against their will during the course of their marriage, whereas another claims that about one-third of women report having "unwanted sex" with their partner. In yet another study of 393 randomly selected women, a date or a spouse was more than three times as likely to rape a woman than was a stranger, a friend, or an acquaintance. Fully 50 percent of the sample reported more than twenty incidents of **marital rape**, and 48 percent indicated that rape was part of the common physical abuse by their husbands. In that study, David Finklehor and Kersti Yllo also found that nearly 75 percent of the women who had been raped by their husbands had successfully resisted at least once; that 88 percent reported that they never enjoyed being forced; and that 22 percent had been sexually victimized as children.[62]

One of the more dramatic changes in rape laws has been the removal of exemptions of husbands from prosecution for rape. As recently as 1985, more than half of the states in the United States still expressly prohibited prosecution for marital rape on the grounds that women had no legal right to say no to sex with their husbands. When a woman said "I do," it apparently also meant "I will...whenever *he* wants to." Although by 1993, all states had declared marital rape a crime "at least where force is used," according to the National Clearinghouse on Marital and Date Rape, as of 1996, the exemption still applies in several states where the husband and wife are living together (not separated), and only five states have extended such protection to unmarried men and women who cohabit. Family researcher Richard Gelles described the scope of this problem in his testimony before the New Hampshire state legislature in 1981, when that state was considering removing the marital exemption from prosecution:

> In reality, marital rape is often *more traumatic* than stranger rape. When you have been intimately violated by a person who is supposed to love and protect you, it can destroy your capacity for intimacy with anyone else. Moreover, many wife

victims are trapped in a reign of terror and experience repeated sexual assaults over a period of years. When you are raped by a stranger you have to live with a frightening memory. *When you are raped by your husband, you have to live with your rapist.*[63]

Marital rape is a significant problem in other countries as well, where husbands remain excluded from prosecution, because a man is legally entitled to do whatever he wants with his property. And wife abuse is also a chronic problem in other countries. In Hong Kong and Quito, Ecuador, for example, as many as 50 percent of all married women are estimated to be regularly beaten by their husbands.[64]

Though domestic violence is certainly a problem in other countries, it also appears that rates of wife abuse in the United States are among the highest in the world. Battery is the major cause of injury to women in the United States. More than two million women are beaten by their partners every year. According to the Bureau of Justice Statistics, 85 percent of all victims of domestic violence are women.

GENDER "SYMMETRY" IN DOMESTIC VIOLENCE?

Despite the overwhelming evidence of the problems of domestic violence against women, we often hear a small chorus of voices shouting about "husband abuse." When one sociologist claims that the abuse of husbands by wives is the most underreported form of domestic violence, suddenly legions of antifeminists trot out such arguments in policy discussions. Some of the studies of "gender symmetry" in domestic violence—a presumption that rates of domestic violence are roughly equal by gender—suggest that women are "as likely" to hit men as men are to hit women and that women commit 50 percent of all spousal murders. These studies provide "facts," such as that 1.8 million women suffered one or more assaults by a husband or boyfriend and that over two million men were assaulted by their wives or girlfriends; that 54 percent of all violence labeled as "severe" was committed by women; or that among teenage dating couples, girls were more violent than boys. (Ironically, the people who claim equivalent rates of domestic violence are often the same people who argue that women and men are biologically different and that women are not biologically aggressive enough to enter the military or serve on police forces.) One obviously confused journalist suggests that because "only" 3–4 percent of women are battered each year, "we ought to consider it the unfortunate behavior of a few crazy men." (If 3–4 percent of all men were stricken with testicular or prostate cancer each year, or were victims of street assault, this same journalist would no doubt consider it a national emergency and try to mobilize the entire medical community or the National Guard—and perhaps both!)[65]

If these data were true, you might ask, why are there no shelters for battered men, no epidemics of male victims turning up in hospital emergency rooms, no legions of battered men coming forward to demand protection? (Well, that's not entirely true. O. J. Simpson did call himself an "abused husband" after he beat up his former wife Nicole. And one shelter for battered men did open in Vancouver, Canada, but closed within two months because no one came to it.) Partly, these pundits tell us, because men who are victims of domestic violence are so ashamed of the humiliation, of the denial of manhood, they are unlikely to come forward and are more likely to suffer in silence the violent ministrations of their wives—a psychological problem that one researcher calls "the **battered husband syndrome**." "Because men have been taught to 'take it like a man' and are ridiculed when they feel that they have been battered by women, women are nine times more likely to report their abusers to the authorities," observe two writers. And partly, the pundits tell us, because the power of the "feminist lobby" is so pervasive, there has been a national cover-up of this demonstrably politically incorrect finding. As one polemicist puts it,

> While repeated studies consistently show that men are victims of domestic violence at least as often as are women, both the lay public and many professionals regard a finding of no sex difference in rates of physical aggression among intimates as surprising, if not unreliable, the stereotype being that men are aggressive and women are exclusively victims.[66]

Such assertions are not supported by empirical research at all, and the inferences drawn from them are even more unwarranted. For example, in the original study of "the battered husband syndrome," sociologist Susan Steinmetz surveyed fifty-seven couples. Four of the wives, but not one husband, reported having been seriously beaten. From this finding, Steinmetz concluded that men simply don't report abuse, that there must be a serious problem of husband abuse, that some 250,000 men were hit every year—this, remember, from a finding that no husbands were abused. By the time the media hoopla over these bogus data subsided, the figure had ballooned to twelve million battered husbands every year![67]

One problem is the questions asked in the research. Those studies that found that women hit men as much as men hit women asked men and women if they had ever, during the course of their relationship, hit their partner. An equal number of women and men answered yes. The number changed dramatically, though, when men and women were asked who initiated the violence (was it offensive or defensive?), how severe it was (did she push him before or after he'd broken her jaw?), and how often the violence occurred. When these three questions were posed, the results looked like what we knew all along: The amount, frequency, severity, and consistency of violence against women are far greater than anything done by women to men—Lorena Bobbitt notwithstanding.[68]

Another problem stems from the question of whom was asked. The studies that found comparable rates of domestic violence asked only one partner about the incident. But studies in which both partners were interviewed separately found large discrepancies between reports from women and from men. The same researchers who found comparable rates have urged that such results be treated with extreme caution, because men underreport severe assaults. (Perhaps it is felt to be equally unmanly to beat up a woman as to be beaten up by one, because "real men" never raise a hand against a woman.)[69]

A third problem results from *when* the informants were asked about domestic violence. The studies that found comparability asked only whether or not any incident occurred in a single year, thus equating a single slap with a reign of domestic terror that may have lasted decades. And, although the research is clear and unequivocal that violence against women increases dramatically after divorce or separation, the research that found comparable results excluded incidents that occurred after separation or divorce. About 76 percent of all assaults take place at that time, though—with a male perpetrator more than 93 percent of the time.[70]

Finally, the research that suggests comparability is all based on the Conflict Tactics Scale (CTS), a scale that does not distinguish between offensive and defensive violence, equating a vicious assault with a woman hitting her husband while he is, for instance, assaulting their children. Nor does it take into account the physical differences between women and men, which lead to women being six times more likely to require medical care for injuries sustained in family violence. Nor does it include the nonphysical means by which women are compelled to remain in abusive relationships (income disparities, fears about their children, economic dependency). Nor does it include marital rape or sexual aggression. As one violence researcher asks, "Can you call two people equally aggressive when a woman punches her husband's chest with no physical harm resulting and a man punches his wife's face and her nose is bloodied and broken? These get the same scores on the CTS."[71]

Supporters of claims about battered men, by the way, rarely dispute the numbers of battered women—they claim only that the number of battered men is equivalent. This is curious, because they typically do not advocate more funding for domestic violence but rather *less* funding for women's programs. Such politically disingenuous efforts have earned the disapproval of even the researcher whose work is used most commonly to support their claims.[72]

Of course, some research suggests that women are fully capable of using violence in intimate relationships, but at nowhere near the same rates or with the same severity. Perhaps as much as 3–4 percent of all spousal violence is committed by women, according to criminologist Martin Schwartz. About one in eight wives reports having ever hit her husband. And when women are violent, they tend to use the least violent tactics and the most violent ones. Women shove, slap, and kick as often as men, Straus and his colleagues found. But they also use guns almost as often as men do.[73]

Domestic violence varies as the balance of power in the relationship shifts. When all the decisions are made by one spouse, rates of spouse abuse—whether committed by the woman or the man—are at their highest levels. Violence against women is most common in those households in which power is concentrated in the hands of the husband. Interestingly, violence against husbands is *also* more common (though much less likely) in homes in which the power is concentrated in the hands of the husband or, in extremely rare cases, in the hands of the wife. Concentration of power in men's hands leads to higher rates of violence, period—whether against women or against men. Rates of wife abuse and husband abuse both plummet as the relationships become increasingly equal, and there are virtually no cases of wives hitting their husbands when all decisions are shared equally, in other words, when the relationships are fully equal.[74]

Women and men do not commit acts of violence at the same rate or for the same reasons. Family violence researcher Kersti Yllo argues that men tend to use domestic violence instrumentally, for the specific purpose of striking fear and terror in their wives' hearts, to ensure compliance, obedience, and passive acceptance of the men's rule in the home. Women, by contrast, tend to use violence expressively, to express frustration or immediate anger—or, of course, defensively, to prevent further injury.

Figure 14.6. In 2009, R&B singer Chris Brown pled guilty to assaulting Rihanna. At the time, the photographs of her bruised and swollen face circulated virally on the Internet, and swayed public opinion. His response? Three years later, he was sporting a tattoo on his neck of a battered woman, a defiant response to critics and a "trophy" image to celebrate his masculinity.

Source: Amanda Marcotte, "What Chris Brown's Tattoo Tells Us About Violence Against Women" available at http://www.rawstory.com/2012/09/what-chris-browns-tattoo-tells-us-about-violence-against-women/. See also Lisa Wade, "Gender, Power, and Chris Brown's Battered Woman Tattoo" available at http://thesocietypages .org/socimages/2012/09/13/gender-power-and-chris-browns-battered-woman-tattoo/. Photo credit: © MJT/ AdMedia/Corbis.

But rarely is women's violence systematic, purposive, and routine. As two psychologists recently put it:

> In heterosexual relationships, battering is primarily something that men do to women, rather than the reverse … There are many battered women who are violent, mostly, but not always, in self-defense. Battered women are living in a culture of violence, and they are part of that culture. Some battered women defend themselves: they hit back, and might even hit or push as often as their husbands do. But they are the ones who are beaten up.[75]

In the results of a survey that simply adds up all violent acts, women and men might appear to be equally violent. But the nation's hospital emergency rooms, battered women's shelters, and county morgues suggest that such appearances are often deadly deceptive.

Violence against women knows no class, racial, or ethnic bounds (tables 14.1a and 14.1b). "Educated, successful, sophisticated men—lawyers, doctors, politicians, business executives—beat their wives as regularly and viciously as dock workers." Yet there are some differences. For example, one of the best predictors of the onset of domestic violence is unemployment. And a few studies have found rates of domestic violence to be higher in African-American families than in white families. One study found that black men hit their wives four times as often as white men did and that black women hit their husbands twice as often as white women did. Although subsequent studies have indicated a decrease in violence among black families, the rates are still somewhat higher than for white families.[76]

Among Latinos the evidence is contradictory: One study found significantly less violence in Latino families than in Anglo families, whereas another found a slightly higher rate. These contradictory findings were clarified by separating different groups of Latinos. Kaufman Kantor and colleagues found that Puerto Rican husbands were about twice as likely to hit their wives as were Anglo husbands (20.4 percent to 9.9 percent) and about ten times more likely than Cuban husbands (2.5 percent). In many cases, however, these racial and ethnic differences disappear when social class is taken into account. Sociologist Noel Cazenave examined the same National Family

Table 14.1a. Lifetime Prevalence of Rape, Physical Violence, and/or Stalking by an Intimate Partner, by Race/Ethnicity—U.S. Women, NISVS 2010

		Hispanic		Non-Hispanic			
			Black	White	Asian or Pacific Islander	American Indian or Alaska Native	Multiracial
Rape	Weighted %	8.4	12.2	9.2	†	†	20.1
	Estimated number of victims*	1,273,000	1,768,000	7,475,000			273,000
Physical violence	Weighted %	35.2	40.9	31.7	†	45.9	50.4
	Estimated number of victims*	5,317,000	5,955,000	25,746,000		399,000	683,000
Stalking	Weighted %	10.6	14.6	10.4	†	†	18.9
	Estimated number of victims*	1,599,000	2,123,000	8,402,000			256,000
Rape, physical violence, and/or stalking	Weighted %	37.1	43.7	34.6	19.6	46.0	53.8
	Estimated number of victims*	5,596,000	6,349,000	28,053,000	1,110,000	400,000	729,000

Note: Race/ethnicity was self-identified. The American Indian or Alaska Native designation does not indicate being enrolled or affiliated with a tribe.

*Rounded to the nearest thousand.

†Estimate is not reported; relative standard error >30 percent or cell size ≤ 20.

Table 14.1b. Lifetime Prevalence of Rape, Physical Violence, and/or Stalking by an Intimate Partner, by Race/Ethnicity—U.S. Men, NISVS 2010

		Hispanic	Non-Hispanic				
			Black	White	Asian or Pacific Islander	American Indian or Alaska Native	Multiracial
Rape	Weighted %	†	†	†	†	†	†
	Estimated number of victims*						
Physical violence	Weighted %	26.5	36.8	28.1	8.4	45.3	38.8
	Estimated number of victims*	4,277,000	4,595,000	21,524,000	428,000	365,000	507,000
Stalking	Weighted %	†	†	1.7	†	†	†
	Estimated number of victims*			1,282,000			
Rape, physical violence, and/or stalking	Weighted %	26.6	38.6	28.2	†	45.3	39.3
	Estimated number of victims*	4,331,000	4,820,000	21,596,000		365,000	513,000

Note: Race/ethnicity was self-identified. The American Indian or Alaska Native designation does not indicate being enrolled or affiliated with a tribe.
*Rounded to the nearest thousand.
†Estimate is not reported; relative standard error >30 percent or cell size ≤ 20.

Violence Survey and found that blacks had *lower* rates of wife abuse than whites in three of four income categories—the two highest and the lowest. Higher rates among blacks were reported only by those respondents in the $6,000–$11,999 income range (which included 40 percent of all blacks surveyed). Income and residence (urban) were also the variables that explained virtually all the ethnic differences between Latinos and Anglos. The same racial differences in spousal murder can be explained by class: Two-thirds of all spousal murders in New York City took place in the poorest sections of the Bronx and Brooklyn.[77]

Of course, gay men and lesbians can engage in domestic violence as well. A recent informal survey of gay victims of violence in six major cities found that gay men and lesbians were more likely to be victims of domestic violence than of antigay hate crimes and just as likely to experience violence as heterosexuals. Over one-fourth of lesbians and gay men (27.9 percent of lesbian and gay adults) reported having experienced IPV (interpersonal violence) in their adult lives. Compare that to the 28.5 percent of heterosexual men and 35.6 percent of heterosexual women in the NISVS (National Intimate Partner and Sexual Violence Survey). And it's even worse if you're bisexual: two in five (40.6 percent) bisexuals experienced violence—the highest percentage of all.

READ ALL ABOUT IT!

Lesbians and gay people have long been targets of violence. In recent years, transgender people have been especially singled out as targets as well, in part because they expose the artificiality of the gender binary and reveal gender to be more fluid, more of a continuum. To some people, this feels like the earth is no longer solidly beneath their feet; they experience a sense of gender vertigo. As Karl Marx once wrote on an entirely different topic, "All that is solid melts into air." This can really make some people angry. Doug Meyer's article "An Intersectional Analysis of Lesbian, Gay, Bisexual and Transgender People's Evaluations of Anti-Queer Violence" asks LGBT people themselves how they understand and interpret that violence. Meyer finds that black and Latino victims of violence often interpret it through a lens of race and ethnicity, somehow betraying their racial and ethnic communities, while white people tend to see the violence entirely in sexual and gender terms.

Intimate partner violence is ultimately about power. For men who abuse their women partners, it is just another way in which they can access and exert power and control. And yet, like rape, domestic violence is most likely to occur not when the man feels most powerful, but rather when he feels relatively powerless. Violence is restorative, a means to reclaim the power that he believes is rightfully his. As one sociologist explains, "abusive men are more likely to batter their spouses and children whenever they feel they are losing power or control over their lives." Another reminds us that "male physical power over women, or the illusion of power, is nonetheless a minimal compensation for the lack of power over the rest of one's life."[78]

CONCLUSION

Violence is epidemic in American society today. The United States is, by far, the most violent industrial nation in the world—despite our nation being the society with the highest rates of incarceration and the only industrialized nation that uses the death penalty to deter violence. Did I say "despite"? Don't I mean "because"?

Violence takes an enormous social toll, not just on its victims, but also in the massive costs of maintaining a legal system, prisons, and police forces. And it takes an incalculable psychic toll—an entire nation that has become comfortable living in fear of violence. (Turn on the evening news in any city in America for the nightly parade of murders, fires, parental abuse, and fistfights masquerading as sports.) "To curb crime we do not need to expand repressive state measures, but we do need to reduce gender inequalities," writes criminologist James Messerschmidt. And assuaging that fear, as criminologist Elizabeth Stanko puts it, "will take more than better outdoor lighting."[79]

Of course, better lighting is a start. And we have to protect women from a culture of violence that so often targets them. But we also have to protect boys "from a culture of violence that exploits their worst tendencies by reinforcing and amplifying the atavistic values of the masculine mystique." After all, it is men who are overwhelmingly the victims of violence—just as men are overwhelmingly its perpetrators.[80]

Often, biological explanations are invoked as evasive strategies. "Boys will be boys," we say, throwing up our hands in helpless resignation. But even if all violence were biologically programmed by testosterone or the evolutionary demands of reproductive success, the epidemic of male violence in America would still beg the political question: Are we going to organize our society so as to maximize this propensity for violence or are we going to take steps to minimize it? These are political questions, and they demand political answers—answers that impel us to find alternative, nonviolent routes for men to express themselves as men.

Frankly, I believe that men are better than that, better than biologically programmed violent and rapacious beasts. A colleague recently devised a way to suggest that men can do better. For Rape Awareness Week at his university, he created hundreds of "splash guards" to be distributed in the men's rooms on campus. (For those who don't know, a splash guard is the plastic grate that is placed in men's public urinals to prevent splatter.) He had thousands made up with a simple and hopeful slogan. It says simply: "You hold the power to stop rape in your hand."

I believe that we can also do far better than we have in reducing violence in our society and in withdrawing our tacit, silent, and thereby complicit support for it. When right-wingers engage in this sort of "male-bashing"—asserting that men are no better than testosterone-crazed violent louts (and that therefore women must leave the workplace and return home to better constrain us)—most men know these slurs to be false. But they are false with a ring of truth to them. Because as long as men remain in their postures of either silent complicity or defensive denial, one might very well get the idea that we do condone men's violence. "All violent feelings," wrote the great nineteenth-century British social critic John Ruskin, "produce in us a falseness in all our impressions of external things." Until we transform the meaning of masculinity, we will continue to produce that falseness—with continued tragic consequences.

KEY TERMS

Acquaintance Rape
Battered Husband
　　Syndrome
Cult of Domesticity

Gendered Violence
Intimate Partner Violence
Male Violence
Marital Rape

Masculine Bravado
Pedophilia
Rape as Recreation
Women's Criminality

Epilogue
"A DEGENDERED SOCIETY"?

The principle which regulates the existing social relations between the two sexes—the legal subordination of one sex to the other—is wrong in itself, and now one of the chief hindrances to human improvement; and…it ought to be replaced by a principle of perfect equality, admitting no power or privilege on the one side, nor disability on the other.

—John Stuart Mill
The Subjection of Women (1869)

In this second decade of a new millennium, we sit perched on a precipice, looking into an uncharted expanse of the future. What kind of society do we want to live in? What will be the gender arrangements of that society?

To see gender differences as intransigent leads also to a political resignation about the possibilities of social change and increased gender equality. Those who proclaim that men and women come from different planets would have us believe that the best we can hope for is a sort of interplanetary détente, an uneasy truce in which we exasperatingly accept the inherent and intractable foibles of the other sex, a truce mediated by ever-wealthier psychological interpreters who can try to decode the sexes' impenetrable language.

I think the evidence is clear that women and men are far more alike than they are different and that we need far fewer cosmic interpreters and far more gender equality to enable both women and men to live the lives they want to live. The future of gender differences is intimately tied to the future of gender inequality. As gender inequality is reduced, the differences between women and men will shrink.

And besides, the interplanetary model of gender differences entirely ignores the historical record. For the past century, we have steadily moved to lessen gender inequality—by removing barriers to women's entry into all arenas of the public sphere, protecting women who have been victimized by men's violent efforts to delay, retard, or resist that entry. And as we have done so, we have found that women can perform admirably in arenas once believed to be suitable only for men and that men can perform admirably in arenas once held to be exclusively women's domain. Don't believe me: Ask those women surgeons, lawyers, and pilots. And ask those male nurses, teachers, and social workers, as well as all those single fathers, if they are capable of caring for their children.

In this book, I've made several arguments about our gendered society. I've argued that women and men are more alike than we are different, that we're not at all from different planets. I've argued that it is gender inequality that produces the differences we do observe and that that inequality also produces the cultural impulse to search for such differences, even when there is little or no basis for them in reality. I've also argued that gender is not a property of individuals, which is accomplished by socialization, but rather a set of relationships produced in our social interactions with one another and within gendered institutions, whose formal organizational dynamics reproduce gender inequality and produce gender differences.

I've also pointed to evidence of a significant gender convergence taking place over the past half-century. Whether we look at sexual behavior, friendship dynamics, efforts to balance work and family life, or women's and men's experiences and aspirations in education or the workplace, we find the gender gap growing ever smaller. (The lone exception to this process, as we saw in the last chapter, is violence.)

To celebrate this gender convergence in behavior and attitudes is not to advocate degendering *people*. A recent book by Judith Lorber makes a case for degendering. She argues that, as one reviewer put it, "degendering reduces gender inequality by eliminating gender difference as a meaningful consequential component of institutions and identities." Such an argument, to my mind, however utopian, still puts the cart before the horse, claiming that eliminating difference will lead to eliminating inequality. But such a model equates equality with sameness—only by flattening all differences will equality be possible. I see it exactly the other way around: Only by eliminating inequality will difference recede until the variations among us—by race, age, ethnicity, sexuality, and, yes, biological sex—will prove largely epiphenomenal. (There *are* some differences, after all, and we should neither ignore nor minimize them.) Just as we know that sameness doesn't automatically lead to equality, so, too, is difference not necessarily incompatible with it.[1]

I don't have much faith, for example, in the ideal of androgyny. Some psychologists have proposed androgyny as a solution to gender inequality and gender differences. It implies a flattening of gender differences, so that women and men will think, act, and behave in some more "neutralized" gender-nonspecific ways. "Masculinity" and "femininity" will be seen as archaic constructs as everyone becomes increasingly "human."

Such proposals take a leap beyond the ultimately defeatist claims of immutable difference offered by the interplanetary theorists. After all, proponents of androgyny at least recognize that gender differences are socially constructed and that change is possible.

But androgyny remains unpopular as a political or psychological option because it would eliminate differences between people, mistaking equality for sameness. To many of us, the idea of sameness feels coercive, a dilution of difference into a bland, tasteless amalgam in which individuals would lose their distinctiveness. It's like Hollywood's vision of communism as a leveling of all class distinctions into a colorless, amorphous mass in which everyone would look, act, and dress the same—as in those advertisements that feature poorly but identically dressed Russians. Androgyny often feels like it would enforce life on a flat and ultimately barren, degendered landscape. Is the only way for women and men to be equal to become the same? Can we not imagine equality based on respect for and embracing of difference?

Fears about androgyny confuse gendered people with gendered traits. It's not that women and men need to be more like each other than we already are but rather that all the psychological traits and attitudes and behaviors that we, as a culture, label as "masculine" or "feminine" need to be redefined. These traits and attitudes, after all, also carry positive and negative values, and it is through this hierarchy, this unequal weighting, that gender inequality becomes so deeply entwined with gender difference. To degender people does not by itself eliminate gender inequality.

In fact, calls for androgyny paradoxically reify the very gender distinctions that they seek to eliminate. Advocates frequently urge men to express more of their "feminine" sides; women, to express more of their "masculine" sides. Such exhortations, frankly, leave me deeply insulted.

Let me give you an example. Some years ago, as I sat in my neighborhood park with my newborn son in my arms, a passerby commented, "How wonderful it is to see men these days expressing their feminine sides." I growled, underneath my conspicuously false smile. Although I tried to be pleasant, what I wanted to say was this: "I'm not expressing anything of the sort, ma'am. I'm being tender and loving and nurturing toward my child. As far as I can tell, I'm expressing my *masculinity*!"

Why, after all, are love, nurturance, and tenderness defined as feminine? Why do I have to be expressing the affect of the other sex in order to have access to what I regard as human emotions? Because I am a man, everything I do expresses my masculinity. And I'm sure my wife would be no less insulted if, after editing a particularly difficult article or writing a long, involved essay, she were told how extraordinary and wonderful it is to see women expressing their masculine sides—as if competence, ambition, and assertiveness were not human properties to which women *and* men could equally have access.

Love, tenderness, nurturance; competence, ambition, assertion—these are *human* qualities, and all human beings—both women and men—should have equal access to them. And when we do express them, we are expressing, respectively, our gender identities, not the gender of the other. What a strange notion, indeed, that such emotions should be labeled as masculine or feminine, when they are so deeply human and when both women and men are so easily capable of a so much fuller range of feelings.

Strange, and also a little sad. "Perhaps nothing is so depressing an index of the inhumanity of the male supremacist mentality as the fact that the more genial human traits are assigned to the underclass: affection, response to sympathy, kindness, cheerfulness," was the way feminist writer Kate Millett put it in her landmark book, *Sexual Politics*, first published in 1969.[2]

So much has changed since then. The gendered world that I inhabit is totally unlike that of my parents. My father could have gone to an all-male college, served in an all-male military, and spent his entire working life in an all-male work environment. Today that world is but a memory. Women have entered every workplace, the military, and its training academies (both federally and state supported), and all but three or four colleges today admit women. Despite persistent efforts from some political quarters to turn back the calendar to the mid-nineteenth century, those changes are permanent; women will not go back to the home where some people think they belong.

These enormous changes will only accelerate in the next few decades. The society of the third millennium will increasingly degender traits and behaviors without degendering people. We will still be women and men, equal yet capable of appreciating our differences, different yet unwilling to use those differences as the basis for discrimination.

Imagine how quickly the pace of that change might accelerate if we continue to degender traits, not people. What if little boys and girls saw their mothers and their fathers go off to work in the morning, with no compromise to their masculinity or femininity? Those little boys and girls would grow up thinking that having a job—being competent, earning a living, striving to get ahead—was something that *grown-ups* did, regardless of whether they were male or female grown-ups. Not something that men did and that women did only with guilt, social approbation, and sporadic and irregular dependence on their fertility. "And when I grow up," those children would say, "I'm going to have a job also."

And when both mothers and fathers are equally loving and caring and nurturing toward their children, when nurture is something that *grown-ups* do—and not something that mothers do routinely and men do only during halftime on Saturday afternoon—then those same children will say to themselves, "And when I get to be a grown-up, I'm going to be loving and caring toward my children."

Such a process may sound naively optimistic, but the signs of change are everywhere around us. In fact, the historical evidence points exactly in that direction. It was through the dogged insistence of that nineteenth-century ideology, the separation of spheres, that two distinct realms for men and women were imposed, with two separate sets of traits and behaviors that accompany each sphere. This was the historical aberration, the anomaly—its departure from what had preceded it and from the "natural" propensity of human beings goes a long way in explaining the vehemence with which it was imposed. Nothing so natural or biologically determined has to be so coercive.

The twentieth century witnessed the challenge to separate spheres, undertaken, in large part, by those who were demoted by its ideological ruthlessness—women. That century witnessed an unprecedented upheaval in the status of women, possibly the most significant transformation in gender relations in world history. From the rights to vote and work, asserted early in the century, to the rights to enter every conceivable workplace, educational institution, and the military in the latter half, women shook the foundations of the gendered society. And at the end of the century they had accomplished half a revolution—a transformation of their opportunities to be workers and mothers.

This half-finished revolution has left many women frustrated and unhappy. For some reason, they remain unable to "have it all"—to be good mothers and also to be effective and ambitious workers. With astonishing illogic, some pundits explain women's frustrations as stemming not from the continued resistance of men, the intransigence of male-dominated institutions to accept them, or the indifference of politicians to enact policies that would enable these women to balance their work and family lives, but rather from the effort of women to expand their opportunities and to claim a full share of humanity. It is a constant source of amazement how many women have full-time jobs exhorting women not to take full-time jobs.

The second half of the transformation of gender is just beginning and will be, I suspect, far more difficult to accomplish than the first. That's because there was an intuitively obvious ethical imperative attached to enlarging the opportunities for, and eliminating discrimination against, women. But the transformation of the twenty-first century involves the transformation of men's lives.

Men are just beginning to realize that the "traditional" definition of masculinity leaves them unfulfilled and dissatisfied. Whereas women have left the home, from which they were "imprisoned" by the ideology of separate spheres, and now seek to balance work and family lives, men continue to search for a way back into the family, from which they were exiled by the same ideology. Some men express their frustration and confusion by hoping and praying for a return to the old gender regime, the very separation of spheres that made both women *and* men unhappy. Others join various men's movements, like Promise Keepers or the Million Man March, or troop off to a mythopoetic men's retreat in search of a more resonant, spiritually fulfilling definition of masculinity.

The nineteenth-century ideology of separate spheres justified gender inequality based on putative natural differences between the sexes. What was normative—enforced by sanction—was asserted to be normal, a part of the nature of things. Women have spent the better part of a century making clear that such an ideology did violence to their experiences, effacing the work outside the home that women actually performed and enforcing a definition of femininity that allowed only partial expression of their humanity.

It did the same for men, of course—valorizing some emotions and experiences, discrediting others. As with women, it left men with only partially fulfilled lives. Only recently, though, have men begun to chafe at the restrictions that such an ideology placed on their humanity.

In the twenty-first century, it might be wise to recall the words of a writer at the turn of the twentieth century. In a remarkable essay written a century ago, in 1917, the New York City writer Floyd Dell spelled out the consequences of separate spheres for both women and men:

> When you have got a woman in a box, and you pay rent on the box, her relationship to you insensibly changes character. It loses the fine excitement of democracy. It ceases to be a companionship, for companionship is only possible in a democracy. It is no longer a sharing of life together—it is a breaking of life apart. Half a life—cooking, clothes and children; half a life—business, politics and baseball. It doesn't make much difference which is the poorer half. Any half, when it comes to life, is very near to none at all.

Like feminist women, Dell understands that these separate spheres that impoverish the lives of both women and men are also built upon gender inequality. (Notice how he addresses his remarks to men who "have got a woman in a box.") Gender inequality produced the ideology of separate spheres, and the ideology of separate spheres, in turn, lent legitimacy to gender inequality. Thus, Dell argues in the opening sentence of his essay that "feminism will make it possible for the first time for men to be free."[3]

The direction of the gendered society in the new century and the new millennium is not for women and men to become increasingly *similar*, but rather for them to become more *equal*, for those traits and behaviors heretofore labeled as masculine and feminine—competence and compassion, ambition and affection—to be labeled as distinctly human qualities, accessible to both women and men who are grown-up enough to claim them. It suggests a form of gender proteanism—a temperamental and psychological flexibility, the ability to adapt to one's environment with a full range of emotions and abilities. The protean self, articulated by psychiatrist Robert Jay Lifton, is a self that can embrace difference, contradiction, and complexity, a self that is mutable and flexible in a rapidly changing world.[4] Such a transformation does not require that men and women become more like each other, but, rather, more deeply and fully themselves.

Notes

CHAPTER ONE

1. John Gray, *Men Are from Mars, Women Are from Venus* (New York: HarperCollins, 1992), p. 5.
2. *J.E.B. v. Alabama*, 114 S. Ct., 1436 (1994).
3. Barbara Risman, *Gender Vertigo* (New Haven: Yale University Press, 1998), p. 25. See also Judith Lorber, *Paradoxes of Gender* (New Haven, CT: Yale University Press, 1994).
4. Catharine Stimpson, *Where the Meanings Are* (New York: Methuen, 1988).
5. See Michael Kimmel, *Manhood in America: A Cultural History* (New York: Free Press, 1996).
6. This story also appears in Kimmel, *Manhood in America*.
7. Torri Minton, "Search for What It Means to Be White" in *San Francisco Chronicle*, May 8, 1998.
8. Simmel is cited in Lewis Coser, "Georg Simmel's Neglected Contributions to the Sociology of Women" in *Signs*, 2(4), 1977, p. 872.
9. Ibid.
10. R. W. Connell, *Gender and Power* (Stanford, CA: Stanford University Press, 1987), p. 183; Erving Goffman, *Stigma* (Englewood Cliffs, NJ: Prentice-Hall, 1963), p. 128.
11. Connell, *Gender and Power*, pp. 183, 188, 187.
12. Cited in Risman, *Gender Vertigo*, p. 141.
13. Carol Tavris, "The Mismeasure of Woman" in *Feminism and Psychology*, 1993, p. 153.
14. Cynthia Fuchs Epstein, *Deceptive Distinctions* (New Haven, CT: Yale University Press, 1988).
15. Alex Witchel, "Our Finances, Ourselves" in *New York Times*, June 4, 1998, p. 13.
16. Ibid.
17. Rosabeth M. Kanter, *Men and Women of the Corporation* (New York: Harper and Row, 1977).
18. Kathleen Gerson, *Hard Choices* (Berkeley: University of California Press, 1985); *No Man's Land* (New York: Basic Books, 1993).
19. Risman, *Gender Vertigo*, p. 70.
20. David Almeida and Ronald Kessler, "Everyday Stressors and Gender Differences in Daily Distress" in *Journal of Personality and Social Psychology*, 75(3), 1998, pp. 670–680.
21. See Nancy Stedman, "In a Bad Mood—for a Good Reason" in *New York Times*, October 24, 1998, for an example of a journalist who actually understood the story.
22. Risman, *Gender Vertigo*, p. 21.
23. Gayle Rubin, "The Traffic in Women" in *Toward an Anthropology of Women*, R. R. Reiter, ed. (New York: Monthly Review Press, 1975), pp. 179–180.
24. Catharine MacKinnon, *Towards a Feminist Theory of the State* (Cambridge: Harvard University Press, 1989), pp. 218–219.

25. Michael Kimmel, Diane Diamond, and Kirby Schroeder, "'What's This About a Few Good Men?' Negotiating Sameness and Difference in Military Education from the 1970s to the Present" in *Masculinities and Education*, N. Lesko, ed. (Thousand Oaks, CA: Sage Publications, 1999), pp. 231–252.

CHAPTER TWO

1. Jerre Levy, cited in Jo Durden-Smith and Diane deSimone, *Sex and the Brain* (New York: Warner Books, 1983), p. 61.

2. Rev. John Todd, *Woman's Rights* (Boston: Lee and Shepard, 1867), p. 26.

3. Barbara Ehrenreich and Deirdre English, *For Her Own Good: 150 Years of the Experts' Advice to Women* (New York: Doubleday, 1979), p. 111.

4. Cited in Carl Degler, *In Search of Human Nature: The Decline and Revival of Darwinism in American Social Thought* (New York: Oxford University Press, 1991), p. 107.

5. Todd, *Woman's Rights*, p. 25.

6. California State Historical Society Library, San Francisco, ms. #2334. For a summary of the way biological arguments were used to exclude women from public participation, see Michael Kimmel, "Introduction," in *Against the Tide: Pro-Feminist Men in the United States, 1776–1990, a Documentary History*, M. Kimmel and T. Mosmiller, eds. (Boston: Beacon, 1992).

7. Cited in Stephen Jay Gould, *The Mismeasure of Man* (New York: W. W. Norton, 1981), pp. 104–105.

8. Edward C. Clarke, *Sex in Education; or, A Fair Chance for the Girls* (Boston: Osgood and Co., 1873), p. 152.

9. See Cynthia Eagle Russet, *Sexual Science: The Victorian Construction of Womanhood* (Cambridge: Harvard University Press, 1989).

10. Newt Gingrich, comments in his course "Renewing American Civilization" at Reinhardt College, January 7, 2005, available at http://lists.asu.edu/cgi-bin/wa?A2=ind9503e&L=christia&D=0&T=0&P=15988, accessed May 24, 2006.

11. There are several important texts that provide good ripostes to the biological arguments. Among them are Ruth Bleir, ed., *Feminist Approaches to Science* (New York: Pergamon, 1986); Lynda Birke, *Women, Feminism and Biology: The Feminist Challenge* (New York: Methuen, 1986). Anne Fausto-Sterling's *Myths of Gender: Biological Theories About Women and Men* (New York: Basic Books, 1985) is indispensible. Deborah Blum, *Sex on the Brain: The Biological Differences Between Men and Women* (New York: Viking, 1997), provides a good summary. Robert Nadeau, *S/He Brain: Science, Sexual Politics and the Myths of Feminism* (New York: Praeger, 1996), illustrates the conservative and antifeminist uses to which this research can so effortlessly be put.

12. E. O. Wilson, *Sociobiology: The New Synthesis*, 2nd ed. (Cambridge: Harvard University Press, 1977).

13. Richard Dawkins, *The Selfish Gene* (New York: Oxford University Press, 1976), p. 152; Edward O. Wilson, *On Human Nature* (Cambridge: Harvard University Press, 1978), p. 167.

14. Anthony Layng, "Why Don't We Act Like the Opposite Sex?" in *USA Today* magazine, January 1993; Donald Symons, "Darwinism and Contemporary Marriage" in *Contemporary Marriage: Comparative Perspectives on a Changing Institution*, K. Davis, ed. (New York: Russell Sage Foundation, 1985), cited in Carl Degler, "Darwinians Confront Gender; or, There Is More to It Than History" in *Theoretical Perspectives on Sexual Difference*, D. Rhode, ed. (New Haven, CT: Yale University Press, 1990), p. 39.

15. Edward Wilson, *Sociobiology: The New Synthesis* (Cambridge: Harvard University Press, 1974).

16. Lionel Tiger, "Male Dominance?" in *New York Times Magazine*, October 25, 1970.

17. See, for example, Judy Stamps, "Sociobiology: Its Evolution and Intellectual Descendents" in *Politics and Life Science*, 14(2), 1995: 191–193.

18. David Buss, *The Evolution of Desire: Strategies of Human Mating* (New York: Basic Books, 1994), but see also Robert Sapolsky, *Monkeyluv* (New York: Scribner, 2006), p. 175. See Martha McCaughey, *The Caveman Mystique: Pop-Darwinism and the Debates over Sex, Violence, and Science* (New York: Routledge, 2007), p. 117.

19. Randy Thornhill and Craig T. Palmer, "Why Men Rape" in *New York Academy of Sciences*, January 2000, p. 30.

20. Randy Thornhill and Craig T. Palmer, *A Natural History of Rape* (Cambridge: MIT Press, 2000), p. 53.

21. Richard Alexander and K. M. Noonan, "Concealment of Ovulation, Parental Care and Human Social Evolution" in *Evolutionary Biology and Human Social Behavior*, N. Chagnon and W. Irons, eds. (North Scituate, MA: Duxbury, 1979), p. 449.

22. Richard Lewontin, "Biological Determinism as a Social Weapon" in *Biology as a Social Weapon*, Ann Arbor Science for the People Editorial Collective, ed. (Minneapolis: Burgess, 1977), p. 15; Stephen Jay Gould, *Ever Since Darwin:*

Reflections in Natural History (New York: W. W. Norton, 1977), p. 254.

23. Sapolsky, *Monkeyluv*, p. 30.

24. Carol Tavris and Carole Wade, *The Longest War* (New York: Harcourt, Brace, 1984).

25. See, for example, Frans de Waal, *Our Inner Ape: A Leading Primatologist Explains Why We Are Who We Are* (New York: Riverhead Books, 2005). De Waal cautions against explaining *any* human behavior strictly from looking at primate behaviors, as they are far too variable and diverse—sort of like humans.

26. Mary McDonald Pavelka, "Sexual Nature: What Can We Learn from a Cross-Species Perspective?" in *Sexual Nature, Sexual Culture*, P. Abrahamson and S. Pinkerton, eds. (Chicago: University of Chicago Press, 1995), p. 22.

27. See Jonah Lehrer, "The Effeminate Sheep—and Other Problems with Darwinian Sexual Selection" in *Seed*, June 2006.

28. Simon LeVay, "Survival of the Sluttiest" at Nerve .com, 2000, available at www.nerve.com.

29. Laurence Gesquiere, Niki Leam, M. Carolina M. Simao, Patrick Onyango, Susan Alberts, and Jeanne Altmann, "Life at the Top: Rank and Stress in Wild Male Baboons" in *Science*, 333(6040), July 15, 2011, pp. 357–360. See also James Gorman, "Baboon Study Shows Benefits for Nice Guys, Who Finish 2nd," in *New York Times*, July 14, 2011.

30. Lloyd DeMause, "Our Forbears Made Childhood a Nightmare" in *Psychology Today*, April 1975.

31. Thornhill and Palmer, "Why Men Rape," pp. 32, 34; see also Thornhill and Palmer, *A Natural History of Rape*. See also my critique of their book, "An Unnatural History of Rape," in Cheryl Travis, ed., *Evolution, Gender, and Rape* (Cambridge: MIT Press, 2003). Even other evolutionary psychologists have dismissed Thornhill and Palmer's apologetics. See Michael Gard and Benjamin Bradley, "Getting Away with Rape" in *Psychology, Evolution and Gender*, 2(3), December 2000, pp. 313–319.

32. See Roy Baumeister, Kathleen Catanese, and Harry Wallace, "Conquest by Force: A Narcissistic Reactance Theory of Rape and Sexual Coercion" in *Review of General Psychology*, 6(10), 2002, pp. 92–135.

33. I. Singer and J. Singer, "Periodicity of Sexual Desire in Relation to Time of Ovulation in Women" in *Journal of Biosocial Science*, 4, 1972, pp. 471–481; see also Elisabeth A. Lloyd, "Pre-theoretical Assumptions in Evolutionary Explanations of Female Sexuality" in *Feminism and Science*, E. F. Keller and H. E. Longino, eds. (New York:

Oxford University Press, 1996); Suzanne Franks, "They Blinded Me with Science: Misuse and Misunderstanding of Biological Theory" in *Fundamental Differences: Feminists Talk Back to Social Conservatives*, Cynthia Burack and Jyl J. Josephson, eds. (Lanham, MD: Rowman and Littlefield, 2005).

34. N. Burley, "The Evolution of Concealed Ovulation" in *American Naturalist*, 114, 1979; Mary McDonald Pavelka, "Sexual Nature," p. 19. See also Sarah Blaffer Hardy, *The Woman That Never Evolved* (Cambridge: Harvard University Press, 1981).

35. Elisabeth Lloyd, *The Case of the Female Orgasm: Bias in the Science of Evolution* (Cambridge: Harvard University Press, 2005).

36. Stephen Beckerman, R. Lizzarralde, C. Ballew, S. Schroeder, C. Fingelton, A. Garrison, and H. Smith, "The Bari Partible Paternity Project: Preliminary Results" in *Current Anthropology*, 39(1), 1998, pp. 164–167.

37. Steven Gangestad, Randy Thornhill, and Christine Garver, "Changes in Women's Sexual Interests and Their Partners' Mate-Retention Tactics Across the Menstrual Cycle: Evidence for Shifting Conflicts of Interest" in *Proceedings of the Royal Society*, 2002. Not surprisingly, Gangestad repudiated the journalist's interpretation, because it's pretty much the mirror image of his argument that it is more in males' interest to be promiscuous and in females' interest to be monogamous. Personal communication, December 16, 2002.

38. See Evelyn Fox Keller, *A Feeling for the Organism: The Life and Work of Barbara McClintock* (San Francisco: W. H. Freeman, 1983).

39. Martha McClintock, "Menstrual Synchrony and Suppression" in *Nature*, 229, January 22, 1971.

40. See Natalie Angier, "Men, Women, Sex, and Darwin" in *New York Times*, February 21, 1999; see also her *Women: An Intimate Geography* (Boston: Houghton, Mifflin, 1999).

41. Paul Ehrlich, *Human Natures: Genes, Cultures, and the Human Prospect* (New York: Penguin, 2002).

42. Emile Durkheim, *The Division of Labor in Society* (New York: Free Press, 1984 [1893]), p. 21; see also Ehrenreich and English, *For Her Own Good*, p. 117. Of course, Durkheim's assertion of the progressive historical divergence could be due not to evolution but rather to women's increased confinement and restriction.

43. James C. Dobson, *Straight Talk to Men and Their Wives* (Dallas: Word Publishing Co., 1991), p. 177; Adam Begley, "Why Men and Women Think Differently" in *Newsweek*, May 12, 1995, p. 51.

44. See Elizabeth Fee, "Nineteenth Century Craniology: The Study of the Female Skull" in *Bulletin of the History of Medicine*, 53, 1979.

45. Turner is cited in *South Side Observer*, April 29, 1896; C. A. Dwyer, "The Role of Tests and Their Construction in Producing Apparent Sex-Related Differences" in *Sex-Related Differences in Cognitive Functioning*, M. Wittig and A. Peterson, eds. (New York: Academic Press, 1979), p. 342.

46. Doreen Kimura's summary of these brain differences, *Sex and Cognition* (Cambridge, MA: MIT Press, 1999), catalogs a large variety of brain differences in spatial, verbal, and other forms of reasoning. She feels comfortable stating that "we can say with certainty that there are substantial stable sex differences in cognitive functions like spatial rotation ability, mathematical reasoning, and verbal memory; and in motor skills requiring accurate targeting and finger dexterity" (p. 181). Because she never tells the reader about the shape of the distribution of these traits, we have no idea whether such differences actually mean anything at all, if they are categorical, or if the distribution is larger among women and among men than it is between women and men—which is the case in virtually every one of these studies. Such is typically the case when authors argue from ideology rather than evidence. A better source is Lesley Rogers, *Sexing the Brain* (New York: Columbia University Press, 2001), which is at least intellectually honest and does not conceal or obscure conflicting information.

47. Norman Geschwind, cited in Durden-Smith and deSimone, *Sex and the Brain*, p. 171. Other influential studies on hormone research include G. W. Harris, "Sex Hormones, Brain Development and Brain Function" in *Endocrinology*, 75, 1965.

48. Ruth Bleier, *Science and Gender: A Critique of Biology and Its Theory on Women* (New York: Pantheon, 1984).

49. A. W. H. Buffery and J. Gray, "Sex Differences in the Development of Spacial and Linguistic Skills" in *Gender Differences: Their Ontogeny and Significance*, C. Ounsted and D. C. Taylor, eds. (London: Churchill Livingston, 1972); Jerre Levy, "Lateral Specialization of the Human Brain: Behavioral Manifestation and Possible Evolutionary Basis" in *The Biology of Behavior*, J. A. Kiger, ed. (Corvallis, Eugene: University of Oregon Press, 1972); see also Fausto-Sterling, *Myths of Gender*, p. 40.

50. Jean Christophe Labarthe, "Are Boys Better Than Girls at Building a Tower or a Bridge at 2 Years of Age?" in *Archives of Disease in Childhood*, 77, 1997, pp. 140–144.

51. Joseph Lurito cited in Robert Lee Hotz, "Women Use More of Brain When Listening, Study Says" in *Los Angeles Times*, November 29, 2000.

52. Durden-Smith and deSimone, *Sex and the Brain*, p. 60.

53. Levy, "Lateral Specialization."

54. Janet Hyde, "How Large Are Cognitive Differences? A Metanalysis" in *American Psychologist*, 26, 1981; Janet Hyde, Elizabeth Fennema, and S. J. Laman, "Gender Differences in Mathematics Performance: A Meta-Analysis" in *Psychological Bulletin*, 107, 1990.

55. Michael Peters, "The Size of the Corpus Callosum in Males and Females: Implications of a Lack of Allometry" in *Canadian Journal of Psychology*, 42(3), 1988; Christine de Lacoste-Utamsing and Ralph Holloway, "Sexual Dimorphism in the Human Corpus Callosum" in *Science*, June 25, 1982; but also see William Byne, Ruth Bleier, and Lanning Houston, "Variations in Human Corpus Callosum Do Not Predict Gender: A Study Using Magnetic Resonance Imaging" in *Behavioral Neuroscience*, 102(2), 1988.

56. See Michael Gurian, *The Wonder of Girls* (New York: Pocket Books, 2002); see also Caryl Rivers, "Pop Science Book Claims Girls Hardwired for Love" in *Women's E-News*, June 29, 2002.

57. See "The Merrow Report," January 8, 2000, "Are Boys in Trouble?" transcript, p. 11.

58. See Larry Cahill, "His Brain, Her Brain" in *Scientific American*, May 2005, pp. 22–29.

59. Simon Baron-Cohen et al., "Sex Differences in the Brain: Implications for Explaining Autism" in *Science*, 310, 2005, pp. 819–823; "Intelligence in Men and Women Is a Gray and White Matter" in *ScienceDaily*, available at http://www.sciencedaily.com/releases/2005/01/050121100142.htm, accessed August 14, 2009.

60. Cited in Le Anne Schreiber, "The Search for His and Her Brains" in *Glamour*, April 1993; Kimura, cited in Rivers, "Pop Science Book."

61. Lise Eliot, *Pink Brain, Blue Brain* (Boston: Houghton, Mifflin, 2009), p. 9.

62. Marcel Kinsbourne, "The Development of Lateralization" in *Biological and Neurological Mechanisms*, H. W. Reese and M. D. Franzen, eds. (Mahwah, NJ: Erlbaum, 1996).

63. Several books are useful summaries of this research, including Dean Hamer and Peter Copeland, *The Science of Desire* (New York: Simon & Schuster, 1994); Simon LeVay, *Queer Science: The Use and Abuse of Research into Homosexuality* (Cambridge: MIT Press, 1996); Lee Ellis and Linda Ebertz, eds., *Sexual Orientation: Toward Biological*

Understanding (New York: Praeger, 1997). Several other works provide valuable rejoinders to the scientific research; see, for example, Vernon Rosario, ed., *Science and Homosexualities* (New York: Routledge, 1997); Timothy Murphy, *Gay Science: The Ethics of Sexual Orientation Research* (New York: Columbia University Press, 1997); John Corvino, ed., *Same Sex: Debating the Ethics, Science and Culture of Homosexuality* (Lanham, MD: Rowman and Littlefield, 1997). A double issue of *Journal of Homosexuality,* 28(1–2), 1995, was devoted to this theme. For a strong dissenting opinion, see William Byne, "Why We Cannot Conclude That Sexual Orientation Is Primarily a Biological Phenomenon" in *Journal of Homosexuality,* 34(1), 1997; William Byne, "Science and Belief: Psychobiological Research on Sexual Orientation" in *Journal of Homosexuality,* 28(2), 1995.

64. Michel Foucault, *The History of Sexuality* (New York: Pantheon, 1978). See also Jonathan Ned Katz, *The Invention of Heterosexuality* (New York: E. P. Dutton, 1993).

65. Gunter Dorner, W. Rohde, F. Stahl, L. Krell, and W. Masius, "A Neuroendocrine Predisposition for Homosexuality in Men" in *Archives of Sexual Behavior,* 4(1), 1975, p. 6.

66. Simon LeVay, "The 'Gay Brain' Revisited" at www .nerve.com/Regulars/Science of Sex/09-05-00/, accessed August 14, 2009; LeVay, "A Difference in Hypothalamic Structure Between Homosexual and Heterosexual Men" in *Science,* 253, August 30, 1991; Simon LeVay, *The Sexual Brain* (Cambridge: MIT Press, 1994); Simon LeVay and Dean Hamer, "Evidence for a Biological Influence in Male Homosexuality" in *Scientific American,* 270, 1994. See also "Born or Bred?" in *Newsweek,* February 24, 1992.

67. P. Yahr, "Sexually Dimorphic Hypothalamic Cell Groups and a Related Pathway That Are Essential for Masculine Copulatory Behavior" in *The Development of Sex Differences and Similarities in Behavior,* M. Haug, R. Whalen, C. Aron, and K. Olsen, eds. (Dordrecht, Netherlands: Kluwer Academic Publishers, 1993), p. 416.

68. See *Chronicle of Higher Education,* November 10, 1995.

69. Ivanka Savic, Hans Berglund, and Per Lindstrom, "Brain Response to Putative Pheromones in Homosexual Men" in *Proceedings of the National Academy of Sciences,* 102(20), May 17, 2005, pp. 7356–7361.

70. Cited in Nicholas Wade, "For Gay Men, an Attraction to a Different Kind of Scent" in *New York Times,*
May 10, 2005, available at http://www.nytimes.com/2005/05/10/science/10smell.html, accessed May 10, 2005.

71. See, for example, Dennis McFadden and Edward G. Pasanen, "Comparison of the Auditory Systems of Heterosexuals and Homosexuals: Click-Evoked Otoacoustic Emissions" in *Proceedings of the National Academy of Sciences,* 95, March 1998, pp. 2709–2713; and McFadden and Pasanen, "Spontaneous Otoacoustic Emissions in Heterosexuals, Homosexuals, and Bisexuals" in *Journal of the Acoustical Society of America,* 105(4), April 1999, pp. 2403–2413; and Dennis McFadden and Craig Champlin, "Comparison of Auditory Evoked Potentials in Heterosexual, Homosexual and Bisexual Males and Females" in *Journal of the Association for Research in Otolaryngology,* 1, 2000, pp. 89–99.

72. Marc Breedlove and Pat McBroom, "Sexual Experience May Affect Brain Structure" at http://www.berkeley.edu/news/berkeleyan/1997/1119/sexexp.html, accessed August 14, 2009; see also Jim McKnight, "Editorial: The Origins of Male Homosexuality" in *Psychology, Evolution and Gender,* 2(3), December 2000, p. 226.

73. See F. Kallmann, "Comparative Twin Study on the Genetic Aspects of Male Homosexuality" in *Journal of Nervous Mental Disorders,* 115, 1952, pp. 283–298. Kallmann's findings may have been an artifact of his sample, which was drawn entirely from institutionalized mentally ill patients—some of whom had been institutionalized because they were gay. See also Richard Lewontin, Steven Rose, and Leon Kamin, *Not in Our Genes: Biology, Ideology and Human Nature* (New York: Pantheon, 1984).

74. J. Michael Bailey and Richard Pillard, "A Genetic Study of Male Sexual Orientation" in *Archives of General Psychiatry,* 48, December 1991; J. Michael Bailey and Richard Pillard, "Heritable Factors Influence Sexual Orientation in Women" in *Archives of General Psychiatry,* 50, March 1993.

75. This is equally a problem in Frederick Whitam, Milton Diamond, and James Martin, "Homosexual Orientation in Twins: A Report on 61 Pairs and Three Triplet Sets" in *Archives of Sexual Behavior,* 22(3), 1993.

76. Richard Pillard and James Weinreich, "Evidence of a Familial Nature of Male Homosexuality" in *Archives of General Psychiatry,* 43, 1986.

77. See Peter Bearman and Hannah Bruckner, "Opposite Sex Twins and Adolescent Same-Sex Attraction" in *American Journal of Sociology,* March 2002.

78. Steven Goldberg, *The Inevitability of Patriarchy* (New York: Simon & Schuster, 1973), p. 93.

79. C. Apicella, A. Dreber, P. Gray, M. Hoffman, A. C. Little, and B.C. Campbell, "Androgens and Competitiveness in Men" in *Journal of Neuroscience, Psychology and Economics*, February 2011, pp. 54–62.

80. C. Eisenegger, M. Naef, R. Snozzi, M. Heinrichs, and E. Fehr, "Prejudice and Truth About the Effect of Testosterone on Human Bargaining Behaviour," in *Nature*, 08711, 2009, pp. 1–6.

81. See James McBride Dabbs (with Mary Godwin Dabbs), *Heroes, Rogues and Lovers: Testosterone and Behavior* (New York: McGraw-Hill, 2000), p. 8; Andrew Sullivan, "The He Hormone" in *New York Times Magazine*, April 2, 2000, p. 48. Dabbs rampages through the literature about testosterone, claiming to be able to predict (cause and effect) behaviors ranging from rape to fraternity keg parties, from choice of occupation to likelihood to commit crimes, simply by the level of testosterone. About the only statement that Dabbs makes that is less than completely hyperbolic is that "sometimes male bluster is hardwired into the brain by early testosterone" (p. 66). Well, at least some people's bluster may be.

82. There is some evidence that AndroGel is dangerous and should not be taken without significant testing. Testosterone may shrink the testes (because they no longer need to produce it) but also may exacerbate prostate cancer, acting like food to a growing tumor. See Jerome Groopman, "Hormones for Men" in *New Yorker*, July 29, 2002, pp. 34–38.

83. Robert Sapolsky, *The Trouble with Testosterone* (New York: Simon & Schuster, 1997), p. 155.

84. Theodore Kemper, *Testosterone and Social Structure* (New Brunswick, NJ: Rutgers University Press, 1990); Arthur Kling, "Testosterone and Aggressive Behavior in Man and Non-human Primates" in *Hormonal Correlates of Behavior*, B. Eleftheriou and R. Sprott, eds. (New York: Plenum, 1975); see also E. Gonzalez-Bono, A. Salvador, J. Ricarte, M. A. Serrano, and M. Arendo, "Testosterone and Attribution of Successful Competition" in *Aggressive Behavior*, 26(3), 2000, pp. 235–240.

85. Anu Aromaki, Ralf Lindman, and C. J. Peter Eriksson, "Testosterone, Aggressiveness and Antisocial Personality" in *Aggressive Behavior*, 25, 1999, pp. 113–123; Sapolsky cited in Richard Lacayo, "Are You Man Enough?" in *Time*, April, 24, 2000.

86. Peter B. Gray, Sonya Kahlenberg, Emily Barrett, Susan Lipson, and Peter T. Ellison, "Marriage and Fatherhood Are Associated with Lower Testosterone in Males" in *Evolution and Human Behavior*, 23, 2002, pp. 193–201; see also the coverage of this study, William Cromie, "Marriage Lowers Testosterone" in *Harvard Gazette*, September 19, 2002; Ellen Barry, "The Ups and Downs of Manhood" in *Boston Globe*, July 9, 2002.

87. See, for example, Jed Diamond, *Male Menopause* (Naperville, IL: Sourcebooks, 1998); and Groopman, "Hormones for Men."

88. See Celina Cohen-Bendahan, Cornelieke van de Beek, and Sheri Berenbaum, "Prenatal Sex Hormone Effects on Child and Adult Sex-Typed Behavior: Methods and Findings" in *Neuroscience and Biobehavioral Reviews*, 29(2), April 2005, pp. 353–384, for a summary of such clinically based studies.

89. John Money and Anke Ehrhardt, *Man and Woman, Boy and Girl* (Baltimore: Johns Hopkins University Press, 1972).

90. Anke Ehrhardt and S. W. Baker, "Fetal Androgens, Human Central Nervous System Differentiation, and Behavior Sex Differences" in *Sex Differences in Behavior*, R. Friedman, R. M. Richart, and R. L. Vande Wiele, eds. (Huntington, NY: Krieger, 1978), p. 49.

91. Fausto-Sterling, *Myths of Gender*, pp. 136–137.

92. Irvin Yalom, Richard Green, and N. Fisk, "Prenatal Exposure to Female Hormones—Effect on Psychosexual Development in Boys" in *Archives of General Psychiatry*, 28, 1973.

93. See John Colapinto, *As Nature Made Him: The Boy Who Was Raised as a Girl* (New York: HarperCollins, 2000), and John Colapinto, "Gender Gap: What Were the Real Reasons Behind David Reimer's Suicide?" in *Slate*, June 3, 2004, available at www.slate.com/id/2101678. Scholarly papers include M. Diamond, "Sexual Identity, Monozygotic Twins Reared in Discordant Sex Roles and a BBC Follow-Up" in *Archives of Sexual Behavior*, 11(2), 1982, pp. 181–185; M. Diamond and H. K. Sigmundson, "Sex Reassignment at Birth: Long Term Review and Clinical Implications" in *Archives of Pediatrics and Adolescent Medicine*, 151, March 1997, pp. 298–304.

94. Shari Roan, "The Basis of Sexual Identity" in *Los Angeles Times*, March 14, 1997, p. E1.

95. See Judith Lorber and Lisa Jean Moore, *Gendered Bodies: Feminist Perspectives* (Palo Alto CA: Roxbury Press, 2006).

96. Gloria Steinem, "If Men Could Menstruate" in *Outrageous Acts and Everyday Rebellions* (New York: Holt, Rinehart and Winston, 1983).

97. Durden-Smith and deSimone, *Sex and the Brain*, p. 92.

98. Gunter Dorner, B. Schenk, B. Schmiedel, and L. Ahrens, "Stressful Events in Prenatal Life of Bisexual and Homosexual Men" in *Explorations in Clinical Endocrinology*, 81, 1983, p. 87. See also Dorner et al., "Prenatal Stress as a Possible Paetiogenic Factor of Homosexuality in Human Males" in *Endokrinologie*, 75, 1983; and G. Dorner, F. Gotz, T. Ohkawa, W. Rohde, F. Stahl, and R. Tonjes, "Prenatal Stress and Sexual Brain Differentiation in Animal and Human Beings," *Abstracts*, International Academy of Sex Research, Thirteenth Annual Meeting, Tutzing, June 21–25, 1987.

99. The other side is presented in a clever article by Gunter Schmidt and Ulrich Clement, "Does Peace Prevent Homosexuality?" in *Journal of Homosexuality*, 28(1–2), 1995.

100. John Stossel, "Just Too Taboo to Talk About" in *Orange County Register*, January 30, 2005, Home section.

101. Terrance Williams, Michelle Pepitone, Scott Christensen, Bradley Cooke, Andrew Huberman, Nicolas Breedlove, Tess Breedlove, Cynthia Jordan, and S. Marc Breedlove, "Finger Length Ratios and Sexual Orientation" in *Nature*, 404, March 30, 2000, p. 455; see also S. J. Robinson, "The Ratio of 2nd to 4th Digit Length and Male Homosexuality" in *Evolution and Human Behavior*, 21, 2000, pp. 333–345. Also see Tim Beneke, "Sex on the Brain" in *East Bay Express*, September 22, 2000, for a superb profile of Breedlove and his research.

102. Marc Breedlove, personal communication with the author, February 13, 2001; see also Susan Rubinowitz, "Report: Index Finger Size May Indicate Homosexuality" in *New York Post*, March 30, 2000.

103. Anthony Bogaert, "Biological Versus Nonbiological Older Brothers and Men's Sexual Orientation" in *Proceedings of the National Academy of Science*, 103(28), July 11, 2006, pp. 10771–10774; see also David Puts, Cynthia Jordan, and S. Marc Breedlove, "O Brother, Where Are Thou? The Fraternal Birth-Order Effect on Male Sexual Orientation" in *Proceedings of the National Academy of Science*, 103(28), July 11, 2006, pp. 10531–10532.

104. See Alice Domurat Dreger, *Hermaphrodites and the Medical Invention of Sex* (Cambridge: Harvard University Press, 1998); Gert Hekma, "'A Female Soul in a Male Body': Sexual Inversion as Gender Inversion in Nineteenth Century Sexology" in *Third Sex, Third Gender*, Gilbert Herdt, ed. (Cambridge: MIT Press, 1993).

105. See Julliane Imperato-McGinley et al., "Steroid 5-Alpha Reductase Deficiency in Man: An Inherited Form of Pseudo-hermaphroditism" in *Science*, 186, 1974; Julliane Imperato-McGinley et al., "Androgens and the Evolution of Male-Gender Identity Among Male Pseudohermaphrodites with 5-Alpha Reductase Deficiency" in *New England Journal of Medicine*, 300, 1979, p. 1235. For an excellent summary of the research, see Gilbert Herdt, "Mistaken Sex: Culture, Biology and the Third Sex in New Guinea" in Herdt, *Third Sex, Third Gender*.

106. Herdt, "Mistaken Sex."

107. Dobson, *Straight Talk*, p. 184.

108. Goldberg, *Inevitability of Patriarchy*, pp. 233–234; see also Fausto-Sterling, *Myths of Gender*, p. 124.

109. A recent effort to use hormone research and evolutionary imperatives is J. Richard Udry, "Biological Limits of Gender Construction" in *American Sociological Review*, 65, June 2000, pp. 443–457. Udry's thesis is elegantly demolished by Eleanor Miller and Carrie Yang Costello, "Comment on Udry" in *American Sociological Review*, 65, June 2000, pp. 592–598.

110. Lewontin et al., *Not in Our Genes*, p. 147.

111. Alice Rossi, *Gender and the Life Course* (Chicago: Aldine, 1982).

112. Darrell Yates Rist, "Are Homosexuals Born That Way?" in *The Nation*, October 19, 1992, p. 427; "Born or Bred?" in *Newsweek*, February 24, 1992.

113. Karen De Witt, "Quayle Contends Homosexuality Is a Matter of Choice, Not Biology" in *New York Times*, September 14, 1992; Ashcroft cited in Eric Alterman, "Sorry, Wrong President" in *The Nation*, February 26, 2001, p. 10. See John Leland and Mark Miller, "Can Gays Convert?" in *Newsweek*, August 17, 1998. Although it is certain that some therapeutic interventions can lead people to change their sexual behavior and sexual object choice, the evidence that people's orientations change is less than convincing.

114. John D'Emilio, *Making Trouble: Essays on Gay History* (New York: Routledge, 1992), p. 187.

115. See, for example, Martin P. Levine, *Gay Macho: The Life and Death of the Homosexual Clone* (New York: New York University Press, 1997); see also John Gagnon and William Simon, *Sexual Conduct* (Chicago: Aldine, 1973).

116. Vera Whisman, *Queer by Choice* (New York: Routledge, 1992).

117. Charlotte Bunch, "Lesbians in Revolt" in *Feminist Frameworks*, A. Jaggar and P. Rothenberg, eds. (New York: McGraw-Hill, 1984), p. 144.

118. LeVay, *Sexual Brain*, p. 6.

119. Ruth Hubbard, "The Political Nature of Human Nature" in *Theoretical Perspectives on Sexual Difference*, Deborah Rhode, ed. (New Haven, CT: Yale University Press, 1990), p. 69.

120. Robert A. Padgug, "On Conceptualizing Sexuality in History" in *Radical History Review*, 20, 1979, p. 9.

121. Richard Hofstadter, *Social Darwinism in American Thought* (New York: Random House, 1944), p. 204.

122. Deena Skolnick Weisberg, Frank C. Keil, Joshua Goodstein, Elizabeth Rawson, and Jeremy Gray, "The Seductive Allure of Neuroscience Explanation" in *Journal of Cognitive Neuroscience*, 20(3), 2008, pp. 470–477.

123. Adam Begley, "Why Men and Women Think Differently" in *Newsweek*, 1995.

CHAPTER THREE

1. See, for example, Karen Sacks, "Engels Revisited: Women, Organization of Production, and Private Property" in *Women, Culture and Society*, M. Rosaldo and L. Lamphere, eds. (Stanford, CA: Stanford University Press, 1974); and *Sisters and Wives: The Past and Future of Sexual Equality* (Westport, CT: Greenwood, 1979).

2. Margaret Mead, *Sex and Temperament in Three Primitive Societies* (New York: William Morrow, 1935). Critics such as Derek Freeman have suggested that Mead, like the biologists she was criticizing, simply found what she was looking for, especially in Samoa, where she apparently fabricated some details. Yet challenges to the core insight in her work in New Guinea, that of cultural variation in gender roles, are unsubstantiated and unconvincing.

3. Mead, *Sex and Temperament*, pp. 29, 35, 57–58, 84, 101, 128.

4. Margaret Mead, *Male and Female* (New York: William Morrow, 1949), p. 69; Mead, *Sex and Temperament*, p. 171.

5. Mead, *Sex and Temperament*, pp. 189, 190, 197; Mead, *Male and Female*, p. 98.

6. Mead, *Sex and Temperament*, p. 228.

7. Adrienne Zihlman, "Woman the Gatherer: The Role of Women in Early Hominid Evolution" in *Gender and Anthropology*, S. Morgen, ed. (Washington, DC: American Anthropological Association, 1989), p. 31.

8. Friedrich Engels, *The Origin of the Family, Private Property and the State* (New York: International Publishers, 1970).

9. Eleanor Leacock, "Women's Status in Egalitarian Society: Implications for Social Evolution" in *Current Anthropology*, 19(2), 1978, p. 252; see also Eleanor Leacock, "Montagnais Women and the Jesuit Program for Colonization" in *Women and Colonization*, M. Etienne and E. Leacock, eds. (New York: Praeger, 1980).

10. Sacks, "Engels Revisited" in *Sisters and Wives*.

11. Marvin Harris, *Cows, Pigs, Wars and Witches: The Riddle of Culture* (New York: Random House, 1974); and Marvin Harris, *Cannibals and Kings* (New York: Random House, 1977).

12. Lionel Tiger and Robin Fox, *The Imperial Animal* (New York: Holt, 1971).

13. Claude Levi-Strauss, *The Elementary Structures of Kinship* (London: Tavistock, 1969); see also Collier and Rosaldo, "Politics and Gender in Simple Societies" in *Sexual Meanings: The Cultural Construction of Gender and Sexuality*, S. B. Ortner and H. Whitehead, eds. (Cambridge: Cambridge University Press, 1981).

14. Barry, Herbert, III, Margaret K. Bacon, and Irvin L. Child, "A Cross-Cultural Survey of Some Sex Differences in Socialization," in *Journal of Abnormal and Social Psychology*, 55, 1957, pp. 327–332.

15. Judith Brown, "A Note on the Division of Labor by Sex," in *American Anthropologist*, 72(5), 1970.

16. Mead, *Male and Female*, pp. 189, 190.

17. Daphne Spain, *Gendered Spaces* (Chapel Hill: University of North Carolina Press, 1992); and Daphne Spain, "The Spatial Foundations of Men's Friendships and Men's Power" in *Men's Friendships*, Peter Nardi, ed. (Newbury Park, CA: Sage Publications, 1992), p. 76.

18. Thomas Gregor, *Mehinaku: The Drama of Daily Life in a Brazilian Indian Village* (Chicago: University of Chicago Press, 1977), p. 255; see also pp. 305–306. In another passage, Gregor recounts a child's game in which a girl pretends to invade the men's house, and the boys pretend to gang rape her (p. 114). See also Thomas Gregor, "No Girls Allowed," *Science*, 82, December 1982.

19. Peggy Reeves Sanday, *Female Power and Male Dominance* (New York: Cambridge University Press, 1981), pp. 75, 128. See also Maria Lepowsky, "Gender in an Egalitarian Society: A Case Study from the Coral Sea" in *Beyond the Second Sex: New Directions in the Anthropology of Gender*, P. R. Sanday and R. G. Goodenough, eds. (Philadelphia: University of Pennsylvania Press, 1990).

20. See Carol Tavris and Carole Wade, *The Longest War* (New York: Harcourt, Brace, 1984), pp. 330–331.

21. See Salman Masood, "Pakistan's High Court Reviewing Officially Ordered Gang Rape" in *New York Times*, June 28, 2005, p. 3.

22. See Peggy Reeves Sanday, *Fraternity Gang Rape* (New York: New York University Press, 1991).

23. John W. Whiting, Richard Kluckhohn, and Albert Anthony, "The Function of Male Initiation Ceremonies at Puberty" in *Readings in Social Psychology*, E. Maccoby, T. M. Newcomb, and E. L. Hatley, eds. (New York: Henry Holt, 1958).

24. Edgar Gregersen, *Sexual Practices* (New York: Franklin Watts, 1983), p. 104.

25. Marc Lacey, "African Activists Urge End to Female Mutilation" in *International Herald Tribune*, February 7, 2003, p. 10.

26. Cited in Rogaia Mustafa Abusharaf, "Unmasking Tradition" in *The Sciences*, March/April 1998, p. 23.

27. AMA, http://www.ama-assn.org/amednews/2012/02/27/prse0302.htm.

28. Frederick Nzwili, "New Ritual Replaces Female Genital Mutilation" in *Women's ENews*, April 10, 2003, www.womensenews.org/article.cfm/dyn/aid/1284.

29. See, for example, Joseph Zoske, "Male Circumcision: A Gender Perspective" in *Journal of Men's Studies*, 6(2), Winter 1998; see also Michael Kimmel, "The Kindest Uncut" in *Tikkun*, 16(3), May 2001.

30. Karen Paige and Jeffrey Paige, *The Politics of Reproductive Ritual* (Berkeley: University of California Press, 1981).

31. Tavris and Wade, *Longest War*, p. 314; see also Paige and Paige, *Politics of Reproductive Ritual*; Fatima Mernissi, *Beyond the Veil: Male-Female Dynamics in a Modern Muslim Society* (New York: Wiley, 1975).

32. Michael Olien, *The Human Myth* (New York: Harper and Row, 1978); M. K. Martin and B. Voorhies, *Female of the Species* (New York: Columbia University Press, 1975).

33. Walter Williams, *The Spirit and the Flesh* (Boston: Beacon Press, 1986).

34. Marc Lacey, "A Lifestyle Distinct: The Muxe of Mexico" in *New York Times*, December 7, 2008.

35. Paula Gunn Allen, "Beloved Women: Lesbians in American Indian Cultures" in *Conditions: Seven: A Magazine of Writing by Women* (self-published, 1981), p. 67.

36. Martin and Voorhies, *Female of the Species*, p. 97.

37. See Jenny Nordberg, "Where Boys Are Prized, Girls Live the Part" in *New York Times*, September 21, 2010, p. 1.

38. Cited in Clyde Kluckhohn, *Mirror for Man* (Greenwich, CT: Greenwood, 1970).

39. Gilbert Herdt, *Guardians of the Flutes* (Chicago: University of Chicago Press, 1981), pp. 1, 165, 282.

40. F. E. Williams, *Papuans of the Trans-Fly* (Oxford: Oxford University Press, 1936), p. 159; see also E. L. Schiefflin, *The Sorrow of the Lonely and the Burning of the Dancers* (New York: St. Martin's Press, 1976); R. Kelly, *Etero Social Structure* (Ann Arbor: University of Michigan Press, 1977); J. Carrier, "Sex Role Preference as an Explanatory Variable in Homosexual Behavior" in *Archives of Sexual Behavior*, 6, 1977; Stephen O. Murray, *Homosexualities* (Chicago: University of Chicago Press, 2000).

41. William Davenport, "Sex in Cross-Cultural Perspective" in *Human Sexuality in Four Perspectives*, F. Beach and M. Diamond, eds. (Baltimore: Johns Hopkins University Press, 1977); see also Gilbert Herdt, ed., *Ritualized Homosexuality in Melanesia* (Berkeley: University of California Press, 1984), p. 66.

42. Gregersen, *Sexual Practices*, p. 257.

43. Ibid.

44. Davenport, "Sex in Cross-Cultural Perspective."

45. Ernestine Friedel, *Women and Men: An Anthropologist's View* (New York: Holt, Rinehart, 1975).

46. Gregersen, *Sexual Practices*.

47. Clyde Kluckhohn, *Mirror for Man* (New York: Whittlesey Houx, 1949); see also Gregersen, *Sexual Practices*.

48. Gregersen, *Sexual Practices*.

49. Nancy Tanner and Adrienne Zihlman, "Women in Evolution" in *Signs*, 1(3), Spring 1976. Nancy Tanner, *Becoming Human* (New York: Cambridge University Press, 1981); Adrienne Zihlman, "Motherhood in Transition: From Ape to Human" in *The First Child and Family Formation*, W. Miller and L. Newman, eds. (Chapel Hill: Carolina Population Center, 1978).

50. Helen Fisher, *The Anatomy of Love* (New York: Norton, 1992), p. 57.

51. Michelle Rosaldo, "The Use and Abuse of Anthropology: Reflections on Feminism and Cross-Cultural Understanding" in *Signs*, 5(3), Spring 1980, p. 393; Bonnie Nardi, review of Peggy Reeves Sanday's *Female Power and Male Dominance Power and Male Dominance* in *Sex Roles*, 8(11), 1982, p. 1159.

52. Marija Gimbutas, *The Goddesses and Gods of Old Europe, 7000–3500 B.C.* (Berkeley: University of California Press, 1982); and Marija Gimbutas, *The Living Goddesses* (Berkeley: University of California Press, 1999). See also Riane Eisler, *The Chalice and the Blade* (New York: HarperCollins, 1987).

53. Eisler, *Chalice and the Blade*, pp. 45, 58.

54. Francis Fukuyama, "Women and the Evolution of World Politics" in *Foreign Affairs*, September 1998, p. 27; see also Lawrence Keely, *War Before Civilization* (New York: Oxford University Press, 1997).

55. Maria Lepowsky, *Fruit of the Motherland: Gender in an Egalitarian Society* (New York: Columbia University Press, 1993), p. 219.

56. Peggy Reeves Sanday, *Women Center: Life in a Modern Matriarchy* (Boston: Beacon, 2002), p. 116.

57. Leacock, "Montagnais Women," p. 200.

CHAPTER FOUR

1. Carol Gilligan, affidavit in *Faulkner v. Jones* (D. Ct., S.C., filed January 7, 1993), p. 3; affidavit on file with the author.

2. Sigmund Freud, "The Dissection of the Psychical Personality" in *New Introductory Lectures on Psychoanalysis* [1933] (New York: W. W. Norton, 1965), p. 74.

3. Sigmund Freud, "The Dissolution of the Oedipus Complex" [1924] in *The Standard Edition of the Complete Psychological Works* (New York: W. W. Norton, 1965), Vol. 19, p. 179.

4. Sigmund Freud, *Letters of Sigmund Freud, 1873–1939*, Ernst Freud, ed. (London: Hogarth Press, 1961), pp. 419–420.

5. See, for example, Jeffrey Masson, *The Assault on Truth* (New York: Farrar, Straus and Giroux, 1984); and Alice Miller, *Thou Shalt Not Be Aware: Society's Betrayal of the Child* (New York: Farrar, Straus and Giroux, 1984) and *For Your Own Good* (New York: Farrar, Straus and Giroux, 1983).

6. Lewis Terman and Catherine Cox Miles, *Sex and Personality* (New York: McGraw-Hill, 1936); see also Henry Minton, "Femininity in Men and Masculinity in Women: American Psychiatry and Psychology Portray Homosexuality in the 1930s" in *Journal of Homosexuality*, 13(1), 1986.

7. George Henry, "Psychogenic Factors in Overt Homosexuality" in *American Journal of Psychiatry*, 93, 1937; cited in Minton, "Femininity in Men," p. 2. Note, however, that Henry's secondary claim is not that these tendencies will simply emerge, but rather that the social *response* to these traits will exaggerate and sustain them; in other words, that overt responses

of homophobia will actually encourage the tendency toward homosexuality.

8. See Peter Wyden and Barbara Wyden, *Growing Up Straight: What Every Thoughtful Parent Should Know About Homosexuality* (New York: Trident Press, 1968).

9. See Jean Piaget, *Plays, Dreams and Imitation in Children* (New York: Norton, 1951), *The Language and Thought of the Child* (London: Routledge, 1952), and *The Moral Judgment of the Child* (New York: Free Press, 1965).

10. Lawrence Kohlberg, "A Cognitive-Developmental Analysis of Children's Sex Role Concepts and Attitudes" in *The Development of Sex Differences*, E. Maccoby, ed. (Stanford, CA: Stanford University Press, 1966); and Lawrence Kohlberg and Edward Zigler, "The Impact of Cognitive Maturity on the Development of Sex Role Attitudes in the Years 4 to 8" in *Genetic Psychology Monographs*, 75, 1967.

11. Albert Bandura and Althea Huston, "Identification as a Process of Incidental Learning" in *Journal of Abnormal and Social Psychology*, 63, 1961; Albert Bandura, Dorothea Ross, and Sheila Ross, "A Comparative Test of the Status Envy, Social Power, and Secondary Reinforcement Theories of Indeificatory Learning" in *Journal of Abnormal and Social Psychology*, 67, 1963; Walter Mischel, "A Social-Learning View of Sex Differences" in Maccoby, *Development of Sex Differences*.

12. See Karen Horney, "On the Genesis of the Castration Complex in Women" in *Psychoanalysis and Women*, J. B. Miller, ed. (New York: Bruner/Mazel, 1973).

13. Bruno Bettelheim, *Symbolic Wounds* (New York: Collier, 1962); Wolfgang Lederer, *The Fear of Women* (New York: Harcourt Brace Jovanovich, 1968).

14. Nancy Chodorow, *The Reproduction of Mothering* (Berkeley: University of California Press, 1978); Jessica Benjamin, *The Bonds of Love* (New York: Pantheon, 1984); Dorothy Dinnerstein, *The Mermaid and the Minotaur* (New York: Harper and Row, 1977); Lillian Rubin, *Intimate Strangers* (New York: Harper and Row, 1983). Three of these writers—Chodorow, Benjamin, and Rubin—have PhDs in sociology and also are practicing therapists, a combination that, in my view, enabled them to explore the social consequences of the individual devaluation of women with rare acuity.

15. Chodorow, *Reproduction of Mothering*; see also Chodorow, "Family Structure and Feminine Personality" in *Women, Culture and Society*,

M. Rosaldo and L. Lamphere, eds. (Stanford, CA: Stanford University Press, 1974).

16. Chodorow, "Family Structure," p. 50.

17. Carol Gilligan, *In a Different Voice* (Cambridge: Harvard University Press, 1982), p. 173.

18. Mary Belenky, Blythe Clinchy, Nancy Goldberger, and Jin Tarule, *Women's Way of Knowing* (New York: Basic Books, 1987); Deborah Tannen, *You Just Don't Understand* (New York: William Morrow, 1990); Robert Bly, *Iron John* (Reading: Addison-Wesley, 1991).

19. See H. Crothers, *Meditations on Votes for Women* (Boston: Houghton, Mifflin, 1914), p. 74.

20. Carol Gilligan, "Reply" in "On *In a Different Voice*: An Interdisciplinary Forum" in *Signs*, 11(2), 1986, p. 327; affidavit of Carol Gilligan in *Faulkner v. Jones*, D. Ct., S.C., filed January 7, 1993, p. 3.

21. Carol Tavris, "The Mismeasure of Woman" in *Feminism and Psychology*, 3(2), 1993, p. 153.

22. Janet Hyde, "The Gender Similarities Hypothesis" in *American Psychologist*, 60, 2005, pp. 581–592.

23. Eleanor Maccoby and Carol Jacklin, *The Psychology of Sex Differences* (Stanford, CA: Stanford University Press, 1974), p. 362.

24. Rosalind Chait Barnett, "Understanding the Role of Pervasive Negative Gender Stereotypes: What Can Be Done?" paper presented at The Way Forward, Heidelberg, Germany, May 2007.

25. Piper Weiss, "Couple Finally Reveals Child's Gender, Five Years After Birth" in *Yahoo! Shine*, January 20, 2012.

26. Joseph Pleck offered a superb summary of these studies in "The Theory of Male Sex Role Identity: Its Rise and Fall, 1936 to the Present" in *In the Shadow of the Past: Psychology Views the Sexes*, M. Lewin, ed. (New York: Columbia University Press, 1984). Much of my summary draws from his essay.

27. Teodor Adorno et al., *The Authoritarian Personality* (New York: Harper and Row, 1950).

28. Qazi Rahman, Suraj Bhanot, Hanna Emrith-Small, Shilan Ghafoor, and Steven Roberts, "Gender Nonconformity, Intelligence, and Sexual Orientation" in *Archives of Sexual Behavior*, February 18, 2011, unpaginated.

29. See Robb Willer, "Overdoing Gender," unpublished manuscript, Department of Sociology, Cornell University, 2005.

30. Walter Miller and E. Guy Swanson, *Inner Conflict and Defense* (New York: Holt, 1960).

31. Talcott Parsons, "Certain Primary Sources and Patterns of Aggression in the Social Structure of the Western World" in *Psychiatry*, 10, 1947, p. 309.

32. Sandra Bem, "The Measurement of Psychological Androgyny" in *Journal of Consulting and Clinical Psychology*, 42, 1974; Sandra Bem, "Androgyny vs. the Tight Little Lives of Fluffy Women and Chesty Men" in *Psychology Today*, September 1975; Sandra Bem, "Beyond Androgyny: Some Presumptuous Prescriptions for a Liberated Sexual Identity" in *The Future of Women: Issues in Psychology*, J. Sherman and F. Denmark, eds. (New York: Psychological Dimensions, 1978). See also Alexandra Kaplan and Mary Anne Sedney, *Psychology and Sex Roles: An Androgynous Perspective* (Boston: Little Brown, 1980), quote is on p. 6; Janet Spence, Robert Helmreich, and Joy Stapp, "The Personal Attributes Questionnaire: A Measure of Sex-Role Stereotypes and Masculinity-Femininity" in *JSAS Catalog of Selected Documents in Psychology*, 4, 1974.

33. Sandra Bem, *Lenses of Gender* (New Haven, CT: Yale University Press, 1993), p. 124.

34. Joseph Pleck, *The Myth of Masculinity* (Cambridge: MIT Press, 1981).

35. See, for example, James M. O'Neil, "Assessing Men's Gender Role Conflict" in *Problem Solving Strategies and Interventions for Men in Conflict*, D. Moorer and F. Leafgren, eds. (Alexandria, VA: American Association for Counseling and Development, 1990); J. M. O'Neil, B. Helms, R. Gable, L. David, and L. Wrightsman, "Gender Role Conflict Scale: College Men's Fear of Femininity" in *Sex Roles*, 14, 1986, pp. 335–350; Joseph Pleck, "The Gender Role Strain Paradigm: An Update" in *A New Psychology of Men*, R. Levant and W. Pollack, eds. (New York: Basic Books, 1995); James Mihalik, Benjamin Locke, Harry Theodore, Robert Cournoyer, and Brendan Lloyd, "A Cross-National and Cross-Sectional Comparison of Men's Gender Role Conflict and Its Relationship to Social Intimacy and Self-Esteem" in *Sex Roles*, 45(1/2), 2001, pp. 1–14.

36. Warren Farrell, *The Myth of Male Power* (New York: Simon & Schuster, 1993), p. 40.

37. That's not to say that Pleck doesn't try valiantly to do so. His "Men's Power over Women, Other Men and in Society" in *Women and Men: The Consequences of Power*, D. Hiller and R. Sheets, eds. (Cincinnati: University of Cincinnati Women's Studies, 1977), takes the theory as far as it will go, which is quite far in my view. But the theory is still unable to theorize both difference and institutionalized gender relations adequately.

38. Jean-Paul Sartre, *Anti-Semite and Jew* (New York: Schocken Press, 1965), p. 60.

CHAPTER FIVE

1. M. Pines, "Civilizing of Genes" in *Psychology Today*, September 1981.

2. Helen Z. Lopata and Barrie Thorne, "On the Term 'Sex Roles'" in *Signs*, 3, 1978, p. 719.

3. Tim Carrigan, Bob Connell, and John Lee, "Toward a New Sociology of Masculinity" in *Theory and Society*, 14, 1985. See also R. W. Connell, *Gender and Power* (Stanford, CA: Stanford University Press, 1987); R. W. Connell, *Masculinities* (Berkeley: University of California Press, 1995); Judith Stacey and Barrie Thorne, "The Missing Feminist Revolution in Sociology" in *Social Problems*, 32(4), 1985, for elaboration and summaries of the sociological critique of sex-role theory.

4. Deborah Rhode, *Speaking of Sex* (Cambridge: Harvard University Press, 1997), p. 42.

5. Stacey and Thorne, "The Missing Feminist Revolution," p. 307.

6. Carrigan, Connell, and Lee, "Toward a New Sociology of Masulinity," p. 587; see also Connell, *Gender and Power*.

7. David Tresemer, "Assumptions Made About Gender Roles" in *Another Voice: Feminist Perspectives on Social Life and Social Science*, M. Millman and R. M. Kanter, eds. (New York: Anchor Books, 1975), p. 323; R. Stephen Warner, David Wellman, and Leonore Weitzman, "The Hero, the Sambo and the Operator: Three Characterizations of the Oppressed" in *Urban Life and Culture*, 2, 1973.

8. Carrigan, Connell, and Lee, "Toward a New Sociology of Masculinity," p. 587.

9. Hannah Arendt, *On Revolution* (New York: Viking, 1976).

10. P. T. Costa and R. R. McCrae, "Age Difference in Personality Structure: A Cluster Analytic Approach" in *Journal of Gerontology*, 31, 1978, pp. 564–570; see also G. E. Valliant, *Adaptations to Life* (Boston: Little Brown, 1978).

11. Elaine Wethington, "Multiple Roles, Social Integration, and Health" in K. Pillemer, P. Moen, E. Wethington, and N. Glasgow, eds., *Social Integration in the Second Half of Life* (Baltimore, MD: Johns Hopkins University Press, 2000).

12. U.S. Bureau of the Census, *United States Census 2000* (Washington, DC: U.S. Department of Commerce, Bureau of the Census, 2000).

13. United Nations, *The World's Women 2010* (New York: United Nations, 2010).

14. Richard Woods, "Women Take Lead as Lifespan Heads for the Happy 100," in *London Times*, October 30, 2005, p. 14.

15. Evelyn Fox Keller, *A Feeling for the Organism* (New York: W. H. Freeman, 1985).

16. Janet Saltzman Chafetz, "Toward a Macro-Level Theory of Sexual Stratification" in *Current Perspectives in Social Theory*, 1, 1980.

17. Erving Goffman, "The Arrangement Between the Sexes" in *Theory and Society*, 4, 1977, p. 316.

18. Rosabeth Moss Kanter, *Men and Women of the Corporation* (New York: Basic Books, 1977). See also Rosabeth Moss Kanter, "Women and the Structure of Organizations: Explorations in Theory and Behavior" in *Another Voice: Feminist Perspectives on Social Life and Social Science*, M. Millman and R. M. Kanter, eds. (New York: Anchor Books, 1975).

19. Joan Acker, "Hierarchies, Jobs, Bodies: A Theory of Gendered Organizations" in *Gender & Society*, 4(2), 1990, p. 146; see also Joan Acker, "Sex Bias in Job Evaluation: A Comparable Worth Issue" in *Ingredients for Women's Employment Policy*, C. Bose and G. Spitze, eds. (Albany: SUNY Press, 1987); "Class, Gender and the Relations of Distribution" in *Signs: Journal of Women in Culture and Society*, 13, 1988; *Doing Comparable Worth: Gender, Class and Pay Equity* (Philadelphia: Temple University Press, 1989); and Joan Acker and Donald R. Van Houten, "Differential Recruitment and Control: The Sex Structuring of Organizations" in *Administrative Science Quarterly*, 19(2), 1974.

20. Acker, "Hierarchies, Jobs, Bodies," pp. 146–147.

21. Judith Gerson and Kathy Peiss, "Boundaries, Negotiation, Consciousness: Reconceptualizing Gender Relations" in *Social Problems*, 32(4), 1985, p. 320.

22. Acker, "Hierarchies, Job, Bodies," p. 258.

23. Candace West and Don Zimmerman, "Doing Gender" in *Gender & Society*, 1(2), 1987, p. 140.

24. Suzanne J. Kessler, "The Medical Construction of Gender: Case Management of Intersex Infants" in *Signs* 16(1), 1990, pp. 12–13.

25. Claudia Dreifus, "Declaring with Clarity When Gender Is Ambiguous" in *New York Times*, May 31, 2005, p. F2.

26. The phrase comes from R. W. Connell; I take it from the title of Barbara Risman, *Gender Vertigo* (New Haven, CT: Yale University Press, 1998).

27. Cited in West and Zimmerman, "Doing Gender," pp. 133–134.

28. It is difficult to accurately estimate how many individuals identify as transgender, as most surveys don't include gender identity questions, or incorrectly include "transgender" as a sexual orientation. Additionally, we have no estimates on the number of people who identify as nonbinary, genderqueer, or gender nonconforming (or any of the other myriad diverse gender identities). The estimate of one million comes from Gary J. Gates,

"How Many People Are Lesbian, Gay, Bisexual and Transgender?" in Williams Institute, 2011.

29. http://www.revelandriot.com/resources/trans-health/

30. Vanessa Vitiello Urquhart, "What the Heck is Genderqueer?" in *Slate*, March 24, 2015, accessed at http://www.slate.com/blogs/outward/2015/03/24/genderqueer_what_does_it_mean_and_where_does_it_come_from.html.

31. Cited in Carey Goldberg, "Shunning 'He' and 'She': They Fight for Respect" in *New York Times*, September 8, 1996, p. 24

32. Harold Garfinkle, *Studies in Ethnomethodology* (Englewood Cliffs, NJ: Prentice Hall, 1967), pp. 128, 132.

33. Kessler, "The Medical Construction of Gender" p. 25.

34. Tannen, *You Just Don't Understand*, pp. 24, 25; see also Deborah Tannen, *Gender and Discourse* (New York: Oxford University Press, 1994).

35. Tannen, *You Just Don't Understand*, p. 181.

36. C. L. Bylund and G. Makoul, "Empathic Communication and Gender in the Physician–Patient Encounter" in *Patient Education and Counseling*, 48(3), 2002, pp. 207–216; J. A. Hall, J. T. Irish, D. L. Roter, C. M. Ehrlich, and L. H. Miller, "Gender in Medical Encounters: An Analysis of Physician and Patient Communication in a Primary Care Setting" in *Health Psychology*, 13(5), 1994, p. 384; J. A. Hall, J. T. Irish, D. L. Roter, C. M. Ehrlich, and L. H. Miller, "Satisfaction, Gender, and Communication in Medical Visits" in *Medical Care*, 32(12), 1994, pp. 1216–1231; D. L. Roter, J. A. Hall, and Y. Aoki, "Physician Gender Effects in Medical Communication: A Meta-analytic Review" in *Jama*, 288(6), 2002, pp. 756–764; D. L. Roter and J. A. Hall, "Physician Gender and Patient-Centered Communication: A Critical Review of Empirical Research" in *Annual Review of Public Health*, 25, 2004, pp. 497–519; H. Sandhu, A. Adams, L. Singleton, D. Clark-Carter, and J. Kidd, "The Impact of Gender Dyads on Doctor–Patient Communication: A Systematic Review" in *Patient Education and Counseling*, 76(3), 2009, pp. 348–355.

37. William O'Barr and Jean F. O'Barr, *Linguistic Evidence: Language, Power and Strategy—The Courtroom* (San Diego: Academic Press, 1995); see also Alfie Kohn, "Girl Talk, Guy Talk" in *Psychology Today*, February 1988, p. 66.

38. Nicholas Groth, Ann Burgess, and Suzanne Sgroi, *Sexual Assault of Children and Adolescents* (San Francisco: Jossey-Bass, 1978).

39. Carol Sheffield, *Feminist Jurisprudence* (New York: Routledge, 1997), p. 203.

40. I will explore the sociology of rape in significantly more detail in chapter 11.

41. West and Zimmerman, "Doing Gender," p. 140; E. P. Thompson, *The Making of the English Working Class* (New York: Pantheon, 1963), p. 11.

42. James Messerschmidt, *Masculinities and Crime* (Lanham, MD: Rowman and Littlefield, 1993), p. 121.

43. Carrigan, Connell, and Lee, "Toward a New Sociology of Masculinity," p. 589; Karen D. Pyke, "Class-Based Masculinities: The Interdependence of Gender, Class and Interpersonal Power" in *Gender & Society*, 10(5), 1996, p. 530.

CHAPTER SIX

1. "Marital Status of People 15 Years and Over, by Age, Sex, Personal Earnings, Race, and Hispanic Origin/1, 2013," in *America's Families and Living Arrangements: 2013: Adults* (Washington, DC: U.S. Census Bureau, 2013); CDC/NCHS National Vital Statistics System, http://www.cdc.gov/nchs/nvss/marriage_divorce_tables.htm; "Table UC1" in *America's Families and Living Arrangements: 2011* (Washington, DC: U.S. Census Bureau, November 2011); "Census Bureau Releases Estimates of Same-Sex Married Couples" (Washington, DC: U.S. Census Bureau, September 2011); "Cohabitation Is Replacing Dating" in *USA Today*, July 17, 2005; National Center for Health Statistics, *Vital Health Statistics*, 23(28), 2010, available from http://www.cdc.; *Current Population Reports*, P70-125 (Washington, DC: U.S. Census Bureau, 2011), available from http://www.census.gov/prod/2011pubs/p70125.pdf; "Table 14" in *Trends in Nonmarital Birth Rate by Age, Race, and Hispanic Origin Births: Final Data for 2012* (Washington, DC: USDHHS, 2012); *America's Families and Living Arrangements: 2013: Children* (Washington, DC: U.S. Census Bureau, 2013).

2. Scott Coltrane, *Gender and Families* (Newbury Park, CA: Pine Forge Press, 1998), pp. 48–49; Stephanie Coontz, *The Way We Really Are: Coming to Terms with America's Changing Families* (New York: Basic Books, 1998), p. 30.

3. On the transformation of the idea of marriage, see, for example, Edward Shorter, *The Making of the Modern Family* (New York: Basic Books, 1977); Arlene Skolnick, *Embattled Paradise: The American Family in an Age of Uncertainty* (New York: Basic Books, 1993); Christopher Lasch, *Women and the Common Life: Love, Marriage and Feminism* (New York: Norton, 1997), especially p. 162. On husbands' brutality, see, for example, Steven Mintz and Susan Kellogg, *Domestic Revolutions: A Social History of the American Family* (New York: Free Press, 1988), p. 58.

4. Mintz and Kellogg, *Domestic Revolutions*, p. 50; see also Page Smith, *Daughters of the Promised*

Land: Women in American History (Boston: Little Brown, 1970); John Demos, "The Changing Faces of Fatherhood: A New Exploration in American Family History" in *Father and Child: Developmental and Clinical Perspectives*, S. Cath, A. Gurwitt, and J. Ross, eds. (Boston: Little Brown, 1982), p. 429.

5. John Demos, *Past, Present, and Personal: The Family and Life Course in American History* (New York: Oxford University Press, 1986), p. 32; see also Tamara Hareven, *Family Time and Industrial Time* (New York: Cambridge University Press, 1982). Tennyson, "The Princess," is cited in Skolnick, *Embattled Paradise*, p. 35.

6. Cited in David Popenoe, *Life Without Father: Compelling New Evidence That Fatherhood and Marriage Are Indispensable for the Good of Children and Society* (New York: Free Press, 1996), p. 95.

7. Gerda Lerner, "The Lady and the Mill Girl: Changes in the Status of Women in the Age of Jackson" in *American Studies Journal*, 10(1), Spring 1969, pp. 7, 9. Theodore Dwight, *The Father's Book* (Springfield, MA: G. and C. Merriam, 1834). See, generally, Michael Kimmel, *Manhood in America: A Cultural History* (New York: Free Press, 1996), chapters 1 and 2.

8. Lasch, *Women and the Common Life*, p. 162.

9. Bonnie Thornton Dill, "Our Mothers' Grief: Racial-Ethnic Women and the Maintenance of Families" in *Journal of Family History*, 13(4), 1988, p. 428.

10. John Gillis, "Making Time for Family: The Invention of Family Time(s) and the Reinvention of Family History" in *Journal of Family History*, 21, 1996; John Gillis, *A World of Their Own Making: Myth, Ritual, and the Quest for Family Values* (New York: Basic Books, 1996).

11. Skolnick, *Embattled Paradise*, p. 33; *Harper's*, cited in John Demos, "Changing Faces of Fatherhood," p. 442; see also Ralph LaRossa, "Fatherhood and Social Change" in *Family Relations*, 37, 1988; and Ralph LaRossa, *The Modernization of Fatherhood: A Social and Political History* (Chicago: University of Chicago Press, 1997); Robert Griswold, *Fatherhood in America: A History* (New York: Basic Books, 1993).

12. Skolnick, *Embattled Paradise*, p. 41; Mintz and Kellogg, *Domestic Revolutions*, p. 110.

13. See Stephen D. Sugarman, "Single Parent Families" in *All Our Families: New Policies for a New Century*, M. Mason, A. Skolnick, and S. Sugarman, eds. (New York: Oxford University Press, 1998), pp. 20–21.

14. See LaRossa, *Modernization of Fatherhood*.

15. Mintz and Kellogg, *Domestic Revolutions*, p. 179; Coontz, *The Way We Really Are*, p. 30; Mintz and Kellogg, *Domestic Revolutions*, p. 237.

16. William Chafe, *The Unfinished Journey: America Since World War II* (New York: Oxford University Press, 1986), p. 125; Morris Zelditch, "Role Differentiation in the Nuclear Family: A Comparative Study" in *Family, Socialization and Interaction Process*, T. Parsons and R. F. Bales, eds. (New York: Free Press, 1955), p. 339.

17. Griswold, *Fatherhood in America*, p. 204; Lasch, *Women and the Common Life*, p. 94; Ruth Schwartz Cowan, *More Work for Mother: The Ironies of Household Technology from the Open Hearth to the Microwave* (New York: Basic Books, 1983), p. 216; Lerner, cited in Skolnick, *Embattled Paradise*, p. 115.

18. See, for example, Barbara Ehrenreich, *The Hearts of Men* (New York: Doubleday, 1983), on the "male revolt" from breadwinner status. Also see Kimmel, *Manhood in America*, especially chapter 7.

19. See Skolnick, *Embattled Paradise*, p. 148.

20. U.S. Census Bureau, *Current Population Survey, 2015 Annual Social and Economic Supplement*, https://www.census.gov/hhes/www/poverty/about/overview/.

21. Anna Quindlen, "Men at Work" in *New York Times*, February 18, 1990.

22. Coontz, *Way We Really Are*, p. 79; Arlene Skolnick, *The Intimate Environment* (New York: HarperCollins, 1996), p. 342; Judith Bruce, Cynthia B. Lloyd, and Ann Leonard, *Families in Focus: New Perspectives on Mothers, Fathers, and Children* (New York: Population Council, 1995); Dirk Johnson, "More and More, the Single Parent Is Dad" in *New York Times*, August 31, 1993, p. 1. See also U.S. Bureau of the Census, *2007 Current Population Survey* (Washington, DC: U.S. Department of Commerce, Bureau of Census, 2007).

23. "Opposite Sex Unmarried Couples by Presence of Biological Children Under 18," in *American Families and Living Arrangements* (Washington, DC: U.S. Census Bureau, 2014).

24. Arlie Hochschild (with Anne Machung), *The Second Shift: Working Parents and the Revolution at Home* (New York: Viking, 1989), p. 258.

25. J. K. Footlick, "What Happened to the Family?" in "The 21st Century Family," special edition, *Newsweek*, Winter–Spring 1990, p. 14.

26. Scott Coltrane, *Family Man: Fatherhood, Housework and Gender Equity* (New York: Oxford University Press, 1996), p. 203; Lillian Rubin, *Worlds of Pain* (New York: Basic Books, 1976), p. 131; Cherlin, "By the Numbers," p. 39; Coltrane, *Family Man*, p. 203.

27. Jessie Bernard, *The Future of Marriage* (New York: World, 1972); Walter R. Gove, "The Relationship Between Sex Roles, Marital Status and Mental Illness" in *Social Forces*, 51, 1972; Walter Gove and M. Hughes, "Possible Causes of the Apparent Sex Differences in Physical Health: An Empirical Investigation" in *American Sociological Review*, 44, 1979; Walter Gove and Jeanette Tudor, "Adult Sex Roles and Mental Illness" in *American Journal of Sociology*, 73, 1973; "The Decline of Marriage" in *Scientific American*, December 1999.

28. Natalie Angier, *New York Times*, 1998, p. 10.

29. See Linda J. Waite and Maggie Gallagher, *The Case for Marriage: Why Married People Are Happier, Healthier and Better Off Financially* (New York: Doubleday, 2000). See also, for example, Hynubae Chun and Injae Lee, "Why Do Married Men Earn More: Productivity or Marriage Selection?" in *Economic Inquiry*, 39(2), April 2001, pp. 307–319; and Leslie Stratton, "Examining the Wage Differential for Married and Cohabiting Men" in *Economic Inquiry*, 40(2), April 2002, pp. 199–212. See also Paula England's review of *The Case for Marriage* in *Contemporary Sociology*, 30(6), 2001.

30. Bebin and statistics cited in Elaine Carey, "Kids Put a Damper on Marital Bliss: Study" in *Toronto Star*, August 15, 1997, pp. A1, A14.

31. Arlie Hochschild, *Second Shift*; Paul Amato and Alan Booth, "Changes in Gender Role Attitudes and Perceived Marital Quality" in *American Sociological Review*, 60, 1995.

32. For example, see "Stress: Relevations sur un mal français" in *le Figaro*, April 15, 2006, p. 46.

33. Pat Mainardi, "The Politics of Housework" in *Sisterhood Is Powerful*, R. Morgan, ed. (New York: Vintage, 1970).

34. Ballard and Foote are cited in Schwartz Cowan, *More Work for Mother*, p. 43; Campbell is cited in Susan Strasser, *Never Done: A History of American Housework* (New York: Pantheon, 1982), p. 62.

35. Johnson, "More and More, the Single Parent Is Dad," p. A15.

36. Kim Parker and Wendy Wang, "Modern Parenthood: Roles of Moms and Dads Converge as They Balance Work and Family," Pew Research Center, March 14, 2013, www.pewsocialtrends.org/2013/03/11/modern-parenthood-roles-of-moms-and-dads-converge-as-they-balance-work-and-family/; "Parental Time Use," Pew Research Center, http://www.pewresearch.org/data-trend/society-and-demographics/parental-time-use/.

37. Arlie Hochschild, "Ideals of Care: Traditional, Postmodern, Cold-Modern and Warm-Modern" in *Social Politics*, Fall 1995, p. 318.

38. Anna Quindlen, cited in Deborah Rhode, *Speaking of Sex* (Cambridge: Harvard University Press, 1997), p. 8.

39. Phyllis Moen and Patricia Roehling, *Career Mystique: Cracks in the American Dream* (Lanham, MD: Rowman and Littlefield, 2004).

40. On men's involvement in family work, see Joseph Pleck, "Men's Family Work: Three Perspectives and Some New Data" in *Family Coordinator*, 28, 1979; "American Fathering in Historical Perspective" in *Changing Men: New Directions in Research on Men and Masculinity*, M. S. Kimmel, ed. (Beverly Hills, CA: Sage Publications, 1987); *Working Wives/Working Husbands* (Newbury Park, CA: Sage Publications, 1985); "Families and Work: Small Changes with Big Implications" in *Qualitative Sociology*, 15, 1992; "Father Involvement: Levels, Origins and Consequences" in *The Father's Role*, 3rd ed., M. Lamb, ed. (New York: John Wiley, 1997).

41. Julie Press and Eleanor Townsley, "Wives' and Husbands' Housework Reporting: Gender, Class and Social Desirability" in *Gender & Society*, 12(2), 1998, p. 214. See also Yun-Suk Lee and Linda J. Waite, "Husbands' and Wives' Time Spent on Housework: A Comparison of Measures" in *Journal of Marriage and the Family*, 67, May 2005, pp. 328–336.

42. Lisa Belkin, "When Mom and Dad Share It All" in *New York Times Magazine*, June 15, 2008, p. 47.

43. Hiromi Ono, "Husbands' and Wives' Resources and Marital Dissolution in the United States," *Journal of Marriage and the Family*, 60, 1998, pp. 674–689; see also Dirk Johnson, "Until Dust Do Us Part" in *Newsweek*, March 25, 2002, p. 41; see also Sanjiv Gupta, "The Effects of Transitions in Marital Status on Men's Performance of Housework" in *Journal of Marriage and the Family*, August 1999.

44. *Ladies Home Journal*, September 1997; John Gray, "Domesticity, Diapers and Dad" in *Toronto Globe and Mail*, June 15, 1996.

45. http://www.time.com/time/magazine/article/0,9171,2084582,00.html.

46. Ibid.

47. Amelia Hill, "Fathers Are Happier When Doing More Housework, Study Says" in *Guardian*, November 4, 2010.

48. Carol Shows and Naomi Gerstel, "Fathering, Class and Gender: A Comparison of Physicians and EMTs" in *Gender & Society* 23(2), 2009, pp. 161–187.

49. See Bart Landry, *Black Working Wives: Pioneers of the American Family Revolution* (Berkeley: University of California Press, 2001); Margaret

Usdansky, "White Men Don't Jump into Chores" in *USA Today*, August 20, 1994; Julia Lawlor, "Blue Collar Dads Leading Trend in Caring for Kids, Author Says" in *New York Times*, April 15, 1998.

50. Cited in Coltrane, *Family Man*, p. 162: see also Scott Coltrane and Michele Adams, "Men's Family Work: Child Centered Fathering and the Sharing of Domestic Labor" in *Working Families: The Transformation of the American Home*, Rosanna Hertz and Nancy Marshall, eds. (Berkeley: University of California Press, 2001).

51. Mick Cunningham, "Parental Influences on the Gendered Division of Housework" in *American Sociological Review*, 66, April 2001, pp. 184–203; see also Janet Simons, "Life with Father" in *Rocky Mountain News*, August 20, 2001.

52. Barbara Vobejda, "Children Help Less at Home, Dads Do More" in *Washington Post*, November 24, 1991, p. A1.

53. Jerry Adler, "Building a Better Dad" in *Newsweek*, June 17, 1996; Tamar Lewin, "Workers of Both Sexes Make Trade-Offs for Family, Study Shows" in *New York Times*, October 29, 1995, p. 25.

54. United Nations, *The World's Women, 1970–1990: Trends and Statistics* (New York: United Nations, 1991).

55. Mette Deding, "Born Familieidyl begynder med Ligestilling" ("Children: The Idyllic Family Begins with Gender Equality") in *Politiken*, April 28, 2007, p. 4.

56. Lewin, "Workers of Both Sexes Make Trade-Offs," p. 25.

57. "Sex, Death, and Football" in *The Economist*, June 13, 1998, p. 18; Robert D. Mintz and James Mahalik, "Gender Role Orientation and Conflict as Predictors of Family Roles for Men" in *Sex Roles*, 34(1–2), 1996, pp. 805–821; Barbara Risman, "Can Men 'Mother'? Life as a Single Father" in *Family Relations*, 35, 1986; see also Caryl Rivers and Rosalind Barnett, "Fathers Do Best" in *Washington Post*, June 20, 1993, p. C5.

58. Alyssa Croft, Toni Schmader, Katharina Block, and Andrew Scott Baron, "The Second Shift Reflected in the Second Generation: Do Parents' Gender Roles at Home Predict Children's Aspiration" in *Psychological Science 25, 7* (2014): 1418–1428 See also Ian Johnston, "Dad, Do the Dishes for the Sake of your Daughter" in *Independent*, May 30, 2014.

59. Andrew Cherlin, "By the Numbers" in *New York Times Magazine*, April 5, 1998, p. 41.

60. Ibid.; Donald Hernandez, "Children's Changing Access to Resources: A Historical Perspective" in *Social Policy Report*, 8(1), Spring 1994, p. 22.

61. Johnson, "Until Dust Do Us Part."

62. Jane R. Eisner, "Leaving the Office for Family Life" in *Des Moines Register*, March 27, 1998, p. 7A.

63. Jay Belsky, "A Reassessment of Infant Day Care," and Thomas Gamble and Edward Zigler, "Effects of Infant Day Care: Another Look at the Evidence," both in *The Parental Leave Crisis: Toward a National Policy*, E. Zigler and M. Frank, eds. (New Haven, CT: Yale University Press, 1988); see also Susan Chira, "Study Says Babies in Child Care Keep Secure Bonds to Mother" in *New York Times*, April 21, 1996. For a handy summary of these data, see "Child Care in the United States, 1972 vs. 1999," a flyer from the National Council of Jewish Women at www.ncjw.org.

64. Susan Chira, "Can You Work and Have Good Happy Kids?" in *Glamour*, April 1998.

65. Cherlin, "By the Numbers."

66. See S. M. Bianchi and Daphne Spain, *American Women in Transition* (New York: Russell Sage Foundation, 1986); E. G. Menaghan and Toby Parcel, "Parental Employment and Family Life: Research in the 1980s" in *Journal of Marriage and the Family*, 52, 1990; Glenna Spitze, "Women's Employment and Family Relations: A Review" in *Journal of Marriage and the Family*, 50, 1988.

67. Philip Blumstein and Pepper Schwartz, *American Couples* (New York: William Morrow, 1983), p. 155; Chira, "Can You Work," p. 269.

68. Joan K. Peters, *When Mothers Work: Loving Our Children Without Sacrificing Our Selves* (Reading, MA: Addison-Wesley, 1997).

69. Popenoe, *Life Without Father*, p. 63; National Center for Health Statistics, "Births, Marriages, Divorces and Deaths for January, 1995" in *Monthly Vital Statistics Report*, 44(1) (Hyattsville, MD: Public Health Service).

70. Popenoe, *Life Without Father*, pp. 6, 34; see also Tamar Lewin, "Is Social Stability Subverted if You Answer 'I Don't'?" in *New York Times*, November 4, 2000, pp. B11, 13; U.S. National Center for Health Statistics, National Vital Statistics Reports (NVSR), *Births: Final Data for 2005*, 56, December 5, 2007; see also Emily Bazelon, "2 Kids + 0 Husbands = Family" in *New York Time Magazine*, February 1, 2009, p. 32.

71. Pittman, cited in Olga Silverstein, "Is a Bad Dad Better Than No Dad?" in *On the Issues*, Winter 1997, p. 15; David Blankenhorn, *Fatherless America: Confronting Our Most Urgent Social Problem* (New York: Basic Books, 1993), p. 30; Robert Bly, *Iron John* (Reading, MA: Addison-Wesley, 1990), p. 96; Popenoe, *Life Without Father*, p. 12. See also Stephen Marche, "Manifesto

of the New Fatherhood" in *Esquire,* June/July 2014, pp. 118–121.

72. Carey Goldberg, "Single Dads Wage Revolution One Bedtime Story at a Time" in *New York Times,* June 17, 2001, pp. A1, 16.

73. Cherlin, "By the Numbers"; Kristin Luker, "Dubious Conceptions: The Controversy over Teen Pregnancy" in *American Prospect,* 5, 1991; Paul Amato and Alan Booth, *A Generation at Risk: Growing Up in an Era of Family Upheaval* (Cambridge: Harvard University Press, 1997), p. 229; P. Amato and J. Gilbreth, "Nonresident Fathers and Children's Well-Being: A Meta-Analysis" in *Journal of Marriage and the Family,* 61, 1999, pp. 557–573.

74. Martin Sanchez-Jankowski, *Islands in the Street: Gangs and American Urban Society* (Berkeley: University of California Press, 1991), p. 39.

75. Blaine Harden, "Finding Common Ground on Poor Deadbeat Dads" in *New York Times,* February 3, 2002, p. 3.

76. David Popenoe, "Evolution of Marriage and Stepfamily Problems" in *Stepfamilies: Who Benefits? Who Does Not?,* A. Booth and J. Dunn, eds. (Hillsdale, NJ: Lawrence Erlbaum, 1994), p. 528.

77. Blankenhorn, *Fatherless America,* p. 96.

78. Ibid., p. 102.

79. http://www.supremecourt.gov/opinions/14pdf/ 14-556_3204.pdf

80. Michael J. Kanotz, "For Better or for Worse: A Critical Analysis of Florida's Defense of Marriage Act" in *Florida State University Law Review,* 25(2), 1998.

81. Gilbert Zicklin, "Deconstructing Legal Rationality: The Case of Lesbian and Gay Family Relationships" in *Marriage and Family Review,* 21(3/4), 1995, p. 55.

82. Cited in *New York Times,* September 27, 1991.

83. Laura Benkov, *Reinventing the Family: Lesbian and Gay Parents* (New York: Crown, 1994); Skolnick, *Intimate Environment,* pp. 293–294; Blumstein and Schwartz, *American Couples*; Lawrence Kurdek, "The Allocation of Household Labor in Gay, Lesbian and Heterosexual Married Couples" in *Families in the United States: Kinship and Domestic Politics,* K. Hansen and A. Ilta Garey, eds. (Philadelphia: Temple University Press, 1998). See also Abbie Goldberg, Juli Anna Smith, and Maureen Perry Jenkins, "The Division of Labor in Lesbian, Gay and Heterosexual New Adoptive Parents" in *Journal of Marriage and the Family,* August 2012.

84. John Gagnon and William Simon, *Sexual Conduct* (Chicago: Aldine, 1973), p. 213.

85. J. Schulenberg, *Gay Parenting* (New York: Doubleday, 1985); F. W. Bozett, ed., *Gay and Lesbian Parents* (New York: Praeger, 1987); Katherine Allen and David H. Demo, "The Families of Lesbians and Gay Men: A New Frontier in Family Research" in *Journal of Marriage and the Family,* 57, 1995; Ann Sullivan, ed., *Issues in Gay and Lesbian Adoption: Proceedings of the Fourth Annual Peirce-Warwick Adoption Symposium* (Washington, DC: Child Welfare League of America, 1995), p. 5; John J. Goldman, "N.J. Gays Win Adoption Rights" in *Los Angeles Times,* December 18, 1997.

86. Nanette Gartrell and Henny Bos, "US National Longitudinal Lesbian Family Study: Psychological Adjustment of 17-Year-Old Adolescents" in *Pediatrics,* 126(1), June 2010; and Nanette Gartrell, Henny Bos, and Naomi Goldberg, "Adolescents of the U.S. National Longitudinal Lesbian Family Study: Sexual Orientation, Sexual Behavior, and Sexual Risk Exposure" in *Archives of Sexual Behavior,* November 2010.

87. Michael Lamb, "Mothers, Fathers, Families and Circumstances: Factors Affecting Children's Adjustment" in *Applied Developmental Science,* 16(2), 2012, pp. 98–111.

88. Judith Stacey, "Gay and Lesbian Families: Queer Like Us" in *All Our Families: New Policies for a New Century,* M. Mason, A. Skolnick, and S. Sugarman, eds. (New York: Oxford University Press, 1998), p. 135. See also Michael Rosenfeld, "Nontraditional Families and Childhood Program Through School," in *Demography,* August 2010, pp. 755–775.

89. Judith Stacey and Timothy J. Biblarz, "(How) Does the Sexual Orientation of Parents Matter?" in *American Sociological Review,* 66, April 2001, pp. 159–183; see also Michael Bronski, "Queer as Your Folks" in *Boston Phoenix,* August 3, 2001; and Erica Goode, "A Rainbow of Differences in Gays' Children" in *New York Times,* July 17, 2001.

90. United Nations, *Demographic Yearbook,* Department for Economic and Social Information and Policy Analysis, Statistical Division, November 1996; United States Bureau of the Census, *Current Population Report: Marital Status and Living Arrangements, March, 1996* (Washington, DC: United States Government Printing Office, 1997); "Divorce, American Style" in *Scientific American,* March 1999.

91. Lawrence Stone, "A Short History of Love" in *Harper's Magazine,* February 1988, p. 32.

92. Constance Ahrons, *The Good Divorce* (New York: HarperCollins, 1994).

93. Demie Kurz, *For Richer, For Poorer: Mothers Confront Divorce* (New York: Routledge, 1995);

Leonore Weitzman, *The Divorce Revolution: The Unexpected Social and Economic Consequences for Women and Children in America* (New York: Free Press, 1985); Patricia A. McManus and Thomas A. DiPrete, "Losers and Winners: The Financial Consequences of Separation and Divorce for Men" in *American Sociological Review*, 66, April 2001, pp. 246–268; Paul Amato, "The Impact of Divorce on Men and Women in India and the United States" in *Journal of Comparative Family Studies*, 25(2), 1994.

94. Popenoe, *Life Without Father*, p. 27; Frank Furstenberg and Andrew Cherlin, *Divided Families: What Happens to Children When Parents Part?* (Cambridge: Harvard University Press, 1991); Debra Umberson and Christine Williams, "Divorced Fathers: Parental Role Strain and Psychological Distress" in *Journal of Family Issues*, 14(3), 1993.

95. Valerie King, "Nonresident Father Involvement and Child Well-Being" in *Journal of Family Issues*, 15(1), 1994; Edward Kruk, "The Disengaged Noncustodial Father: Implications for Social Work Practice with the Divorced Family" in *Social Work*, 39(1), 1994.

96. Judith Wallerstein and J. Kelly, *Surviving the Breakup: How Children and Parents Cope with Divorce* (New York: Basic Books, 1980); Judith Wallerstein and Susan Blakeslee. *Second Chances: Men, Women, and Children a Decade After Divorce* (New York: Ticknor and Fields, 1989), p. 11; Judith Wallerstein, Julia Lewis, and Sandra Blakeslee, *The Unexpected Legacy of Divorce: A 25 Year Landmark Study* (New York: Hyperion, 2000).

97. For criticism of Wallerstein's study, see, for example, Andrew Cherlin, "Generation Ex-" in *Nation*, December 11, 2000; Katha Pollitt, "Social Pseudoscience" in *Nation*, October 23, 2000, p. 10 (and subsequent exchange, December 4, 2000); Thomas Davey, "Considering Divorce" in *American Prospect*, January 1–15, 2001; Walter Kirn, "Should You Stay Together for the Kids?" in *Time*, September 25, 2000; and Elisabeth Lasch-Quinn, "Loving and Leaving" in *New Republic*, May 6, 2002.

98. Andrew Cherlin, "Going to Extremes: Family Structure, Children's Well-Being and Social Science" in *Demography*, 36(4), November 1999, p. 425.

99. See E. Mavis Heatherington and John Kelly, *For Better or for Worse: Divorce Reconsidered* (New York: W. W. Norton, 2002); Leonard Beeghley, *What Does Your Wife Do? Gender and the Transformation of Family Life* (Boulder, CO: Westview Press, 1996), p. 96; Donna Ruane Morrison and Andrew Cherlin, "The Divorce Process and Young Children's Well-Being: A Prospective Analysis" in *Journal of Marriage and the Family*, 57(3), 1995; Amato, "Impact of Divorce."

100. Joan B. Kelly, "Mediated and Adversarial Divorce: Respondents' Perceptions of Their Processes and Outcomes" in *Mediation Quarterly*, 24, Summer 1989, p. 125.

101. J. Block, J. Block, and P. F. Gjerde, "The Personality of Children Prior to Divorce: A Prospective Study" in *Child Development*, 57, 1986; Skolnick, *Embattled Paradise*, p. 212; for British study, see Jane Brody, "Problems of Children: A New Look at Divorce" in *New York Times*, June 7, 1991.

102. Amato and Booth, *Generation at Risk*, pp. 201, 230, 234; Paul Amato and Alan Booth, "The Legacy of Parents' Marital Discord: Consequences for Children's Marital Quality" in *Journal of Personality and Social Psychology*, 81(4), 2001, pp. 627–638; see also Amato, "Impact of Divorce"; "The Implications of Research Findings on Children in Stepfamilies" in *Stepfamilies: Who Benefits? Who Does Not?*, A. Booth and J. Dunn, eds. (Hillsdale, NJ: Lawrence Erlbaum, 1994); "Single-Parent Households as Settings for Children's Development, Well-Being and Attainment: A Social Networks/Resources Perspective" in *Sociological Studies of Children*, 7, 1995; Paul Amato and Alan Booth, "Changes in Gender Role Attitudes and Perceived Marital Quality" in *American Sociological Review*, 60, 1995; Paul Amato, Laura Spencer Loomis, and Alan Booth, "Parental Divorce, Marital Conflict, and Offspring Well-Being During Early Adulthood" in *Social Forces*, 73(3), 1995. "Low conflict," by the way, is unhappy but not physically violent.

103. B. Berg and R. Kelly, "The Measured Self-Esteem of Children from Broken, Rejected and Accepted Families" in *Journal of Divorce*, 2, 1979; R. E. Emery, "Interparental Conflict and Children of Discord and Divorce" in *Psychological Bulletin*, 92, 1982; H. J. Raschke and V. J. Raschke, "Family Conflict and the Children's Self-Concepts" in *Journal of Marriage and the Family*, 41, 1979; J. M. Gottman and L. F. Katz, "Effects of Marital Discord on Young Children's Peer Interaction and Health" in *Developmental Psychology*, 25, 1989; D. Mechanic and S. Hansell, "Divorce, Family Conflict and Adolescents' Well-Being" in *Journal of Health and Social Behavior*, 30, 1989; Paul Amato and Juliana Sobolewski, "The Effects of Divorce and Marital Discord on Adult Children's Psychological Well-Being" in *American Sociological Review*, 66, December 2001, pp. 900–921.

104. Block, Block, and Gjerde, "The Personality of Children"; president of council cited in Coontz, *Way We Really Are*, p. 108.

105. Coontz, *Way We Really Are*, p. 83.
106. Amato and Booth, *Generation at Risk*, p. 207; see also Susan Jekielek, "The Relative and Interactive Impacts of Parental Conflict and Marital Disruption on Children's Emotional Well-Being," paper presented at the annual meeting of the American Sociological Association, New York, 1996; Carl Degler, *At Odds: Women and the Family in America from the Revolution to the Present* (New York: Oxford University Press, 1980); Terry Arendell, "Divorce American Style" in *Contemporary Sociology*, 27(3), 1998, p. 226. See also Terry Arendall, *Mothers and Divorce: Legal, Economic and Social Dilemmas* (Berkeley: University of California Press, 1986); "After Divorce: Investigations into Father Absence" in *Gender & Society*, December 1992; *Fathers and Divorce* (Newbury Park, CA: Sage Publications, 1995).
107. Griswold, *Fatherhood in America*, p. 263; Nancy Polikoff, "Gender and Child Custody Determinations: Exploding the Myths" in *Families, Politics and Public Policy: A Feminist Dialogue on Women and the State*, I. Diamond, ed. (New York: Longman, 1983), pp. 184–185; Robert H. Mnookin, Eleanor Maccoby, Catherine Albiston, and Charlene Depner, "Private Ordering Revisited: What Custodial Arrangements Are Parents Negotiating?" in *Divorce Reform at the Crossroads*, S. Sugarman and H. Kaye, eds. (New Haven, CT: Yale University Press, 1990), especially p. 55; Eleanor Maccoby and Robert Mnookin, *Dividing the Child: Social and Legal Dilemmas of Custody* (Cambridge: Harvard University Press, 1992), especially p. 101.
108. Maccoby, quoted in Johnson, "More and More, the Single Parent Is Dad," p. A15; Furstenberg and Cherlin, *Divided Families*; Frank Furstenberg, "Good Dads–Bad Dads: Two Faces of Fatherhood" in *The Changing American Family and Public Policy*, A. Cherlin, ed. (Lanham, MD: Urban Institute Press, 1988); William J. Goode, "Why Men Resist" in *Rethinking the Family: Some Feminist Questions*, B. Thorne and M. Yalom, eds. (New York: Longman, 1982).
109. Amato and Booth, *Generation at Risk*, p. 74.
110. See, for example, Joan Kelly, "Longer-Term Adjustments of Children of Divorce" in *Journal of Family Psychology*, 2(2), 1988, p. 131; D. Leupnitz, *Child Custody: A Study of Families After Divorce* (Lexington, KY: Lexington Books, 1982); D. Leupnitz, "A Comparison of Maternal, Paternal and Joint Custody: Understanding the Varieties of Post-Divorce Family Life" in *Journal of Divorce*, 9, 1986; V. Shiller, "Loyalty Conflicts and Family Relationships in Latency Age Boys: A Comparison of Joint and Maternal Custody" in *Journal of Divorce*, 9, 1986.
111. Kelly, "Longer-Term Adjustments," p. 136; Crowell and Leeper, *America's Fathers and Public Policy*, p. 27.
112. For more about the U.S. fatherhood movement, see Anna Gavanas, *Fatherhood Politics in the United States* (Urbana: University of Illinois Press, 2004).
113. Cited in Richard Gelles, *The Violent Home* (Beverly Hills, CA: Sage Publications, 1972), p. 14.
114. Elizabeth Thompson Gershoff, "Corporal Punishment by Parents and Associated Child Behaviors and Experiences: A Meta-Analytic and Theoretical Review" in *Psychological Bulletin*, 128(4), 2002, pp. 539–579. Gershoff's critics suggest that the negative effects are the result of "inept harsh parenting" and not specifically spanking. See Diana Baumrind, Robert Larzelere, and Philip A. Cowan, "Ordinary Physical Punishment: Is It Harmful?" in *Psychological Bulletin*, 128(4), 2002, pp. 580–589.
115. Abraham Bergman, Roseanne Larsen, and Beth Mueller, "Changing Spectrum of Child Abuse" in *Pediatrics*, 77, 1986.
116. Murray Straus, Richard Gelles, and Suzanne Steinmetz, *Behind Closed Doors: Violence in the American Family* (New York: Anchor, 1981), p. 94; see also Murray Straus, *Beating the Devil Out of Them* (New York: Jossey-Bass, 1994).
117. Richard Gelles, *Family Violence* (Newbury Park, CA: Sage Publications, 1987), p. 165.
118. Skolnick, *Intimate Environment*, p. 426.
119. *Harvard Men's Health Watch*, 2(11), June 1998.
120. David H. Demo, "Parent-Child Relations: Assessing Recent Changes" in *Journal of Marriage and the Family*, 54(1), 1990, p. 224.
121. Hochschild, *Second Shift*, p. 269.
122. Cited in Quindlen, "Men at Work."
123. Frank Furstenberg, "Can Marriage Be Saved?" in *Dissent*, Summer 2005, p. 80.
124. Andrew Greeley, "The Necessity of Feminism" in *Society* 30(6), September 1993, pp. 13–14.
125. Lasch, *Women and the Common Life*, p. 119.
126. Coltrane, *Family Man*, pp. 223–225.

CHAPTER SEVEN

1. In M. G. Lord, *Forever Barbie: The Unauthorized Biography of a Real Doll* (New York: William Morrow, 1994).
2. Deborah Rhode, *Speaking of Sex* (Cambridge: Harvard University Press, 1997), p. 56.

3. Edward C. Clarke, *Sex in Education; or, A Fair Chance for the Girls* (Boston: Osgood, 1873), pp. 128, 137.

4. W. W. Ferrier, *Origin and Development of the University of California* (Berkeley: University of California Press, 1930); see also Myra Sadker and David Sadker, *Failing at Fairness: How Schools Shortchange Girls* (New York: Simon & Schuster, 1994), p. 22.

5. Henry Fowle Durant, "The Spirit of the College" [1977], reprinted in Michael S. Kimmel and Thomas Mosmiller, *Against the Tide: Pro-Feminist Men in the United States, 1776–1990, a Documentary History* (Boston: Beacon Press, 1992), p. 132.

6. Henry Maudsley, "Sex in Mind and in Education" [1874] in *Desire and Imagination: Classic Essays in Sexuality*, R. Barreca, ed. (New York: Meridian, 1995), pp. 208–209.

7. Sadker and Sadker, *Failing at Fairness*, p. 14. These stereotypes can break down when complicated by other, racially based stereotypes; for example, Asian American girls are expected to like math and science more than are white girls.

8. David Karp and William C. Yoels, "The College Classroom: Some Observations on the Meanings of Student Participation" in *Sociology and Social Research*, 60(4), 1976; American Association of University Women, *How Schools Shortchange Girls: A Study of Major Findings on Girls and Education* (Washington, DC: American Association of University Women, 1992), p 68; Sadker and Sadker, *Failing at Fairness*, p. 5.

9. Sadker and Sadker, *Failing at Fairness*, pp. 42–43.

10. Peggy Orenstein, *Schoolgirls* (New York: Doubleday, 1994), pp. 11, 12.

11. Jenny Soffel, "Gender Bias Fought at Egalia Preschool in Stockholm, Sweden" in *Huffington Post*, June 26, 2011, www.huffintonpost.com/2011/06/26/gender-bias-egalia-preschool_n_884866.html.

12. American Association of University Women, *Hostile Hallways: The AAUW Survey on Sexual Harassment in America's Schools* (Washington, DC: American Association of University Women, 1993); Sandler, cited in Sadker and Sadker, *Failing at Fairness*, p. 111.

13. See, for example, William Pollack, *Real Boys: Rescuing Our Sons from the Myths of Boyhood* (New York: Random House, 1998).

14. Christine Hoff Sommers, *The War Against Boys* (New York: Scribner's, 1999); Sommers, cited in Debra Viadero, "Behind the 'Mask of Masculinity'" in *Education Week*, May 13, 1998; Thompson, cited in Margaret Combs, "What About the Boys?" in *Boston Globe*, June 26, 1998. For more of this backlash argument, see Michael Gurian, *The Wonder of Boys* (New York: Jeremy Tarcher/Putnam, 1997); and Judith Kleinfeld, "Student Performance: Male Versus Female" in *Public Interest*, Winter 1999. For dissenting opinions, see my review of Gurian, "Boys to Men . . .," in *San Francisco Chronicle*, January 12, 1997; Martin Mills, "What About the Boys?" and R. W. Connell, "Teaching the Boys" in *Teachers College Record*.

15. Carol Gilligan, *In a Different Voice*; Lyn Mikel Brown and Carol Gilligan, *Meeting at the Crossroads* (New York: Ballantine, 1992).

16. Pollack, cited in Viadero, "Behind the Mask."; see also Pollack, *Real Boys*.

17. Shelley Correll, "Gender and the Career Choice Process: The Role of Biased Self-Assessments" in *American Journal of Sociology*, 106(6), pp. 1691–1730.

18. Ibid.

19. Wayne Martino, "Masculinity and Learning: Exploring Boys' Underachievement and Under-representation in Subject English" in *Interpretation*, 27(2), 1994; "Boys and Literacy: Exploring the Construction of Hegemonic Masculinities and the Formation of Literate Capacities for Boys in the English Classroom" in *English in Australia*, 112, 1995; "Gendered Learning Experiences: Exploring the Costs of Hegemonic Masculinity for Girls and Boys in Schools" in *Gender Equity: A Framework for Australian Schools* (Canberra: Publications and Public Communications, Department of Urban Services, ACT Government, 1997). Catharine Stimpson, quoted in Tamar Lewin, "American Colleges Begin to Ask, Where Have All the Men Gone?" in *New York Times*, December 6, 1998.

20. Wayne Martino, "Gendered Learning Experiences," pp. 133, 134.

21. Martain Mac an Ghaill, *The Making of Men: Masculinities, Sexualities and Schooling* (Buckingham, UK: Open University Press, 1994), p. 59; David Gillborne, *Race, Ethnicity and Education* (London: Unwin Hyman, 1990), p. 63; James Coleman, *The Adolescent Society* (New York: Harper and Row, 1961). "Report: Girls Are Smarter Than Boys" in *Stockton Record*, September 20, 2003. Thanks to Lisa Jones for her help in tracking down this article.

22. Sui-fong Lam, et al., "Do Girls and Boys Perceive Themselves as Equally Engaged in School?

The Results of an International Study from 12 Countries" in *Journal of School Psychology*.

23. Cited in David Macleod, *Building Character in the American Boy* (Madison: University of Wisconsin Press, 1983), p. 49.

24. William McFee, letter to the editor, *Nation*, July 20, 1927, p. 2.

25. Brendan Koerner, "Where the Boys Aren't" in *U.S. News & World Report*, February 8, 1999; Lewin, "American Colleges Begin to Ask"; Michael Fletcher, "Degrees of Separation" in *Washington Post*, June 25, 2002; Jamilah Evelyn, "Community Colleges Start to Ask, Where Are the Men?" in *Chronicle of Higher Education*, June 28, 2002; Ridger Doyle, "Men, Women and College" in *Scientific American*, October 1999.

26. Joel Best, *Stat-Spotting* (Berkeley: University of California Press, 2008), p. 95.

27. Cited in Tamar Lewin, "At Colleges, Women Are Leaving Men in the Dust" in *New York Times*, July 9, 2006.

28. Mary Beth Marklein, "College Gender Gap Widens: 57% Are Women" in *USA Today*, October 19, 2005, available at http://www.usatodavy.com/news/education/2005-10-19-male-college-cover_x.htm.

29. http://nces.ed.gov/programs/crimeindicators/crimeindicators2010/figures/figure_07_1.asp.

30. "Boys will be boys" are, not so incidentally, the last four words of Hoff Sommers's antifeminist creed.

31. Cited in Michael S. Kimmel, "The Struggle for Gender Equality: How Men Respond" in *Thought and Action: The NEA Higher Education Journal*, 8(2), 1993.

32. Richard Kim, "Eminem—Bad Rap?" in *Nation*, March 13, 2001, p. 4. In his film *8 Mile*, and in subsequent albums, Eminem goes out of his way to repudiate his earlier homophobia.

33. T. R. Nansel, M. Overpeck, R. S. Pilla, W. J. Ruan, B. Simons-Moore, and P. Scheidt, "Bullying Behaviors Among U.S. Youth: Prevalence and Association with Psychosocial Adjustment" in *Journal of the American Medical Association*, 285(16), 2001, pp. 2094–2100; S. P. Limber, P. Cunningham, V. Florx, J. Ivey, M. Nation, S. Chai, and G. Melton, "Bullying Among School Children: Preliminary Findings from a School-Based Intervention Program," paper presented at the Fifth International Family Violence Research Conference, Durham, NH, June 1997; Juvonen Jaana, Sandra Graham, and Mark Schuster, "Bullying Among Young Adolescents: The Strong,

the Weak and the Troubled" in *Pediatrics*, 112(6), December 2003, pp. 1231–1237.

34. "Fear of Classmates" in *USA Today*, April 22, 1999, p. A1; "Half of Teens Have Heard of a Gun Threat at School" in *USA Today*, November 27, 2001, p. 6D.

35. This section draws on Michael Kimmel and Matthew Mahler, "Adolescent Masculinity, Homophobia, and Violence: Random School Shootings, 1982–2001" in *American Behavioral Scientist*, 46(10), June 2003.

36. Actually, somebody did. Tom DeLay, the Texas congressman, blamed day care, the teaching of evolution, and "working mothers who take birth control pills." Don't ask; I don't get it either! (See "The News of the Weak in Review" in *Nation*, November 15, 1999, p. 5.)

37. J. Adams and J. Malone, "Outsider's Destructive Behavior Spiraled into Violence" in *Louisville Courier Journal*, March 18, 1999; J. Blank, "The Kid No One Noticed" in *U.S. News & World Report*, December 16, 1998, p. 27.

38. N. Gibbs and T. Roche, "The Columbine Tapes" in *Time*, December 20, 1999, p. 40; D. Cullen, "The Rumor That Won't Go Away" in *Salon*, April 24, 1999, available at http://www.salon.com/news/feature/1999/04/24/rumors/index.html.

39. Eric Pooley, "Portrait of a Deadly Bond" in *Time*, May 10, 1999, pp. 26–27.

40. Catell, cited in William O'Neil, *Divorce in the Progressive Era* (New Haven, CT: Yale University Press, 1967), p. 81; Admiral F. E. Chadwick, "The Woman Peril" in *Educational Review*, February 1914, p. 47; last cited in Sadker and Sadker, *Failing at Fairness*, p. 214.

41. United States Department of Education, 1996.

42. National Science Foundation, "Characteristics of Doctoral Students," cited in Linda Schliebenger, *Has Feminism Changed Science?* (Cambridge: Harvard University Press, 1999), p. 34.

43. See Scott Jaschik, "Disparate Burden" in *Inside Higher Ed*, March 21, 2005, www.insidehighered.com/news/2005/03/21/care, accessed March 31, 2005.

44. Cornelius Riordan, "The Future of Single-Sex Schools" in *Separated by Sex: A Critical Look at Single-Sex Education for Girls* (Washington, DC: American Association of University Women Educational Foundation, 1998), p. 54.

45. Orenstein, *Schoolgirls*, p. 27.

46. Elizabeth Tidball, "Perspectives on Academic Women and Affirmative Action," *Educational Record*, 54(2), 1973.

47. Cynthia Fuchs Epstein, *Deceptive Distinctions* (New Haven: Yale University Press, 1991).

48. Faye Crosby et al., "Taking Selectivity into Account, How Much Does Gender Composition Matter? A Reanalysis of M. E. Tidball's Research" in *National Women's Studies Association Journal*, 6, 1994; see also Cynthia Fuchs Epstein, "The Myths and Justifications of Sex Segregation in Higher Education: VMI and the Citadel" in *Duke Journal of Gender Law and Policy*, 4, 1997; and Cynthia Fuchs Epstein, "Multiple Myths and Outcomes of Sex Segregation" in *New York Law School Journal of Human Rights*, 14, 1998.

49. Christopher Jencks and David Riesman, *The Academic Revolution* (New York: Doubleday, 1968), pp. 298, 300. Despite his own findings, see also David Riesman, "A Margin of Difference: The Case for Single-Sex Education" in *Social Roles and Social Institutions: Essays in Honor of Rose Laub Coser*, J. R. Blau and N. Goodman, eds. (Boulder, CO: Westview Press, 1991). Riesman supported the continuation of VMI's and the Citadel's single-sex policy.

50. Carol Tavris, *The Mismeasure of Woman* (New York: Simon & Schuster, 1992), p. 127; R. Priest, A. Vitters, and H. Prince, "Coeducation at West Point" in *Armed Forces and Society*, 4(4), 1978, p. 590.

51. Fuchs Epstein, "Multiple Myths and Outcomes," p. 191.

52. See Margaret Talbot, "Sexed Ed" in *New York Times Magazine*, September 22, 2002.

53. VMI I, 766 F. Supp., p. 1435; VMI V, 116 S. Ct. 2264, Brief for Petitioner; see also Valorie K. Vojdik, "Girls' Schools After VMI: Do They Make the Grade?" in *Duke Journal of Gender Law and Policy*, 4, 1997, p. 85; Fuchs Epstein, "Myths and Justifications," p. 108.

54. *Faulkner v. Jones*, 858 F. Supp. 552 1994; Citadel Defendants' Proposed Findings of Fact, p. 1434.

55. Josiah Bunting quote in Citadel case. Cited in Vojdik, "Girls' Schools After VMI," p. 76. (As someone who began his college career at an all-male college and later transferred to a co-educational one, I could readily testify that men at the single-sex school were far more distracted by the absence of women than were the men at the co-educational school by their presence! With no women around, most of the young men couldn't stop thinking about them!)

56. John Dewey, "Is Coeducation Injurious to Girls?" in *Ladies Home Journal*, June 11, 1911, p. 60.

57. Thomas Wentworth Higginson, "Sex and Education" in *Woman's Journal*, 1874, editorial, p. 1, reprinted in *History of Woman Suffrage*, S. B. Anthony and E. C. Stanton, eds. (New York: Ayer, 1974).

58. See www.singlesexschools.org.

59. Diane Halpern, Lise Eliot, Rebecca Bigler, Richard Fabes, Laura Hanish, Janet Hyde, Lynn Liben, Carol Lynn Martin, "The Pseudoscience of Single-Sex Schooling" in *Science*, 333, September 23, 2011, pp. 1706–1707.

60. Mike Bowler, "All-Male, All-Black, All Learning" in *Baltimore Sun*, October 15, 1995; Susan Estrich, "For Girls' Schools and Women's College, Separate Is Better" in *New York Times*, May 22, 1994.

61. See Kim Gandy, "Segregation Won't Help" in *USA Today*, May 10, 2002.

62. "Harlem Girls School vs. the Three Stooges" in *New York Observer*, March 30, 1998, p. 4.

63. Pamela Haag, "Single-Sex Education in Grades K–12: What Does the Research Tell Us?" in *Separated by Sex: A Critical Look at Single-Sex Education for Girls* (Washington, DC: American Association of University Women Educational Foundation, 1998), p. 34; Valerie Lee, "Is Single-Sex Secondary Schooling a Solution to the Problem of Gender Inequity?" in *Separated by Sex* p. 43; Riordan, "Future of Single-Sex Schools," p. 53; Connie Leslie, "Separate and Unequal?" in *Newsweek*, March 23, 1998, p. 55; Clark, cited in Charles Whitaker, "Do Black Males Need Special Schools?" in *Ebony*, March 1991, p. 18.

64. Amanda Datnow, Lea Hubbard, and Elisabeth Woody, *Is Single Gender Schooling Viable in the Public Sector? Lessons from California's Pilot Program* (Toronto: Ontario Institute for Studies in Education, 2001).

65. Sadker and Sadker, *Failing at Fairness*, pp. 125–126.

66. See Don Sabo, Kathleen Miller, Merrill Melnick, Michael Farrell, and Grace Barnes, "High School Athletic Participation and Adolescent Suicide: A Nationwide Study" in *International Review for the Sociology of Sport*, 40(1), 2005, pp. 5–23; Don Sabo, Kathleen Miller, Merrill Melnick, and Leslie Haywood, *Her Life Depends on It: Sport, Physical Activity and the Health and Well-Being of American Girls* (East Meadow, NY: Women's Sports Foundation, 2004); Don Sabo, Kathleen Miller, Merrill Melnick, Michael Farrell, and Grace Barnes, "High School Athletic Participation, Sexual Behavior and Adolescent Pregnancy: A Regional Study" in *Journal of Adolescent Health*, 25(3), 1999, pp. 207–216.

67. "The Attack on Women's Sports" in *New York Times*, February 17, 2003, p. A22.

68. See, for example, Christine Stolba, "We've Come the Wrong Way Baby" in *Women's Quarterly*,

Spring 2002. On the other side, see the "Title IX FAQ Packet," published by the Women's Equity Resource Center at www.edc.org/womensequity.

CHAPTER EIGHT

I thank the three anonymous reviewers engaged by the press; their comments improved this chapter enormously.

1. Front page, *New York Post*, June 17, 1991.
2. Ari Goldman, "Cardinal Said God Is a Man? Not Really" in *New York Times*, June 22, 1991.
3. See, for example, Louis Henry Morgan, *Ancient Society* (1877); Frederich Engels, *The Origin of the Family, Private Property and the State* (1902); and Lester Ward, *Pure Sociology* (1903).
4. I take this from Claire Renzetti and Robert Curran, *Women, Men and Society*, 5th ed. (Boston: Allyn and Bacon, 2003), p. 333.
5. See, for example, Karen McCarthy, *Mam Lola: A Voudou Priestess in Brooklyn* (Berkeley: University of California Press, 1991).
6. At least in theory. In practice, organizationally, Buddhism rehearses many of the inequalities its actual doctrines caution against. See, for example, Wendy Cadge, "Gendered Religious Organizations: The Case of Theravada Buddhism in America" in *Gender and Society*, 8(6), 2004.
7. Carol Christ, "Heretics and Outsiders: The Struggle Over Female Power in Western Religion" in *Feminist Frontiers*, Laurel Richardson and Verta Taylor, eds. (Reading, MA: Addison-Wesley, 1983), pp. 93–94.
8. Yvonne Y. Haddad, "Islam, Women and Revolution in Twentieth Century Arab Thought" in *Women, Religion and Social Change*, Y. Y. Haddad and E. B. Findley, eds. (Albany: SUNY Press, 1985).
9. Leonard Swidler, "Jesus Was a Feminist" [1973], available at http://www.gods wordtowomen.org/feminist.htm, accessed August 1, 2009.
10. Cited in Haddad, "Islam, Women and Revolution," p. 294.
11. Kristen Moulton, "Southern Baptists Say Women Should 'Submit Graciously' to Their Husbands," Associated Press, June 10, 1998, available at http://www.encyclopedia.com/doc/1PI-19752545.html, accessed August 1, 2009.
12. Christian Smith, *Christian America? What Evangelicals Really Want* (Berkeley: University of California Press, 2002).
13. Orthodox Judaism is only one of the three major branches of Judaism. Conservative and Reform Judaism are significantly less "orthodox" and more egalitarian.
14. John Todd, *Women's Rights* (Boston: Lee and Shepard, 1867), p. 25.
15. Samuel B. May, "The Rights and Condition of Women," reprinted in *Against the Tide: Pro-Feminist Men in the United States, 1776–1990*, Michael Kimmel and Thomas Mosmiller, eds. (Boston: Beacon, 1992), pp. 94–97.
16. Debra Kaufman, *Rachel's Daughters: Newly Orthodox Jewish Women* (New Brunswick, NJ: Rutgers University Press, 1991), p. 8.
17. Tova Hartman and Naomi Marmon, "Lived Regulations, Systemic Attributions: Menstrual Separation and Ritual Immersion in the Experience of Orthodox Jewish Women" in *Gender & Society*, 18, June 2004, pp. 389–408.
18. Jen'nan Ghazal Read and John Bartkowski, "To Veil or Not to Veil?" in *Gender & Society*, 14(3), 2000, pp. 395–417; Etsuko Maruoka, "Veiled Passion: Negotiation of Gender, Race and Religiosity Among Young Muslim American Women," PhD dissertation, Department of Sociology, SUNY Stony Brook, 2008.
19. Rosine J. Perelberg, "Quality, Asymmetry, and Diversity: On Conceptualization of Gender" in *Gender and Power in Families*, R. J. Perelberg and A. Miller, eds. (London: Routledge, 1990), p. 45.
20. Cited in Mary Daly, *Beyond God the Father* (Boston: Beacon, 1973), 44.
21. Butch Hancock, cited in *The Education of Shelby Knox: Sex Lies, and Education*, Marion Lipschutz and Rose Rosenblatt, dir. (New York: Women Make Movies, 2005).
22. Table available on p. 96 of http://religions.pewforum.org/pdf/report2-religious-landscape-study-full.pdf. See also "Muslim Americans: Middle Class and Mostly Mainstream," Pew Research Center, 2007.
23. The actual Jewish prayer is "I thank thee, O Lord, that thou has not created me a woman." Hindu Code also cited in Daly, *Beyond God the Father*, p. 132.
24. Andrew Kohut and Melissa Rogers, *Americans Struggle with Religion's Role at Home and Abroad* (Washington, DC: Pew Forum on Religion and Public Life, 2002).
25. See Alan Miller and John Hoffman, "Risk and Religion: An Explanation of Gender Differences in Religiosity" in *Journal for the Scientific Study of Religion* 34(1), 1995, pp. 63–75; current data from the General Social Survey, 2006.

26. George Gallup and J. Castelli, *The People's Religion* (New York: Macmillan, 1989); Cheryl Townsend Gilkes, "Together and in Harness: Women's Traditions in the Sanctified Church" in *Signs*, 10, 1985, pp. 678–699; Pew Forum on Religion and Public Life, *U.S. Religious Landscape Survey* (Washington, DC: Pew Research Center, February 2008).

27. Orestes Hastings and D. Michael Lindsay, "Rethinking Religious Gender Differences: The Case of Elite Women" in *Sociology of Religion*, 2013, pp. 1–25.

28. This is not always the work of men. One recent fundamentalist group called "True Womanhood" seeks to undo all the gains of feminism since the 1960s and return women to submissive subordination as an expression of their freedom to choose. See Kathryn Joyce, "Women's 'Liberation' Through Submission: An Evangelical Anto-Feminism Is Born" at www.altemet.org/story/121603, accessed August 1, 2009.

29. See http://www.ats.edu/Resources/Documents/AnnualDataTables/2007–08AnnualDataTables.pdf; see also http://www.elca.org/Who-We-Are/Welcome-to-the-ELCA/Quick-Facts.aspx, accessed August 1, 2009.

30. Peter Steinfels, "Vatican Says the Ban on Women as Priests Is 'Infallible' Doctrine" in *New York Times*, November 19, 1995.

31. Bill Frogameni, "Vatican Justice" in *Ms.*, Winter 2009, p. 16.

32. "Women Clergy: A Growing and Diverse Community" in *Religion Link*, August 4, 2014, http://www.religionlink.com/source-guides/women-clergy-a-growing-and-diverse-community/.

33. Angela Bonavoglia, *Good Catholic Girls* (New York: HarperCollins, 2006).

34. Kevin Christiano, William Swatos, and Peter Kivisto, eds., *Sociology of Religion: Contemporary Developments* (Lanham, MD: Rowman and Littlefield, 2002). See also Bonavoglia, *Good Catholic Girls*.

35. See also Ruth Wallace, *They Call Her Pastor: A New Role for Catholic Women* (Albany: SUNY 1992), and *They Call Him Pastor: Married Men in Charge of Catholic Parishes* (New York: Paulist Press, 2003).

36. Cited in Ann Douglas, *The Feminization of American Culture* (New York: Knopf, 1977), pp. 17, 97, 101, 113. Much of the material in this section is adapted from my book *Manhood in America: A Cultural History*, 2nd ed. (New York: Oxford University Press, 2006), pp. 116–120.

37. Cited in Ted Ownby, *Subduing Satan: Religion, Recreation and Manhood in the Rural South* (Chapel Hill: University of North Carolina Press, 1991), p. 14.

38. Cited in Roger Bruns, *Preacher: Billy Sunday and Big-Time American Evangelicism* (New York: Norton, 1992), p. 137.

39. Cited in Bruns, *Preacher*, pp. 16, 121, 122, 138; William G. McLaughlin, *Billy Sunday Was His Real Name* (Chicago: University of Chicago Press, 1955), p. 175.

40. Cited in Frances Fitzgerald, *Cities on a Hill* (New York: Simon and Schuster, 1986), p. 166.

41. Randy Phillips, "Spiritual Purity" in *The Seven Promises of a PromiseKeeper* (Colorado Springs: Focus on the Family, 1994), pp. 79–80.

42. See Sharon Mazer, "The Power Team: Muscular Christianity and the Spectacle of Conversion" in *Drama Review*, 38(4), Winter 1994, pp. 162, 169.

43. Molly Worthen, "Who Would Jesus Smack Down?" in *New York Times Magazine*, January 11, 2009, p. 22.

44. See my *Manhood in America*, p. 206; see also Laurie Beth Jones, *Jesus CEO: Using Ancient Wisdom for Visionary Leadership* (New York: Hyperion, 1994).

45. In Worthen, "Who Would Jesus Smack Down?," p. 23.

46. Swidler, "Jesus Was a Feminist."

47. Charlotte Perkins Gilman, *His Religion and Hers* (New York: Century, 1923), p. 154.

48. Ibid., p. 202.

49. Ibid., p. 206.

50. Ibid., pp. 217, 237.

51. Ibid., p. 46.

52. Ibid., p. 20.

53. Ibid., p. 259.

54. Ibid., pp. 255, 292.

55. Mary Daly, *The Church and the Second Sex* (Boston: Beacon Press, 1968), p. 74; see also Cullen Murphy, *The Word According to Eve* (Boston: Houghton, Mifflin, 1998).

56. See Elizabeth Fiorenza, *In Memory of Her: A Feminist Theological Reconstruction of Christian Origins* (New York: Crossroads, 1983); and Susan Farrell, "Women-Church and Egalitarianism: Revisioning 'in Christ There Is No More Distinctions Between Male and Female'" in *The Power of Gender in Religion*, G. A. Weatherly and S. A. Farrell, eds. (New York: McGraw-Hill, 1996).

57. The classic and still unsurpassed argument like this is Linda Nochlin, "Why Have There Been No

Great Women Artists?" *ARTnews,* January 1971, pp. 22–39, 67–71.

58. Laurel Kendall, *Shamans, Housewives, and Other Restless Spirits: Women in Korean Ritual Life* (Honolulu: University of Hawaii Press, 1985); quoted in Susan Starr Sered, *Priestess Mother Sacred Sister: Religions Dominated by Women* (New York: Oxford University Press, 1992), p. 18.

59. Charlene Spretnak, "Introduction" in *The Politics of Women's Spirituality,* Charlene Spretnak, ed. (New York: Doubleday, 1982), p. xii.

60. Mary Daly, *Pure Lust* (Boston: Beacon, 1984), p. xii.

61. See also Starhawk, *Dreaming in the Dark: Magic, Sex, and Politics* (Boston: Beacon, 1997), and *The Spiral Dance: A Rebirth of the Ancient Religion of the Goddess,* 20th anniversary ed. (New York: HarperCollins, 1999). A good guide to this tradition is Margot Adler's *Drawing Down the Moon: Witches, Druids, Goddess-Worshippers and Other Pagans in America Today* (New York: Penguin, 1986).

62. Mary Daly, *Beyond God the Father* (Boston: Beacon Press, 1973), p. 13.

63. Cited in Daly, *Beyond God the Father,* p. 13.

CHAPTER NINE

1. Bureau of Labor Statistics, U.S. Department of Labor, Current Population Survey.

2. "Latest Annual Data Women of Working Age, 2013," Bureau of Labor Statistics, U.S. Department of Labor, Current Population Survey.

3. See Felice Schwartz, "Management Women and the New Facts of Life" in *Harvard Business Review,* January–February 1989.

4. Bureau of Labor Statistics, U.S. Department of Labor, 2013.

5. Jerry Jacobs, 1993, see GS2, FN3, p. 318.

6. Taylor, cited in Ashley Montagu, *The Natural Superiority of Women* (New York: Anchor, 1952), p. 28; *Workplace 2000,* cited in Rosalind Barnet and Caryl Rivers, *She Works/He Works* (New York: Simon & Schuster, 1992), p. 64.

7. Michael Kimmel, *Manhood in America: A Cultural History* (New York: Free Press, 1996); Willard Gaylin, *The Male Ego* (New York: Viking, 1992), cited also in Michael Kimmel, "What Do Men Want?" in *Harvard Business Review,* November–December 1993.

8. Gaylin, *Male Ego,* p. 64.

9. Peg Tyre and Daniel McGinn, "She Works, He Doesn't" in *Newsweek,* May 12, 2003, pp. 45–53.

10. Marc Feigen-Fasteau, *The Male Machine* (New York: Dell, 1974), p. 120.

11. See Patricia Yancey Martin, "'Mobilizing Masculinities': Women's Experiences of Men at Work" in *Organization,* 8(4), 2001, pp. 587–618.

12. Cited in Londa Schiebinger, *Has Feminism Changed Science?* (Cambridge: Harvard University Press, 1999), p. 76.

13. See Arlie Hochschild, *The Managed Heart* (Berkeley: University of California Press, 1982).

14. Katha Pollitt, "Killer Moms, Working Nannies" in *Nation,* November 24, 1997.

15. U.S. Bureau of Labor Statistics, "Inflation Calculator," www. bls. gov/data/inflation_ calculator.htm.

16. Catherine Rampell, "As Layoffs Surge, Women May Pass Men in Job Force" in *New York Times,* February 5, 2009.

17. John Baden, "Perverse Consequences (P.C.) of the Nanny State" in *Seattle Times,* January 17, 1996; Del Jones, "Hooters to Pay $3.75 Million in Sex Suit" in *USA Today,* October 1, 1997, p. 1A.

18. David S. Pedulla, "The Positive Consequences of Negative Stereotypes: Race, Sexual Orientation, and the Job Application Process" in *Social Psychology Quarterly,* 77(1), 2014, pp. 75–94.

19. Barbara Reskin, "Sex Segregation in the Workplace" in *Women and Work: A Handbook,* P. Dubeck and K. Borman, eds. (New York: Garland, 1996), p. 94; see also Barbara Reskin, ed., *Sex-Segregation in the Workplace: Trends, Explanations, Remedies* (Washington, DC: National Academy Press, 1984); Barbara Reskin, "Bringing the Men Back In: Sex Differentiation and the Devaluation of Women's Work" in *Gender and Society,* 2(1), 1988; and Barbara Reskin and Patricia Roos, eds., *Job Queues, Gender Queues: Explaining Women's Inroads into Male Occupations* (Philadelphia: Temple University Press, 1990).

20. Padavic and Reskin, *Women and Men at Work,* pp. 65, 67; see also Andrea Beller and Kee-Ok Kim Han, "Occupational Sex Segregation: Prospects for the 1980s" in Reskin, *Sex-Segregation in the Workplace,* p. 91.

21. "2013 Household Data Annual Average," Bureau of Labor Statistics, U.S. Department of Labor, Table 39.

22. Current Population Survey, 2007, U.S. Department of Labor, Bureau of Labor Statistics. Earlier data from Dana Dunn, "Gender-Segregated Occupations" in *Women and Work,* P. Dubeck and K. Borman, eds. (New York: Garland, 1996), p. 92.

23. Margaret Mooney Marini and Mary C. Brinton, "Sex Typing in Occupational Socialization" in Reskin, *Sex-Segregation in the Workplace*, p. 224; Jerry A. Jacobs, *Revolving Doors: Sex Segregation and Women's Careers* (Stanford, CA: Stanford University Press, 1989), p. 48.

24. "Tables of Employment and Earnings, 2009–2013," Bureau of Labor Statistics, U.S. Department of Labor.

25. Samuel Cohn, *The Process of Occupational Sex-Typing: The Feminization of Clerical Labor in Great Britain* (Philadelphia: Temple University Press, 1985).

26. Yilu Zhao, "Women Soon to Be Majority of Veterinarians" in *New York Times*, June 9, 2002, p. 24.

27. Katharine Donato, "Programming for Change? The Growing Demand Among Computer Specialists" in *Job Queues, Gender Queues: Explaining Women's Inroads into Male Occupations*, B. Reskin and P. Roos, eds. (Philadelphia: Temple University Press, 1990), p. 170.

28. Charlotte Perkins Gilman, *His Religion and Hers* [1923], edited with a new introduction by Michael Kimmel (Walnut Creek, CA: Altamira Press, 2003), p. 72.

29. Michelle Arthur, Robert Del Campo, and Harry Van Buren III, "The Impact of Gender-Differentiated Golf Course Structures on Women's Networking Abilities," paper presented at the Academy of Management meeting, Anaheim, California, August 10, 2008.

30. William Bielby and James Baron, "Undoing Discrimination: Job Integration and Comparable Worth" in *Ingredients for Women's Employment Policy*, C. Bose and G. Spitze, eds. (Albany: SUNY Press, 1987), p. 226; Reskin, "Bringing the Men Back In," p. 64.

31. Kristen Schilt and Matthew Wiswall, "Before and After: Gender Transitions, Human Capital, and Workplace Experiences" in *B.E. Journal of Economic Analysis & Policy* 8(1), 2008, available at http://www.bepress.com/bejeap/vol8/iss1/art39, accessed August 1, 2009.

32. *EEOC v. Sears, Roebuck and Co.*, 628 F. Supp. 1264 (N.D. Ill. 1986); 839 F. 2d 302 (7th Cir. 1988).

33. Asra Q. Nomani, "A Fourth Grader's Hard Lesson: Boys Earn More Money Than Girls" in *Wall Street Journal*, July 7, 1995, p. B1.

34. Census 2000, http://www.census.gov/Press-Release/www/2002/demoprofiles.html, accessed August 14, 2009; see also Ronnie Steinberg, "How Sex Gets into Your Paycheck" in *Women's VU*, 20(2), 1997, p. 1.

35. Elizabeth Becker, "Study Finds a Growing Gap Between Managerial Salaries for Men and Women" in *New York Times*, January 24, 2002, p. 18; Shannon Henry, "Wage Gap Widens" in *Washington Post*, January 23, 2002.

36. Joyce Sterling and Nancy Reichman, "Gender Penalties Revisited," cited in Jim Dunlap, "Will Women Ever Be Equal?" in *National Jurist*, November 2004.

37. Mary Corcoran, Greg Duncan, and Michael Ponza, "Work Experience, Job Segregation and Wages" in Reskin, *Sex-Segregation in the Workplace*; p. 188; Michelle Budig and Paula England, "The Wage Penalty for Motherhood" in *American Sociological Review*, 66, 2001, pp. 204–225.

38. Timothy Judge and Beth Livingston, "Is the Gap More Than Gender? A Longitudinal Analysis of Gender, Gender Role Orientation and Earnings" in *Journal of Applied Psychology*, 93(5), 2008, pp. 994–1012.

39. Becker, "Study Finds Growing Gap Judith Lorber, "Women and Medical Sociology: Invisible Professionals and Ubiquitous Patients" in *Another Voice*, M. Millman and R. M. Kanter, eds. (Garden City, NY: Anchor, 1975), p. 82.

40. Sarah Portlock, "Gender Wage Gap in Eight Charts" in *Wall Street Journal*, April 14, 2015, http://blogs.wsj.com/economics/2015/04/14/the-gender-wage-gap-in-eight-charts.

41. Cited in Julie Mathaei, *An Economic History of Women in America* (New York: Schocken, 1982), p. 192.

42. Lynn Martin, *A Report on the Glass Ceiling Initiative* (Washington, DC: U.S. Department of Labor, 1991), p. 1.

43. "The Conundrum of the Glass Ceiling" in *The Economist*, July 21, 2005.

44. *Good for Business: Making Full Use of the Nation's Human Capital* (Washington, DC: U.S. Government Printing Office, 1995); Ruth Simpson, "Does an MBA Help Women?—Career Benefits of the MBA" in *Gender, Work and Organization*, 3(2), April, 1996, p. 119.

45. Warren Farrell, *The Myth of Male Power* (New York: Simon & Schuster, 1993), pp. 105–106.

46. Rosabeth Moss Kanter, *Men and Women of the Corporation* (New York: Basic Books, 1977), p. 209.

47. Ibid. pp. 216, 221, 230.

48. Lynn Zimmer, "Tokenism and Women in the Workplace: The Limits of Gender-Neutral Theory" in *Social Problems*, 35(1), 1988, p. 64;

Nina Toren and Vered Kraus, "The Effects of Minority Size on Women's Position in Academia" in *Social Forces*, 65, 1987, p. 1092.

49. Christine Williams, "The Glass Escalator: Hidden Advantages for Men in the 'Female' Professions" in *Social Problems*, 39(3), 1992; *Still a Man's World: Men Who Do "Women's Work"* (Berkeley: University of California Press, 1995); see also Marie Nordberg, "Constructing Masculinity in Women's Worlds: Men Working as Pre-school Teachers and Hairdressers" in *NORA: Nordic Journal of Women's Studies*, 10(1), 2002, pp. 26–37.

50. Williams, "Glass Escalator," p. 296.

51. Ibid.; Alfred Kadushin, "Men in a Woman's Profession" in *Social Work*, 21, 1976, p. 441.

52. Heidi Hartmann, "Capitalism, Patriarchy and Job Segregation by Sex" in *Signs*, 1(3), 1976, p. 139.

53. Cited in Deborah Rhode, *Speaking of Sex: The Denial of Gender Equality* (Cambridge: Harvard University Press, 1997), p. 144.

54. See Catharine MacKinnon, *Sexual Harassment of Working Women* (Cambridge: Harvard University Press, 1977).

55. *Henson v. Dundee*, 682 F.2d, 897, p. 902.

56. "Sexual Harassment in the Workplace," available at http://www.sexualharassmentsupport.org/SHorkplace.html, accessed August 1, 2009.

57. Susan Crawford, "Sexual Harassment at Work Cuts Profits, Poisons Morale" in *Wall Street Journal*, April 19, 1993, p. 11F; Elizabeth Stanko, *Intimate Intrusions* (London: Routledge, 1985); E. Couric, "An NJL/West Survey, Women in the Law: Awaiting Their Turn" in *National Law Journal*, December 11, 1989; 1997 study by Klein Associates.

58. Ellen Neuborne, "Complaints High from Women in Blue Collar Jobs" in *USA Today*, May 3–6, 1996.

59. De'Ann Weimer, "Slow Healing at Mitsubishi" in *U.S. News & World Report*, September 22, 1997, pp. 74, 76.

60. Rhode, *Speaking of Sex*, p. 28.

61. Stanko, *Intimate Intrusions*, p. 61.

62. I am grateful to Erin Smith at the University of Texas at Dallas for bringing this to my attention.

63. Crawford, "Sexual Harassment at Work Cuts Profits," p. 11F.

64. "Snapshot," in *USA Today*, April 5, 2006.

65. Jennifer Hicks, "Number of Discrimination Suits Soar in *IMDiversity*, October 29, 2012, " at http://www.imdiversity.com/Villages/Careers/articles/hicks_discrimination_suits_soar.asp.

66. Steinberg, "How Sex Gets into Your Paycheck," p. 2.

67. See Barbara Reskin and Irene Padavic, *Women and Men at Work* (Thousand Oaks, CA: Pine Forge Press, 1995).

68. Sara Evans and Barbara Nelson, *Wage Justice: Comparable Worth and the Paradox of Technocratic Reform* (Chicago: University of Chicago Press, 1989), p. 13; Barbara Reskin, "Bringing the Men Back In."

69. Cited in Rhode, *Speaking of Sex*, pp. 165, 169.

70. See, for example, Felice Schwartz and Gigi Anders, "The Mami Track" in *Hispanic*, July 1993.

71. Richard Bernstein, "Men Chafe as Norway Ushers Women into Boardroom" in *New York Times*, January 12, 2006; Thomas Fuller and Ivar Ekman, "The Envy of Europe" in *International Herald Tribune*, September 17–18, 2005, p. 19; Mari Teigen, "The Universe of Gender Quotas" in *NIKK*, 3, 2002, pp. 4–8.

72. Nicola Clark, "The Norwegian Experiment" in *International Herald Tribune Magazine*, special issue, "The Female Factor," 2010.

73. See *The Week*, p. 36.

74. See Roy D. Adler, "Women in the Executive Suite Correlate to High Profits" in *Harvard Business Review*, November 2001; Roy D. Adler, "Profit, Thy Name Is . . . Woman?" in *Miller-McCune Magazine*, March–April 2009.

75. Karen Oppenheim Mason, "Commentary: Strober's Theory of Occupational Sex Segregation" in *Sex-Segregation in the Workplace: Trends, Explanations, Remedies*, B. Reskin, ed. (Washington, DC: National Academy Press, 1984), p. 169.

76. Stephanie Coontz, *The Way We Never Were* (New York: Basic Books, 1999), p. 52.

77. See Sylvia Ann Hewlett, *Creating a Life: Professional Women and the Quest for Children* (New York: Talk Miramax Books, 2002); Sylvia Ann Hewlett, "Executive Women and the Myth of Having It All" in *Harvard Business Review*, April 2002, pp. 66–73. But see also the enormous critical response from feminists, including Katha Pollitt, "Backlash Babies" in *Nation*, May 13, 2002; and Garance Franke-Ruta, "Creating a Lie" in *American Prospect*, 13(12), July 1, 2002.

78. See, for example, C. E. Miree and I. H. Frieze, "Children and Careers: A Longitudinal Study of the Impact of Young Children on Critical Career Outcomes of MBAs" in *Sex Roles*, 41, 1999, pp. 787–808; J. E. Olson, I. H. Frieze, and E. G. Detlefsen, "Having It All? Combining Work and Family in a Male and Female Profession" in *Sex Roles*, 23, 1990, pp. 515–533. See also the summary of this research in Maureen Perry-Jenkins,

Rena Repetti, and Ann Crouter, "Work and Family in the 1990s" in *Journal of Marriage and the Family*, 62(4), 2000, pp. 981–998.

79. See Lisa Belkin, "Tony Blair's Baby: Some Decisions Last Longer" in *New York Times*, April 12, 2000, p. G1; Ellen Goodman, "Well Done, Mrs. Blair" in *Boston Globe*, April 14, 2000.

80. Scott Coltrane, "The Risky Business of Paternity Leave" in *Atlantic*, December 2013; Liza Mundy, "The Daddy Track," in *Atlantic*, January 2014, pp. 15–18.

81. Sarah Hall, "Fathers 'Scared' to Ask for Flexible Hours" in *Guardian*, January 14, 2003; Erika Kirby and Kathleen Krone, "'The Policy Exists but You Can't Really Use It': Communication and the Structuration of Work-Family Policies" in *Journal of Applied Communication Research*, 30(1), 2002, pp. 50–77.

82. Faye Crosby, *Spouse, Parent, Worker: On Gender and Multiple Roles* (New Haven, CT: Yale University Press, 1990); Joan Peters, *When Mothers Work: Loving Our Children Without Sacrificing Ourselves* (New York: Addison-Wesley, 1997).

CHAPTER TEN

1. Sara Wheaton, "Iron My Shirt" in *New York Times*, January 8, 2008, available at http://thecaucus.blogs.nytimes.com/2008/01/07/iron-my-shirt/.

2. "Worldwide Guide to Women in Leadership," available at http://www.guide2womenleaders.com/Female_Leaders.htm.

3. "Men or Women: Who's the Better Leader?," Pew Research Center, August 25, 2008, http://pewresearch.org/pubs/932/men-or-women-whos-the-better-leader.

4. Deborah Rhode, *Speaking of Sex* (Cambridge: Harvard University Press, 1997), p. 7.

5. http://www.cawp.rutgers.edu/research/reports/PoisedtoRun.pdf.

6. Cited in Stephen J. Ducat, *The Wimp Factor*, p. 174.

7. Some parts of this section are drawn from the third edition of my book *Manhood in America* (New York: Oxford University Press, 2010).

8. His impeachment trial came because he was accused of lying to the special prosecutor of the case when he said that he "did not have sexual relations with that woman." However, it appears that President Clinton and Monica Lewinsky's sexual trysts involved "everything but" sexual intercourse, and instead were based on other sexual acts. In a survey published by the *Journal of the American Medical Association*, most Americans apparently agreed with him, saying that "sex" is defined only by penile-vaginal intercourse. Therefore, it appears that he was telling the truth, at least according to public opinion, if not according to the spirit of the law (cf. Stephanie Sanders and June Machover Reinisch, "Would You Say 'Had Sex' If . . ." in *JAMA*, 281, January 20, 1999).

9. Front-page headline in the *New York Sun*, July 13, 2004; see also Katha Pollitt, "The Girlie Vote" in *Nation*, September 27, 2004, p. 12; Kenneth Walsh, "What the Guys Want" in *U.S. News and World Report*, September 20, 2004, pp. 22–23; Frank Rich, "How Kerry Became a Girlie-Man" in *New York Times*, September 5, 2004, section 2, pp. 1, 18; George Will, "The Politics of Manliness" in *Washington Post, January 19, 2004.*

10. Cited in Richard Goldstein, "Neo-Macho Man," *Nation*, March 24, 2003, http://www.thenation.com/article/new_macho_men. See also Frank Rich, "How Kerry Became a Girlie-Man."

11. See Jackson Katz, "It's the Masculinity Stupid: A Cultural Studies Analysis of Media, the Presidency and Pedagogy" in *Handbook of Cultural Politics and Education*, Zeus Leonardo, ed. (Rotterdam, Netherlands: Sense Publishers, 2010).

12. "The Macho Factor" in *Orlando Sentinel*, September 1, 2008, p. A18.

13. Susan Faludi, "Think the Gender War Is Over? Think Again" in *New York Times*, June 15, 2008.

14. http://www.bhurt.com/barackandcurtis.php.

15. Susan Faludi, "Think the Gender War Is Over?"

16. Elwood Watson, *Pimps, Wimps, Studs, Thugs, and Gentlemen: Essays on Media Images of Masculinity* (Jefferson, NC: McFarland and Company, 2009), p. 1.

17. Frank Rudy Cooper, "Our First Unisex President? Black Masculinity and Obama's Feminine Side" in *Denver University Law Review*, 86, 2009, pp. 633–661.

18. http://www.cbsnews.com/2100-201_162-1753947.html.

19. Jody Heymann, Alison Earle, and Jeffrey Hayes, *The Work, Family, and Equity Index* (Boston: Project on Global Working Families, 2004).

20. These data come from the 2011 National Transgender Discrimination Survey, available at http://equity.lsnc.net/2011/03/a-report-of-the-national-transgender-discrimination-survey/.

21. Kate Johnson and Albert Garcia, " 'Male stewardess' just didn't fly," *Los Angeles Times*, September 27, 2007.

22. Mrinhalini Sinha, "Gender and Imperialism: Colonial Policy and the Ideology of Moral Imperialism in Late Nineteenth Century Bengal" in *Changing Men: New Directions in Research on Men*

and Masculinity, Michael Kimmel, ed. (Newbury Park, CA: Sage Publications, 1987), p. 223.

23. Frantz Fanon, *Black Skin, White Masks* [1952] (New York: Grove Press, 1971), p. 165.

24. Xan Rice, Katherine Marsh, Tom Finn, Harriet Sherwood, Angelique Chrisafis, and Robert Booth, "Women Have Emerged as Key Players in the Arab Spring" in *Guardian*, April 22, 2011, http://www.theguardian.com/world/2011/apr/22/women-arab-spring.

25. "Taliban Shave Men for Listening to Music in Buner" in *Islamization Watch*, April 26, 2009, http://islamizationwatch.blogspot.com/2009/04/taliban-shave-men-for-listening-to.html.

26. http://www.smh.com.au/world/were-here-for-sam-mullet-to-get-revenge-saga-of-the-amish-beard-snatchers-20111013-1lmn5.html.

CHAPTER ELEVEN

1. Ben Hubbard, "Young Saudis Find Freedom on Smartphones" in *New York Times,* May 24, 2015, p. 11.

2. Winda Benedetti, "Were Video Games to Blame for the Massacre?" MSNBC.com, April 20, 2007, available at www.msnbc.com/id/18220228.html.

3. Victoria J. Rideout, Ulla G. Foehr, Donald F. Roberts, "Generation M2: Media in the Lives of 8- to 18-Year-Olds," 2010, Kaiser Family Foundation, https://kaiserfamilyfoundation.files.wordpress.com/2013/01/8010.pdf.

4. Ibid.

5. See, for example, http://www.readwriteweb.com/archives/people_do_read_they_just_do_it_online.php; statistics on family book buying from www.JenkinsGroupInc.com.

6. See Leonore Weitzman and Diane Russo, *The Biased Textbook: A Research Perspective* (Washington, DC: Research Center on Sex Roles and Education, 1974).

7. Leonore Weitzman, Deborah Eifler, Elizabeth Hokada, and Catheine Ron, "Sex Role Socialization in Picture Books for Preschool Children" in *American Journal of Sociology*, 77(6), 1972.

8. Rhode, *Speaking of Sex*, p. 56.

9. Angela M. Gooden and Mark A. Gooden, "Gender Representation in Notable Children's Picture Books: 1995–1999" in *Sex Roles*, 45(1/2), July 2001, pp. 89–101; Janice McCabe, Emily Fairchild, Liz Grauerholz, Bernice Pescosolido, Daniel Tope, "Gender I Twentieth-Century Children's Books: Patterns of Disparity in Titles and Central Characters" in *Gender & Society*, 25(2), April 2011, pp. 197–226.

10. *National Television Violence Study* (Thousand Oaks, CA: Sage Publications, 1998), Vol. 2, p. 97. I will return to this issue in the last chapter.

11. Parents Television Council, *Media Violence: An Examination of Violence, Graphic Violence, and Gun Violence in the Media 2012–2013*.

12. Parents Television Council, *Women in Peril: A Look at TV's Disturbing New Storyline Trend, 2004–2009*.

13. Kay Bussey and Albert Bandura, "Social Cognitive Theory of Development and Differentiation" in Psychological Review, 106, 1999, pp. 676–713.

14. Paul McGhee and Terry Frueh, "Television Viewing and the Learning of Sex-Role Stereotypes" in Sex Roles, 6(2), 1980, pp. 179–188.

15. John Consoli, "What Women Don't Want? Soap Operas" in *Adweek*, November 1, 2004; Betty Goodwin, "Cable Channels Take Aim at Women" in *Television Week*, November 5, 2005.

16. See Stuart Elliott, "NBC Looks Beyond TV for a Prime Time Revival" in *New York Times*, May 16, 2006, p. C10; Alec Foge, "Searching for the Elusive Male" in *Mediaweek*, September 5, 2005; Betty Goodwin, "Programmers Cast a Wide Net" in *Television Week*, November 7, 2005.

17. See Zondra Hughes, "Prime-Time 2005: More Stars, More Soul, More Sensation" in *Ebony*, October 2005.

18. James Fenimore Cooper, *The Last of the Mohicans* (New York: Harper and Row, 1965), pp. 26, 132.

19. See, for example, Scott Mebus, *Booty Nomad* (New York: Hyperion, 2004); Benjamin Kunkel, *Indecision* (New York: Random House, 2005); Kyle Smith, *Love Monkey* (New York: HarperCollins, 2005).

20. See Amy Beth Aronson, *Taking Liberties: Early American Women's Magazines and Their Readers* (Westport, CT: Praeger, 2002), p. 3; Betty Friedan, *The Feminine Mystique* (New York: Dell Publishing, 1983), pp. 15–79.

21. Friedan, *Feminine Mystique*, p. 36.

22. Aronson, *Taking Liberties*, p. 3; see also, for example, Tanya Modeski's characterization of women soap opera fans as "egoless receptacles." See Tanya Modeski, "The Search for Tomorrow in Today's Soap Operas" in *Loving with a Vengeance: Mass-Produced Fantasies for Women* (Hamden, CT: Shoestring Press, 1982).

23. Marjorie Ferguson, *Forever Feminine: Women's Magazines and the Cult of Femininity* (London: Gower, 1983), p. 3.

24. Gaye Tuchman, Arlene Daniels, and James Benit, eds., *Hearth and Home: Images of Women in the Mass Media* (New York: Oxford University Press, 1978); Jean Kilbourne, "Killing Us Softly," available from the Media Education Foundation, www.mef.org; Naomi Wolf, *The Beauty Myth* (New York: William Morrow, 1991).

25. Media Research Center, *Landmark Study Reveals Women's Magazines Are Left-Wing Political Weapon* (Alexandria, VA: Author).

26. Christina Hoff Sommers, "The Democrats' Secret Woman Weapon: In the Pages of Glossy Women's Magazines, the Party's Line Is in Fashion" *in Washington Post*, January 13, 1997, p. 22.

27. Danielle Crittenden, *What Our Mothers Didn't Tell Us: Why Happiness Eludes the Modern Woman* (New York: Simon & Schuster, 1999), pp. 20–21.

28. Aronson, *Taking Liberties.*

29. Laramie Taylor, "All for Him: Articles About Sex in American Lad Magazines" in *Sex Roles*, 52(3/4), 2005, p. 155.

30. Tim Adams, "New Kid on the Newsstand" in *Observer*, January 23, 2005.

31. Circulation figures cited in David Brooks, "The Return of the Pig" in *Atlantic Monthly*, April 2003.

32. Adams, "New Kid on the Newsstand."

33. Spil Games, *State of the Industry 2013*, http://auth-83051f68-ec6c-44e0-afe5-bd8902acff57.cdn.spilcloud.com/v1/archives/1384952861.25_State_of_Gaming_2013_US_FINAL.pdf; *2014 Essential Facts About the Computer and Video Game Industry*, http://www.theesa.com/wp-content/uploads/2014/10/ESA_EF_2014.pdf; *The State of Gaming 2014*, http://www.bigfishgames.com/daily/infographic/state-of-video-game-industry/#intro.

34. Video game data are drawn from Michel Marriott, "The Color of Mayhem" in *New York Times*, August 12, 2004, p. G3; www.idsa.com; www.digiplay.org.uk; http://www.theesa.com/facts/pdfs/ESA_EF_2011.pdf

35. See, for example, M. D. Griffiths, Mark N. O. Davies, and Darren Chappell, "Online Computer Gaming: A Comparison of Adolescent and Adult Gamers" in *Journal of Adolescence*, 10, 2003; James D. Ivory, "Still a Man's Game: Gender Representations in Online Reviews of Video Games" in *Mass Communication and Society*, 9(1), 2006.

36. "Cloudburst of Ghoul Slayers" in *Economist*, November 26, 2005, p. 54.

37. Jeff Grubb, "Gaming Advocacy Group: The Average Gamer Is 31, and Most Play on a Console" in *Venture Beat*, April 29, 2014, http://venturebeat.com/2014/04/29/gaming-advocacy-group-the-average-gamer-is-31-and-most-play-on-a-console/.

38. William Lugo, interview, February 2, 2005.

39. Interview with Nina Huntemann, November 1, 2005. *Game Over* is available from the Media Education Foundation.

40. See Derek Burrill, "Watch Your Ass: The Structure of Masculinity in Video Games," unpublished manuscript, University of California at Riverside, 2005.

41. The one game in which relationships exist is *Sims*, because the game makes it possible for same-sex characters to live together, share a bed, kiss, have a baby, and so on (Nina Huntemann, personal communication, December 19, 2005). And, of course, *Sims* is the one game that "real guys" can't stand! No doubt there will soon be a campaign by Focus on the Family against this particular game.

42. See, for example, Helen Kennedy, "Lara Croft: Feminist Icon or Cyberbimbo?" in *Game Studies*, 2(2), December 2002.

43. Seth Schiesel, "The Year in Gaming: Readers Report" in *New York Times*, December 31, 2005, p. B21; Edward Castronova, *Synthetic Worlds* (Chicago: University of Chicago Press, 2005).

44. Jessica Williams, "Facts That Should Change the World: America Spends $10bn Each Year on Porn" in *New Statesman*, June 7, 2004.

45. Larry Flynt, "Porn World's Sky Isn't Falling—It Doesn't Need a Condom Rule" in *Los Angeles Times*, April 23, 2004.

46. Ogi Ogasa and Sai Gaddam, *A Billion Wicked Thoughts: What the Internet Tells Us About Sexual Relationships* (New York: Plume, 2011).

47. Stacy L. Smith and Ed Donnerstein, "The Problem of Exposure: Violence, Sex, Drugs and Alcohol" in *Kid Stuff: Marketing Sex and Violence to America's Children*, Diane Ravitch and Joseph Viteritti, eds. (Baltimore: Johns Hopkins University Press, 2003), p. 83.

48. Pamela Paul, *Pornified* (New York: St. Martin's, 2006).

49. John Stoltenberg, "Pornography and Freedom" in *Men Confront Pornography*, M. Kimmel, ed. (New York: Crown, 1990), p. 64.

50. Lillian Rubin, *Erotic Wars* (New York: Farrar, Straus and Giroux, 1991), p. 102.

51. Tom Cayler, ". . . Those Little Black Dots," reprinted in Kimmel, *Men Confront Pornography*, p. 52.

52. William Lugo, interview, February 5, 2005.

53. M. Duggan, "It's a Woman's (Social Media) World," Pew Research Center, 2013, http://www.pewresearch.org/fact-tank/2013/09/12/its-a-womans-social-media-world/, accessed May 2015; following data and charts are from Michael Patterson, "Social Media Demographics to Inform a Better Segmentation Strategy," May 4, 2015, http://sproutsocial.com/insights/new-social-media-demographics/.

54. Deborah Fallows, *How Women and Men Use the Internet* (Washington, DC: Pew Internet and American Life Project, 2005).

55. Ibid.

56. Eszter Hargittai and Steven Shafter, "Differences in Actual and Perceived Online Skills: The Role of Gender" in *Social Science Quarterly*, 87(2), June 2006, pp. 432–448.

57. Jeffrey Jones, "Six in 10 Americans Are Pro Football Fans," Gallup Poll, February 4, 2005.

58. *Brandweek*, September 29, 2003.

59. http://www.fsta.org.

CHAPTER TWELVE

1. Cited in Drury Sherrod, "The Bonds of Men: Problems and Possibilities in Close Male Relationships" in *The Making of Masculinities: The New Men's Studies*, H. Brod, ed. (Boston: Allen and Unwin, 1987), p. 230; cited in Lillian Rubin, *Intimate Strangers* (New York: Harper and Row, 1983), p. 59.

2. Mary Wollstonecraft, *A Vindication of the Rights of Women* [1792] (London: Penguin, 1969), p. 56; Simone de Beauvoir, *The Second Sex* (New York: Vintage, 1959), p. 142.

3. Lionel Tiger, *Men in Groups* (New York: Vintage, 1969).

4. Jack Balswick, "The Inexpressive Male: A Tragedy of American Society" in *The Forty-Nine Percent Majority*, D. David and R. Brannon, eds. (Reading, MA: Addison-Wesley, 1976); Mirra Komorovsky, *Blue Collar Marriage* (New York: Vintage, 1964); Joseph Pleck, "The Male Sex Role: Definitions, Problems and Sources of Change" in *Journal of Social Issues*, 32(3), 1976, p. 273.

5. Robert Lewis, "Emotional Intimacy Among Men" in *Journal of Social Issues*, 34, 1978; see also Pleck, "The Male Sex Role."

6. Paul Wright, "Men's Friendships, Women's Friendships and the Alleged Inferiority of the Latter" in *Sex Roles*, 8(1), 1982, p. 3; Daniel Levinson, *The Seasons of a Man's Life* (New York: William Morrow, 1978), p. 335.

7. Francesca Cancian, "The Feminization of Love" in *Signs*, 11, 1986; and *Love in America: Gender and Self-Development* (Cambridge: Cambridge University Press, 1987).

8. Simone Schnall, Kent Harber, Jeanine Stefanucci, and Dennis Proffiytt, "Social Support and the Perception of Geographical Slant" in *Journal of Experimental Social Psychology*, 44, 2008, pp. 1246–1255.

9. See S. E. Taylor, L. C. Klein, B. P. Lewis, T. L. Gruenwald, R. A. R. Gurung, and J. A. Updegraff, "Biobehavioral Female Responses to Stress: Tend and Befriend, Not Fight or Flight" in *Psychological Review*, 107(3), 2000, pp. 411–429.

10. Sharon Brehm, *Intimate Relationships* (New York: Random House, 1985), p. 346.

11. Mayta Caldwell and Letitia Peplau, "Sex Differences in Same-Sex Friendships" in *Sex Roles*, 8(7), 1982; Beth Hess, "Friendship" in *Aging and Society*, M. Riley, M. Johnson, and A. Foner, eds. (New York: Russell Sage, 1972); Erina MacGeorge, Angela Graves, Bo Feng, Seth Gillihan, and Brant Burleson, "The Myth of Gender Cultures: Similarities Outweigh Differences in Men's and Women's Provision of and Responses to Supportive Communication" in *Sex Roles*, 50(3/4), February 2004, pp. 143–175.

12. Lynne Davidson and Lucille Duberman, "Friendship: Communication and Interactional Patterns in Same-Sex Dyads" in *Sex Roles*, 8(8), 1982, p. 817.

13. Lillian Rubin, *Just Friends* (New York: Harper and Row, 1985), pp. 60–61, 62–63; Rubin, *Intimate Strangers*, pp. 130, 135.

14. Brehm, *Intimate Relationships*; Wright, "Men's Friendships"; Davidson and Duberman, "Friendship"; R. Bell, *Worlds of Friendship* (Beverly Hills, CA: Sage Publications, 1981).

15. Karen Walker, "'I'm Not Friends the Way She's Friends': Ideological and Behavioral Constructions of Masculinity in Men's Friendships" in *Masculinities*, 2(2), 1994, p. 228; Rubin, *Intimate Strangers*, p. 104. On the impact of the telephone more generally, see Claude Fischer, *To Dwell Among Friends* (Chicago: University of Chicago Press, 1982).

16. Stuart Miller, *Men and Friendship* (Boston: Houghton, Mifflin, 1983).

17. Graham Allen, *Friendship—Developing a Sociological Perspective* (Boulder, CO: Westview, 1989), p. 66.

18. Wright, "Men's Friendships," p. 19.

19. N. L. Ashton, "Exploratory Investigation of Perceptions of Influences on Best-Friend Relationships" in *Perception and Motor Skills*, 50, 1980; Shavaun Wall, Sarah M. Pickert, and Louis V. Paradise, "American Men's Friendships: Self-Reports on Meaning and Changes" in *Journal of Psychology*, 116, 1984.

20. Helen Hacker, "Blabbermouths and Clams: Sex Differences in Self-Disclosure in Same-Sex and Cross-Sex Friendship Dyads" in *Psychology of Women Quarterly*, 5(3), Spring 1981.

21. Scott Swain, "Men's Friendship with Women: Intimacy, Sexual Boundaries, and the Informant Role" in *Men's Friendships*, P. Nardi, ed. (Newbury Park, CA: Sage Publications, 1992), pp. 84, 77. For a more general review of this literature,

see Eleanor Maccoby and Carol Jacklin, *The Psychology of Sex Differences* (Stanford, CA: Stanford University Press, 1974).

22. Barbara Bank, "Friendships in Australia and the United States: From Feminization to a More Heroic Image" in *Gender & Society*, 9(1), 1995, p. 96.

23. Theodore F. Cohen, "Men's Families, Men's Friends: A Structural Analaysis of Constraints on Men's Social Ties" in Nardi, *Men's Friendships*, p. 117; Allen, *Friendship*, p. 75.

24. Shanette Harris, "Black Male Masculinity and Same Sex Friendships" in *Western Journal of Black Studies*, 16(2), 1992, p. 77.

25. Ibid., pp. 78, 81; see also Clyde W. Franklin II, "'Hey Home'—'Yo, Bro': Friendship Among Black Men" in Nardi, *Men's Friendships*.

26. Helen M. Reid and Gary Alan Fine, "Self-Disclosure in Men's Friendships: Variations Associated with Intimate Relations" in Nardi, *Men's Friendships*; Jeanne Tschann, "Self-Disclosure in Adult Friendship: Gender and Marital Status Differences" in *Journal of Social and Personal Relationships*, 5, 1988; Wright, "Men's Friendships," pp. 16–17.

27. April Bleske-Rechek, Erin Somers, Cierra Micke, Leah Erickson, Lindsay Matteson, Corey Stocco, Brittany Schumacher, and Laura Ritchie, "Benefit or Burden? Attraction in Cross-Sex Friendship" in *Journal of Social and Personal Relationships*, 29(5), 2012, pp. 569–596.

28. Rubin, *Intimate Strangers*, pp. 154, 150.

29. Gerald Suttles, "Friendship as a Social Institution" in *Social Relationships*, G. McCall, M. McCall, N. Denzin, G. Suttles, and S. Kurth, eds. (Chicago: Aldine, 1970), p. 116.

30. Miller, *Men and Friendship*, pp. 2, 3; Rubin, *Intimate Strangers*, p. 103.

31. Niobe Way, *Deep Secrets: Boys' Friendships and the Crisis of Connection* (Cambridge: Harvard University Press, 2011), pp. 15, 20.

32. On experiment, see Lillian Faderman, *Surpassing the Love of Men* (New York: Columbia University Press, 1981); quote from Scott Swain, "Covert Intimacy," pp. 83–84.

33. Peter Nardi and Drury Sherrod, "Friendship in the Lives of Gay Men and Lesbians" in *Journal of Social and Personal Relationships*, 11, 1994; Rubin, *Intimate Strangers*, p. 105.

34. Cited in Rubin, *Intimate Strangers*, p. 130.

35. Peter Nardi, "The Politics of Gay Men's Friendships" in *Men's Lives*, 4th ed., M. Kimmel and M. Messner, eds. (Boston: Allyn and Bacon, 1998), p. 250.

36. Rubin, *Intimate Strangers*, pp. 58, 159, 205.

37. Sherrod, "Bonds of Men," p. 231.

38. Rubin, *Intimate Strangers*, p. 206.

39. Sherrod, "Bonds of Men," p. 221; E. Anthony Rotundo, "Romantic Friendships: Male Intimacy and Middle-Class Youth in the Northern United States, 1800–1900" in *Journal of Social History*, 23(1), 1989, p. 21.

40. Foucault cited in Nardi, *Men's Friendships*, p. 184; Lynne Segal, *Slow Motion: Changing Masculinities, Changing Men* (New Brunswick, NJ: Rutgers University Press, 1990), p. 139.

41. Lawrence Stone, "Passionate Attachments in the West in Historical Perspective" in *Passionate Attachments: Thinking About Love,* W. Gaylin and E. Person, eds. (New York: Free Press, 1988), p. 33; Francesca Cancian, *Love in America*, p. 70.

42. Stone, "Passionate Attachments," p. 28.

43. Ibid., p. 32; Michael Gordon and M. Charles Bernstein, "Mate Choice and Domestic Life in the Nineteenth Century Marriage Manual" in *Journal of Marriage and the Family*, November 1970, pp. 668, 669.

44. William J. Goode, "The Theoretical Importance of Love" in *American Sociological Review*, 24(1), 1959.

45. Cited in Cancian, *Love in America*, pp. 19, 21, 23; see also Mary Ryan, *The Cradle of the Middle Class: The Family in Oneida County, N.Y., 1790–1865* (New York: Cambridge University Press, 1981).

46. Cancian, *Love in America*, p. 121; Carol Tavris, *The Mismeasure of Woman* (New York: Simon & Schuster, 1992), p. 263; Rubin, *Intimate Strangers*.

47. Lillian Rubin, *Worlds of Pain* (New York: Basic Books, 1976), p. 147.

48. Robin Simon and Leda Nath, "Gender and Emotion in the United States: Do Men and Women Differ in Self-Reports of Feelings and Expressive Behavior?" in *American Journal of Sociology*, 109(5), pp. 1137–1176.

49. Elaine Hatfield, "What Do Women and Men Want from Love and Sex?" in *Changing Boundaries*, E. Allegier and N. McCormick, eds. (Mountain View, CA: Mayfield, 1983).

50. William Kephart, "Some Correlates of Romantic Love" in *Journal of Marriage and the Family*, 29, 1967; Kenneth Dion and Karen Dion, "Correlates of Romantic Love" in *Journal of Consulting and Clinical Psychology*, 41, 1973; Charles Hill, Zick Rubin, and Letitia Anne Peplau, "Breakups Before Marriage: The End of 103 Affairs" in *Divorce and Separation: Context, Causes and Consequences*, G. Levinger and O. C. Moles, eds. (New York: Basic Books, 1979); Charles Hobart, "Disillusionment in

Marriage and Romanticism" in *Marriage and Family Living*, 20, 1958; Charles Hobart, "The Incidence of Romanticism During Courtship" in *Social Forces*, 36, 1958; David Knox and John Spoakowski, "Attitudes of College Students Toward Love" in *Journal of Marriage and the Family*, 30, 1968; George Theodorson, "Romanticism and Motivation to Marry in the United States, Singapore, Burma and India" in *Social Forces*, 44, 1965.

51. Dion and Dion, "Correlates of Romantic Love"; Zick Rubin, "Measurement of Romantic Love" in *Journal of Personality and Social Psychology*, 16(2), 1970; Arlie Hochschild, "Attending to, Codifying and Managing Feelings: Sex Differences in Love," paper presented at the annual meeting of the American Sociological Association, August 1975; Eugene Kanin, Karen Davidson, and Sonia Scheck, "A Research Note on Male-Female Differentials in the Experience of Heterosexual Love" in *Journal of Sex Research*, 6, 1970, p. 70.

52. Hill, Rubin, and Peplau, "Breakups Before Marriage."

53. Kephart, "Some Correlates of Romantic Love."

54. http://www.thedailybeast.com/articles/2012/02/02/republicans-have-more-orgasms-according-to-match-com-sex-survey.html and http://www.usatoday.com/news/health/wellness/story/2012–02-02/Survey-gives-a-snapshot-of-singles-in-America/52922248/1.

55. Susan Sprecher, E. Aron, E. Hatfield, A. Cortese, E. Potapava, and A. Levitskaya, "Love: American Style, Russian Style, and Japanese Style," paper presented at the Sixth Annual Conference on Personal Relationships, Orono, Maine, 1992.

56. Susan Sprecher and Maura Toro-Morn, "A Study of Men and Women from Different Sides of Earth to Determine if Men Are from Mars and Women Are from Venus in Their Beliefs About Love and Romantic Relationships" in *Sex Roles*, 46(5/6), March 2002, pp. 131–147.

57. Cathy Greenblat, personal communication. This research has not yet been published.

58. Tavris, *Mismeasure of Woman*, p. 284.

59. Cancian, "Feminization of Love," pp. 705, 709.

60. Rubin, *Just Friends*, p. 41.

CHAPTER THIRTEEN

1. It is ironic, perhaps, that some of these developments that have made us more aware of our bodies have also enabled us to change (surgery) or conceal (Internet) them.

2. Naomi Wolf, *The Beauty Myth* (New York: William Morrow, 1991), pp. 10, 184.

3. See Emili Vesilind, "Fashion's Invisible Woman" in *Los Angeles Times*, March 1, 2009, http://www.latimes.com/features/lifestyle/la-ig-size1-2009mar01,0,2345629.story, accessed August 1, 2009.

4. http://www.raderprograms.com/causes-statistics/media-eating-disorders.html; and Edward Lovett, "Most Models Meet Criteria for Anorexia; Size 6 Is Plus Size: Magazine" in ABC News, January 12, 2012, http://abcnews.go.com/blogs/headlines/2012/01/most-models-meet-criteria-for-anorexia-size-6-is-plus-size-magazine/.

5. See Debra Gimlin, *Body Work: Beauty and Self-Image in American Culture* (Berkeley: University of California Press, 2002), p. 5; "How to Get Plump" in *Harper's Bazaar*, August 1908, p. 787; Mary Pipher, *Reviving Ophelia* (New York: Ballantine, 1996); M. E. Collins, "Body Figure Perceptions and Preferences Among Preadolescent Children" in *International Journal of Eating Disorders*, 10, 1991, pp. 199–208; A. Gustafson-Larson and R. Terry, "Weight-Related Behaviors and Concerns of Fourth Grade Children" in *Journal of the American Dietetic Association*, 92(7), 1992, pp. 818–822; see also www.healthywithin.com/STATS.htm, August 14, 2009.

6. J. I. Hudson, E. Hiripi, H. G. Pope Jr., and R. C. Kessler, "The Prevalence and Correlates of Eating Disorders in the National Comorbidity Survey Replication" in *Biological Psychiatry*, 61, 2007, pp. 348–358; T. D. Wade, A. Keski-Rahkonen, and J. Hudson, "Epidemiology of Eating Disorders," in *Textbook in Psychiatric Epidemiology*, 3rd ed., M. Tsuang and M. Tohen, eds., pp. 343–360 (New York: Wiley, 2011).

7. "Europe Targets Eating Disorders," available at http://news.bbc.uk/1/hi/health/197334.stm; and "Eating Disorders Factfile," available at http://news.bbc.co.uk/1/hi/health/medical_notes/187517.stm.

8. See A. Furnham and N. Alibhai, "Cross-Cultural Differences in the Perception of Female Body Shapes" in *Psychological Medicine*, 13(4), 1983, pp. 829–837; D. B. Mumford, "Eating Disorders in Different Cultures" in *International Review of Psychiatry*, 5(1), 1993, pp. 109–113; N. Shuriquie, "Eating Disorders: A Transcultural Perspective" in *Eastern Mediterranean Health Journal*, 5(2), 1999, pp. 354–360, also available at http://www.emro.who.int/Publications/EMHJ/0502/20.htm. I am grateful to Lisa Machoian for her help in obtaining this material.

9. Sonni Efron, "Eating Disorders on the Increase in Asia in *Dimensions Magazine*," available at http://www.dimensionsmagazine.com/news/asia/html, accessed August 14, 2009.

10. http://thesocietypages.org/socimages/2011/03/19/push-up-bikini-tops-at-abercrombie-kids/.

11. Their report can be accessed at www.apa.org/pi/wpo/sexualization.html.

12. Deborah Gregory, "Heavy Judgment" in *Essence*, August 1994, pp. 57–58; G. B. Schreiber, K. M. Pike, D. E. Wilfley, and J. Rodin, "Drive for Thinness in Black and White Preadolescent Girls" in *International Journal of Eating Disorders*, 18(1), 1995, pp. 59–69.

13. See Susan Bordo, *The Male Body* (New York: Farrar, Straus and Giroux, 2000).

14. Harrison Pope, Katharine Phillips, and Roberto Olivardia, *The Adonis Complex: The Secret Crisis of Male Body Obsession* (New York: Free Press, 2000).

15. Denis Campbell, "Body Image Concerns Men More Than Women" in *Guardian*, January 6, 2012, http://www.guardian.co.uk/lifeandstyle/2012/jan/06/body-image-concerns-men-more-than-women.

16. Cited in Richard Morgan, "The Men in the Mirror" in *Chronicle of Higher Education*, September 27, 2002, p. A53.

17. Tracy McVeigh, "Skinny Male Models and New Fashions Fuel Eating Disorders Among Men" in *Guardian*, May 16, 2010, http://www.guardian.co.uk/society/2010/may/16/skinny-models-fuel-male-eating-disorders.

18. Trent Petrie, Christy Greenleaf, Jennifer Carter, and Justine Reel, "Psychosocial Correlates of Disordered Eating Among Male Collegiate Athletes" in *Journal of Clinical Sport Psychology*, 1(4), December 2007, pp. 340–357; see also Trent Petrie, Christy Greenleaf, Jennifer Carter, and Justine Reel, "Prevalence of Eating Disorders and Disordered Eating Behaviors Among Male Collegiate Athletes" in *Psychology of Men & Masculinity*, 9(4), October 2008, pp. 267–277.

19. Pope et al., *Adonis Complex*.

20. Douglas Quenqua, "Muscular Body Image Lures Boys into Gym, and Obsession" in *New York Times*, November 19, 2012, pp. 1, 13; R. J. DiClemente, J. M. Jackson, V. Hertzberg, and P. Seth, "Steroid Use, Health Risk Behaviors and Adverse Health Indicators Among U.S. High School Students" in *Family Medicine and Medical Science Research*, 3(127), 2014.

21. Gina Kolata, "With No Answers on Risks, Steroid Users Still Say 'Yes'" in *New York Times*, December 2, 2002, pp. A1, 19, NYTimes.com./2011/12/18/opinion/sunday

22. See, for example, Christine Webber, "Eating Disorders," available at http://netdoctor.co.uk/diseases/facts/eatingdisorders.htm, accessed August 14, 2009.

23. See http://seattletimes.nwsource.corn/html/living/2008829680_barbie09.html, accessed August 1, 2009.

24. M. L. Armstrong, A. E. Roberts, J. R. Koch, J. C. Saunders, D. C. Owen, and R. R. Anderson, "Motivation for Contemporary Tattoo Removal: A Shift in Identity," in *Archives of Dermatology*, 144(7), 2008, pp. 879–884.

24. Shari Roan, "Social Stigma Drives Some Women to Remove Tattoos" in *Los Angeles Times*, July 21, 2008, available at http://latimesblogs.latimes.com/booster_shots/2008/07/social-stigma-d.html, accessed August 14, 2009.

26. http://www.plasticsurgery.org/Documents/news-resources/statistics/2011-statistics/2011_Stats_Full_Report.pdf.

27. See the website of the American Society of Plastic Surgeons at http:///www.plasticsurgery.org/mediactr/92sexdis.html, accessed August 14, 2009.

28. See Lynne Luciano, *Looking Good: Male Body Image in Modern America* (New York: Hill and Wang, 2001).

29. Gimlin, *Body Work*, p. 102.

30. See Sam Fields, "Penis Enlargement Surgery," availabe at www.4-men.org/penisenlargementsurgery.html; and Randy Klein, "Penile Augmentation Surgery," in *Electronic Journal of Human Sexuality*, 2, March 1999, chapter 2, p. 1; chapter 5, pp. 8–9.

31. Letter testimonials to Dr. E. Douglas Whitehead, available at www.penile-enlargement-surgeon.com/diary.html, accessed August 14, 2009.

32. Amy Chozcik, "Virgin Territory: U.S. Women Seek a Second First Time" in *Wall Street Journal*, December 15, 2005.

33. See David L. Matlock, *Sex by Design* (Los Angeles: Demiurgus Press, 2004); see also www.drmatlock.com, accessed June 2, 2006.

34. Jules Michelet, cited in Darlaine C. Gardetto, "The Social Construction of the Female Orgasm, 1650–1890," paper presented at the annual meeting of the American Sociological Association, Atlanta, 1988, p. 18.

35. Cited in Barbara Ehrenreich and Deidre English, *For Her Own Good: 150 Years of Medical Advice to Women* (New York: Anchor, 1974).

36. Alfred Kinsey, Wendall Pomeroy, and Charles Martin, *Sexual Behavior in the Human Female* (Philadelphia: W. B. Saunders, 1953), p. 376.

37. Pauline Bart, "Male Views of Female Sexuality: From Freud's Phallacies to Fisher's Inexact Test," paper presented at the Second National Meeting of the Special Section of Psychosomatic Obstetrics and Gynecology, Key Biscayne, Florida, 1974, pp. 6–7.

38. Lillian Rubin, *Erotic Wars* (New York: Farrar, Straus and Giroux, 1991), pp. 28, 42; Billy Crystal, quoted in *Week*, May 10, 2002, p. 17.

39. Catharine MacKinnon, *Only Words* (Cambridge: Harvard University Press, 1996), p. 185.

40. The best recent work on this dilemma for girls is Deborah Tolman, *Dilemmas of Desire: Teenage Girls Talk About Sexuality* (Cambridge: Harvard University Press, 2002).

41. Stephanie Sanders and June Machover Reinisch, "Would You Say 'Had Sex'

42. Emmanuel Reynaud, *Holy Virility*, R. Schwartz, trans. (London: Pluto Press, 1983), p. 41.

43. See, for example, Carol Tavris, *The Mismeasure of Woman* (New York: Simon & Schuster, 1992); Harriet Lerner, *Women in Therapy* (New York: Harper and Row, 1989), chapter 2.

44. Laumann et al., *Social Organization of Sexuality*, p. 135.

45. Michael Kimmel and Rebecca Plante, "Sexual Fantasies and Gender Scripts: Heterosexual Men and Women Construct Their Ideal Sexual Encounters" in *Gendered Sexualities*, vol. 6 of *Advances in Gender Research*, ed. Patricia Gagné and Richard Tewksbury (Amsterdam: JAI Press, 2002).

46. See also E. Barbara Hariton and Jerome Singer, "Women's Fantasies During Sexual Intercourse: Normative and Theoretical Implications" in *Journal of Consulting and Clinical Psychology*, 42(3), 1974; Daniel Goleman, "Sexual Fantasies: What Are Their Hidden Meanings?" in *New York Times*, February 28, 1983; Daniel Goleman, "New View of Fantasy: Much Is Found Perverse?" in *New York Times*, May 7, 1991; Robert May, *Sex and Fantasy: Patterns of Male and Female Development* (New York: W. W. Norton, 1980); David Chick and Steven Gold, "A Review of Influences on Sexual Fantasy: Attitudes, Experience, Guilt and Gender" in *Imagination, Cognition and Personality*, 7(1), 1987–1988; Robert A. Mednick, "Gender Specific Variances in Sexual Fantasy" in *Journal of Personality Assessment*, 41(3), 1977; Diane Follingstad and C. Dawne Kimbrell, "Sexual Fantasies Revisited: An Expansion and Further Clarification of Variables Affecting Sex Fantasy Production" in *Archives of Sexual Behavior*, 15(6), 1986; Danielle Knafo and Yoram Jaffe, "Sexual Fantasizing in Males and Females" in *Journal of Research in Personality*, 18, 1984.

47. Robert Stoller, *Porn* (New Haven, CT: Yale University Press, 1991), p. 31.

48. For a review of the empirical literature on pornography, see Michael Kimmel and Annulla Linders, "Does Censorship Make a Difference? An Aggregate Empirical Analysis of Pornography and Rape" in *Journal of Psychology and Human Sexuality*, 8(3), 1996.

49. Rubin, *Erotic Wars*, p. 102; Carol Tavris and Carole Wade, *The Longest War* (New York: Harcourt Brace, 1984), p. 111.

50. Philip Blumstein and Pepper Schwartz, *American Couples* (New York: William Morrow, 1983), p. 279; Pepper Schwartz and Virginia Rutter, *The Gender of Sexuality* (Thousand Oaks, CA: Pine Forge Press, 1998), pp. 60–61. Of course, there are also systematic gender biases in the reporting of sexual experiences: Men tend to overstate their experiences, and women tend to understate theirs. So such wide discrepancies should be viewed with a skeptical eye.

51. Blumstein and Schwartz, *American Couples*, p. 234.

52. Laumann et al., *Social Organization of Sexuality*, p. 347.

53. Stevi Jackson, "The Social Construction of Female Sexuality" in *Feminism and Sexuality: A Reader*, S. Jackson and S. Scott, eds. (New York: Columbia University Press, 1996), p. 71.

54. Charlene Muehlenhard, "'Nice Women' Don't Say Yes and 'Real Men' Don't Say No: How Miscommunication and the Double Standard Can Cause Sexual Problems" in *Women and Therapy*, 7, 1988, pp. 100–101.

55. See Dwight Garner, "Endurance Condoms" in *New York Times Magazine*, December 15, 2002, p. 84.

56. See Jeffrey Fracher and Michael Kimmel, "Hard Issues and Soft Spots: Counseling Men About Sexuality" in *Handbook of Counseling and Psychotherapy with Men*, M. Scher, M. Stevens, G. Good, and G. Eichenfeld, eds. (Newbury Park, CA: Sage Publications, 1987).

57. Cited in Susan Bordo, *The Male Body*, p. 61. There is actually some evidence of Viagra-related violence against women and a sort of sexual "road rage."

58. See Bruce Handy, "The Viagra Craze" in *Time*, May 4, 1998, pp. 50–57; Christopher Hitchens, "Viagra Falls" in *Nation*, May 25, 1998, p. 8.

59. Rubin, *Erotic Wars*, p. 13; on rates of change in sexual activity, see A. C. Grunseit, S. Kippax, M. Baldo, P. A. Aggleton, and G. Slutkin, "Sexuality, Education and Young People's Sexual Behavior: A Review of Studies," manuscript from UNAID, 1997.

60. Amber Hollibaugh, "Desire for the Future: Radical Hope in Passion and Pleasure" in Jackson and Scott, *Feminism and Sexuality: A Reader*; Rubin, *Erotic Wars*, pp. 5, 46.

61. On rates of masturbation, see Laumann et al., *Social Organization of Sexuality*, p. 86; Schwartz and Rutter, *Gender of Sexuality*, p. 39. On sexual

attitudes, see Laumann et al., *Social Organization of Sexuality*, p. 507.

62. Tamar Lewin, "One in Five Teenagers Has Sex Before 15, Study Finds" in *New York Times*, May 20, 2003.

63. Laumann et al., *Social Organization of Sexuality*; Schwartz and Rutter, *Gender of Sexuality*, p. 165.

64. *Newsweek*, December 9, 2002, pp. 61–71.

65. Peter S. Bearman and Hannah Bruckner, "Promising the Future: Virginity Pledges and First Intercourse" in *American Journal of Sociology*, 106(4), 2001, pp. 859–912; see also Alan Guttmacher Institute, "Why Is Teenage Pregnancy Declining? The Role of Abstinence, Sexual Activity and Contraceptive Use," 1996, available at www.agi.org; see also Ceci Connolly, "Teen Pledges Barely Cut STD Rates, Study Says" in *Washington Post*, March 19, 2005, p. A3.

66. See Barbara Risman and Pepper Schwartz, "After the Sexual Revolution: Gender Politics in Teen Dating" in *Contexts*, 1(1), 2002, pp. 16–24.

67. Willard Waller, "The Rating and Dating Complex" in *American Sociological Review*, 2, October 1937, pp. 727–734.

68. "'Hookups': Characteristics and Correlates of College Students' Spontaneous and Anonymous Sexual Experiences" in *Journal of Sex Research*, 37(1), February 2000, pp. 76–88.

69. Interview conducted for my book *Guyland: The Perilous World Where Boys Become Men* (New York: HarperCollins, 2008), p. 210.

70. Norval Glenn and Elizabeth Marquardt, *Hooking Up, Hanging Out, and Hoping for Mr. Right: College Women on Dating and Mating Today* (New York: Institute for American Values, 2001).

71. Laumann et al., *Social Organization of Sexuality*; see also Schwartz and Rutter, *Gender of Sexuality*, pp. 102–103; see Sam Janus, *The Janus Report on Sexual Behavior* (New York: John Wiley, 1993), pp. 315–316; Blumstein and Schwartz, *American Couples*; see also Lynne Segal, ed., *New Sexual Agendas* (New York: New York University Press, 1997), p. 67.

72. Gina Kolata, "Women and Sex: On This Topic, Science Blushes" in *New York Times*, June 21, 1998, p. 3; young woman cited in Rubin, *Erotic Wars*, p. 14.

73. Rubin, *Erotic Wars*, p. 120.

74. Laura Sessions Stepp, "Study: Half of All Teens Have Had Oral Sex" in *Washington Post*, September 15, 2005; Sharon Jayson, "Teens Define Sex in New Ways" in *USA Today*, October 18, 2005.

75. Cited in Rubin, *Erotic Wars*, p. 58; Mary Koss, L. A. Goodman, A. Browne, L. F. Fitzgerald, G. P. Keita, and N. F. Russo, *No Safe Haven: Male Violence Against Women at Home, at Work, and in the Community* (Washington, DC: American Psychological Association, 1994).

76. Mary Koss, P. T. Dinero, C. A. Seibel, and S. L. Cox, "Stranger and Acquaintance Rape: Are There Differences in the Victim's Experience?" in *Psychology of Women Quarterly*, 12(1), 1988.

77. Laumann et al., *Social Organization of Sexuality*, p. 336; see also Koss et al., *No Safe Haven*.

78. Ronald F. Levant, "Nonrelational Sexuality in Men" in *Men and Sex: New Psychological Perspectives*, R. Levant and G. Brooks, eds. (New York: John Wiley, 1997), p. 270.

79. See, for example, J. O. Billy, G. K. Tanfer, W. R. Grady, and D. H. Klepinger, "The Sexual Behavior of Men in the United States" in *Family Planning Perspectives*, 25(2), 1993; Laumann et al., *Social Organization of Sexuality*.

80. Gary Brooks, *The Centerfold Syndrome* (San Francisco: Jossey-Bass, 1995), and "The Centerfold Syndrome" in *Men and Sex: New Psychological Perspectives*, R. Levant and G. Brooks, eds. (New York: John Wiley, 1997). See also Levant, "Nonrelational Sexuality," p. 19; Joni Johnston, "Appearance Obsession: Women's Reactions to Men's Objectification of Their Bodies" in Levant and Brooks, *Men and Sex*, pp. 79, 101.

81. Glenn Good and Nancy B. Sherrod, "Men's Resolution of Nonrelational Sex Across the Lifespan" in Levant and Brooks, *Men and Sex*, pp. 189, 190.

82. See Good and Sherrod, "Men's Resolution of Nonrelational Sex," p. 186.

83. Peter Wyden and Barbara Wyden, *Growing Up Straight: What Every Thoughtful Parent Should Know About Homosexuality* (New York: Trident Press, 1968).

84. Richard Green, *The "Sissy Boy" Syndrome* (New Haven, CT: Yale University Press, 1986).

85. George Gilder, *Men and Marriage* (Gretna, LA: Pelican Publishers, 1985).

86. Joe Jackson, "Real Men"; for a sociological investigation of the gender organization of clone life, see Martin P. Levine, *Gay Macho: The Life and Death of the Homosexual Clone*, M. S. Kimmel, ed. (New York: New York University Press, 1998).

87. Cited in Steve Chapple and David Talbot, *Burning Desires: Sex in America* (New York: Doubleday, 1989), p. 356.

88. G. Clarke, "Conforming and Contesting with (a) Difference: How Lesbian Students and Teachers Manage Their Identities" *International Studies in Sociology of Education*, 6(2), 1996, 191–209.

89. Alan Bell and Martin Weinberg, *Homosexualities* (New York: Simon & Schuster, 1978); William Masters, Virginia Johnson, and Richard Kolodny, *Human Sexuality* (New York: Harper and Row, 1978); Blumstein and Schwartz, *American Couples*, p. 317.

90. American Psychological Association, "Equal Level of Commitment and Relationship Satisfaction Found Among Gay and Heterosexual Couples" in *Science News*, January 23, 2008, http://www.sciencedaily.com/releases/2008/01/080122101929.htm.

91. Data from Blumstein and Schwartz, *American Couples*; woman is quoted in Bell and Weinberg, *Homosexualities*, p. 220.

92. Masters, Johnson, and Kolodny, *Human Sexuality*.

93. Ken Plummer, *Sexual Stigma: An Interactionist Account* (New York: Routledge, 1975), p. 102.

94. Gerald Davison and John Neale, *Abnormal Psychology: An Experimental-Clinical Approach* (New York: John Wiley, 1974), p. 293.

95. See Jeni Loftus, "America's Liberalization in Attitudes Toward Homosexuality, 1973–1998" in *American Sociological Review*, 66, October 2001, pp. 762–782.

96. Muehlenhard, "Nice Women Don't Say Yes"; John Gagnon and Stuart Michaels, "Answer No Questions: The Theory and Practice of Resistance to Deviant Categorization," unpublished manuscript, 1989, p. 2. On the impact of homophobia on heterosexual men's lives, see also Richard Goldstein, "The Hate That Makes Men Straight" in *Village Voice*, December 22, 1998.

97. See Laumann et al., *Social Organization of Sexuality*, pp. 82–84, 98, 177, 192, 302–309, 518–529.

98. Rubin, *Erotic Wars*, p. 165.

99. Julia Heiman, J. Scott Long, Shawna N. Smith, William A. Fisher, Michael S. Sand, and Raymond C. Rosen, "Sexual Satisfaction and Relationship Happiness in Midlife and Older Couples in Five Countries" in *Archives of Sexual Behavior*, 40, 2011, pp. 741–753.

100. "Does Equality Produce a Better Sex Life?" in *Newsday*, April 19, 2006; see Edward O. Laumann, Anthony Paik, Dale Glasser, Jeong-Han Kang, Tianfu Wang, Bernard Levinson, Edson Moreira, Anfredo Nocolosi, and Clive Gingell, "A Cross-National Study of Subjective Sexual Well-Being Among Older Women and Men: Findings from the Global Study of Sexual Attitudes and Behaviors" in *Archives of Sexual Behavior*, 35(2), April 2006, pp. 145–161.

101. See John Gottman, *Why Marriages Succeed or Fail* (New York: Simon & Schuster, 1995).

102. See on these changes generally, Levine, *Gay Macho*.

103. World Health Organization, "Adults and Children Estimated to Be Living with HIV/AIDS as of End 2002," http://www.who.int/hiv/facts/plwha_m.jpg, accessed August 14, 2009.

104. Michele Landsberg, "U.N. Recognizes Women Double Victims of AIDS" in *Toronto Star*, July 1, 2001.

105. World Health Organization, "Adults and Children Estimated."

106. Lawrence K. Altman, "Swift Rise Seen in H.I.V. Cases for Gay Blacks" in *New York Times*, June 1, 2001, p. A1.

107. See Michael Kimmel and Martin Levine, "A Hidden Factor in AIDS: 'Real' Men's Hypersexuality" in *Los Angeles Times*, June 3, 1991. Of course, the route taken by women to high-risk behaviors is also gendered. Whereas men are often eager to demonstrate manhood by engaging in such high-risk behaviors, women typically become IV drug users in the context of a "romantic" relationship or as part of a sexual initiation. And some women are also exposed to risk from HIV by male sexual partners who lie to them about their HIV status. I am grateful to Rose Weitz for pointing this out to me.

108. See Will Courtenay, "Engendering Health: A Social Constructionist Examination of Men's Health Beliefs and Behaviors" in *Psychology of Men and Masculinity*, 1(1), 2000, pp. 4–15; "Men's Health," editorial in *British Medical Journal*, January 13, 1996, pp. 69–70. For more about men's health specifically, see *Men's Health on the Internet*, M. Sandra Wood and Janet M. Coggan, eds. (Binghamton, NY: Haworth Information Press, 2002).

109. Will H. Courtenay, "College Men's Health: An Overview and a Call to Action" in *Journal of American College Health*, 46(6), 1998; see also Lesley Doyal, "Sex, Gender and Health: The Need for a New Approach" in *British Medical Journal*, November 3, 2001, pp. 1061–1063.

110. Linda Villarosa, "As Black Men Move into Middle Age, Dangers Rise" in *New York Times*, September 23, 2002, pp. F1, 8.

111. See Diana Jean Schemo, "Study Calculates the Effects of College Drinking in the U.S." in *New York Times*, April 10, 2002, p. A21; Jodie Morse, "Women on a Binge" in *Time*, April 1, 2002, pp. 57–61; Barbara Ehrenreich, "Libation as Liberation?" in *Time*, April 1, 2002, p. 62.

112. See Judith Lorber, *Gender and the Social Construction of Illness* (Newbury Park, CA: Pine Forge Press, 1997).

113. Amartya Sen, "The Many Faces of Gender Inequality" in *New Republic*, September 17, 2001, pp. 35–40.

114. See, for example, "Whatever Happened to Men's Health?" published by Men's Health America, www.egroups.com/group/menshealth, accessed August 14, 2009.

CHAPTER FOURTEEN

1. *Youth and Violence: Psychology's Response*, Vol. 1 (Washington, DC: American Psychological Association Commission on Violence and Youth, 1993); "Saving Youth from Violence" in *Carnegie Quarterly*, 39(1), Winter 1994.

2. Federal Bureau of Investigation, *Uniform Crime Report* (2013), table 42: "Arrests by Sex."

3. National Academy of Sciences, cited in Michael Gottfredson and Travis Hirschi, *A General Theory of Crime* (Stanford, CA: Stanford University Press, 1990), p. 145. See also Steven Barkan, "Why Do Men Commit Almost All Homicides and Assault?" in *Criminology: A Sociological Understanding* (Englewood Cliffs, NJ: Prentice Hall, 1997); *Masculinities and Violence*, Lee Bowker, ed. (Thousand Oaks, CA: Sage Publications, 1998).

4. See James Q. Wilson and Richard Herrnstein, *Crime and Human Nature* (New York: Simon & Schuster, 1985), p. 121. For descriptions of various biological theories of violence, see also chapter 2.

5. I summarize these arguments in chapter 2.

6. Judith Lorber, *Paradoxes of Gender* (New Haven CT: Yale University Press, 1994), p. 39. On the sociology of men's violence, see especially Michael Kaufman, *Cracking the Armour: Power, Pain and the Lives of Men* (Toronto: Viking, 1993); and Michael Kaufman, "The Construction of Masculinity and the Triad of Men's Violence" in *Men's Lives*, 4th ed., M. Kimmel and M. Messner, eds. (Boston: Allyn and Bacon, 1997); see also Jackson Toby, "Violence and the Masculine Ideal: Some Qualitative Data" in *Annals of the American Academy of Political and Social Science*, 364, March 1966.

7. Barbara Ehrenreich, *Blood Rites: Origins and History of the Passions of War* (New York: Metropolitan Books, 1997), pp. 45, 127.

8. Signe Howell and Roy Willis, *Societies at Peace* (New York: Routledge, 1983).

9. Howell and Willis, *Societies at Peace*, p. 38.

10. See, for example, D. Stanistreet, C. Bambra, and A. Scott-Samuel, "Is Patriarchy the Source of Men's Higher Mortality?" in *Journal of Epidemiology and Community Health*, 59, 2005, pp. 873–876.

11. See also Elizabeth Stanko, *Everyday Violence* (London: Pandora, 1990), p. 71.

12. A. Cooper and E. L. Smith, *Homicide in the U.S. Known to Law Enforcement, 2011* (Washington, DC: U.S. Department of Justice, Bureau of Justice Statistics, 2013), http://www.bjs.gov/index.cfm?ty=pbdetail&iid=4863.

13. Fox Butterfield, *All God's Children: The Bosket Family and the American Tradition of Violence* (New York: Avon, 1995), p. 329. *Bureau of Justice Statistics*, 2007.

14. Butterfield, *All God's Children*, p. 325; see also Wray Herbert, "Behind Bars" in *U.S. News & World Report*, March 23, 1998, p. 33. See also Jay Livingston, "Crime and Sex: It's a Man's World" in *Crime and Criminology*, 2nd ed. (Englewood Cliffs, NJ: Prentice Hall, 1996).

15. See Public Safety Performance Project, "One in 100: Behind Bars in America 2008," Pew Charitable Trusts, February 28, 2008, http://www.pewcenteronthestates.org/uploadedFiles/One-in-100.pdf, accessed August 1, 2009.

16. Cited in June Stephenson, *Men Are Not Cost Effective* (Napa, CA: Diemer, Smith, 1991), p. 248.

17. Joe Sharkey, "Slamming the Brakes on Hot Pursuit" in *New York Times*, December 14, 1997, p. 3.

18. Centers for Disease Control and Prevention, "Youth Violence: Facts at a Glance," http://www.cdc.gov/ViolencePrevention/pdf/YV-DataSheet-a.pdf.

19. Freda Adler, *Sisters in Crime* (New York: McGraw-Hill, 1975), p. 10; Rita Simon, *Women and Crime* (Washington, DC: U.S. Government Printing Office, 1975), p. 40.

20. See Patricia Pearson, *When She Was Bad: Violent Women and the Myth of Innocence* (New York: Viking, 1998); see also Larissa MacFarquhar, "Femmes Fatales" in *New Yorker*, March 9, 1998, pp. 88–91.

21. Malcolm Feely and Deborah L. Little, "The Vanishing Female: The Decline of Women in the Criminal Process" in *Law and Society Review*, 25(4), 1991, p. 739.

22. Darrell J. Steffensmeier, "Trends in Female Crime: It's Still a Man's World" in *The Criminal Justice System and Women*, B. R. Price and N. J. Sokoloff, eds. (New York: Clark, Boardman, 1982), p. 121.

23. John O'Neil, "Homicide Rates Fall Among Couples" in *New York Times*, October 23, 2001, p. E8.

24. Erich Goode, personal communication, December 5, 2002; Jerome Skolnick, personal communication, December 5, 2002; see also Erich Goode, *Deviant Behavior*, 5th ed. (Englewood Cliffs, NJ: Prentice Hall), p. 127; and Kathleen Daly, *Gender*

Crime and Punishment (New Haven, CT: Yale University Press, 1994).

25. See Laura Dugan, Daniel Nagin, and Richard Rosenfeld, "Explaining the Decline in Intimate Partner Homicide: The Effects of Changing Domesticity, Women's Status and Domestic Violence Resources" in *Homicide Studies* 3(3), 1999, pp. 187–214; and Richard Rosenfeld, "Changing Relationships Between Men and Women: A Note on the Decline in Intimate Partner Homicide" in *Homicide Studies*, 1(1), 1997, pp. 72–83; Chris Huffine, personal communication.

26. Jack Katz, *Seductions of Crime: Moral and Sensual Attractions in Doing Evil* (New York: Basic Books, 1988), p. 71.

27. Jack Katz, *Seductions of Crime*, p. 247; see also James Messerschmidt, *Masculinities and Crime* (Lanham, MD: Rowman and Littlefield, 1993), especially p. 107; and Jody Miller, "The Strengths and Limits of 'Doing Gender' for Understanding Street Crime" in *Theoretical Criminology*, 6(4), 2002, pp. 433–460.

28. Darrell Steffensmeier and Ellie Allan, "Criminal Behavior: Gender and Age" in *Criminology: A Contemporary Handbook*, J. F. Sheley, ed. (Mountain View, CA: Wadsworth, 1995), p. 85.

29. David Adams, "Biology Does Not Make Men More Aggressive Than Women" in *Of Mice and Women: Aspects of Female Aggression*, K. Bjorkvist and P. Niemela, eds. (San Diego: Academic Press, 1992), p. 14; see also Pearson, *When She Was Bad*. But see also Coramae Richey Mann, *When Women Kill* (Albany: State University of New York Press, 1996).

30. Adam Fraczek, "Patterns of Aggressive-Hostile Behavior Orientation Among Adolescent Boys and Girls" in Bjorkvist and Niemala, *Of Mice and Women: Aspects of Female Aggression*, K. Bjorkvist and P. Niemela, eds.; Kirsti M. J. Lagerspetz and Kaj Bjorqvist, "Indirect Aggression in Boys and Girls" in *Aggressive Behavior: Current Perspectives*, L. R. Huesmann, ed. (New York: Plenum, 1994).

31. Vappu Viemero, "Changes in Female Aggression over a Decade" in Bjorkvist and Niemala, *Of Mice and Women*, p. 105.

32. See, for example, Rachel Simmons, *Odd Girl Out: The Hidden Culture of Aggression in Girls* (New York: Harcourt, 2002); Rosalind Wiseman, *Queen Bees and Wannabes: A Parents' Guide to Helping Your Daughter Survive Cliques, Gossip, Boyfriends, and Other Realities of Adolescence* (New York: Crown, 2002); Sharon Lamb, *The Secret Lives of Girls: Sex, Play, Aggression and Their Guilt* (New York: Free Press, 2002). See also Margaret Talbot, "Mean Girls"

in *New York Times Magazine*, February 24, 2002, pp. 24–29, 40, 58, 64–65; and Carol Tavris, "Are Girls Really as Mean as Books Say They Are?" in *Chronicle of Higher Education*, July 5, 2002, pp. B7–9.

33. Simmons, *Odd Girl Out*.

34. See, for example, Ann Donahue, "Population of Female Inmates Reaches Record" in *USA Today*, July 21, 1997; Steffensmeier and Allen, "Criminal Behavior," p. 85.

35. Helen Caldicott, *Missile Envy* (New York: William Morrow, 1984); Barbara Ehrenreich, "The Violence Debate Since Adam and Eve" in *Test the West: Gender Democracy and Violence* (Vienna: Federal Minister of Women's Affairs, 1994), p. 34.

36. R. W. Connell, "Masculinity, Violence and War" in *Men's Lives*, 3rd ed., M. Kimmel and M. Messner, eds. (Boston: Allyn and Bacon, 1995), p. 129.

37. David Halberstam, *The Best and the Brightest* (New York: Random House, 1972), p. 531.

38. Maureen Dowd, "Rummy Runs Wampant" in *New York Times*, October 30, 2002, p. A29.

39. Cited in Brian Easlea, *Fathering the Unthinkable: Masculinity, Scientists and the Nuclear Arms Race* (London: Pluto Press, 1983), p. 117; see also his "Patriarchy, Scientists and Nuclear Warriors" in *Beyond Patriarchy: Essays by Men on Pleasure, Power and Change*, M. Kaufman, ed. (Toronto: Oxford University Press, 1987); I. F. Stone, "Machismo in Washington" in *Men and Masculinity*, J. Pleck and J. Sawyer, eds. (Englewood Cliffs, NJ: Prentice Hall, 1974); Carol Cohn, "'Clean Bombs' and Clean Language" in *Women, Militarism and War: Essays in History, Politics and Social Theory*, J. B. Elshtain, ed. (Savage, MD: Rowman and Littlefield, 1990), p. 137.

40. Cohn, "'Clean Bombs,'" p. 35.

41. Wayne Ewing, "The Civic Advocacy of Violence" in *Men's Lives*, M. Kimmel and M. Messner, eds. (New York: Macmillan, 1989).

42. Jackson's mother, cited in Butterfield, *All God's Children*, p. 11; see also *The Civilization of Crime*, Eric A. Johnson and Eric H. Monkkonen, eds. (Urbana: University of Illinois Press, 1996); David Courtwright, *Violent Land: Single Men and Social Disorder from the Frontier to the Inner City* (Cambridge: Harvard University Press, 1997). Also see the trilogy by Richard Slotkin, *Regeneration Through Violence: The Mythology of the American Frontier, 1600–1860* (New York: Atheneum, 1973); *The Fatal Environment: The Myth of the Frontier in the Age of Industrialization* (New York: Atheneum, 1985); *Gunfighter Nation: The Myth of the Frontier in Twentieth Century America* (New York: Atheneum, 1992).

43. Margaret Mead, *And Keep Your Powder Dry* (New York: William Morrow, 1965), pp. 151, 157.

44. J. Adams Puffer, *The Boy and His Gang* (Boston: Houghton, Mifflin, 1912), p. 91.

45. James Gilligan, *Violence* (New York: Putnam, 1996).

46. Butterfield, *All God's Children*, pp. 206–207; Kit Roane, "New York Gangs Mimic California Original" in *New York Times*, September 14, 1997, p. A37; others cited in Jack Katz, *Seductions of Crime*, pp. 88, 107; Vic Seidler, "Raging Bull" in *Achilles Heel*, 5, 1980, p. 9; Hans Toch, "Hypermasculinity and Prison Violence" in *Masculinities and Violence*, L. Bowker, ed. (Newbury Park, CA: Sage Publications, 1998), p. 170.

47. Data from *New York Times*, August 25, 1997; U.S. Department of Justice, *Family Violence*, 1997; Reva Siegel, "The 'Rule of Love': Wife Beating as Prerogative and Privacy" in *Yale Law Journal*, 105(8), June 1996; Deborah Rhode, *Speaking of Sex: The Denial of Gender Inequality* (Cambridge: Harvard University Press, 1997), p. 108; Stephenson, *Men Are Not Cost Effective*, p. 285; see also Neil Websdale and Meda Chesney-Lind, "Doing Violence to Women: Research Synthesis on the Victimization of Women" in Bowker, *Masculinities and Violence*, L. Bowker, ed.

48. Peggy Reeves Sanday, *Female Power and Male Dominance* (New York: Cambridge University Press, 1981); quote from Larry Baron and Murray Straus, "Four Theories of Rape: A Macrosociological Analysis" in *Social Problems*, 34(5), 1987, p. 481.

49. "By the Numbers" in *Nation,* June 23/30, 2014, p. 4.

50. See, for example, Diana Scully, *Understanding Sexual Violence: A Study of Convicted Rapists* (New York: HarperCollins, 1990); Diana Russell, *Rape in Marriage* (New York: Macmillan, 1982), and *Sexual Exploitation* (Beverly Hills, CA: Sage Publications, 1984); Rhode, *Speaking of Sex*, pp. 119–120; Allan Johnson, "On the Prevalence of Rape in the United States" in *Signs*, 6(1), 1980, p. 145. For more on this, see also Diana Scully and J. Marolla, "'Riding the Bull at Gilley's': Convicted Rapists Describe the Rewards of Rape" in *Social Problems*, 32, 1985.

51. National Center for Injury Prevention and Control, *National Intimate Partner and Sexual Violence Survey: 2010 Summary Report*, http://www.cdc.gov/ViolencePrevention/pdf/NISVS_Report2010-a.pdf.

52. U.S. Department of Justice, "Child Rape Victims, 1992" (NCJ-147001), June 1994; Eugene Kanin, "False Rape Allegations" in *Archives of Sexual Behavior*, 23(1), 1994.

53. Johnson, "On the Prevalence of Rape," p. 145; Scully, *Understanding Sexual Violence*, p. 53.

54. Mary Koss, Christine A. Gidycz, and Nadine Misniewski, "The Scope of Rape: Incidence and Prevalence of Sexual Aggression and Victimization in a National Sample of Higher Education Students" in *Journal of Consulting and Clinical Psychology*, 55(2), 1987. Bonnie Fisher, Francis Cullen, and Michael Turner, *National Social Victimization of College Women* (Washington, DC: United States Department of Justice, OJP, 2000).

55. Dean G. Kilpatrick, Heidi S. Resnick, Kenneth J. Ruggiero, Lauren M. Conoscenti, Jenna McCauley. *Drug-Facilitated, Incapacitated, and Forcible Rape: A National Study (NCJ 219181)*, National Institute of Justice, May 2007. NCJ 219181, https://www.ncjrs.gov/pdffiles1/nij/grants/219181.pdf. NCJ221153, https://www.ncjrs.gov/pdffiles1/nij/grants/221153.pdf.

56. John Briere and Neil Malamuth, "Self-Reported Likelihood of Sexually Aggressive Behavior: Attitudinal Versus Sexual Explanations" in *Journal of Research in Personality*, 17, 1983; Todd Tieger, "Self-Rated Likelihood of Raping and Social Perception of Rape" in *Journal of Research in Personality*, 15, 1991.

57. J. L. Herman, "Considering Sex Offenders: A Model of Addiction" in *Signs*, 13, 1988; Bernard Lefkowitz, *Our Guys* (Berkeley: University of California Press, 1997); Don Terry, "Gang Rape of Three Girls Leaves Fresno Shaken and Questioning" in *New York Times*, April 28, 1998; see also Jane Hood, "'Let's Get a Girl': Male Bonding Rituals in America" in *Men's Lives*, 4th ed., M. Kimmel and M. Messner, eds. (Boston: Allyn and Bacon, 1997).

58. Scully, *Understanding Sexual Violence*, pp. 74, 140, 159, 166.

59. Tim Beneke, *Men on Rape* (New York: St. Martin's Press, 1982), p. 81.

60. See Mary P. Koss, Christine Gidycz, and Nadine Misniewski, "The Scope of Rape," and Scott Boeringer, "Pornography and Sexual Aggression: Associations of Violence and Nonviolent Depictions with Rape and Rape Proclivity" in *Deviant Behavior*, 15, 1994, pp. 289–304.

61. Murray Straus, Richard Gelles, and Suzanne Steinmetz, *Behind Closed Doors* (Garden City, NY: Anchor Books, 1981).

62. Diana Russell, *Rape in Marriage* (New York: Macmillan, 1982); David Finklehor and Kersti Yllo, *License to Rape: Sexual Abuse of Wives* (Newbury Park, CA: Sage Publications, 1985), pp. 217, 208. On marital rape generally, see also Raquel Kennedy Bergen, "Surviving Wife Rape: How Women Define and Cope with the Violence" in *Violence Against Women*, 1(2), 1995, pp. 117–138;

and the special issue of *Violence Against Women,* 5(9), September 1999, she edited; Raquel Kennedy Bergen, *Wife Rape: Understanding the Response of Survivors and Service Providers* (Thousand Oaks, CA: Sage Publications, 1996); Anne L. Buckborough, "Family Law: Recent Developments in the Law of Marital Rape" in *Annual Survey of American Law,* 1989; "To Have and to Hold: The Marital Rape Exemption and the Fourteenth Amendment" in *Harvard Law Review,* 99, 1986.

63. Gelles, cited in Joanne Schulman, "Battered Women Score Major Victories in New Jersey and Massachusetts Marital Rape Cases" in *Clearinghouse Review,* 15(4), 1981, p. 345.

64. Ehrenreich, "Violence Debate," p. 30.

65. Armin Brott, "The Battered Statistic Syndrome" in *Washington Post,* July 1994.

66. R. L. McNeely and G. Robinson-Simpson, "The Truth About Domestic Violence: A Falsely Framed Issue" in *Social Work,* 32(6), 1987.

67. Susan Steinmetz, "The Battered Husband Syndrome" in *Victimology,* 2, 1978; M. D. Pagelow, "The 'Battered Husband Syndrome': Social Problem or Much Ado About Little?" in *Marital Violence,* N. Johnson, ed. (London: Routledge and Kegan Paul, 1985); Elizabeth Pleck, Joseph Pleck, M. Grossman, and Pauline Bart, "The Battered Data Syndrome: A Comment on Steinmetz's Article" in *Victimology,* 2, 1978; G. Storch, "Claim of 12 Million Battered Husbands Takes a Beating" in *Miami Herald,* August 7, 1978; Jack C. Straton, "The Myth of the 'Battered Husband Syndrome'" in *Masculinities,* 2(4), 1994; Kerrie James, "Truth or Fiction: Men as Victims of Domestic Violence?" in *Australian and New Zealand Journal of Family Therapy,* 17(3), 1996; Betsy Lucal, "The Problem with 'Battered Husbands'" in *Deviant Behavior,* 16, 1995, pp. 95–112.

    After the first edition of this book was published, I became increasingly distressed that social science research was being so badly misused for political ends. So I undertook an attempt to thoroughly investigate the case of "gender symmetry." See Michael Kimmel, "Gender Symmetry in Domestic Violence: A Substantive and Methodological Research Review" in *Violence Against Women,* 8(11), November 2002, pp. 1332–1363. Useful data can be found in Callie Marie Rennison, *Intimate Partner Violence and Age of Victim, 1993–1999* (Washington, DC: U.S. Department of Justice, Bureau of Justice Statistics, 2001).

68. See Kerrie James, "Truth or Fiction," which found the same results in a sample of Australian and New Zealand couples.

69. J. E. Stets and Murray Straus, "The Marriage License as a Hitting License: A Comparison of Assaults in Dating, Cohabiting and Married Couples" in *Journal of Family Violence,* 4(2), 1989; J. E. Stets and Murray Straus, "Gender Differences in Reporting Marital Violence and Its Medical and Psychological Consequences" in *Physical Violence in American Families,* M. Straus and R. Gelles, eds. (New Brunswick, NJ: Transaction Publishers, 1990).

70. Bureau of Justice Statistics, *Family Violence.*

71. Glanda Kaufman Kantor, Jana Janinski, and E. Aldorondo, "Sociocultural Status and Incidence of Marital Violence in Hispanic Families" in *Violence and Victims,* 9(3), 1994; and Jana Janinski, "Dynamics of Partner Violence and Types of Abuse and Abusers," available at http://www.nnfr.org/nnfr/research/pv_ch1.html; Kersti Yllo, personal communication.

72. See Richard Gelles, "Domestic Violence: Not an Even Playing Field," and "Domestic Violence Factoids," both available from Minnesota Center Against Violence and Abuse, www.mincava.umn.edu. See also Kimmel, "'Gender Symmetry.'"

73. Bachman and Saltzman, "Violence Against Women," p. 6; Straus and Gelles, *Physical Violence in American Families.* Given that Schwartz's estimate of the actual rates is exactly the same as that used earlier by journalist Armin Brott, I wonder if he would say that we ought to consider this "the unfortunate behavior" of a few crazy women.

74. See, for example, Kersti Yllo, "Through a Feminist Lens: Gender, Power, and Violence" in *Current Controversies on Family Violence,* R. J. Gelles and D. Loseke, eds. (Thousand Oaks, CA: Sage Publications, 1993).

75. Neil Jacobson and John Gottman, *When Men Batter Women* (New York: Simon & Schuster, 1998), p. 36.

76. C. Saline, "Bleeding in the Suburbs" in *Philadelphia Magazine,* March 1984, p. 82; Straus et al., *Behind Closed Doors;* R. L. Hampton, "Family Violence and Homicides in the Black Community: Are They Linked?" in *Violence in the Black Family: Correlates and Consequences* (Lexington, MA: Lexington Books, 1987); R. L. Hampton and Richard Gelles, "Violence Towards Black Women in a Nationally Representative Sample of Black Families" in *Journal of Comparative Family Studies,* 25(1), 1994.

77. Noel Cazenave and Murray Straus, "Race, Class, Network Embeddedness and Family Violence: A Search for Potent Support Systems" in Straus and

Gelles, *Physical Violence in American Families*; Pam Belluck, "Women's Killers Are Very Often Their Partners" in *New York Times*, March 31, 1997, p. B1.

78. Cited in Stephenson, *Men Are Not Cost Effective*, p. 300; Dorie Klein, "Violence Against Women: Some Considerations Regarding Its Causes and Elimination" in *The Criminal Justice System and Women*, B. Price and N. Sokoloff, eds. (New York: Clark Boardman, 1982), p. 212.

79. James Messerschmidt, *Masculinities and Crime* (Totowa, NJ: Rowman and Littlefield, 1993), p. 185; Elizabeth Stanko, "The Image of Violence" in *Criminal Justices Matters*, 8, 1992, p. 3.

80. Myriam Miedzian, *Boys Will Be Boys: Breaking the Link Between Masculinity and Violence* (New York: Doubleday, 1991), p. 298.

EPILOGUE

1. See Judith Lorber, *Breaking the Bowls: Degendering and Feminist Change* (New York: W. W. Norton, 2005); and Lisa Brush, review of Lorber in *Contemporary Sociology*, 35(3), 2006, p. 246.

2. Kate Millett, *Sexual Politics* (New York: Random House, 1969).

3. Floyd Dell, "Feminism for Men" in *The Masses*, February 1917, reprinted in *Against the Tide: Profeminist Men in the United States, 1776–1990 (A Documentary History)*, M. S. Kimmel and T. Mosmiller, eds. (Boston: Beacon Press, 1992).

4. Robert Jay Lifton, *The Protean Self* (New York: Basic Books, 1994). See also Cynthia Fuchs Epstein, "The Multiple Realities of Sameness and Difference: Ideology and Practice" in *Journal of Social Issues*, 53(2), 1997.

Sources for Chapter Opening Art

Chapter 2   © GraphicaArtis/Corbis

Chapter 3   © Emilie CHAIX/Photononstop/Corbis

Chapter 4   Northern Sun Merchandising

Chapter 5   Brent Stirton/Getty Images
Purestock/Getty Images RF

Chapter 6   Office of the Governor of Alaska

Chapter 7   © Design Pics Inc / Alamy Stock Photo
© Corbis

Chapter 8   © 1991 The New York Post

Chapter 9   TinaImages/Shutterstock

Chapter 10   Photo by Joe Raedle/Getty Images

Chapter 11   Courtesy of Dr. Elizabeth Bell

Chapter 12   Marili Forastieri
© Stock Connection Blue/Alamy Stock Photo

Chapter 13   AP Photo/Remy de la Mauviniere
Photo by Alan Oxley/BIPs/Getty Images

Chapter 14   © Reuters/Corbis

Index

Abbott, John S. C., 156
Abercrombie Kids, 399
Abortion, 63, 160, 180, 188,
 420, 468
Ackard, Diann M., 426
Acker, Joan, 130–131, 133
Acquaintance rape, 470
Addams, Jane, 156
Adler, Freda, 458
Adler, Roy Douglas, 306
Adolescence/adolescents.
 See Youth
Adonis Complex, 401
Adoption studies, 41–42
Advertising, 345, 350–351
Affective individualism, 154
Affirmative action, 121, 197, 305
Afghanistan
 gender inequality in, 78
 sexual assault of female troops
 in, 468
Africa
 AIDS-HIV in, 442
 circumcision in, 71, 73
 market economy of, 65
African Americans
 AIDS-HIV in, 442
 body image issues in, 399–400
 brain research, 33
 domestic violence and, 478, 479
 education and, 218, 231, 232
 family life of, 159
 feminism and, 340
 friendship and, 382–383
 health and, 444
 homicide rate in, 453
 housework division in, 169
 incarceration rate for, 455
 lesbianism in, 187
 the media and, 354
 out-of-wedlock births in,
 152, 180
 politics and, 316f, 317

religion and, 244, 246, 248
sexuality and, 332–333, 438
wages of, 281, 282, 283f,
 286t, 286f
women's position compared
 with, 120, 270
in the workplace, 262, 264,
 270–272, 273, 287, 292
Age
 criminal offenders by, 456f
 divorce and, 190
 friendship and, 383
 gender and, 125–127
 homicide rates by, 457f
 media and, 345
 midlife crisis, 124–125
 sexuality and, 439
 of video gamers, 360
 violence and, 456
 wages and, 284, 285
Age of Consent Act of
 1891, 332
Agents of socialization, 123
Aggravated assault, 449
Aggression. See Violence/
 aggression
Agnes (trans woman), 140–142
Ahrons, Constance, 188
AIDS-HIV, 39–40, 73, 127, 422,
 441–444, 446
 prevalence and distribution of,
 442, 443f
 sex education effect on rates
 of, 421
Alexander, Richard, 27
Alexithymia, 431
Allen, Paula Gunn, 78
Allen, Woody, 418–419
Alliance theory, 66
Almeida, David, 13
5-Alpha reductase, 51, 138
Alyha, 78
Amato, Paul, 190, 193

America as a Civilization
 (Lerner), 159
American Academy of
 Pediatrics, 198
American Association of
 University Women
 (AAUW), 208, 212, 232
American Civil Liberties
 Union, 232
American Psychiatric
 Association, 48, 90, 101
American Psychological
 Association, 399, 449
American Religous
 Landscape, 246
American Society of Plastic and
 Reconstructive Surgeons
 (ASPRS), 405, 406
American Sociological
 Association, 56
The American Woman's Home
 (Beecher and Stowe), 155
Amherst College, 219
Amish cult, 336, 337f
Amygdala, 37
Anal sex, 424
Anal stage of psychosexual
 development, 88–89
Anaphrodisiacs, 439
Anderson, Cameron, 267
Androgenital syndrome
 (AGS), 45–46
Androgyny, 110–111, 484–485
Andropause, 45
Angier, Natalie, 163
Animist religions, 235
Anorexia nervosa, 399, 401, 402
Anorgasmia, 432
Anterior hypothalamus, 40
Anthony, Albert, 71
Anthony, Susan B., 206
Anthropomorphic
 hyperbole, 29, 55

Antifeminists, 341
Antipornography feminism, 339, 415
Antisocial personality disorder, 45
Aphrodisiacs, 83
Arab Spring, 333, 335
Aranda people, 81
Arapesh people, 60, 62f, 437–438
Arendt, Hannah, 122
Argentina, female heads of state in, 312
Aristotle, 374
Arizona State University, 165
Aronson, Amy, 357, 358
Arquette, Rosanna, 126
Arrest rates, 449, 460
Arson, 456
Arthur, Michelle, 278–279
As Nature Made Him: The Boy Who Was Raised as a Girl (Colapinto), 47
Ashcroft, John, 53
Asian Americans
    cosmetic surgery and, 408
    religion and, 248
    wages of, 283f, 286t, 289f
    in the workplace, 273
Assaults, 449
Associated Press poll on ordination of women, 249
Association of Theological Schools, 248
Atlas, Charles, 400
Attention deficit disorder, 213
Auchus, Richard, 139
Augustine, Saint, 243
Australia
    AIDS-HIV in, 442
    child care sharing in, 171
    female heads of state in, 312
    importance of economic prosperity in, 26
    teen birth rates in, 179f
    the workplace in, 291
Austria, sexuality in, 440
The Authoritarian Personality (Adorno, et al.), 107
Authoritarianism, 107–108, 109
Avengers T-shirts, 107
Aymara people, 236

Babcock, Barbara Allen, 305
Baboons, 28–29, 451
Baby boom, 158, 162
Bacha posh, 78
Bachelet, Michelle, 312
Bailey, J. Michael, 41–42, 53
Ball, Edward, 8
Ballard, Martha, 166
Bambara people, 83
Bangladesh
    female heads of state in, 312
    female legislators in, 313
Bank, Barbara, 381
Bank of Montreal, 292
"Barack and Curtis" (campaign video), 321–322
Barbie, 204, 401, 404
Bari people, 31–32
Barnett, Rosalind Chait, 106, 145, 178

Baron, James, 279–280
Baron-Cohen, Simon, 38
Bartkowski, John, 241
Bates, Vincent M., 33
Bathroom discrimination, 129–130, 129f, 327, 328, 330f
"Battered husband syndrome," 475
Baumeister, Roy, 30
"Beards, Breasts, and Bodies" (Dozier), 437
Bearman, Peter, 42, 422
Beauty, 408
Beauty myth, 396–404
    defined, 398
    standards for men, 400–403
    standards for women, 396–400
The Beauty Myth (Wolf), 357
Beauvoir, Simone de, 375, 462
Bebin, Mary, 165
Bechdel, Alison, 356
Beckwith, Jonathan, 38
Beecher, Catharine, 155
Behan, Peter, 34, 35, 43
Belgium
    sexuality in, 440
    the workplace in, 291
Bell, Shannon Elizabeth, 331
"Beloved women," 78
Bem, Sandra, 110–111
Bem Sex Role Inventory (BSRI), 110, 110t
Benedict XVI, Pope, 234, 249
Beneke, Tim, 472
Benevolent exploitation, 269
Bengal, colonialism in, 332
Benjamin, Jessica, 97
Benokraitis, Nicole, 269
Berdache. *See* Two-spirit people
Bergman, Abraham, 198
Bernard, Jessie, 163, 256, 345, 352
Best, Joel, 217
"Best interests of the child" standard, 195, 196
Bethlehem Steel Corporation, 286
Bettelheim, Bruno, 97
Bible, 237, 238, 246, 256–257
Bielby, William, 279–280
Bin Laden, Osama, 336
Binge eating, 401, 402
Biological determinism, 19–57. *See also* Brain; Evolutionary theory; Hormones
    central premise of, 2–3
    culture and, 58–59
    differential socialization compared with, 4
    primary areas of research on, 23
    social constructionism compared with, 114–115, 128
Biological essentialism, 52–54
Biological principle, 24
Birdwhistell, Raymond, 153
Birth control, 188
    Catholics and, 239
    debate on coverage for, 324–325
    liberating effects of, 63, 420
    restrictions on, 160, 180
    virginity pledges and, 424

Birth weight, brain development and, 35–36
Bisexuals, 81–82, 404, 479
Black Skin, White Masks (Fanon), 332
Blackwell, Elizabeth, 248
Blackwell, Samuel, 248
Blair, Cherie, 308–309
Blair, Tony, 308–309
Blankenhorn, David, 180, 181, 183
Bleier, Ruth, 35
Block, Jack, 193
Block, Jeanne, 193
Bly, Robert, 181
Bobbitt, Lorena, 415, 475
Body, 396–447. *See also* Health; Sexuality
    changing, 404–407
    politicization of the, 240–241
    standards for men, 400–403
    standards for women, 396–400
Body piercing, 404
Boeringer, Scott, 473
Bogaert, Anthony, 50
Bolivia, female heads of state in, 312
"Bona fide occupational qualification" standard, 271
Bonobos, 28
Books
    children's, 348–350
    novels, 355–357
Booth, Alan, 193
Boston College, 169
Bourgeois, Roy, 250
Boushey, Heather, 302
Boxer, Barbara, 276
Boy Scouts, 216
Boy-centered stories, 350
Brady, Tom, 370
Brain
    friendship differences and, 376
    of gay people, 38–41, 53–54
    gender differences in, 2, 3, 23, 33–38
    gray and white matter of, 38
    hemispheric function in, 34–36, 43, 52
    LeBon's theory of, 22
    video games' effects on, 364
Brain, Robert, 388
Brandon, Teena, 137f
Brawdy, Tawnya, 212
Bray, Robert, 53
Brazil
    corporal punishment banned in, 198
    female heads of state in, 312
    sexuality in, 440
Breasts
    augmentation of, 398, 405
    concern with appearance of, 396–398
Breedlove, Marc, 41, 49–50
Brehm, Sharon, 377
Brescoll, Victoria, 315
Bridges, Tristan, 469
Bridget Jones's Diary (Fielding), 356
Brines, Julie, 175
Brodkin, Karen, 58–59, 65
Bromances, 385
Brontë, Charlotte, 264
Brontë sisters, 6

Brooks, Gary, 431
Brooks, Tim, 354
Brown, Antoinette, 248
Brown, Chris, 477f
Brown v. Board of Education of Topeka, 232, 270
Browning, Robert, 373
Bruckner, Hannah, 42
Bryn Mawr College, 226, 227
Bryson, Bethany, 353–354
Buddhism, 236, 243, 246, 257
Buffery, A. W. H., 35
Bulimia, 399, 401, 402
Bullying, 219, 220–221, 457
Bunch, Charlotte, 54
Bundchen, Gisele, 398
Bunting, Josiah, III, 229, 341
Burka/burqa, 240, 340
Bush, George H. W., 317, 322, 323f, 462
Bush, George W., 176, 231, 317, 318, 319, 462
Business Week survey on wages, 287
Buss, David, 26, 429
Byron, Lord, 373, 374

Caldwell, Mayta, 377
A Call to Men, 342
Cambridge University, 186
Campbell, Helen, 166
Canada
    child care sharing in, 171
    divorce rate in, 189t
    female heads of state in, 312
    housework division in, 168
    marriage rate in, 189t
    sexuality in, 440
    teen birth rate in, 179f
    the workplace in, 291
Cancian, Francesca, 389, 394
Capital punishment, 465, 480
Capitalism, 63–65
Caplan, Paula, 101
Caplow, Theodore, 159
Carlson, Daniel L., 175
Carlson, Tucker, 322
Carneal, Michael, 222
Carter, Betty, 195
Carter, Jimmy, 128, 305, 462
Castration, 44
Castration complex, 89, 96
Castronova, Edward, 363
Catalyst Pyramid, 290f
Catholic Church, 239
    gap between priests and Catholics in, 249f
    gender difference and inequality in, 245
    gender gap in religiosity, 246
    homosexuality and, 243, 244
    pedophile priest scandal in, 249, 469–470
    women's ordination prohibited in, 248–250
Cattell, J. McKeen, 223–224
"Caveman Masculinity" (McCaughey), 25
Cayler, Tom, 366
Cazenave, Noel, 478–479

Celibacy, 243, 249, 250
Census Bureau, U.S., 188, 272, 287
Center for Talent Innovation, 167
Center for Work and Family (Boston College), 169
Centerfold syndrome, 431
Centers for Disease Control, 466
Chafe, William, 157
Chaga people, 82
Charlie Hebdo, terrorist attack on, 362
Chaudhary, N., 64
Chenchu people, 83
Cher, 126
Cherlin, Andrew, 178, 180, 192, 196
Cherokee Indians, 78
Chicago, homicide rate in, 457f
Chick flicks, 345
Chick lit, 345, 356
Child abuse, 197–199, 458, 460
Child allowance, 175
Child care, 325
    culture and, 62, 67–68
    day care "problem," 177–179
    fathers and, 67–68, 154–155, 166, 169–176, 171f
    gendered politics of, 165–177
    historical perspective on, 154–155
    political office entry and, 314
    separation of housework from, 176
Child custody, 195–197
Child support, 182, 196
Children. *See also* Family; Fathers/fatherhood; Mothers/motherhood; Parents/parenting; Youth
    average time spent on activities, 170f
    in cohabiting households, 161
    decline in number of, 160
    decline in well-being of, 200
    divorce and, 152, 190–195, 194f
    evolutionary theory on nurturing of, 28
    of gay and lesbian couples, 185–187
    as homicide victims, 458, 460
    housework performed by, 170
    investing in the future of, 200–201
    isolated, 115
    marital happiness decline and, 164, 165
    the media and, 347, 348–352
    minutes spent engaged with by family structure, 185f
    out-of-wedlock births, 152, 180–181
    parental violence against, 197–199, 458, 460
    parents' sex life hindered by, 439, 440f
    percentage living with both parents, 160
    percentage who do activities, 348f
    as a political issue, 323
    sexual abuse of, 458, 469–470
    violence among, 460
    women's career growth stymied by, 308
    women's wages decreased by, 285
Chile
    female heads of state in, 312
    views of "traditional" family in, 162
Chimpanzees, 28

China
    leg lengthening in, 408
    love in, 393
    the workplace in, 268
Cho, Seung-Hui, 344
Chodorow, Nancy, 97, 98, 387
Christ, Carol, 238
Christian Marriage and Religion Research Institute, 244
Christian Science, 253
Christianity, 234, 257
    evangelical, 239, 243, 244, 250, 253
    gender differences and inequality in, 240
    homosexuality and, 244
    Muscular, 251–252, 253–254, 256
    sexuality and, 243, 244
The Cinderella Complex (Dowling), 11–12
Circumcision, 70–73
    female, 71–73, 71f
    male, 70–71, 72–73, 465
Citadel, 99, 229, 297
City Slickers (film), 124f
Civil Rights Act of 1964, 297, 304
Civil Rights Act of 1991, 292
Clancy, Tom, 355
Clark, Kenneth, 232
Clarke, Edward, 22, 205
Class. *See* Social class
Cleaver, Eldridge, 333
Clerical work, gender composition of, 277–278
Clinton, Bill, 318, 319–320, 412, 462
Clinton, Hillary, 311–312, 318, 320, 321f
Clitoridectomy, 46, 71. *See also* Female circumcision
Clitoris, 31, 89, 96
Code of Manu, 245
Co-education, 205–206, 230
Cognitive development theories
    feminist criticism of, 98–101
    overview of, 94–96
Cognitive filters, 94, 95, 96
Cohabitation, 152, 161, 175
Cohen, Dov, 466
Cohen, Ted, 382
Cohn, Carol, 463
Cohn, Samuel, 278
Colapinto, John, 47
Coleman, James, 215–216
Colgate, Florence, 397
College
    actual and projected numbers for enrollment, 218f
    gender disparities in, 216–219
    hazing in, 221
    hook-up culture on campuses, 424–426
    sexual assaults on campuses, 430, 468, 470
    sexual behavior of men in, 472–473
    single-sex, 227–230
    teachers' gender, 225–227
    transgender protection on campus, 328
    women's, 206, 225–227
Collegial exclusion, 269
Colonialism, 332–333

Colonization, 69
Color-coding of boys and girls, 23, 97
Coltrane, Scott, 67–68, 162, 201
Columbia University, 217
Columbine High School shootings, 221, 222–223
"Coming of Age and Coming Out Ceremonies Across Cultures" (Herdt), 80
Coming of Age in Samoa (Mead), 60
Commission on Opportunity in Athletics, 233
Commission on Violence and Youth, 449
Communication, gendered, 142–145
Companionate marriage, 388, 389
Comparable-worth criteria, 290, 304
Complex or undetermined intersex, 138
Compositional fallacy, 281
Compulsive masculinity, 109
Computer programming, gender composition of, 278
Condescending chivalry, 269
Confirmation bias, 125
Conflict Tactics Scale (CTS), 476
Confucianism, 257
Congenital adrenal hyperplasia (CAH), 49, 138
Connell, R. W., 10–11, 119
Connery, Sean, 126
Conservative Judaism, 248
Considerate domination, 269
Coontz, Stephanie, 164, 307
Cooper, Anderson, 267
Cooper, Frank Rudy, 322
Cooper, James Fenimore, 355–356
Cooper, Kieran, 106
Coppen, Alec, 48
Cornell University, 51
Corporal punishment, 154, 197–198, 199
Corpus callosum, 37
Correll, Shelley, 214, 215
Cose, Ellis, 444
Cosmetic surgery, 398, 405–408, 405*f*
Costa Rica, female heads of state in, 312
Cottingham, Marci, 276, 277
Coulter, Ann, 354
Courtenay, Will H., 444
Couvade, 73, 74*f*
Covenant marriage, 194–195
Craniology, 34
Crichton, Michael, 355
Crime
    fatherlessness and, 181, 182
    gender of, 453–457
    women and, 458–461
Crittenden, Danielle, 358
Croatia, female heads of state in, 312
Crockett, Davy, 317
Crosby, Faye, 310
Cross-dressing, 135, 138
Crow Indians, 76
The Crying Game (film), 135
Crystal, Billy, 411
Cubans, domestic violence and, 478
Cult of compulsive masculinity, 109
Cult of domesticity, 458

Culture, 58–86
    division of labor and, 61–63, 68, 69
    friendship and, 388
    gender definition variations in, 59–61
    gender dimorphic and polymorphic, 51
    gender fluidity and, 75–78, 80
    love and, 392–393
    masculinity and femininity defined by, 3, 4, 58, 59, 60–61, 65, 67, 116
    rape and, 68, 69–70
    rituals of gender in, 70–75, 80
    sexual diversity and, 80–83
    sexuality and, 82–83, 437–438
    values of cross-cultural research, 86
    violence and, 59, 60–61, 451
Cunnilingus, 417, 425, 429
"Cutting Through Words" (ritual), 73

The Da Vinci Code (Brown), 237
Dabbs, James, 43
"Daddy days," 200
"Daddy track," 132, 172, 309
Dalton, Katherine, 29
Daly, Mary, 256, 258
Daniels, Susanne, 353
Darwin, Charles, 20, 21–22, 24
Date rape, 473
Dating, 26, 390, 424, 425
Davenport, William, 82
Davidson, Lynne, 377–378
Davis, Alexander, 353–354
Davis v. Monroe County Board of Education, 212
Dawkins, Richard, 24
Day care "problem," 177–179
Dean, Craig, 185
"Deceptive distinctions," 11–13, 218
Declaration of Sentiments, 341
Defense of Marriage Act (DOMA), 183
Degendering, 484–486
Del Campo, Robert, 278–279
Dell, Floyd, 487–488
Deloitte Global Center for Corporate Governance, 291
"Delusional Dominating Personality Disorder (DDPD)", 101, 102*f*
Demo, David, 200
Democracy in America (Tocqueville), 1
Democratic Party, 247, 315, 316*f*, 317, 318, 441
Demos, John, 154–155
Denmark
    child care sharing in, 171
    female heads of state in, 312
    out-of-wedlock births in, 181
Dentistry, gender composition of, 273, 276*f*
Depression, 38
The Descent of Man (Darwin), 21
Descent theory, 65–66
DeSimone, Diane, 36
Dewey, John, 87, 229–230
Diagnostic and Statistical Manual of Mental Disorders (DSM), 48, 101
Diamond, Milton, 47
Diaz v. Pan American World Airways, 280, 328
Dickens, Charles, 6

Dickinson, Emily, 166
Differential socialization, 2
    biological determinism compared with, 4
    central premise of, 3–4
    occupational sex segregation and, 273
Digit ratio studies, 49–50
Dinnerstein, Dorothy, 97
Discourse on Friendship (Taylor), 375
Division of labor. *See* Gendered division of labor
Divorce, 188–195, 200, 341, 392. *See also* Child custody
    best predictors of, 190
    gender differences in impact of, 189–191
    historical perspective on, 156–157
    rates of, 152, 153, 162, 188, 189*t*
    religion and, 240
    remarriage following, 152, 163, 188
    violence against women following, 475–476
"Do It All for Your Public Hairs" (Mora), 403
Dobesova, Michaela, 450
Dobson, James, 52
Dog attacks, based on sex of walker, 450
"Doing" gender, 133–142, 147, 459
"Doing Gender" (West and Zimmerman), 133
"Doing Gender, Determining Gender" (Westbrook and Schilt), 136
Domestic violence, 339, 474–480. *See also* Intimate partner violence
    arrest rates for, 449
    against children, 197–199, 458, 460
    against men, 458, 460, 474–477
Donato, Katharine, 278
Dorner, Gunter, 39, 48–49
Double bind, 286
Double standard. *See* Sexual double standard
Douglas, Michael, 125
Douglass, Frederick, 312, 341
Dowling, Colette, 11–12
Dozier, Raine, 437
Drinking, 444–446
Driscoll, Mark, 253
Drunk driving, 444, 455, 459
DTR (Define the Relationship) conversation, 425
Duberman, Lucille, 377–378
Duke University, 226, 320
Dunn, David, 364
Dupont Corporation, 172
Durant, Henry Fowle, 204, 206
Durden-Smith, Jo, 36
Durkheim, Emile, 33
Duster, Troy, 56
Dwight, Theodore, 156
Dyble, Mark, 64
Dyslexia, 213

Eagleton Institute of Politics (Rutgers University), 314
Earle, Alison, 305
East Bay society, 82

Eastwick, Paul, 26
Eating disorders, 399–400, 401–402
Ecofeminism, 257–258
Education, 204–233, 270, 280, 327–328.
    See also College
    athletics equality in, 232–233
    boys' performance and behavior in,
        213–219
    bullying issue, 219, 220–221
    co-education, 205–206, 230
    divorce and, 190
    toward gender equality in, 231–232
    gender policing in, 219–223
    the gendered classroom in, 206–213
    "hidden curriculum" in, 205, 216
    for manhood, traditional, 205–206
    school shootings, 221–223, 344, 448
    single-sex schools/classrooms, 227–232
    teachers' gender, 223–227, 224t
    wages and, 282, 284
    women discouraged from pursuing, 22,
        34, 205–206
    women encouraged to pursue, 87,
        204, 206
Education Act of 1972, 232
Education Department, U.S., 348
Education Sector, 217
Edwards, John, 319
EEOC v. Sears, 280–281
Egalia School, 209
Ego, 88, 89
Egypt, social movements in, 334
Ehrenreich, Barbara, 446, 451
Ehrhardt, Anke, 45–46
Ehrlich, Paul, 32
Eisenberg, Marla, 426
Eisenegger, Christoph, 43
Eisler, Riane, 84–85
Elder abuse, 458, 460
Eliot, Lise, 35, 38
Ellis, Amy, 211f
Ellison, Peter, 45
Ellison v. Brady, 301
Elsesser, Kim, 267
Ely, Robin, 292, 294
Emerson, Ralph Waldo, 114
Emily's List, 315
Eminem, 220
Emotion work, 266–267
Emotional intimacy, 375
Emphasized femininity, 11, 15, 119
Endocrinological research, 23. *See also*
    Hormones
Engels, Friedrich, 63
Engineering, gender differences in, 216,
    217f, 225
England. *See* Great Britain/United
    Kingdom
England, Paula, 270
Entrapment (film), 126
Episcopal Church, 248
Epstein, Cynthia Fuchs, 11, 52, 218
Equal Employment Opportunity
    Commission (EEOC), 271, 280–281,
    286, 297, 298, 299, 303, 304
Equal Marriage Rights Fund, 185
Equal Pay Act of 1963, 286

Equal Rights Amendment, 339
Erectile dysfunction, 420
Estrogen
    the gay brain and, 41
    gender differences and, 43, 46, 48
    life expectancy and, 126
    in males, 3, 43
Etero people, 81
Ethic of care, 98–100
Ethic of justice, 98–100
Ethiopia, life expectancy gap in, 127
Ethnocentrism, 82
European Medical Association, 399
Europe/European Union
    AIDS-HIV in, 442
    child care in, 178
    child support in, 196
    corporal punishment banned in, 198
    female heads of state in, 312
    religion in, 254
    the workplace in, 273, 306
Evangelical Christianity, 239, 243, 244,
    250, 253
Eve's Rib (Pool), 37
Evolutionary imperative, 24–27
Evolutionary psychology, 23, 27–32,
    416, 429
    anthropomorphic language
        used in, 29
    central premise of, 26
    as a "just-so story," 31
Evolutionary success, 27
Evolutionary theory, 20–33, 450–451.
    See also Evolutionary imperative;
        Evolutionary psychology;
        Sociobiology
Expressive roles, 109, 158

Facebook, 143, 267, 309, 367, 369
Fagan, Pat, 244
Failing at Fairness (Sadker and Sadker),
    207, 208–209
Fallon, Conan, 354
Falwell, Jerry, 252
Families and Work Institute, 169, 172
Family, 151–203. *See also* Children;
        Domestic violence; Fathers/
        fatherhood; Housework; Marriage;
        Mothers/motherhood; Nuclear
        family
    brief history of, 154–163
    "constructed problems" of
        contemporary, 177–187
    of the future, 199–203
    gay and lesbian, 183–187
    gender socialization and, 12–13
    love in, 394
    resilience of, 152
    "traditional," 157–158, 159, 162–163
    types of households (2012), 161t
    withdrawal of public support from, 160
    work and (*see under* Work/workplace)
Family and Divorce Mediation Council of
    Greater New York, 194
Family and Medical Leave Act of 1993,
    305–306
Family Research Council, 178

Family values, 151, 152, 153, 154, 162,
    200, 305
Family wage, 154
Family-friendly workplace policies,
    175–176, 200, 290, 306, 325
Fanon, Franz, 332
Farrell, Warren, 112, 122, 292–293
Fatherless America (Blankenhorn), 181
Fatherlessness, 181–183, 188
The Father's Book (Dwight), 156
"Father's rights" organizations, 196
Fathers/fatherhood, 308–310
    absent, 181–183, 188
    of babies born to teen mothers, 180
    in Bari people, 31–32
    child abuse and, 198
    child care and, 67–68, 154–155, 166,
        169–176, 171f
    child custody and, 195–197
    cognitive development theories on, 98
    culture and, 61, 67–68
    "daddy track" and, 132, 172, 309
    declining importance of, 156
    divorce and, 190
    grandfathers and, 116
    historical perspective on, 154–155, 156,
        158–159
    housework and, 166, 169, 171
    psychosexual development theory on,
        89, 90, 98
    single fathers, 13, 153, 161, 181
    stay-at-home fathers, 164, 173–174
    testosterone decrease and, 45
Fausto-Sterling, Anne, 23, 35, 46
FBI, 466
Fellatio, 417, 429
Felmlee, Diane, 382
Female circumcision, 71–73, 71f
Female genital mutilation (FGM), 72, 73
Female Power and Male Dominance
    (Sanday), 235
Feminine mystique, 154
The Feminine Mystique
    (Friedan), 159, 357
Femininities, 10, 112, 118
Femininity
    aging and, 126
    cultural definitions of, 3, 4, 58, 59,
        60–61, 65, 116
    education and, 220
    emphasized, 11, 15, 119
    globalization and, 331
    hormonal influences on, 43
    through the life course, 123
    M-F test, 91–93, 107
    plural meanings of, 10–11
    psychosexual development theory
        on, 90, 98
    redefining, 485, 487, 488
    sex-role theory on, 107–113, 117–119
    sexuality and, 411
    social constructionist perspective on,
        116–117
    the workplace and, 266
Feminism/feminists
    basic beliefs of, 339
    biological essentialism and, 52

Feminism/feminists (*Continued*)
cognitive development theories
vs., 98–101
crime blamed on, 458
divorce blamed on, 190
eco-, 257–258
family values debate and, 154
fatherlessness blamed on, 182
first wave of, 337
focus of scholarship, 5–6
lesbianism and, 338, 434
liberal, 339, 340
the media and, 353
men and, 340–342, 488
multicultural, 340
politics and, 336–342
pornography opposed by, 339, 415
on power, 121
psychosexual development theory
vs., 94, 96–98
radical, 339–340, 415
religion and, 234, 239, 255–258
second wave of, 338, 357
sex roles expanded by, 120
sexuality and, 179, 421, 424
third wave of, 338
on the traditional family, 159
women's magazines criticized by, 357
Feminist anthropology, 84–85
Feminization of poverty, 181
Feminized love, 376, 390–391, 394, 420
Fennema, E., 210*f*
"Feral children," 115
Ferguson, Marjorie, 357
Fernandez de Kirchner, Cristina, 312
Fielding, Helen, 356
Fincham, Frank, 426
Fineman, Martha, 197
Finkel, Eli, 26
Finklehor, David, 473
Finland
female heads of state in, 312
importance of economic prosperity
in, 26
violence in, 460
First-wave feminism, 337
Fisher, Helen, 84
Fisher, Terri D., 413
Fisk, N., 46
Fitzgerald, Louise, 300
Fluke, Sandar, 324
Flynn, Frank, 267
Flynt, Larry, 364
Focus on the Family, 52, 94
Fonda, Jane, 126
Foote, Mary Hallock, 166
Ford, Harrison, 125–126
Ford, Maggie, 232
Forster, E. M., 395
Fortune 100 companies, 287
Fortune 500 companies, 287, 301, 306
Foucault, Michel, 39, 389
Fourteenth Amendment, 326
Fox, Robin, 26, 65–66
France
ban on religious head coverings in
schools, 241, 242

divorce rate in, 188, 189*t*
life expectancy gap in, 127
marriage rate in, 189*t*
sexuality in, 439*f*
teen birth rate in, 179*f*
views of "traditional" family in, 162
the workplace in, 291, 306
Franklin, Christine, 212
Frederick II, Emperor, 115
Freedman, David, 29
Freud, Sigmund, 19, 39, 87–91, 93, 94,
260, 332, 451. *See also* Post-Freudian
theories; Psychosexual development
theory
Friedan, Betty, 159, 357
Friedel, Ernestine, 82
Friedman, Howard, 444
Friendly harassment, 269
Friends (television program), 418
"Friends with benefits," 424, 426, 427*f*
Friendship, 374–389, 394–395
cross-sex, 381, 382, 383–384, 386–387
factors other than gender affecting,
382–387
gender differences in, 376–382
gender of, 374–376
historical gendering of, 387–389
Frost, Robert, 203
Frustration-aggression hypothesis, 30, 451
Fukuyama, Francis, 85
Full faith and credit clause of the
Constitution, 183
Functionalism, 62
Fundamentalism, 247
Fur trade, 65
Furstenberg, Frank, 196, 200–201

Gagnon, John, 437, 469
Galinsky, Ellen, 169
Gallup Polls, 162
Galupo, M. Paz, 384
Game Over (documentary), 362
Gamergate, 362
Gandhi, Indira, 128, 455
Gang rape, 69, 70, 146, 471
Garfinkle, Harold, 140–142
Gates, Bill, 344
Gay gene, search for, 41–42, 53
Gay liberation movement, 120, 433–434
Gay men
AIDS-HIV in, 441–442
brain research on, 39–41, 54
in the clergy, 248, 249
domestic violence and, 479
eating disorders and, 401
family life and, 183–187
food claimed to produce, 46
friendship and, 386–387
gender conformity in, 54, 432–435
genetic research on, 41–42, 53
hormones and, 48–50
religion, manhood, and, 254
tattoos and, 404
violence against, 480
in the workplace, 271–272
Gaylin, Willard, 265
Gelles, Richard, 199, 473

Gender. *See also* Men; Women
aging and, 125–127
of crime, 453–457
depoliticization of, 119
"doing," 133–142, 147, 459
of friendship, 374–376
homicide rates by, 457, 457*f*
increasing visibility of, 5–9
as an institution, 127–133
through the life course, 122–125
life expectancy by, 445*f*
love and, 389–390
as a "managed property," 147
as plural, 118
politics of, 322–327
as relational, 118
rituals of, 70–75, 80
sex distinguished from, 3
as situational, 119
Gender: An Ethnomethodological Approach
(Kessler and McKenna), 134
Gender conformity. *See also* Gender
nonconformity
in education, 209, 219–223
homosexuality as, 54, 432–437
rape and, 471
in the workplace, 266
Gender convergence
in health, 444
increase in, 484
in the media, 368–370
in sexuality, 426–432
Gender development, 87–113. *See also*
Cognitive development theories;
Psychosexual development theory;
Sex-role theory
differences in, 101–106
M-F test of, 91–93, 107
Gender differences. *See also*
Interplanetary theory of gender
difference
among *vs.* between the sexes, 10, 14, 36,
101, 112, 281
biological explanations for, 54–57
brain research on, 2, 3, 23, 33–38
culture and, 58–86
as "deceptive distinctions," 11–13, 218
developmental, 101–106
divorce and, 189–191
evolutionary theory on, 20–23, 25
the family and, 200, 203
in friendship, 376–382
future of, 483, 484–485
gender inequality and, 4–5, 59, 484–485
in the hookup culture, 425–426
hormonal influences on, 2–3, 42–48
institutions and, 129–131, 132–133, 147
love and, 391
as mean differences, 13–15, 14*f*
the media and, 345, 347, 348, 352
politics of, 15–16
primary theories on reasons for, 1–5
religion and, 20, 238–244, 245, 248
in sexuality, 412–417
social constructionist perspective on, 5,
129–131, 132–133, 147
social media and, 367

Gender dimorphic cultures, 51
Gender discrimination
    biological explanations for, 23
    in education, 212–213
    in religion, 258
    against transgender persons, 327–328
    in the workplace, 268, 270–272,
        292–293, 304
Gender diversity. *See* Sexual diversity
Gender fluidity, 75–78, 80
Gender gap
    in education, 214
    in elected officials, 312–315
    narrowing of, 484
    in religiosity, 245–247, 246*f*, 251, 255
    in sexuality, 416, 420–421
    in violence, 460
    in voting, 315–317
    in wages (*see* Wage gap)
    in the workplace, 263*f*
Gender identity
    biological explanations for, 42, 47
    cognitive development theories of,
        94–96
    hormonal influences on, 43, 45
    institutions and, 127
    M-F test, 91–93, 107
    psychosexual development theory of,
        87–88, 89–91, 96
    rigid notions of, 105
    sex-role theory on, 106–109, 127, 133
    social constructionist perspective
        on, 127
Gender inequality
    biological explanations for, 20, 54–55
    circumcision linked to, 71
    cosmetic surgery and, 406, 407
    culture and, 58, 68, 78
    differential socialization and, 4
    divorce and, 188–190
    domestic violence and, 199
    in education, 207–209, 214, 219–220
    eliminating, 483–485
    the family and, 200, 203
    gender differences and, 4–5, 59,
        484–485
    health and, 446
    hunter-gatherers inaccurately
        blamed for, 64
    institutions and, 127, 129, 132–133, 147
    love and, 391
    the media and, 345, 347, 352
    religion and, 236, 238–244, 245, 248, 259
    in same-sex relationships,
        neutralization of, 185
    separation of spheres and, 487–488
    sexuality and, 411, 426, 430
    social constructionist perspective on, 5,
        127, 129, 132–133, 147
    social media and, 367
    violence and, 452, 460–461
    warfare, bonding, and, 65–66
    in the workplace, 132–133, 268–270,
        296–297, 303–307
Gender inversion, 54
Gender Neutral Job Comparison
    System, 304

Gender neutrality
    consequences of illusion of, 8
    of institutions, presumed, 127, 131, 133
    of joint child custody, apparent, 197
    in the workplace, assumption of, 15–16
Gender nonconformity, 140. *See also*
        Gender conformity
    homosexuality seen as, 90, 93
    sex-role theory on, 108
    in the workplace, 266
"Gender Penalties Revisited" (study), 284
Gender policing, 219–223
Gender polymorphic cultures, 51
Gender queer (GQ) identity, 138–140, 327
Gender reassignment, 134
Gender roles. *See* Sex-role theory
"Gender Rules" (Felmlee), 382
"Gender Similarities Hypothesis"
        (Hyde), 104
Gender socialization
    family experiences and, 12–13
    fashion and, 107
    through the life course, 122–123
Gender stereotypes, 15
    education and, 229
    the media and, 350–351, 353
    psychosexual development theory
        and, 90
    sexual orientation and, 39
    in video games, 362–363
    in the workplace, 268, 281, 287, 292
Gendered division of labor, 2
    culture and, 61–63, 68, 69
    evolutionary theory on, 25–26
    in hunting-and-gathering societies,
        62, 375
    prevalence of, 260–262
    private property and, 63
Gendered love. *See* Love, gendered
Gendered political divide, 318
Gendered processes, 130–131
Gendered violence. *See* Violence,
        gendered
"Gender-fuck" identity, 327
Genes/genetics
    anthropomorphic hyperbole on, 55
    "gay gene" research, 41–42, 53
    limits to influence of, 32
    sexuality and, 28
Genital mutilation
    female, 72, 73
    male, 70, 71
Genital reconstruction surgery, 406–407
Germany
    divorce rate in, 188, 189*t*
    female heads of state in, 312
    marriage rate in, 189*t*
    sexuality in, 439*f*, 440
    teen birth rate in, 179*f*
    views of "traditional" family in, 162
    the workplace in, 291
Gerson, Judith, 132
Gerson, Kathleen, 12, 201–202
Geschwind, Norman, 34, 35, 43
Gesquiere, Laurence, 29
Gettler, Lee, 67
G.I. Joe, 401, 402*f*

Gilder, George, 433
Gilligan, Carol, 98–101, 144, 214
Gilligan, James, 456, 465
Gillis, John, 156
Gilman, Charlotte Perkins, 256, 257, 278
Gimbutas, Marija, 84
Gingrich, Newt, 23, 162, 313
Girl-centered stories, 350
Girl-watching, 374
"Glass ceiling," 270, 286, 287, 290–293,
        295, 303, 306
    circumstances fostering, 290–291
    in politics, 311, 312
Glass Ceiling Commission, 287, 292, 297
"Glass cellar," 293
"Glass escalator," 295–296
Globalization, 331, 333
Gnostic Gospels, 257
God. *See* Religion
Goddess traditions, 84–85, 235–238, 258
Goffman, Erving, 10, 130
Goldberg, Steven, 43, 52, 58
Goldilocks dilemma, 398
Goldspink, David, 126
Golf courses, study of, 278–279
Good, Glenn, 431
The Good Divorce (Ahrons), 188
"Good Guys with Guns" (Stroud), 453
Goode, William J., 390
Google, 309
Gordon, George. *See* Byron, Lord
Gore, Al, 318, 319*f*
Gore, Tipper, 319*f*
Gorillas, 28
Gottfredson, Michael, 449
Gottman, John, 300
Gould, Stephen Jay, 28
Grabar-Kitarovic, Kolinda, 312
Grandfathers, 116
Grateful Dad (workshops), 170
Gray, John, 1, 35, 37, 190, 306
Great Britain/United Kingdom
    child care sharing in, 171
    crime by age and gender in, 456*f*
    divorce rate in, 188, 189*t*
    eating disorders in, 399
    female heads of state in, 312
    homicide rate in, 453
    housework division in, 169
    importance of economic prosperity
        in, 26
    marriage rate in, 189*t*
    teen birth rate in, 179
    the workplace in, 291, 306
Great Goddess, 235
Great Mother, 236, 256
Great Recession of 2008, 302
Greek mythology, 236
Greeley, Andrew, 201
Green, Richard, 46, 433
Greenblat, Cathy, 393
Gregor, Thomas, 68, 69
Griffin, Susan, 471
Growing Up Straight (Wyden and
        Wyden), 432
Grybauskaité, Dalia, 312
Guevadoches, 51

Gun ownership, 453
Gurian, Michael, 37
"Gyn/Ecology," 258

Hacker, Andrew, 215
Hacker, Helen, 120
Hafen, Christopher A., 33
Halim, May Ling, 105
Hall, G. Stanley, 205
Hamlet (Shakespeare), 448
Han, Hongyun, 208
Hannah, Daryl, 126
Hanson, Sarah, 175
Hardy, Thomas, 6–7
Harlan, Heather, 125
Harrington, Brad, 169
Harris, Eric, 222–223
Harris, Mark, 125
Harris, Marvin, 65
Harris, Shanette, 383
Harris poll on sexual harassment, 298
Harris v. Forklift, 301
Harrison, William Henry, 317
Hartmann, Heidi, 296
Harvard Business School, 292, 294
Harvard Humanitarian Initiative, 467
Harvard Medical School, 38
Harvard Men Against Rape, 342
Harvard University, 226
Hate crimes, 328
Havlicek, Zdenek, 450
Hawthorne, Nathaniel, 355
Hayes, Jeffrey, 305
Hazing, 221
Health, 441–447
    gendered, 444–447
    sex and, 441–444
Health, Education, and Welfare
    Department, U.S., 350
Health care coverage, 324–325
Heath High School shooting, 222
Hedberg, Allan, 456
Hegemonic masculinity, 10, 15, 119
The Heidi Chronicles (Wasserstein), 387
Heiman, Julia, 426
Helbig, Marcel, 224
Hemicastration, 71
Hemingway, Ernest, 355
Herdt, Gilbert, 51, 80–81
Heresy, 237
Hermaphrodites. *See* Intersexuality/
    intersexed persons
Hess, Amanda, 244
Hess, Beth, 377
Hewlett, Sylvia, 308
Heymann, Jody, 305
"Hidden curriculum," 205, 216
Higginson, Thomas Wentworth, 230
High Fidelity (Hornby), 356
High-speed chases, 456
Hijab, 242–243, 242*f*
Hijra community, 79*f*
Hill, Anita, 297–298, 304
Hilton, Phil, 359
Hinduism, 236, 244, 245, 247
Hirschi, Travis, 449
His Religion and Hers (Gilman), 256

Hispanics/Latino/as
    domestic violence and, 478, 479
    education and, 218, 232
    health and, 444
    incarceration rate for, 455
    politics and, 316*f*, 317
    puberty meaning in, 403
    religion and, 244, 248
    sexuality and, 438–439
    wages of, 281, 282, 283*f*, 288*f*, 289*f*
    in the workplace, 262, 273, 287
Historically black churches, 244, 246
HIV-AIDS. *See* AIDS-HIV
Hochschild, Arlie, 165, 167, 266
Hofstadter, Richard, 55–56
Homicide, 85, 453–455, 456, 466
    arrest rates for, 449
    child victims of, 458, 460
    of intimates, by sex of victim, 467*f*
    rate of, 453, 454*f*, 455*f*, 457*f*
    spousal, 460, 474, 479
    women as perpetrators of, 458–459
Homophobia, 185
    friendship in men and, 375,
        384–386, 389
    in schools, 220, 222
    sex-role theory on, 108, 109
    sexual behavior affected by, 436–437
Homosexuality. *See also* Bisexuals; Gay
        men; Lesbians; LGBT community
    in the animal kingdom, 28, 80
    biological essentialism on, 52–54
    brain research on, 38–41, 53–54
    co-education viewed as a risk factor
        for, 205
    "conversion" movement and, 53
    culture and, 80–82
    declassified as a mental illness, 90, 101
    emergence as a distinct identity, 39
    food claimed to produce, 46
    as gender conformity, 54, 432–437
    gender inversion linked to, 54
    genetic research on, 41–42, 53
    hormones and, 48–50
    M-F test, 93
    pedophilia distinguished form, 470
    psychosexual development theory on,
        88, 90–91
    religion and, 243–244
    ritualized, 80–81
    sex-role theory and, 118, 119
    "warning signs" of, 94
Homosocial reproduction, 265
Hong Kong, sexuality in, 439*f*
Hooking up, 424–426
Hooters restaurant chain, 271
Hopkins, Ann, 291–292
Hopkins v. Price Waterhouse, 291–292
Hormones, 23. *See also* Estrogen;
        Testosterone
    gender differences and, 2–3, 42–48
    homosexuality and, 48–50
    intersexuality and, 50–51
Hornby, Nick, 356
Horney, Karen, 96
Hostile environment sexual
        harassment, 299

Housework
    decrease in time spent on, 168, 176
    in gay and lesbian households, sharing
        of, 185
    gendered politics of, 165–177
    men's happiness increased by, 169
    overreporting of, 167
    separate domains of, 166–167
    separation of child care from, 176
    sex life and, 175
Hubbard, Ruth, 55
Hughes, Karen, 176
Hughes, Langston, 260
Humbolt University, 48
Hummer, Tom A., 364
Hungary, views of "traditional" family
    in, 162
Hunting-and-gathering societies, 64*f*,
        83–84, 85
    child care in, 67
    division of labor in, 62, 375
    gender equality in, 64
    separation of spheres in, 25–26
Huntmann, Nina, 362
Hurlbert, Anya, 23
Hurt, Byron, 321–322
Hussein, Saddam, 463
Hwame, 78
Hyde, Janet, 36, 101, 104, 210*f*
Hymenoplasty, 407
Hypermasculinity, 67, 108, 294
Hypothalamus, 39, 40, 41

Iceland, female heads of state in, 312
Id, 88
Imperato-McGinley, Julliane, 51
Impulsive hyperindividualism, 116
Imus, Don, 322
In a Different Voice (Gilligan), 98–100
Incarceration. *See* Prisons/incarceration
Income. *See also* Wages/earnings/salaries
    divorce and, 190
    education and, 219*t*
    inequality in, 268–270, 281
    mathematics scores by, 211*f*
India
    female heads of state in, 312
    importance of economic prosperity
        in, 26
    religion in, 245
    views of "traditional" family in, 162
Indiana University, 31, 364
Indiana University School of
        Medicine, 36
Indonesia, female heads of state in, 312
Industrialization, 156, 195, 388, 389
The Inevitability of Patriarchy
        (Goldberg), 52
Infanticide, 29, 30, 458, 460
    female, 60, 65, 81
    male, 61
Infibulation, 71. *See also* Female
    circumcision
Infidelity, 416
Inheritance, 63–65
Initiation rituals, 70, 78, 97
Instagram, 367, 369

Institute for Experimental Endocrinology (Humbolt University), 48
Institutions
  gender as, 127–133
  the media as a gendered, 345–346
  the media as a gendering, 346–348
  religion as a gendered, 247–250
  social constructionist perspective on, 127–133, 147
  the state as a gendered, 329–336
  violence and, 127–128, 461–463
Instrumental roles, 109, 158
"Intermediate scrutiny" standard, 271, 326
Internet
  gender differences in use of, 369
  pornography on, 363, 364, 365
  social media, 366–367, 367f, 368f
Interplanetary theory of gender difference, vii, 1–2, 4, 11, 145, 190, 373, 483, 484
  in education, 204
  importance of, 14–15
  sexuality and, 410, 411
  in the workplace, 306
Interruptions, 144
Intersexuality/intersexed persons (hermaphrodites), 142
  categories of, 138
  "gay brain" theory on, 54
  hormone studies on, 50–51
  incidence of, 134, 139
  pseudohermaphrodites, 58, 138
Intimate partner violence, 199, 466, 480. *See also* Domestic violence
Intimate relationships. *See* Friendship; Love
Invisibility
  of masculinity, 6–9, 131
  of privilege, 7–9
  of tokens, 294
  of workplace inequality, 296
IQ tests, 34
Iran
  hostage crisis, 128
  social movements in, 333, 335
  women's progress in, 334
Iraq
  sexual assault of female troops in, 468
  U.S. invasion of, 462
  women's progress in, 334
Ireland, female heads of state in, 312
"Iron Maiden," 398
"Is Coeducation Injurious to Girls?" (Dewey), 87
Isabelle (isolated child), 115
Islam, 234, 340
  female circumcision in, 72
  gender differences and inequality in, 238, 240, 241, 242–243, 245
  gender gap in religiosity, 246
  homosexuality and, 243
  purdah in, 73, 75, 398
  social movements and, 334–336
Isolated children, 115
Israel
  female heads of state in, 312
  Orthodox Judaism in, 241, 335–336

Italy
  divorce rate in, 189t
  homicide rate in, 453
  marriage rate in, 189t
  sexuality in, 439f
  the workplace in, 291

Jacklin, Carol, 101
Jackson, Andrew, 317, 462, 464
Jackson, Joe, 433
Jacobs, Jerry, 264
Jacobs, John, 253
Jahjaga, Atifete, 312
Jamaica, female heads of state in, 312
James, Henry, Jr., 7
James, Henry, Sr., 251
Janssen, Erick, 416
Japan
  divorce rate in, 189t
  eating disorders in, 399
  housework division in, 168
  love in, 392–393
  marriage rate in, 189t
  sexuality in, 427, 439f, 440, 441
  teen birth rate in, 179f
  views of "traditional" family in, 162
  the workplace in, 303
Japan Family Planning Association, 427
Al-Jazeera, 243
JBC Men, 253
Jefferson, Thomas, 317
Jehovah's Witnesses, 243, 246
Jencks, Christopher, 228
Jenson, Lois, 299
Jesus, 237, 249
  concern for women, 238
  efforts to remasculinize, 251, 252, 253–255
  feminist views attributed to, 255–256
Jesus, CEO, 254
Jewett, Milo, 206
Jobs Related Almanac, 293
Johns Hopkins University, 192
Johns Hopkins University Medical Center, 47
Johnson, Allan, 470
Johnson, Lyndon, 462
Johnson, Virginia, 434, 435
Johnston, Levi, 151–152
Johnston, Sherry, 151
Joint child custody, 196–197
Journal of the American Medical Association (JAMA)
  on bullying, 220
  on sexuality, 412
Judaism, 234, 236, 335–336
  clergywomen in, 248
  gender differences and inequality in, 240, 241–242, 245
  gender gap in religiosity, 246, 247
  homosexuality and, 243
Jude the Obscure (Hardy), 6
Judge, Timothy, 285
Junia, 238
Justice Department, U.S., 470

"Just-so stories"
  gender-equal societies as, 85
  sociobiology and evolutionary psychology as, 31
  war-homosexuality link as, 49

Kadushin, Alfred, 296
Kalnin, Andrew, 364
Kane, Jonathan, 210, 211f
Kanter, Rosabeth Moss, 12, 130, 294–295
Kantor, Kaufman, 478
Karoshi, 303
Katz, Jack, 459
Kaufman, Debra, 241
Kellaway, Lucy, 306
Kellogg Foundation, 444
Kendall, Laurel, 257
Kennedy, John F., 367
Keraki people, 81
Kerry, John, 319, 322
Kessel, Neil, 48
Kessler, Ronald, 13
Kessler, Suzanne, 134, 142
Kessler-Harris, Alice, 281
Kilbourne, Jean, 357
"Killing Us Softly" (Kilbourne), 357
Kimura, Doreen, 38
King, Larry, 344
Kinsbourne, Marcel, 38
Kinsey, Alfred, 42, 83, 205, 410, 413, 426, 438
Kinship system, 109
Kinsley, Michael, 305
Kirby, Erika, 310
Klebold, Dylan, 222–223
Klein, Randy, 406
Kluckhohn, Clyde, 80, 83
Kluckhohn, Richard, 71
Kohlberg, Lawrence, 94–95, 98
Komorovsky, Mirra, 375
Koniag people, 80
Konigsberg, Ruth, 168
Korea
  cosmetic surgery in, 405
  female heads of state in, 312
  religion in, 257
Kornrich, Sabino, 175
Kosovo, female heads of state in, 312
Koss, Mary, 430, 470, 472–473
Kronenberger, William, 364
Kruk, Edward, 191
Ku Klux Klan, 254
!Kung bushmen, 85

Labarthe, Jean Christophe, 35
Labor Statistics, U.S. Bureau of, 168
Lad lit, 345, 356–357
Ladd, Everett C., 316
Ladd, Katie, 254
Ladies Home Journal poll on housework, 168
Lamb, Michael, 186
Lamon, S., 210f
LaMunyon, Craig W., 33
Landmann, Andreas, 224
Lango people, 80
Langurs, 28

Larceny-theft, 459
Lasch, Christopher, 201
The Last of the Mohicans (Cooper), 355
Latino/as. *See* Hispanics/Latino/as
"Latte pappas," 171
Latvia, female heads of state in, 312
Laumann, Edward, 441, 469
Law of the excluded middle, 11
Laws of nature, 21
Laxton, Beck, 106
Layng, Anthony, 24
Leacock, Eleanor, 65
Lean In (Sandberg), 267, 303
"Lean In Together" campaign, 303
Leaning in, 292, 303
LeBon, Gustav, 22
Lee, Robert E., 356
Lefkowitz, Bernard, 471
Leg lengthening, 408
Lepowsky, Maria, 85
Lerner, Gerda, 155
Lerner, Max, 159
Lesbians
    African-American, 187
    "bed death" in, 434
    brain research on, 39, 41
    in the clergy, 248
    domestic violence and, 479
    family life and, 183–187
    feminism and, 338, 434
    friendship and, 386–387
    gender conformity in, 54, 432,
        433, 434–435
    genetic research on, 42
    hormonal studies on, 50
    psychosexual development theory
        on, 90
    tattoos and, 404
    violence against, 480
Lesotho, parental leave not offered in,
    305, 325
Lessing, Doris, 373
Leupp, Katrina, 175
Levant, Ronald, 431
LeVay, Simon, 28, 39–40, 53, 55
Lever, Janety, 267
Levine, Martin, 432
Levinson, Daniel, 376
Levi-Strauss, Claude, 66
Levy, Jerre, 35, 36
Lewinsky, Monica, 318, 412
Lewis, C. S., 375
Lewis, Robert, 375
Lewontin, Richard, 27–28
LGBT community, 326–327
Liberal feminism, 339, 340
Liberated sexism, 269
Liberia
    female heads of state in, 312
    parental leave not offered in, 305, 325
Libya, social movements in, 335
Life expectancy, 126–127, 163, 173,
    444, 445f
"Life Satisfaction Across Nations" (York
    and Bell), 331
Life Without Father (Popenoe), 181
Lifetime Television, 353, 354

Lifton, Robert Jay, 488
Limbaugh, Rush, 324–325, 354
Lincoln, Abraham, 317
Lindberg, Sara, 211f
Ling, Yazhu, 23
Linn, Marcia, 211f
Lithuania, female heads of state in, 312
Livingston, Beth, 285
Lloyd, Elisabeth, 31
Locker room syndrome, 406
Long, James, 22–23
Loomis, Laura Spencer, 193
Lopata, Helena, 117
Lorber, Judith, 76, 285, 451, 484
Lotus, 292
Love, 30, 373, 387–395
    feminized, 376, 390–391, 394, 420
    gender and, 389–390
    gendered, American style, 390–394
    historical gendering of, 387–389
Lugo, William, 361, 366
Lutheran Church, 248
Lyle, Katy, 212
Lynch, Dennis, 406
Lynching, 332
Lynd, Helen, 159
Lynd, Robert, 159

M Butterfly (film), 135
Macaques, 28
Maccoby, Eleanor, 101, 195–196
Mace, R., 64
Machihembra, 51
MacKinnon, Catharine, 297, 411
Mad Men (television program), 268, 269
Magazines, 357–359
Mai, Mukhtar, 69
Mainardi, Pat, 165–166
Malaysia, sexuality in, 439f
Male and Female (Mead), 60
Male bonding, 65–66, 68, 81, 374
Male domination, 3
    biological essentialism on, 52
    bonding and, 65–66
    circumcision linked to, 71, 72
    culture and, 59f, 63–66, 69, 83–85
    the family and, 200
    housework and, 166
    in nonhuman primates, 28
    politics of, 15–16
    prevalence of, 2
    private property and, 63–65
    psychosexual development theory
        on, 98
    rape and, 69, 146
    religion and, 235, 245, 257
    warfare and, 65–66
Male gaze, 406, 407
Male menopause, 45
Male Sex Role Identity model, 111
Male Sex Role Strain model, 111
Malinowski, Bronislaw, 438
Malleus Maleficarum, 243
Malta, female heads of state in, 312
Mandel, Ruth, 314
The Manhood of the Master (Sunday), 251
The Manliness of Christ (Sunday), 251

The Manly Christ (Sunday), 251
"Manly-hearted women," 78
Manson, Marilyn, 135
Marbles, Jenna, 368
Marcotte, Amanda, 477f
Marind-anim people, 81
Marital rape, 473–474, 476
Mark, Kristen P., 416
Market economy, 65
Marquesa people, 82
Marriage. *See also* Divorce; Same-sex
        marriage
    companionate, 388, 389
    covenant, 194–195
    culture and, 60
    decline in happiness of, 200
    education and, 208
    friendship and, 383
    gendered, 163–165
    historical perspective
        on, 154, 157
    housework inequality increased
        by, 168
    love and, 389–390, 392, 393–394
    median age at first, 157, 160, 160f
    percentage by gender, 188
    percentage of never-married persons,
        153f, 161
    "Plan B" for, 201–202
    private property and, 63–65
    rape in, 473–474, 476
    rates of, 152, 153, 157, 189t
    religion and, 239, 240
    resilience of, 153
    sex and, 163, 175, 426, 428f, 435,
        439–440, 440f
    testosterone depressed by, 45
    working mothers happier in, 178
Mars and Venus in the Workplace
    (Gray), 306
Martin, Lynn, 299
Martineau, Harriet, 58
Martino, Wayne, 209, 215
Maruoka, Etsuko, 242
Marvel Comics, 107
Marx, Karl, 63, 480
Marx, Patricia, 405
Mary Magdalene, 237
Masai people, 83
Masculine bravado, 452
Masculinities, 10, 112, 118
Masculinity
    aging and, 126
    AIDS-HIV and, 442–444
    compulsive, 109
    cultural definitions of, 3, 4, 58, 59,
        60–61, 65, 67, 116
    current debate about, 9
    education and, 220
    globalization and, 331
    hegemonic, 10, 15, 119
    hormonal influences on, 43
    hyper-, 67, 108, 294
    invisibility of, 6–9, 131
    through the life course, 123
    M-F test, 91–93, 107
    plural meanings of, 10–11

of politics, 317–320
psychosexual development theory on, 98
redefining, 485, 487, 488
religion and, 251
sex-role theory on, 107–113, 117–119
social constructionist perspective on, 116–117
violence and, 451, 452, 464, 465
war and, 462–463
the workplace and, 265–266, 293, 294
Masculinization of sex, 409, 420
Mason, Karen Oppenheim, 307
Mason, Katherine, 400
Massachusetts State Department of Education, 211
Masters, William, 434, 435
Masturbation, 413, 421, 422f, 431, 438
Mate guarding, 32
"Maternal instinct," 29, 60
Maternity leave, 200. *See also* Parental leave
Mathematics, gender differences in, 11–12, 36, 204, 210–211f, 214–215, 226t, 231, 232
Mathews, Vincent, 364
Matriarchal religions, 236. *See also* Goddess traditions
Matrilinearity, 85
Mattox, William R., 178
Maudsley, Henry, 206
Maume, David, 295
Maxim, 358–359
May, Samuel B., 240
McCain, John, 320
McCartney, Bill, 253
McCaughey, Martha, 25
McClintock, Barbara, 128
McClintock, Martha, 32
McGraw, Phil (Dr. Phil), 344, 354
McKenna, Wendy, 134
McKibbin, William, 33
McMillan, Laurie, 368
McNeil, Mike, 271
Mead, Margaret, 60–61, 62f, 67, 151, 437–438, 464
Mead, Sara, 217–218
Media, 343–370
children and, 347, 348–352
convergence and equality increase in, 368–370
as a gendered institution, 345–346
as a gendering institution, 346–348
pervasiveness of, 343–344
pornographic (*see* Pornography)
print, 355–360
social, 366–367, 367f, 368f
television (*see* Television)
video games, 344, 360–363, 361f, 364
Media Education Foundation, 362
Media Research Center, 358
Medial zone of the hypothalamus, 39
Medved, Caryn, 164
Mehinaku people, 68
Meir, Golda, 128, 455

Men. *See also* Fathers/fatherhood; Gender entries; Male domination; Masculinity
adornment of, 74
AIDS-HIV in, 442–444
arrest rates for, 449
body image issues in, 400–403
body politicization and, 241
brain research findings, 33–38
cosmetic surgery for, 405, 406
divorce impact on, 191
as domestic violence victims, 458, 460, 474–477
eating disorders in, 401–402
educated women valued by, 208
education for manhood, traditional, 205–206
in the family, historical perspective on, 154–163
feminism and, 340–342, 488
gender politics and, 340–342
life expectancy of, 126–127
marriage benefits, 163–164, 392
married, percentage of, 188
never-married, 153f, 161
power and, 121–122
rape of, 30, 466
religious re-engagement of, 251–255
retirement and, 126
sexual harassment of, 298, 301, 303
sexual peak myth, 123–124, 439–440
stress, reactions to, 13, 37–38, 165, 376–377
in teaching, 223, 224, 225, 226
tokenism and, 295–296
top 12 reasons for having sex, 429
wage decline for, 269–270, 281–282
workplace discrimination claims of, 271, 292–293
"Men and Women Are from Earth" (Barnett and Rivers), 145
Men and Women of the Corporation (Kanter), 12, 294–295
"Men as Women and Women as Men" (Lorber), 76
Men Can Stop Rape (MCSR), 342
Men's Health, 175, 359, 400, 441
Men's huts, 68, 85
"Men's liberation," 375
Menstruation, 21, 26, 29, 31, 32, 48, 82, 241
Merit Systems Protection Board, U.S., 301
Merkel, Angela, 312
Mertz, Janet, 210, 211f
Messerschmidt, James, 147, 480
Meston, Cindy, 429
Meyer, Doug, 480
M-F test, 91–93, 107
Michaels, Stuart, 437, 469
Michelet, Jules, 410
Michels, Robert, 469
Middle East
female circumcision in, 72
gender fluid cultures in, 78
sexuality in, 439
Middletown, 159
Midlife crisis, 124–125
Migliano, A. B., 64

Mikvah, 241
Miles, Catherine Cox, 91, 92, 93, 107
Milhausen, Robin R., 416
Military. *See also* Citadel; Virginia Military Institute
transgender persons banned from service, 328
women in, 23, 63, 326
Mill, John Stuart, 483
Miller, Amanda, 175
Miller, Claire Cain, 225
Miller, Monica, 361
Miller, Stuart, 384–385
Miller, Walter, 108–109
Millett, Kate, 485
Million Man March, 487
Mills, C. Wright, 114
Minangkabau people, 85
Minyan, 240
Miranda, V., 261
Miss America pageant, 398
Miss Universe pageant, 328, 329f
MIT, 217
Mitsubishi Motor Corporation, 299
MMORPG (massively multiplayer online role-playing games), 360, 363
Mnookin, Robert, 195–196
Mocumbi, Pascoal, 442
Mohammed, 238
Mohave Indians, 78
"Mommy track," 132, 305, 309
Mondale, Walter, 462
Money, John, 45–46, 47
Mongolia, life expectancy gap in, 127
Monkeys, 44
Monogamy
in the animal kingdom, 28
evolutionary theory on, 24–25, 28, 32
in gay men and lesbians, 435
male bonding and, 66
private property and, 65
Monopolization behavior, 32
Monotheism, 234, 236, 240, 243, 248
Monroe, Marilyn, 398
Montaigne, Michel, 374–375
Montana Men Against Rape, 342
Moore, Zachary T., 413
Mora, Richard, 403
Morgan, Robin, 339
Mormons, 243
Mortality gap, 446
Mosier, Kristine, 364
"Mother to Son" (Hughes), 260
Mothers/motherhood
in Bari people, 31–32
child abuse and, 198
child care and, 154–155, 166, 169
child custody and, 195–197
child-to-parent violence and, 199
cognitive development theories on, 98
culture and, 60–61
day care "problem" and, 178–179
divorce and, 190–191
gender socialization and, 12–13
historical perspective on, 154, 156
housework and, 166
infanticide and, 29, 458, 460

Mothers/motherhood (*Continued*)
"maternal instinct" belief, 29, 60
"mommy track" and, 132, 305, 309
psychosexual development theory on, 89, 90, 97–98
sex-role theory on, 109
single mothers, 13, 152, 157, 181–183
as sole "calling," 156
teenage, 179–181, 179*f*, 422
workplace participation rate, 262, 263*f*, 264*f*
Muehlenhard, Charlene, 418
Mullet, Sam, 336, 337*f*
Multicultural feminism, 340
Mundugumor people, 60–61, 62*f*
Muscle dysmorphia, 401, 403
Muscular Christianity, 251–252, 253, 255, 256
Muslims. *See* Islam
Muxe, 76–77
The Myth of Masculinity (Pleck), 111

Nadle, 76
Nangurai, Priscilla, 73
Nardi, Bonnie, 84
Nardi, Peter, 386
National Academy of Sciences, 182, 449
National Assessment of Educational Progress, 227
National Association for Single Sex Public Education, 230
National Clearinghouse on Marital and Date Rape, 473
National College Women Sexual Victimization Study, 470
National Committee on Pay Equity, 282
National Congregations Study, 250
National Family Violence Survey, 478–479
National Gay and Lesbian Task Force, 53
National Health and Social Life Survey, 244
National Institute for Mental Health, 178
National Institutes of Health, 138, 177
National Intimate Partner and Sexual Violence Survey (NISVS), 466, 468, 478*f*, 479, 479*f*
National Nursing Shortage Reform and Patient Advocacy Act, 276
National Organization for Men Against Sexism (NOMAS), 342
National Organization for Women, 232
National Pay Inequity Awareness Day, 282
The National Report on Work and Family, 306
National Study of the Changing Workforce, 295
National Survey of Families and Households, 168
National Television Violence Study, 351
National Transgender Discrimination Survey, 327–328
National Woman Suffrage Association, 337
Nation-state, 63, 65
Native American cultures, 76, 77–78, 80, 83
A Natural History of Rape (Thornhill and Palmer), 27
Natural selection, 21, 22

Nature *vs.* nurture debate, 2–5, 23, 47. *See also* Biological determinism; Differential socialization
Navajo Indians, 76
Nell (film), 115
Nelson, Mariah Burton, 370
Neolithic societies, 84–85
Netherlands
child care sharing in, 171
divorce rate in, 189*t*
marriage rate in, 189*t*
teen birth rate in, 179*f*
the workplace in, 291
Neuebauer, Martin, 224
Neumark-Sztainer, Dianne, 426
Neurosis, 88
"New lad" magazines, 358–359
New Testament, 237, 238
New York University, 34
New Zealand
AIDS-HIV in, 442
female heads of state in, 312
the workplace in, 291
Newsweek poll on spousal earnings, 266
Nielsen, Arrah, 285
Nigeria, religion in, 245
Nisbett, Richard, 466
Noah, Joakim, 370
Non-binary (NB) identity, 138–140
Nonrelational sex, 431–432
Noonan, K. M., 27
NORC sex survey, 417, 421
North County (film), 299
Northeastern University, 225
Norway
female heads of state in, 312
importance of economic prosperity in, 26
life expectancy gap in, 127
out-of-wedlock births in, 181
parental leave policies in, 200
the workplace in, 291, 306
Novels, 355–357
Nuclear family
emergence of, 63–65
idealization of, 157–158
love expression in, 394
percentage of children living in, 160
women's status and, 67
Nursing, gender composition of, 276–277

Oakley, Ben, 222
Obama, Barack, 311, 320, 321–322
O'Barr, William, 145
Obesity, 400–401
O'Byrne, Rachel, 468
Occupational sex segregation, 132–133, 272–281
Occupational system, 109
O'Connor, John Cardinal, 234
Oedipal crisis, 89, 98, 109, 451
Oedipus the King (Sophocles), 89
"On Friendship" (Montaigne), 374–375
"On the Genesis of the Castration Complex in Women" (Horney), 96
On the Origin of Species (Darwin), 21
Online College Social Life Survey, 425

Oral sex, 83, 416–417, 424, 426–427, 428–430, 439
Oral stage of psychosexual development, 88
Orenstein, Peggy, 209, 227
Organization for Economic Cooperation and Development (OECD), 261, 268
Orgasm, 244, 410, 412, 425–426, 432
cultural differences in, 82
evolutionary theory on, 31, 33
faking, 427–428
increased attention to, 409
political affiliation and, 441
simultaneous, 419
vaginal, myth of, 421
Orgasm gap, 425–426
The Origin of the Family, Private Property and the State (Engels), 63
Original sin, 243, 249, 256
Orthodox Judaism, 240, 241–242, 243, 245, 248, 335–336
Osten-Sacken, Thomas von der, 72
Out-of-wedlock births, 152, 180–181
"Overdoing Gender" (Willer), 108
Overing, Joanna, 452
Ovulation, 31, 32, 81
Own, Jesse, 426
Oxfam, 467
Oxytocin, 37, 376–377

Pachamama, 236
Packwood, Robert, 299
Padgug, Robert, 55
Page, A., 64
Paige, Jeffrey, 73, 75
Paige, Karen, 73, 75
Pakistan
female heads of state in, 312
life expectancy gap in, 127
Palin, Bristol, 151–152
Palin, Sarah, 151–152, 320–321
Palin, Todd, 151
Palmer, Craig, 27, 30, 467
Paltrow, Gwyneth, 125
Paoletti, Jo, 97
Papua New Guinea, parental leave not offered in, 305, 325
Parental leave, 175, 200, 305, 308–310, 325
Parents/parenting. *See also* Children; Family; Fathers/fatherhood; Mothers/motherhood; Single parents/parenting
child-to-parent violence and, 197
evolutionary theory on, 28
gay and lesbian, 185–187
gender expectations of children, 170
historical perspective on, 154
parent-to-child violence and, 197–199, 458, 460
Park Geun-hye, 312
Parsons, Talcott, 109, 158
Pascoe, C. J., 106
Passages (Sheehy), 124
Paternity leave, 175, 200, 309. *See also* Parental leave
Paul, Pamela, 365
Paul, Saint, 239, 240, 257

Pay Equity Act of 1963, 304
Pay-equity schemes, 304
Pearson, Patricia, 458
Pedophilia, 249, 469–470
Pedulla, David, 271–272
Peiss, Kathy, 132
Penile enlargement surgery, 406
Penis, 50, 134, 412, 419
Penis envy, 89, 96–97
Penn State University, 390
Peplau, Letitia, 377
Pepperdine University, 306
Perelberg, Rosine, 243
A Perfect Murder (film), 125
"Performing Gender on YouTube"
    (Wotanis and McMillan), 368
Persad-Bissessar, Kamla, 312
Peters, Joan, 179, 310
Petersen, Jennifer, 211*f*
Petty, Tom, 466
Pew Forum on Religion and Public
    Life, 244
Pew Research Center for the People and
    the Press, 168, 244
Phallic stage of psychosexual
    development, 89
Phallocentrism, 365, 412, 418
Phelan, Jo, 190
Philippines, female heads of state in, 312
*A Physician's Counsels to Woman in Health
    and Disease* (Taylor), 20–21
Piaget, Jean, 94
Piaroas, 452
Pillard, Richard, 41–42, 53
"Pink Frilly Dresses and the Avoidance of
    All Things 'Girly'" (Halim), 105
Pinterest, 367
Pipher, Mary, 300
Pittenger, Mary-Jo, 413
Pittman, Frank, 181
Plante, Rebecca, 414
Plato, 374
Playboy Bunnies, 271
Pleck, Joseph, 111, 375
Plummer, Ken, 436
PMS. *See* Premenstrual syndrome
Poland
    female heads of state in, 312
    religion in, 245
"The Policy Exists but You Can't Really
    Use it" (Kirby), 310
Politicization of the body, 240–241
Politics, 311–342
    of biological essentialism, 52–54
    deep voices preferred by voters, 320
    of gender, 322–327
    of gender difference, 15–16
    gender gap in elected officials, 312–315
    gender gap in voting, 315–317
    of housework and child care, 165–177
    life satisfaction and participation in, 331
    of male domination, 15–16
    masculinity of, 317–320
    men and gender issues, 340–342
    of PMS, 48
    redressing the gendered realm
        of, 336–340

sex and, 440–441
social movements and, 333–336,
    333*f*, 334*f*
the state as a gendered institution,
    329–336
survey on women leaders, 313*f*
talk time, by gender, 314–315
transgender persons and the law,
    327–328
The Politics of Reproductive Ritual (Paige
    and Paige), 73
Pollack, William, 214
Pollitt, Katha, 267, 356
Polo ad campaign, 214
Polygamy/polygyny, 60, 61
Polyvocality, 358
Pool, Robert, 37
Pope, Harrison, 401
Popenoe, David, 181, 182, 190
Pornified (Paul), 365
Pornography, 344, 363–366
    feminist opposition to, 339, 415
    perceptions and attitudes influenced
        by, 365
    pervasiveness of, 365
    size of U.S. industry, 363
    women as consumers of, 363
Portugal, female heads of state in, 312
Pospisilova, Dagmar, 450
Post-Freudian theories, 94–96
Poverty, 157, 160, 181, 182
Power
    domestic violence and, 476, 480
    institutions and, 127, 128
    invisiblity of, 9
    rape and, 146, 472, 473
    sex-role theory on, 119, 120
    sexuality and, 417
    social constructionist perspective
        on, 121–122
Power Team, 253
Powerlessness and rape, 472, 473
Preca, Marie Louise Coleiro, 312
Pregnancy discrimination, 304, 305
Pregnancy Discrimination Act of 1978, 305
Premature ejaculation, 418–419
Premenstrual dysphoric disorder, 101
Premenstrual syndrome (PMS), 48, 59, 101
Presidential campaigns/elections, 317–322
Primary sex characteristics, 134–135
Primates, nonhuman, 28–29, 39, 44
"The Princess" (Tennyson), 155
Princeton University, 217, 226
Print media, 355–360
Prisons/incarceration, 30, 453, 455, 480
Private Lessons (film), 126
Private property, male domination
    and, 63–65
Privilege, invisibility of, 7–9
Prohibition, 251
Promiscuity
    in the animal kingdom, 28
    evolutionary theory on, 24–25, 27,
        28, 31–32
    in gay men, 184–185
Promise Keepers, 253, 341, 487
Protected classes, 326

Protestantism, 240, 244, 246, 248,
    250, 251, 255–256
Prozac, 37
Pseudohermaphrodites, 58, 138
Psychology Today study on male body
    image, 401
Psychosexual development theory, 87–91
    feminist challenges to, 94, 96–98
    overview of, 88–91
Psychosis, 88
Puberty, 42–43, 51, 403
Publix Super Markets, Inc., 287
Puerto Ricans, domestic violence and, 478
Pulpit and Pew study, 250
Purdah, 73, 75, 398
Pyke, Karen, 147

Al Qaeda, 336
Quayle, Dan, 53
Quechua people, 236
Quid pro quo sexual harassment, 298–299
Quindlen, Anna, 167
Quinn, Beth, 374
Quinn, Jane Bryant, 12
Quinn, Zoe, 362
Quota systems, 306
Qur'an, 238

Race and ethnicity. *See also* specific racial
        and ethnic groups
    beauty standards and, 397, 408
    biological theories on, 22
    brain research and, 33
    domestic violence and, 478–479,
        478*f*, 479*f*
    education and, 218, 219*t*, 231, 232, 270
    friendship and, 382–383
    health and, 444
    life expectancy by, 444, 445*f*
    marriage and, 161
    the media and, 345, 353, 354
    politics and, 316–317, 316*f*
    sex-role theory on, 108, 109, 118, 120
    sexual orientation and, 187
    sexuality and, 332–333, 438–439
    transgenderism and, 328
    wages by, 282, 283*f*, 286
    the workplace and, 270–271, 287, 295
"Race suicide," 157
Racism, 22, 33, 108, 109, 270–271,
    332–333, 382–383, 397
Radcliff College, 227
Radiant devaluation, 269
Radical feminism, 339–340, 415
Rahman, Qazi, 108
Ralph Lauren ad campaign, 214
Ramadan, 238
Randall, Tony, 125
Random Hearts (film), 126
Rape, 467–474
    acquaintance, 470
    arrest rates for, 449
    Cleaver on, 333
    cross-cultural explanations of, 68,
        69–70
    date, 473
    by fathers, 468

Rape (*Continued*)
gang rape, 69, 70, 146, 471
incidence of, 431, 466
intimate partner, 478f, 479f
male victims of, 30, 466
marital, 473–474, 476
by "normal" men, 470–473
pornography and, 415
"reproductive strategy" argument, 27,
29–30, 69, 70, 145–146, 467, 470
social constructionist perspective
on, 145–147
women's status and, 68, 146, 468
in the workplace, 298
Rape Awareness Week, 481
Rape cultures/rape-prone societies, 468
Rape-as-recreation model, 467
Rate My Professor (website), 225
"The Rating and Dating Complex"
(Waller), 390
Rating-dating-mating complex, 390,
424, 425
Ratzinger, Joseph Cardinal.
See Benedict XVI, Pope
Rawlings, William, 164
Raye, Martha, 125
Read, Jen'nan Ghazal, 241
Reading
gender differences in, 35–36
percentage of students at the
proficient level, 349f
Reagan, Ronald, 462
Reality makeover shows, 353–354
"Reasonable woman" standard, 301
Reay, Diane, 209
Reddit, 309, 367
Reebok International, 292
Reed, Sarah, 187
Reflexive passivity, 116
Reform Judaism, 248
Reimer, Bruce, 47
Reiner, William, 134
Religion, 234–259
clergy of, 248–250
gender differences and, 20, 238–244,
245, 248
gender inequality and, 236, 238–244,
245, 248, 259
gender of God, 234, 238
as a gendered institution, 247–250
historical gendering of, 235–238
monotheistic, 234, 236, 240, 243, 248
re-engaging men in, 251–255
woman-centered spirituality, 238,
255–258
Religiosity
gender gap in, 245–247, 246f, 251, 255
same-sex marriage and, 244
The Reproduction of Mothering
(Chodorow), 98
Reproductive strategies, 24–25, 31–32.
See also Rape, "reproductive strategy"
argument
Reproductive success, 24–25, 27, 30
Republican Party, 183–184, 247, 315, 316,
317, 318, 441
Reskin, Barbara, 272

Resnick, Michael, 426
Retirement, 126
Reverse discrimination, 121, 233, 296, 341
Revirgination.net, 407
Reynaud, Emmanuel, 412
Rezac, Petr, 450
Rhode, Deborah, 119, 205, 300
Riche, Martha Farnsworthe, 170
Richmond, Geri, 266
Riesman, David, 228
"The Rights and Conditions of Women"
(May), 240
Risman, Barbara, 12–13, 173, 424
Ritual purification, 241
Ritualized homosexuality, 80–81
Rituals of gender, 70–75, 80. *See also*
Initiation rituals
Rivera, Mariano, 370
Rivers, Caryl, 145
Robbery, 449, 459
Rockettes, 271
Rogers, Laura, 353–354
Rohypnol, 83
Roman mythology, 236
Romney, Mitt, 322, 323f
Roosevelt, Franklin Delano, 97, 317
Roosevelt, Theodore, 157, 216, 317, 462
Roper Center, 316
Rosaldo, Michelle, 84
Rossi, Alice, 52
Rousseff, Dilma, 312
Rubin, Gayle, 14
Rubin, Lillian, 162
on friendship, 378, 383, 385, 386,
387–388, 394–395
on love, 391
on pornography, 365
on psychosexual development theory, 97
on sexuality, 411, 416, 421, 427–428, 439
Rudman, Laurie, 190
Ruskin, John, 481
Russia
divorce rate in, 188
incarceration rate in, 453
love in, 392–393
the workplace in, 273
Rutgers University, 314
Rutz, Jim, 46
Rwandan genocide, 467

Sabo, Don, 232
Sacks, Karen. *See* Brodkin, Karen
Sadker, David, 207, 208
Sadker, Myra, 207, 208
Safe sex, 441–442
Salini, G. D., 64
Sambia culture, 80–81
"Sambo theory of oppression," 120
Same-sex marriage, 80, 152, 153, 315,
326–327
current legal status in U.S., 184f
increasing support for, 187, 187f
"problem" of, 183–185
religion and, 244, 245f
Sammy and Rosie Get Laid (film), 418
Sanchez-Janowski, Martin, 182
Sanday, Peggy Reeves, 68, 69, 70, 85, 235, 467

Sandberg, Sheryl, 267, 303
Santeria, 235
Sapolsky, Robert, 28, 44, 45
Sarkeesian, Anita, 362
Sartre, Jean-Paul, 113
Sasha (gender-neutral child), 106
Sassler, Sharon, 175
Saturday Night Live (television program),
135–136
Saudi Arabia
female legislators in, 313
media in, 343
women's progress in, 334
Savage, Mike, 354
Savic, Ivanka, 41
Sax, Linda, 218–219
Scarborough, Joe, 322
Schilt, Kristen, 136, 280
Schmidt, Benjamin, 225
School. *See* Education
Schroeder, Pat, 314
Schwartz, Andrew, 143
Schwartz, Christine, 208
Schwartz, Martin, 476
Schwartz, Pepper, 424
Schwarzenegger, Arnold, 319
Science, gender differences in, 214–215,
217f, 226, 226t, 227, 231, 232
Scully, Diana, 471, 472
Searching for Debra Winger (film), 126
Sears, 280–281
Seasons of a Man's Life
(Levinson et al.), 124
The Second Sex (Beauvoir), 375
"Second shift," 165, 173, 176
Secondary sex characteristics, 134–135
Second-wave feminism, 338, 357
Seelye, L. Clark, 206
Segal, Lynne, 389
Seguino, Stephanie, 235
Seidler, Vic, 465
Selective serotonin reuptake inhibitors, 37
Semenya, Caster, 139
Sen, Amartya, 446
Senate bill 739, 276
Seneca Falls Women's Convention, 336, 341
Senegal, female heads of state in, 312
"Separate but equal" standard, 229, 232
Separation of spheres, 201, 223, 261, 486,
487–488
declining support for, 162
evolutionary theory on, 25–26
friendship and, 388, 389
historical perspective on, 155–156,
157, 158
love and, 389, 390
male domination and, 166
Serotonin, 37–38
Sesame Street (television program), 350
Seton, Ernest Thompson, 216
The Seven Promises of a Promise Keeper
(McCartney), 253
Sevre-Duszynska, Janice, 250
Sex (biological), 3
Sex and Personality (Terman and Miles), 91
*Sex and Temperament in Three Primitive
Societies* (Mead), 60, 62f

Sex discrimination. *See* Gender discrimination
Sex education, 180, 420–421, 422
Sex in Education: or; A Fair Chance for the Girls (Clarke), 22
Sex segregation
  in cultural ritual practices, 68, 81
  in education, 206–207
  occupational, 132–133, 272–281
  in religion, 248, 258
  in social media, 367
  women's status and, 68, 81
Sexism, 269, 311–312, 356
Sex-role theory, 106–113
  on institutions, 127, 128, 131
  limitations of, 110–113, 117–120, 122
  M-F test and, 91
  overview of, 107–110
  on political office and gender, 313–314
Sexual abuse, 458, 469–470
Sexual agency, 179, 421, 431
Sexual ambiguity, 137–138
Sexual assault, 430–431, 468, 469, 470. *See also* Rape
Sexual customs, 82–83
Sexual diversity, 80–83
Sexual division of labor. *See* Gendered division of labor
Sexual double standard, 409–412
Sexual entitlement, 425
Sexual harassment
  hostile environment form, 299-300
  legal standard of, 301
  of men, 298, 301, 303
  quid pro quo form, 298–299
  in schools, 211–212, 212*f*
  in the workplace, 268, 297–303, 304
"Sexual Harassment and Masculinity" (Quinn), 374
Sexual orientation. *See also* Gay men; Homosexuality; Lesbians
  birth order and, 50
  brain research on, 38–41
  hormones and, 48
  psychosexual development theory on, 89–91, 96
  race and, 187
  sexuality and, 54
Sexual Politics (Millett), 485
"Sexual psychologies," 24–25
Sexual response, 410
Sexual revolution, 409–410, 420, 432
Sexual socialization, 417–420
Sexual terrorism, 146
Sexuality, 409–444
  adult convergence in, 426–432
  age of first intercourse, 409, 421
  behaviors in, percentage performing, 423*t*
  best and worst, by country, 438*f*, 439*f*
  culture and, 82–83, 437–438
  factors other than gender affecting, 437–441
  fantasies about, 413–416
  friendship and, 381, 382, 383–384
  gender as organizing principle of, 54
  health and, 441–444

hooking up, 424–426
housework impact on, 175
infidelity in, 416
love and, 387–389, 390, 393
marriage and, 163, 175, 426, 428*f*, 435, 439–440, 440*f*
masculinization of, 409, 420
in nonhuman primates, 28–29
problems, evaluation for, 419–420
racism and, 332–333
religion and, 243, 244
sexual peak myth, 123–124, 439–440
sexual socialization and, 417–420
sociobiology on, 24–25, 31–32
time spent thinking about, 413
top 12 reasons for having sex, 429
virginity pledges and, 422–424
in youth, 179–180, 409*f*, 411, 417–418, 421, 428–430
Sexually transmitted diseases (STDs), 422, 424. *See also* AIDS-HIV
Shackelford, Todd, 33
Shakers, 255
Shakespeare, William, 19, 448
Shaktism, 236
Shamanism, 257
Shavante people, 452
Sheffield, Carol, 146
Shelton, Beth Ann, 170
Sherrod, Drury, 386
Sherrod, Nancy, 431
Shilts, Randy, 53
Shoplifting, 459
Sibling violence, 198–199, 458
Silicon Valley companies, 309
Simmel, Georg, 8
Simmons, Martin, 382–383
Simmons, Rachel, 460–461
Simon, Rita, 458
Simpson, O. J., 474
Simpson-Miller, Portia, 312
Singapore, sexuality in, 439*f*
Single parents/parenthood
  fathers as, 13, 153, 161, 181
  increase in, 160–161, 181
  mothers as, 13, 152, 157, 181–183
  social problems associated with, 152
Singles in America Survey, 392
Single-sex schools/classrooms, 227–232
Sioux Indians, 78
Siriono people, 83
Sirleaf, Ellen Johnson, 312
Siwans, 81
Skolnick, Arlene, 193, 199
Skynyrd, Lynyrd, 466
Smith, D., 64
Smith College, 206, 226, 227
"Smurfette Principle," 356
Snake Goddess, 237*f*
Snapchat, 369
Social class
  child care and, 169
  divorce and, 190
  domestic violence and, 478–479
  education and, 228
  family life and, 156
  friendship and, 383

health and, 444
housework and, 169
sexuality and, 438
weight and, 399
work and, 178
Social constructionist (sociological) perspective, 5, 53, 114–148
  central premise of, 10
  on communication, 142–145
  on gender through the life course, 122–125
  on institutions, 127–133, 147
  overview of, 116–117
  on power, 121–122
  on rape, 145–147
Social Darwinism, 21–23, 24, 55–56
Social media, 366–367, 367*f*, 368*f*
"Social men," 78
Social psychology of sex roles, 106–113
Socialization. *See* Differential socialization; Gender socialization; Sexual socialization
Society in America (Martineau), 58
Sociobiology, 23, 24–32
  anthropomorphic language used in, 29
  criticism of arguments, 27–32
  as a "just-so story," 31
  on separation of spheres, 25–26
  on sexuality, 24–25, 31–32
Sociological perspective. *See* Social constructionist perspective
Solberg, Erna, 312
Solomon, Robert, 394
Sommers, Christina Hoff, 213, 358
Sophocles, 89
South, violence in, 464, 465, 466
South Korea
  cosmetic surgery in, 405
  female heads of state in, 312
Southern Baptist Convention, 239, 249
Soy products, 46
Spain
  importance of economic prosperity in, 26
  sexuality in, 440
  views of "traditional" family in, 162
  the workplace in, 291
Spain, Daphne, 68
Spanking, 197–198
Speed-dating, 26
Sperm, 29, 33
The Spirit and the Flesh (Williams), 76
"The Spirit of the College" (Durant), 204
Splenium, 37
Sports, 232–233, 354, 360, 361, 369–370
Spretnak, Charlene, 258
Spur Posse, 146
"Squaw Jim and His Squaw" (photo), 77*f*
Sri Lanka
  female heads of state in, 312
  life expectancy gap in, 127
Stacey, Judith, 186
Stalking, 466, 478*f*, 479*f*
Standards of female beauty, 396–400
Stanford University, 44, 91, 290
Stanko, Elizabeth, 480
Stanton, Elizabeth Cady, 259

State University of New York at Stony Brook, 226, 242
Steinem, Gloria, 48
Steinmetz, Susan, 475
Stereotypes
gay, 39, 271–272
gender (*see* Gender stereotypes)
racial, 272, 321–322
Stern, Howard, 354
Steroid use, 403
Stickups, 459
Stimpson, Catharine, 5, 215
Stoller, Robert, 140
Stoltenberg, John, 365
Stone, I. F., 462–463
Stone, Lawrence, 188, 389
Stonewall riots, 433
Stossel, John, 49
Stowe, Harriet Beecher, 155
Straujuma, Laimdota, 312
Straus, Murray, 197, 198–199, 473
Stress, 13, 37–38, 45, 49, 165, 173, 376–377
"Strict scrutiny" standard, 270–271, 326
The Stronger Women Get, the More Men Love Football (Nelson), 370
Stroud, Angela, 453
Structuralist-functionalist school of social science, 157–158
Stryker, Susan, 140
The Subjection of Women (Mill), 483
Subjective objectification, 269
Subtle sexism, 269
Sudan, female legislators in, 313
Sulimani, Faizah, 334
Sumerau, Ed, 255
Summer of '42 (film), 126
Summers, Alicia, 361
Summers, Lawrence, 210, 226
Sunday, Billy, 251–252, 252f, 253, 256
Super-ego, 88
Supportive discouragement, 269
Supreme Court decisions
on educational equality, 229, 232, 280, 341
on gender discrimination, 271
on gender-sex distinction, 3
on racial discrimination, 270–271
on same-sex marriage, 183, 187
on sexual harassment, 212, 301, 303
on workplace discrimination, 270–271, 280–281, 291–292
Surviving the Breakup (Wallerstein), 191
Swain, Scott, 380
Swanson, E. Guy, 108–109
Swaziland
life expectancy gap in, 127
parental leave not offered in, 305, 325
Sweden
child care sharing in, 171
corporal punishment banned in, 198
divorce rate in, 188, 189t
housework division in, 168
marriage rate in, 189t
out-of-wedlock births in, 181
parental leave policies in, 200
the workplace in, 306

Swidler, Leonard, 238, 255
The Symbolic Annihilation of Women by the Mass Media (Tuchman), 357
Symons, Donald, 24–25
Szydlo, Beata, 312

Tadpole (film), 126
Tahrir Square, 333f
Taiwan
female heads of state in, 312
views of "traditional" family in, 162
Take Back the Night, 342
Talackova, Jenna, 329f
Taliban, 240, 334, 335, 336
Tanala people, 80
Tannen, Deborah, 144, 145
Tatlow, Didi Kirsten, 268
Tattoos, 404, 407f
Tavris, Carol, 11, 28, 228–229, 391, 394
Taylor, Jeremy, 375
Taylor, Mary, 264
Taylor, W. C., 20–21
Tchambuli people, 61, 62f
Teachers, 223–227
Tebow, Tim, 253f, 253–254
Technical virgins, 412
Teena, Brandon, 137f
Teenage mothers, 179–181, 179f, 422
Teenagers. *See* Youth
Telephone, gender differences in use of, 378, 381
Television, 360
children and, 347, 350–351
gender and, 352–354
reality makeover shows on, 353–354
sexism on, 356
Teller, Edward, 461
The Tempest (Shakespeare), 19
The Ten Commandments (film), 236
Tennyson, Alfred Lord, 155
Tent revivals, 252
Terman, Lewis, 91, 92, 93, 107
Testosterone (androgens)
in females, 3, 43
gender differences and, 43–46, 48
homosexuality and prenatal levels of, 39, 40, 41, 48–50
intersexuality and, 51
life expectancy and, 126
the male brain and, 34, 35, 43
permissive effect of, 44–45
stress and, 45, 376
violence and aggression and, 4, 43–45, 450–451
Testosterone and Social Structure (Kemper), 44
"Testosterone Rules" (Sapolsky), 44
Thailand, sexuality in, 439f
Thatcher, Margaret, 128, 455
Third genders, 76
Third-wave feminism, 338
Thomas, Clarence, 297–298, 301, 304
Thomas, Kristin Scott, 126
Thompson, E. P., 147
Thompson, J., 64
Thompson, Jack, 344
Thompson, Michael, 213

Thonga people, 82, 83
Thorne, Barrie, 117, 352
Thornhill, Randy, 27, 30, 467
Tibetan Buddhism, 236
Tidball, Elizabeth, 227–228
Tiger, Lionel, 26, 65–66, 375, 387
Tisch, Ann Rubenstein, 232
Title VII, 297, 304
Title IX, 212, 232–233, 370
Tobago, female heads of state in, 312
Toch, Hans, 465
Tocqueville, Alexis de, 1, 156
Todd, Evan, 222
Todd, John, 20, 21, 240
Tokenism, 294–297
Tolkien, J. R. R., 355
Tolman, Deborah, 411
Tomboys, 45–46, 433
Tonne, Hilde, 306
Tootsie (film), 135
Torah, 240
Toys, gender-coded, 103–104, 103f, 105f, 106, 351, 360
"Traditional" family, 157–158, 159, 162–163
Trans World Airlines (TWA), 271
Transgenderism/transgender persons, 77, 138–142
birth certificate laws in the U.S., 141f
diversity of, 138–140
friendship and, 384
law as gender politics, 327–328
number of in U.S., 138
sexuality and, 437
violence against, 328, 480
wage shift in, 280
Transvestites, 138
Tresemer, David, 120
Trinidad, female heads of state in, 312
Trobriand Islanders, 83, 438
Troiden, Richard, 432
"Trouble talk," 377
Trow, Martin, 225
True gonadal intersex, 138
"The Truth About Boys and Girls" (Eliot), 35
Tsai Ing-wen, 312
Tsongas, Paul, 172
Tuchman, Gaye, 357
Tukano-Kubeo people, 83
Tulane Men Against Rape, 342
Tumblr, 367
Tunisia, social movements in, 335
Turkey, religion in, 245
Turner, R., 34
Twin studies, 41–42, 53
Twitter, 367
Two-spirit people (berdache), 76, 77, 77f

UCLA, 45
"The Unequal Weight of Discrimination" (Mason), 400
United Arab Emirates, female legislators in, 313
United Kingdom. *See* Great Britain/ United Kingdom
United Nations Declaration of 1985, 339

United Nations Demographic
    Yearbook, 188
United States
    AIDS-HIV in, 442
    beauty standards in, 397–398
    child support in, 196
    circumcision practiced in, 70, 73
    compared with other cultures, 60, 61
    cosmetic surgery in, 405
    day care not supported in, 177, 178
    divorce rate in, 188, 189t
    eating disorders in, 399
    family history, 154–163
    gender dimorphic view in, 51
    health in, 446–447
    homicide rate in, 453–455, 456,
        457, 457f
    incarceration rate in, 453, 461, 480
    life expectancy in, 127
    love in, 390–394
    marriage in, 189t
    masculinity in, 9
    math-gender correlation in, 210
    media in, 343
    out-of-wedlock births in, 181
    paid parental leave not offered in, 175,
        200, 305, 309, 325
    politics in, 312–313
    pornography sales in, 363
    rape in, 468
    religion in, 242–243, 245–247, 248, 250
    sexuality in, 83, 423t, 438, 440
    teen birth rates in, 179, 179f
    transgender birth certificate laws
        in, 141f
    video game popularity in, 360
    violence in, 449, 450, 453–455,
        462–463, 464–465, 466, 480
    wages in, 284, 288–289f
    the workplace in, 268–270, 272, 273,
        291, 305, 308
University of California at Berkeley, 205
University of California at Riverside, 444
University of California Irvine, 38
University of Chicago, 441, 469
University of Cincinnati, 295
University of Illinois, 300
University of London, 108
University of Michigan, 205
University of New Mexico, 278
University of Pennsylvania, 70, 226
University of Rochester, 206
University of Texas, 429
University of Vermont, 235
University of Virginia, 376
University of Washington, 300
University of Wisconsin, 36, 168
Uwer, Thomas, 72

Vagina Monologues (play), 342
Van Buren, Harry, 278–279
Van Buren, Martin, 317–318
Vanatinai people, 85
Vassar, Matthew, 206
Vassar College, 206, 226, 227
"Veiled Submission" (Bartkowski and
    Read), 241

Veterinary medicine, gender
    composition of, 278
Viagra, 325, 420
Video games, 344, 360–363, 361f, 364
Vietnam War, 319, 321, 462–463
Vinicius, L., 64
Violence/aggression, 9, 403, 448–481.
    See also Domestic violence
    culture and, 59, 60–61, 451
    evolutionary theory on, 27, 450–451
    feminist theory on, 98
    gender gap in, 460
    gendered, 452, 461–463, 464–465
    institutions and, 127–128, 461–463
    male-to-male, 452–453
    the media and, 344, 351
    pornography and, 344, 415
    regional differences in, 466
    in schools, 220–223, 344, 448
    social constructionist perspective
        on, 127–128
    testosterone and, 4, 43–45, 450–451
    against transgender persons,
        328, 480
    against women, 59, 68, 342, 351, 451,
        452–453, 465–474
    by women, 43, 48, 60–61, 460–461
    youth, 403, 449, 456
Virginia Military Institute (VMI), 99,
    100f, 229, 280, 297, 341
Virginia Tech shootings, 344
Virginity, 32, 407, 412, 421, 428
Virginity pledges, 422–424
Viziova, Petra, 450
Voodoo, 235
Voting, gender gap in, 315–317

Wade, Carole, 28
Wade, Lisa, 477f
Wage gap, 278, 281–286
    cartoon explaining, 282f
    consistency of, 284
    "feminist fiction" claim, 285
Wages/earnings/salaries, 272–286
    activism for equality in, 286
    annual median for different
        groups, 286t
    dollar-for-dollar comparison by
        gender, 288f
    family wage, 154
    gender ideologies about, 266
    gender inequality in, 268–270
    the "glass ceiling" and, 286–287
    median, by gender and race, 283f
    occupational sex segregation and,
        272–281
    remedies for inequality in, 304
    for teachers, 223, 224, 225
    women's as a percentage of men's,
        283f, 284f
Waite, Linda, 163
Wajed, Sheikh Hasina, 312
Wales, criminal offenders in, 456t
"Walk a Mile in Her Shoes"
    campaigns, 342
Walker, Karen, 378
Wall, Shavaun, 379

Wall Street Journal
    on income discrimination, 281
    on women as colleagues, 296–297
Waller, Willard, 390, 424, 425
Wallerstein, Judith, 191–192
Wang, Yang, 364
The War Against Boys (Sommers), 213
Warfare, 68, 127, 451, 461–463
    "gender" of, 455
    male domination and, 65–66
    rape and, 146
    religious justifications for, 256
    testosterone levels and, 49
Warner, R. Stephen, 120
Wasserstein, Wendy, 387
Watson, James, 53
Watson, John, 157
Watts, Jonathan, 408
Way, Niobe, 385
Weber, Max, 398
Weight
    obesity, 400–401
    tyranny of slenderness, 398–400
Weinrich, James, 42
Weisberg, Deena Skolnick, 56
Weitzman, Leonore, 190, 348–350
Welfare reform legislation, 178
Wellesley College, 206, 226
West, Candace, 133–134, 147
Westbrook, Laurel, 136
Western Wall, 240
Wethington, Elaine, 125
Wharton, Edith, 7
When Harry Met Sally (film), 381, 382
"Where Does Gender Come From?"
    (Fausto-Sterling), 23
Whisman, Vera, 54
Whitcomb, Dale, 301
White House Conference on Children, 157
White House Fellows, study of, 247
White Ribbon Campaign, 341–342
Whites
    domestic violence and, 479
    education and, 218
    health and, 444
    homicide rate in, 453
    housework division in, 169
    incarceration rate for, 455
    the media and, 354
    never-married, 161
    out-of-wedlock births in, 152, 181
    politics and, 316–317, 316f
    sexuality and, 438–439
    wages of, 281, 282, 283f, 286, 286t
    in the workplace, 262, 272, 287
Whiting, John W., 71
Whitman, Walt, 374
"Who Takes the Floor and Why?"
    (Brescoll), 315
Wicca, 258
Widows and widowers, 163
Willer, Robb, 108
Williams, Alex, 174
Williams, Caroline, 211f
Williams, Christine, 295–296
Williams, Walter, 76
Wilson, Edward, 24, 25–26

Winfield, Adia Harvey, 295
Winfrey, Oprah, 19, 354, 400
Winger, Debra, 126
Wingfield, Nick, 362
Wiswall, Matthew, 280
Witchcraft and witches, 237–238, 243, 258
Wodaabe people, 74
Wolf, Naomi, 318, 357, 398
Wolfgang, Marvin, 456
Wollstonecoft, Mary, 375
Womb envy, 97
Women. *See also* Femininity; Feminism/
    feminists; Gender entries; Mothers/
    motherhood
  African Americans' position compared
    with, 120, 270
  AIDS-HIV in, 442
  arrest rates for, 449, 460
  beauty standards for, 396–400
  body politicization and, 240
  brain research findings, 33–38
  criminality in, 458–461
  cultures dominated by, 61, 84
  divorce impact on, 191
  education discouraged for, 22, 34,
    205–206
  education encouraged for, 87, 204, 206
  education in valued by men, 208
  in the family, historical perspective
    on, 154–163
  "frigidity" in, 410, 420
  as heads of state, 312
  life expectancy of, 126–127
  marriage impact on happiness,
    163–164, 392
  married, percentage of, 188
  in the military, 23, 63, 326
  in military schools, 99, 100*f*, 229, 280,
    297, 341
  never-married, 153*f*, 161
  pornography consumption by, 363
  power and, 121–122
  retirement and, 126
  sexual peak myth, 123–124, 439–440
  sports enjoyed by, 369–370
  status of, 66–69, 81, 146, 173,
    396–397, 468
  stress, reactions to, 13, 37–38, 165,
    376–377
  suffrage for, 20, 21, 104, 240, 315, 337,
    341, 398
  tattoos and, 404
  top 12 reasons for having sex, 429
  violence against, 59, 68, 342, 351, 451,
    452–453, 465–474
  violence by, 43, 48, 60–61, 460–461
"Women as a Minority Group"
    (Hacker), 120
Women's spirituality, 238, 255–258
"Women's work," 155, 166, 201, 223
Woodham, Luke, 222, 448, 451
Woodhull, Victoria, 312
Working Woman study of sexual
    harassment, 301
Work/workplace, 260–310
  ancestral occupations in, 262, 264
  dual-earner couples in, 265, 266
  family life and, 154, 155–156, 157, 160,
    164, 165, 169, 172, 175–176, 176*f*,
    177–179, 200, 225–227, 305, 307–310
  family-friendly policies in, 175–176,
    200, 290, 306, 325
  friendship and, 382
  gender composition changes in,
    262–265
  gender differences in, 12, 15–16, 130,
    132–133
  gender discrimination in, 268, 270–272,
    292–293, 304
  gender ideology persistence in, 265–270
  gender of bosses in, 267, 295
  "glass ceiling" in (*see* "Glass ceiling")
  "glass cellar" in, 293
  "glass escalator" in, 295–296
  hazardous occupations in, 279, 293
  hours worked by gender, 261
  job loss and growth by gender, 302
  male domination in, 15–16
  occupational deaths in, 293, 293*f*
  occupational sex segregation
    in, 132–133, 272–281
  professional sector, 262–264, 273
  quota systems in, 306
  remedies for inequality in, 303–307
  sexual harassment in, 268,
    297–303, 304
  ten most common occupations for
    men, 275*t*
  ten most common occupations for
    women, 274*t*
  tokenism in, 294–297
  wages in (*see* Wages/earnings/salaries)
World Cyber Games, 360–361
World Health Organization, 71
World War II, 157, 261, 467
Worlds of Pain (Rubin), 428
"Worship" (Emerson), 114
Wotanis, Lindsey, 368
Wright, Paul, 379
Wyden, Barbara, 432
Wyden, Peter, 432

Xanith, 78
XX intersex, 138
XY intersex, 138

Yahoo, 309
Yale University, 226
Yalom, Irvin, 46
Yankelovitch survey on job
    dissatisfaction, 265
Yanomamö people, 81
Yapese people, 82
Yarborough, Jeannette, 407
Yeats, William Butler, 214
Yemen, social movements in, 334, 335
Yllo, Kersti, 473, 476
York, Richard, 331
Yoruba, 235
You Just Don't Understand (Tannen),
    144, 145
Young, Iris, 398
Young, Neil, 466
Young Women's Leadership School,
    231–232
Youth
  aggression, hormones and, 43
  body image issues in, 399, 400, 403
  cultural rituals of, 81, 388
  gender gap in, 214
  gender socialization in, 123
  sexual socialization in, 417–418
  sexuality in, 179–180, 409*f*, 411,
    417–418, 421, 428–430
  teenage mothers, 179–181, 179*f*, 422
  violence in, 403, 449, 456
  virginity pledges and, 422–424
  working mothers and, 178
Youth and Violence (report), 449
YouTube, 368
Yurok people, 83

Zande people, 82
Zeta-Jones, Catherine, 126
Zihlman, Adrienne, 62
Zimmerman, Don, 133–134, 147